Beginning

CSS

Cascading Style Sheets for Web Design

Second Edition

Richard York

Wiley Publishing, Inc.

Beginning CSS: Cascading Style Sheets for Web Design, Second Edition

Published by
Wiley Publishing, Inc.
10475 Crosspoint Boulevard
Indianapolis, IN 46256
www.wiley.com

Copyright © 2007 by Wiley Publishing, Inc., Indianapolis, Indiana

Published simultaneously in Canada

ISBN: 978-0-470-09697-0

Manufactured in the United States of America

10 9 8 7 6 5 4 3 2 1

For general information on our other products and services or to obtain technical support, please contact our Customer Care Department within the U.S. at (800) 762-2974, outside the U.S. at (317) 572-3993 or fax (317) 572-4002.

Library of Congress Cataloging-in-Publication Data
York, Richard, 1978–
   Beginning CSS : cascading style sheets for Web design / Richard York. — 2nd ed.
     p. cm.
   Includes index.
   ISBN 978-0-470-09697-0 (paper/website)
  1. Web sites—Design. 2. Cascading style sheets. I. Title.
   TK5105.888.Y67 2007
   006.7—dc22

               2007008853

Wiley also publishes its books in a variety of electronic formats. Some content that appears in print may not be available in electronic books.

To my own cousin Ryan Wood

In the words of Ryan's favorite comedian, Dave Chappelle,
"I'm rich, bitch!"

Rest in peace, brother. We love you and we miss you.

About the Author

Richard York is a web application developer for Trilithic, Inc., a company specializing in test equipment for the telecommunications industry. He wrote his first book, *Beginning CSS: Cascading Style Sheets for Web Design* (Wrox Press), in 2004.

Richard began his web development career taking courses at Indiana University–Purdue University Indianapolis. Since college, he has continued a self-imposed curriculum, mastering various technologies used in web development including HTML/XHTML, CSS, JavaScript, PHP, and MySQL. An avid supporter of open source software, he has written an open source webmail application for PHP PEAR and is currently working on an open source PHP library and framework called Hierophant, which he hopes to release in 2007.

Richard maintains a personal website at `http://www.richard-york.com` where you can learn more about his professional and personal interests.

Credits

Senior Acquisitions Editor
Jim Minatel

Development Editor
Brian MacDonald

Technical Editor
Alexei Gorkov

Technical Reviewers
Robert Searing
Marybeth Fullmer

Copy Editor
Mildred Sanchez

Editorial Manager
Mary Beth Wakefield

Production Manager
Tim Tate

Vice President and Executive Group Publisher
Richard Swadley

Vice President and Executive Publisher
Joseph B. Wikert

Project Coordinator
Heather Kolter

Graphics and Production Specialists
Carrie A. Foster
Denny Hager
Joyce Haughey
Alicia B. South
Ronald Terry

Quality Control Technician
John Greenough

Proofreader
Sossity R. Smith

Indexer
Aptara

Anniversary Logo Design
Richard Pacifico

Contents

Contents

Contents

Contents

Contents

Acknowledgments

As I wrote this book, so much has happened. Through the course of about 10 months, many people have been instrumental in making this happen, either directly or indirectly. I owe my success to all of you.

I'd like to thank my boss at Trilithic, Karalee Slayton. I appreciate all the encouragement, understanding, and help you've given me along the way. And I have just one more thing to say, shhhhhhhht!

I'd like to thank Marybeth Fulmer, my colleague and friend. Thanks for always being willing to listen and help.

I want to thank again, Jim Minatel from Wiley, for giving me the opportunity to write for Wrox again. Thanks for listening to all my wild ideas, and for being willing to take the risks on all the new things we've done with this book.

A great big thanks to Brian MacDonald, my development editor. I appreciate your patience and understanding, and you've been truly great to work with. This book owes much to your meticulous attention to every detail.

I'd also like to thank my tech editor, Alexei Gorkov. Your incredible attention to detail has been a tremendous asset on this project.

I want to thank my friends and family, who have been very supportive through some very difficult times: my aunt, Brenda; my uncle, Johnny; my cousins, Amanda, Kimberly, and Amy. Be strong, but don't be afraid to talk about your son, your brother, and my cousin, Ryan. Let's always keep in mind the good times, and the good things that happened, and not dwell on the bad. We can't change what happened, but we can keep his memory alive. Here's to you. Here's to me...

I want to thank Richelle Brown. You are a truly awesomely good friend. As we enter the year of our Paul, 5AP, I'm very proud of all of your accomplishments as of late. Egg-cellent! Keep your nose up. Let's find another Paul McCartney show so we can reset the Paul clock.

Thanks to my parents, John and Tammy. Thanks for your help and support. I love you.

And finally, I want to thank my best friend, Lisa Ratliff. I'm very sorry that I haven't been there for you. I should have been. There are so many things that I should have said and done, but didn't. I regret that we grew apart. Thanks for listening and thanks for understanding. Despite our ups and downs, you should know that I will always be here for you, and I will always love you. Snotface.

Introduction

Cascading style sheets (CSS) are the modern standard for website presentation. When combined with a structural markup language such as HTML, XHTML, or XML (though not limited to these), cascading style sheets provide Internet browsers with the information that enables them to present all the visual aspects of a web document. Cascading style sheets apply things such as borders, spacing between paragraphs, headings or images, control of font faces or font colors, background colors and images, textual effects such as underlined or strike-through text, layering, positioning, and a number of other presentational effects. CSS controls the presentational aspects of a web page's design, whereas HTML, XHTML, or XML controls the structure of a web page, which means little more than determining that certain text is a heading, other text is a paragraph, still other text is a list of hyperlinks, and so on. CSS provides enhanced and precise visual rendering; markup languages such as HTML provide meaning and structure.

Beginning CSS: Cascading Style Sheets for Web Design, Second Edition covers all the details required to combine CSS with HTML, XHTML, or XML to create rich, aesthetically powerful designs. Throughout the book, I focus on combining CSS with XHTML specifically because XHTML is the standard hailed by Internet standards bodies as the successor to HTML and the present and future of website design. CSS and XHTML allow a web document to be presented with less code, resulting in a significantly smaller file size and greatly increased ease of maintenance. CSS also enables the presentation of a web document to be centralized, which allows for the look and feel of an entire website to be written and centralized in one or a few simple documents, which makes updating a website a breeze. With only a few simple edits to a single document, the look and feel of an entire website can be completely changed.

By using modern standards like CSS and XHTML, you can drastically reduce the cost of building and maintaining a website when compared to legacy HTML-only pages. You can also greatly reduce the amount of physical bandwidth and hard disk space required, resulting in immediate long-term benefits for any website.

In this book, I also discuss how to style XML documents with CSS — XML being a more advanced markup language with multipurpose applications. XML will play an increasingly larger role in the production of XHTML documents in the future.

What's New in the Second Edition

This second edition of *Beginning CSS* features a near-complete overhaul of the content from the first edition. I listened to what my readers had to say about the first edition and took that feedback to create the most comprehensive introduction on CSS available on the market. Throughout this book, you see CSS broken down into simple examples that focus on a single concept at a time. This allows you to better understand how and why something works, since you aren't presented with a lot of irrelevant code, and you can better see the bits and pieces that come together that make something work. While these examples may not be particularly pretty, they are extremely valuable learning tools that will help you master cascading style sheets.

Introduction

To enhance the learning experience, I've presented most of the source code examples in syntax-colored code, a special feature in this book. Syntax coloring is a feature that you commonly see in fancy development software, such as Zend Studio (used to develop PHP), or Microsoft's Visual Studio (used to develop ASP, C#, and so on), and other software used by professional programmers every day. Syntax coloring is used in these software suites to make programming easier and more intuitive, and I think that it offers tremendous benefits in teaching as well. It allows you to see what the different bits and pieces are in source code, since each of the different bits and pieces has a different coloring to identify its purpose. It helps you to distinguish the building blocks of code more easily, and if you use similar development software to write your CSS and HTML documents, you'll also find that you make fewer mistakes and typos, since syntax coloring also helps you to write code that is more bug free.

I've also added annotations to many of the source code examples to highlight important, not-to-be-forgotten bits of information, and to visually point out concepts that are discussed in the surrounding text.

This edition also features every screenshot from a browser in color, a first for Wrox. Presenting the browser screenshots in color makes it easier for you to compare your results with what you see in the book.

This book also approaches CSS development from a browser-neutral point of view, and provides all the information that you need to get a good healthy start on professional cross-browser, cross-platform website design with IE 6, IE 7, Firefox 2, Opera 9, and Safari 2, which will allow you to reach over 99 percent of the web browsing public.

You also see comprehensive coverage of bugs, and workarounds for the IE 6 and IE 7 web browsers. Long a thorn in the side of CSS developers, making CSS work in IE 6 can be quite a chore without detailed knowledge of its quirks and shortcomings. I have covered throughout this book many of the hacks and nonstandard workarounds that you may need to develop compatible CSS content in IE 6. IE 7 features many great improvements to CSS support, and though they are much fewer than its predecessor, you still need a few tricks to make your web page shine in Microsoft's latest browser. I have covered the workarounds that you'll need to make your pages work just as well in IE 7 as they do in all the other popular browsers. In addition, you'll find the quick reference in Appendix B updated to reflect all of IE 7's new CSS support.

Along with better coverage of Internet Explorer, I've also greatly improved coverage of Mac OS X browsers, Safari, Firefox, and Opera. You'll see that Mac browsers are equally represented among their Windows brethren.

I had so much new content that I've even written an additional chapter that will appear online, on the Wrox website, which you'll be able to download for free. In this chapter I discuss additional workarounds for IE 6, and walk you through putting all of the knowledge that you've learned throughout the book together in a real-life web page.

You can visit the book's web page at:

```
http://www.wrox.com/go/beginning_css2e
```

The following sections tell you what *Beginning CSS: Cascading Style Sheets for Web Design, Second Edition* covers, whom this book is intended for, how it is structured, what equipment you need to use it, where you can go if you have a problem or question, and the conventions used in writing it.

Whom Is This Book For?

This book's primary audience is anyone seeking to learn how to use cascading style sheets to present web documents. Because cascading style sheets are used to control the presentational layout of a web document, people from backgrounds in art, graphic design, or those who prepare print layouts for publishing will feel at home using CSS. Regardless of your background, CSS is a simple and powerful language designed so that anyone can understand and use it.

To get the most out of this book, you need some experience with markup languages like HTML or XHTML. If you are completely new to website design and development, I recommend you begin learning web programming with Jon Duckett's *Beginning Web Programming with HTML, XHTML, and CSS*. Jon Duckett's book provides a complete overview of website development and design for the complete beginner, whereas *Beginning CSS: Cascading Style Sheets for Web Design, Second Edition* focuses specifically on the role of CSS in website design.

Throughout this book, I present all of the material you need to become comfortable with writing CSS from scratch.

What Does This Book Cover?

This book covers portions of the CSS Level 1, 2, 2.1, and 3 specifications. These specifications are created by an independent, not-for-profit Internet standards organization called the World Wide Web Consortium (W3C) that plans and defines how Internet documents work. The majority of the book is written using what is defined in the CSS Level 2.1 specification.

This book leads you through how to write CSS so that it is compatible with all of the most popular web browsers. I have focused on all of the following popular browsers:

- ❑ Microsoft Internet Explorer 6 for Windows
- ❑ Windows Internet Explorer 7 for Windows XP Service Pack 2, Windows Server 2003, Windows XP Professional 64 bit, and Windows Vista
- ❑ Safari 2 for Mac OS X 10.4 (Tiger)
- ❑ Mozilla Firefox 2 for Mac OS X, Windows, and Linux
- ❑ Opera 9 for Mac OS X, Windows, and Linux

The preceding browsers make up over 99 percent of the web browser market share at the time of this writing. For your convenience, this book also includes an integrated CSS feature reference throughout the book, as well as notes on browser compatibility. A CSS reference is also included in Appendix B.

How This Book Is Structured

This book is divided into three parts. The following explains each of these three parts in detail, and what each chapter covers.

Introduction

Part I: The Basics

Throughout Chapters 1 through 4 you learn the founding principles of CSS-based web design.

❑ **Chapter 1, "Introducing Cascading Style Sheets":** In this first chapter, I talk about what CSS is, why it exists, who created it, where it is maintained, and how it has evolved. I also discuss some of the basic differences among the various CSS specifications—CSS Level 1, CSS Level 2, CSS Level 2.1, and CSS Level 3—and how these specifications define what CSS is. You also learn more about each of the most popular browsers in use today, how to obtain them, and write your first CSS-enabled document. I also show you how to install Internet Explorer 6 and Internet Explorer 7 side-by-side on the same computer for testing.

❑ **Chapter 2, "The Essentials":** This chapter introduces the basics of CSS. Now that you have seen an example CSS document, this chapter introduces CSS rules and how selectors and declarations are combined to create rules. I demonstrate the various methods used to include CSS in a document. I explain how keywords are used in CSS to create predefined behavior, and how strings are used in CSS to refer to font names in a style sheet. I present the various units of measurement that CSS supports. Finally, I talk about the different ways of specifying color.

❑ **Chapter 3, "Selectors":** Chapter 2 introduced the concept of selectors. In Chapter 3 I talk about complex selectors, and how you apply style to a portion of a document based on its context within the document or user-initiated events.

❑ **Chapter 4, "The Cascade and Inheritance":** In Chapter 4, you learn about how to override styles, how precedence works in a style sheet, and how some styles can be considered more important than others, concepts that come together to define the *cascade* in *cascading style sheets*. You also learn how once you set some styles in a document, those styles can be inherited to other parts of a document depending on the context in which they are applied.

Part II: Properties

Throughout Chapters 5 through 12, you learn about properties that are used to manipulate the presentation of a document.

❑ **Chapter 5, "Text Manipulation":** In Chapter 5, I present the various properties that CSS provides for text manipulation. These properties provide effects such as controlling the amount of space between the letters of words, controlling the amount of space between the words of a paragraph, controlling text alignment, underlining, overlining, or strike-through text. I also show how to control the case of text by making text all lowercase, uppercase, or capitalized.

❑ **Chapter 6, "Fonts":** After you have seen the properties that CSS provides for text manipulation in Chapter 5, Chapter 6 presents the CSS properties you can use to manipulate the presentation of fonts. These effects include applying bold text, setting a font face, setting the font size, setting an italic font, as well as learning to use a property that enables you to specify all CSS's font effects in one single property.

❑ **Chapter 7, "The Box Model":** Chapter 7 elaborates on a design concept fundamental to CSS design: The Box Model. You learn how the box model plays an important role in determining layout dimensions. Using the margin, border, padding, width, and height properties, you can control how much space elements within a document occupy, how much space separates them, whether there are borders around them, whether scroll bars should be included. I also discuss a

CSS phenomenon known as margin collapsing, which is what happens when top or bottom margins come into direct contact with other top or bottom margins in a web document.

❑ **Chapter 8, "CSS Buoyancy: Floating and Vertical Alignment":** In Chapter 8, I discuss `float` and `clear`, two properties used to control the flow of layout in a web document and often used to flow text beside images. I also discuss the `vertical-align` property, which is used to create effects like subscript or superscript text, as well as to control vertical alignment in table cells.

❑ **Chapter 9, "List Properties":** In this chapter, I look at the properties CSS provides to control presentation of ordered and unordered lists. This discussion includes the options CSS provides for predefined list markers, custom list markers, and the position of list markers.

❑ **Chapter 10, "Backgrounds":** In Chapter 10, I present the properties CSS provides to control backgrounds in a web page. This includes properties that set a background color or background image, as well as those that control the position of a background, the tiling of a background, and whether a background remains fixed in place as a web page is scrolled or remains static. Finally, the chapter shows you how to use a property that combines all these individual effects into a single property.

❑ **Chapter 11, "Positioning":** I discuss four different types of positioning: static, relative, absolute, and fixed. You use positioning primarily to layer portions of a document. I also describe some of the practical uses for positioning, such as creating a multicolumn layout.

❑ **Chapter 12, "Tables":** In Chapter 12, I present the different properties that CSS provides for styling (X)HTML tables. The properties presented in this chapter let you control the spacing between the cells of a table, the placement of the table caption, and whether empty cells are rendered. I also look in detail at the available tags and options that (X)HTML provides for structuring tabular data.

Part III: Advanced CSS and Alternative Media

Throughout Chapters 13, 14, and 15 you learn about how to use CSS to make documents for printing, and another kind of document altogether, XML.

❑ **Chapter 13, "Styling for Print":** In this chapter, I discuss what steps to take to use CSS to provide alternative style sheets to create a printer-friendly version of a web document.

❑ **Chapter 14, "XML":** In this chapter, I show how you can use CSS to style XML content. This chapter focuses specifically on the CSS `display` property and how you use this property to change the behavior of tags in an XML or HTML/XHTML document.

❑ **Chapter 15, "The Cursor Property":** In this chapter, I show you how you can change the user's mouse cursor using CSS, how you can customize the mouse cursor, and what browsers support which cursor features.

❑ **Chapter 16, "Dean Edwards's 'IE7'":** In this chapter I talk about one alternative to many of the hacks and workarounds that you need for IE6. I talk about how to install an HTTP server for your website, and how to install and use Dean Edwards's "IE7" JavaScript, which is a collection of IE6 hacks and workarounds designed to make "IE6" feature compatible with its successor. This chapter is available online only, on the Wrox website at `www.wrox.com/go/beginning_css2e`.

❑ **Appendixes:** Appendix A contains the answers to chapter exercises. Appendix B, "CSS Reference," provides a place for you to look up CSS features and browser compatibility on the fly. Appendix C, "CSS Colors," provides a reference of CSS named colors. Appendix D, "Browser Rendering Modes," provides a reference for the browser rendering modes invoked by the presence or absence of a Document Type Declaration (discussed in Chapter 7).

What Do You Need to Use This Book?

To make use of the examples in this book, you need the following:

- ❑ Several Internet browsers to test your web pages
- ❑ Text-editing software

Designing content for websites requires being able to reach more than one type of audience. Some of your audience may be using different operating systems or different browsers other than those you have installed on your computer. This book focuses on the most popular browsers available at the time of this writing.

I discuss how to obtain and install each of these browsers in greater detail in Chapter 1. The examples in this book also require that web page source code be composed using text-editing software. Chapter 1 also discusses a few different options for the text-editing software available on Windows or Macintosh operating systems.

Conventions

To help you get the most from the text and keep track of what's happening, I've used a number of conventions throughout the book:

> Boxes like this one hold important, not-to-be-forgotten information that is directly relevant to the surrounding text.

Tips, hints, tricks, and asides to the current discussion are offset and placed in italics like this.

As for styles in the text:

- ❑ I *highlight* important words when I introduce them.
- ❑ I show keyboard strokes like this: Ctrl+A.
- ❑ I show URLs and code within the text in a special monofont typeface, like this: `persistence.properties`.
- ❑ I present code in the following two ways:

```
In code examples, I highlight new and important code with a gray background.
```

```
The gray highlighting is not used for code that's less important in the present
context, or has been shown before.
```

Source Code

As you work through the examples in this book, you may choose either to type the code yourself or use the source code files that accompany the book. All the source code used in this book is available for download at www.wrox.com/go/beginning_css2e. When you arrive at the site, simply click the Download Code link on the book's detail page to obtain all the source code for the book.

> *Because many books have similar titles, you may find it easiest to search by ISBN; this book's ISBN is 978-0-470-09697-0.*

After you download the code, just decompress it with your favorite compression tool. Alternatively, you can go to the main Wrox code download page at www.wrox.com/dynamic/books/download.aspx to see the code available for this book and all other Wrox books.

Errata

We make every effort to ensure that there are no errors in the text or in the code. However, no one is perfect, and mistakes do occur. If you find an error in one of our books, like a spelling mistake or faulty piece of code, we would be very grateful for your feedback. By sending in errata you may save another reader hours of frustration; at the same time, you will be helping us provide even higher quality information.

To find the errata page for this book, go to www.wrox.com and locate the title using the Search box or one of the title lists. Then, on the book details page, click the Book Errata link. On this page, you can view all errata that has been submitted for this book and posted by Wrox editors. A complete book list including links to each book's errata is also available at www.wrox.com/misc-pages/booklist.shtml.

If you don't spot "your" error on the Book Errata page, go to www.wrox.com/contact/techsupport.shtml and complete the form there to send us the error you have found. We'll check the information and, if appropriate, post a message to the book's errata page and fix the problem in subsequent editions of the book.

p2p.wrox.com

For author and peer discussion, join the P2P forums at p2p.wrox.com. The forums are a web-based system for you to post messages relating to Wrox books and related technologies and interact with other readers and technology users. The forums offer a subscription feature to e-mail you topics of interest of your choosing when new posts are made to the forums. Wrox authors, editors, other industry experts, and your fellow readers are present on these forums.

At http://p2p.wrox.com you will find a number of different forums that will help you not only as you read this book, but also as you develop your own applications. To join the forums, just follow these steps:

1. Go to p2p.wrox.com and click the Register link.
2. Read the terms of use and click Agree.

3. Complete the required information to join as well as any optional information you wish to provide and click Submit.

4. You will receive an e-mail with information describing how to verify your account and complete the joining process.

You can read messages in the forums without joining P2P; but, in order to post your own messages, you must join.

After you join, you can post new messages and respond to messages other users post. You can read messages at any time on the Web. If you would like to have new messages from a particular forum e-mailed to you, click the Subscribe to this Forum icon by the forum name in the forum listing.

For more information about how to use the Wrox P2P, be sure to read the P2P FAQs for answers to questions about how the forum software works, as well as answers to many common questions specific to P2P and Wrox books. To read the FAQs, click the FAQ link on any P2P page.

Part I
The Basics

Introducing
Cascading Style Sheets

Cascading style sheets is a language intended to simplify website design and development. Put simply, CSS handles the *look and feel* of a web page. With CSS, you can control the color of text, the style of fonts, the spacing between paragraphs, how columns are sized and laid out, what background images or colors are used, as well as a variety of other visual effects.

CSS was created in language that is easy to learn and understand, but it provides powerful control over the presentation of a document. Most commonly, CSS is combined with the markup languages HTML or XHTML. These markup languages contain the actual text you see in a web page — the hyperlinks, paragraphs, headings, lists, and tables — and are the glue of a web document. They contain the web page's data, as well as the CSS document that contains information about what the web page should look like, and JavaScript, which is another language that provides dynamic and interactive functionality.

HTML and XHTML are very similar languages. In fact, for the majority of documents today, they are pretty much identical, although XHTML has some strict requirements about the type of syntax used. I discuss the differences between these two languages in detail in Chapter 2, and I also provide a few simple examples of what each language looks like and how CSS comes together with the language to create a web page. In this chapter, however, I discuss the following:

- ❑ The W3C, an organization that plans and makes recommendations for how the web should function and evolve
- ❑ How Internet documents work, where they come from, and how the browser displays them
- ❑ An abridged history of the Internet
- ❑ Why CSS was a desperately needed solution
- ❑ The advantages of using CSS

The next section takes a look at the independent organization that makes recommendations about how CSS, as well as a variety of other web-specific languages, should be used and implemented.

Who Creates and Maintains CSS?

Creating the underlying theory and planning how cascading style sheets should function and work in a browser are tasks of an independent organization called the World Wide Web Consortium, or W3C. The W3C is a group that makes recommendations about how the Internet works and how it *should* evolve. I emphasize *should*, because the World Wide Web Consortium has no control over the implementation of the standards that it defines. The W3C is comprised of member companies and organizations that come together to create agreed-upon standards for how the web should function. Many prominent companies and organizations are W3C members, including Microsoft, Adobe, The Mozilla Foundation, Apple, Opera Software, and IBM. The W3C oversees the planning of several web languages including CSS, HTML, XHTML, and XML, all of which are mentioned in this book.

CSS is maintained through a group of people within the W3C called the CSS Working Group. The CSS Working Group creates documents called *specifications*. When a specification has been discussed and officially ratified by W3C members, it becomes a recommendation. These ratified specifications are called *recommendations* because the W3C has no control over the actual implementation of the language. Independent companies and organizations create that software.

The specifications created by the W3C are not limited only to web browsers; in fact, the specifications can be used in a variety of software, including word processor and spreadsheet applications, as well as by different types of hardware devices, such as PDAs and cell phones. For that reason, the software implementing a specification is referred to by the W3C as the *user agent,* which is a generic term that encompasses all the different types of software that implement W3C specifications.

The W3C merely recommends that a language be implemented in a certain way to ensure that the language does what is intended no matter which operating system, browser, or other type of software is being used. The goal of this standardization is to enable someone using the Netscape browser, for example, to have the same Internet experience as someone using Internet Explorer, and likewise, for developers to have a common set of tools to accomplish the task of data presentation. Were it not for web standards, developing documents for the web might require an entirely different document for a given user agent. For example, Internet Explorer would require its own proprietary document format, while Mozilla Firefox would require another. Common community standards provide website developers with the tools they need to reach an audience, regardless of the platform the audience is using.

As I write this, CSS comes in four different versions, each newer version building on the work of the last. The first version is called CSS level 1, and became a W3C recommendation in 1996. The second version, CSS level 2, became a W3C recommendation in 1998. The third version, CSS level 2.1, is currently a working draft, downgraded from a candidate recommendation since I wrote the first edition of this book in 2004. A *candidate recommendation* is the status the W3C applies to a specification when it feels the specification is complete and ready to be implemented and tested. After the specification has been implemented and tested by at least a few of the member companies, the candidate recommendation is then more likely to become a full recommendation. A *working draft* is the status the W3C applies to an ongoing work, which is subject to change. The fourth version of CSS is called CSS level 3, and many portions of it are still in development. Although portions of CSS are officially subject to change by the W3C standards body, I may discuss these features anyway if at least one browser maker has implemented the feature in question. I preface any such discussion with the warning that these features are still under development and could be subject to change.

This book discusses the portions of CSS available in browsers at the time of this writing — that includes most of CSS 2 and CSS 2.1, and a little of CSS 3. Some portions of CSS 2.1 contradict CSS 2 and are not yet implemented in any browser. Where appropriate throughout the book and before introducing a new CSS feature, I reference the W3C specification in which that CSS feature is documented by including the phrase *Documented in CSS* followed by the version number. Later in this chapter, I discuss the browsers that you need to test and build CSS-enabled web documents.

You can find the W3C website at `www.w3.org`. Go there to find documents that browser makers refer to when they are looking to implement languages such as CSS into a browser or other software. Be advised, these specifications lean heavily toward the technical side. They aren't intended as documentation for people who use CSS; rather, they are aimed at those who write programs that interpret CSS. Despite the heavily technical nature of the W3C specification documents, many web developers refer to the W3C documents as end-user documentation anyway, since it is the most complete resource.

Now that you know a little about who is responsible for planning and outlining the development of CSS, the next section describes how a web document makes its way into your browser.

How the Internet Works

As you probably already know, the Internet is a complex network of computers. Most of what goes on behind the scenes is of little interest to the person developing content for a website, but it is important to understand some of the fundamentals of what happens when you type an Internet address into your browser. Figure 1-1 shows a simple diagram of this process.

At the top of the diagram in Figure 1-1, you see a computer labeled *server-side* and a computer labeled *client-side.* The diagram is by no means an exhaustive or complete picture of what happens when you type in an Internet address, but it serves the purpose of illustrating the portions of the process that the aspiring web designer needs to understand. The server-side computer houses the documents and data of the website and is generally always running so that the website's visitors can access the website at any time of day. The client-side computer is, of course, your own computer.

The server-side computer contains HTTP server software that handles all the incoming requests for web pages. When you type an Internet address into a browser, the browser sends out a request that travels through a long network of computers that act as relays for that request until the address of the remote (server-side) computer is found. After the request reaches the HTTP server, the HTTP server sees what it is you are trying to find, searches for the page on the server's hard drive, and responds to the request you've made, sending the web page that you expect. That response travels back through another long chain of computers until your computer is found. Your browser then opens the response and reads what the HTTP server has sent back to it. If that server has sent an HTML document or another type of document that your browser can interpret, it reads the source code of that document and processes it into a displayable web page.

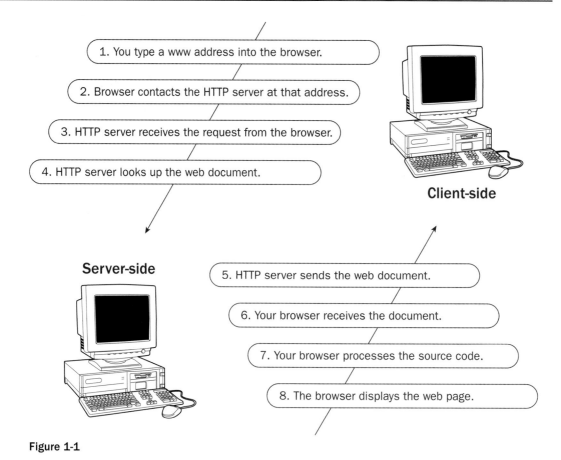

1. You type a www address into the browser.

2. Browser contacts the HTTP server at that address.

3. HTTP server receives the request from the browser.

4. HTTP server looks up the web document.

Client-side

Server-side

5. HTTP server sends the web document.

6. Your browser receives the document.

7. Your browser processes the source code.

8. The browser displays the web page.

Figure 1-1

This is where CSS enters the picture. If CSS is present in the document, the CSS describes what the HTML page should look like to the browser. If the browser understands the CSS, it processes the web page into something you can see and interact with. If the browser understands only some of the CSS, it generally ignores what it doesn't understand. If the browser doesn't understand CSS at all, it usually displays a plain-looking version of the HTML document.

How CSS Came to Be

During the mid-1990s, use of the Internet exploded. At that time, HTML was the only option for presenting a web page. As the Internet began to be used by more regular folks (as opposed to government, educational institutions, and researchers, as in the early days), users began demanding more control over the presentation of HTML documents. A great quandary arose — clearly HTML alone was not good enough to make a document presentable. In fact, not only was it not good enough, HTML alone simply wasn't suited for the job. HTML did not have the functionality that professional publishing required and had no way of making magazine- or newspaper-like presentations of an electronic document.

At the time, style sheets were not a new invention. In fact, style sheets were part of the plan from the beginning of HTML in 1990. Unfortunately, however, no standardized method of implementing style sheets was ever outlined, leaving this function up to the various browsers. In 1994, Tim Berners-Lee founded the World Wide Web Consortium, and a few days later, Håkon Wium Lie published his first draft of Cascading HTML Style Sheets. This draft was a proposal for how HTML documents could be styled using simple declarations.

Of those that responded to Håkon's draft of Cascading HTML Style Sheets was Bert Bos, who was working on a style sheet proposal of his own. The two joined forces and came up with cascading style sheets. They dropped HTML from the title, realizing that CSS would be better as a general style sheet language, applicable to more than one type of document. CSS caused some controversy at its inception because part of the underlying fundamentals of the new style sheet language was that it created a balance between the browser's style sheet, the user's style sheet, and the author's style sheet. Some simply didn't like the idea that the user could have control over the presentation of a web document. Ultimately, however, the Internet community accepted CSS.

Among CSS supporters was Microsoft, who pledged support for the new style sheet language in its Internet Explorer web browser. Netscape, on the other hand, another popular web browser at the time, remained skeptical about CSS and went forward with a style sheet language of its own called JavaScript Style Sheets, or JSSS. Ultimately, Netscape's style sheets were not successful. Eventually, because of a series of bad decisions and setbacks on the part of Netscape as a whole and Netscape's management, Netscape ultimately began losing market share, and Microsoft's Internet Explorer (IE) browser grew more and more popular. At IE's peak, it held 95 to 98 percent of the browser market share. Although IE has since lost market share to the likes of Mozilla Firefox and Safari, at the time of this writing, IE is still the dominant browser, most firms putting IE's market share at 50 to 85 percent, depending on the website's audience. Mainstream sites will see upward of 85 percent, but technical websites may see around 50 percent. Your own website's browser statistics will depend largely on the content of your site. One such site to reference for statistics is `http://www.upsdell.com/BrowserNews/stat.htm`. However, keep in mind the quote, "There are lies, damn lies — and statistics" — Disraeli (later made famous by Mark Twain).

During the time that CSS was being planned, browsers began allowing HTML features that control presentation of a document into the browser. This change is the primary reason for much of the bloated and chaotic source code in the majority of websites operating today on the Internet. Even though HTML was never supposed to be a presentational language, it grew to become one. Unfortunately, by the time CSS level 1 was made a full W3C recommendation in 1996, the seed had already been planted. Presentational HTML had already taken root in mainstream website design and continues today.

However, all is not lost. Today, the most popular browsers have fantastic support for cascading style sheets. Ironically, the browser exhibiting the least support is Microsoft's Internet Explorer for Windows, which still has plenty of CSS support to do away with most presentational HTML design. More ironic still, among the browsers with the best CSS support is Netscape's browser, and its open source offspring, Mozilla Firefox. This may beg the question: If Microsoft was such an avid supporter of cascading style sheets in the beginning, why is Microsoft's browser the least standards-compliant today? The answer is that Microsoft did indeed follow through with its promise for CSS support, and it was the most comprehensive and impressive implementation of CSS even up to the release of Internet Explorer 6 in 2001. Even so, CSS implementation in Internet Explorer has declined since the release of Internet Explorer 5. We can only speculate as to why Microsoft's browser declined in its support for CSS.

In the next section, I talk about the different types of browsers that you'll need to work through the examples for this book.

Browsers

Because CSS is a standard web language, many browsers support it. Therefore, it stands to reason that the aspiring web designer would want to harness that standardization to reach the largest audience possible, regardless of operating system or platform. In this section I provide an overview of each of these browsers, and where you can look to obtain a new version of that browser. Together, the following browsers combined comprise over 99 percent of the browser market share for the majority of websites in operation today:

❑ Internet Explorer 6 and 7 for Windows

❑ Mozilla Firefox for Windows, Mac, and Linux

❑ Opera for Windows, Mac, and Linux

❑ Safari for Mac OS X

In the next section, I discuss Internet Explorer 6 and 7 for Windows.

Internet Explorer

Internet Explorer is Microsoft's flagship browser that comes preloaded with the Windows operating system. The current stable version, as of this writing, is version 7.

Internet Explorer 7

Late in 2004, after the first edition of this book was published, Microsoft finally began work on a new version of Internet Explorer. IE 7 includes stronger security, tabbed browsing, and other goodies for users, and for developers — improvements to IE's support for CSS!

IE 7 comes just over five years after the release of IE 6, which was released in 2001. IE 7 is a fantastic improvement over IE 6, but it still doesn't quite meet the level of CSS present in competing browsers like Apple's Safari browser, or Mozilla Firefox. Although it doesn't exhibit the best CSS support, there is hope that future versions of IE will make significant progress in this area. Internet Explorer developers, and even Bill Gates, have publicly stated that Microsoft has returned to a more frequent release cycle for Internet Explorer, and we can expect new versions of Internet Explorer every year for the foreseeable future. Microsoft has even gone so far as to admit that it made a mistake by waiting too long to release a new version of IE.

Even though IE 7 is finally here, it will be years still before it achieves sufficient market penetration that web developers can officially dump support for IE 6. Because of IE 6's deficiencies, many are chomping at the bit for that time to come. In the meantime, we'll have to continue to support it and work around its shortcomings.

IE 7 is available for the following operating systems:

❏   Windows XP Service Pack 2

❏   Windows XP Pro 64-bit Edition

❏   Windows Server 2003

❏   Windows Vista

You can obtain IE 7 from Microsoft's website at `http://www.microsoft.com/ie`.

Internet Explorer 6

At the time of this writing Internet Explorer 6 is still the top dog with its browser market share between 50 and 85 percent, depending on the website's audience (see my discussion of Internet Explorer's market share in the section titled "How CSS Came to Be" earlier in this chapter). If you don't already have IE 6, you can obtain it from `http://www.microsoft.com/windows/ie/ie6/default.mspx`.

Installing Multiple Versions of Internet Explorer for Testing

At the time of this writing, you cannot install IE 7 alongside IE 6 on the same copy of Windows. For development, you need a way to test IE 6 and IE 7 both, since you'll have visitors to your website on both browsers. The following are a few ways to do this.

❏   Use PC virtualization/emulation software such as Virtual PC (a product made by Microsoft), which allows you to install and run different versions of Windows (or other operating systems, such as Linux) from within Windows or Mac OS X. Essentially, you can load up a new instance of Windows from your Windows desktop, and have that instance of Windows run in a window, independently. For example, Figure 1-2 shows a screenshot of me running Windows XP and IE 6 from my Mac OS X desktop, using the open source software Q, which lets me install and run Windows from within Mac OS X.

❏   Another option is setting up two different physical computers, one with IE 6 installed, and the other with IE 7.

❏   If you're feeling particularly adventurous, you can set up two installations of Windows on the same computer, although for this discussion, this method is a bit too advanced for me to adequately cover here. If you'd like to learn more about installing Windows more than once on the same computer, more information about that can be found at `http://www.microsoft.com/windowsxp/using/setup/learnmore/multiboot.mspx`.

Figure 1-2 shows two instances of Windows XP running in Parallels Desktop for Mac; one is running IE 6, and the other is running IE 7.

Most people prefer to keep it simple, and have all of their development tools at their fingertips. That makes the virtualization/emulation method the most attractive, in lieu of actually being able to install IE 6 alongside IE 7. I discuss this method in further detail in the next section.

Figure 1-2

Installing Windows Using PC Virtualization/Emulation Software

Today many companies make PC virtualization or emulation software, which allows you to run an entire operating system from a window on your desktop in the manner illustrated in Figure 1-2. More or less, it's like having multiple computers all consolidated into one. You can boot up a virtual computer, with all default settings so you can test your web pages. Here are some of the titles available.

❑ **VMWare, Player:** Available for free from `http://www.vmware.com/products/player/` for Windows and Linux.

❑ **Virtual PC:** Made by Microsoft, available for $129 from `http://www.microsoft.com/windows/virtualpc` (the price does not include a license for running Windows in the Virtual PC). Requires Windows or a PowerPC-based Mac.

❑ **Q** (pictured in Figure 1-2): Available for free from `http://www.kberg.ch/q`. If you're using Mac OS X, Q is available as a universal application (it runs on both PowerPC-based and Intel-based Macs).

❑ **Parallels:** Available for $49.99 from `http://www.parallels.com` for Windows, Mac (PowerPC and Intel-based), and Linux.

The best software for installing Windows from another operating system is software that uses *virtualization*. Without going into the technical details, software using virtualization runs much faster. The other, slower, much slower, in fact, method is *emulation*. Parallels and VMWare use virtualization, whereas, at the time of this writing, Microsoft's Virtual PC and "Q" both use emulation. Your computer will also need serious horsepower to run two operating systems at the same time; see each respective website for the system requirements of each of the aforementioned solutions. In my experience, software like this works best with at least 1GB of RAM and about a 2 GHz processor.

Without the ability to install and work with Windows virtually using software such as VMWare, your last resort is to uninstall IE 7 every time you need to test in IE 6, which can throw a pretty big wrench in the testing process. Currently, the virtual machine solution is the one officially sanctioned and recommended by Microsoft for testing in multiple versions of Internet Explorer. The IE team has responded to requests from web developers for the ability to install and run multiple versions of Internet Explorer side-by-side, and have said they are looking at the problem, but have not yet publicly announced a solution or released software to remedy the problem.

Internet Explorer for PowerPC Mac OS X

For PowerPC Macintosh users, I recommend not using or testing in IE for Mac. The capabilities and bugs of IE for Windows and IE for Mac are very different. IE for the Macintosh has better support for CSS (compared to IE 6), but it is an entirely different browser. The name may be the same, but the browsers are very different. In fact, Microsoft has completely dropped support for IE for Mac, having stopped development with a public announcement made in 2003, and having completely stopped support in 2005. It has less than a tenth of a percent of market share, if that much, and it does not run on Apple's Intel-based Macs.

For Mac users, I recommend Apple's own Safari or a Gecko browser, such as Camino or Mozilla Firefox, which I discuss further in the coming sections. If you don't have Internet Explorer for Windows, you still can work through most exercises and examples presented in this book, but if you are serious about website design, you will need to find a way to test your websites in Internet Explorer on Windows, since it has the majority of market share, and will enjoy that status far into the foreseeable future.

For news on what is transpiring in the world of Internet Explorer development, you might like to check out the Internet Explorer Team's blog at `http://blogs.msdn.com/ie`. New IE features and news of anything relating to Internet Explorer are announced on the IE Team blog.

The Gecko Browsers: Mozilla Firefox, Netscape, Camino

Gecko was created in January 1998. At that time, Netscape announced that it was making its browser free to its users and that its browser would be *open source*, meaning that its source code would be freely available for modification and distribution. This led to the creation of Mozilla; at the time Mozilla was the organization charged with developing and managing the Netscape code base. America Online later purchased Netscape, and until July 2003 Mozilla remained a part of Netscape. In July 2003, the Mozilla Foundation was created, making Mozilla an independent, not-for-profit corporation. When the Netscape browser became open source, its rendering engine, the part of the browser software responsible for making the source code of a web page into something you can see and interact with, was given the name Gecko.

Gecko is the foundation that a whole suite of browsers relies on to do the behind-the-scenes work of rendering web pages. Gecko is included in AOL for Mac OS X, Camino, Netscape 6, Netscape 7, Netscape 8, Mozilla Suite, Mozilla Sea Monkey, and Mozilla Firefox.

Netscape's browser market share has greatly diminished, whereas Mozilla Firefox continues to gain in popularity, occupying the number-two spot at between 5 and 30% market share (again, depending on the website's audience). Netscape's (and other Gecko browsers, for that matter) market share is charted by most statistics at less than one percent.

The following table shows the relationship between other Gecko browsers and Mozilla Firefox. This table illustrates the version of the underlying Gecko engine that each browser has in common with Firefox. Each of these browsers can be expected to render a web page identically and have the same capabilities in the area of CSS and document layout as the version of Firefox cited.

Other Gecko Browser	Firefox
Netscape 8.1	Firefox 1.5
Netscape 8.0	Firefox 1.0
Netscape 7.2	Firefox 0.9
Camino 1.0	Firefox 1.5
SeaMonkey 1.0 (formerly Mozilla Suite)	Firefox 1.5
Mozilla Suite 1.8	Firefox 1.0
Mozilla Suite 1.7	Firefox 0.9
Mozilla Suite 1.6	Firefox 0.8

Netscape 8.0 and 8.1 both feature the ability to switch between IE and Gecko for rendering a web page from within the Netscape browser, so essentially it is both Internet Explorer and Gecko in the same browser. The version of Internet Explorer in Netscape 8.0 and 8.1 is the same as the version of IE installed on the system. Netscape uses Gecko by default, but may try to "automatically" select the best rendering engine to use for a given website.

You can see that Firefox 0.9 and Mozilla Suite 1.7 can be expected to behave identically where CSS and design layout is concerned.

Because gecko browsers share the same brain (and because of Firefox's popularity), for the remainder of this book, I cite only Firefox when referring to a Gecko browser.

Depending on which Gecko browser you happen to like, you can obtain Gecko browsers from the following places:

❑ **Mozilla Firefox for Windows, Mac, and Linux:** Available from `http://www.mozilla.com/firefox`

❑ **Netscape for Windows:** Available from `http://www.netscape.com/download`

❑ **Camino for Mac:** Available from `http://www.caminobrowser.org/`

❑ **SeaMonkey for Windows, Mac, and Linux:** Available from `http://www.mozilla.org/projects/seamonkey/`

Safari

The next browser that I discuss is Safari, which is based on Konqueror, an open source browser available for Linux operating systems. The rendering engine used in the Safari and Konqueror web browsers is called KHTML. While Konqueror and Safari both have KHTML in common, Safari is a fork of KHTML (a *fork* means they shared the exact same source code at one point, but now each is developed independently), and features found in Safari may not necessarily appear in Konqueror and vice versa. Despite this, the two browsers render documents very similar to one another. Apple develops Safari, independently of Konqueror, and is the browser included with Macintosh OS X operating systems. Before Safari, Internet Explorer for Mac and Gecko had been dominant on the Mac.

For the purpose of this book, I note Safari compatibility when appropriate. Safari is available only for Mac OS X and can be obtained from `www.apple.com/safari`. Konqueror is only available for Linux (and any operating system in which KDE, the K Desktop Environment, runs) at the time of this writing; it can be found at `www.konqueror.org`.

Opera

Opera is a lesser-known, Norwegian-based company. Opera users are fewer, accounting for only a few percent market share by most statistical estimates. Again, that figure can be much higher or lower depending on a website's audience. Also be aware that Opera and Mozilla Firefox browsers can be configured to identify themselves to a website as Microsoft Internet Explorer browsers. This, of course, can distort statistical analysis. This spoofing is done because websites often create content targeting Microsoft Internet Explorer and Netscape specifically, leaving everyone else out in the cold — even though third-party browsers like Mozilla Firefox and Opera probably support the required functionality.

At the time of this writing, the current version of the Opera browser is 9.0. You can download this browser for free from `www.opera.com`. The Opera browser is available for Windows, Macintosh, Linux, and a variety of other platforms.

Writing CSS

To write CSS, just as is the case when writing HTML source, you will need a text editor. WYSIWYG (What You See Is What You Get) editors such as Microsoft Word aren't ideally suited for CSS because the environment is not ideal for the composition of source code. WYSIWYG programs often have features like AutoCorrection and line wrapping; a plain text editor is more appealing precisely because it does not have these automatic features. Furthermore, the more automated WYSIWYG editors are designed to write the source code for you behind the scenes, so you don't have complete control over the structure and formatting of the source code. In contrast, a plain text editor doesn't insert anything into the source code beyond what you type into the text editor.

The Windows Notepad program is one example of a text editor that is ideal for composing source code. To launch Notepad, choose Start ➪ Run and then type **Notepad** in the Open text box. You can also use Microsoft FrontPage, but FrontPage is best used in *view source* mode where you can edit the source code directly instead of via the WYSIWYG interface. The same holds true for Macromedia Dreamweaver.

On Mac OS X, the Notepad equivalent is TextEdit, which can be found in the Mac OS X Applications folder.

If Notepad or TextEdit is just too basic for your taste, a text editor that highlights markup and CSS syntax might suit your needs better. The following are full-featured alternative text editors for Windows:

❑ Crimson Editor: `www.crimsoneditor.com` (free)

❑ HTML-kit: `www.chami.com/html-kit` (free)

Here are some alternative text editors that work with Mac OS X:

❑ CreaText: `http://createext.sourceforge.net` (free)

❑ BBEdit: `www.barebones.com` (shareware)

If you're using Linux, you're probably already familiar with the different text editors that come bundled with the various distributions.

You must create HTML files with the `.html` extension. If you use Notepad or TextEdit, beware of your files being saved with a `.txt` extension, which will not result in the HTML file you were going for.

To ensure that your files are saved properly on Windows, choose Start ➪ Run and type **Explorer** (or right-click Start and choose Explore from the pop-up menu) to open Windows Explorer. After Windows Explorer is open, choose Tools ➪ Folder Options to open the Folder Options window, click the View tab, and uncheck the Hide Extensions for Known File Types box (see Figure 1-3). Then click OK.

HTML files are not the only file type in which the document extension is important; other file types require specific extensions as well. Those file types are covered later in this chapter.

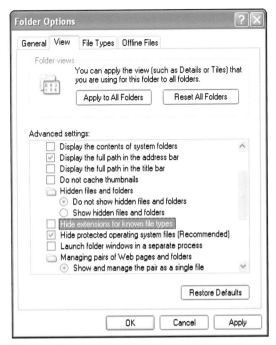

Figure 1-3

On Mac OS X, open Finder, and go to Finder ⇨ Preferences. Select the Advanced tab, and check the box for Show All File Extensions, which is depicted in Figure 1-4.

Figure 1-4

Armed with a browser and a text editor, in the next section I present an example of what CSS can do.

Your First CSS-Enabled Document

The following example is designed to introduce you to what CSS is capable of. It is designed to help you get your feet wet and get straight down to the business of writing style sheets.

You can find the images and source code for the following example at www.wrox.com. *While you can obtain the source code from* www.wrox.com, *I recommend that you type out the example so that you can get used to writing the syntax, and take in the different bits that come together in the example.*

Try It Out   **Creating a CSS-Enabled Document**

Example 1-1. To write your first CSS-enabled document, follow these steps.

1.   In your text editor of choice, enter the following markup:

```
<!DOCTYPE html PUBLIC "-//W3C//DTD XHTML 1.0 Strict//EN"
"http://www.w3.org/TR/xhtml1/DTD/xhtml1-strict.dtd">
<html xmlns='http://www.w3.org/1999/xhtml' xml:lang='en'>
  <head>
    <meta http-equiv="Content-Type" content="text/html; charset=UTF-8" />
    <title>The Gas Giants</title>
    <link rel='stylesheet' type='text/css' href='solar_system.css' />
    <script type='text/javascript'>
      var fixpng = function($img) {};
    </script>
<!--[if lt IE 7]>
    <link rel='stylesheet' type='text/css' href='solar_system.ie.css' />
    <script type='text/javascript'>
    // This fixes PNG transparency in IE
    var fixpng = function($img)
    {
      var $html =
        '<span ' +
          (($img.id)?    "id='"  + $img.id + "' "    : '') +
          (($img.className)? "class='" + $img.className + "' " : '') +
          (($img.title)?   "title='" + $img.title + "' "   : '') +
          'style="' +
            'display: inline-block;' +
            'width: ' + $img.width + 'px;' +
            'height: ' + $img.height + 'px;' +
            "filter:progid:DXImageTransform.Microsoft.AlphaImageLoader(" +
            "src='" + $img.src + "', sizingMethod='scale'); " +
          $img.style.cssText + '" ';

      if ($img.getAttribute('mouseoversrc'))
      {
        $html += "mouseoversrc='" + $img.getAttribute('mouseoversrc') + "' ";
      }

      if ($img.getAttribute('mouseoutsrc'))
      {
        $html += "mouseoutsrc='" + $img.getAttribute('mouseoutsrc') + "' ";
      }

      $html += '></span>';

      $img.outerHTML = $html;
```

```
      }
    </script>
<![endif]-->
  </head>
  <body>
    <!--
        Image reuse guidelines:
        http://www.nasa.gov/multimedia/guidelines/index.html
    -->
<div id='solar-system'>
  <div class='planet jupiter'>
    <img src='images/jupiter.png'
       alt='Jupiter'
       class='planet'
       onload='fixpng(this);' />
    <div class='planet-copy'>
      <h1>Jupiter</h1>
      <ul>
        <li><b>Distance from the Sun:</b> 78,412,020 km</li>
        <li><b>Equatorial Radius:</b> 71,492 km</li>
        <li><b>Volume:</b> 1,425,500,000,000,000 km<sup>3</sup></li>
        <li><b>Mass:</b> 1,898,700,000,000,000,000,000,000 kg</li>
        <li>
<a href='http://solarsystem.jpl.nasa.gov/planets/profile.cfm?Object=Jupiter'>
  More Facts
</a>
        </li>
      </ul>
      <img src='images/symbols/jupiter.png'
         alt='Mythological Symbol for Jupiter'
         onload='fixpng(this);' />
    </div>
  </div>
  <div class='planet saturn'>
    <img src='images/saturn.png'
       alt='Saturn'
       class='planet'
       onload='fixpng(this);'/>
    <div class='planet-copy'>
      <h1>Saturn</h1>
      <ul>
        <li><b>Distance from the Sun:</b> 1,426,725,400 km</li>
        <li><b>Equatorial Radius:</b> 60,268 km</li>
        <li><b>Volume:</b> 827,130,000,000,000 km<sup>3</sup></li>
        <li><b>Mass:</b> 568,510,000,000,000,000,000,000 kg</li>
        <li>
<a href='http://solarsystem.jpl.nasa.gov/planets/profile.cfm?Object=Saturn'>
  More Facts
</a>
        </li>
      </ul>
      <img src='images/symbols/saturn.png'
```

```
              alt='Mythological Symbol for Saturn'
              onload='fixpng(this);' />
        </div>
      </div>
      <div class='planet uranus'>
        <img src='images/uranus.png'
          alt='Uranus'
          class='planet'
          onload='fixpng(this);' />
        <div class='planet-copy'>
          <h1>Uranus</h1>
          <ul>
            <li><b>Distance from the Sun:</b> 2,870,972,200 km</li>
            <li><b>Equatorial Radius:</b> 25,559 km</li>
            <li><b>Volume:</b> 69,142,000,000,000 km<sup>3</sup></li>
            <li><b>Mass:</b> 86,849,000,000,000,000,000,000,000 kg</li>
            <li>
<a href='http://solarsystem.jpl.nasa.gov/planets/profile.cfm?Object=Uranus'>
   More Facts
</a>
            </li>
          </ul>
          <img src='images/symbols/uranus.png'
            alt='Mythological Symbol for Uranus'
            onload='fixpng(this);' />
        </div>
      </div>
      <div class='planet neptune'>
        <img src='images/neptune.png'
          alt='Neptune'
          class='planet'
          onload='fixpng(this);' />
        <div class='planet-copy'>
          <h1>Neptune</h1>
          <ul>
            <li><b>Distance from the Sun:</b> 4,498,252,900 km</li>
            <li><b>Equatorial Radius:</b> 24,764 km</li>
            <li><b>Volume:</b> 62,526,000,000,000 km<sup>3</sup></li>
            <li><b>Mass:</b> 102,440,000,000,000,000,000,000,000 kg</li>
            <li>
<a href='http://solarsystem.jpl.nasa.gov/planets/profile.cfm?Object=Neptune'>
   More Facts
</a>
            </li>
          </ul>
          <img src='images/symbols/neptune.png'
            alt='Mythological Symbol for Neptune'
            onload='fixpng(this);'/>
        </div>
      </div>
    </div>
  </body>
</html>
```

2. Save the preceding file in a new folder of its own as `index.html`.

3. Create a new, blank document in your text editor, and enter the following CSS:

```css
body {
  margin: 0;
  padding: 0;
  background: #000 url('images/backgrounds/star.png') no-repeat fixed;
  font: 12px sans-serif;
}
a {
  text-decoration: none;
  color: lightblue;
}
a:hover {
  color: yellow;
}
div#solar-system {
  position: relative;
  height: 575px;
  margin: 50px 0 0 0;
  border-top: 1px solid #000;
  border-bottom: 1px solid #000;
  background: #000 url('images/backgrounds/star_darker.png') no-repeat fixed;
  overflow: auto;
  white-space: nowrap;
}
div.planet {
  position: absolute;
  top: 0;
  left: 0;
  bottom: 25px;
}
div.jupiter img.planet {
  margin: 75px 0 0 40px;
}
div.saturn {
  left: 900px;
}
div.uranus {
  left: 1900px;
}
div.uranus img.planet {
  margin: 175px 0 0 100px;
}
div.neptune {
  left: 2750px;
}
div.neptune img.planet {
  margin: 175px 0 0 200px;
}
div.planet img {
  float: left;
  margin-top: 20px;
}
```

```
    }
div.planet-copy {
    color: white;
    padding: 10px;
    margin-left: 520px;
    background: #000 url('images/backgrounds/star_darker_still.png') no-repeat
fixed;
    position: absolute;
    top: 0;
    bottom: 0;
    left: 0;
    border-left: 1px solid #000;
    border-right: 1px solid #000;
}
div.planet-copy h1 {
    border-bottom: 1px solid #000;
    margin: 0 -10px;
    padding: 0 10px;
}
div.planet-copy ul {
    list-style: none;
}
```

4. Save the preceding CSS in the same folder where you saved `index.html`, as `solar_system.css`.

5. Enter the following CSS in a new document in your text editor:

```
div.planet {
    height: expression(document.getElementById('solar-system').offsetHeight - 25);
}
div.planet-copy {
    height: expression(document.getElementById('solar-system').offsetHeight - 45);
}
```

6. Save the preceding document in the same folder as `index.html` and `solar_system.css`, as `solar_system.ie.css`. The preceding source code results in the image in Figure 1-5, when loaded into Safari on Mac OS X.

    To see how `index.html` looks in other browsers, you can load it up by going to the File menu of the browser you'd like to view it in, and then select Open or Open File, and then locate `index.html` on your hard disk.

How It Works

Example 1-1 is an introduction to a little of what CSS is capable of. This example is designed to get your hands dirty up front with CSS, as a preview of what you can expect throughout the rest of the book. With each new chapter, I introduce and explain each of the nuts and bolts that come together to make examples like the preceding one. In Figure 1-5, you can see that CSS can be used to specify background images, and other aesthetic aspects of an XHTML document. I continue to revisit and explain the CSS that resulted in Figure 1-5 throughout the book.

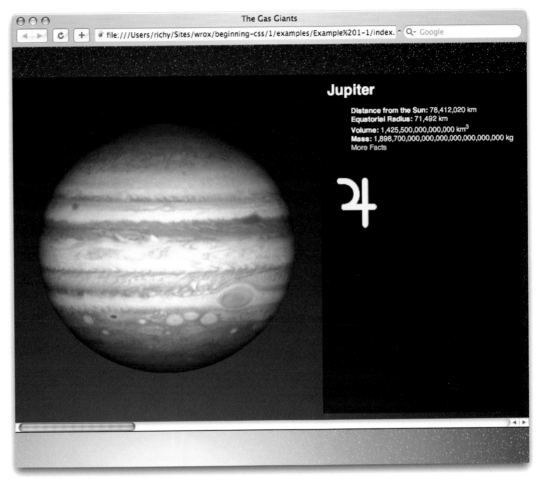

Figure 1-5

You might also note that Example 1-1 took some additional handy work to make it come out the same in Internet Explorer, as it did in Safari, Firefox, and Opera. Throughout this book, you also learn the hacks and workarounds that you need to make CSS-enabled web pages compatible with IE 6.

Advantages of Using CSS

By using cascading style sheets for the presentation of a web document, you can substantially reduce the amount of time and work spent on composing not only a single document, but an entire website. Because more can be done with less, cascading style sheets can reduce the amount of hard disk space that a website occupies, as well as the amount of bandwidth required to transmit that website from the server to the browser. Cascading style sheets have the following advantages:

❏ The presentation of an entire website can be centralized to one or a handful of documents, enabling the look and feel of a website to be updated at a moment's notice. In legacy HTML documents, the presentation is contained entirely in the body of each document. CSS brings a much needed feature to HTML: the separation of a document's structure from its presentation. CSS can be written independently of HTML.

❏ Users of a website can compose style sheets of their own, a feature that makes websites more accessible. For example, a user can compose a high-contrast style sheet that makes content easier to read. Many browsers provide controls for this feature for novice users, but it is CSS nonetheless.

❏ Browsers are beginning to support multiple style sheets, a feature that allows more than one design of a website to be presented at the same time. The user can simply select the look and feel that he or she likes most. This could only be done previously with the aid of more complex programming languages.

❏ Style sheets allow content to be optimized for more than one type of device. By using the same HTML document, different versions of a website can be presented for handheld devices such as PDAs and cell phones or for printing.

❏ Style sheets download much more quickly because web documents using CSS take up less hard disk space and consume less bandwidth. Browsers also use a feature called *caching*, a process by which your browser will download a CSS file or other web document only once, and not request that file from the web server again unless it's been updated, further providing your website with the potential for lightning-fast performance.

Cascading style sheets allow the planning, production, and maintenance of a website to be simpler than HTML alone ever could be. By using CSS to present your web documents, you curtail literally days of development time and planning.

Summary

Cascading style sheets are the very necessary solution to a cry for more control over the presentation of a document. In this chapter, you learned the following:

❏ The World Wide Web Consortium plans and discusses how the Internet should work and evolve. CSS is managed by a group of people within the W3C called the CSS Working Group. This group of people makes recommendations about how browsers should implement CSS itself.

❏ The Internet is a complex network of computers all linked together. When you request a web document, that request travels through that network to a computer called an HTTP server that runs software. It sends a response containing the page you requested back through the network. Your browser receives the response and turns it into something you can see and interact with.

❏ CSS answers a need for a style sheet language capable of controlling the presentation of not only HTML documents, but also several types of documents.

❏ Internet Explorer 6, Gecko, Opera, and KHTML browsers make up the majority of browsers in use today, with Internet Explorer 6 being the world's most popular browser.

❏ CSS has many advantages. These include being accessible, applicable to more than one language; applicable to more than one type of device, and allowing a website to be planned, produced, and maintained in much less time. CSS also enables a website to take up significantly less hard disk space and bandwidth than formerly possible.

Now that you have the tools to write CSS, and have seen a little of what CSS can do, in Chapter 2, I begin talking about the bits and pieces that come together in a CSS document to define the CSS language.

The Essentials

In Chapter 1 you received a taste of what CSS is capable of in Example 1-1, a web page that contains the four gas giant planets of our solar system and some facts about them. In this chapter, I begin the process of drilling down into CSS syntax. Throughout Chapter 2, I take an exacto knife to the `solar_system.css` style sheet that you wrote for Example 1-1, and explore what makes CSS work. I begin this discussion with CSS rules.

CSS Rules

As you dissect a style sheet, it can be broken down into progressively smaller bits. From large to small, it goes like this:

- ❏ Style sheet
- ❏ Rule
- ❏ Selector
- ❏ Declaration
- ❏ Property
- ❏ Value

In between, some special characters are used to mark the beginning and ending of one bit from another. Figure 2-1 shows a CSS rule.

The highlighted is a complete stylesheet rule.

```
body {
    margin: 0;
    padding: 0;
    background: #000 url('images/backgrounds/star.png') no-repeat fixed;
    font: 12px sans-serif;
}
```

A rule begins with a selector, followed by a left curly brace, "{", then one or more declarations, and the rule ends with a right curly brace "}".

Figure 2-1

You can set the layout of the rule according to your preferences; you can add line breaks and spacing to make CSS readable, sensible, and organized:

```
body {
    margin: 0;
    padding: 0;
    background: #000 url('images/backgrounds/star.png') no-repeat fixed;
    font: 12px sans-serif;
}
```

Or you can scrunch it all together:

```
body {margin: 0; padding: 0; background: #000 url('images/backgrounds/star.png')
no-repeat fixed; font: 12px sans-serif;}
```

Like HTML, CSS can use white space and line breaks for purposes of readability. The interpreter reading the CSS doesn't care how much white space appears in the style sheet or how many line breaks are used. Humans, however, must often add some sort of structure to prevent eyestrain, and to increase maintainability and productivity.

Within a rule, the bit that chooses what in the HTML document to format is called a selector.

Selectors

In CSS, a *selector* is the HTML element or elements to which a CSS rule is applied. Put simply, the selector tells the browser what to format. The simple selector that you saw in the last section is called a type selector; it merely references an HTML element. The selector portion of a CSS rule is highlighted in Figure 2-2.

The selector precedes the first curly brace.

```
body {
    margin: 0;
    padding: 0;
    background: #000 url('images/backgrounds/star.png') no-repeat fixed;
    font: 12px sans-serif;
}
```

Figure 2-2

body is written in the style sheet without the left and right angle brackets, < >. This rule applies the CSS properties: margin, padding, background, and font to the <body> element. I talk more about what these properties do in Chapters 6, 7, and 10.

Declarations

Declarations are enclosed within curly braces to separate them from selectors. A *declaration* is the combination of a CSS property and value. Figure 2-3 highlights the property and value portions of a declaration.

```
                    This is the property.
body {
    margin: 0;            A colon separates the property and value.
    padding: 0;
    background: #000 url('images/backgrounds/star.png') no-repeat fixed;
    font: 12px sans-serif;
}                                 From the colon to the semi-colon is the value.
```

Figure 2-3

The property appears before the colon, and the colon is used to separate the property from the value. Declarations are used to describe. What would the CSS be like if I used CSS to describe myself? It might look like the following

```
richard {
    mood: content;
    height: 6.1ft;
    weight: auto;
    hair: brown;
    eyes: hazel;
    belly: full;
}
```

A declaration is a complete instruction for styling a property of an HTML element. The whole declaration appears highlighted in Figure 2-4.

```
                          The declaration is the combination of a property
body {                    and value.
    margin: 0;
    padding: 0;
    background: #000 url('images/backgrounds/star.png') no-repeat fixed;
    font: 12px sans-serif;
}                    Each declaration ends with a semi-colon.
```

Figure 2-4

A declaration always ends with a semi-colon.

When more than one declaration or selector appears in the same rule, they are said to be *grouped*.

Grouping Selectors

You can group multiple selectors together in a single rule by providing a comma after each selector; this is illustrated in Figure 2-5. The result is that a rule applies to more than one selector at a time.

```
h1, h2, h3, h4, h5, h6 {
    font-family: sans-serif;
    color: maroon;
    border-bottom: 1px solid rgb(200, 200, 200);
}
```

A rule may contain more than one selector. This allows a rule to reference more than one HTML element at once. Each selector is separated by a comma.

Figure 2-5

The rule in Figure 2-5 applies to the HTML elements, <h1>, <h2>, <h3>, <h4>, <h5>, and <h6>. Try it for yourself.

Try It Out   Grouping Selectors

Example 2-1. To see how a selector is used to select HTML elements in the body, follow these steps.

1. Fire up your favorite text editor and type the following XHTML:

```
<!DOCTYPE html PUBLIC "-//W3C//DTD XHTML 1.0 Strict//EN"
"http://www.w3.org/TR/xhtml1/DTD/xhtml1-strict.dtd">
<html xmlns='http://www.w3.org/1999/xhtml' xml:lang='en'>
    <head>
        <meta http-equiv='Content-Type' content='text/html; charset=UTF-8' />
        <title>Selectors and Grouping</title>
        <style type='text/css'>
            h1, h2, h3, h4, h5, h6 {
                font-family: sans-serif;
                color: maroon;
                border-bottom: 1px solid rgb(200, 200, 200);
            }
        </style>
    </head>
    <body>
        <h1>Style Sheet</h1>
        <h2>Rule</h2>
        <h3>Selector</h3>
        <h4>Declaration</h4>
        <h5>Property</h5>
        <h6>Value</h6>
    </body>
</html>
```

2. Save this as `Example_2-1.html`.

3. Fire up your favorite browser and load the file. Figure 2-6 shows how CSS selects the different headings in the body of the HTML document to apply style.

Figure 2-6

How It Works

In Figure 2-6 you see the hierarchy of a style sheet, drilling down from the whole style sheet to the value of a property. In Example 2-1, you included a single CSS rule with a selector that provides properties for all six HTML heading elements, <h1>, <h2>, <h3>, <h4>, <h5>, and <h6>. The selector contains three declarations that provide the browser with information about how to style the aforementioned heading elements. The browser is told to give each heading text colored maroon in the sans-serif font face, and a bottom border that's gray, solid, and one pixel thick.

CSS Comments

As is the case with HTML, comment text can be added to style sheets as well. In a multipage template, this helps you remember which CSS rule applies to what or why it was added in the first place. CSS supports multiline comments that begin with a forward slash and an asterisk (/*) and terminate with an asterisk and a forward slash (*/). This is illustrated in Figure 2-7.

```
Comments begin with a forward
slash, followed by an asterisk.
                                Comments end with an asterisk,
/* This is a comment! */        followed by a forward slash.
body {
    margin: 0;          Comment text appears in the middle.
    padding: 0;
    background: #000 url('images/backgrounds/star.png') no-repeat fixed;
    font: 12px sans-serif;
}
```

Figure 2-7

CSS comments provide a mechanism that allows you to insert notes about what the styles in the style sheet do and why they were added. The design of a website can get complicated, and often it's helpful to make notes that help you remember why you added one thing or another. The following are some examples of what you can do with comments.

❑ Comments can appear inside of a rule, as illustrated in Figure 2-8.

```
body {
    /* This is a comment! */        Comment text can appear
    margin: 0;                      inside of a rule.
    padding: 0;
    background: #000 url('images/backgrounds/star.png') no-repeat fixed;
    font: 12px sans-serif;
}
```

Figure 2-8

❑ Comments can appear inside of a declaration, as demonstrated in Figure 2-9.

```
body {                      Comment text can appear
    margin: 0;              within a declaration.
    padding: 0;
    background: #000 url('images/backgrounds/star.png') no-repeat fixed;
    font: /* This is a comment! */ 12px sans-serif;
}
```

Figure 2-9

❑ Comments can span multiple lines, as shown in Figure 2-10.

```
/*
 * Sometimes you have       Comments can also span multiple lines.
 * note to say!             Beginning each line with an asterisk is not
 */                         required, but is common practice among
body {                      experienced programmers.
    margin: 0;
    padding: 0;
    background: #000 url('images/backgrounds/star.png') no-repeat fixed;
    font: 12px sans-serif;
}
```

Figure 2-10

❑ Comments can be used to disable portions of a style sheet, as shown in Figure 2-11.

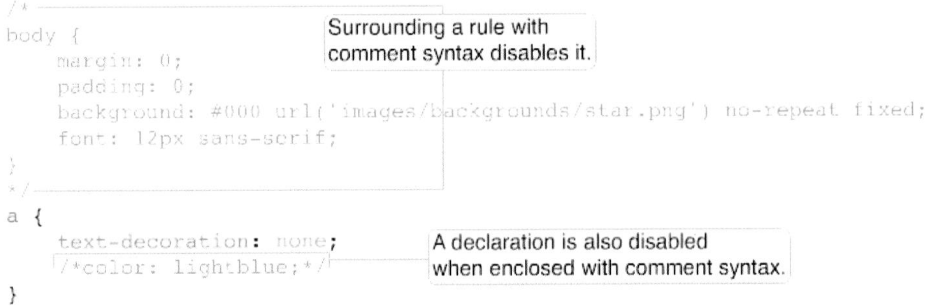

```
/*
body {
    margin: 0;
    padding: 0;
    background: #000 url('images/backgrounds/star.png') no-repeat fixed;
    font: 12px sans-serif;
}
*/

a {
    text-decoration: none;
    /*color: lightblue;*/
}
```

Surrounding a rule with comment syntax disables it.

A declaration is also disabled when enclosed with comment syntax.

Figure 2-11

Disabling portions of a style sheet can be useful if you are trying to track down problematic styles, or if you are simply experimenting with different effects.

Values

CSS can become quite complex in terms of what it allows a property's value to be. Figure 2-5 illustrates some, but not all, of the potential types of values that you see in CSS. In the coming sections I discuss each of the different types of values that CSS allows in greater detail, beginning with keyword values.

Keywords

A *keyword* value is used to invoke a predefined function. For example, red, green, and blue are CSS keywords, red, green and blue; all have a predefined purpose. Color keywords can be used on any property that accepts a color value. Figure 2-12 shows some examples of keywords in a style sheet.

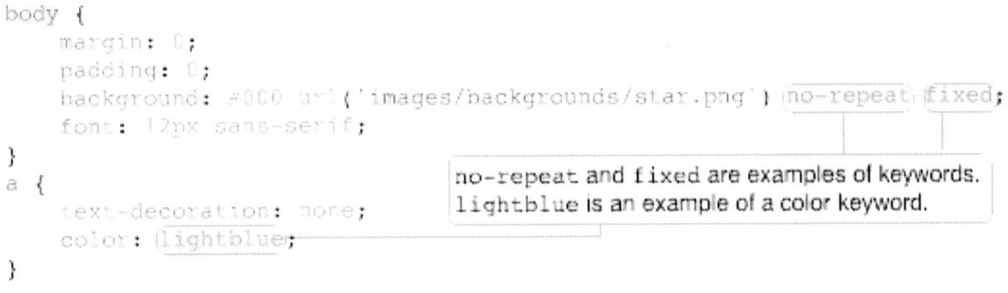

```
body {
    margin: 0;
    padding: 0;
    background: #000 url('images/backgrounds/star.png') no-repeat fixed;
    font: 12px sans-serif;
}
a {
    text-decoration: none;
    color: lightblue;
}
```

no-repeat and fixed are examples of keywords.
lightblue is an example of a color keyword.

Figure 2-12

The keywords in Figure 2-12 are no-repeat, fixed, and lightblue. no-repeat and fixed provide the browser with instructions for how to render the background image. lightblue is a keyword that tells the browser what color the text of hyperlinks should be.

Many types of keywords are used in CSS, and sometimes a single keyword can have different meanings depending on the element to which it is applied. The auto keyword, for example, is used by CSS to apply some default style or behavior, and its meaning depends on the way it's used, and what property it is used with. Try the auto keyword in this example.

Try It Out   **Adding auto width to a Table**

Example 2-2. To see the effects of the auto keyword as applied to a `<table>` element, follow these steps.

1. Enter the following XHTML-compliant markup.

```
<!DOCTYPE html PUBLIC "-//W3C//DTD XHTML 1.0 Strict//EN"
                  "http://www.w3.org/TR/xhtml1/DTD/xhtml1-strict.dtd">
<html xmlns='http://www.w3.org/1999/xhtml' xml:lang='en'>
    <head>
        <meta http-equiv='Content-Type' content='text/html; charset=UTF-8' />
        <title>Auto width on tables</title>
        <style type='text/css'>
            table {
                width: auto;
                background: black;
                color: white;
            }
        </style>
    </head>
    <body>
        <table>
            <tbody>
                <tr>
                    <td>How will this table react to auto width?</td>
                </tr>
            </tbody>
        </table>
    </body>
</html>
```

2. Save the preceding markup as `Example_2-2.html`, and then load it into a browser. Figure 2-13 shows `width: auto;` applied to the `<table>` element.

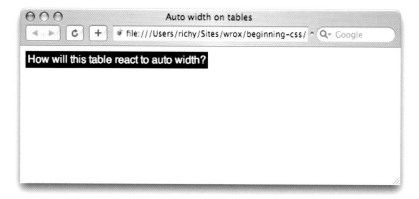

Figure 2-13

How It Works

In Figure 2-13, you can see that the table expands only enough to accommodate the text within it.

When `width: auto;` is applied to a `<table>` element, it invokes a different mechanism for width measurement than when it is applied to a `<div>` element. Next, see what happens when auto width is applied to a `<div>` element.

Try It Out   Applying auto width to a div

Example 2-3. To see the effects of the `auto` keyword as applied to a `<div>` element, follow these steps.

1.   Enter the following document:

```
<!DOCTYPE html PUBLIC "-//W3C//DTD XHTML 1.0 Strict//EN"
                      "http://www.w3.org/TR/xhtml1/DTD/xhtml1-strict.dtd">
<html xmlns='http://www.w3.org/1999/xhtml' xml:lang='en'>
    <head>
        <meta http-equiv='Content-Type' content='text/html; charset=UTF-8' />
        <title>Auto width on divs</title>
        <style type='text/css'>
            div {
                width: auto;
                background: black;
                color: white;
            }
        </style>
    </head>
    <body>
        <div>How will this div react to auto width?</div>
    </body>
</html>
```

2.   Save the preceding markup as `Example_2-3.html`. Figure 2-14 shows `width: auto;` applied to the `<div>` element.

Figure 2-14

How It Works

All elements with a `width` property have an `auto` value by default, but not all elements behave the same way when `auto width` is applied. The `<table>` element, for instance, only expands horizontally to accommodate its data, which is a method called *shrink-to-fit*. A `<div>` element, on the other hand, expands horizontally as far as there is space, which is called *expand-to-fit*.

I've added a background for each element in Examples 2-2 and 2-3 so that you can see its width. The border outlines the edges of each element, showing exactly how much space each element occupies. You learn more about how width works in Chapter 7, "The Box Model."

Keywords always invoke some special, predefined behavior. Another example I can present is with the CSS border property: A border may take three separate keywords that define how it appears when the browser renders it:

```
border: thin solid black;
```

This example defines a property with three keyword values: `thin`, `solid`, and `black`. Each value refers to a different characteristic of the border's appearance: `thin` refers to its measurement, `solid` to its style, and `black` to its color.

Sometimes you have need of including content from a style sheet or referencing a file path or including a font name that has spaces in its name or referencing an HTML element's attribute value. To accomplish these tasks, CSS supports a type of value called strings.

Strings

A *string* is any sequence of characters. For example, "Hello, World" is a string. In most programming languages and in CSS, strings are enclosed within either single or double quotation marks. A string is what is known as a data type. *Data types* are used to classify information. Integers, real numbers, and strings are examples of data types. Strings may contain text, numbers, symbols — any type of character. An integer can be a number that has a positive or negative value, and can only be a whole number, no decimals. A real number can have decimal places. These data types are made to conform to their defined rules by the language. Whereas a string can contain any character, real numbers are expected to be whole numbers or decimals; a string cannot appear where a real number is expected, and a real number cannot appear where an integer is expected, and so on.

One use of strings in CSS is to specify a font that contains spaces in its name.

```
font-family: "Times New Roman", Times, serif;
```

Font faces with spaces in the name are enclosed with quotations to keep the program that interprets CSS from getting confused. The quotes act as marking posts for where the font face's name begins and ends. You see more about how fonts work in Chapter 6, "Fonts."

Strings may also be used to include content in an HTML document from a style sheet. Try including content from a style sheet for yourself.

Try It Out   **Including Content from a Style Sheet**

Example 2-4. To include content from a style sheet, follow these steps.

1. Type in the following document:

```
<!DOCTYPE html PUBLIC "-//W3C//DTD XHTML 1.0 Strict//EN"
                "http://www.w3.org/TR/xhtml1/DTD/xhtml1-strict.dtd">
<html xmlns='http://www.w3.org/1999/xhtml' xml:lang='en'>
    <head>
        <meta http-equiv='Content-Type' content='text/html; charset=UTF-8' />
        <title>Generated content</title>
        <style type='text/css'>
            div {
                font-family: sans-serif;
            }
            div::before {
                content: "I said, \"Hello, world!\"";
                background: black;
                color: white;
                margin-right: 25px;
            }
        </style>
    </head>
    <body>
        <div>The world said, "Hello, yourself!"</div>
    </body>
</html>
```

2. Save the document as `Example_2-4.html`.

3. Open the example with Safari, Firefox, or Opera—IE 6 and IE 7 don't support this feature. Figure 2-15 shows that the string "I said, "Hello, world!"" is inserted into the `<div>` element using the `content` property.

Figure 2-15

How It Works

You included the string "I said, "Hello, world!"" in the HTML document by using the CSS `content` property.

────────────

Strings may contain any sequence of characters of any length (at least up to whatever arbitrary limit a browser may have defined) — even quotation marks are allowed. However, strings may contain quotation marks only if they're *escaped* using another special character, the backslash character. When you *escape* quotation marks, you tell the browser: "Ignore the quotation mark; it is part of the string." The backslash is used to quote Foghorn Leghorn in the following code:

```
div {
    content: "Foghorn said: \"Get away from me son, you bother me.\"";
}
```

As an escape character, a backslash is included to tell the browser to ignore only the quotation mark that appears directly after it. The same backslash character is used to escape single quotes as well, if the string is enclosed by single quotes:

```
div {
    content: 'Foghorn said: \'Get away from me son, you bother me.\'';
}
```

The browser also ignores the single quotes in the middle with the use of the backslash character before the quote mark. Quotation marks do not have to be escaped if single quotes are used within a string enclosed by double quotes or vice versa. In this example

```
div {
    content: "Foghorn said: 'Get away from me son, you bother me.'";
}
```

the single quotes do not have to be escaped because double quotes enclose the string.

Length and Measurement

There are two kinds of lengths used in CSS: relative and absolute. *Absolute* lengths are not dependent on any other measurement. An absolute measurement retains its length regardless of the environment (operating system, browser, or screen resolution of a computer monitor) in which it is applied. *Relative* lengths, on the other hand, depend on the environment in which they're used, such as the computer monitor's screen resolution or the size of a font.

Absolute measurements are defined based on real-world units such as inches, centimeters, points, and so on. These measurements have been used for centuries in the print industry, and one would be accustomed to finding them on a ruler.

Absolute Measurement

CSS supports a variety of real-world measurements. Each absolute length unit supported by CSS is defined in the following table.

Unit Abbreviation	Description
in	Inches
cm	Centimeters
mm	Millimeters
pt	Points, 1 point is equal to 1/72nd of an inch
pc	Picas, 1 pica is equal to 12 points

Absolute lengths are not intended for the computer screen; they are intended for where a physical measurement is necessary. For example, printing a document requires real-word measurements. When you are composing a web document, you want the printable version of that document to be made using lengths that are reliable for the print environment.

On the other hand, when absolute measurements are applied to the computer screen, some inconsistencies surface.

The Pitfalls of Onscreen Absolute Measurement

Coding real-world physical lengths into a computer isn't as easy as it may seem. When applied to a computer screen, physical measurements are based on pixels. *Pixels* are tiny dots that a computer monitor uses to create the image you see, and the number of pixels displayed depends on the monitor's screen resolution. For example, a computer monitor set to an 800×600 screen resolution displays 800 pixels horizontally and 600 pixels vertically for a possibility of 480,000 total pixels.

Windows defines one inch as 96 pixels, by default. The definition of an inch as 96 pixels depends on an operating system display setting called DPI, or dots per inch. The DPI setting of an operating system is a user-configurable setting for defining the number of dots (or pixels) that make up an inch.

In the earlier days of the web, Macintosh and Windows had different DPI settings; a Mac's default DPI was 72 and Windows' was 96. Today all modern browsers, including those on the Macintosh, have standardized on Windows' 96 DPI measurement as the de facto default standard for DPI. While this de facto standardization makes for a greater likelihood of consistency, because the DPI setting can be customized, absolute measurement cannot be relied upon for onscreen layout. For example, Firefox still includes a setting in its font options menu for the DPI to either 72 or 96 DPI, and it's possible to change the DPI setting through other means, such as within Windows display settings control panel.

Figure 2-16 shows Firefox 1.5's DPI setting, a setting that has since been eliminated from Firefox 2.0, since Macs just use the same DPI setting as Windows these days.

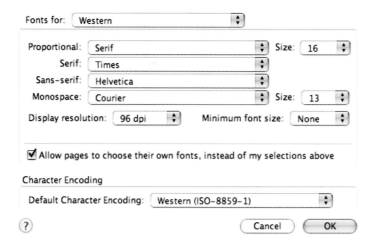

Figure 2-16

In the next two examples, you set up an experiment to see how the DPI can affect absolute measurements in CSS, and ultimately discover the reason why absolute measurements are not suited for onscreen layout purposes.

Try It Out   **Testing 96 DPI Equals an Inch**

Example 2-5. To see a side-by-side comparison of pixels to inches, follow these steps.

1.   Enter the following document:

```
<!DOCTYPE html PUBLIC "-//W3C//DTD XHTML 1.0 Strict//EN"
"http://www.w3.org/TR/xhtml1/DTD/xhtml1-strict.dtd">
<html xmlns='http://www.w3.org/1999/xhtml' xml:lang='en'>
    <head>
        <meta http-equiv='Content-Type' content='text/html; charset=UTF-8' />
        <title>Pixels to Inches</title>
        <style type='text/css'>
            div {
                background: #000;
                border: 1px solid rgb(128, 128, 128);
                color: white;
                font: 9px monospace;
                margin: 15px;
                text-align: center;
            }
            div#inches {
                width: 1in;
                height: 1in;
            }
            div#pixels {
```

```
                width: 96px;
                height: 96px;
            }
        </style>
    </head>
    <body>
        <div id='inches'>&lt;-- 1 Inch --&gt;</div>
        <div id='pixels'>&lt;-- 96 Pixels --&gt;</div>
    </body>
</html>
```

2. Save the document you just created as `Example_2-5.html`.

3. Open the document in your browser of choice. Figure 2-17 shows two `<div>` elements: The top `<div>` element has a height and width of 1 inch, and the bottom `<div>` has a height and width of 96 pixels. Both have a black background with white text for clarity. Switching the screen resolution from 800 × 600 pixels to 1280 × 1024 shows that the measurement of 1 inch remains the same as the 96-pixel measurement.

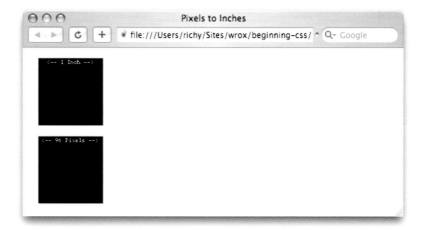

Figure 2-17

How It Works

By default, browsers conform to the Windows default of 96 dots per inch for the onscreen definition of what an inch is.

Obviously, since absolute measurement is not well suited for onscreen layout, there must surely be another, right? Yes! The other method of measurement in CSS is relative measurement.

Relative Measurement

Relative measurement is better suited for the purpose of onscreen layout. The following table defines the four types of relative measurement that CSS allows.

Unit Abbreviation	Description
em	Length relevant to the nearest font size.
ex	The x-height of the relevant font (height of the letter x).
px	Pixels, relative to the viewing device, for example, a computer monitor.
%	Percentage measurement; how percentage length is calculated depends on what property it is being applied to.

The em and ex units are measured relative to the font size of a document, pixels use the real pixels of the monitor's screen resolution, and percentage measurement depends on what property it is being applied to. In the coming sections you explore each type of relative measurement in greater detail.

Measurement Based on the Font Size

Measurement in em is currently the most favored of relative measurement for onscreen layout, for most measurements. A measurement that is relative to the font size allows for designs that scale up and down gracefully with the user's font size preferences.

Try It Out   Comparing em to Pixels

Example 2-6. To see how the em measurement compares to pixel measurement, follow these steps.

1.   Enter the following XHTML document:

```
<!DOCTYPE html PUBLIC "-//W3C//DTD XHTML 1.0 Strict//EN"
                      "http://www.w3.org/TR/xhtml1/DTD/xhtml1-strict.dtd">
<html xmlns='http://www.w3.org/1999/xhtml' xml:lang='en'>
    <head>
        <meta http-equiv='Content-Type' content='text/html; charset=UTF-8' />
        <title>Em Measurement Comparison to Pixels</title>
        <style type='text/css'>
            body {
                font: 1em sans-serif;
            }
            p {
                background: rgb(234, 234, 234);
                border: 1px solid rgb(200, 200, 200);
            }
            p#em-measurement {
                width: 12em;
                padding: 1em;
            }
            p#px-measurement {
                width: 192px;
                padding: 16px;
            }
```

```
        </style>
    </head>
    <body>
        <p id='em-measurement'>
            This paragraph is 12em wide, with a 1em padding.
        </p>
        <p id='px-measurement'>
            This paragraph is 192 pixels wide, with 16 pixels of
            padding.
        </p>
    </body>
</html>
```

2. Save the preceding document as `Example_2-6.html`, and load it up in your favorite browser. When Example 2-6 is loaded up, you should see something like that in Figure 2-18.

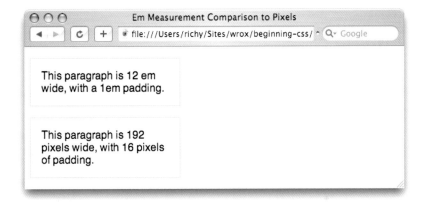

Figure 2-18

How It Works

In Figure 2-18 you see that 12em is the same measurement as 192 pixels. When the font size is set to 16 pixels (the default in all modern browsers). So with the em unit, you can layout a whole web page that scales with the user's font size preference.

All modern browsers provide a mechanism for scaling the font size up or down to the user's preference. On the Mac, ⌘-+ increases the size of the text, and on Windows, it's Ctrl-+. Figure 2-19 shows what happens when the text is scaled up in Safari or Firefox with Example 2-6 loaded.

In Figure 2-19, you see that the 12em measurement no longer matches the 192-pixel measurement when the text is scaled up. IE 7 and Opera do not display the effect the same as seen in Figure 2-19, however, since they scale everything, even the size of a pixel.

Figure 2-20 shows what happens when text is scaled down.

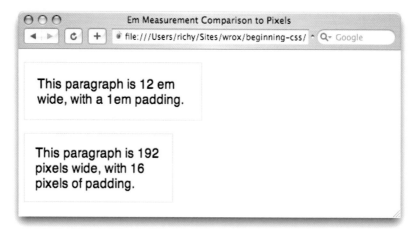

Figure 2-19

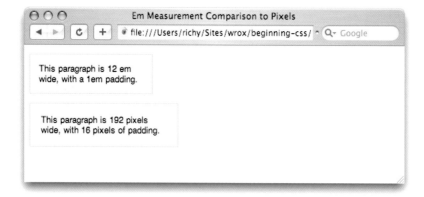

Figure 2-20

In Figure 2-20, the opposite of what you observed in Figure 2-19 has happened; the top paragraph is now smaller than the paragraph with a 192-pixel width. Em measurement lets you layout a web page with the font size preferences of the end user in mind, which in turn makes your website more accessible to people with visual disabilities. Again, IE 7 and Opera do not display the effect the same as shown in Figure 2-20, since they scale all content, which many would argue is much better than having designers trying to design scalable websites with features like the em unit. The IE 7 and Opera approach takes designers out of the equation and puts users in charge, which is much better for accessibility.

Like the em unit, the ex unit is based on font size, but unlike the em unit, the ex unit is based on the height of the lowercase letter "x."

Measurements Based on the Height of the Lowercase Letter x

The *ex* measurement, also known as *x-height*, is (like the em) based on the font size. However, the ex measurement is relative to the height of the lowercase letter *x*. The ex measurement is another unit of measurement derived from typography.

Like measurement in inches, the ex measurement is unreliable, but for different reasons. Because it is difficult to determine the actual height of the lowercase letter *x* for a given font, most browser creators take a shortcut in implementing the ex measurement. Instead of relying on the height of the lowercase letter *x*, ex measurement is defined by taking the measurement of half of 1em, or 0.5em. Because of its inconsistencies, ex measurement is yet another unit of measure to be avoided when designing for display on a computer monitor.

Pixel Measurements

As you may have guessed from the discussion in this chapter about absolute measurements, pixels, the *px* measurement, are measured relative to the computer monitor's settings. This measurement depends on the resolution of the user's monitor. For instance, a 1px measurement viewed at a resolution of 800 × 600 is larger than a 1px measurement viewed at a resolution of 1024 × 768.

Pixels are easiest to understand when they specify the width and height of an image because most images are created based on the number of pixels they contain. This type of image is known as a *bitmap* image. Examples of bitmap images are the J-PEG, GIF, and PNG image formats. These image formats store information about an image by the pixel, and those are mapped together to create the image that you see. To illustrate my point, Figure 2-21 is a screenshot of Safari's window controls from the upper left-hand corner of Figure 2-20 while zoomed to the maximum of 1600% in Photoshop. At this level of detail the pixels are clearly visible as individual squares, and it becomes easier to imagine what a pixel is, since you're actually seeing them.

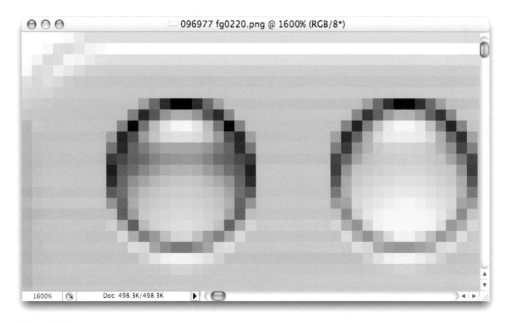

Figure 2-21

Keeping the image portrayed in Figure 2-21 in mind, when you measure in pixels with CSS, the individual pixels are as wide as the squares you see in Figure 2-21, which can be larger or smaller depending on the screen resolution setting of your monitor.

Pixel measurements have some advantages and disadvantages. Pixel measurements use the actual pixels on your computer monitor. Although that is often fine for screen display, it is not as precise when it comes to printing documents. The size of a pixel can change depending on many factors, among which are monitor size and resolution and the fine-tuning settings that stretch and shrink the display output. Therefore, defining a pixel measurement for print leaves lots of room for browser inconsistencies. How big is a pixel in the real world? It simply isn't a constant measurement for physical length the same way that centimeters are. This is an area best suited for the absolute units that I discussed earlier in the chapter. I discuss this issue further in Chapter 13, "Styling for Print."

> Use the right tool for the job! Pixels should be used for measurements where a user's font size preference won't be a factor, and where a real-world, absolute length wouldn't be superior, such as for print. An example of a good place to use pixels would be for the width of a border around a box.

The last type of relative measurement that CSS has to offer is percentage measurement.

Percentage Measurements

Percentage measurements are always dependent on something else; therefore, percentage measurements are also a form of relative measurement. The behavior of a percentage measurement changes depending on the element to which the measurement is being applied. Try applying a percentage width yourself.

Try It Out   Experimenting with Percentage Measurement

Example 2-7. To see how percentage measurement works, follow these steps.

1.   Enter the following markup into your text editor.

```
<!DOCTYPE html PUBLIC "-//W3C//DTD XHTML 1.0 Strict//EN"
"http://www.w3.org/TR/xhtml1/DTD/xhtml1-strict.dtd">
<html xmlns='http://www.w3.org/1999/xhtml' xml:lang='en'>
    <head>
        <meta http-equiv='Content-Type' content='text/html; charset=UTF-8' />
        <title>Experimenting with Percentage Measurement</title>
        <style type='text/css'>
            div {
                width: 100%;
                background: black;
                color: white;
            }
        </style>
    </head>
    <body>
        <div>What happens when I apply a 100% width?</div>
    </body>
</html>
```

2. Save the document as `Example_2-7.html`, and load it up into your favorite browser. When you load Example 2-7 into a browser, you should see something like Figure 2-22.

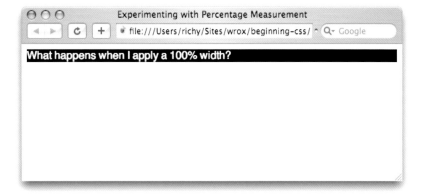

Figure 2-22

How It Works

Percentage measurement works differently depending on what property it is applied to; you'll continue to see examples of this throughout this book. In Example 2-7, you applied the declaration `width: 100%;` to the `<div>` element, and when loaded into a browser you see that the `<div>` element expands for the whole width of the window. If you've been paying attention, you might have noted that this result is identical to the one you observed for Example 2-3, earlier in this chapter. Yes, when applied this way, the `width: auto;` declaration and the `width: 100%;` declaration produce identical results; however, there are fundamental differences between these two completely different methods of specifying width. The percentage method used here calculates the width of the `<div>` element based on its parent element. In this case, the parent element is the `<body>` element, and the width of the `<div>` is set to 100% of the width of the `<body>` element, no ifs, ands, or buts. Although you may not see why auto width is different at this point, it is, and that is a topic that is much too big to get into right now. You learn more about the differences between auto width and percentage width in Chapter 7, "The Box Model."

Because it's a presentational language, most of CSS is affected in some way by length and units of measurement. The fundamental unit for all measurements when you design for display on a computer monitor is the pixel, because computers display images in pixels. You can define lengths relative to font sizes, using em units as the most practical and consistent solution. Absolute lengths, on the other hand, are better suited for print because of the multitude of inconsistencies that occur when absolutes are used for presentations on a computer monitor. In the next section, I continue the discussion of CSS property values with a look at how CSS interprets numbers.

Numbers

CSS allows numbers as values for several properties. Two types of numbers are accepted by CSS: *integers* and *real numbers.* Like strings, integers and real numbers are data types and are often used in CSS for the measurement of length. The first type, integer, is expected to be exclusively a whole number, meaning no decimals are allowed.

Integers

In CSS, an integer may be preceded by a plus (+) or minus (-) to indicate the sign. Although some properties do not accept negative values, many do. As you can see in the following example, one property that allows negative values is the margin property.

Setting a Negative Margin

Example 2-8. To see what happens when the margin property has a negative value, follow these steps.

1.   Enter the following markup:

```
<!DOCTYPE html PUBLIC "-//W3C//DTD XHTML 1.0 Strict//EN"
"http://www.w3.org/TR/xhtml1/DTD/xhtml1-strict.dtd">
<html xmlns='http://www.w3.org/1999/xhtml' xml:lang='en'>
    <head>
        <meta http-equiv='Content-Type' content='text/html; charset=UTF-8' />
        <title>Setting a Negative Margin</title>
        <style type='text/css'>
            div {
                background: black;
                color: white;
                margin: -10px 0 0 -15px;
                font: 12px sans-serif;
            }
        </style>
    </head>
    <body>
        <div>What happens when I apply a negative margin?</div>
    </body>
</html>
```

2.   Save the markup that you entered as `Example_2-8.html`, and load it into your favorite browser. You should see something like what you see in Figure 2-23.

Figure 2-23

How It Works

From Figure 2-23, you can see that the position of the `<div>` element has been altered by the addition of the negative margin. It has been moved a little off-screen on the left and just a tad off-screen on the top. This is one example of how you can use an integer in CSS. You learn more about how the margin property works in Chapter 7, "The Box Model."

Real Numbers

Real numbers can have a decimal value, and decimal values increase the precision of measurements in CSS. As was the case for integers, real numbers in CSS can also be preceded by plus (+) or minus (–) to indicate the number's sign. The value 1.2em, for example, means 1.2 times the font size. As in mathematics, a positive sign is assumed if no sign is present. If I have a declaration that says `margin-left: -1.2em;`, this causes an element to shift to the left 1.2 times the font size.

CSS provides some basic and reasonable rules for the specification of integers and real numbers in property values. CSS is also very flexible with how colors are specified, a topic I discuss in the following section.

Colors

CSS has a number of options for specifying colors, ranging from a 216-color, web-safe palette to the full range of colors available in the RGB format, a total of 16,777,216 colors! More specifically, those options are as follows:

- ❑ **Color keywords:** These enable you to specify a color by its name.
- ❑ **RGB values:** These enable you to specify a color via a Red, Green, Blue representation, which provides access to millions of colors.
- ❑ **RGB Percentage:** This option is the same as RGB but uses percentages.
- ❑ **RGBA (RGB with Alpha channel [available in CSS 3]):** The RGB palette is used with the addition of an alpha channel to specify transparency.
- ❑ **Hexadecimal:** This enables you to specify a color by a special hexadecimal number.
- ❑ **Shorthand Hexadecimal:** This is a shortened representation of hexadecimal numbers; it is limited to a special 216-color, web-safe palette.

Each method is a means of accomplishing the same thing: specifying a color. You can use these methods to specify text color, border color, or background color. Next, you see what each of these methods looks like when used in the context of a style sheet rule.

Color Keywords

The first method for specifying color, mentioned previously, is to use a color keyword. This is the most intuitive method because all you need to do is reference the name of the color itself. Here are some examples:

```
div {
    color: black;
    background-color: red;
    border: thin solid orange;
}
```

This rule applies to any <div> element contained in the document. I have specified that each <div> element should have black text, a red background, and a thin, solid orange border around the element. In this example, black, red, and orange are color keywords, so a color keyword is simply the name of the color.

In CSS 3, 147 colors are named. Browser support for these colors is very good. I have found only a single color not supported by IE 6. That color is lightgray, spelled with an *a*; however, the browser does support lightgrey, spelled with an *e*. This is an obscure bug that arises because Internet Explorer allows only the British spelling of *grey* and not the American English *gray*. The CSS specification supports both spellings of gray. Firefox, Opera, and Safari support all 147 named colors.

A complete table of CSS-supported color keywords is available in Appendix C.

RGB Colors

RGB stands for Red, Green, and Blue. These are the primary colors used to display the color of pixels on a computer monitor. When you use these three colors in various combinations, it is possible to create every color of the rainbow. This is done through different colored lights either overlapping each other or appearing side by side in different intensities to display color. RGB is also known as *luminous* or *additive* color. Luminous means that RGB uses light in varying intensities to create color, and additive means colors are added to one another to produce the colors of the spectrum. Many computer monitors are capable of displaying millions of colors: 16,777,216 colors, in fact. CSS RGB color is specified using a special three-number syntax, with each one representing a color channel. This first number is red, the second green, and the third blue:

```
body {
    background-color: rgb(128, 128, 128);
}
```

This produces the same color as the CSS color keyword gray. Equal amounts of all three channels form a variation of gray, where 0, 0, 0 is black and 255, 255, 255 is white.

Here's another example:

```
body {
    background-color: rgb(135, 206, 235);
}
```

This produces the same color as the CSS color keyword skyblue. The number 135 refers to the red channel, 206 to the green channel, and 235 to the blue channel. RGB values may also be represented using percentages:

```
body {
    background-color: rgb(50%, 50%, 50%);
}
```

This also produces the same color as the CSS color keyword gray.

CSS 3 is to introduce one more variation on the RGB scheme, with RGBA. This specification includes an alpha channel, which is used to make an element transparent. The alpha channel of RGBA is specified in the same manner as regular RGB with the A indicating how transparent the color is, with 0 being fully opaque, and 255 being fully transparent. No browser supports the RGBA specification yet.

RGB color is also often specified in hexadecimal format.

Hexadecimal Colors

Hexadecimal colors have been around nearly as long as the World Wide Web has been. *Hexadecimal* refers to a numbering scheme that uses 16 characters as its base, expressed in a combination of letters and numbers. The decimal numbering system, on the other hand, uses 10 numbers as its base. A hexadecimal system uses 0-9 for the first 10 digits and A-F to represent the remaining 6 digits. Letter *A* corresponds to the number 10, *B* to 11, *C* to 12, and so on up to 15, which is represented by *F*. Hexadecimal values are another way of expressing an RGB value. For instance, #FFFFFF refers to white, which is expressed in RGB as 255, 255, 255. To switch from RGB values to hexadecimal, each channel is converted to its hexadecimal equivalent, so each 255 becomes FF in hexadecimal. To calculate the hexadecimal value, divide the RGB number by 16. The result is the first hexadecimal digit. The remainder from the division becomes the second hexadecimal digit. The RGB value 255 divided by 16 equals 15 with a remainder of 15. In hexadecimal, the number "15" is represented by "F", so applying this formula results in FF. The process is repeated for each RGB color channel, so the hexadecimal notation of 255, 255, 255 is FF, FF, FF or #FFFFFF. In CSS, hexadecimal colors are included just as RGB or color keywords are, as shown in the following example.

```
div {
    color: #000000;
    background-color: #FF0000;
    border: thin solid #FFA500;
}
```

#000000 is the hexadecimal representation of black; the same as RGB 0, 0, 0 or simply the `black` color keyword. #FF0000 is a hexadecimal representation of red, or RGB 255, 0, 0, or the `red` color keyword. Finally, #FFA500 is a hexadecimal representation of orange, or RGB 255, 165, 0, or the `orange` color keyword.

Short Hexadecimal and Web-Safe Colors

There are 216 web-safe colors. A *web-safe color* is a hexadecimal color comprised of any combination of the following: FF, CC, 99, 66, 33, 00, for a potential of 216 colors. These colors were originally identified and given their web-safe name by Lynda Weinman, a graphic and web design guru and author of numerous graphic and web design books. These 216 colors were identified as colors safe for cross-platform, cross-browser use on computer systems capable of displaying only 256 colors; in other words, 8-bit systems. There are 216 colors, minus 40 colors reserved for use by operating systems. Different operating systems, such as Macintosh OS and Windows OS, do not reserve the same 40 colors, so these 40 colors cannot be relied upon. If you attempt to use a color outside of the 216-color palette on a system capable of displaying only 256 colors, the operating system may attempt to display the color through a process called dithering. *Dithering* is a process in which the operating system attempts to mix two colors that it is capable of displaying to get the requested color. While today the majority of computers are comfortably able to display millions of colors, there is still one audience that is using devices that aren't capable of displaying that many colors, and that is people using cell phones and other small screen devices to access the web.

Figure 2-24 shows a normal image.

Figure 2-25 shows the dithered image.

Figure 2-24

Figure 2-25

If you look at these two figures together, you should be able to see the effects of dithering. The image in Figure 2-26 is pixelated and grainy; the image in Figure 2-25 is smooth and fluid.

Dithering causes all sorts of nasty things to happen to an image or solid color. In some cases a grid appears on a solid background where the operating system attempts to display the color using two colors.

Hexadecimal notation is capable of expressing all 16,777,216 colors allowed by RGB. If a color outside the web-safe palette is used, this leads to dithering. Short hexadecimal notation, on the other hand, allows only the 216-color, web-safe palette:

```
div {
    color: #000;
    background-color: #F00;
    border: thin solid #FFA500;
}
```

Only FF, CC, 99, 66, 33, and 00 are allowable in the web-safe palette, so the notation for these can be simplified. FF becomes simply F, CC becomes C, 99 becomes 9, and so on. A single digit rather than two represents the pair. So in this example, #000 refers to black and #F00 refers to red. #FFA500 is not representable in short hexadecimal notation because A5 cannot be simplified to a single digit. Only pairs in which both numbers have the same value can be converted to short hexadecimal notation.

Although in the past the web-safe pallet was frequently necessary for designers, today advanced graphic cards capable of displaying millions of colors have become so common that the number of 8-bit systems capable of displaying only 256 colors has fallen dramatically. Today, it is safer to design creatively with color. The browser-safe pallet is not yet completely dead — it still has a place in designing web content for display on PDAs and cell phones, most of which are limited to 256 colors.

The URI

CSS uses a special term — URI (Universal Resource Indicator) — when the location of a resource or data file must be specified. The acronym *URI* is related to two other acronyms, URL (Universal Resource Locator), and URN (Universal Resource Name). The ideas behind both of these specifications are combined to get the URI, the term used in the W3C CSS specifications. URIs are most used in CSS for two purposes:

❏ The inclusion of style sheets

❏ The inclusion of background images

The URI is referenced using a special method, as shown in the following example:

```
background: url(mypicture.jpg);
```

The url() syntax is used to enclose the URI of the file being referenced. In this example, *mypicture.jpg* must exist in the same directory as the style sheet. If the style sheet is named *mystyle.css* and it's located at http://www.example.com/styles/mystyle.css, the *mypicture.jpg* file must also exist in the *styles* directory, where its path is http://www.example.com/styles/mypicture.jpg. The complete, absolute path or the shortened relative paths are both acceptable references to the file. I address this topic again in Chapter 10, "Backgrounds," where I discuss the background property and the syntax it allows.

Including CSS in a Document

CSS is very flexible regarding how you call it in a document. You can include CSS in a document in four ways:

❑ CSS can be included in a document by using embedded style sheets, which are included between `<style>` and `</style>` tags directly in an HTML document, as demonstrated in Figure 2-26. These tags must appear between the `<head>` and `</head>` tags.

```
<!DOCTYPE html PUBLIC "-//W3C//DTD XHTML 1.0 Strict//EN"
                      "http://www.w3.org/TR/xhtml1/DTD/xhtml1-strict.dtd">
<html xmlns='http://www.w3.org/1999/xhtml' xml:lang='en'>
    <head>
        <meta http-equiv='Content-Type' content='text/html; charset=UTF-8' />
        <title>Selectors and Grouping</title>
        <style type='text/css'>
            h1, h2, h3, h4, h5, h6 {
                font-family: sans-serif;
                color: maroon;
                border-bottom: 1px solid rgb(200, 200, 200);
            }
        </style>
    </head>
    <body>
        <h1>Style Sheet</h1>
        <h2>Rule</h2>
        <h3>Selector</h3>
        <h4>Declaration</h4>
        <h5>Property</h5>
        <h6>Value</h6>
    </body>
</html>
```

Embedded style sheets appear between the `<style>` and `</style>` tags, and must appear between the `<head>` and `</head>` tags.

Figure 2-26

❑ CSS can be included in its own document and linked to an HTML document by using the `<link>` element, shown in Figure 2-27.

```
<!DOCTYPE html PUBLIC "-//W3C//DTD XHTML 1.0 Strict//EN"
                      "http://www.w3.org/TR/xhtml1/DTD/xhtml1-strict.dtd">
<html xmlns='http://www.w3.org/1999/xhtml' xml:lang='en'>
    <head>
        <meta http-equiv='Content-Type' content='text/html; charset=UTF-8' />
        <title>Selectors and Grouping</title>
        <link rel='stylesheet' type='text/css' href='stylesheet.css' />
    </head>
    <body>
        <h1>Style Sheet</h1>
        <h2>Rule</h2>
        <h3>Selector</h3>
        <h4>Declaration</h4>
        <h5>Property</h5>
        <h6>Value</h6>
    </body>
</html>
```

External style sheets are included via the `<link>` element. Like embedded style sheets, the type, text/css, is also required. The rel attribute, or relationship attribute must be stylesheet, and the path to the CSS file is included in the href attribute.

Figure 2-27

❑ CSS can be imported from within another style sheet by using an @import rule, as shown in Figure 2-28.

```
@import('/path/to/stylesheet.css');

h1, h2, h3, h4, h5, h6 {
    font-family: sans-serif;
    color: maroon;
    border-bottom: 1px solid rgb(200, 200, 200);
}
```

@import rules are used to include a stylesheet from within a stylesheet. @import rules must appear first at the top of a style sheet, before other style sheet rules.

Figure 2-28

❑ CSS can be included directly in an element in an HTML document by using inline styles with the style attribute, as shown in Figure 2-29.

```
<h4 style='font-family: sans-serif; color: maroon;'>Heading</h4>
```

Inline styles are applied directly to an element using the style attribute. Only declarations may appear as the attribute's value.

Figure 2-29

Each method has its own particular usefulness. The upcoming sections describe how you can use each of these methods to include CSS in an HTML document.

Including an Embedded Style Sheet

You use the <style></style> tag set to include embedded style sheets directly in the document. You can include HTML comment tags if you want to hide style sheet rules from non-equipped browsers. Since HTML's early days, HTML has supported the capability of adding comment text to a document. Comment text gives the web author the ability to add notes to a project so he can recall why he did something in a certain way or to mark the sections of a document. In HTML, you add a comment by typing a left angle bracket, an exclamation mark, two dashes, at least one space, and then the comment text itself. You close the comment by typing at least one space, two more dashes, and the right angle bracket. Here's what a comment looks like:

```
<!-- Hi. I'm comment text. -->
```

In the context of an embedded style sheet, comments have a special meaning. Because they appear inside the <style></style> tags, they tell browsers that don't support CSS to ignore the text that appears between them. Modern CSS-equipped browsers, on the other hand, read the sequence of <style>, followed by <!--, and know that style sheet rules appear there. This allows CSS to be hidden from browsers that are incapable of interpreting it. The following snippet shows how you can use comment tags to hide CSS from older browsers:

```
<style type='text/css'>
    <!--
```

```
            body, td {
                color: blue;
            }
        -->
    </style>
```

Older browsers simply ignore any CSS rules defined inside the HTML comments.

For the `<style>` tag to be strictly formed XHTML syntax, a `type` attribute is required for the `<style>` tag. This is intended to tell the browser what type of syntax follows. For the purposes of CSS, the `type` attribute appears in the `<style>` tag with a value of `text/css`, as shown in the preceding block of code.

The next section describes how CSS can be written in its own document and included in an HTML or XHTML document.

Linking to External Style Sheets

The authors of CSS recognized that HTML-template creation is a common need. As such, the W3C body made recommendations that allow external style sheets to be included in a document from within HTML or XHTML by use of the `<link>` element or from within a style sheet itself using the `@import` rule. External style sheets are the preferred method of CSS inclusion in a web document. External style sheets can be cached by the user's browser. This frees the user, who no longer needs to download the web page or website's style sheet on every page request. This also ensures that documents load very quickly, which is another feature of CSS that conserves expensive bandwidth.

Here's a demonstration of the `<link>` element method:

```
<link rel='stylesheet' href='/path/to/stylesheet.css' type='text/css' />
```

The following attributes are required to use the `<link>` element for linking to a CSS document:

- ❑ `rel`: Defines the relation between the external document and the calling document. In this case, the relation is that the external document is the style sheet for the calling document.

- ❑ `href`: Like the anchor tag, `<a>`, `href` stands for hyperlink reference. It accepts an absolute or relative path to the style sheet document.

- ❑ `type`: Refers to the MIME type of the external file.

An *absolute* path means the complete path to the file. For instance, `http://www.example.com` is an absolute path. A *relative* path triggers the application to find the document relative to the requesting document. So if the example file's URL is `http://www.example.com/example.html` and the CSS document is stored in the *stylesheets* directory as *stylesheet.css*, the relative path included in `<link>` is stylesheets/ `stylesheet.css` and the absolute path to the document is `http://www.example.com/stylesheets/` `stylesheet.css` or `/stylesheets/stylesheet.css`.

A style sheet is really easy to set up, and I discuss this in the next section.

How to Structure an External CSS Document

External style sheets are essentially the same thing as embedded style sheets; the key difference is that no markup exists in a CSS file. When you create an external, independent CSS document, it must be created using the `.css` file extension.

An external CSS document may contain nothing but CSS rules or comments. A CSS document cannot contain any markup; see how this is done in the following Try It Out.

Try It Out   **Linking to an External Style Sheet**

Example 2-9. To link to an external style sheet, follow these steps.

1. Enter the following XHTML document:

```
<!DOCTYPE html PUBLIC "-//W3C//DTD XHTML 1.0 Strict//EN"
                      "http://www.w3.org/TR/xhtml1/DTD/xhtml1-strict.dtd">
<html xmlns='http://www.w3.org/1999/xhtml' xml:lang='en'>
    <head>
        <meta http-equiv='Content-Type' content='text/html; charset=UTF-8' />
        <title>Selectors and Grouping</title>
        <link rel='stylesheet' type='text/css' href='stylesheet.css' />
    </head>
    <body>
        <h1>Style Sheet</h1>
        <h2>Rule</h2>
        <h3>Selector</h3>
        <h4>Declaration</h4>
        <h5>Property</h5>
        <h6>Value</h6>
    </body>
</html>
```

2. Save the XHTML document as `Example_2-9.html`.

3. In a new document, enter the following CSS:

```
h1, h2, h3, h4, h5, h6 {
    font-family: sans-serif;
    color: maroon;
    border-bottom: 1px solid rgb(200, 200, 200);
}
```

4. Save the CSS as `stylesheet.css` in the same folder that `Example_2-9.html` was saved in.

5. Load up the document in a browser. You should see output that looks like Figure 2-6.

How It Works

The embedded style sheet between the `<style>`... `</style>` tags has been replaced with an external style sheet by placing the rules inside the embedded style sheet into their own document, saving that document with a `.css` file extension, and then linking to the new file by including the `<link>` element in the XHTML document. One of the benefits of an external style sheet is that it allows the same style rules to be applied to as many documents as the author wishes. This is one of the key benefits of CSS-based design. An external style sheet offers flexibility to the author that saves both time and resources.

Importing Style Sheets

You can also link to an external style sheet by using the @import rule. Here's a demonstration:

```
<style type='text/css'>
    @import url(path/to/cssdoc.css);
</style>
```

This example uses the `<style></style>` method but includes the @import notation. It's very straightforward: Plug in the @import rule followed by the `url()`, which may contain an absolute or relative path.

The @import method is not supported by older browsers, and it is sometimes used as a hack to hide styles from browsers that would crash horribly if these styles were present. One such browser is Netscape Navigator 4, which has horrible CSS support and has been known to lock up when certain styles are present.

The next section describes how styles can be included inline, directly on elements, by using the `style` attribute.

Inline Styles

The last method for including CSS in a document is from within the XHTML elements themselves. Sometimes it doesn't make sense to clutter your external or embedded style sheets with a rule that will be used on only one element in one document. This is where the `style=""` attribute comes into play; it's demonstrated by the following markup:

```
<table style="border: 1px solid black; margin: auto;">
    <tr>
        <td style="text-align: right; font-size: 18pt;">
            Some text aligned left.
        </td>
    </tr>
</table>
```

This method allows for the text to be formatted from within the document and may be applied to any rendered element.

The following Try It Out demonstrates how the `style` attribute is used to add styles directly to the elements of a web document.

Try It Out   Including CSS Using the style Attribute

Example 2-10. To use the `style` attribute to apply styles directly to the elements of a document, follow these steps.

1.   Return to your text editor and enter the following XHTML:

```
<!DOCTYPE html PUBLIC "-//W3C//DTD XHTML 1.0 Strict//EN"
                  "http://www.w3.org/TR/xhtml1/DTD/xhtml1-strict.dtd">
<html xmlns='http://www.w3.org/1999/xhtml' xml:lang='en'>
    <head>
        <meta http-equiv='Content-Type' content='text/html; charset=UTF-8' />
        <title>Selectors and Grouping</title>
        <link rel='stylesheet' type='text/css' href='stylesheet.css' />
    </head>
    <body style='font-family: sans-serif; color: maroon;'>
        <h1 style='border-bottom: 1px solid rgb(200, 200, 200);'>
            Style Sheet
        </h1>
        <h2 style='border-bottom: 1px solid rgb(200, 200, 200);'>
            Rule
        </h2>
        <h3 style='border-bottom: 1px solid rgb(200, 200, 200);'>
            Selector
        </h3>
        <h4 style='border-bottom: 1px solid rgb(200, 200, 200);'>
            Declaration
        </h4>
        <h5 style='border-bottom: 1px solid rgb(200, 200, 200);'>
            Property
        </h5>
        <h6 style='border-bottom: 1px solid rgb(200, 200, 200);'>
            Value
        </h6>
    </body>
</html>
```

2.   Save the preceding document as `Example_2-10.html`

3.   Load up Example 2-10 in your favorite browser. You should see output like that in Figure 2-6.

How It Works

Note that the output is identical to output of the earlier example shown in Figure 2-6. The `style` attribute allows CSS declarations to be included directly in the XHTML element. The `style` attribute, however, is not as dynamic as a style sheet. It gives you no way to group repetitive rules or declarations. The `style` attribute should only be used when a more efficient method is not available (if, for example, the element to be styled does not appear on multiple pages).

Summary

Throughout this chapter you learned about the bits and pieces that make CSS work. You learned the following:

❑   Style sheets are made up of rules.

❑   Rules are made up of selectors and declarations.

- ❏ Declarations are made up of properties and values.

- ❏ Values can be keywords, lengths, colors, strings, integers, real numbers, or URIs.

- ❏ The em measurement is better for onscreen layout. Absolute units such as inches and centimeters are better for print layout. The pixel unit should be used where the user's font size preference won't be a factor.

- ❏ Dithering is a method of mixing known colors to simulate an unknown one.

- ❏ RGB is additive color. The colors red, green, and blue are added to each other in varying intensities to produce every color on the rainbow.

- ❏ Hexadecimal color is just another way of expressing RGB color.

- ❏ Short hexadecimal is a way of expressing web-safe colors.

- ❏ The URI is used to include style sheets and background images (external documents) in CSS.

- ❏ Style sheets can be embedded directly in an HTML document with the `<style>` element.

- ❏ A style sheet can appear in its own document, and linked to from an HTML document using the `<link>` element, or linked from a style sheet using the `@import` rule.

- ❏ Styles can be included inline, directly in an HTML element using the `style` attribute.

Chapter 3 continues the discussion with selectors.

Exercises

1. Style sheets are made of what?

2. What's the difference between when `width: auto;` is applied to a `<table>` as opposed to a `<div>` element?

3. Complete the sequence: Declaration, Property, _____

4. Convert the color RGB(234, 123, 45) to hexadecimal.

5. What is the shortened hexadecimal notation of #FFFFFF?

6. When does dithering occur?

7. If I have a style sheet located at `http://www.example.com/stylesheet.css`, and a web page located at `http://www.example.com/index.html`, what markup would I include in index.html to include `stylesheet.css` via a relative path?

Selectors

In this chapter, you learn about the different types of selectors that CSS supports. In Chapter 2, you learned about the type selector, which is a selector that applies style sheet declarations by using the HTML element's name. "Selectors" is an area of CSS that I discuss that has spotty support with regards to IE 6. To those ends, as I introduce each section, if a selector is not supported by IE 6, I note that. IE 7 features much better selector support, and in fact supports nearly all of the selectors discussed in this chapter, but there are a few selectors that IE 7 doesn't support. This is also noted where appropriate. Other browsers such as Mozilla Firefox, Safari, and Opera all have excellent support for the selectors discussed in this chapter. With each example, I note what browser you should use to view the example, and which browsers the example won't work with.

You may wonder why I bother discussing selectors that don't work in IE 6. I chose to include the selectors with at least some browser support, because each reader's needs and development requirements are different. If you are, for instance, developing a corporate intranet-based application in which you have full control over the browser the end user is using, your needs are different from someone who is developing a publicly-accessible Internet website. Someone developing a corporate intranet site can, for instance, choose Mozilla Firefox as their development platform, rather than IE 6, or that corporation may choose to upgrade to IE 7. In short, not everyone has the same end-user requirements for browser usage, and this book is written with that in mind.

You can also use JavaScript applications that enable a greater spectrum of CSS support in IE 6. *JavaScript* is a programming language that you can use to create scripts that are included in an HTML document in much the same way as CSS. JavaScript opens up possibilities that HTML and CSS alone aren't capable of. Using JavaScript technology, you can give IE 6 CSS capabilities that are impossible without it. When you use JavaScript, most of the very same examples that you encounter in this chapter that don't work in IE 6, can work in IE 6 flawlessly and reliably, and without the end user having to upgrade IE 6 or take any other action. I discuss how you, too, can harness this incredibly useful, and seemingly magical, technology in Chapter 16, available at www.wrox.com/go/beginning_css2e. The best part is, you need no experience programming JavaScript to use the technology that I present in Chapter 15. So, if you feel discouraged by IE 6's lack of support for many of these useful selectors, continue on; there are hackadelic methods yet to be discussed.

You may also wish to see more practical applications of the features presented in this chapter. If that is the case, I provide some real-world projects at the end of this book that help you to put CSS into a real-world context. As is the case throughout this book, I present all the bits and pieces of the language with proof-of-concept examples, and then later in the book you see how to put it all together with some real, skill-building projects. Alternatively, you may also be interested in my book *CSS Instant Results* (Wrox, 2006), an intermediate-level CSS book that focuses on real-world projects exclusively.

I begin the discussion of selectors with the most common and widely supported selectors, class and id selectors.

Class and ID Selectors

Class and id selectors are the most widely supported selectors. In fact, they are as widely supported as the type selector introduced in Chapter 2. There are two types of selectors. The class attribute is more generic, meaning it may encompass many elements in a given document, even elements of different types or purposes. On the other hand, you can use the id attribute only once per document. The name id tells you that the id must be unique. Besides using it in CSS, you can also use an element's id to access it via a scripting language like JavaScript. You can also link to the location of the element with an id name using anchors. Anchors are appended to URLs to force a browser to go to a specific place in a document. So the id attribute serves more than one purpose. Think of it as an element's address inside a document — no two addresses can be the same. The discussion continues with class selectors.

Class Selectors

Figure 3-1 is an example of a class name selector.

```
.planet {
    position: absolute;
    top: 0;
    left: 0;
    bottom: 15px;
}
```

A dot begins a class name selector in the style sheet. The class name is a name that you make up. The class name is typically only comprised of letters, numbers, or hyphens.

Figure 3-1

The class name selector begins with a dot, followed by the class name itself, which you choose. Typically, the class name is comprised of letters, numbers, and hyphens only, since this provides the best compatibility with older browsers. Class names also cannot include spaces. In Figure 3-2, you see the element that the class name planet applies style to in the HTML document.

```
<div class='planet'>
    <img src='images/jupiter.png' alt='Jupiter' />
</div>
```

The class name is included in the HTML
document using the class attribute.

Figure 3-2

The dot appearing before the class name in the CSS rule tells CSS that you are referencing a class selector. The dot does not need to appear in the class attribute value itself; in fact it cannot, because the value of the class attribute is just the class name itself.

When used in this context, the type of element doesn't matter. In other words, you can also apply the class to other elements, as is illustrated in Figure 3-3.

```
<div class='planet'>
    <img src='images/jupiter.png' alt='Jupiter' class='planet' />
</div>
```

Class names don't have to be specific to a type of
element. The <div> element and the <img> element
can both have a class name of *planet*, if desired.

Figure 3-3

The same rule applies to the <img> element as applies to the <div> element. Both now have an absolute position, offset from the top zero pixels, offset from the left of zero pixels, and offset from the bottom of 15 pixels. What if you wanted to give both the <div> and <img> element the same class name, but have a style sheet rule that applies to <div> elements, but not <img> elements? You can do that, too. Limiting a class selector to a type of element is demonstrated in Figure 3-4.

Append a class selector with a type selector to limit the
style sheet rule to a certain type of element.

```
div.planet {
    position: absolute;
    top: 0;
    left: 0;
    bottom: 15px;
}
```

Figure 3-4

In Figure 3-4, you see the combination of two types of selectors that you are already familiar with, the type selector from Chapter 2, and the class selector. When you append a type selector to a class selector, you limit the scope of the style sheet rule to only that type of element. In Figure 3-4, the rule is limited so that it only applies to <div> elements, causing it to no longer apply to <img> elements, or any other type of element for that matter. You can still create additional rules that reference other elements, such as a new rule that only applies to <img /> elements with a class name of *planet*, such as img.planet, but the rule that you see in Figure 3-4 applies exclusively to <div> elements with a class name of *planet*.

Elements can also be assigned more than one class name. Figure 3-5 shows an example of this.

```
<div class='planet jupiter'>
    <img src='images/jupiter.png' alt='Jupiter' class='planet' />
</div>
```

Multiple class names can be applied to a single element.
Each class name must be separated by a single space.

Figure 3-5

The value of this `class` attribute actually contains two class names: `planet` and `jupiter`. Each class name in the attribute is separated by a space. In the corresponding style sheet, the two classes may be referenced by two separate rules, as illustrated in Figure 3-6.

```
div.planet {
    position: absolute;
    top: 0;
    bottom: 15px;
}
div.jupiter {
    left: 0;
}
```

The `<div>` with both `planet` and `jupiter` class names can be referenced by two separate rules.

Figure 3-6

The two style sheet rules in Figure 3-6 result in the `<div>` element with both `planet` and `jupiter` class names receiving the declarations of both rules.

The class names may also be chained together in the style sheet, as shown in Figure 3-7.

```
div.planet.jupiter {
    left: 0;
}
```

Class names can be chained to one another to reference an element that has multiple class name values.

Figure 3-7

The preceding rule applies only to elements that reference both class names in their `class` attribute.

IE 6 interprets chained class names per the CSS 1 specification, which did not allow chained class names in the style sheet. In IE 6, only the last class name in the chain is recognized. In the preceding example, IE 6 would interpret the `.planet.jupiter` selector as `.jupiter` only. This has been fixed in IE 7.

Whereas classes are meant to reference more than one element, ids are meant to reference only one element in a document.

ID Selectors

id selectors are unique identifiers; an id is meant to be unique, defined once per document. Like class selectors discussed in the previous section, a special character precedes id selectors in a style sheet. To reference an id, you precede the id name with a hash mark (or pound sign, #). Like class names, this name cannot contain spaces. You should use names that only include letters, numbers, and spaces for compatibility with the older browsers. You see how this is done in Figure 3-8.

```
#jupiter {
    left: 0;
}
```
An id selector begins with a hash mark (or, if you prefer, the pound sign "#"), then, like the class selector, the hash mark is followed by the id name of the element.

Figure 3-8

Since there's only one Jupiter in the solar system, Jupiter lends itself as a good example of the concept of an id selector. Just as there is only one Jupiter in the solar system, the id name jupiter can be used only once in a document, on one element.

Browsers are forgiving of multiple id names per document as far as style sheets are concerned. However, using an id name more than once in a document can cause conflicts with other applications of unique id names. For example, id names can be used to link to a location within a document (as HTML anchors), or when referencing an element by id name from JavaScript. When you have an id name appearing more than once in the HTML document, on more than one element, the browser won't know which one you're linking to, or which one you want to refer to from JavaScript, and will have to guess. It's best to just use the id name for its intended purpose, just once per document.

An id name must be unique in so far as other id names are concerned. An id name may be repeated as a class name, should you want to do so.

The element can then be defined in the document using the id attribute. This is demonstrated in Figure 3-9.

```
<div id='jupiter'>
    <img src='images/jupiter.png' alt='Jupiter' class='planet' />
</div>
```
The id name is included in the HTML document using the id attribute.

Figure 3-9

You can make both class and id selectors more specific by appending the name of the element to the beginning of the selector. For instance, if in the last examples you only want <div> elements for each rule, the selector will look like what you see in Figure 3-10.

```
div#jupiter {
    left: 0;
}
```
Like class selectors, an id selector can be prepended with a type selector to make the selector apply only to a certain type of element.

Figure 3-10

Now each rule is applied only to `<div>` elements that contain the corresponding class and id names. You may wonder why this is useful for an id selector, since an `id` element has to be unique in a document. Appending the selector with the type of element is useful in situations where one style sheet applies to more than one HTML document, where it's possible that you have a unique id in one of those documents that applies to for instance, an `<img />` element, but in another, separate document, that unique id name applies to a `<div>` element. Of course, it's best practice to avoid situations like that by making each element's `id` name unique, even in different documents, to avoid confusion. Sometimes, it can't be avoided. The other reason this is useful is that it makes the style sheet more intuitive and easier to follow. When you are reading a style sheet and see the id name *jupiter* but no type selector, that id can apply to any element in the document and would require you to scan the whole document from top to bottom without any other search criteria. With the type selector appended, you can narrow the search; if the element is a `<div>` element, then you know that the id selector doesn't apply to images, links, paragraphs, and so on.

Although the `id` must be unique, in these examples you can name only one element `jupiter`. The CSS style sheet, however, may contain as many references to that `id` as are necessary. The uniqueness rule only applies to naming the elements, not the references to them. You can apply classes, on the other hand, to as many elements in the body as necessary.

Now that you've had a proper introduction to the different types of things that id and class name selectors are capable of, try the following proof-of-concept exercise that lets you see how id and class selectors work.

Try It Out   **Class and ID Selectors**

Example 3-1. To see how class and id selectors work, follow these steps.

1. Enter the following markup into your text editor:

```
<!DOCTYPE html PUBLIC "-//W3C//DTD XHTML 1.0 Strict//EN"
                      "http://www.w3.org/TR/xhtml1/DTD/xhtml1-strict.dtd">
<html xmlns='http://www.w3.org/1999/xhtml' xml:lang='en'>
    <head>
        <title>Class and ID Selectors</title>
        <link rel='stylesheet' type='text/css' href='Example_3-1.css' />
    </head>
    <body>
        <p class='container'>
            A class represents something that you can have more than one of.
            You aptly name your class to reflect the type of item that you
            may or may not have more than one of.  The class name for this
            paragraph is <i>container</i>. It could very well be that you
            have many containers, or just one.
        </p>
        <p class='container box'>
            You can chain together class names within the class attribute.
            From a purely semantic standpoint, the class names may or may
            not have a relationship with each other.  Here, the class names
            are <i>container</i> and <i>box</i>. It could be said that boxes
            and containers are related, since <i>box</i> is a type of
            <i>container</i>.
```

```
            </p>
            <p class='container tank'>
                It is wise to put thought behind the naming conventions you use
                within a document.  Here, <i>tank</i> is another type of
                <i>container</i>. All containers have some properties in common.
                Dimensions, color, volume, etc.  But some containers may have
                properties that are unique to that container. Perhaps it has a
                different color, or capacity, or is intended to hold a different
                kind of material.
            </p>
            <p class='container' id='container-1234'>
                An id is used but once per document.  Semantically speaking, the
                id should be able to identify uniquely, and be descriptive.
                You may have several containers, but only one container has the id
                <i>1234</i>.  Since only one container is named <i>1234</i>, it
                becomes easier to find that container among the others.
            </p>
        </body>
    </html>
```

2.   Save the preceding document as `Example_3-1.html`.

3.   Enter the following style sheet into your text editor:

```
body {
    font-family: sans-serif;
}
p.container {
    border: 1px solid rgb(29, 179, 82);
    background: rgb(202, 222, 245);
    padding: 10px;
    width: 245px;
    height: 245px;
    float: left;
    margin: 10px;
}
p.box {
    border: 1px solid rgb(69, 199, 115);
    background: rgb(164, 201, 245);
}
p.tank {
    border: 1px solid rgb(107, 214, 145);
    background: rgb(124, 180, 245);
    clear: left;
}
p#container-1234 {
    border: 1px solid rgb(154, 232, 181);
    background: rgb(82, 157, 245);
}
```

4.   Save the preceding style sheet as `Example_3-1.css`. Figure 3-11 shows what Example 3-1 looks like when rendered in Safari. You should see something similar in Firefox, IE 6, IE 7, and Opera.

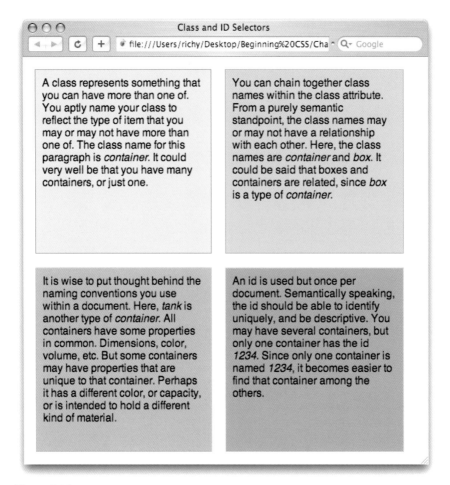

A class represents something that you can have more than one of. You aptly name your class to reflect the type of item that you may or may not have more than one of. The class name for this paragraph is *container*. It could very well be that you have many containers, or just one.

You can chain together class names within the class attribute. From a purely semantic standpoint, the class names may or may not have a relationship with each other. Here, the class names are *container* and *box*. It could be said that boxes and containers are related, since *box* is a type of *container*.

It is wise to put thought behind the naming conventions you use within a document. Here, *tank* is another type of *container*. All containers have some properties in common. Dimensions, color, volume, etc. But some containers may have properties that are unique to that container. Perhaps it has a different color, or capacity, or is intended to hold a different kind of material.

An id is used but once per document. Semantically speaking, the id should be able to identify uniquely, and be descriptive. You may have several containers, but only one container has the id *1234*. Since only one container is named *1234*, it becomes easier to find that container among the others.

Figure 3-11

How It Works

In Example 3-1, you put your newly acquired class and id selector skills to use. The following is a rule-by-rule review of the relevant `class` and `id` styles you applied in `Example_3-1.css`.

First, you created a rule that is applied to all four <p> elements, since all four <p> elements have a class name of `container`. You were able to select all four elements because each <p> element in the document has a `container` class name in the value of the `class` attribute that appears on all four <p> elements.

```
p.container {
    border: 1px solid rgb(29, 179, 82);
    background: rgb(202, 222, 245);
    padding: 10px;
    width: 245px;
```

```
        height: 245px;
        float: left;
        margin: 10px;
    }
```

Since the preceding rule applied to all four `<p>` elements, it set common properties such as dimensions using the `width`, `height`, `padding`, `border`, and `margin` properties. You learn more about these properties in Chapter 7, "The Box Model." For now, just examine how the `p.container` selector is working to select the elements, rather than the actual styling being applied.

In the next rule, you selected the next `<p>` element that also has two class names, `box` and `container`.

```
    p.box {
        border: 1px solid rgb(69, 199, 115);
        background: rgb(164, 201, 245);
    }
```

Although you could have chained the class names in the style sheet by using the selector `p.container` `.box`, you avoid doing this since there are known problems with this approach in IE 6. IE 6, on the other hand, supports just fine multiple class names in the `class` attribute. Referencing just the `box` class name allows you to select the element, too. You give the element a slightly richer shade of light blue, and a slightly lighter green border than was specified in the previous rule, which referenced all four `<p>` elements by the class name, `container`. You see that the `background` and `border` declarations set here overrode the previously set background and border declarations in the first container rule; you'll learn more about this in Chapter 4, "The Cascade and Inheritance."

In the next rule, you set properties on the `<p>` element with both the class names `container` and `tank`. Again, you gave the element an even richer light blue background (compared to the last rule, which was applied to the `<p>` element with `container` and `box` class names).

```
    p.tank {
        border: 1px solid rgb(107, 214, 145);
        background: rgb(124, 180, 245);
        clear: left;
    }
```

In the last rule, you used an id selector to select the fourth `<p>` element, which has an `id` attribute set with a value of `container-1234`. For the fourth `<p>` element, there is an even richer still light blue background, and an even lighter green border around it.

```
    p#container-1234 {
        border: 1px solid rgb(154, 232, 181);
        background: rgb(82, 157, 245);
    }
```

Now that you have worked through this simple, proof-of-concept demonstration of class and id selectors for yourself, continue to the next section, which discusses the universal, or wildcard selector.

The Universal Selector

The *universal selector* is an asterisk. When used alone, the universal selector tells the CSS interpreter to apply the CSS rule to all elements in the document. Figure 3-12 shows what a universal selector looks like.

```
* {
    border: 1px solid black;
}
```

An asterisk is a wildcard selector or *universal selector*. When included alone, all elements in the document are selected.

Figure 3-12

This rule is applied to all elements contained in the document. The universal selector applies to everything, including form input fields and tables of data. It applies style to any and every element present in a document.

Try It Out **The Universal Selector**

Example 3-2. To see how the universal selector works, follow these steps.

1. Enter the following markup into your text editor:

```
<!DOCTYPE html PUBLIC "-//W3C//DTD XHTML 1.0 Strict//EN"
                      "http://www.w3.org/TR/xhtml1/DTD/xhtml1-strict.dtd">
<html xmlns='http://www.w3.org/1999/xhtml' xml:lang='en'>
    <head>
        <title>Class and ID Selectors</title>
        <link rel='stylesheet' type='text/css' href='Example_3-2.css' />
    </head>
    <body>
        <h1>Universal Selectors</h1>
        <p>
            Universal selectors are wildcard selectors.
        </p>
        <p>
            When a universal selector is used alone, all elements
            within a document are selected.
        </p>
        <p>
            Even form elements are selected.
        </p>
        <form method='post' action='Example_3-2.html'>
            <fieldset>
                <legend>Feedback Form</legend>
                <table>
                    <tbody>
```

```
                               <tr>
                                   <td><label for='topic'>Topic:</label></td>
                                   <td><input type='text'
                                              name='topic'
                                               id='topic'
                                            value='Universal Selectors'
                                             size='25' />
                                   </td>
                               </tr>
                               <tr>
                                   <td><label for='feedback'>Feedback:</label></td>
                                   <td>
<textarea cols='55' rows='10' name='feedback' id='feedback'>
Universal selectors have some practical applications.
For instance, when debugging styles you can select
all elements and apply a border to see dimensions.
This could help you identify rogue elements causing
undue disorder in a document.
</textarea>
                                   </td>
                               </tr>
                           </tbody>
                       </table>
                   </fieldset>
               </form>
           </body>
       </html>
```

2. Save the preceding document as `Example_3-2.html` and load it into your favorite browser.

3. Enter the following CSS into a new document in your text editor.

```
body {
    font-family: sans-serif;
}
* {
    border: 1px solid yellowgreen;
    color: green;
    padding: 5px;
    font-weight: normal;
    font-size: 12px;
}
```

4. Save the preceding styles as `Example_3-2.css`. After loading Example 3-2 into your browser, you should see output similar to that of Figure 3-13.

Figure 3-13

Figure 3-13 shows the results from Mac Firefox. Safari 2.0 produces similar results; the difference being only the font color is applied to the form elements. Safari 2.0 does not support custom styling of form elements very well. However, later versions have made progress in this area. IE 6 and IE 7 also differ slightly from the output here, in that the <label> elements are missing the top border, which is because of a bug in IE. While the results are not perfect from browser to browser, you get the idea of what the universal selector does.

How It Works

The concepts at play in Example 3-2 are very simple; the universal selector is included in the style sheet as an asterisk. The declarations in the rule that follow the asterisk are applied to all of the elements that appear in the document, provided that element is allowed to have the property in question applied. For instance, the <tbody> and <tr> elements do not accept most visual styles (borders, padding, and dimensions, for example). The universal selector, alone, doesn't have much practical application, although as previously mentioned, it can be helpful for debugging styles and highlighting element dimensions in complex documents. By applying a border to all elements, you are able to immediately see the space an element occupies.

The universal selector can also be used with other kinds of selectors, such as contextual selectors, also known as descendant selectors.

Descendant Selectors

Descendant selectors apply style based on whether one element is a descendant of another. In CSS, *descendant* means an element that is a child, grandchild, great grandchild, and so on, of another element. This type of relationship is referred to as an *ancestral* relationship. Take for example the document in Figure 3-14. If you were looking to map the ancestral relationship between the elements in Figure 3-14, you would see a tree like that in Figure 3-15.

```
<!DOCTYPE html PUBLIC "-//W3C//DTD XHTML 1.0 Strict//EN"
                      "http://www.w3.org/TR/xhtml1/DTD/xhtml1-strict.dtd">
<html xmlns='http://www.w3.org/1999/xhtml' xml:lang='en'>
    <head>
        <title>Tree</title>
    </head>
    <body>
        <div id='heading'>
            <h1>Ancestral Relationships Among HTML Elements</h1>
            <p>
                A study of lineage in angle-bracket documents.
            </p>
        </div>
        <div id='body'>
            <p>
                Heritage is important in HTML documents.  One element
                that all elements have in common is the
                <span class='inline-code'>&lt;html&gt;</span>.
            </p>
            <p>
                Ancestral relationships affect another CSS feature,
                <i>inheritance</i>, which I discuss in Chapter 4.
            </p>
            <p>
                <a href='http://p2p.wrox.com'>Wrox P2P</a> is a great
                place to go when you have technical questions.
            </p>
        </div>
    </body>
</html>
```

Figure 3-14

As a web designer, you get used to visualizing markup documents as a tree. Perhaps not as a real tree, as you see in Figure 3-15, but visualizing the lineage of an element. The concept of ancestral relationships between elements is a fundamental cornerstone to web development, and as you read on throughout this chapter and Chapter 4, you'll see that ancestral relationships play a large role in CSS development.

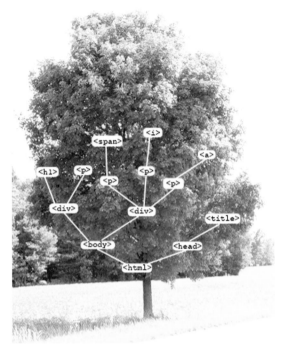

Figure 3-15

Descendant selectors apply style based on the lineage of an element. Keeping in mind the markup presented in Figure 3-14, one example of a descendant selector appears in Figure 3-16.

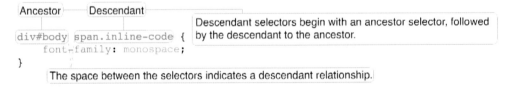

Figure 3-16

Descendant selectors are used to select an element based on the context it appears in the document. In the example code in Figure 3-16, you select a <span> element with an `inline-code` class name, and apply the `monospace` font to it, but only if the `inline-code` <span> element is a descendant of the <div> element with a `body` id name.

Descendant selectors aren't limited to just two elements; you can include more elements in the ancestral lineage, if it suits your needs. Each selector in a descendant selector chain must be separated by a space. This is demonstrated in code in Figure 3-17.

```
div#body p span.inline-code {
    font-family: monospace;
}
```

You can include as many elements in the lineage as you want to. Each selector in a descendant selector chain must be separated by a space.

Figure 3-17

In fact, the entire lineage from the eldest ancestor, the `<html>` element, down through the generations to the element you want to select, can be included in a descendant selector chain.

Descendant selectors can also be combined with the universal selector. You can see an example of this in Figure 3-18.

```
div#body * {
    border: 1px solid orange;
}
```

The universal selector can be used as part of a descendant selector.

Figure 3-18

The universal selector can appear in any part of a descendant selector. When it is included, it is a wildcard. In Figure 3-18, you select all descendants of the *body* `<div>` element.

Because descendant selectors are part of the oldest CSS 1 specification, they are the widest supported contextual selector. The upcoming sections (through to the section titled "Attribute Selectors") are CSS 2 selectors, which are not supported by IE 6.

In the CSS level 1 specification, descendant selectors are referred to as contextual selectors. *The name change was made in the CSS level 2 specification. The name change likely resulted from new selectors in CSS 2, several of which can also be considered contextual because their selection is based on the context in which the target element appears in the document.*

Try It Out   **Descendant Selectors**

Example 3-3. To see how descendant selectors work, follow these steps.

1.   Enter the following markup into your text editor:

```
<!DOCTYPE html PUBLIC "-//W3C//DTD XHTML 1.0 Strict//EN"
                "http://www.w3.org/TR/xhtml1/DTD/xhtml1-strict.dtd">
<html xmlns='http://www.w3.org/1999/xhtml' xml:lang='en'>
    <head>
        <title>Descendant Selectors</title>
        <link rel='stylesheet' type='text/css' href='Example_3-3.css' />
    </head>
    <body>
        <h1>Descendant Selectors</h1>
        <p>
            Descendant selectors apply styles based on ancestral relationships.
```

73

> The first descendant example I present applies style to the
> <span class='code'><span></span> element named <em>code</em>,
> which is a descendant of <span class='code'><p></span> elements.
> To do this, the selector <span class='code'>p span.code</span> is used.
> </p>
> <p>
> Using CSS, styles can be applied to any number of documents. Since
> this is the case, there may be <span class='code'><span></span>
> elements with a class name of <em>code</em> in several documents, but
> have different styles applied depending on the context it appears,
> which is the exact situation the inventors of the descendant
> selector had in mind when it was conceived.
> </p>
> <p class='note'>
> The note text is given different styles. To do this another descendant
> selector is used. This time the selector is <span class='code'>p.note
> span.code</span>
> </p>
> </body>
> </html>

2. Save the preceding document as `Example_3-3.html`.

3. Enter the following CSS in a new document in your text editor:

```css
body {
    font-face: sans-serif;
}
h1 {
    margin: 5px;
}
p {
    border: 1px solid rgb(200, 200, 200);
    background: rgb(234, 234, 234);
    padding: 5px;
    margin: 5px;
}
p.note {
    background: yellow;
    border: 1px solid gold;
}
span.code {
    font-family: monospace;
    padding: 0 10px;
}
p span.code {
    background: yellow;
}
p.note span.code {
    background: lightyellow;
}
```

4. Save the preceding CSS as `Example_3-3.css`. This example results in the output you see in Figure 3-19.

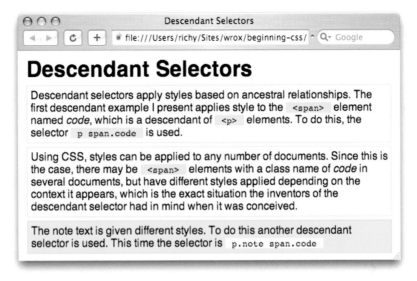

Figure 3-19

How It Works

Descendant selectors apply style based on an ancestral relationship. The first example of descendant selectors that you see in Example 3-3 is p span.code. This selector selects <span> elements with class names of *code*, but only when they appear as descendants of <p> elements. That is to say, when a <span> element exists in the document and it has a class name of code, and it is the child, grandchild, great grandchild, and so on, of a <p> element, those elements receive a yellow background.

The second example of descendant selectors in Example 3-3 is p.note span.code, where two type and class selectors are included in a descendant selector. In this selector any <p> elements appearing in the document with a class name of note that have descendant <span> elements, which have a class name of code, receive lightyellow backgrounds.

Descendant selectors allow you to apply style based on ancestral relationships. In the next section, you see a similar selector, the direct child selector, which also applies style based on an ancestral relationship, but a narrower, more specific ancestral relationship, parent and child.

Direct Child Selectors

Direct child selectors operate much like descendant selectors in that they also rely on an ancestral relationship to decide where to apply style. Descendant selectors, however, are more ambiguous because they apply to any descendant of an element; the descendant can be a grandchild or a great-grandchild, or a great-great-grandchild, and so on. Direct child selectors apply only to immediate children of the element. This is achieved by introducing a new syntax for the selector. Figure 3-20 is an example of a direct child selector.

IE 6 does not support direct child selectors natively; see this book's website at www.wrox.com/go/beginning_css2e for compatibility help.

```
p > span.inline-code {
    font-family: monospace;
}
```

Like descendant selectors, direct child selectors are chained together, but instead of a space, a greater-than symbol (or right angle bracket) is used to separate each element in the selector.

Figure 3-20

In Figure 3-20 you see that the greater than sign (or right angle bracket), >, is used in the style sheet to select an element in the HTML document. In Figure 3-20, you see a parent/child relationship in the direct child selector, p > span.inline-code. In order to apply the declaration font-family: monospace;, the <span> element with the class name inline-code, must be the child of a <p> element.

Direct child selectors are selectors that depend on the context that an element appears in a document. The context in this case is a parent/child relationship. Like descendant selectors, a direct child selector chain can have as many elements as you like; an example of this is shown in Figure 3-21.

```
div#body > p > span.inline-code {
    font-family: monospace;
}
```

You can include as many elements in a direct child selector chain as necessary.

Figure 3-21

In Figure 3-21, you see two parent/child relationships represented in one selector. The <p> element is a direct child of the <div> with an id name of body and the <span> with a class name of inline-code is a direct child of the <p> element.

You can also mix selectors, if you have need of it. Figure 3-22 shows mixing descendant selectors with direct child selectors.

Direct child and descendant selectors can be mixed together.

```
div#body > p span.inline-code {
    font-family: monospace;
}
```

Figure 3-22

In fact, you can mix and match selectors in pretty much any way imaginable — direct child selectors with descendant selectors, with universal selectors. CSS is very flexible in this regard, provided browser support for the selector exists.

Try It Out   **Direct Child Selector**

Example 3-4. To see how the direct child selectors work, follow these steps.

1. Using the markup in `Example_3-3.html`, make the following highlighted changes:

```
<!DOCTYPE html PUBLIC "-//W3C//DTD XHTML 1.0 Strict//EN"
                    "http://www.w3.org/TR/xhtml1/DTD/xhtml1-strict.dtd">
<html xmlns='http://www.w3.org/1999/xhtml' xml:lang='en'>
    <head>
        <title>Direct Child Selectors</title>
        <link rel='stylesheet' type='text/css' href='Example_3-4.css' />
    </head>
    <body>
        <h1><ins>Direct Child</ins> <del>Descendant</del> Selectors</h1>
        <p>
            <ins>Direct Child</ins> <del>Descendant</del> selectors apply styles
            based on <ins>parent/child</ins> <del>ancestral</del> relationships.
            The first <ins>direct child</ins> <del>descendant</del> example I
            present applies style to the
            <span class='code'>&lt;span&gt;</span> element named <em>code</em>,
            which is a <del>descendant</del> <ins>child</ins> of
            <span class='code'>&lt;p&gt;</span> elements.
            To do this, the selector <span class='code'>p <ins>&gt;</ins>
            span.code</span> is used.
        </p>
        <p>
            Using CSS, styles can be applied to any number of documents.  Since
            this is the case, there may be <span class='code'>&lt;span&gt;</span>
            elements with a class name of <em>code</em> in several documents, but
            have different styles applied depending on the context it appears,
            which is the exact situation the inventors of the <del>descendant</del>
            <ins>child</ins> selector had in mind when it was conceived.
        </p>
        <p class='note'>
            The note text is given different styles.  To do this another
            <del>descendant</del> <ins>direct child</ins>
            selector is used, this time the selector is
            <span class='code'>p.note <ins>&gt;</ins> span.code</span>
        </p>
    </body>
</html>
```

2. Save the preceding markup document as `Example_3-4.html`.

3. Using the style sheet that you made for Example 3-3, `Example_3-3.css`, make the following highlighted changes.

```
body {
    font-face: sans-serif;
}
h1 {
    margin: 5px;
}
```

```
del {
    color: crimson;
}
ins {
    color: forestgreen;
}
p {
    border: 1px solid rgb(200, 200, 200);
    background: rgb(234, 234, 234);
    padding: 5px;
    margin: 5px;
}
p.note {
    background: yellow;
    border: 1px solid gold;
}
span.code {
    font-family: monospace;
    padding: 0 10px;
}
p > span.code {
    background: yellow;
}
p.note > span.code {
    background: lightyellow;
}
```

4. Save the preceding style sheet as `Example_3-4.css`. The preceding example results in the rendered document pictured in Figure 3-23.

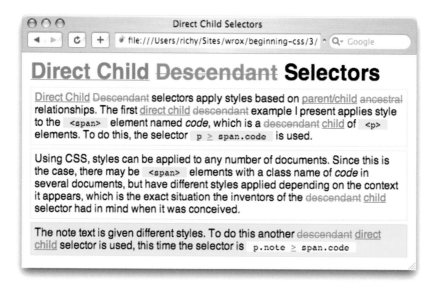

Figure 3-23

How It Works

As is illustrated in Example 3-4, the direct child selector is pretty similar to the descendant selector. In most situations you can get away with using a descendant selector where a child selector could be used and vice versa, the only difference being the direct child must be a parent/child relationship, and the descendant selector can be a more ambiguous ancestral relationship. Using a descendant selector, you have greater compatibility since IE 6 does not support the direct child selector (at least, not without a workaround, which you can find in Chapter 16, available at www.wrox.com/go/beginning_css2e).

There are some situations where a descendant selector would not be desired, and a direct child selector would come in handy, or it wouldn't exist. Those situations are a bit too complex to explain properly here, in addition to being rare.

In Example 3-4, you see that the direct child selector uses a greater than sign (>) within the selector to indicate the parent/child relationship, whereas the descendant selector you saw in Example 3-3 uses space between selectors to indicate an ancestral relationship, which is not limited to parent/child, but could indicate grandparent/grandchild, great-grandparent/great-grandchild, and so on.

Selecting a child element based on the element's parent can be helpful. These contextual selectors allow developers to define fewer class and id names in a markup document, and instead select elements based on the context they appear in a document. In the next section I present another contextual selector, the direct adjacent sibling combinator (its official name), or *next sibling* for short (because that's just too long!).

Next Sibling Selector

The official name of the selector I discuss in this section, according to the W3C is the *adjacent sibling combinator*. I think that's too long and complicated, so I've shortened it to just *next sibling*. The next sibling selector selects, surprise, an element's next sibling. Looking back on the markup in Figure 3-14, the markup in Figure 3-24 is a demonstration of what a next sibling selector looks like in a style sheet.

> IE 6 does not support next sibling selectors natively; see this book's website at www.wrox.com/go/ beginning_css2e for compatibility help.

A next sibling selector uses a plus sign to illustrate the sibling relationship between two elements.

```
div#heading + div#body {
    border: 1px solid rgb(200, 200, 200);
}
```

Figure 3-24

In Figure 3-24, you see that a plus sign is used to denote the sibling relationship between two elements. You may be thinking to yourself at this point, *well that's just fine and dandy, but what's the practical application? Can't you just reference the* div#body *alone and get the same result? Why do you need a next sibling selector?* I'm glad you asked. This selector can be useful in certain situations, such as when you have several HTML documents that reference the same style sheet. In some of these documents, the <div> with an id name of heading and the <div> with an id name of body are siblings, and they appear in the source one right after the other. In other documents these two elements may not be siblings. Naturally, if you have different template requirements in these theoretical two different kinds of documents, you may like to have a way to reference the ones where these elements are siblings explicitly, and that is one example of a practical application of the next sibling selector. Also, as I mentioned in the previous section, "Direct Child Selectors," sometimes you want to avoid creating new id and class names. In some situations when you use the next sibling selector, you can potentially avoid creating new class and id names.

In the following proof-of-concept example, you try out the next sibling selector for yourself.

Try It Out   Next Sibling Selector

Example 3-5. To see how the next sibling selector works, follow these steps.

1. Enter the following markup into your text editor:

```
<!DOCTYPE html PUBLIC "-//W3C//DTD XHTML 1.0 Strict//EN"
                      "http://www.w3.org/TR/xhtml1/DTD/xhtml1-strict.dtd">
<html xmlns='http://www.w3.org/1999/xhtml' xml:lang='en'>
    <head>
        <title>Next Sibling Selectors</title>
        <link rel='stylesheet' type='text/css' href='Example_3-5.css' />
    </head>
    <body>
        <h1>Next Sibling Selectors</h1>
        <p>
            The next sibling selector (or adjacent sibling combinator as
            it's officially called) allows you to select an element based on
            its sibling.  This paragraph has a lightyellow background and
            darkkhaki text.
        </p>
        <p>
            This paragraph has a yellowgreen background and green text.
        </p>
        <p>
            This paragraph has no colored background, border, or text.
        </p>
    </body>
</html>
```

2. Save the preceding markup as Example_3-5.html.

3. Enter the following CSS into your text editor:

```
body {
    font: 12px sans-serif;
}
p {
    padding: 5px;
}
h1 + p {
    background: lightyellow;
    color: darkkhaki;
    border: 1px solid darkkhaki;
```

```
    }
h1 + p + p {
    background: yellowgreen;
    color: green;
    border: 1px solid green;
}
```

4. Save the style sheet as `Example_3-5.css`. Once loaded into your next sibling selector supporting browser, you should see something like that in Figure 3-25.

Figure 3-25

How It Works

The next sibling selector applies a style based on a sibling relationship. The following is a review of the
relevant styles that you applied in `Example_3-5.css`.

The first style you applied in `Example_3-5.css` is applied to the first paragraph in `Example_3-5.html`.
The selector `h1 + p` means that if a `<p>` element is the next, directly adjacent sibling to an `<h1>` element,
apply the declarations in this rule.

```
h1 + p {
    background: lightyellow;
    color: darkkhaki;
    border: 1px solid darkkhaki;
}
```

The rule only applies when a `<p>` element is the directly adjacent sibling of an `<h1>` element.

In the second rule, you have a more complex next sibling selector. It says that if a `<p>` element is the
directly adjacent sibling of another `<p>` element, which in turn is the directly adjacent sibling to an `<h1>`
element, apply the declarations in the rule.

```
h1 + p + p {
    background: yellowgreen;
```

```
      color: green;
      border: 1px solid green;
}
```

Just as the direct child selector allows you to apply a style based on a parent/child relationship, next sibling selectors allow you to apply style based on a sibling relationship.

Sometimes, it's useful to have a selector that can apply styles based on the existence or value of an element's attributes.

Attribute Selectors

Attribute selectors are used to apply style sheet declarations based on the presence of attributes or attribute values of an HTML element.

> *IE 6 does not support attribute selectors natively; see this book's website at www.wrox.com/go/ beginning_css2e for compatibility help.*

Figure 3-26 is an example of an attribute selector that applies a style sheet rule based on the presence of an attribute.

```
img[alt] {
    border: 1px solid blue;
}
```

The attribute is included in the selector surrounded by square brackets. This rule applies if the alt attribute is set on `<img>` elements (the value is irrelevant)

Figure 3-26

In Figure 3-26, if the `alt` attribute is set on `<img>` elements, those `<img>` elements receive a blue border. Detecting the presence of an `alt` attribute is good practice, since the `alt` attribute is required on all `<img>` elements per the HTML 4.01 specification. When the rule in Figure 3-26 is used, `<img>` elements that don't have a blue border need an `alt` attribute applied.

You are not limited to detecting the presence of an attribute; there are several types of attribute selectors, and CSS is capable of detecting attributes based on the following criteria:

❑   The presence of an attribute

❑   The value of an attribute

❑   Whether one of several possible values is present in an attribute

❑   Whether the attribute value begins with a specific string

❑   Whether the attribute value ends with a specific string

❑   Whether the attribute value contains a specific string anywhere in the value, be it at the beginning, end, or middle

The following sections examine each type of attribute selector in greater depth and provide examples of the syntax for each.

Selection Based on the Value of an Attribute

Attribute value selectors delegate style declarations based on an attribute's presence and value. In Figure 3-27, you see an example of what the syntax looks like to select an element based on an attribute's presence and value.

```
input[type="text"] {
    background: blue;
    color: white;
    border: 3px solid royalblue;
}
```

Attribute selectors can select elements based on the value of an attribute contained within an element.

```
<input type='text' name='first_name' value='Richard' size='25' />
```

Attribute Selectors

⊖ ○ ○

◀ ▶ | C | + | file:///Users/richy/Sites/wrox/beginning-css/3/figures/ | Q▾ Google

Feedback Form

First Name: **Richard**

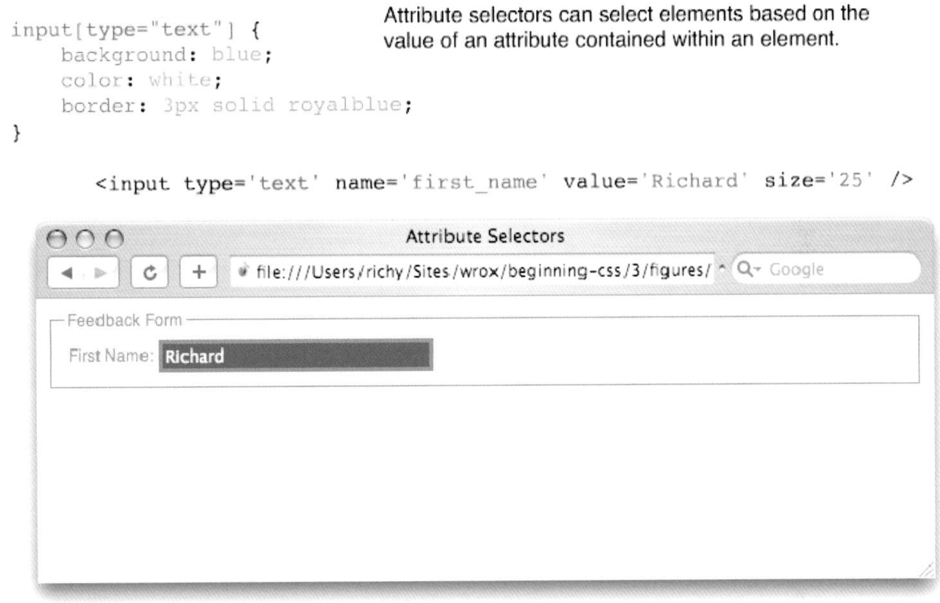

Figure 3-27

In Figure 3-27, you see how to select a text `<input>` element based on the presence of the attribute `type` and a value of `text`.

You are not limited to the presence of only one attribute. An element may also be selected based on the presence and value of multiple attributes, which you see an example of in Figure 3-28.

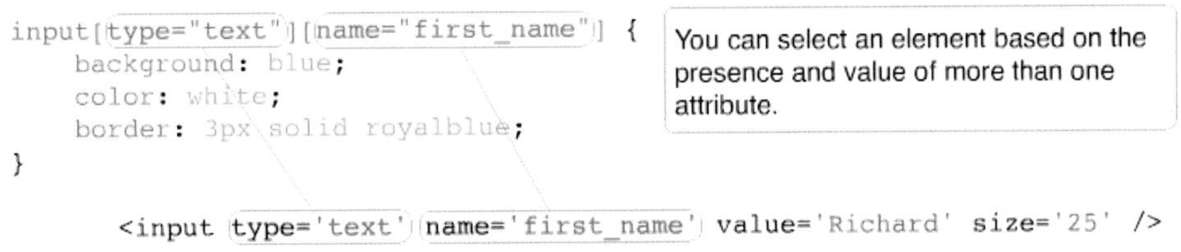

```
input[type="text"][name="first_name"] {
    background: blue;
    color: white;
    border: 3px solid royalblue;
}
```

You can select an element based on the presence and value of more than one attribute.

```
<input type='text' name='first_name' value='Richard' size='25' />
```

Figure 3-28

In Figure 3-28, you see a rule that selects an element based on the presence and value of two attributes: the type and name attributes. In Figure 3-28, when the type attribute is text and the name attribute is first_name, the declarations in the rule are applied to that element. Attribute selectors let you avoid the need of setting class or id selectors when they are otherwise unnecessary.

In the following example, you try out attribute value selectors for yourself.

Try It Out   **Attribute Value Selectors**

Example 3-6. To see how attribute value selectors work, follow these steps.

1.   Enter the following markup into your text editor:

```
<!DOCTYPE html PUBLIC "-//W3C//DTD XHTML 1.0 Strict//EN"
                  "http://www.w3.org/TR/xhtml1/DTD/xhtml1-strict.dtd">
<html xmlns='http://www.w3.org/1999/xhtml' xml:lang='en'>
    <head>
        <title>Attribute Selectors</title>
        <link rel='stylesheet' type='text/css' href='Figure_3-28.css' />
    </head>
    <body>
        <form method='post' action='Example_3-3.html'>
            <fieldset>
                <legend>Feedback Form</legend>
                <table>
                    <tbody>
                        <tr>
                            <td>
                                <label for='first-name'>First Name:</label>
                            </td>
                            <td>
                                <input type='text'
                                       name='first_name'
                                       id='first-name'
                                       value='Richard'
                                       size='25' />
                            </td>
                        </tr>
                        <tr>
                            <td>
                                <label for='last-name'>Last Name:</label>
                            </td>
                            <td>
                                <input type='text'
                                       name='last_name'
                                       id='last-name'
                                       value='York'
                                       size='25' />
                            </td>
                        </tr>
                        <tr>
                            <td>
                                <label for='account-password'>Password:</label>
                            </td>
                            <td>
```

```
                              <input type='password'
                                     name='password'
                                     id='account-password'
                                     size='25'
                                     value='mypass' />
                        </td>
                    </tr>
                </tbody>
            </table>
        </fieldset>
    </form>
</body>
</html>
```

2. Save the markup as `Example_3-6.html`.

3. Enter the following CSS into a new document in your text editor:

```css
* {
    font: 12px sans-serif;
    padding: 5px;
    color: royalblue;
}
fieldset {
    border: 3px solid rgb(234, 234, 234);
    background: rgb(244, 244, 244);
}
label {
    display: block;
    text-align: right;
    width: 100px;
}
label, legend {
    background: gold;
    border: 1px solid rgb(75, 75, 75);
    color: rgb(75, 75, 75);
}
input[type='text'] {
    background: blue;
    color: lightblue;
    border: 3px solid lightblue;
}
input[type='text'][name='last_name'] {
    background: forestgreen;
    color: yellowgreen;
    border: 3px solid yellowgreen;
}
input[type='password'][name='password'] {
    background: crimson;
    color: pink;
    border: 3px solid pink;
}
```

4. Save the CSS as `Example_3-6.css`. Figure 3-29 shows what Example 3-6 looks like rendered in a browser that supports attribute selection based on value.

Figure 3-29

How It Works

In Example 3-6, you saw an example of the attribute selector. This type of attribute selector makes a selection based on the value of an attribute in the HTML document. Following is a review of the relevant rules in Example 3-6.

The first selector applies to all `<input>` elements that have a `type="text"` attribute. (Keep in mind that the quoting style can be either single or double quotes in either place; it doesn't matter which. Use what makes sense to you.)

```
input[type='text'] {
    background: blue;
    color: lightblue;
    border: 3px solid lightblue;
}
```

Two elements in the document match the criteria: the *First Name* and the *Last Name* `<input>` fields of the form. The preceding rule is applied only to the First Name field though, since the last name field has a rule of its own that overrides the preceding rule. The concept of overriding one rule with another is called the cascade, and you learn more about the cascade in Chapter 4. So, the preceding rule applies to this markup:

```
<input type='text' name='first_name' id='first-name' value='Richard' value='25' />
```

The preceding markup appears all on one line, whereas in the original `Example_3-6.html`, it was spread out over several lines to accommodate the width constraints of this printed text.

The preceding `<input>` field receives a blue background, the text within is colored `lightblue` via the `color` property, and a border, three pixels wide, solid and also `lightblue` goes around it.

The next rule applies to the Last Name field; it receives a `forestgreen` background, `yellowgreen` text, and a border three pixels wide, solid, and also `yellowgreen`.

```
input[type='text'][name='last_name'] {
    background: forestgreen;
    color: yellowgreen;
    border: 3px solid yellowgreen;
}
```

In the preceding rule you select the `<input>` element based on the value of *two* attributes: the `type` attribute and the `name` attribute.

Finally, in the last rule you select the `<input>` element with a `type="password"` attribute, and like the last rule, you select the element based on the value of two attributes, the `type` and `name` attributes.

```
input[type='password'][name='password'] {
    background: crimson;
    color: pink;
    border: 3px solid pink;
}
```

While selecting an attribute based on a value is useful, you can also select an attribute based on just part of the value. These are called attribute substring selectors.

Attribute Substring Selectors

Taking the flexibility of attribute selectors even further, the selectors in the following sections choose elements based on whether a particular string appears at the beginning of an attribute's value, at the end of an attribute's value, or anywhere inside an attribute's value. A string that appears inside another string is referred to as a *substring*. You can select an element based on what appears at the beginning of an attribute's value.

Selection Based on Attribute Values That Begin with a String

The first type of substring attribute selector chooses elements with an attribute value that begins with a particular string. You see an example of this in Figure 3-30.

In Figure 3-30, the rule selects `<a>` elements that have an `href` attribute. When the value of the `href` attribute begins with *ftp://*, the rule selects all of the FTP links in a web page and gives them a floppy disk icon in the background, 20 pixels of left padding so that the text of the link doesn't overlap the floppy disk icon image, and colors them `crimson`.

A caret character, followed by an equals sign indicates that only the beginning of the attribute value is being matched.

```
a[href^="ftp://"] {
    background: blue;
    color: white;
    border: 3px solid royalblue;
}
```

```
<a href='ftp://ftp.example.com/'>Company FTP Server</a>
```

Figure 3-30a

Figure 3-30b

This attribute substring selector introduces the caret (^) character in the selector syntax, which indicates that the attribute value begins with *ftp://*. Each `href` attribute prefixed with *ftp://* is then styled according to the declarations defined in the rule.

Another example of this syntax in action is to match all e-mail links in a page, and you can see an example of this in Figure 3-31.

```
a[href^="mailto:"] {
    background: url('envelope.png') no-repeat left center;
    padding-left: 25px;
    color: royalblue;
    text-decoration: none;
}
        <a href="mailto:webmaster@example.com">Email the webmaster!</a>
```

Figure 3-31a

Figure 3-31b

When the selector is a[href^="mailto:"] you match all e-mail links within a document.

Just as you can match values that appear at the beginning of a string, you can also match values that appear at the end of a string.

Selection Based on Attribute Values That End with a String

The next substring attribute selector chooses elements with attributes whose value ends with a string. An example of this appears in Figure 3-32.

To match a string that appears at the end of an attribute's value, you use a dollar sign, followed by the equals sign.

```
a[href$=".html"] {
    background: url('firefox.png') no-repeat left center;
    padding-left: 25px;
    color: blue;
    text-decoration: none;
}
            <a href='home.html'>Go back to the home page.</a>
```

Figure 3-32a

Figure 3-32b

The selector of the preceding rule uses the dollar sign to signify that the selector matches the end of the attribute value. This changes all links that end in an .html suffix to blue, with a Firefox document icon, 25 pixels of left padding, and no underline.

The href attribute's value ends with the string .html, so it receives a text color of blue. Conversely, this principle does not apply to the href attribute of the following <a> element:

```
<a href='http://www.example.com/index.php'>A PHP Page</a>
```

The attribute's value in this example ends with a .php suffix, so it does not receive a text color of `blue`, and a Firefox document icon, 25 pixels of left padding, and the underline are removed.

You've seen how to select an attribute's value based on what appears at the beginning and at the end of the attribute's value. The next section describes how to select an attribute's value based on the value being anywhere: at the beginning, the end, or anywhere in between.

Selection Based on Attribute Values That Contain a String

The final type of attribute substring selector is a wildcard attribute substring selector. It selects an element that contains an attribute whose value contains a string anywhere in the value: at the beginning, the end, or anywhere in the middle. This attribute substring selector uses an asterisk in the syntax to indicate that the selector is looking anywhere inside the value, as shown in Figure 3-33.

Figure 3-33a

Figure 3-33b

This matches any URL that contains a .php extension regardless of whether the URL contains anchors or query strings.

All that after the question mark is called the *query string,* which holds special meaning for programming languages such as PHP, ASP, Perl, and others. What that does isn't important. What is important is that using this style sheet rule, the selector finds the .php extension even though it is in the middle of the value. The selector also finds the .php value if it appears at the beginning or the end of the URL:

```
<a href='http://www.example.com/index.php'>A .php page</a>
```

The markup presented in Figure 3-33 and in the preceding example both receive a Thunderbird icon, 25 pixels of left padding, `steelblue` text, and the underline removed.

In the following example, you experiment with attribute substring selectors.

Try It Out   Attribute Substring Selectors

Example 3-7. To see how attribute substring selectors work, follow these steps.

1. Enter the following markup:

```
<!DOCTYPE html PUBLIC "-//W3C//DTD XHTML 1.0 Strict//EN"
                  "http://www.w3.org/TR/xhtml1/DTD/xhtml1-strict.dtd">
<html xmlns='http://www.w3.org/1999/xhtml' xml:lang='en'>
    <head>
        <title>Attribute Substring Selectors</title>
        <link rel='stylesheet' type='text/css' href='Example_3-7.css' />
    </head>
    <body>
        <h1>Proof-of-Concept: Attribute Substring Selectors</h1>
        <ul>
            <li><a href='index.html'>HTML Page Link</a></li>
            <li><a href='document.pdf'>PDF Link</a></li>
            <li><a href='ftp://www.example.com/'>FTP Link</a></li>
            <li><a href='http://www.example.com/#note'>Anchor Link</a></li>
        </ul>
    </body>
</html>
```

2. Save the preceding markup as `Example_3-7.html`.

3. Enter the following style sheet:

```
body {
    font: 14px sans-serif;
}
h1 {
    font-size: 16px;
}
ul {
    list-style: none;
}
li {
    margin: 5px 0;
}
a {
    padding-left: 20px;
```

```
}
a[href^="ftp://"] {
    color: goldenrod;
    background: url('save.png') no-repeat left center;
}
a[href*="#"] {
    color: cadetblue;
    background: url('anchor.png') no-repeat left center;
}
a[href$=".html"] {
    color: dodgerblue;
    background: url('firefox.png') no-repeat left center;
}
a[href$=".pdf"] {
    color: red;
    background: url('pdf.png') no-repeat left center;
}
```

4. Save the preceding style sheet as `Example_3-7.css`. The preceding markup and style sheet result in the rendered output that you see in Figure 3-34.

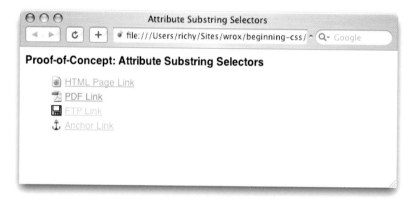

Figure 3-34

How It Works

In Example 3-7, you see how to select an attribute based on just a small portion of its value. The following is a review of the relevant attribute substring selectors.

The first attribute substring rule that you applied styles the FTP link. The selector `a[href^="ftp://"]` applies the style because the href attribute value in the HTML begins with the characters `ftp://`. To select only the beginning of the string, you used a caret character followed by the equals sign.

```
a[href^="ftp://"] {
    color: goldenrod;
    background: url('save.png') no-repeat left center;
}
```

The second attribute substring selector that you applied styles the anchor link. The selector a[href*="#"] finds the special hash mark (or pound sign) within the value of the href attribute in the HTML, http://www.example.com/#note. The hash character can appear anywhere in that value, and the rule still would apply cadetblue colored text and the anchor.png image to the background.

```
a[href*="#"] {
    color: cadetblue;
    background: url('anchor.png') no-repeat left center;
}
```

The third attribute substring selector that you applied styles the plain old HTML document link. Because the value of the href attribute ends in .html, the color dodgerblue is applied as the text color, and the firefox.png image is applied to the background.

```
a[href$=".html"] {
    color: dodgerblue;
    background: url('firefox.png') no-repeat left center;
}
```

The last attribute substring rule that you applied was just like the last, only now you are styling links to PDF documents. When the value of the href attribute ends in .pdf, the link is colored red, and given a PDF icon as the background image.

```
a[href$=".pdf"] {
    color: red;
    background: url('pdf.png') no-repeat left center;
}
```

In the next section you begin to explore a different type of selector, pseudo-element selectors.

Pseudo-Elements :first-letter and :first-line

Pseudo-elements represent certain aspects of a document not easily modifiable with plain markup. Pseudo-elements may be used to modify the formatting of the first letter of a paragraph, or the first line of a paragraph, for example.

The pseudo-elements :first-letter and :first-line refer to the first letter and first line of an element containing text. When you design a website, it is helpful to have control over how you present content. With the :first-letter and :first-line pseudo-elements, you can control the formatting of the first letter and first line of a paragraph completely from CSS. You may add an increased font size or other font effects, apply a background color or image, or use just about any text effect supported by CSS and the browser.

You can apply pseudo-elements to a specific element, via a selector, or to all elements. Figure 3-35 shows an example of styling the first letter of a paragraph using the :first-letter pseudo-element.

> To select the first letter of an element, you append another selector with :first-letter.

```
p:first-letter {
    background: crimson;
    color: pink;
    font: 55px "Monotype Corsiva";
}
```

Figure 3-35a

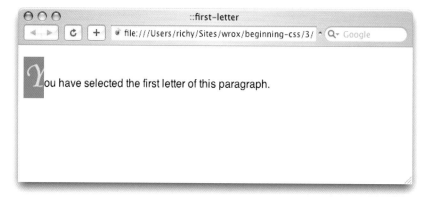

Figure 3-35b

In Figure 3-35, you see that to select the first letter in the paragraph, "Y", you use a :first-letter pseudo-element.

> **CSS 3 changes pseudo-element syntax to use a double colon (::) preceding each pseudo-element. For example, p::first-letter refers to the first letter of a paragraph instead of p:first-letter. This syntax distinguishes pseudo-elements from pseudo-classes, which use single colon syntax, as in a:hover, which is a reference to a pseudo-class.**

IE 6 appears to support the double-colon syntax without any problems, but IE 7 does not support this syntax, which is why I present the single colon syntax here. CSS includes more pseudo-elements than those mentioned here; I've selected only those that have the most browser compatibility and support. See Appendix B for additional pseudo-elements.

The following Try It Out shows you what the :first-letter and :first-line pseudo-elements look like in a style sheet and demonstrates some of the textual effects you can apply.

Try It Out   **:first-letter and :first-line Pseudo-Elements**

Example 3-8. To see how the :first-letter and :first-line pseudo-elements work, follow these steps.

1.   Enter the following markup:

```
<!DOCTYPE html PUBLIC "-//W3C//DTD XHTML 1.0 Strict//EN"
                      "http://www.w3.org/TR/xhtml1/DTD/xhtml1-strict.dtd">
<html xmlns='http://www.w3.org/1999/xhtml' xml:lang='en'>
    <head>
        <title>Pseudo-Element Selectors</title>
        <link rel='stylesheet' type='text/css' href='Example_3-8.css' />
    </head>
    <body>
        <p class='quote'>
            You see, wire telegraph is a kind of a very, very long cat.
            You pull his tail in New York and his head is meowing in Los
            Angeles. Do you understand this? And radio operates exactly
            the same way: you send signals here, they receive them there.
            The only difference is that there is no cat.
        </p>
        <p class='byline'>
            - Albert Einstein
        </p>
    </body>
</html>
```

2.   Save the preceding markup as Example_3-8.html.

3.   Enter the following style sheet:

```
p {
    color: darkblue;
    border: 1px solid lightblue;
    padding: 2px;
    font: 14px sans-serif;
}
p.quote:first-letter {
    background: darkblue;
    color: white;
    font: 55px "Monotype Corsiva";
    float: left;

    margin-right: 5px;
}
p.quote:first-line {
    font-weight: bold;
    letter-spacing: 3px;
}
p.byline {
    text-align: right;
    font-style: italic;
    font-size: 10px;
    border: none;
}
```

4. Save the preceding style sheet as `Example_3-8.css`. The markup and CSS that you entered should look something like Figure 3-36 when rendered in a browser.

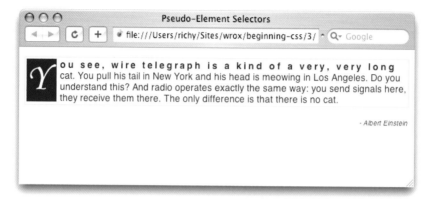

Figure 3-36

How It Works

In Example 3-8 you see an example of both the `:first-letter` and `:first-line` pseudo-elements. The following is a review of the relevant style sheet rules in `Example_3-8.css`. In the following rule, you styled the first letter of the `<p>` element with a class name of `quote`. To select the first letter of the `<p>` element, "Y", you used the selector `p.quote:first-letter`.

```
p.quote:first-letter {
    background: darkblue;
    color: white;
    font: 55px "Monotype Corsiva";
    float: left;
margin-right: 5px;
}
```

As shown in Figure 3-36, the first letter of the Einstein quote received a `darkblue` background, `white` text, a large 55-pixel font size, and the font face *Monotype Corsiva*. It's floated to the left so that subsequent lines wrap around it. It's given five pixels of right margin.

Then, the first line of the quote receives additional styling. It's selected with the selector `p.quote::first-line`, and given bold text, in addition to each letter in the line being spaced three pixels apart.

```
p.quote::first-line {
    font-weight: bold;
    letter-spacing: 3px;
}
```

In the next section, I present another type of selector, pseudo-class selectors.

Pseudo-Classes

Pseudo-classes are used to represent dynamic events, a change in state, or a more general condition present in the document that is not easily accomplished through other means. This may be the user's mouse rolling over or clicking on an element. In more general terms, pseudo-classes style a specific state present in the target element. This state may be hovering your mouse cursor over an element, or visiting a hyperlink. Pseudo-classes allow the author the freedom to dictate how the element should appear under either condition. Unlike pseudo-elements, pseudo-classes have a single colon before the pseudo-class property.

Dynamic Pseudo-Classes

The following are considered dynamic pseudo-classes. They are a classification of elements that are only present after certain user actions have or have not occurred:

- ❑ :link: signifies unvisited hyperlinks
- ❑ :visited: indicates visited hyperlinks
- ❑ :hover: signifies an element that currently has the user's mouse pointer hovering over it
- ❑ :active: signifies an element on which the user is currently clicking

The first two dynamic pseudo-classes that I discuss are :link and :visited.

:link and :visited

The :link pseudo-class refers to an unvisited hyperlink, whereas :visited, of course, refers to visited hyperlinks. These two pseudo-classes are used to separate styles based on user actions. An unvisited hyperlink may be blue, whereas a visited hyperlink may be purple. Those are the default styles your browser applies. Using dynamic pseudo-classes it is possible to customize those styles.

Figure 3-37 demonstrates how these pseudo-classes are applied.

In Figure 3-37, unvisited links are styled with the :link dynamic pseudo-class. They receive meduimblue colored text. Visited links, on the other hand have magenta colored text.

For obvious reasons, the :link *and* :visited *pseudo-classes apply only to <a> elements.]*

```
a:link {
    color: mediumblue;
}
a:visited {
    color: magenta;
}
```

Like pseudo-elements, to include a pseudo-class in a style sheet, you add the pseudo-class to the end of the element you'd like it applied to. Here, unvisited links are mediumblue, and visited links are magenta.

Figure 3-37a

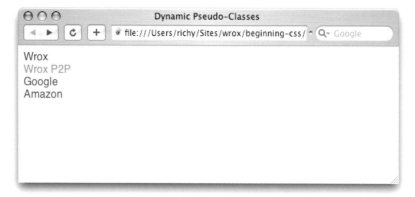

Figure 3-37b

The order in which the :link and :visited dynamic pseudo-classes appear in the style sheet is important and has to do with the cascade, which I discuss in Chapter 4. If the :link pseudo-class is defined after the :visited pseudo-class in the style sheet, the :link pseudo-class takes precedence. The declarations with the :link pseudo-class override those defined for the :visited pseudo-class. As you see in Chapter 4, this has to do with how specific the selector is; in this example, the specificity is the same.

> A mnemonic device used to remember the order in which dynamic pseudo-classes (as applied to links) must appear in style sheets is LoVe HAte, or :link, :visited, :hover and :active.

:hover

The :hover pseudo-class refers to an element over which the user's mouse pointer is currently hovering. While the user's mouse pointer is over the element, the specified style is applied; when the user's mouse pointer leaves the element, it returns to the previously specified style. The :hover pseudo-class is applied in the same way that the :link and :visited pseudo-classes are applied. An example of this appears in Figure 3-38.

In Figure 3-38, when the user's mouse hovers over an <a> element, the text within the <a> element is underlined.

```
a:link {
    color: mediumblue;
}
a:visited {
    color: magenta;
}
a:hover {
    text-decoration: underline;
}
```

When the user's mouse cursor hovers over an <a> element, the text is underlined.

Figure 3-38a

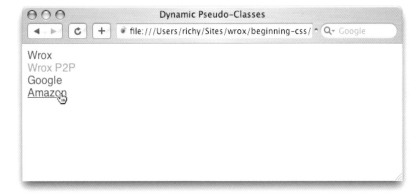

Figure 3-38b

In IE 6, the :hover *pseudo-class applies only to hyperlinks (which is incorrect under the CSS 2 specification), whereas other browsers recognize the* :hover *pseudo-class on any rendered element, per the CSS 2 specification. This problem is fixed in IE 7.*

:active

The :active pseudo-class refers to an element that the user is currently clicking and holding down the mouse button on. The specified style remains in place while the user holds down the mouse button, and the element does not return to its original state until the user releases the mouse button. You can see an example of this in Figure 3-39.

In Figure 3-39 you see the :active pseudo-class in action. When the user clicks on an <a> element, while the mouse button is held down, and before it is released, the element is said to be *active*, in which case the styles in the :active pseudo-class rule are applied.

In IE 6 and IE 7, :active *applies only to hyperlinks; whereas, other browsers allow it to be applied to any element.*

```
a:link {
    color: mediumblue;
}
a:visited {
    color: magenta;
}
a:hover {
    text-decoration: underline;
}
a:active {
    color: crimson;
}
```

> When the user clicks on an <a> element, at the time the click begins to the time the user releases the mouse button, the element is said to be active.

Figure 3-39a

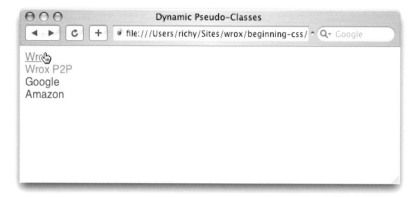

Figure 3-39b

Now that you have been introduced to dynamic pseudo-class selectors, you can try them out for yourself in the following example.

Dynamic Pseudo-Class Selectors

Example 3-9. To try out dynamic pseudo-class selectors, follow these steps.

1. Enter the following markup into your text editor:

```
<!DOCTYPE html PUBLIC "-//W3C//DTD XHTML 1.0 Strict//EN"
                      "http://www.w3.org/TR/xhtml1/DTD/xhtml1-strict.dtd">
<html xmlns='http://www.w3.org/1999/xhtml' xml:lang='en'>
    <head>
        <title>Dynamic Pseudo-Class Selectors</title>
        <link rel='stylesheet' type='text/css' href='Example_3-9.css' />
    </head>
    <body>
        <h1>Proof-of-Concept: Dynamic Pseudo-Class Selectors</h1>
        <ul>
            <li><a href='http://www.wrox.com/'>Wrox</a></li>
            <li><a href='http://p2p.wrox.com/'>Wrox P2P</a></li>
            <li><a href='http://www.google.com/'>Google</a></li>
            <li><a href='http://www.amazon.com/'>Amazon</a></li>
        </ul>
    </body>
</html>
```

2. Save the preceding markup as `Example_3-9.html`.

3. Enter the following CSS into your text editor:

```
body {
    font: 14px sans-serif;
}
h1 {
    font-size: 16px;
}
```

```
ul {
    list-style: none;
}
li {
    margin: 5px 0;
}
a:link {
    color: steelblue;
}
a:visited {
    color: darkorchid;
}
a:hover {
    color: orange;
}
a:active {
    color: crimson;
}
```

4. Save the preceding style sheet as `Example_3-9.css`. Upon completion of the HTML and CSS files, you should see output in your browser like that in Figure 3-40.

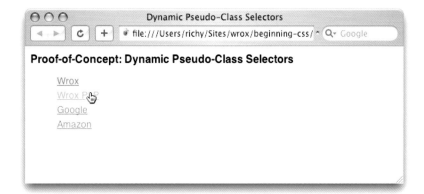

Figure 3-40

How It Works

In Example 3-9, you tried out the dynamic pseudo-classes for yourself. In Example 3-9 there were four dynamic pseudo-classes in use.

The first dynamic pseudo-class that you used styles unvisited links. Unvisited links receive the color `steelblue`.

```
a:link {
    color: steelblue;
}
```

The second dynamic pseudo-class that you used styles visited links. Visited links receive the color `darkorchid`.

```
a:visited {
    color: darkorchid;
}
```

The third selector that you used, the :hover dynamic pseudo-class, applies styles when the user's mouse cursor hovers over a link. When a user's mouse cursor comes over a link, the link is colored orange.

```
a:hover {
    color: orange;
}
```

Last, you used the :active dynamic pseudo-class, which applies style when the user clicks and holds down the mouse button on a link. When the user clicks and holds down the mouse button, the link is colored crimson.

```
a:active {
    color: crimson;
}
```

The last pseudo-class that I discuss in this chapter is the :first-child structural pseudo-class.

The first-child Structural Pseudo-Class

Much like the direct child and next sibling selectors earlier in this chapter, structural pseudo-classes are used to refer to an element's position in a document. The :first-child structural pseudo-class applies only when an element is the first child of another element.

IE 6 does not support the :first-child structural pseudo-class. See this book's website at www.wrox.com/go/beginning_css2e for compatibility help.

In Figure 3-41, you see an example of the :first-child structural pseudo-class. Try it out for yourself in the following example.

```
p:first-child {
    background: moccasin;
    border: 1px solid tan;
}
```

The :first-child structural pseudo-class is used to select the first child of another element.

```
<body>
    <p>
        The selector applies to this element, because it is the
        first child.
    </p>
    <p>
        It does not apply to this element, because it is not the
        first chld.
    </p>
</body>
</html>
```

Figure 3-41a

102

Figure 3-41b

Try It Out   The first-child Structural Pseudo-Class

Example 3-10. To see how the `:first-child` structural pseudo-class works, follow these steps.

1.   Enter the following markup into your text editor:

```
<!DOCTYPE html PUBLIC "-//W3C//DTD XHTML 1.0 Strict//EN"
                    "http://www.w3.org/TR/xhtml1/DTD/xhtml1-strict.dtd">
<html xmlns='http://www.w3.org/1999/xhtml' xml:lang='en'>
    <head>
        <title>:first-child</title>
        <link rel='stylesheet' type='text/css' href='Example_3-10.css' />
    </head>
<body>
        <h1>Abridged Beatles Discography</h1>
        <table>
            <thead>
                <tr>
                    <th>Album</th>
                    <th>Year</th>
                </tr>
            </thead>
            <tbody>
                <tr>
                    <td>Please Please Me</td>
                    <td>March 1963</td>
                </tr>
                <tr>
                    <td>With The Beatles</td>
                    <td>November 1963</td>
                </tr>
                <tr>
                    <td>A Hard Day's Night</td>
                    <td>July 1964</td>
                </tr>
                <tr>
```

```
                    <td>Beatles For Sale</td>
                    <td>December 1964</td>
                </tr>
                <tr>
                    <td>Help!</td>
                    <td>August 1965</td>
                </tr>
                <tr>
                    <td>Rubber Soul</td>
                    <td>December 1965</td>
                </tr>
                <tr>
                    <td>Revolver</td>
                    <td>August 1966</td>
                </tr>
                <tr>
                    <td>Sgt. Pepper's Lonely Hearts Club Band</td>
                    <td>June 1967</td>
                </tr>
                <tr>
                    <td>Magical Mystery Tour</td>
                    <td>November 1967</td>
                </tr>
                <tr>
                    <td>The Beatles (a.k.a. 'The White Album')</td>
                    <td>November 1968</td>
                </tr>
                <tr>
                    <td>Yellow Submarine</td>
                    <td>January 1969</td>
                </tr>
                <tr>
                    <td>Abbey Road</td>
                    <td>September 1969</td>
                </tr>
                <tr>
                    <td>Let It Be</td>
                    <td>May 1970</td>
                </tr>
            </tbody>
        </table>
    </body>
</html>
```

2. Save the preceding as `Example_3-10.html`.

3. Enter the following CSS into your text editor:

```
body {
    font-size: 12px sans-serif;
}
table {
    background: slateblue;
    color: #fff;
    width: 100%;
```

```
        border-collapse: collapse;
        border: 1px solid mediumslateblue;
    }
    td {
        border: 1px solid darkslateblue;
        padding: 2px;
    }
    th {
        background: lightsteelblue;
        color: darkslateblue;
        font-size: 18px;
        text-align: left;
    }
    table tbody tr:first-child td {
        background: mediumslateblue;
    }
```

4. Save the CSS you entered as `Example_3-10.css`. The markup and CSS you entered should look something like what you see in Figure 3-42.

Figure 3-42

How It Works

In Example 3-10, you entered in a table containing some information about albums made by The Beatles. In the style sheet you applied a variety of styles, and among them was an example of the `:first-child` structural pseudo-class.

```
table tbody tr:first-child td {
    background: mediumslateblue;
}
```

The preceding rule applies a mediumslateblue background to the cells of the first row of the table. It does this because of the tr:first-child selector, when <tr> is the first child of the <tbody> element, which is in turn a descendant of a <table> element. The descendant <td> elements of the <tr> element receive each a mediumslateblue background.

Summary

CSS selectors provide a flexible and diverse array of options for applying style to a document. CSS 2 greatly expanded the options made available in CSS 1, with the direct child, attribute value, and next sibling selectors, and CSS 3 has again expanded selector options with selectors like the attribute substring selectors.

In this chapter you learned the following:

❑   Selectors may also be user-defined using the class and/or id attributes.

❑   The universal selector applies style to all conceivable page elements.

❑   Descendant selectors apply style based on document hierarchy and ancestral relationships.

❑   Using child selectors makes the methodology created for descendant selectors more specific.

❑   Direct adjacent sibling combinators (that's a mouthful), or as I have termed them, next sibling selectors, apply style if two elements, appearing back to back in a document as siblings, have the same parent.

❑   Attribute selectors delegate style depending on the presence of attributes or attribute values.

❑   Pseudo-elements are used for situations where it would be difficult to use real markup, such as in the styling of the first letter or first line of a paragraph.

❑   Dynamic pseudo-classes are used to style a change in state; examples include visited hyperlinks, rolling the mouse cursor over an element, or actively clicking on an element.

In Chapter 4, I begin discussing concepts also fundamental to CSS, the cascade and inheritance.

Exercises

1.   Does the selector body * apply to <input> elements (assuming an <input> element appears between the <body> and </body> tags)?

2.   In the following HTML document, do the selectors li a and li > a refer to the same element(s)? Can those selectors be used interchangeably? What type of selector is each? Which one is better to use and why?

```
<!DOCTYPE html PUBLIC "-//W3C//DTD XHTML 1.0 Strict//EN"
                "http://www.w3.org/TR/xhtml1/DTD/xhtml1-strict.dtd">
<html xmlns='http://www.w3.org/1999/xhtml' xml:lang='en'>
    <head>
```

```
            <title>Dynamic Pseudo-Class Selectors</title>
            <link rel='stylesheet' type='text/css' href='Example_3-9.css' />
        </head>
        <body>
            <h1>Proof-of-Concept: Dynamic Pseudo-Class Selectors</h1>
            <ul>
                <li><a href='http://www.wrox.com/'>Wrox</a></li>
                <li><a href='http://p2p.wrox.com/'>Wrox P2P</a></li>
                <li><a href='http://www.google.com/'>Google</a></li>
                <li><a href='http://www.amazon.com/'>Amazon</a></li>
            </ul>
        </body>
    </html>
```

3. Given the HTML document in question 2, does the selector ul + h1 apply? What is the official name of that selector?

4. If you wanted to apply a style based on an HTML attribute's value, what would the selector look like?

5. If you were to style an element based on the presence of an HTML attribute, what would the selector look like?

6. What special character must you include in an attribute value selector to style an element based on what appears at the beginning of an attribute's value? What does a sample selector using that character look like?

7. How many class names can one element have?

8. What special character must you include in an attribute value selector to style an element based on what appears at the end of an attribute's value? What does a sample selector using that character look like?

9. If you wanted to style a link a different color when the user's mouse hovers over it, what might the selector look like?

4

The Cascade and Inheritance

In Chapter 3, I discussed the various types of selectors that CSS supports. In this chapter, now that you have some understanding of the basic nuts and bolts that make up CSS, you continue along that path with the cascade and inheritance. In CSS, inheritance and the cascade are as fundamental as selectors, lengths, and properties. In fact, the importance of precedence is implied by the name of the language itself: cascading style sheets. *Cascading* is a term used to describe precedence. Because CSS declarations can appear more than once for a single element, the CSS specification includes a set of guidelines defining which declarations can take precedence over others and how this is decided. In this chapter, I discuss the following:

❑ The *cascade* and how style sheets and some selectors take precedence over others

❑ Inheritance and why the values of some properties are inherited and some are not

❑ The !important rule and how to force precedence

❑ Custom style sheets and how to override website styles with them

The Cascade

Style sheets can come from more than one place. A style sheet can originate from any of the following sources:

❑ From the browser (default look and feel)

❑ From the user visiting the website (a user-defined style sheet)

❑ From the web page itself (the website's author)

Because a style sheet can originate from more than one source, it is necessary to establish an order of precedence to determine which style sheet applies style for the page the user is seeing. The first style sheet comes from the browser, and this style sheet applies some default styles for a web page, such as the default font and text color, how much space is applied between each line of text, and how much space is applied between each letter of text. In a nutshell, it controls the look and feel of the web page by controlling the behavior of each element when no styles are specified.

A style sheet can also be applied by a user visiting the website via a user-defined style sheet, which is discussed later in this chapter. This allows the user to specify his or her own look and feel. This aspect of CSS makes the web more accessible: A user with visual disabilities can write a style sheet to accommodate his or her needs, or the browser can provide options that generate the user's style sheet behind the scenes. No knowledge of CSS is required.

Finally, the author of the web page can specify a style sheet (of course). The precedence of each style sheet is as follows:

❑ The browser's style sheet is the weakest.

❑ The user's style sheet takes precedence over the browser's style sheet.

❑ The author's style sheet is the strongest and takes precedence over the user's and the browser's style sheets.

The (X)HTML `style` attribute is more important than styles defined in any style sheet.

You might be wondering what kind of styles does the browser apply? Figure 4-1a demonstrates this.

```
<!DOCTYPE html PUBLIC "-//W3C//DTD XHTML 1.0 Strict//EN"
                     "http://www.w3.org/TR/xhtml1/DTD/xhtml1-strict.dtd">
<html xmlns='http://www.w3.org/1999/xhtml' xml:lang='en'>
    <head>
        <title>Default Styles</title>
    </head>
    <body>
        <h1>Default Styles</h1>
        <p>
            Browsers apply default styles to some elements.
        </p>
        <p>
            Examples include:
        </p>
        <ul>
            <li>
                Margin or padding is applied to the &lt;body&gt; element.
            </li>
            <li>
                Margin is applied to heading elements &lt;h1&gt; through
                &lt;h6&gt;
            </li>
            <li>Margin is applied to &lt;p&gt; elements.</li>
            <li>Margin or padding is applied to the &lt;ul&gt; element.</li>
        </ul>
    </body>
</html>
```
Figure 4-1a

This results in the output in Figure 4-1b.

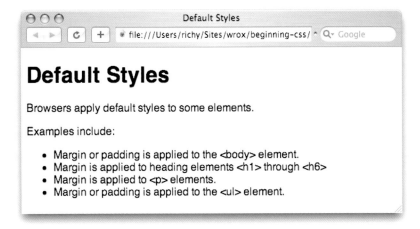

Figure 4-1b

In Figure 4-1b, you can see an example of some of the default styles that a browser applies. One example is the spacing between the heading "Default Styles" and the text in the paragraph that follows. The unordered list (<ul> element) has a bullet before each list item (the <li> element).

Figure 4-2a demonstrates a style sheet that removes the default styles shown in Figure 4-1b.

```
body {
    margin: 0;
    padding: 0;
}
h1 {
    margin: 0;
    font-weight: normal;
    font-size: 16px;
}
p {
    margin: 0;
}
ul {
    margin: 0;
    padding: 0;
    list-style: none;
}
```

On the <body> element, some browsers apply margin, while others apply padding. I talk about the difference between these two properties in Chapter 7.

Figure 4-2a

The style sheet in Figure 4-2a is applied to the markup in Figure 4-1a, which results in the output in Figure 4-2b.

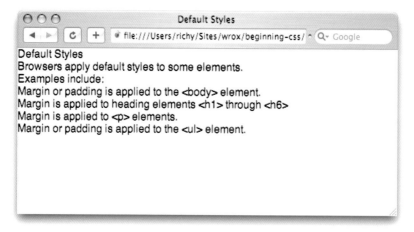

Figure 4-2b

When you compare Figure 4-2b with Figure 4-1b, you get an idea of what kinds of styles a browser applies by default. The browser applies spacing between elements and depending on the element, that spacing can be controlled by either the margin or the padding property. You learn more about those two properties in Chapter 7, "The Box Model." Figure 4-2 demonstrates, however, that it is possible to override the browser's default styles. Overriding the default styles is made possible by the cascade.

The cascade sets the order of precedence, and in Figure 4-2, it says that my style sheet rules (the author's) have stronger precedence (are more important) than the browser's built-in style sheet rules.

By and large, there are only two situations that a web designer will ever encounter in composing a style sheet: overriding the browser's default styles, and overriding styles set in other style sheets within the same website, that is, overriding the web designer's own styles set elsewhere in the same document.

In CSS, the precedence is determined by how specific a selector is. That is to say a vague selector has less precedence than a more specific selector. In the next section, I discuss how to find out how specific a selector is using a simple, easy-to-remember formula.

Calculating the Specificity of a Selector

In addition to style sheet precedence, an order of precedence exists for the selectors contained in each style sheet. This precedence is determined by how specific the selector is. For instance, an id selector is the most specific, and the universal selector is the most general. Between these, the specificity of a selector is calculated using the following formula:

❑   Count 1 if the styles are applied from the (X)HTML style attribute, and 0 otherwise; this becomes variable a.

❑   Count the number of ID attributes in the selector; the sum is variable b.

❑ Count the number of attributes, pseudo-classes, and class names in a selector; the sum is variable c.

❑ Count the number of element names in the selector; this is variable d.

❑ Ignore pseudo-elements.

Concatenate each number together to get the specificity of the selector. *Concatenate* is a programming term that means *glue together*. In this case if I concatenate a, b, c, and d I get *abcd*, instead of the sum of a, b, c, and d, which I might refer to as e. Following are some examples.

Selector	Selector Type	Specificity
*	Universal Selector	0000 ($a = 0, b = 0, c = 0, d = 0$)
li	Element Name	0001 ($a = 0, b = 0, c = 0, d = 1$)
ul li	Element Name	0002 ($a = 0, b = 0, c = 0, d = 2$)
div h1 + p	Element Name	0003 ($a = 0, b = 0, c = 0, d = 3$)
input[type='text']	Element Name + Attribute	0011 ($a = 0, b = 0, c = 1, d = 1$)
.someclass	Class Name	0010 ($a = 0, b = 0, c = 1, d = 0$)
div.someclass	Element Name + Class Name	0011 ($a = 0, b = 0, c = 1, d = 1$)
div.someclass.someother	Element Name + Class Name + Class Name	0021 ($a = 0, b = 0, c = 2, d = 1$)
#someid	ID Name	0100 ($a = 0, b = 1, c = 0, d = 0$)
div#someid	Element Name + ID Name	0101 ($a = 0, b = 1, c = 0, d = 1$)
style (attribute)	style (attribute)	1000 ($a = 1, b = 0, c = 0, d = 0$)

I have included the leading zeros in the specificity chart to clarify how concatenation works, but these are actually dropped. To determine the order of precedence, simply determine the highest number. The selector with the highest number wins. Consider the example in Figure 4-3a.

```
body {
    font-size: 24px;
}
p#none {
    background: none;
}
p {
    background: yellow;
}
```

The <p> element with id name none, doesn't get a yellow background, because its specificity is 101, which is much higher than the general <p> element selector's specificity of 1.

Figure 4-3a

Apply the CSS in Figure 4-3a to the markup in Figure 4-3b.

```
<!DOCTYPE html PUBLIC "-//W3C//DTD XHTML 1.0 Strict//EN"
                      "http://www.w3.org/TR/xhtml1/DTD/xhtml1-strict.dtd">
<html xmlns='http://www.w3.org/1999/xhtml' xml:lang='en'>
    <head>
        <title>Specificity</title>
        <link rel='stylesheet' type='text/css' href='096977%20fg0403.css' />
    </head>
    <body>
        <p>
            This paragraph has a yellow background.
        </p>
        <p  id='none'>
            This paragraph doesn't have a yellow background,
            because the id selector is more specific than the
            element selector.
        </p>
    </body>
</html>
```

Figure 4-3b

The result looks like the output shown in Figure 4-3c.

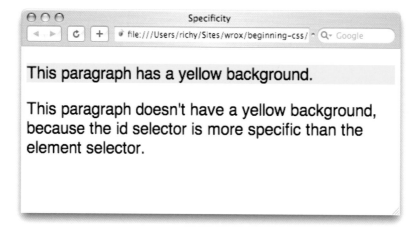

Figure 4-3c

In Figure 4-3, you see an example of precedence via the selector's specificity. In Figure 4-3a, a rule is set for all <p> elements to have a yellow background. Because the selector is vague, it has a low specificity. Using the table at the beginning of this section, you find that the selector

```
p {
    background: yellow;
}
```

has a specificity of 1, which is very low. The <p> element with id name none is set to have no background, and because it has a higher specificity than the other selector, which again using the table at the beginning of this section you find the specificity to be 101, results in the <p> element with id name none having no background.

In Figure 4-3, you can see that the order that the rules appeared in the style sheet does not matter; the rules can swap places in the style sheet and the outcome would be the same. So you might be asking yourself, does the order matter? Sometimes, it does matter, but only when there are two rules of the same specificity. Consider the example in Figure 4-4a.

```
body {
    font-size: 24px;
}
p {
    background: none;
}
p {
    background: yellow;
}
```

If two or more selectors have the same specificity, the last one wins.

Figure 4-4a

Apply the style sheet in Figure 4-4a to the markup in Figure 4-4b.

```
<!DOCTYPE html PUBLIC "-//W3C//DTD XHTML 1.0 Strict//EN"
                "http://www.w3.org/TR/xhtml1/DTD/xhtml1-strict.dtd">
<html xmlns='http://www.w3.org/1999/xhtml' xml:lang='en'>
    <head>
        <title>Specificity</title>
        <link rel='stylesheet' type='text/css' href='096977%20fg0404.css' />
    </head>
    <body>
        <p>
            This paragraph has a yellow background.
        </p>
        <p>
            This paragraph also has a yellow background.
        </p>
    </body>
</html>
```

Figure 4-4b

The result is shown in Figure 4-4c.

Figure 4-4c

In Figure 4-4c, you see that when two or more selectors have the same specificity, the last one wins.

When an (X)HTML `style` attribute is applied, it is considered the most specific of any selector on the page. That's because according to the CSS specification, it is defined as having a specificity all of its own, that is higher than any other. The `style` attribute has a specificity of 1000. Because the `style` attribute appears after any styles appearing in style sheets, it also takes precedence over the all other selectors. Therefore, the `style` attribute takes precedence over all other rules.

Try It Out   Experimenting with Specificity

Example 4-1. Follow these steps to experiment with specificity.

1.   Enter the following markup into your text editor:

```
<!DOCTYPE html PUBLIC "-//W3C//DTD XHTML 1.0 Strict//EN"
                "http://www.w3.org/TR/xhtml1/DTD/xhtml1-strict.dtd">
<html xmlns='http://www.w3.org/1999/xhtml' xml:lang='en'>
    <head>
        <title>Specificity</title>
        <link rel='stylesheet' type='text/css' href='Example_4-1.css' />
    </head>
    <body>
        <p>
            Specificity is determined by how specific the selector is.
            <span id='specific'>A specific selector wins</span>
            over a <span>more general one</span>.
        </p>
        <p>
            Order isn't important until there are one or more elements
            of the same specificity referring to the same element.  In
            which case, <span>the last one wins</span>.
        </p>
    </body>
</html>
```

2.   Save the preceding document as `Example_4-1.html`.

3. Enter the following CSS into your text editor:

```
body {
    font: 14px sans-serif;
}
span#specific {
    background: pink;
}
span {
    background: red;
}
span {
    background: yellow;
}
```

4. Save the preceding style sheet as `Example_4-1.css`. Example 4-1 results in the output you see in Figure 4-5.

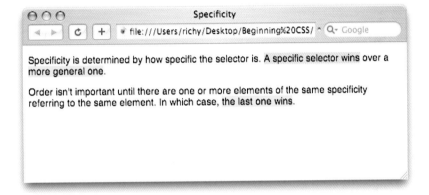

Figure 4-5

How It Works

In Example 4-1, you saw an example of the cascade in action. In the markup there are three `<span>` elements, and one has an id name of `specific`. It gets a `pink` background because the selector `span#specific` has a specificity of 101, which is more specific than the subsequent selectors, which each have a specificity of 1.

```
span#specific {
    background: pink;
}
```

Then there are two additional rules in the style sheet, each with the same specificity of 1. The last selector wins, since both selectors have the same specificity of 1, which in turn results in the last two `<span>` elements in the markup getting `yellow` backgrounds.

```
span {
    background: red;
}
```

```
span {
    background: yellow;
}
```

In the next section, I describe how you can override specificity by including special syntax within a CSS declaration.

!important Rules

Along with the need for the cascade in CSS came the need to override it. This is where !important rules come in. The !important syntax appears within a declaration, after the property value and before the semi-colon that terminates the declaration. Two components make up this syntax: an exclamation mark, used here as a delimiter, and the important keyword. A *delimiter* marks the ending of one thing and the beginning of another. Here the exclamation mark signals the end of the declaration. The important keyword must appear next, followed by a semicolon to terminate the declaration; this is demonstrated in Figure 4-6a.

```
body {
    font-size: 24px;
}
p {
    background: lightblue !important;
}
p {
    background: none;
}
```

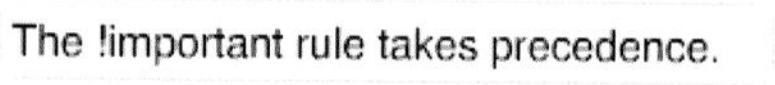

The !important rule takes precedence.

Figure 4-6a

A declaration containing the !important rule, like the preceding one, takes precedence over any other declaration. The CSS in Figure 4-6a is combined with the markup in Figure 4-6b.

```
<!DOCTYPE html PUBLIC "-//W3C//DTD XHTML 1.0 Strict//EN"
                     "http://www.w3.org/TR/xhtml1/DTD/xhtml1-strict.dtd">
<html xmlns='http://www.w3.org/1999/xhtml' xml:lang='en'>
    <head>
        <title>Specificity, !important</title>
        <link rel='stylesheet' type='text/css' href='096977%20fg0406.css' />
    </head>
    <body>
        <p>
            This paragraph has a lightblue background.
        </p>
        <p>
            This paragraph also has a lightblue background.
        </p>
    </body>
</html>
```

Figure 4-6b

The result of Figure 4-6a and Figure 4-6b result in the output in Figure 4-6c.

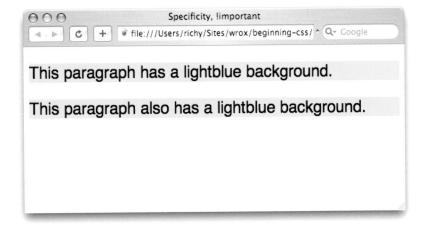

Figure 4-6c

In Figure 4-6, you see the same example as you saw in Figure 4-4 — two selectors for <p> elements with different background declarations. In Figure 4-4, the last selector won because both selectors have the same specificity. In Figure 4-6, the first selector includes the !important syntax, which causes the cascade to be overridden, and thus makes the background of both <p> elements in the XHTML document lightblue.

The !important rule also takes precedence over the style attribute. Figure 4-7 is an example of this.

```
body {
    font: 24px sans-serif;          The !important rule takes precedence over the
}                                    (X)HTML style attribute.
p {
    background: pink !important;
}
```

Figure 4-7a

The CSS in Figure 4-7a is combined with the markup in Figure 4-7b.

```
<!DOCTYPE html PUBLIC "-//W3C//DTD XHTML 1.0 Strict//EN"
                "http://www.w3.org/TR/xhtml1/DTD/xhtml1-strict.dtd">
<html xmlns='http://www.w3.org/1999/xhtml' xml:lang='en'>
    <head>
        <title>Specificity, !important</title>
        <link rel='stylesheet' type='text/css' href='096977%20fg0407.css' />
    </head>
    <body>
        <p>
            This paragraph has a pink background.
        </p>
        <p style='background: lightblue;'>
            This paragraph also has a pink background.
        </p>
    </body>
</html>
```

Figure 4-7b

The CSS in Figure 4-7a and the markup in Figure 4-7b result in the output in Figure 4-7c.

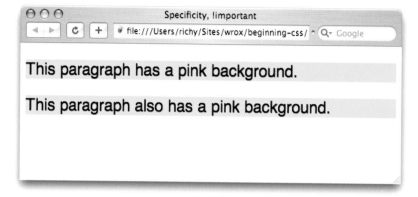

Figure 4-7c

In Figure 4-7c, you see that the background for both paragraphs is pink, despite one of the two paragraphs having a declaration setting the background of that <p> element to lightblue, which demonstrates to you that the !important rule takes precedence over even the style attribute.

If more than one !important rule appears in a style sheet, and the style sheet has the same origin — that is, both rules come from the author's style sheet or both come from the user's style sheet — the latter rule wins out over any specified previously.

Try It Out   **Working with !important Rules**

Example 4-2. Follow these steps to experiment with specificity.

1.   Enter the following markup into your text editor:

```
<!DOCTYPE html PUBLIC "-//W3C//DTD XHTML 1.0 Strict//EN"
                "http://www.w3.org/TR/xhtml1/DTD/xhtml1-strict.dtd">
<html xmlns='http://www.w3.org/1999/xhtml' xml:lang='en'>
    <head>
        <title>Specificity, !important</title>
        <link rel='stylesheet' type='text/css' href='Example_4-2.css' />
    </head>
    <body>
        <p>
            !important rules are used to override specificity.  The
            !important syntax causes a selector to have
            <span id='precedence'>
                greater precedence than those without it.
            </span>
            It also
            <span style='background: lightblue'>
                has greater precedence than the (x)HTML style attribute.
            </span>
        </p>
    </body>
</html>
```

2. Save the preceding document as `Example_4-2.html`.

3. Enter the following CSS into your text editor:

```
body {
    font: 14px sans-serif;
}
span#precedence {
    background: lightyellow;
}
span {
    background: orange !important;
}
```

4. Save the preceding style sheet as `Example_4-2.css`. Example 4-2 results in the output shown in Figure 4-8.

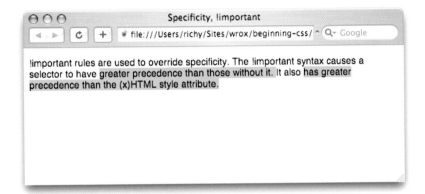

Figure 4-8

How It Works

In Example 4-2, you see how the `!important` rule overrides precedence. Because the following declaration contains the `!important` syntax, it causes the background of all the `<span>` elements to be orange.

```
span {
    background: orange !important;
}
```

So far you've seen precedence, a concept that decides how the browser applies styles based on the importance of the selector. In the next section, I talk about inheritance, which is how the browser applies certain styles to an element and all that element's children.

Inheritance

CSS is designed to simplify web document creation, enabling a property to be applied to all elements in a document. To put it another way, after a property has been applied to a particular element, its children retain those property values as well. This behavior is called *inheritance*.

121

Many properties in CSS are inheritable; some are not. Where it is supported and appropriate, inheritance makes writing style sheets a snap. For the most part, two types of properties can be inherited: text and font properties. Figure 4-9 shows an example of inheritance.

```
body {
    font-size: 24px;
}
div {
    color: crimson;
    text-align: right;
    border: 1px solid crimson;
    padding: 10px;
}
```

Properties that are inheritable, such as the color or the text-align properties, are inherited by all of the element's children.

Figure 4-9a

The CSS in Figure 4-9a is combined with the markup in Figure 4-9b.

```
<!DOCTYPE html PUBLIC "-//W3C//DTD XHTML 1.0 Strict//EN"
                      "http://www.w3.org/TR/xhtml1/DTD/xhtml1-strict.dtd">
<html xmlns='http://www.w3.org/1999/xhtml' xml:lang='en'>
    <head>
        <title>Inheritance</title>
        <link rel='stylesheet' type='text/css' href='096977%20fg0409.css' />
    </head>
    <body>
        <div>
            <h1>Inheritance</h1>
            <p>
                Some properties in CSS are inherited to children elements
                as you can see here.  The &lt;h1&gt; heading and the
                &lt;p&gt; element inherit color and alignment from the
                &lt;div&gt;, but not the border and the padding.
            </p>
        </div>
    </body>
</html>
```

Figure 4-9b

The CSS in Figure 4-9a and the markup in Figure 4-9b result in the output in Figure 4-9c.

In the preceding code, the rule is applied to the <div> element, and the color and text-align properties are inherited by the <h1> and <p> elements contained within the <div> element. The advantage of inherited properties is that you don't have to specify a property again for each nested element. On the other hand, the border and the padding properties are not inherited, since it is not likely a web designer would desire those properties to be inherited. Figure 4-10 shows what Figure 4-9 would look like if the border and padding properties were inherited.

Figure 4-9c

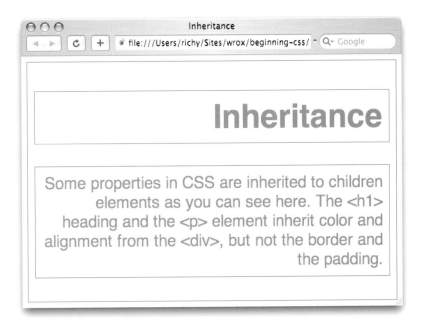

Figure 4-10

In Figure 4-10, you see that some properties, such as border and padding, are not inherited because inheriting would not be appropriate. Most of the time, you want these to be set only on a selected element and not on that selected element's children elements. I discuss the border and padding properties in more detail in Chapter 7, "The Box Model."

Inheritance for each property is outlined in Appendix B.

Try It Out   **Working with Inheritance**

Example 4-3. Follow these steps to experiment with inheritance.

1.   Enter the following markup into your text editor:

```
<!DOCTYPE html PUBLIC "-//W3C//DTD XHTML 1.0 Strict//EN"
                    "http://www.w3.org/TR/xhtml1/DTD/xhtml1-strict.dtd">
<html xmlns='http://www.w3.org/1999/xhtml' xml:lang='en'>
    <head>
        <title>Inheritance</title>
        <link rel='stylesheet' type='text/css' href='Example_4-3.css' />
    </head>
    <body>
        <p>
            In CSS, some properties are inherited, such as the color, font,
            and text properties.  Other properties, such as border, margin,
            and padding, are not inherited, since it wouldn't be
            practical.
        </p>
    </body>
</html>
```

2.   Save the preceding document as Example_4-3.html.

3.   Enter the following CSS into your text editor:

```
body {
    font: 14px sans-serif;
    color: darkslateblue;
    border: 5px dashed darkslateblue;
    margin: 10px;
    padding: 10px;
    text-align: center;
}
```

4.   Save the preceding style sheet as Example_4-3.css. Example 4-3 results in the output shown in Figure 4-11.

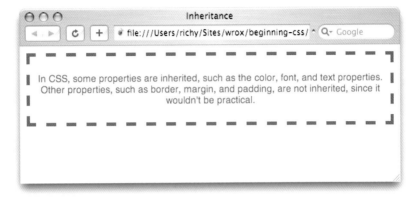

Figure 4-11

How It Works

In Example 4-3, you see an example of inheritance. In the style sheet, the properties `font`, `color`, and `text-align` are inherited by the <p> element, while the `border`, `margin`, and `padding` properties are not inherited.

```
body {
    font: 14px sans-serif;
    color: darkslateblue;
    border: 5px dashed darkslateblue;
    margin: 10px;
    padding: 10px;
    text-align: center;
}
```

Summary

Inheritance and the cascade are fundamental to CSS. Inheritance makes controlling the effects of property values a breeze, because each property is defined either to inherit or not, as is appropriate to its purpose. The cascade provides some rules for precedence to determine which styles win when multiple style sheets and rules containing the same declarations come into play. Precedence is determined by a simple formula that calculates which selector wins. In this chapter you learned the following:

❑ Some properties are inherited, which reduces redundancy in the document by eliminating the need for declarations to be written multiple times.

❑ Some properties are not inherited, which also reduces redundancy by preventing the effects of declarations from being applied to the element's descendants.

❑ The cascade provides both some ground rules and a simple formula to determine the precedence of style sheets and selectors.

Now that you know the background of CSS, Chapter 5 introduces you to CSS's text manipulation properties.

Exercises

1. In the following style sheet, determine the specificity of each selector.

```
ul#hmenu ul.menu {
    margin: 0;
    padding: 0;
    list-style: none;
    position: absolute;
    top: 35px;
    left: 0;
    width: 100%;
    visibility: hidden;
    text-align: left;
    background: rgb(242, 242, 242);
    border: 1px solid rgb(178, 178, 178);
    border-right: 1px solid rgb(128, 128, 128);
    border-bottom: 1px solid rgb(128, 128, 128);
}
ul#hmenu li li:hover {
    background: rgb(200, 200, 200);
}
ul#hmenu ul.menu ul.menu {
    top: -1px;
    left: 100%;
}
ul#hmenu li#menu-204 ul.menu ul.menu,
ul#hmenu li#menu-848 ul.menu ul.menu ul.menu ul.menu,
ul#hmenu li#menu-990 ul.menu ul.menu {
    left: auto;
    right: 100%;
}
ul#hmenu > li.menu.eas + li.menu.eas ul.menu ul.menu ul.menu ul.menu {
    right: auto;
    left: 100%;
}
li.menu,
li.menu-highlight {
    position: relative;
}
ul.menu li a {
    text-decoration: none;
    color: black;
    font-size: 12px;
    display: block;
    width: 100%;
    height: 100%;
}
ul.menu li a span {
    display: block;
```

```
        padding: 3px 10px;
    }
ul.menu span.arrow {
        position: absolute;
        top: 2px;
        right: 10px;
        width: 11px;
        height: 11px;
        background: url('/images/arrow.gif') no-repeat;
    }
```

2.   According to the following style sheet, what color is the link?

```
a.context:link {
        color: blue;
    }
a.context:visited {
        color: purple;
    }
a.context:hover {
        color: green;
    }
a.context:active {
        color: red;
    }
```

3.   According to the following style sheet, what color is the link?

```
a.context:visited {
        color: purple;
    }
a.context:hover {
        color: green;
    }
a.context:active {
        color: red;
    }
a.context:link {
        color: blue;
    }
```

4.   According to the following style sheet, what color is the link?

```
a.context:link {
        color: blue;
    }
a.context:visited {
        color: purple !important;
    }
a.context:hover {
        color: green;
    }
a.context:active {
        color: red;
    }
```

Part II
Properties

Text Manipulation

In Chapter 4, you learned how certain properties in CSS are inherited and how the cascade determines which style rules are the most important. In this and subsequent chapters, I begin an in-depth look at the individual properties of CSS and how these come together to style a document.

In this chapter, I look specifically at properties that manipulate the presentation of text. You can manipulate text in a variety of ways, from the length of space between letters in words of text, to the length of space between the words of a sentence, to the spacing between sentences in a paragraph, to how much space is used to indent the text contained in a paragraph.

I cover the various CSS text-manipulation properties:

❑ The `letter-spacing` property and how it is used to add or subtract space between the letters that make up a word

❑ The `word-spacing` property and how it is used to add or subtract space between the words of a sentence

❑ The `text-indent` property and how it is used to indent the text of a paragraph

❑ The `text-align` property and how it is used to align the text of a document

❑ The `text-decoration` property and how it is used to underline, overline, and strikethrough text

❑ The `text-transform` property and how it is used to capitalize text or convert text to uppercase or lowercase letters

❑ The `white-space` property and how it is used to control the flow and formatting of text

The text manipulation properties of CSS allow you to design the layout of a document in much the same way as you use a word processing application.

The letter-spacing Property

The letter-spacing property, as I have demonstrated briefly in previous chapters, controls the amount of space between the letters. The following table shows its allowable values.

Property	Value
letter-spacing	normal | <length> Initial value: normal

The letter-spacing property is a simple property that accepts a length as its value. A <length> value is any length value supported by CSS, as I discussed in Chapter 2. A normal value is the default value, and is determined by the font that's being used. This value is equal to a zero length value.

Figure 5-1a shows an example of the letter-spacing property.

```
h4 {
    font: 18px sans-serif;        The letter-spacing property, oddly enough, adjusts
    letter-spacing: 10px;         spacing between letters. It takes a length value.
    background: lightyellow;
    color: saddlebrown;
    margin-bottom: 0;
    border-bottom: 1px solid khaki;
}
p {
    color: darkkhaki;
    margin-top: 0;
    font-size: 14px;
}
```

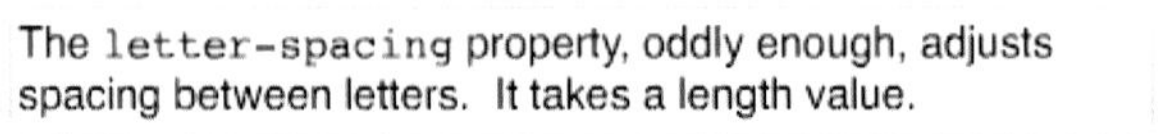

Figure 5-1a

In Figure 5-1a, you see how the letter-spacing property would be specified; Figure 5-1b shows the corresponding markup.

Figure 5-1c shows the rendered output of the CSS in Figure 5-1a and the markup in Figure 5-1b in the Safari browser.

The letter-spacing property may have either a positive or negative value. When given a negative value, letters are rendered closer together. Figure 5-2a shows an example of this.

```
<!DOCTYPE html PUBLIC "-//W3C//DTD XHTML 1.0 Strict//EN"
                      "http://www.w3.org/TR/xhtml1/DTD/xhtml1-strict.dtd">
<html xmlns='http://www.w3.org/1999/xhtml' xml:lang='en'>
    <head>
        <title>letter-spacing</title>
        <link rel='stylesheet' type='text/css' href='096977%20fg0501.css' />
    </head>
    <body>
        <h4>Wide Letter Spacing</h4>
        <p>
            In this example the space between letters in the header is
            set to 10 pixels.
        </p>
    </body>
</html>
```

Figure 5-1b

Figure 5-1c

```
h4 {
    font: 18px sans-serif;
    letter-spacing: -1px;
    background: lightyellow;
    color: saddlebrown;
    margin-bottom: 0;
    border-bottom: 1px solid khaki;
}
p {
    color: darkkhaki;
    margin-top: 0;
    font-size: 14px;
}
```

If a negative value is supplied, the letters of the target element are rendered closer together.

Figure 5-2a

The CSS in Figure 5-2a is combined with the markup in Figure 5-2b.

```
<!DOCTYPE html PUBLIC "-//W3C//DTD XHTML 1.0 Strict//EN"
                "http://www.w3.org/TR/xhtml1/DTD/xhtml1-strict.dtd">
<html xmlns='http://www.w3.org/1999/xhtml' xml:lang='en'>
    <head>
        <title>letter-spacing</title>
        <link rel='stylesheet' type='text/css' href='096977%20fg0502.css' />
    </head>
    <body>
        <h4>Narrow Letter Spacing</h4>
        <p>
            In this example the space between letters in the header is
            set to -1 pixels.
        </p>
    </body>
</html>
```

Figure 5-2b

Figure 5-2c shows the rendered output of Figures 5-2a and 5-2b.

Figure 5-2c

As you can see in Figure 5-2c, the letters of the paragraph are condensed together because the value of the `letter-spacing` property is a negative value.

You can use the `letter-spacing` property to add or subtract space between letters. In the following example, you try the `letter-spacing` property out for yourself.

The letter-spacing Property

Example 5-1. To see the `letter-spacing` property in action, follow these steps.

1. Enter the following markup:

```
<!DOCTYPE html PUBLIC "-//W3C//DTD XHTML 1.0 Strict//EN"
                "http://www.w3.org/TR/xhtml1/DTD/xhtml1-strict.dtd">
<html xmlns='http://www.w3.org/1999/xhtml' xml:lang='en'>
    <head>
        <title>letter-spacing</title>
        <link rel='stylesheet' type='text/css' href='Example_5-1.css' />
    </head>
    <body>
        <h4>Letter Spacing</h4>
        <p>
            The <span class='code'>letter-spacing</span> property can take either a
            positive or negative length value.  The higher the value, the
            <span class='higher'>farther apart the letters</span>; the lower the
            value, <span class='lower'>the closer together the letters</span>.
        </p>
    </body>
</html>
```

2. Save the preceding markup as `Example_5-1.html`.

3. Enter the following CSS:

```
body {
    font: 14px sans-serif;
}
h4 {
    border-bottom: 1px solid green;
    margin-bottom: 3px;
}
p {
    margin: 0;
}
.code {
    font-family: monospace;
}
.higher,
.lower {
    letter-spacing: 5px;
    background: lavender;
    color: midnightblue;
}
.lower {
    letter-spacing: -1px;
}
```

4. Save the preceding CSS as `Example_5-1.css`. The preceding example results in the rendered output in Figure 5-3.

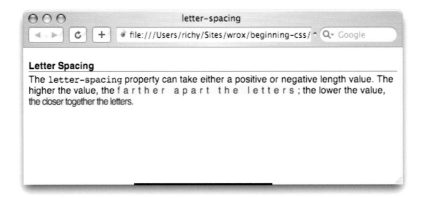

Figure 5-3

How It Works

In Example 5-1, you typed in an example of the `letter-spacing` property, so that you could see it work in a browser for yourself. You applied two relevant style sheet rules. The first rule refers to elements with class names `higher` and `lower`. Both elements initially receive a `letter-spacing` value of five pixels, a `lavender` background, and `midnightblue` text. The `letter-spacing` value of five pixels causes the letters to be spaced farther apart.

```
.higher,
.lower {
    letter-spacing: 5px;
    background: lavender;
    color: midnightblue;
}
```

In a subsequent rule, you apply another `letter-spacing` value for the element with class name *lower*; it receives a value of negative one pixel. This causes the letters in that element to be spaced close together. This new rule overrides the `letter-spacing` style set in the previous rule for elements with class name *lower*.

```
.lower {
    letter-spacing: -1px;
}f
```

In the next section, I present a property similar to the `letter-spacing` property, the `word-spacing` property.

The word-spacing Property

The `word-spacing` property, in essence, functions identically to the `letter-spacing` property. However, (of course) instead of controlling the space between letters, the `word-spacing` property controls the space between words. The following table shows its allowable values.

Property	Value
word-spacing	normal | <length> Initial value: normal

To demonstrate the effect of the `word-spacing` property, consider the style sheet rule in Figure 5-4a.

```
h4 {
    font: 18px sans-serif;          Like the letter-spacing property, larger values of the
    word-spacing: 25px;             length supplied to the word-spacing property results in
    background: mistyrose;          words spaced farther apart.
    color: crimson;
    margin-bottom: 0;
    border-bottom: 1px solid pink;
}
p {
    color: crimson;
    margin-top: 0;
    font-size: 14px;
}
```

Figure 5-4a

The style sheet in Figure 5-4a is coupled with the markup in Figure 5-4b.

```
<!DOCTYPE html PUBLIC "-//W3C//DTD XHTML 1.0 Strict//EN"
                      "http://www.w3.org/TR/xhtml1/DTD/xhtml1-strict.dtd">
<html xmlns='http://www.w3.org/1999/xhtml' xml:lang='en'>
    <head>
        <title>word-spacing</title>
        <link rel='stylesheet' type='text/css' href='096977%20fg0504.css' />
    </head>
    <body>
        <h4>Wide Word Spacing</h4>
        <p>
            In this example the space between words in the header is
            set to 25 pixels.
        </p>
    </body>
</html>
```

Figure 5-4b

Figure 5-4a and Figure 5-4b together result in the output shown in Figure 5-4c; 25 pixels of space now separate each word of the <h4> element.

Figure 5-4c

Additionally, like the `letter-spacing` property, the `word-spacing` property can contain a negative value. If given a negative value, the effects are less space between each word. This is demonstrated in CSS in Figure 5-5a.

```
h4 {
    font: 18px sans-serif;        Like the letter-spacing property, lower values
    word-spacing: -5px;           of the length supplied to the word-spacing property
    background: mistyrose;        result in words spaced closer together.
    color: crimson;
    margin-bottom: 0;
    border-bottom: 1px solid pink;
}
p {
    color: crimson;
    margin-top: 0;
    font-size: 14px;
}
```

Figure 5-5a

Again, the CSS in Figure 5-5a is combined with the markup in Figure 5-5b.

```
<!DOCTYPE html PUBLIC "-//W3C//DTD XHTML 1.0 Strict//EN"
                "http://www.w3.org/TR/xhtml1/DTD/xhtml1-strict.dtd">
<html xmlns='http://www.w3.org/1999/xhtml' xml:lang='en'>
    <head>
        <title>word-spacing</title>
        <link rel='stylesheet' type='text/css' href='096977%20fg0505.css' />
    </head>
    <body>
        <h4>Narrow Word Spacing</h4>
        <p>
            In this example the space between words in the header is
            set to -5 pixels.
        </p>
    </body>
</html>
```

Figure 5-5b

The CSS in Figure 5-5a and the markup in Figure 5-5b result in the output depicted in Figure 5-5c.

Figure 5-5c

As you did with the letter-spacing property in Example 5-1, in the following Try It Out you experiment with the word-spacing property for yourself.

Try It Out   **The word-spacing Property**

Example 5-2. To see the word-spacing property in action for yourself, follow these steps.

1.   Enter the following markup into your text editor:

```
<!DOCTYPE html PUBLIC "-//W3C//DTD XHTML 1.0 Strict//EN"
                "http://www.w3.org/TR/xhtml1/DTD/xhtml1-strict.dtd">
<html xmlns='http://www.w3.org/1999/xhtml' xml:lang='en'>
    <head>
        <title>word-spacing</title>
        <link rel='stylesheet' type='text/css' href='Example_5-2.css' />
    </head>
    <body>
        <h4>Word Spacing</h4>
        <p>
            The <span class='code'>word-spacing</span> property can take either a
            positive or negative length value.  The higher the value, the
            <span class='higher'>farther apart the words</span>; the lower the
            value, <span class='lower'>the closer together the words</span>.
        </p>
    </body>
</html>
```

2.   Save the preceding markup as Example_5-2.html.

3. Enter the following CSS into your text editor:

```
body {
    font: 14px sans-serif;
}
h4 {
    border-bottom: 1px solid pink;
    margin-bottom: 3px;
}
p {
    margin: 0;
}
.code {
    font-family: monospace;
}
.higher,
.lower {
    word-spacing: 15px;
    background: mistyrose;
    color: crimson;
}
.lower {
    word-spacing: -5px;
}
```

4. Save the preceding CSS as `Example_5-2.css`. The preceding markup and CSS results in the output shown in Figure 5-6.

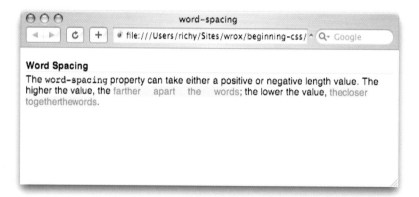

Figure 5-6

How It Works

In Example 5-2, you experimented with the `word-spacing` property. Example 5-2 is nearly identical to Example 5-1, the only difference being that you are modifying the space between words, rather than the space between letters. Following is a recap of the relevant rules.

The first rule you applied to elements with class names `higher` and `lower`, just as you did in Example 5-1. This time you applied the `word-spacing` property with a value of 15 pixels, meaning that 15 pixels of space separate the words contained within the element. This is coupled with a `mistyrose` background, and `crimson` text.

```
.higher,
.lower {
    word-spacing: 15px;
    background: mistyrose;
    color: crimson;
}
```

Then, in a subsequent rule you applied a different `word-spacing` value to elements with a `lower` class name. This time space is subtracted from between words, five pixels in fact.

```
.lower {
    word-spacing: -5px;
}
```

Now that you have seen how to control the space between letters and words, the next section describes how to indent text within a paragraph.

Indenting Paragraph Text Using text-indent

Indenting text in CSS is done using the `text-indent` property. The `text-indent` property identifies the first line of text of a paragraph and inserts the specified length before the first line of text, thus indenting the text. The following table shows this property's allowed values.

Property	Value
text-indent	<length> | <percentage>
	Initial value: 0

The `text-indent` property accepts either a normal length value or a percentage value. Figure 5-7a demonstrates the text-indent property with a normal length value in pixels applied.

```
p {
    color: saddlebrown;
    background: lightyellow;
    border: 1px solid khaki;
    padding: 10px;
    text-indent: 25px;
}
```

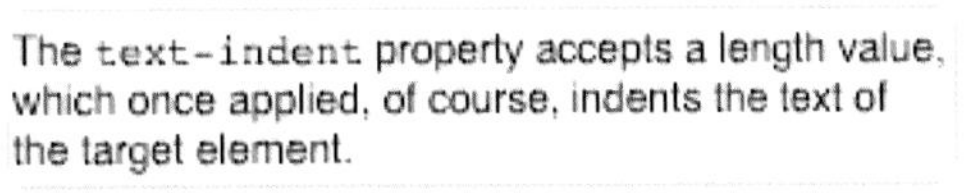

The `text-indent` property accepts a length value, which once applied, of course, indents the text of the target element.

Figure 5-7a

Figure 5-7a is combined with the markup in Figure 5-7b.

```
<!DOCTYPE html PUBLIC "-//W3C//DTD XHTML 1.0 Strict//EN"
                      "http://www.w3.org/TR/xhtml1/DTD/xhtml1-strict.dtd">
<html xmlns='http://www.w3.org/1999/xhtml' xml:lang='en'>
    <head>
        <title>text-indent</title>
        <link rel='stylesheet' type='text/css' href='096977%20fg0507.css' />
    </head>
    <body>
        <p>
            "There are two ways of constructing a software design; one way is
            to make it so simple that there are obviously no deficiencies,
            and the other way is to make it so complicated that there are no
            obvious deficiencies. The first method is far more difficult."
            - C. A. R. Hoare
        </p>
    </body>
</html>
```

Figure 5-7b

Figure 5-7c shows the result of the preceding rule and markup.

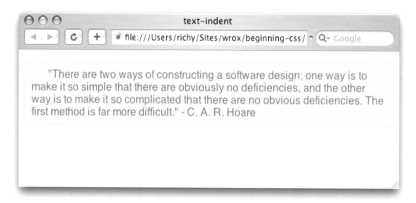

Figure 5-7c

Figure 5-7 demonstrates the most common use of the `text-indent` property, with a normal length value, used to indent the text of the target element. The `text-indent` property can also accept a percentage width. This is demonstrated in the rule in Figure 5-8a.

Figure 5-8a is combined with the markup from Figure 5-7b, to get the output you see in Figure 5-8b.

The percentage width assigned by the `text-indent` property depends on the width of the `<p>` element's parent element. In this example, the parent element is the `<body>` element. By default, the `<body>` element's width expands horizontally, filling the entire browser window.

```
p {
    color: saddlebrown;
    background: lightyellow;
    border: 1px solid khaki;
    padding: 10px;
    text-indent: 10%;
}
```

If you desire, you can also use a percentage value for the text-indent property.

Figure 5-8a

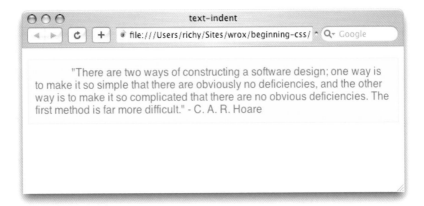

Figure 5-8b

For instance, if the <p> element were to be assigned a fixed width of 200 pixels, since the indentation for the <p> element is based on the width of the <body> element, which is more than 200 pixels, let's say for this example it's 800 pixels wide. Given a 10% indention, the indention of the first line of the <p> element would be 80 pixels, rather than 20 pixels, since 10% of 800 is 80.

Like the letter-spacing and word-spacing properties, the text-indent property can also accept a negative value. Figure 5-9a shows an example of the text-indent property with a negative value.

```
p {
    color: saddlebrown;
    background: lightyellow;
    border: 1px solid khaki;
    padding: 25px;
    text-indent: -10px;
}
```

When you provide a negative value to the text-indent property, the text of the target element is reverse indented.

Figure 5-9a

The CSS rule in Figure 5-9a is combined with the markup from Figure 5-7b. Safari (or your browser of choice) gives you the output in Figure 5-9b.

Figure 5-9b shows that the text is shifted the other way.

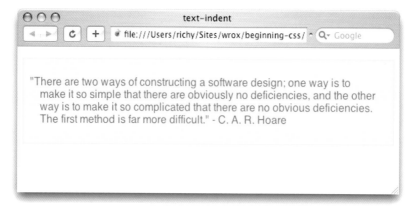

Figure 5-9b

Now that you've seen some examples of the `text-indent` property, in Example 5-3, you experiment with it for yourself.

Try It Out   Applying the text-indent Property

Example 5-3. To experiment with the `text-indent` property, follow these steps.

1. Enter the following markup into your editor. (Don't want to type out the "lipsum" dummy text? Visit `http://www.lipsum.com/`.)

```
<!DOCTYPE html PUBLIC "-//W3C//DTD XHTML 1.0 Strict//EN"
                "http://www.w3.org/TR/xhtml1/DTD/xhtml1-strict.dtd">
<html xmlns='http://www.w3.org/1999/xhtml' xml:lang='en'>
    <head>
        <title>text-indent</title>
        <link rel='stylesheet' type='text/css' href='Example_5-3.css' />
    </head>
    <body>
        <h4>Indenting Text With CSS</h4>
        <p>
            Text can be indented by a positive length value, as is demonstrated
            by the following paragraph.
        </p>
        <p class='indent-example' id='indent'>
            Lorem ipsum dolor sit amet, consectetur adipisicing elit, sed
            do eiusmod tempor incididunt ut labore et dolore magna aliqua.
            Ut enim ad minim veniam, quis nostrud exercitation ullamco
            laboris nisi ut aliquip ex ea commodo consequat. Duis aute
            irure dolor in reprehenderit in voluptate velit esse cillum
            dolore eu fugiat nulla pariatur. Excepteur sint occaecat
            cupidatat non proident, sunt in culpa qui officia deserunt mollit
            anim id est laborum.
        </p>
        <p>
            Text can be indented via a percentage value, as is demonstrated
```

```
            by the following paragraph.
        </p>
        <p class='indent-example' id='indent-percentage'>
            Lorem ipsum dolor sit amet, consectetur adipisicing elit, sed
            do eiusmod tempor incididunt ut labore et dolore magna aliqua.
            Ut enim ad minim veniam, quis nostrud exercitation ullamco
            laboris nisi ut aliquip ex ea commodo consequat. Duis aute
            irure dolor in reprehenderit in voluptate velit esse cillum
            dolore eu fugiat nulla pariatur. Excepteur sint occaecat
            cupidatat non proident, sunt in culpa qui officia deserunt mollit
            anim id est laborum.
        </p>
        <p>
            Finally, text can be reverse indented by providing a negative
            length value, which is demonstrated by the following paragraph.
        </p>
        <p class='indent-example' id='indent-reverse'>
            Lorem ipsum dolor sit amet, consectetur adipisicing elit, sed
            do eiusmod tempor incididunt ut labore et dolore magna aliqua.
            Ut enim ad minim veniam, quis nostrud exercitation ullamco
            laboris nisi ut aliquip ex ea commodo consequat. Duis aute
            irure dolor in reprehenderit in voluptate velit esse cillum
            dolore eu fugiat nulla pariatur. Excepteur sint occaecat
            cupidatat non proident, sunt in culpa qui officia deserunt mollit
            anim id est laborum.
        </p>
    </body>
</html>
```

2. Save the preceding markup as `Example_5-3.html`.

3. Enter the following CSS into your text editor:

```
body {
    font: 14px sans-serif;
}
p {
    padding: 5px 25px;
}
p#indent {
    text-indent: 25px;
}
p#indent-percentage {
    text-indent: 10%;
}
p#indent-reverse {
    text-indent: -25px;
}
p.indent-example {
    background: lightyellow;
    border: 1px solid darkkhaki;
}
```

4. Save the preceding CSS as `Example_5-3.css`. The CSS and markup of Example 5-3 result in the output you see in Figure 5-10.

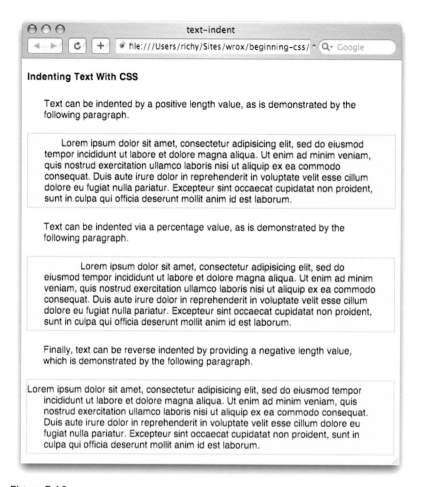

Figure 5-10

How It Works

In Example 5-3 you tried three different methods of indenting text via CSS's text-indent property. Following is a review of the relevant styles you applied.

In the first rule in which you applied the text-indent property, you applied a length value of 25 pixels.

```
p#indent {
    text-indent: 25px;
}
```

In the second rule you indented the text 10% of the parent element of the <p> element with id name *indent-percentage*, which would be the <body> element. So the 10% value is 10% of the width of the <body> element.

```
p#indent-percentage {
    text-indent: 10%;
}
```

In the third rule, you reverse indented the <p> element with id name *indent-reverse,* which resulted in the first line being indented 25 pixels to the left.

```
p#indent-reverse {
    text-indent: -25px;
}
```

In the next section, I discuss the `text-align` property.

Aligning Text with the text-align Property

The purpose of the `text-align` property is simple: It aligns text! The following table outlines each of the possible values for the `text-align` property.

Property	Value
text-align	left | right | center | justify
	Initial value: left

The text-align property should be fairly straightforward and obvious in its purpose. Figures 5-11a, 5-11b, and 5-11c demonstrate what the different keyword values of the text-align property do.

```
body {
    font: 12px sans-serif;
    color: darkslateblue;
}
h1 {
    font: 14px sans-serif;
    margin: 0;
    border-bottom: 1px solid steelblue;
}
p {
    padding: 10px;
}
p#left {
    text-align: left;
}
p#center {
    text-align: center;
}
p#right {
    text-align: right;
}
p#justify {
    text-align: justify;
}
```

The `text-align` property takes one of four values, `left`, `center`, `right` or `justify`.

Figure 5-11a

147

The CSS in Figure 5-11a is combined with the markup in Figure 5-11b.

```
<!DOCTYPE html PUBLIC "-//W3C//DTD XHTML 1.0 Strict//EN"
                      "http://www.w3.org/TR/xhtml1/DTD/xhtml1-strict.dtd">
<html xmlns='http://www.w3.org/1999/xhtml' xml:lang='en'>
    <head>
        <title>text-align</title>
        <link rel='stylesheet' type='text/css' href='096977%20fg0511.css' />
    </head>
    <body>
        <h1>Mitch Hedberg Quotes</h1>
        <p id='left'>
            "Fettuccine alfredo is macaroni and cheese for adults."
        </p>
        <p id='right'>
            "Rice is great if you're really hungry and want to eat two
            thousand of something."
        </p>
        <p id='center'>
            "I'm lactose intolerant, so I eat my cereal with a fork."
        </p>
        <p id='justify'>
            "When I went to England to tell this joke, I had to find out if
            they knew who Smokey the Bear was. But they didn't. In England,
            Smokey the Bear is not the forest fire prevention representative.
            They have Smacky the Frog. It's just like a bear, but it's a
            frog. I think it's a better system, I think we should adopt it.
            Because bears can be mean, but frogs are always cool. Never has
            there been a frog hopping toward me, and I thought "Man, I'd
            better play dead. Here comes that frog..." You never say 'here
            comes that frog' in a nervous manner. It's always optimistic.
            "Hey, here comes that frog, all right. Maybe he'll settle near
            me, and I can pet him, and stick him in a mayonnaise jar, with a
            stick and a leaf, to recreate his natural environment."
        </p>
    </body>
</html>
```

Figure 5-11b

The CSS and markup from Figures 5-11a and 5-11b result in the output observed in Figure 5-11c.

In Figure 5-11c, there are no surprises; left aligns text left, right, to the right, and center to the middle. You may not, however, be familiar with the justify keyword. In Figure 5-11c, you can see that the text is lined up on the left and on the right; spacing between words on the line is adjusted automatically so that both the beginning and the end of each line are lined up. To put this in perspective, Figure 5-12 shows the same code, but with the text-align: justify; declaration removed.

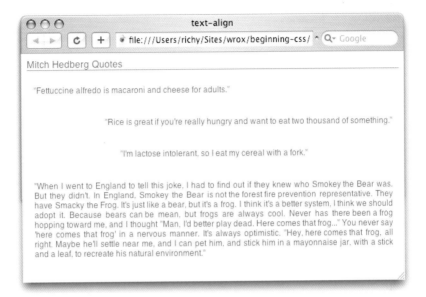

Figure 5-11c

Figure 5-12

In Figure 5-12 you can see that the ends of each line are no longer lined up.

The text-decoration Property

The text-decoration property applies underlining, overlining, and strikethrough to text. The following table outlines the text-decoration property and the values it allows.

Property	Value
text-decoration	none | [underline || overline || line-through || blink Initial value: none

Safari and IE do not support the blink *keyword.*

Because this property is a little more complicated than those covered previously, a simple explanation of its use is warranted.

To demonstrate the various styles available using this property, consider the example in Figure 5-13a.

The CSS in Figure 5-13a is combined with the markup in Figure 5-13b.

Figure 5-13c shows the various effects provided by the text-decoration property as specified by the preceding code.

However, this is not all that is possible with the text-decoration property. This notation

```
[ underline || overline || line-through || blink ]
```

means that the text-decoration property can accept one or more of these values. To specify more than one value, each value is separated by a single space. Take for example the code in Figure 5-14a.

```
body {
    font: 12px sans-serif;
}
.underline, .overline, .line-through, .blink {
    color: darkred;
    background: mistyrose;
}
.underline {
    text-decoration: underline;
}
.overline {
    text-decoration: overline;
}
.line-through {
    text-decoration: line-through;
}
.blink {
    text-decoration: blink;
}
```

The text-decoration property takes from one to four keyword values. Those can be any combination of underline, overline, line-through, or blink.

Figure 5-13a

```
<!DOCTYPE html PUBLIC "-//W3C//DTD XHTML 1.0 Strict//EN"
                     "http://www.w3.org/TR/xhtml1/DTD/xhtml1-strict.dtd">
<html xmlns='http://www.w3.org/1999/xhtml' xml:lang='en'>
    <head>
        <title>text-decoration</title>
        <link rel='stylesheet' type='text/css' href='096977%20fg0513.css' />
    </head>
    <body>
        <p>
            As of CSS 2.1, the text-decoration property supports four
            different styles, <span class='underline'>underline</span>,
            <span class='overline'>overline</span>,
            <span class='line-through'>line-through</span> and
            <span class='blink'>blink</span>.  IE and Safari, thankfully, do
            not support the annoying <span class='blink'>blink</span> style.
            Although if you must have it, it can be done with JavaScript.
        </p>
    </body>
</html>
```

Figure 5-13b

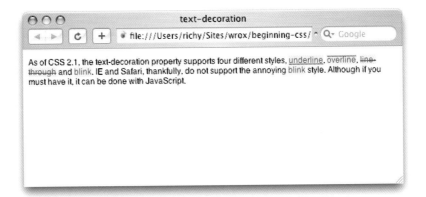

Figure 5-13c

```
body {
    font: 12px sans-serif;
}
.underover, .overthrough, .underoverthrough {
    color: darkred;
    background: mistyrose;
}
.underover {
    text-decoration: underline overline;
}
.overthrough {
    text-decoration: overline line-through;
}
.underoverthrough {
    text-decoration: underline overline line-through;
}
```

> To specify more than one
> text-decoration style, you just
> separate each keyword with a single
> space.

Figure 5-14a

The CSS in Figure 5-14a is combined with the markup in Figure 5-14b.

```
<!DOCTYPE html PUBLIC "-//W3C//DTD XHTML 1.0 Strict//EN"
                      "http://www.w3.org/TR/xhtml1/DTD/xhtml1-strict.dtd">
<html xmlns='http://www.w3.org/1999/xhtml' xml:lang='en'>
    <head>
        <title>text-decoration</title>
        <link rel='stylesheet' type='text/css' href='096977%20fg0514.css' />
    </head>
    <body>
        <p>
            text-decoration styles can be combined. For instance, you can
            have <span class='underover'>text that is underlined and
            overlined</span>.  You can have
            <span class='overthrough'>text that is overlined with a line
            through</span>.  You can even have
            <span class='underoverthrough'>text that is underlined,
            overlined, with a line-through</span>.  <b>Why</b> you would want
            to do this is another question altogether.
        </p>
    </body>
</html>
```

Figure 5-14b

The code in Figures 5-14a and 5-14b result in the output shown in Figure 5-14c.

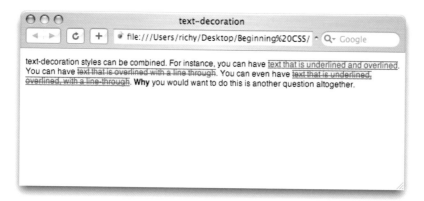

Figure 5-14c

The notation for the text-decoration property indicates that it can accept up to four values. Those values can be any combination of underline, overline, line-through, and blink. The values none or inherit can be used *instead of* any of those four values; so if either the value none or inherit is used, only that lone value may appear.

Try It Out   **Applying the text-decoration Property**

Example 5-4. To experiment with the `text-decoration` property, follow these steps.

1. Enter the following markup into your text editor:

```
<!DOCTYPE html PUBLIC "-//W3C//DTD XHTML 1.0 Strict//EN"
                 "http://www.w3.org/TR/xhtml1/DTD/xhtml1-strict.dtd">
<html xmlns='http://www.w3.org/1999/xhtml' xml:lang='en'>
    <head>
        <title>text-decoration</title>
        <link rel='stylesheet' type='text/css' href='Example_5-4.css' />
    </head>
    <body>
        <h4>CSS's text-decoration Property</h4>
        <p>
            CSS supports four text-decoration styles, officially.  Those are
            <span class='underline example'>underline</span>,
            <span class='overline example'>overline</span>,
            <span class='line-through example'>line-through</span>,
            and <span class='blink example'>blink</span>.  IE and Safari do not
            support the extremely useless <span class='blink example'>blink</span>
            keyword.
        </p>
        <p>
            It is also possible to combine text-decoration styles. You can
            for instance <span class='underover example'>underline and overline
            text</span>, <span class='underthrough example'>underline and
            line-through text</span>, or <span class='overthrough example'>overline
            and line-through text</span>, though it is unlikely you'd ever want to.
        </p>
    </body>
</html>
```

2. Save the preceding markup as `Example_5-4.html`.

3. Enter the following CSS into your text editor:

```
body {
    font: 14px sans-serif;
}
p {
    padding: 5px 25px;
    background: lightblue;
    border: 1px solid black;
}
span.underline {
    text-decoration: underline;
}
span.overline {
    text-decoration: overline;
}
span.line-through {
    text-decoration: line-through;
}
span.blink {
```

```
        text-decoration: blink;
    }
    span.underover {
        text-decoration: underline overline;
    }
    span.underthrough {
        text-decoration: underline line-through;
    }
    span.overthrough {
        text-decoration: overline line-through;
    }
    span.example {
        background: mistyrose;
    }
```

4. Save the preceding CSS as `Example_5-4.css`. The aforementioned CSS and markup result in the output in Figure 5-15.

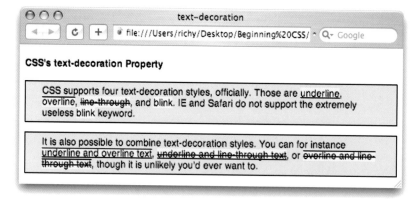

Figure 5-15

How It Works

In Example 5-4 you applied various styles of the `text-decoration` property. The first four rules are pretty straightforward; you created a separate rule for each of the four individual styles of the `text-decoration` property, `underline`, `overline`, `line-through`, and `blink`.

```
span.underline {
    text-decoration: underline;
}
span.overline {
    text-decoration: overline;
}
span.line-through {
    text-decoration: line-through;
}
span.blink {
    text-decoration: blink;
}
```

In the next three style sheet rules, you applied some combinations of styles. The `text-decoration` property allows you to specify more than one style at the same time, if you have need of doing that. Each keyword value must be separated by a single space.

```
span.underover {
    text-decoration: underline overline;
}
span.underthrough {
    text-decoration: underline line-through;
}
span.overthrough {
    text-decoration: overline line-through;
}
```

In the next section, I discuss the `text-transform` property, which allows you to control the case of text via CSS.

The text-transform Property

The `text-transform` property exists purely to manipulate the case of text, for instance, to capitalize or make all characters uppercase or all characters lowercase. The following table shows the `text-transform` property and its possible values.

Property	Value
text-transform	capitalize | uppercase | lowercase | none
	Initial value: none

Consider the CSS in Figure 5-16a.

```
body {
    font: 12px sans-serif;
}
#capitalize {
    text-transform: capitalize;
}
#uppercase {
    text-transform: uppercase;
}
#lowercase {
    text-transform: lowercase;
}
```

The `text-transform` property can take one of four values, `capitalize`, `uppercase`, `lowercase`, or `none`.

Figure 5-16a

This CSS is combined with the markup in Figure 5-16b.

```
<!DOCTYPE html PUBLIC "-//W3C//DTD XHTML 1.0 Strict//EN"
                      "http://www.w3.org/TR/xhtml1/DTD/xhtml1-strict.dtd">
<html xmlns='http://www.w3.org/1999/xhtml' xml:lang='en'>
    <head>
        <title>text-transform</title>
        <link rel='stylesheet' type='text/css' href='096977%20fg0516.css' />
    </head>
    <body>
        <p id='capitalize'>every word of this statement is captitalized.</p>
        <p id='uppercase'>every letter in this statement is in uppercase.</p>
        <p id='lowercase'>EVERY LETTER IN THIS STATEMENT IS IN LOWERCASE.</p>
    </body>
</html>
```

Figure 5-16b

Figure 5-16c shows that the text-transform property overrides the case of the text, no matter how it appears in the source code.

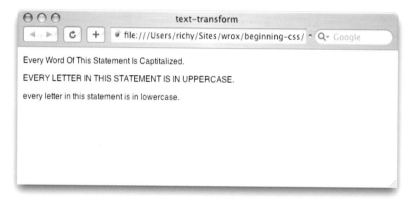

Figure 5-16c

In the first paragraph, even though in the source the sentence appears in all lowercase, if you apply the text-transform: capitalize; declaration, each word of the sentence is capitalized. Likewise, in the next paragraph, even though the source code contains all lowercase letters, with the addition of the text-transform: uppercase; declaration, each word of the sentence appears in all uppercase letters in the rendered output. In the last paragraph, each word appears in uppercase in the markup source code, but with the addition of the text-transform: lowercase; declaration, each word of the sentence appears in all lowercase in the actual output rendered by the browser.

Now that you've seen an example of what the text-transform property does, in the following example you try out the text-transform property for yourself.

Try It Out   **Apply the text-transform Property**

Example 5-5. To get a feel for the `text-transform` property, follow these steps.

1.   Enter the following markup into your text editor:

```
<!DOCTYPE html PUBLIC "-//W3C//DTD XHTML 1.0 Strict//EN"
                      "http://www.w3.org/TR/xhtml1/DTD/xhtml1-strict.dtd">
<html xmlns='http://www.w3.org/1999/xhtml' xml:lang='en'>
    <head>
        <title>text-transform</title>
        <link rel='stylesheet' type='text/css' href='Example_5-5.css' />
    </head>
    <body>
        <h4>Manipulating Case With the text-transform Property</h4>
        <p>
            You can control the case of text using CSS. For instance,
            you can make <span class='lower example'>UPPERCASE TEXT
            LOWERCASE</span> or <span class='upper example'>lowercase
            text uppercase</span>, or you can just
            <span class='capitalize example'>capitalize every word
            in a sentence</span>.
        </p>
    </body>
</html>
```

2.   Save the preceding markup as `Example_5-5.html`.

3.   Enter the following CSS into your text editor:

```
body {
    font: 14px sans-serif;
}
p {
    padding: 5px 25px;
    background: mistyrose;
    border: 1px solid orange;
}
span.lower {
    text-transform: lowercase;
}
span.upper {
    text-transform: uppercase;
}
span.capitalize {
    text-transform: capitalize;
}
span.example {
    background: pink;
}
```

4.   Save the preceding CSS as `Example_5-5.css`. The aforementioned CSS and markup result in the output in Figure 5-17.

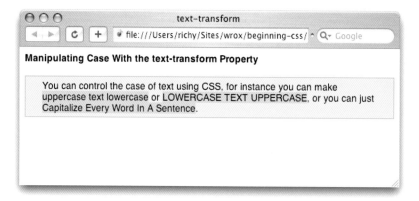

Figure 5-17

How It Works

In Example 5-5, you tried out the different methods that CSS provides for manipulating the case of text in a document. Following are the relevant three rules. In the first rule, you made the uppercase text in the `<span>` element with class name *lower*, lowercase.

```
span.lower {
    text-transform: lowercase;
}
```

In the second rule, you made the lowercase text in the `<span>` element with class name `upper` all uppercase.

```
span.upper {
    text-transform: uppercase;
}
```

In the third rule, you capitalized each word of the all-lowercase text in the `<span>` element with class name `capitalize`.

```
span.capitalize {
    text-transform: capitalize;
}
```

In the next section, I present CSS's `white-space` property, which controls whether or not spaces and line breaks in the source code are recognized, and whether or not text wraps automatically.

The white-space Property

The `white-space` property allows you to control text formatting in the source code of the web document. The following table outlines the possible keyword values of the `white-space` property as of CSS 2.

Property	Value
white-space	normal | pre | nowrap
	Initial value: normal

IE 6 and IE 7 support white-space: pre; *only in standards rendering mode. For more information on rendering modes, see Chapter 7, "The Box Model."*

Figure 5-18a is an example of the white-space: pre; declaration.

I've specified a monospace font for clarity. The CSS in Figure 5-18a is combined with the markup in Figure 5-18b.

```
body {
    font: 16px sans-serif;
}
p {
    white-space: pre;
}
span.quote {
    color: purple;
}
span.author {
    font-size: 12px;
}
```

The pre keyword of the white-space property causes spacing and line breaks in the source code to be preserved.

Figure 5-18a

```
<!DOCTYPE html PUBLIC "-//W3C//DTD XHTML 1.0 Strict//EN"
                      "http://www.w3.org/TR/xhtml1/DTD/xhtml1-strict.dtd">
<html xmlns='http://www.w3.org/1999/xhtml' xml:lang='en'>
    <head>
        <title>white-space</title>
        <link rel='stylesheet' type='text/css' href='096977%20fg0518.css' />
    </head>
    <body>
<p>
    <span class='quote'>From the moment I picked up
your book until I laid it down,
I was convulsed with laughter.
Some day I intend reading it.</span>

                <span class='author'>- Groucho Marx</span>
</p>
    </body>
</html>
```

Figure 5-18b

The result looks like Figure 5-18c.

Figure 5-18c

In the source code for the output shown in Figure 5-18c, I've added spaces before each line and line breaks. With the `white-space: pre;` declaration, those spaces and line breaks are preserved in the browser's rendered output.

By default, the browser will collapse the extra spaces between words and ignore the line breaks, which is the behavior of the `white-space: normal;` declaration. The `white-space: pre;` declaration preserves that extra space and keeps the line breaks where they appear in the source code. Under normal circumstances, if there is too much text to appear on a single line, the extra text overflows onto the following line or lines. The `white-space: nowrap;` declaration prevents that overflow from happening and forces the text to stay on one line, unless an HTML line break `<br />` element is encountered. That forces a line break. Figure 5-19a is an example of this.

```
body {
    font: 12px sans-serif;
}
p {
    white-space: nowrap;
}
```

The `nowrap` keyword prevents text from wrapping onto new lines automatically, unless an explicit (X)HTML line break `<br />` is included.

Figure 5-19a

The CSS in Figure 5-19a is combined with the markup in Figure 5-19b.

Figure 5-19c shows that the text has flowed off the screen to the right because there is more text than can fit on the screen.

Compare the output in Figures 5-18c and 5-19c to that in Figure 5-20 where no `white-space` property is applied. That is, applying the `white-space: normal;` declaration is the same as applying no white-space property, because `normal` is the initial value of the `white-space` property.

```
<!DOCTYPE html PUBLIC "-//W3C//DTD XHTML 1.0 Strict//EN"
                      "http://www.w3.org/TR/xhtml1/DTD/xhtml1-strict.dtd">
<html xmlns='http://www.w3.org/1999/xhtml' xml:lang='en'>
    <head>
        <title>white-space</title>
        <link rel='stylesheet' type='text/css' href='096977%20fg0519.css' />
    </head>
    <body>
<p>
    From the moment I picked up
    your book until I laid it down,
    I was convulsed with laughter.
    Some day I intend reading it.

                    - Groucho Marx
</p>
    </body>
</html>
```

Figure 5-19b

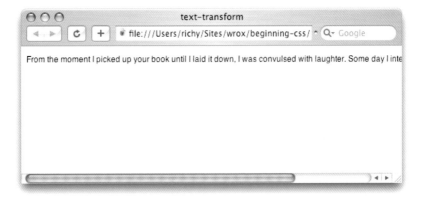

Figure 5-19c

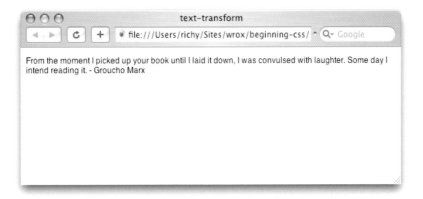

Figure 5-20

Now that you've had an overview of what the white-space property is, the following Try It Out gives you an opportunity to test the white-space property for yourself.

Try It Out   **Applying the white-space Property**

Example 5-6. Follow these steps to see the white-space property in action for yourself.

1.   Enter the following markup into your text editor. Again, the dummy text in the example can be copied from http://www.lipsum.com/.

```
<!DOCTYPE html PUBLIC "-//W3C//DTD XHTML 1.0 Strict//EN"
                    "http://www.w3.org/TR/xhtml1/DTD/xhtml1-strict.dtd">
<html xmlns='http://www.w3.org/1999/xhtml' xml:lang='en'>
    <head>
        <title>white-space</title>
        <link rel='stylesheet' type='text/css' href='Example_5-6.css' />
    </head>
    <body>
        <h4>Controlling white-space With CSS</h4>
        <p>
            CSS provides a property for controlling how the white-space
            in the source code is handled.  When you use the pre keyword
            with the white-space property, for example, all the spaces
            and line breaks in the source code are preserved, as is
            demonstrated by the following paragraph.
        </p>
        <p id='pre' class='example'>
            Lorem ipsum dolor sit amet, consectetuer adipiscing elit.
            Vestibulum nisl tortor, vehicula eu, eleifend a, tincidunt ac,
            erat. Ut ut turpis. Nullam urna odio, tempor eget, egestas at,
            luctus tristique, felis. Donec eget velit. Vestibulum
            scelerisque felis in dolor.
        </p>
        <p>
            You can also prevent text from wrapping automatically. This is
            done using the nowrap keyword in conjunction with the white-space
            property, as is demonstrated by the following paragraph.
        </p>
        <p id='nowrap' class='example'>
            Lorem ipsum dolor sit amet, consectetuer adipiscing elit. Vestibulum
            nisl tortor, vehicula eu, eleifend a, tincidunt ac, erat. Ut ut turpis.
            Nullam urna odio, tempor eget, egestas at, luctus tristique, felis.
            Donec eget velit. Vestibulum scelerisque felis in dolor.
        </p>
    </body>
</html>
```

2.   Save the preceding markup as Example_5-6.html.

3. Enter the following CSS into your text editor:

```
body {
    font: 14px sans-serif;
}
p {
    padding: 5px;
}
p#pre {
    white-space: pre;
}
p#nowrap {
    white-space: nowrap;
}
p.example {
    background: lightyellow;
    border: 1px solid darkkhaki;
}
```

4. Save the preceding CSS as `Example_5-6.css`. The aforementioned CSS and markup result in the output in Figure 5-21.

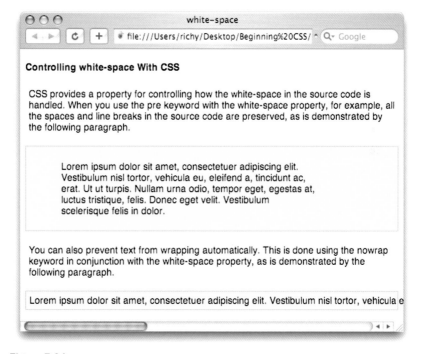

Figure 5-21

How It Works

In Example 5-6 you tried out two keywords of the white-space property. Following is a review of the two relevant rules. In the first rule, you applied the pre keyword of the white-space property. The pre keyword causes all spacing and line breaks in the source code to be preserved in the rendered output.

```
p#pre {
    white-space: pre;
}
```

In the second rule, you applied the nowrap keyword of the white-space property, which prevents the text of the <p> element with id name nowrap from wrapping.

```
p#nowrap {
    white-space: nowrap;
}
```

Summary

In this chapter, I discussed a variety of CSS text-manipulation properties, which include the following:

- ❑ The letter-spacing property, which is used to specify the length of space between letters
- ❑ The word-spacing property, which is used to specify the length of space between words
- ❑ The text-indent property, which is used to indent text
- ❑ The text-align property, which is used to align the text of a document
- ❑ The text-decoration property, which is used to apply decorative styling to text, such as underlining, overlining, strikethrough, or blinking text
- ❑ The text-transform property, which is used to control the case of text regardless of what case is used in the document's source code
- ❑ The white-space property, which is used to control text formatting as it relates to how the text appears in the document's source code

Chapter 6 continues along the same vein of text manipulation, with a discussion of the font properties in CSS.

Exercises

1. If you wanted to reduce the spacing between letters, how would it be done? Provide an example declaration.

2. How would you produce the output you see in Figure 5-22? Provide the declaration.

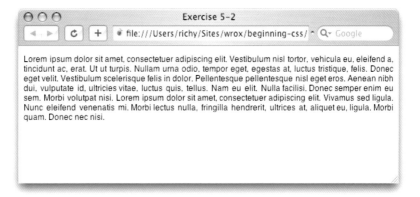

Figure 5-22

3. When indenting text in a paragraph, how is a percentage value calculated?

4. What are the keywords that CSS offers for changing the case of text within an element?

5. If you wanted to preserve line breaks and spacing as formatted in the source code, what would the CSS declaration be?

6. What browsers do not support the annoying `blink` keyword?

7. If you wanted to put a line over a section of text, rather than underlining it, what property and keyword would you use?

Fonts

Chapter 5 presented a variety of text manipulation properties. This chapter continues the discussion of text manipulation with CSS's font manipulation properties. CSS includes a variety of properties that change the face, size, and style of a font. This chapter covers:

- ❑ The `font-family` property and how it is used to change the face of a font
- ❑ The `font-style` property and how it is used to make a font italic or oblique
- ❑ The `font-variant` property, a property similar to the `text-transform` property presented in Chapter 5, and how this property is used to create a small-caps effect
- ❑ The `font-weight` property and how it is used to increase or decrease how bold or light a font appears
- ❑ The `font-size` property and how it is used to increase or decrease the size of a font
- ❑ The `font` property and how it is used as shorthand to specify a number of other font properties

I begin the discussion of CSS's font properties with the `font-family` property.

Specifying Fonts with the font-family Property

The `font-family` property is used to specify fonts. The following table outlines the `font-family` property and the values that it allows.

Property	Value
font-family	[[<family-name> | <generic-family>] [, <family-name>| <generic-family>]*]
	Initial value: Varies depending on the browser or user agent.

Figure 6-1a is an example of the basic use of the `font-family` property.

```
body {
    color: royalblue;
    font-size: 24px;
}
p#times-new-roman {
    font-family: "Times New Roman";     Fonts with spaces in the name must be
}                                       enclosed in quotations.
p#arial {
    font-family: Arial;                 Fonts without spaces in the name do not
}                                       require quotations.
```

Figure 6-1a

The rules in Figure 6-1a are combined with the markup in Figure 6-1b.

```
<!DOCTYPE html PUBLIC "-//W3C//DTD XHTML 1.0 Strict//EN"
                      "http://www.w3.org/TR/xhtml1/DTD/xhtml1-strict.dtd">
<html xmlns='http://www.w3.org/1999/xhtml' xml:lang='en'>
    <head>
        <title>font-family</title>
        <link rel='stylesheet' type='text/css' href='096977%20fg0601.css' />
    </head>
    <body>
        <p id='times-new-roman'>
            Times New Roman
        </p>
        <p id='arial'>
            Arial
        </p>
    </body>
</html>
```

Figure 6-1b

The CSS and markup in Figures 6-1a and 6-1b result in the output in Figure 6-1c.

Figure 6-1c

The example is pretty straightforward. Times New Roman is applied to the first paragraph with the id name `times-new-roman`, and Arial is applied to the second paragraph, with id name `arial`. There is one fundamental difference between the two: Times New Roman appears enclosed in double quotes. The name of the font itself contains white space, and so enclosing the name of the font in quotes prevents the browser from getting confused. The second example, which specifies an Arial font, does not appear enclosed in quotes because no white space appears in the name of the font.

The notation for the `font-family` property can accept one or more fonts for its value, which is what is meant by the repetition of the syntax in the notation and the presence of the asterisk. The asterisk indicates that the syntax may be repeated one or more times, and a comma is used to separate each font name provided. You can specify two types of fonts. The first is documented as `<family-name>` in the preceding table. The `<family-name>` notation refers to fonts installed on the user's computer, which means that the available fonts depend on the user's operating system and the fonts available to that operating system. The `<generic-family>` notation refers to a small subset of predefined fonts that can be expected to always be available; this is discussed shortly.

Font Families

The available font families that can be specified vary depending on the operating system. Using a default installation, Windows does not provide the same fonts as Mac OS X, for instance. Furthermore, the available fonts also vary depending on the programs installed on the user's computer. For instance, Microsoft Office installs a number of extra fonts in addition to those that ship with Mac OS X or Windows. In fact, with the exception of a few fonts, Mac OS X with Microsoft Office installed provides pretty much the same fonts as installed on Windows. Without Microsoft Office installed, however, many Windows fonts are not available on the Mac platform.

It is for this reason, the possibility of font inconsistencies, that the `font-family` property is dynamic. It can accept more than one font as its value. The browser will use the first font provided that is installed and available on the end user's computer. The browser will fall back to the next font in the list in the event that previous fonts are not available. So subsequent fonts in the list are called *fallback fonts*. This capability is provided because it is difficult to foresee which fonts will be available on the user's computer.

It is best to test your web page on several different platforms using different browsers on different operating systems to ensure that your fonts are working as you intend them to. Providing fallback fonts ensures consistency of fonts. Take for example the rule in Figure 6-2a.

```
body {
    font-size: 24px;
}
p {
    font-family: "Californian FB", AppleMyungjo;
}
```

A list of fonts can be supplied to the `font-family` property. Fonts after the first font are called fallback fonts, which are only used in the event that previous fonts are not available. A comma is used to separate each font in the list.

Figure 6-2a

The CSS in Figure 6-2a is combined with the markup in Figure 6-2b.

```
<!DOCTYPE html PUBLIC "-//W3C//DTD XHTML 1.0 Strict//EN"
                      "http://www.w3.org/TR/xhtml1/DTD/xhtml1-strict.dtd">
<html xmlns='http://www.w3.org/1999/xhtml' xml:lang='en'>
    <head>
        <title>font-family</title>
        <link rel='stylesheet' type='text/css' href='096977%20fg0601.css' />
    </head>
    <body>
        <p>
            This text appears in Californian FB, if Californian FB is
            available.  If Californian FB is not available, AppleMyungjo is
            used.
        </p>
    </body>
</html>
```

Figure 6-2b

The CSS and markup in Figure 6-2a and Figure 6-2b produce the results shown in Figure 6-2c.

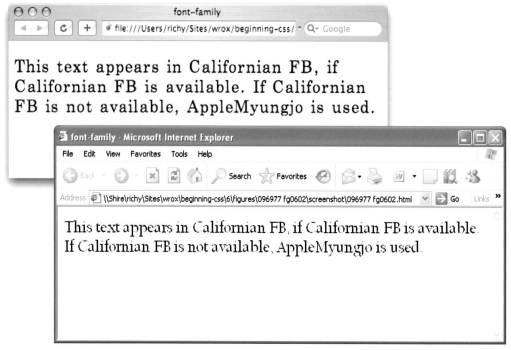

Figure 6-2c

In the example in Figure 6-2, two fonts are specified as the value of the `font-family` property. This allows you to specify a fallback font. In this case, if Californian FB (common to Windows computers) is not installed on the user's computer, the browser attempts to display the AppleMyungjo font (common to Macintosh computers). If neither font is available, the browser uses its default font, which is the same as the font used when no font is specified and varies depending on the browser. The `font-family` allows a potentially unlimited list of fonts to be specified, meaning that you can specify as many fonts as you'd like to fall back on. It may also be possible that you do not have any of these fonts, since certain software packages such as Microsoft Office, and Adobe Creative Suite install various fonts along with the software; fonts available will vary from computer to computer.

The effect of the following code is that the browser goes through the list of comma-separated fonts until it finds one that it is capable of displaying:

```
p {
    font-family: Arial, Shruti, "Microsoft Sans Serif", Tahoma, Mangal, Helvetica;
}
```

CSS provides a couple of generic fonts, serif, sans-serif, monospace, fantasy, and cursive, that you can always rely on being installed.

Generic Font Families

As I mentioned in the previous section, the available fonts vary from operating system to operating system. They can vary even more with individual user's computer systems because even more fonts can be installed along with certain programs. The only way to maintain consistency displaying from platform to platform is to provide either a list of font families (so a fallback font can be called upon if the desired font is not installed) or to specify a generic font. Generic fonts are a set of basic fonts that are available regardless of the user's operating system.

The following table outlines the generic font family names defined in CSS.

Generic Font	Resembles
serif	Times, Times New Roman
sans-serif	Helvetica, Arial
cursive	Zapf-Chancery
fantasy	Western
monospace	Courier, Courier New

Generic fonts are often mapped, by the browser, to other fonts that already exist on the system. For example, on Windows, IE maps the sans-serif font to Arial and the serif font to Times New Roman. In fact some browsers provide user-configurable generic fonts. In Firefox, for example, you can set the font used for the serif, sans-serif, cursive, fantasy, and monospace generic fonts.

The generic font names display fonts similarly in different browsers and operating systems. Figure 6-3 shows generic font output in various browsers, as they appear by default.

Figure 6-3

Figure 6-3 shows how various browsers render generic fonts. From the output shown in those figures, you can see that generic font rendering is not exactly identical between browsers and platforms. Fonts that display consistently are serif, sans-serif, and monospace. Because of the wildly varying differences in rendering of the fantasy and cursive fonts, designers seldom use these two fonts.

In the notation for the `font-family` property documentation, `<generic-family>` refers to the possible specification of a generic font name. Often a generic font is included as a last fallback option, as shown in the following rule:

```
p {
    font-family: Arial, Shruti, Tahoma, Mangal, Helvetica, sans-serif;
}
```

The addition of *sans-serif* to the end of the font list for the `font-family` property means that as a last resort, if none of the other fonts specified are installed on the user's computer, the generic sans-serif font should be used.

Use the following Try It Out to experiment with the `font-family` property for yourself.

Try It Out   Applying the font-family Property

Example 6-1. Follow these steps to experiment with the `font-family` property.

1.   Write the following markup in your text editor:

```
<!DOCTYPE html PUBLIC "-//W3C//DTD XHTML 1.0 Strict//EN"
                    "http://www.w3.org/TR/xhtml1/DTD/xhtml1-strict.dtd">
<html xmlns='http://www.w3.org/1999/xhtml' xml:lang='en'>
    <head>
        <title>font-family</title>
        <link rel='stylesheet' type='text/css' href='Example_6-1.css' />
    </head>
    <body>
        <p>
            The font-family property allows you to specify a
            <span class='font1'>font face</span>.
            It has the built-in ability of allowing you to
            <span class='font2'>specify fallback fonts</span>,
            <span class='font3'>
                fonts that are used when your first choice
                (or choices) aren't installed on the end user's OS
            </span>.
            Even though, these days, because of the dominance of the
            <span class='font4'>Windows platform</span>,
            cross-platform fonting is less of an issue.
        </p>
    </body>
</html>
```

2.   Save `Example_6-1.html`.

3. Write the following CSS in your text editor:

```css
body {
    font: 14px sans-serif;
    line-height: 30px;
}
span {
    background: mistyrose;
    border: 1px solid pink;
}
span.font1 {
    font-family: "Perpetua Titling MT", serif;
}
span.font2 {
    font-family: "Baskerville Old Face", serif;
}
span.font3 {
    font-family: "Lucida Bright", monospace;
}
span.font4 {
    font-family: Herculanum, "Eras Demi ITC", sans-serif;
}
```

4. Save the CSS as `Example_6-1.css`. The results of these modifications are shown in Figure 6-4.

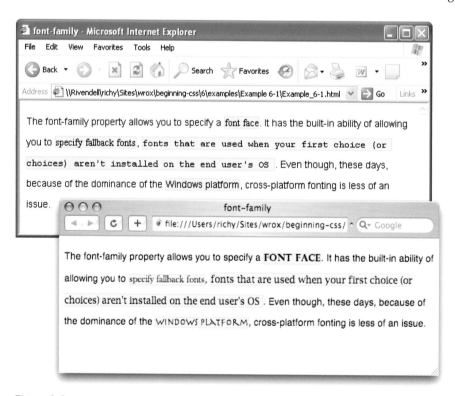

Figure 6-4

How It Works

In Example 6-1, you made use of four examples of the `font-family` property. Following is a review of each of the four relevant rules.

The first example of the `font-family` property you used was applied to the `<span>` element with class name `font1`. It is given the *Perpetua Titling MT* font face, which is enclosed in quotations because the font name contains spaces. As you can see in the screenshot of Safari and IE 6 in Figure 6-4, this font works on both Mac and Windows platforms.

```
span.font1 {
    font-family: "Perpetua Titling MT", serif;
}
```

In the second example, you specify the *Baskerville Old Face* font, which is again present on both Mac OS X and Windows.

```
span.font2 {
    font-family: "Baskerville Old Face", serif;
}
```

In the third example, you specify the *Lucida Bright* font, and like the previous two, this font is present on both Mac OS X and Windows. The generic font, *monospace*, is specified as a fallback font, just in case Lucida Bright is not installed on the end user's OS.

```
span.font3 {
    font-family: "Lucida Bright", monospace;
}
```

Finally, in the last example you encounter a font that is not shared between Mac and Windows, *Herculanum*, which is installed on Mac OS X. On Windows, the browser falls back to *Eras Demi ITC*, and if neither of those fonts are present, the browser falls back to the generic *sans-serif* font.

```
span.font4 {
    font-family: Herculanum, "Eras Demi ITC", sans-serif;
}
```

In the next section, I discuss how to make text italic or oblique with the font-style property.

The font-style Property

The `font-style` property is used to switch between styles provided by a particular font. Those styles are italic or oblique, and they are a part of the font itself. The following table outlines the possible values for the `font-style` property.

Property	Value
font-style	normal | italic | oblique
	Initial value: normal

The italic and oblique values are, with most fonts, indistinguishable in how they render. Consider the example in Figure 6-5a.

```
body {
    font-size: 24px;
}
p {
    margin: 0;
}
p#italic {
    font-style: italic;
}
p#oblique {
    font-style: oblique;
}
```

For the majority of fonts, the italic and oblique styles are rendered identically.

Figure 6-5a

Combine the rules in Figure 6-5a with the markup in Figure 6-5b.

```
<!DOCTYPE html PUBLIC "-//W3C//DTD XHTML 1.0 Strict//EN"
                      "http://www.w3.org/TR/xhtml1/DTD/xhtml1-strict.dtd">
<html xmlns='http://www.w3.org/1999/xhtml' xml:lang='en'>
    <head>
        <title>font-style</title>
        <link rel='stylesheet' type='text/css' href='096977%20fg0605.css' />
    </head>
    <body>
        <p>
            This font is normal.
        </p>
        <p id='italic'>
            This font is italic.
        </p>
        <p id='oblique'>
            This font is oblique.
        </p>
    </body>
</html>
```

Figure 6-5b

Figure 6-5c shows that the oblique and italic values are identical.

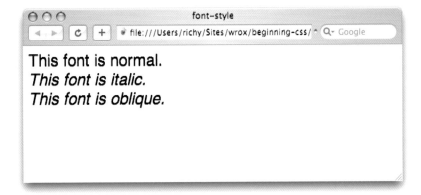

Figure 6-5c

This test of the oblique and italic values shows that if the font has an italic style, that italic style is used when either the italic or oblique values are specified, there is no difference between the two values. This behavior is identical when viewed in IE, Opera, or Firefox. In my experience, because it is identical to the italic style, and the browser will automatically select the italic style if a font has no oblique style and vice versa, I have never seen the oblique style actually used in real-world sites.

However, not all fonts have an italic style or an oblique style. Consider the example in Figure 6-6, which demonstrates what happens when a font has neither an italic nor an oblique style.

```
body {
    font-size: 24px;
}
p {
    margin: 0;
    font-family: "Monotype Corsiva";
}
p#italic {
    font-style: italic;
}
p#oblique {
    font-style: oblique;
}
```

Some fonts do not have an italic nor an oblique style. The results differ from browser to browser when an italic or an oblique style is specified for fonts that do not have these styles

Figure 6-6a

Combine the style sheet in Figure 6-6a with the markup in Figure 6-6b.

```
<!DOCTYPE html PUBLIC "-//W3C//DTD XHTML 1.0 Strict//EN"
                      "http://www.w3.org/TR/xhtml1/DTD/xhtml1-strict.dtd">
<html xmlns='http://www.w3.org/1999/xhtml' xml:lang='en'>
    <head>
        <title>font-style</title>
        <link rel='stylesheet' type='text/css' href='096977%20fg0606.css' />
    </head>
    <body>
        <p>
            This font is normal.
        </p>
        <p id='italic'>
            This font is italic.
        </p>
        <p id='oblique'>
            This font is oblique.
        </p>
    </body>
</html>
```

Figure 6-6b

Figure 6-6c shows *Monotype Corsiva,* a font that has neither an italic style nor an oblique style — it has only one style.

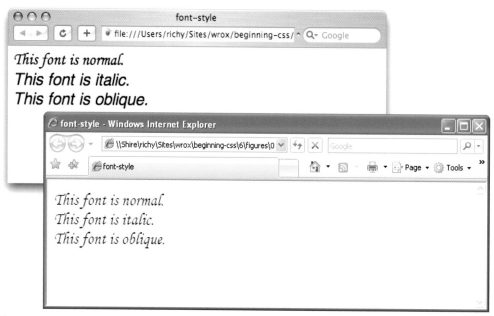

Figure 6-6c

In Figure 6-6c, you can see that Safari and IE treat fonts that do not have an italic or an oblique style differently. Safari falls back on the default font, rather than rendering the font. IE just ignores the italic and oblique styles and goes ahead and renders the font.

In the following Try It Out you experiment with the `font-style` property.

Try It Out   **Applying the font-style Property**

Example 6-2. Follow these steps to try out the `font-style` property.

1.   Write the following markup in your text editor:

```
<!DOCTYPE html PUBLIC "-//W3C//DTD XHTML 1.0 Strict//EN"
                    "http://www.w3.org/TR/xhtml1/DTD/xhtml1-strict.dtd">
<html xmlns='http://www.w3.org/1999/xhtml' xml:lang='en'>
    <head>
        <title>font-style</title>
        <link rel='stylesheet' type='text/css' href='Example_6-2.css' />
    </head>
    <body>
        <p>
            When it comes to the font-style property,
            <span class='oblique'>oblique</span> and
            <span class='italic'>italic</span> are interchangeable.
        </p>
        <p class='naught'>
            Some fonts have neither an oblique nor an italic style.
            Safari differs from IE, Firefox, and Opera on what to do
            when one of these is encountered.
        </p>
    </body>
</html>
```

2.   Save the preceding markup as `Example_6-2.html`.

3.   Write the following CSS in your text editor:

```
body {
    font: 14px sans-serif;
    line-height: 30px;
}
span {
    background: yellow;
    border: 1px solid gold;
}
span.oblique {
    font-style: oblique;
}
span.italic {
    font-style: italic;
}
p.naught {
```

```
    font-family: "Monotype Corsiva";
    font-style: italic;
}
```

4. Save the preceding CSS as `Example_6-2.css`. The example results in the output in Figure 6-7.

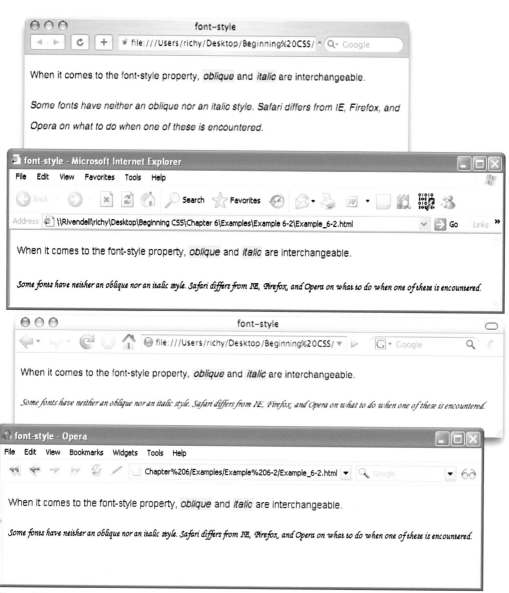

Figure 6-7

How It Works

In Example 6-2 you experimented a bit with the `font-style` property. You found that browsers use the `italic` and `oblique` style interchangeably, as evidenced by the following two rules.

First you applied the `oblique` font style to the `<span>` element with class name `oblique`.

```
span.oblique {
    font-style: oblique;
}
```

Then you applied the `italic` font-style to the `<span>` element with class name `italic`. In Figure 6-7 you can see that the rendered output of the `italic` and the `oblique` style are indistinguishable.

```
span.italic {
    font-style: italic;
}
```

Finally, in the last example you specified a font with neither an oblique nor an italic style, *Monotype Corsiva*. In Figure 6-7, you can see that Safari differs from IE, Firefox, and Opera in what it does when a font with neither an `italic` nor an `oblique` style is set to either `italic` or `oblique`. Safari ignores the font altogether, while IE, Firefox, and Opera just ignore the `italic` or `oblique` style.

```
p.naught {
    font-family: "Monotype Corsiva";
    font-style: italic;
}
```

In the next section, I introduce the `font-variant` property.

The font-variant Property

The `font-variant` property provides an effect that is only slightly different from that of the `text-transform: uppercase;` declaration presented in Chapter 5. The following table outlines the `font-variant` property and its possible values.

Property	Value
font-variant	normal | small-caps Initial value: normal

The `font-variant: small-caps;` declaration causes letters to appear in uppercase but scaled slightly smaller than capitalized letters. Consider the example in Figure 6-8a.

```
body {
    font-size: 24px;
    text-align: center;
}
p {
    margin: 0;
}
p#uppercase {
    margin-top: 15px;
    text-transform: uppercase;
    color: crimson;
}
p#small-caps {
    font-variant: small-caps;
    margin-bottom: 15px;
    color: crimson;
}
```

The small-caps style offers a style similar to the text-transform: uppercase; declaration, the difference being the small-caps style results in lowercase letters being slightly scaled down uppercase letters.

Figure 6-8a

Combine the style sheet in Figure 6-8a with the markup in Figure 6-8b.

```
<!DOCTYPE html PUBLIC "-//W3C//DTD XHTML 1.0 Strict//EN"
                      "http://www.w3.org/TR/xhtml1/DTD/xhtml1-strict.dtd">
<html xmlns='http://www.w3.org/1999/xhtml' xml:lang='en'>
    <head>
        <title>font-variant</title>
        <link rel='stylesheet' type='text/css' href='096977%20fg0608.css' />
    </head>
    <body>
        <p>
            Sunday! Sunday! Sunday!
        </p>
        <p>
            Wrox Press Presents
        </p>
        <p id='uppercase'>
            Uppercase
        </p>
        <p>
            vs.
        </p>
        <p id='small-caps'>
            Small Caps
        </p>
        <p>
            A fight to the <b>DEATH</b>!
        </p>
        <p>
            <em>We'll sell you the whole seat, but you'll only need the
            edge!</em>
        </p>
    </body>
</html>
```

Figure 6-8b

The result is shown in Figure 6-8c.

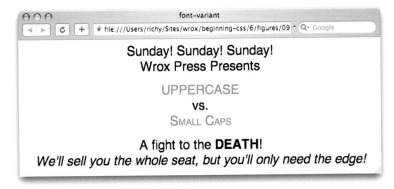

Figure 6-8c

Figure 6-8c shows that when compared side by side with the `text-transform: uppercase;` declaration, the effect of the `font-variant: small-caps;` declaration is obvious. The capitalized letter maintains its case and size, but all lowercase letters are displayed as capital letters scaled slightly smaller than any *real* capital letters appearing in the markup's source code.

The next section continues the discussion of font manipulation properties with the `font-weight` property.

The font-weight Property

The `font-weight` property provides the functionality to specify how bold a font is. The following table outlines the `font-weight` property and the values that it allows.

Property	Value
font-weight	normal | bold | bolder | lighter | 100 | 200 | 300 | 400 | 500 | 600 | 700 | 800 | 900
	Initial value: normal

As you can see in the preceding table, the `font-weight` property has several values. Despite all of these different values being available for the `font-weight` property, in real-world web design, a font is either bold or it isn't. That is to say, in real-world web design, the only two values that matter in the preceding table are the `normal` and `bold` values.

In the preceding table, you can see that CSS allows for up to nine different variations of bold, from 100, being very light, to 900, being very bold. The reasoning behind there being several possible values for the `font-weight` property is in professional typography, designers are likely to have access to fonts with nine different variations of bold. However, these high-end professional fonts aren't available by default on any operating system, and in order to make use of the 100 through 900 values, you'd need to purchase a professional font package. Purchase of a font package that contains nine different variations of bold can be quite expensive. The average price tag for a font package (one single font) with this many variations is on average about $300.

Setting aside the values of the `font-weight` property that you're extremely unlikely to ever have need of, there are two uses for the `font-weight` property: to make text bold, or to make bold text normal. This is demonstrated in Figure 6-9a.

```
h4 {
    font-weight: normal;
}
p {
    font-weight: bold;
}
```

To remove bold formatting from an element that is bold by default, such as the <h4> through <h6> elements, set the value of the `font-weight` property to normal. Conversely, to apply bold formatting, set the value of the `font-weight` property to bold.

Figure 6-9a

The CSS in Figure 6-9a is combined with the markup in Figure 6-9b.

```
<!DOCTYPE html PUBLIC "-//W3C//DTD XHTML 1.0 Strict//EN"
                      "http://www.w3.org/TR/xhtml1/DTD/xhtml1-strict.dtd">
<html xmlns='http://www.w3.org/1999/xhtml' xml:lang='en'>
    <head>
        <title>font-weight</title>
        <link rel='stylesheet' type='text/css' href='096977%20fg0609.css' />
    </head>
    <body>
        <h4>When everything is dark, and you want to make it light.</h4>
        <p>When everything is light, and you want to make it dark.</p>
    </body>
</html>
```

Figure 6-9b

The CSS and markup in Figure 6-9a and Figure 6-9b result in the output in Figure 6-9c.

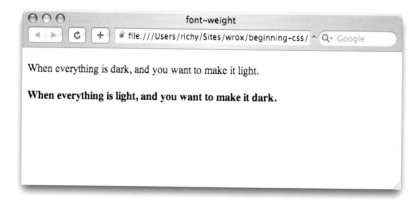

Figure 6-9c

In Figure 6-9a, you see two elements in the body of the document, an <h4> element and a <p> element. The <h4> element is formatted bold by default. To take away the bold formatting, you simply include the `font-weight: normal;` declaration. The text within <p> elements is not bold by default. To make that text bold, you use the `font-weight: bold;` declaration.

Now that you have seen how to make font bold, or not, depending on the element, the next section describes how to use the `font-size` property.

The font-size Property

The `font-size` property is, of course, used to control the size of fonts. The following table outlines the `font-size` property and its possible values.

Property	Value
font-size	<absolute-size> | <relative-size> | <length> | <percentage> Initial value: medium

The bad news, as I mentioned in Chapter 2 in the discussion of CSS length units, is the number of caveats and fallbacks attached to each measurement. Some are better suited for screen and some are better suited for print, and not all length units are interpreted consistently on different browsers. The same is true of the keyword values for the `font-size` property that I discuss in the following sections.

Absolute Font Sizes

The <absolute-size> value notation of the `font-size` property refers to one of seven keyword values. Absolute values for the `font-size` property are defined using keywords that range from xx-large to xx-small. The following table outlines the absolute values and their relation to HTML heading sizes as of CSS 2.0.

Absolute Keyword	xx-small	x-small	small	medium	large	x-large	xx-large
HTML Heading	n/a	<h6>	<h5>	<h4>	<h3>	<h2>	<h1>

These keywords specify the font size based on a scaling factor of 1.2. *Scaling factor* is the ratio between two shapes. The scaling factor is determined by multiplying the font size by 1.2 to determine the next font size relative to the previous one. For instance, if a font size of 16 pixels is assumed for the medium keyword value, the large keyword would be approximately 20 pixels, rounding up from 19.2 because 16 multiplied by 1.2 equals 19.2.

These keywords exist for sizing fonts relative to the browser user's font-size preferences. The browser precalculates the value of each keyword depending on those preferences. The name *absolute* is somewhat misleading because each keyword is *relative* to the user's font-size preferences. The actual length unit size of each keyword varies depending on a number of factors, such as:

❑ The browser's default font size

❑ The user's font size preferences

❑ The font family being used

Despite all of these variables, this is one place where the three browsers, IE, Firefox, Safari, and Opera, seem to be consistent.

Figure 6-10 shows each absolute font size in relation to the default HTML heading size and a size specified in points.

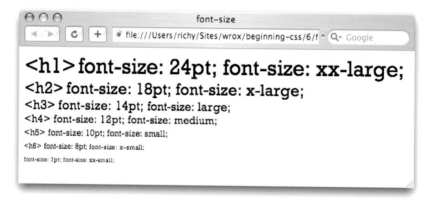

Figure 6-10

Although this association between font size keywords and length units works for the Rockwell font I used in Figure 6-10, the point sizes depicted are approximations and might not be the same point unit values when another font is used. If you increase or decrease the size of the text using the zoom feature of the browser, you'd notice that the point sizes change in response to the absolute keyword values if you are using IE 7, Safari, Opera, or Firefox. However, IE 6 ignores the user's adjustments to font size preferences on font sizes specified in points (or any other absolute length unit, like inches or centimeters). Therefore, the point sizes do not change with the size of the absolute keywords when adjustments to the user's font size preferences are made. You can make adjustments in the size of the font in Internet Explorer from the View ⇨ Text Size menu. In IE 7, Windows Opera, and Windows Firefox, changes to font size can be made by pressing Ctrl-+ (The control key and the plus sign key) or Ctrl--- (The control key and the minus sign key), or from the View ⇨ Text Zoom menu. Safari, Mac Opera, and Mac Firefox use the shortcut, ⌘-+ (Command, plus sign key), or ⌘--- (Command, minus key).

Relative font-size keywords, covered in the following section, are closely associated with the absolute font size keywords.

Relative Font Sizes

The `<relative-size>` notation of the `font-size` property refers to two values: `larger` and `smaller`. When either of these two values is used, the font size is determined by the values appearing in the table for absolute size keywords discussed in the previous section. Take, for instance, the example in Figure 6-11a.

```
body {
    font-size: medium;
}
p#larger {
    font-size: larger;
}
p#larger span {
    font-size: 20px;
}
p#smaller {
    font-size: smaller;
}
p#smaller span {
    font-size: 12px;
}
span {
    background: mistyrose;
}
```

> The smaller and larger keywords cause a decrease or increase in size by a scaling factor of 1.2.

Figure 6-11a

Combine the CSS in Figure 6-11a with the markup in Figure 6-11b.

```
<!DOCTYPE html PUBLIC "-//W3C//DTD XHTML 1.0 Strict//EN"
                 "http://www.w3.org/TR/xhtml1/DTD/xhtml1-strict.dtd">
<html xmlns='http://www.w3.org/1999/xhtml' xml:lang='en'>
    <head>
        <title>font-size</title>
        <link rel='stylesheet' type='text/css' href='096977%20fg0611.css' />
    </head>
    <body>
        <p>
            The larger and smaller keywords of the font-size property
            function using the scaling factor of 1.2.
        </p>
        <p id='larger'>
            This font is 1.2 times the default font, or 20 pixels.<br />
            <span>Evidenced by this point-of-reference.</span>
        </p>
        <p id='smaller'>
            This font is 1.2 smaller than the default size, or pixels.<br />
            <span>Evidenced by this point-of-reference.</span>
        </p>
    </body>
</html>
```

Figure 6-11b

The results are shown in Figure 6-11c.

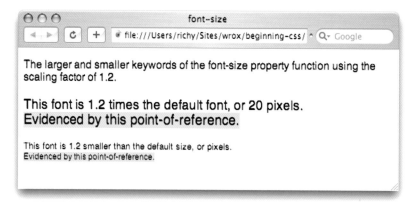

Figure 6-11c

Figure 6-11 demonstrates how the next value in the absolute font-size keyword table is chosen. Because the font for the <body> element is made medium in size with the `font-size: medium;` declaration, when `font-size: larger;` is applied to the <p> element, the browser chooses the next larger value in the absolute keyword table and applies a font size that is the same as would be generated by the `font-size: large;` declaration. If the value is specified with a length unit — say, for instance, as pixels — the browser simply applies a 1.2 scaling factor to that size to get the larger size.

Figure 6-12 shows how a font size specified as 16 pixels gets increasingly larger when `font-size: larger;` is applied to descendant elements.

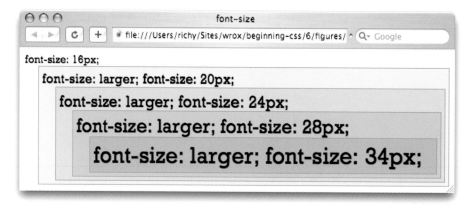

Figure 6-12

In contrast to the `font-size: larger;` declaration, Figure 6-13 shows what happens when the `font-size: smaller;` declaration is used instead.

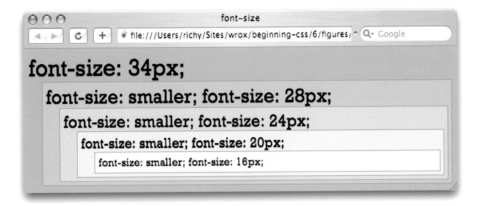

Figure 6-13

The `font-size: smaller;` declaration performs the same scaling factor changes that the `font-size: larger;` declaration does, but does them in reverse.

Percentage Font Sizes

Percentage font sizes work much like the em units discussed in Chapter 2. Consider the example in Figure 6-14a.

```
span {
    background: mistyrose;
    font-size: 150%;
}
span span {
    background: pink;
    font-size: 125%;
}
```

> When specifying a font size by percentage, a value larger than 100% results in a font size larger than the parent element, or browser default. A value of 100% means no change in font size.

Figure 6-14a

Combine the CSS in Figure 6-14a with the markup in Figure 6-14b.

The result is shown in Figure 6-14c.

Figure 6-14c shows that percentage values are based on the element's ancestry. The font size for the `<p>` element is the default font size, which is `medium` or typically 16 pixels. The font size of the first `<span>` element is made 50% larger than the font size of its parent element, the `<p>` element. Assuming the default font size is 16 pixels, that makes the font size of the first `<span>` element 24 pixels. Then, the nested, child `<span>` element is made 25% bigger than the font size of its parent `<span>` element, which comes to 30 pixels.

```
<!DOCTYPE html PUBLIC "-//W3C//DTD XHTML 1.0 Strict//EN"
                      "http://www.w3.org/TR/xhtml1/DTD/xhtml1-strict.dtd">
<html xmlns='http://www.w3.org/1999/xhtml' xml:lang='en'>
    <head>
        <title>font-size</title>
        <link rel='stylesheet' type='text/css' href='096977%20fg0614.css' />
    </head>
    <body>
        <p>
            Percentage font sizes apply a font size relative to the
            parent element's font size.  For example,<br />
            <span>
                This font size is 50% bigger than that of the
                &lt;p&gt; element.<br />
                <span>
                    This font is 25% bigger than the font used
                    for the parent &lt;span&gt; element.
                </span>
            </span>
        </p>
    </body>
</html>
```

Figure 6-14b

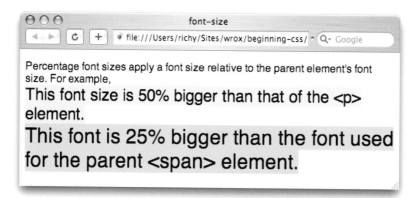

Figure 6-14c

A percentage font size measurement might also be used to decrease the size of a font. Take, for instance, the CSS in Figure 6-15a.

```
span {
    background: mistyrose;
    font-size: 75%;
}
span span {
    background: pink;
    font-size: 75%;
}
```

When specifying a font size by percentage, a value smaller than 100% results in a font size smaller than the parent element, or browser default.

Figure 6-15a

The CSS in Figure 6-15a is combined with the markup in Figure 6-15b.

```
<!DOCTYPE html PUBLIC "-//W3C//DTD XHTML 1.0 Strict//EN"
                    "http://www.w3.org/TR/xhtml1/DTD/xhtml1-strict.dtd">
<html xmlns='http://www.w3.org/1999/xhtml' xml:lang='en'>
    <head>
        <title>font-size</title>
        <link rel='stylesheet' type='text/css' href='096977%20fg0615.css' />
    </head>
    <body>
        <p>
            The same principle can be applied to make font sizes smaller
            by percentage. For example,<br />
            <span>
                This font size is 25% smaller than that of the
                &lt;p&gt; element.<br />
                <span>
                    This font is 25% smaller than the font used
                    for the parent &lt;span&gt; element.
                </span>
            </span>
        </p>
    </body>
</html>
```
Figure 6-15b

The result is shown in Figure 6-15c.

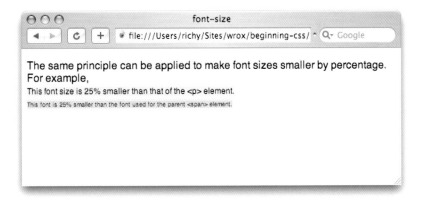

Figure 6-15c

As you saw in Figure 6-14c, Figure 6-15c shows how percentage fonts can be used to make a font smaller. Again assuming the default font size is 16 pixels, the child <span> element is made 25% smaller than the font of the <p> element, which comes to 12 pixels. Then the nested <span> element is made 25% smaller than its parent <span> element, which comes to 9 pixels.

Now that you've had an overview of how the font-size property works, you can try out the font-size property firsthand.

Try It Out   Applying a Font Size

Example 6-3. Follow these steps to try out the `font-size` property.

1.   In your text editor, type the following markup:

```
<!DOCTYPE html PUBLIC "-//W3C//DTD XHTML 1.0 Strict//EN"
                      "http://www.w3.org/TR/xhtml1/DTD/xhtml1-strict.dtd">
<html xmlns='http://www.w3.org/1999/xhtml' xml:lang='en'>
    <head>
        <title>font-size</title>
        <link rel='stylesheet' type='text/css' href='Example_6-3.css' />
    </head>
    <body>
        <p>
            The font-size property supports a variety of methods for
            specifying a font size. For example, there
            are seven different absolute size keywords, which set the
            font size relative to the user's font size preference.
        </p>
        <ul>
            <li style='font-size: xx-small;'>xx-small</li>
            <li style='font-size: x-small;'>x-small</li>
            <li style='font-size: small;'>small</li>
            <li style='font-size: medium;'>medium</li>
            <li style='font-size: large;'>large</li>
            <li style='font-size: x-large;'>x-large</li>
            <li style='font-size: xx-large;'>xx-large</li>
        </ul>
        <p>
            You can also make fonts
            <span style='font-size: larger;'>larger</span> or
            <span style='font-size: smaller;'>smaller</span> by way
            of the <span style='font-size: larger;'>larger</span> or
            <span style='font-size: smaller;'>smaller</span> keywords.
        </p>
        <p>
            You can make fonts
            <span style='font-size: 150%;'>50% larger</span>
            or <span style='font-size: 75%;'>25% smaller</span> by way
            of percentages.
        </p>
        <p>
            You can even make a font
            <span style='font-size: 1.5em;'>50% larger</span>
            or <span style='font-size: 0.75em;'>25% smaller</span> by way
            of em units.
        </p>
    </body>
</html>
```

2.   Save the markup as `Example_6-3.html`.

3.   In a new document in your text editor, write the following CSS:

```
body {
    font: 16px sans-serif;
}
span {
    background: mistyrose;
}
```

4. Save the preceding CSS as `Example_6-3.css`. The results of these modifications can be seen in Figure 6-16.

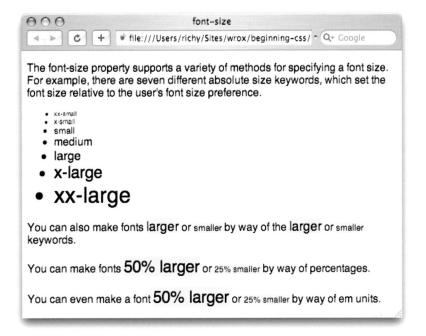

Figure 6-16

How It Works

In Example 6-3, you tried a variety of different methods of setting a font size. You began by typing out all seven absolute font sizes, from `xx-small` to `xx-large`.

Next you experimented with three different ways of adjusting a font size relative to the parent element or browser default font size. You began with the `larger` and `smaller` keywords. The `larger` keyword makes the font size 1.2 times larger, and the `smaller` keyword makes the font size 1.2 times smaller.

```
<p>
    You can also make fonts
    <span style='font-size: larger;'>larger</span> or
    <span style='font-size: smaller;'>smaller</span> by way
    of the <span style='font-size: larger;'>larger</span> or
    <span style='font-size: smaller;'>smaller</span> keywords.
</p>
```

Next, you experimented with percentage font size. A percentage value larger than 100 results in a larger font size, while a percentage value under 100 results in a smaller font size.

```
<p>
    You can make fonts
    <span style='font-size: 150%;'>50% larger</span>
    or <span style='font-size: 75%;'>25% smaller</span> by way
    of percentages.
</p>
```

The em unit is pretty much identical to the percentage font size, except you can use the em unit on any element, not just font sizes (such as defining the width of a <div>; more on this in Chapter 7). You get identical results when using em units as you did with the percentage size.

```
<p>
    You can even make a font
    <span style='font-size: 1.5em;'>50% larger</span>
    or <span style='font-size: 0.75em;'>25% smaller</span> by way
    of em units.
</p>
```

The next section examines a special shorthand property used to specify several font properties in one.

The font Shorthand Property

The font property is a shorthand property that allows you to write several font-related properties in a single property. The following table outlines the font property and the values that it allows.

Property	Value
font	[<'font-style'> || <'font-variant'> || <'font-weight'>]? <'font-size'> [/ <'line-height'>]? <'font-family'>] caption | icon | menu | message-box | small-caption | status-bar

The notation for the font property is somewhat more complicated than those presented in previous examples. For now, just ignore the caption, icon, menu, message-box, small-caption, and status-bar values — these are called system fonts, and I discuss them in the next section.

The font Properties

As for the first part of the notation, here's a breakdown of each portion:

```
[ <'font-style'> || <'font-variant'> || <'font-weight'> ]?
```

This indicates that either a `font-style`, `font-variant`, or `font-weight` value can be provided. The question mark indicates that this part is optional; you don't have to include a `font-style`, `font-variant`, or a `font-weight`. The double vertical bars in the notation indicates that each value is optional, and they also indicate that any combination of the three can appear. You can include just a `font-style`, just a `font-variant`, just a `font-weight`, all three, or any combination of the three.

The next part indicates that a font size must be specified:

```
<'font-size'>
```

The font size is not optional, so a `font-size` value must always be provided.

The next part indicates that a `line-height` (discussed in Chapter 7) may be specified, but because a question mark follows it, the line height is optional:

```
[ / <'line-height'> ]?
```

The forward slash in the notation indicates that if a line height is specified, a forward slash must separate the `font-size` and `line-height` properties. The question mark after the closing square bracket indicates that this portion of the syntax is optional.

The last portion indicates that a `font-family` must be specified:

```
<'font-family'>
```

So at the very least, a `font-size` value and a `font-family` value must be specified. Now that you understand the notation, Figure 6-17a is an example of this property including all its optional values.

```
p {
    font-style: italic;
    font-variant: small-caps;
    font-weight: bold;
    font-size: 1.5em;
    line-height: 3em;
    font-family: sans-serif;
    color: forestgreen;
}
```

The font shorthand property facilitates the specification of six different properties in just one.

The preceding rule can be collapsed into the following rule.

```
p {
    font: italic small-caps bold 1.5em/3em sans-serif;
    color: forestgreen;
}
```

Figure 6-17a

The CSS in Figure 6-17a is combined with the markup in Figure 6-17b.

```
<!DOCTYPE html PUBLIC "-//W3C//DTD XHTML 1.0 Strict//EN"
                      "http://www.w3.org/TR/xhtml1/DTD/xhtml1-strict.dtd">
<html xmlns='http://www.w3.org/1999/xhtml' xml:lang='en'>
    <head>
        <title>font</title>
        <link rel='stylesheet' type='text/css' href='096977%20fg0617.css' />
    </head>
    <body>
        <p>
            The font property in all its unmolested glory.
        </p>
        <p>
            Looks like a font you would find in a comic book.
        </p>
    </body>
</html>
```

Figure 6-17b

The result is shown in Figure 6-17c.

Figure 6-17c

This rule includes all the values possible with the font property shorthand. Figure 6-17 shows that this rule makes the font italic, small-caps, bold, 1em in size with a 1.5em line-height and a sans-serif font. I haven't discussed the line-height property yet because this property is discussed in Chapter 7, but essentially the line-height property accepts a normal length value, which sets the height for each line of text.

In contrast to the example in Figure 6-17, the example in Figure 6-18a shows the font property with a minimal set of values.

```
p {
    font: 32px "Monotype Corsiva";
    color: darkslateblue;
}
```

You must specify at least a `font-size` and `font-family`; all other values are optional.

Figure 6-18a

The CSS in Figure 6-18a is combined with the markup in Figure 6-18b.

```
<!DOCTYPE html PUBLIC "-//W3C//DTD XHTML 1.0 Strict//EN"
                      "http://www.w3.org/TR/xhtml1/DTD/xhtml1-strict.dtd">
<html xmlns='http://www.w3.org/1999/xhtml' xml:lang='en'>
    <head>
        <title>font</title>
        <link rel='stylesheet' type='text/css' href='096977%20fg0618.css' />
    </head>
    <body>
        <p>
            The font property with a minimal set of values is just a
            size and font-family.
        </p>
    </body>
</html>
```

Figure 6-18b

The result is shown in Figure 6-18c.

Figure 6-18c

The notation indicates that at least a font size and a font family must be provided, as is reflected in the preceding example. Figure 6-18c shows output with a Monotype Corsiva font 32px in size.

Here are a few more possible variations of the font property:

```
font: bold 1.2em Arial, sans-serif;
```

This makes the font bold and 1.2em in size. Then, like the font-family property, the font property accepts a list of fonts. I've specified an Arial font, which is common. If that font isn't found on the user's computer, the generic sans-serif font is used. The following is another variation of the font property:

```
font: italic 1.2/2em "Times New Roman", Times, serif;
```

The preceding rule makes the font italic and 1.2em in size with a 2em line height. Those specifications are followed by a list of font families.

Now that you've had an overview of the font shorthand property, you can try out the font property for yourself in the following Try It Out.

Try It Out   **Applying the font Property**

Example 6-4. Follow these steps to try out the font property.

1.   In your text editor, type the following markup:

```
<!DOCTYPE html PUBLIC "-//W3C//DTD XHTML 1.0 Strict//EN"
                     "http://www.w3.org/TR/xhtml1/DTD/xhtml1-strict.dtd">
<html xmlns='http://www.w3.org/1999/xhtml' xml:lang='en'>
    <head>
        <title>font</title>
        <link rel='stylesheet' type='text/css' href='Example_6-4.css' />
    </head>
    <body>
        <p>
            The font shorthand property lets you combine up to six
            different properties in one single property.
        </p>
        <p class='font1'>
            You can make text that's bold, 24 pixels in size,
            and sans-serif.
        </p>
        <p class='font2'>
            You can make text that's italic, bold, small-caps,
            24 pixel sans-serif, which looks like a comic
            book font.
        </p>
        <p class='font3'>
            Or you can just keep it simple, 16 pixels and
            monospace.
        </p>
    </body>
</html>
```

2. Save the markup as `Example_6-4.html`.

3. In a new document in your text editor, write the following CSS:

```
body {
    font: 16px sans-serif;
}
p.font1 {
    font: bold 24px sans-serif;
}
p.font2 {
    font: italic bold small-caps 24px sans-serif;
}
p.font3 {
    font: 16px monospace;
}
```

4. Save the preceding CSS as `Example_6-4.css`. The results of these modifications are shown in Figure 6-19.

The font shorthand property lets you combine up to six different properties in one single property.

You can make text that's bold, 24 pixels in size, and sans-serif.

YOU CAN MAKE TEXT THAT'S ITALIC, BOLD, SMALL-CAPS, 24 PIXEL SANS-SERIF, WHICH LOOKS LIKE A COMIC BOOK FONT.

`Or you can just keep it simple, 16 pixels and monospace.`

Figure 6-19

How It Works

In Example 6-4, you saw four examples of the font shorthand property. The first example sets the font for the whole document, 16px, sans-serif. Because the font property is inherited, the font will stay 16px and sans-serif unless specified otherwise for a child element.

```
body {
    font: 16px sans-serif;
}
```

You then set the font to be bold, 24px, sans-serif for the <p> element with class name font1.

```
p.font1 {
    font: bold 24px sans-serif;
}
```

Next you made the font italic, bold, small-caps, 24px, and sans-serif for the <p> element with class name font2.

```
p.font2 {
    font: italic bold small-caps 24px sans-serif;
}
```

Finally, you set the font to 16px, monospace for the <p> element with class name font3.

```
p.font3 {
    font: 16px monospace;
}
```

In the next section I talk about system fonts, which are fonts that you can use to style a web page based on an end user's operating system fonts.

System Fonts

System fonts are keywords that refer to a font predefined by the user's operating system. The following table outlines each available system font.

Font Name	Font Description
Caption	Refers to the font used for captioned controls.
Icon	Refers to the font used to label icons like those found on the desktop.
Menu	Refers to the font used in menus, drop-down menus, and menu lists.
message-box	The font used in dialog boxes.
small-caption	The font used for labeling small controls.
status-bar	The font used in window status bars.

System fonts may only be set as a whole when a system font is specified using the font shorthand property, the font-family, font-size, font-weight properties, and all other aspects of font display are set at once.

The CSS in Figure 6-20a is combined with the markup in Figure 6-20b.

Figure 6-20c shows what system fonts look like in various browsers on various operating systems.

```
p#caption {
    font: caption;
}
p#icon {
    font: icon;
}
p#menu {
    font: menu;
}
p#message-box {
    font: message-box;
}
p#small-caption {
    font: small-caption;
}
p#status-bar {
    font: status-bar;
}
```

System fonts can be used to style fonts in a
web document the same as they are for various
components of the user's operating system.

Figure 6-20a

```
<!DOCTYPE html PUBLIC "-//W3C//DTD XHTML 1.0 Strict//EN"
                      "http://www.w3.org/TR/xhtml1/DTD/xhtml1-strict.dtd">
<html xmlns='http://www.w3.org/1999/xhtml' xml:lang='en'>
    <head>
        <title>system fonts</title>
        <link rel='stylesheet' type='text/css' href='096977%20fg0620.css' />
    </head>
    <body>
        <p id='caption'>
            This is the caption font.
        </p>
        <p id='icon'>
            This is the icon font.
        </p>
        <p id='menu'>
            This is the menu font.
        </p>
        <p id='message-box'>
            This is the message-box font.
        </p>
        <p id='small-caption'>
            This is the small-caption font.
        </p>
        <p id='status-bar'>
            This is the status-bar font.
        </p>
    </body>
</html>
```

Figure 6-20b

Figure 6-20c demonstrates each of the system fonts. From left to right and top to bottom the screenshots
in Figure 6-20c are Safari, Windows XP IE 6, Windows Vista IE 7, Mac Opera 9, Ubuntu Linux Firefox 1.5,
Windows XP Opera 9, Mac Firefox 1.5, Windows XP Firefox 1.5.

Figure 6-20c

System fonts are intended to allow a web designer to set fonts based on a user's font preferences as defined for his or her operating system. While system fonts sound great in theory, Figure 6-20c shows that system fonts are a bit of a hit and miss proposition. They don't work in IE 7 on Windows Vista, in Firefox on Ubuntu Linux, or in Safari on Mac OS X. Because system fonts can't be relied upon absolutely, it may be better to just define font styles for yourself.

Additionally, different aspects of system fonts can be overridden via the cascade by specifying the different font properties after a font declaration with a system font value. This is demonstrated by the following rule:

```
p {
    font: caption;
    font-size: 2em;
    font-style: italic;
}
```

In the preceding example, the font size and font style replace those specified for the system font.

Summary

This chapter demonstrated several properties CSS provides for manipulating font display. These properties allow both simple and complex control over how fonts are presented to the end user. In this chapter you learned:

- How to specify the font face using the `font-family` property.

- How to make the font style oblique or italic with the `font-style` property.

- How to style the small-caps effect using the `font-variant` property.

- How to control the lightness and boldness of a font using the `font-weight` property.

- How to take advantage of specifying a font size that adjusts based on the user's font size preferences with the `font-size` property and absolute keywords.

- How to increase the size of a font based on the font size of an element's parent using relative keywords, percentage font sizes, or em units with the `font-size` property.

- How to combine the various font properties into one using the `font` shorthand property.

After learning some of CSS's simpler properties for text manipulation in Chapter 5 and going over font manipulation in this chapter, you now learn about the CSS box model in Chapter 7.

Exercises

1. Why aren't the values of the `font-weight` property `100` through `900`, `bolder`, and `lighter` used in real-world web design?

2. If "Font A" is supported on Mac OS X, and "Font B" is supported on Windows XP, and "Font C" is supported on Linux, what style would you write so that one of the three would always be used in the absence of one of the others?

3. If you want to make text italic, what are two possible declarations for doing that?

4. What's the difference between the `font-variant: small-caps;` and `text-transform: uppercase;` declarations?

5. How could the following rules be better written?

```
p {
    font-family: Arial, sans-serif;
    font-weight: bold;
    font-size: 24px;
    color: crimson;
}
p.copy {
    font-style: italic;
    font-weight: bold;
    line-height: 2em;
}
p#footer {
```

```
        font-size: 12px;
        line-height: 2em;
        font-family: Helvetica, Arial, sans-serif;
    }
```

6. What's wrong with the following rule?

```
p {
    font-size: 24;
}
```

7. If you include the declaration `font-size: larger;` in a style sheet rule, how much larger would the text be?

8. Would the declaration `font-size: 75%;` make the font size larger or smaller?

The Box Model

In this chapter, I discuss one of the most important concepts in CSS-based web design, the box model. The box model is a set of rules that dictate how width, height, padding, borders, and margin are measured on HTML elements.

In this chapter, I discuss:

- ❏ The CSS box model
- ❏ CSS box model properties, padding, margins, borders, width, and height
- ❏ Controlling line height
- ❏ Establishing minimum and maximum dimensions
- ❏ Overflowing content

The next section begins with an overview of what the box model is.

Overview

The CSS box model is a collection of properties that define the amount of space around an element, its dimensions, its margins, its borders, and padding between text content and the borders. In Figure 7-1, you see a diagram of the box model.

In Figure 7-1 you see what the different components that come together to make the box model look like. Around the outside of an element is space called the *margin*, inside of the margin is the *border*, inside of the border is the *padding*, and inside of the padding is the content of the element. Figure 7-2 takes the box model in Figure 7-1 and reproduces it in an (X)HTML document with CSS.

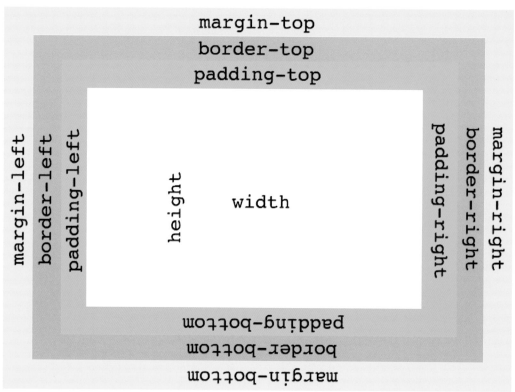

Figure 7-1

```
body {
    margin: 0;
    padding: 0;
}
div#box-wrapper {
    background: #ff0;
    border: 1px solid #fff;
}
div#box {
    border: 20px solid #ff0;
    margin: 20px;
    padding: 20px;
    background: #ff9;
}
div#box-inner {
    background: #fff;
    color: rgb(244, 244, 244);
}
```

Margin is invisible; you set the background of the parent element here, so that you see where it is applied.

The background color is applied from the outside border edge and includes the padding and content area. To give the content area a different background, so you can see the padding area, you included another element and gave it a white background (#fff).

Figure 7-2a

The CSS in Figure 7-2a is combined with the markup in Figure 7-2b.

```
<!DOCTYPE html PUBLIC "-//W3C//DTD XHTML 1.0 Strict//EN"
                      "http://www.w3.org/TR/xhtml1/DTD/xhtml1-strict.dtd">
<html xmlns='http://www.w3.org/1999/xhtml' xml:lang='en'>
    <head>
        <title>box model</title>
        <link rel='stylesheet' type='text/css' href='096977%20fg0702.css' />
    </head>
    <body>
        <div id='box-wrapper'>
            <div id='box'>
                <div id='box-inner'>
                    Lorem ipsum dolor sit amet, consectetuer adipiscing
                    elit. Proin consectetuer neque ac eros. Vivamus vel
                    nibh. Vestibulum aliquam neque a nisi. Nullam eu
                    turpis. Proin mi. Cras dictum semper felis. Maecenas
                    porttitor neque at dolor. Integer vel libero vitae
                    ante lobortis tristique. Morbi sapien diam, tristique
                    sed, placerat pharetra, luctus eget, neque.
                    Pellentesque leo mauris, sollicitudin a, malesuada
                    vitae, varius vitae, quam. Cras eget tellus vel nunc
                    dapibus pharetra.

                    Phasellus varius tincidunt quam. Maecenas viverra
                    mattis orci. Etiam porttitor luctus ligula. Ut ac
                    nibh. In commodo imperdiet sapien. Nulla vel sapien
                    sed mauris euismod pharetra. Quisque eu ante eget
                    pede tristique tincidunt. Curabitur eu erat eu libero
                    aliquam placerat. Pellentesque felis erat, cursus
                </div>
            </div>
        </div>
    </body>
</html>
```

Figure 7-2b

The result of the CSS in Figure 7-2a and the markup in Figure 7-2b is shown in Figure 7-2c.

In Figure 7-2a, you can see how space around an element is controlled with the three properties, margin, border, and padding. All three of these properties are specified on the <div> element with id name box. Then to highlight the presence of these properties, you included two additional elements, one wrapping the <div> element named box, where the element is given id name box-wrapper, and one wrapping the content within the element, where the element is given the id name box-inner.

The element box-wrapper is given a yellow background of #ff0. This is because margins don't have backgrounds themselves; therefore, in order to highlight the margin area, an element needs to wrap around the element with margin applied to it, and be given a different background color. The area that is the darkest yellow (#ff0) is the margin area of the box element. The box-wrapper also has a one-pixel, solid, white border applied to it. This is to prevent box model behavior that arises in some circumstances called *margin collapsing*. You'll learn more about margin collapsing later in this chapter; for now, just disregard that border.

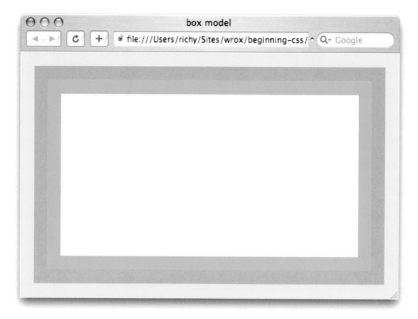

Figure 7-2c

The `border` can have its own color separate from the background, so you specified the `border` as `border: 20px solid #ff6;`. This yellow is slightly lighter than that used for the `margin` area. The `padding` is the area between the inside border edge and the outside edge of the content of the element. Since the padding and content area actually have the same background color, you included another `<div>` element with id name `box-inner`. The `box-inner` element is given a white background (`#fff`) to highlight only the content area.

In the coming sections, I pick apart the various properties that comprise the box model in CSS, beginning with margin.

Margin

The `margin` property applies space outside the box, between the box and the browser window, or between the box and the other elements in the document. The following table shows the various margin properties.

Property	Value
Margin	[<length>	<percentage>	auto] {1,4}
margin-top margin-right margin-bottom margin-left	<length>	<percentage>	auto

The margin property is a shorthand property for the four individual margin properties, margin-top, margin-right, margin-bottom, and margin-left.

Margin Property with Four Values

Figure 7-3 shows a comparison between the individual margin properties and the margin shorthand property with four values.

```
body {
    margin: 0;
    padding: 0;
}
div {
    width: 100px;
    height: 100px;
    background: mistyrose;
    border: 1px solid pink;
}
div#top-right-bottom-left {
    margin-top: 10px;
    margin-right: 10px;
    margin-bottom: 10px;
    margin-left: 10px;
}
div#top-right-bottom-left-1 {
    margin: 10px 10px 10px 10px;
}
```

Margin for each side can be specified individually, or written using the margin property, which provides the ability to specify margin for all four sides in just a single property.

margin-top   margin-right   margin-bottom   margin-left

Figure 7-3a

The CSS in Figure 7-3a is combined with the markup in Figure 7-3b.

```
<!DOCTYPE html PUBLIC "-//W3C//DTD XHTML 1.0 Strict//EN"
                      "http://www.w3.org/TR/xhtml1/DTD/xhtml1-strict.dtd">
<html xmlns='http://www.w3.org/1999/xhtml' xml:lang='en'>
    <head>
        <title>box model</title>
        <link rel='stylesheet' type='text/css' href='096977%20fg0702.css' />
    </head>
    <body>
        <div id='top-right-bottom-left'></div>
        <div id='top-right-bottom-left-1'></div>
    </body>
</html>
```

Figure 7-3b

The CSS in Figure 7-3a and the markup in Figure 7-3b result in the output you see in Figure 7-3c.

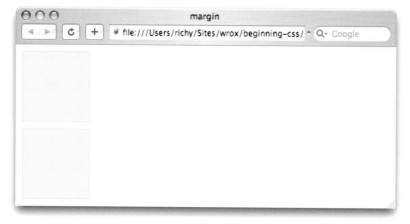

Figure 7-3c

In Figure 7-3, you see how the four individual margin properties can be used to specify the margin of an element, and how those four individual properties can be consolidated into a single margin shorthand property.

> **Box model shorthand properties are always specified in order clockwise from the top: top, right, bottom, and left**—for example: margin: 10px 10px 10px 10px;.

In Figure 7-3, you specified 10 pixels of margin around both <div> elements, but used two different ways of doing it. Figure 7-4 shows the output of Figure 7-3 with the margin area highlighted yellow.

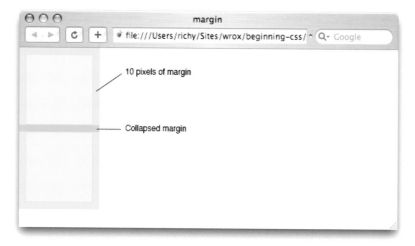

Figure 7-4

In Figure 7-4, the 10 pixels of margin on each side of each <div> element appears in yellow. Also take note of the orange area, which is 10 pixels of margin, rather than 20, as you might have expected. This is caused by margin collapsing, which I discuss later in this section.

Margin Property with Three Values

In Figure 7-3, you saw an example of specifying margin using four values, but you can also specify only three values for the margin shorthand property. This is demonstrated in Figure 7-5.

```
body {
    margin: 0;
    padding: 0;
}
div {
    width: 100px;
    height: 100px;
    background: mistyrose;
    border: 1px solid pink;
}
div#top-rightleft-bottom {
    margin-top: 15px;
    margin-right: 5px;
    margin-bottom: 10px;
    margin-left: 5px;
}
div#top-rightleft-bottom-1 {
    margin: 15px 5px 10px;
}
```

When the left and right margins are the same, but the top and botttom margins are different for the same element, you can use the margin property with three values.

| margin-top | margin-right | margin-bottom |
| | margin-left | |

Figure 7-5a

The CSS in Figure 7-5a is combined with the markup in Figure 7-5b.

```
<!DOCTYPE html PUBLIC "-//W3C//DTD XHTML 1.0 Strict//EN"
                "http://www.w3.org/TR/xhtml1/DTD/xhtml1-strict.dtd">
<html xmlns='http://www.w3.org/1999/xhtml' xml:lang='en'>
    <head>
        <title>box model</title>
        <link rel='stylesheet' type='text/css' href='096977%20fg0705.css' />
    </head>
    <body>
        <div id='top-rightleft-bottom'></div>
        <div id='top-rightleft-bottom-1'></div>
    </body>
</html>
```

Figure 7-5b

The source code in Figure 7-5a and Figure 7-5b results in the output you see in Figure 7-5c.

Figure 7-5c

In Figure 7-5, you see how when you have the same margin value for the left and right margins, and different values for the top and bottom margins, the solution is to use the margin shorthand property with three values.

> **Box model shorthand properties with three values always follow the convention top, right and left, bottom — for example:** margin: 15px 5px 10px;.

Figure 7-6 shows the different margin areas of Figure 7-5 highlighted.

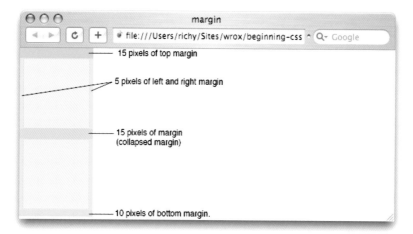

Figure 7-6

In Figure 7-6, you see the margin area highlighted for each <div> element appearing in Figure 7-5. Take note of the collapsed margin, which I talk about later in this chapter.

Margin Property with Two Values

Naturally, the margin shorthand property also supports two values. When two values are specified, the first value refers to the top and bottom sides, and the second value refers to the right and left sides. This is demonstrated in Figure 7-7.

```
body {
    margin: 0;
    padding: 0;
}
div {
    width: 100px;
    height: 100px;
    background: mistyrose;
    border: 1px solid pink;
}
div#topbottom-rightleft {
    margin-top: 15px;
    margin-right: 5px;
    margin-bottom: 15px;
    margin-left: 5px;
}
div#topbottom-rightleft-1 {
    margin: 15px 5px;
}
```

When two margin values are specified, the first value refers to the top and bottom sides, whereas the second value refers to the right and left sides.

```
margin-top          margin-right
margin-bottom       margin-left
```

Figure 7-7a

The CSS in Figure 7-7a is combined with the markup in Figure 7-7b.

```
<!DOCTYPE html PUBLIC "-//W3C//DTD XHTML 1.0 Strict//EN"
                      "http://www.w3.org/TR/xhtml1/DTD/xhtml1-strict.dtd">
<html xmlns='http://www.w3.org/1999/xhtml' xml:lang='en'>
    <head>
        <title>margin</title>
        <link rel='stylesheet' type='text/css' href='096977%20fg0707.css' />
    </head>
    <body>
        <div id='topbottom-rightleft'></div>
        <div id='topbottom-rightleft-1'></div>
    </body>
</html>
```

Figure 7-7b

The CSS in Figure 7-7a and the markup in Figure 7-7b result in the output you see in Figure 7-7c.

In Figure 7-7, you see what happens when just two values are supplied to the margin shorthand property.

Figure 7-7c

Box model shorthand properties with two values always follow the convention top and bottom, right and left—for example: margin: 15px 10px;.

Margin Property with One Value

You can specify just one value for the margin property, which simultaneously sets all four sides of an element's margin. An example of the margin shorthand property with just one value appears in Figure 7-8.

```
body {
    margin: 0;
    padding: 0;
}
div {
    width: 100px;
    height: 100px;
    background: mistyrose;
    border: 1px solid pink;
}
div#toprightbottomleft {
    margin-top: 10px;
    margin-right: 10px;
    margin-bottom: 10px;
    margin-left: 10px;
}
div#toprightbottomleft-1 {
    margin: 10px;
}
```

When one value is specified for the margin shorthand property, the value is applied to all four sides.

margin-top
margin-right
margin-bottom
margin-left

Figure 7-8a

The CSS in Figure 7-8a is combined with the markup in Figure 7-8b.

```
<!DOCTYPE html PUBLIC "-//W3C//DTD XHTML 1.0 Strict//EN"
                      "http://www.w3.org/TR/xhtml1/DTD/xhtml1-strict.dtd">
<html xmlns='http://www.w3.org/1999/xhtml' xml:lang='en'>
    <head>
        <title>margin</title>
        <link rel='stylesheet' type='text/css' href='096977%20fg0708.css' />
    </head>
    <body>
        <div id='toprightbottomleft'></div>
        <div id='toprightbottomleft-1'></div>
    </body>
</html>
```

Figure 7-8b

The resulting screenshot appears in Figure 7-8c.

Figure 7-8c

In Figure 7-8 you see how all four sides can be set with just one `margin` property and keyword value, as opposed to four.

> Box model shorthand properties with one value always set the property for all sides of the box.

Margin Collapsing

In CSS, *margin collapsing* occurs when the top or bottom margin of one element comes into contact with the top or bottom margin of another element. The concept is simple: The smaller of the two margins is reduced to zero; if both element margins are the same length, then one of the margins is reduced to zero. Margin collapsing is demonstrated in Figure 7-9.

```
body {
    margin: 0;
    padding: 0;
}
div {
    width: 100px;
    height: 100px;
    background: lightyellow;
    border: 1px solid gold;
}
div#top {
    margin: 10px 20px;
}
div#bottom {
    margin: 20px;
}
```

Margins collapse where two margins come into contact with each other.

The larger of the two margins wins; the smaller margin is made as though it doesn't exist at all.

Figure 7-9a

You combine the CSS in Figure 7-9a with the markup in Figure 7-9b.

```
<!DOCTYPE html PUBLIC "-//W3C//DTD XHTML 1.0 Strict//EN"
                      "http://www.w3.org/TR/xhtml1/DTD/xhtml1-strict.dtd">
<html xmlns='http://www.w3.org/1999/xhtml' xml:lang='en'>
    <head>
        <title>margin</title>
        <link rel='stylesheet' type='text/css' href='096977%20fg0709.css' />
    </head>
    <body>
        <div id='top'></div>
        <div id='bottom'></div>
    </body>
</html>
```

Figure 7-9b

The source code in the preceding two figures results in what you see in Figure 7-9c.

In Figure 7-9, you see the most common form of margin collapsing; the top margin of one element comes into contact with the bottom margin of another element. When this happens, the element with the bigger margin wins.

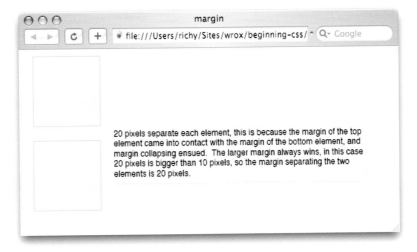

20 pixels separate each element, this is because the margin of the top element came into contact with the margin of the bottom element, and margin collapsing ensued. The larger margin always wins, in this case 20 pixels is bigger than 10 pixels, so the margin separating the two elements is 20 pixels.

Figure 7-9c

Margin collapsing also happens when an element is contained inside of another element. It doesn't matter where the two margins come into contact, even an element inside of another element will margin collapse with its parent if the two margins come into contact. An example of this appears in Figure 7-10.

```
body {
    margin: 0;
    padding: 0;
}
div {
    width: 100px;
    height: 100px;
}
div#parent {
    margin: 10px 20px;
    background: yellow;
}
div#child {
    margin: 20px;
    background: lightyellow;
    border: 1px solid gold;
}
```

When a child element's margin comes into contact with a parent element's margin, margin collapsing is triggered.

As was the case with adjacent sibling elements, the bigger margin is the one that is applied. The margin is always applied to the parent element, and the child's margin always collapses.

Figure 7-10a

The CSS in Figure 7-10a is included in the markup in Figure 7-10b, and that results in the output you see in Figure 7-10c.

217

```
<!DOCTYPE html PUBLIC "-//W3C//DTD XHTML 1.0 Strict//EN"
                      "http://www.w3.org/TR/xhtml1/DTD/xhtml1-strict.dtd">
<html xmlns='http://www.w3.org/1999/xhtml' xml:lang='en'>
    <head>
        <title>margin</title>
        <link rel='stylesheet' type='text/css' href='096977%20fg0710.css' />
    </head>
    <body>
        <div id='parent'>
            <div id='child'>
            </div>
        </div>
    </body>
</html>
```

Figure 7-10b

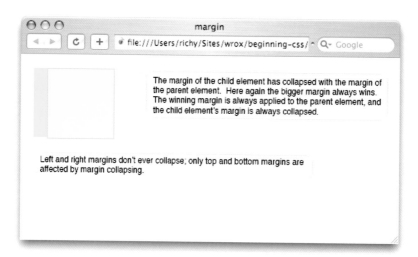

Figure 7-10c

In Figure 7-10, you see how margin collapsing works between a parent and child element. If a child's margin comes into direct contact with the margin of a parent, the margins collapse. Like the example in Figure 7-9 that contained adjacent sibling margins collapsing, the larger margin is the winning margin. The winning margin is always applied to the parent element, and the child element's margin always collapses. In this scenario, margin collapsing can be stopped if you prevent the two margins from coming into contact with one another. You can prevent the two margins from coming into contact with one another by applying padding or a border to the parent element. An example of this appears in Figure 7-11.

The CSS in Figure 7-11a is included in the markup in Figure 7-11b to get the output that you see in Figure 7-11c.

In Figure 7-11, you see how to stop margin collapsing from happening. You must give the parent element a border or padding to prevent the top and bottom margin of the child element from coming into contact with the top and bottom margin of the parent element.

```
body {
    margin: 0;
    padding: 0;
}
div {
    width: 100px;
    height: 100px;
}
div#parent {
    margin: 10px 20px;
    background: yellow;
    border: 1px solid gold;
}
div#child {
    margin: 20px;
    background: lightyellow;
    border: 1px solid gold;
}
```

When you apply a border or padding to the parent element, margin collapsing is prevented. Margin collapsing only happens when the top or botttom margin of one element comes into contact with the top or bottom margin of another element.

Figure 7-11a

```
<!DOCTYPE html PUBLIC "-//W3C//DTD XHTML 1.0 Strict//EN"
                       "http://www.w3.org/TR/xhtml1/DTD/xhtml1-strict.dtd">
<html xmlns='http://www.w3.org/1999/xhtml' xml:lang='en'>
    <head>
        <title>margin</title>
        <link rel='stylesheet' type='text/css' href='096977%20fg0711.css' />
    </head>
    <body>
        <div id='parent'>
            <div id='child'>
            </div>
        </div>
    </body>
</html>
```

Figure 7-11b

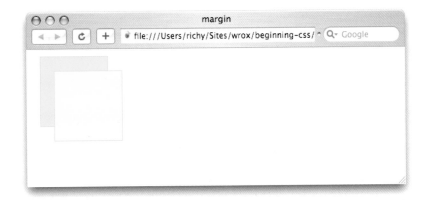

Figure 7-11c

Horizontally Aligning Elements with the Margin Property

The margin property has one other useful function: It can be used to center or align elements. An example of this concept appears in Figure 7-12.

```css
body {
    margin: 10px;
    padding: 0;
}
div {
    width: 50px;
    height: 50px;
    background: rgb(218, 220, 243);
    border: 1px solid rgb(154, 157, 203);
}
div#left {
    margin: 10px auto 10px 0;
}
div#center {
    margin: 10px auto;
}
div#right {
    margin: 10px 0 10px auto;
}
```

The auto keyword is used in conjunction with the margin property for aligning an element to the left, center, or right.

Figure 7-12a

The CSS you see in Figure 7-12a is included in the markup in Figure 7-12b; this results in what you see in Figure 7-12c.

```html
<!DOCTYPE html PUBLIC "-//W3C//DTD XHTML 1.0 Strict//EN"
                      "http://www.w3.org/TR/xhtml1/DTD/xhtml1-strict.dtd">
<html xmlns='http://www.w3.org/1999/xhtml' xml:lang='en'>
    <head>
        <title>margin</title>
        <link rel='stylesheet' type='text/css' href='096977%20fg0712.css' />
    </head>
    <body>
        <div id='left'>
        </div>
        <div id='center'>
        </div>
        <div id='right'>
        </div>
    </body>
</html>
```

Figure 7-12b

In Figure 7-12, you see a technique that is used to align elements in a document via the combination of the auto keyword with the left or right margin of an element. The margin that is specified must be either the left or the right margin, because the auto keyword is ignored when applied to the top or bottom margin. The element is not aligned vertically, as you might expect.

220

Figure 7-12c

Aligning Elements in IE 6 and IE 7 in Quirks Rendering Mode

Every modern browser today supports what's called the DOCTYPE switch, a method of selecting the rendering mode of your browser based on the Document Type Declaration that appears at the top of an (X)HTML document. If you structure your documents like the example you see here in this book, you'll never encounter quirks rendering mode, but if you are working with legacy websites that must maintain backward compatibility with the web of yesterday, chances are you'll encounter a quirks mode site sooner or later. Appendix D, "Browser Rendering Modes," shows a listing of Document Type Declarations that trigger quirks rendering mode, and as such, I won't reiterate that here.

If you encounter quirks mode, you'll also discover that some CSS features don't work in quirks mode, but do work in standards mode. Aligning an element using the auto keyword in conjunction with the margin property is one such quirks mode incompatibility. In IE, this feature is only implemented in standards mode. Whereas the example that you see in Figure 7-12 will work fine in IE, it won't work if you change the Document Type Declaration to a quirks mode invoking DOCTYPE. The CSS from Figure 7-12a is combined with the markup that you see in Figure 7-13a to get the result you see in Figure 7-13b.

```
<!DOCTYPE HTML PUBLIC "-//W3C//DTD HTML 4.0 Transitional//EN">
<html>
    <head>
        <title>margin</title>
        <link rel='stylesheet' type='text/css' href='096977%20fg0712.css'>
    </head>
    <body>
        <div id='left'>
        </div>
        <div id='center'>
        </div>
        <div id='right'>
        </div>
    </body>
</html>
```

Figure 7-13a

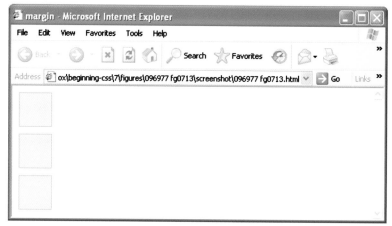

Figure 7-13b

In Figure 7-13, you see what happens when quirks rendering mode is invoked and the auto keyword of the margin property used. IE 6 (and IE 7) ignore the auto keyword in quirks mode (they work fine in standards mode). To work around this problem, you can use an IE bug to your advantage. A demonstration of this appears in Figure 7-14.

```
body {
    margin: 10px;
    padding: 0;
}
div div {
    width: 50px;
    height: 50px;
    background: rgb(218, 220, 243);
    border: 1px solid rgb(154, 157, 203);
    text-align: left;
}
div#left {
    text-align: left;
}
div#center {
    text-align: center;
}
div#right {
    text-align: right;
}
```

IE (against the standards) can use the text-align property for aligning elements. This technique does not work in other browsers.

Figure 7-14a

The CSS in Figure 7-14a is included in the markup in Figure 7-14b to get the output that you see in Figure 7-14c.

```
<!DOCTYPE HTML PUBLIC "-//W3C//DTD HTML 4.0 Transitional//EN">
<html>
    <head>
        <title>margin</title>
        <link rel='stylesheet' type='text/css' href='096977%20fg0714.css'>
    </head>
    <body>
        <div id='left'>
            <div></div>
        </div>
        <div id='center'>
            <div></div>
        </div>
        <div id='right'>
            <div></div>
        </div>
    </body>
</html>
```

Figure 7-14b

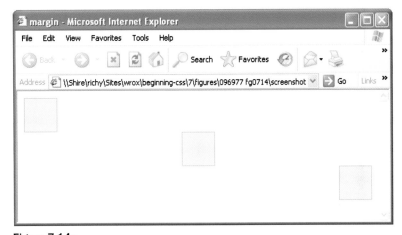

Figure 7-14c

In Figure 7-14, you see how the `text-align` property can help you align elements in IE in quirks mode. Wherever possible, I recommend setting the Document Type Declaration to a standards mode DOCTYPE, which will allow you to use the standard method of aligning elements. The technique that you see here can also be easily combined with the margin method, which is common for aligning elements in IE 5.5, which has no standards rendering mode and does not support the margin method of alignment.

Vertical alignment of an element requires *layering* (also called positioning) an element, and because of this I discuss vertical alignment of elements in Chapter 11, "Positioning."

Try It Out   **Applying Margin**

Example 7-1. To recap the margin property, follow these steps.

1.   Enter the following markup in your text editor:

```
<!DOCTYPE html PUBLIC "-//W3C//DTD XHTML 1.0 Strict//EN"
                      "http://www.w3.org/TR/xhtml1/DTD/xhtml1-strict.dtd">
<html xmlns='http://www.w3.org/1999/xhtml' xml:lang='en'>
    <head>
        <title>margin</title>
        <link rel='stylesheet' type='text/css' href='Example_7-1.css' />
    </head>
    <body>
        <p>
            The margin shorthand property can accept from one to four values.
            When all four values are provided, each is provided in order clockwise,
            beginning with the top property.  Box model properties are
            always specified in order clockwise.
        </p>
        <div class='margin-wrapper'>
            <div id='margin'></div>
        </div>
        <p>
            You can also specify margin via one of the four separate margin
            properties: margin-top, margin-right, margin-bottom, and margin-left.
        </p>
        <div class='margin-wrapper'>
            <div id='margin-properties'></div>
        </div>
        <p>
            When three values are supplied to the margin shorthand property,
            the top is the first value, the right and left sides are the second
            value, and the bottom is the third value.
        </p>
        <div class='margin-wrapper'>
            <div id='margin-three'></div>
        </div>
        <p>
            When two values are supplied to the margin shorthand property,
            the top and bottom are the first value, right and left sides are the
            second value.
        </p>
        <div class='margin-wrapper'>
            <div id='margin-two'></div>
        </div>
        <p>
            When one value is supplied to the margin shorthand property, all four
            sides are specified with that one value.
        </p>
        <div class='margin-wrapper'>
            <div id='margin-one'></div>
```

```
        </div>
        <p>
            If the auto keyword is supplied for the left or right margins, the
            element that margin is applied to is aligned horizontally.
        </p>
        <div class='margin-wrapper alignment'>
            <div id='margin-left'></div>
            <div id='margin-center'></div>
            <div id='margin-right'></div>
        </div>
        <p>
            Margin collapsing happens when the top or bottom margin of one element
            comes into contact with the top or bottom margin of another element.
            The smaller of the two margins is eliminated; if they are equal size,
            then one margin is still eliminated.  This happens with adjacent
            siblings.
        </p>
        <div class='margin-wrapper'>
            <div id='top'></div>
            <div id='bottom'></div>
        </div>
        <p>
            Margin collapsing also happens between parent and child elements.
        </p>
        <div class='margin-wrapper'>
            <div id='parent'>
                <div id='child'></div>
            </div>
        </div>
    </body>
</html>
```

2. Save the preceding document as `Example_7-1.html`.

3. Enter the following CSS in a new document in your text editor:

```
body {
    font: 12px sans-serif;
}
div.margin-wrapper {
    background: lightyellow;
    border: 1px solid gold;
    float: left;
    margin: 5px;
}
p {
    clear: left;
    margin: 5px;
}
div.margin-wrapper div {
    background: khaki;
    border: 1px solid black;
```

```
        width: 25px;
        height: 25px;
}
div#margin {
    margin: 4px 6px 8px 10px;
}
div#margin-properties {
    margin-top: 2px;
    margin-right: 4px;
    margin-bottom: 6px;
    margin-left: 8px;
}
div#margin-three {
    margin: 2px 10px 4px;
}
div#margin-two {
    margin: 2px 10px;
}
div#margin-one {
    margin: 2px;
}
div.alignment {
    float: none;
}
div#margin-left {
    margin-right: auto;
}
div#margin-center {
    margin: 0 auto;
}
div#margin-right {
    margin-left: auto;
}
div#top {
    margin: 5px;
}
div#bottom {
    margin: 5px;
}
div#parent {
    margin: 5px;
    border: none;
    background: crimson;
}
div#child {
    margin: 5px;
}
```

4. Save the CSS document as `Example_7-1.css`. The preceding example results in the output that you see in Figure 7-15.

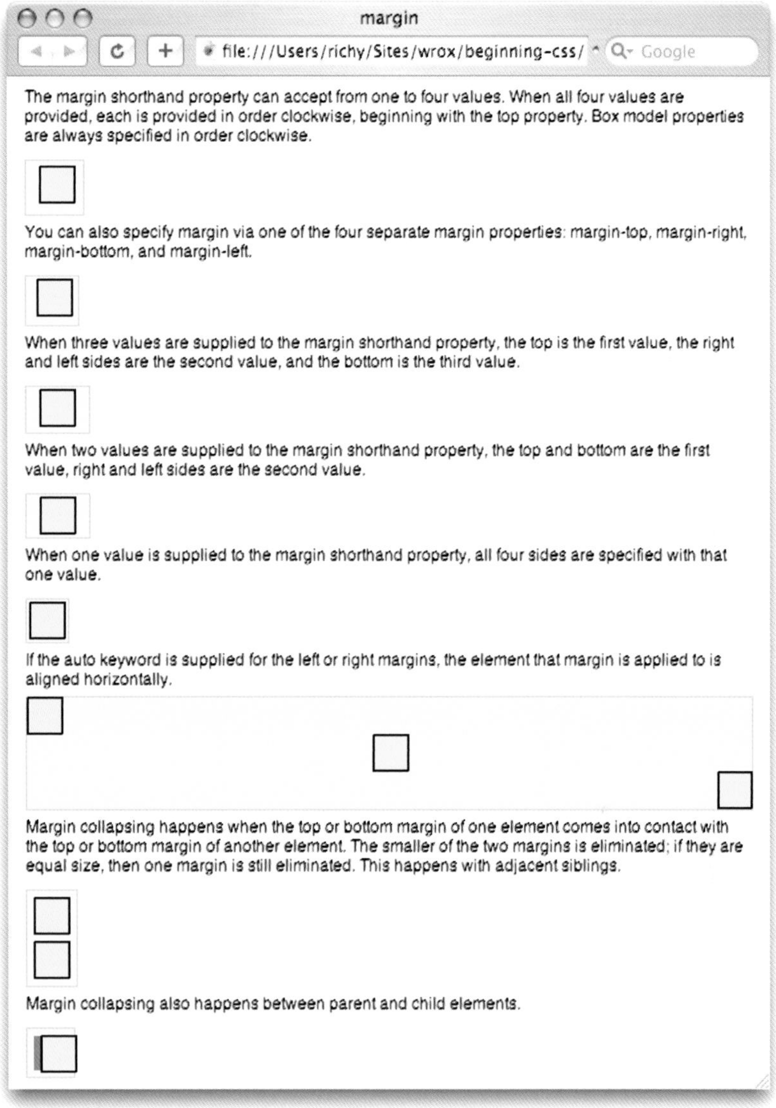

Figure 7-15

How It Works

In Example 7-1, you recapped the margin property. You begin with an example of the margin shorthand property with values for all four sides of a box. Because each example has a wrapping `<div>` element around it, you can see the amount of space that the margin occupies. In the first example you set all four margin values; you can see what happened in Figure 7-16.

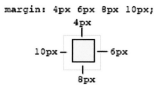

Figure 7-16

In the second example, you set each margin value via the separate margin properties, which are illustrated in Figure 7-17.

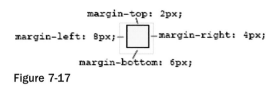

Figure 7-17

In the next example, you set the margin shorthand property with three values. The first value sets the value for the top margin, the second value sets the left and right margins, and the third value sets the bottom margin. The result is illustrated in Figure 7-18.

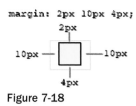

Figure 7-18

Figure 7-19 is an example of the margin shorthand property with two values. When only two values are specified, the first value sets both the top and bottom margins, and the second value sets the left and right margins.

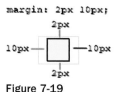

Figure 7-19

Figure 7-20 is an example of the margin property with just one value. When only one value is set, all four margin values are set at once.

margin: 2px;

Figure 7-20

Next, you did an example of horizontally aligning elements with the margin property. You did this by setting either the left or right margin, or both, to auto. An example of horizontal alignment using the margin property appears in Figure 7-21.

Figure 7-21

In the next example you see margin collapsing in action. When the bottom margin of the element with id name top came into contact with the top margin of the element with id name bottom, margin collapsing occurred. Instead of 10 pixels separating the top and bottom elements, one margin is collapsed, and only 5 pixels separate each element. An example of this appears in Figure 7-22.

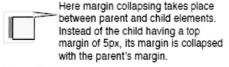

Figure 7-22

In the final example, you see how to create margin collapsing between parent and child elements. Just as was the case in the previous example of adjacent sibling elements where the bottom margin of the top sibling collapsed with the top margin of the bottom sibling, when a child's top or bottom margin comes into contact with the top or bottom margin of its parent element, margin collapsing also takes place. An example of this appears in Figure 7-23.

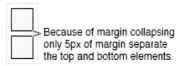

Figure 7-23

In the next section I discuss the next box model property, borders.

Borders

Borders appear between the `margin` and `padding` in the box model depicted in Figure 7-1. It's obvious that borders put lines around boxes. Applying borders usually makes the other box model properties easier to see. The following sections examine each individual border property.

border-width

The `border-width` properties all control the width of a box border in some fashion. The following table outlines each `border-width` property.

Property	Value
border-top-width border-right-width border-bottom-width border-left-width	<border-width> Initial value: medium
border-width A <border-width> value refers to one of the following: thin | medium | thick | <length>	<border-width> {1,4} Initial value: medium

The individual `border-top-width`, `border-right-width`, `border-bottom-width`, and `border-left-width` properties exist for setting the width of the individual sides of a box. Each of these properties can be combined into the single `border-width` shorthand property.

Borders aren't allowed to have percentage values; however, they are capable of accepting any length measurement supported by CSS (em, pixel, centimeter, and so on). In addition to length units, the border width may also be specified using one of three keywords: `thin`, `medium`, and `thick`. Figure 7-24 shows the rendered output of these three keywords.

The CSS in Figure 7-24a is combined with the markup in Figure 7-24b.

```
div {
    padding: 3px;
    border-color: black;
    border-style: solid;
    background: mistyrose;
    margin: 5px;
}
div#thin {
    border-width: thin;
}
div#medium {
    border-width: medium;
}
div#thick {
    border-width: thick;
}
```

The `border-width` property can take a length value or one of three keyword values: `thin`, `medium`, and `thick`.

Figure 7-24a

```
<!DOCTYPE html PUBLIC "-//W3C//DTD XHTML 1.0 Strict//EN"
                      "http://www.w3.org/TR/xhtml1/DTD/xhtml1-strict.dtd">
<html xmlns='http://www.w3.org/1999/xhtml' xml:lang='en'>
    <head>
        <title>border-width</title>
        <link rel='stylesheet' type='text/css' href='096977%20fg0724.css' />
    </head>
    <body>
        <div id='thin'>thin</div>
        <div id='medium'>medium</div>
        <div id='thick'>thick</div>
    </body>
</html>
```

Figure 7-24b

When loaded into a browser, you should see output like that in Figure 7-24c resulting from the CSS and markup in Figures 7-24a and 7-24b.

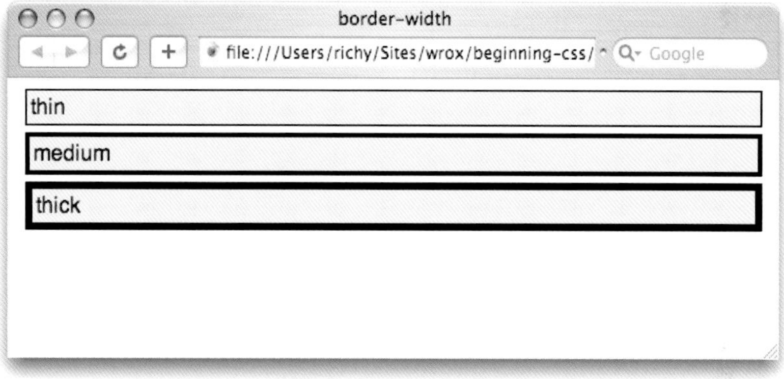

Figure 7-24c

In Figure 7-24, you see what the three keyword values (thin, medium, and thick) of the border-width property look like. The border-width property can also take an arbitrary length value; an example of this appears in Figure 7-25.

The CSS in Figure 7-25a is combined with the markup in Figure 7-25b.

Figure 7-25c shows the rendered output of Figure 7-25a and Figure 7-25b.

In Figure 7-25, you see that the border-width property with a length value can be specified in a variety of ways. You can use the individual border-width properties, border-top-width, border-right-width, border-bottom-width, and border-left-width, or you can use the border-width short-hand property. Like the margin property that you examined in the last section, it can take from one to four values for specifying the border width of each side of the box.

```
div {
    padding: 3px;
    border-color: khaki;
    border-style: solid;
    background: lightyellow;
    margin: 5px;
    float: left;
    width: 50px;
    height: 50px;
}
div#properties {
    border-top-width: 2px;
    border-right-width: 4px;
    border-bottom-width: 8px;
    border-left-width: 10px;
}
div#four {
    border-width: 2px 4px 8px 10px;       border-left-width
}
border-top-width              border-bottom-width

            border-right-width

div#three {
    border-width: 2px 4px 8px;
}
border-top-width   border-right-width    border-bottom-width
                   border-left-width

div#two {
    border-width: 8px 4px;
}
  border-top-width       border-right-width
  border-bottom-width   border-left-width

div#one {
    border-width: 4px;
}
            border-top-width
            border-right-width
            border-bottom-width
            border-left-width
```

Like the margin property, the border-width property is a shorthand property that can accept one to four length values. The width of each side can also be specified via individual properties.

Figure 7-25a

```
<!DOCTYPE html PUBLIC "-//W3C//DTD XHTML 1.0 Strict//EN"
                      "http://www.w3.org/TR/xhtml1/DTD/xhtml1-strict.dtd">
<html xmlns='http://www.w3.org/1999/xhtml' xml:lang='en'>
    <head>
        <title>border-width</title>
        <link rel='stylesheet' type='text/css' href='096977%20fg0725.css' />
    </head>
    <body>
        <div id='properties'></div>
        <div id='four'></div>
        <div id='three'></div>
        <div id='two'></div>
        <div id='one'></div>
    </body>
</html>
```

Figure 7-25b

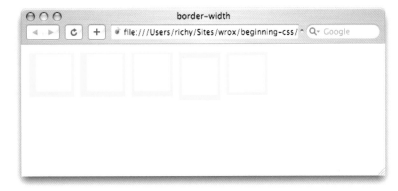

Figure 7-25c

In the next section I discuss the border-style property, and how it is used to change the style of border.

border-style

You use the border-style property to specify the style of border to be used. The border-style property is very similar to the border-width property presented in the previous section in that it uses an identical syntax to specify the style of border to be used for each side of the box. The following table outlines the border-style family of properties.

Property	Value
border-style A <border-style> value refers to one of the following: none | hidden | dotted | dashed | solid | double | groove | ridge | inset | outset	<border-style> {1,4} Initial value: none
border-top-style border-right-style border-bottom-style border-left-style	<border-style> Initial value: none

Like the border-width property, the border-style property is also a shorthand property, which combines the individual border-top-style, border-right-style, border-bottom-style, and border-left-style properties into the single border-style property. Figure 7-26 shows the rendered representation of each of the border-style keywords.

The CSS in Figure 7-26a is included in the markup in Figure 7-26b.

```
div {
    padding: 3px;
    border-color: crimson;
    border-width: 3px;
    margin: 5px;
    float: left;
    width: 50px;
    height: 50px;
}

div#hidden {border-style: hidden;}
div#dotted {border-style: dotted;}
div#dashed {border-style: dashed;}
div#solid  {border-style: solid; }
div#double {border-style: double;}
div#groove {border-style: groove;}
div#ridge  {border-style: ridge; }
div#inset  {border-style: inset; }
div#outset {border-style: outset;}
div#none   {border-style: none;  }
```

The border-style property supports 10 different border styles.

Figure 7-26a

```
<!DOCTYPE html PUBLIC "-//W3C//DTD XHTML 1.0 Strict//EN"
                      "http://www.w3.org/TR/xhtml1/DTD/xhtml1-strict.dtd">
<html xmlns='http://www.w3.org/1999/xhtml' xml:lang='en'>
    <head>
        <title>border-style</title>
        <link rel='stylesheet' type='text/css' href='096977%20fg0726.css' />
    </head>
    <body>
        <div id='hidden'>hidden</div>
        <div id='dotted'>dotted</div>
        <div id='dashed'>dashed</div>
        <div id='solid'>solid</div>
        <div id='double'>double</div>
        <div id='groove'>groove</div>
        <div id='ridge'>ridge</div>
        <div id='inset'>inset</div>
        <div id='outset'>outset</div>
        <div id='none'>none</div>
    </body>
</html>
```

Figure 7-26b

You should get something like the output in Figure 7-26c from the code in Figures 7-26a and 7-26b.

In Figure 7-26, you can see what each border style looks like in each of the major browsers, Safari, IE 6, IE 7, Firefox 2, and Opera.

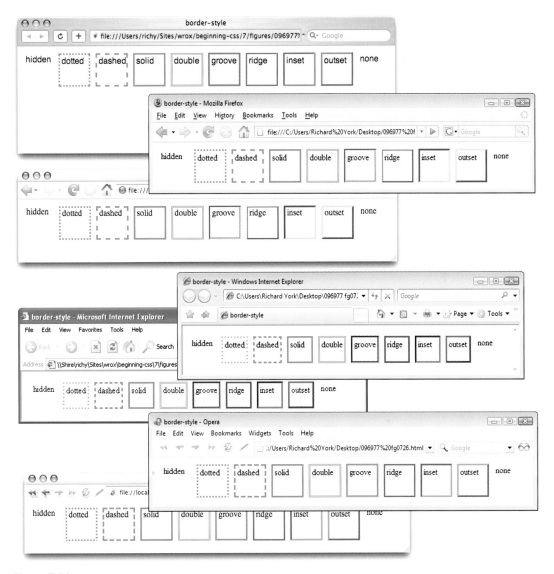

Figure 7-26c

Like the border-width property, the border-style property can accept up to four values to specify the style for each side of the box. The rules for specifying styles for different sides of the box are the same as the border-width property of the previous section, but instead of the length, like this:

```
border-width: 2px 4px 6px 8px;
```

There would be a border style, for example:

```
border-style: hidden dotted dashed solid;
```

As is the case for the `margin` and `border-width` properties, the shorthand is specified as top, right, bottom, and left, and `border-style` also supports the three-value, two-value, and one-value shorthand syntax as the `border-width` and `margin` properties.

border-color

The `border-color` property is another shorthand property. Like the `border-style` and `border-width` properties, you can use `border-color` to control how a border is styled. The `border-color` property, as you may have guessed, specifies the border color for each side of the box. The following table outlines the `border-color` family of properties.

Property	Value
border-color	[<color> | transparent] {1,4} Initial value: the value of the 'color' property
border-top-color border-right-color border-bottom-color border-left-color	<color> | transparent Initial value: the value of the 'color' property

IE 6 and IE 7 do not support the `transparent` keyword as applied to border color; in IE the `transparent` keyword is rendered as black.

Like `border-style`, `margin`, and `border-width`, the `border-color` property can accept up to four values. This property accepts a `<color>` value, meaning that it can accept a color keyword, a hexadecimal value, short hexadecimal value, or an RGB value; any color value accepted by the `color` property is also acceptable to the `border-color` properties.

> **When the `border-color` property is not specified, the `border-color` is the same color as specified for the `color` property.**

Now that you've seen an overview of what is possible with borders, the upcoming sections discuss the border shorthand properties.

Border Shorthand Properties

The `border-top`, `border-right`, `border-bottom`, `border-left`, and `border` properties combine the `border-width`, `border-style`, and `border-color` properties into single properties for each side of the box, or all sides of the box. The following table outlines the possible values for these five properties.

Property	Value
border-top border-right border-bottom border-left	\<border-width> || \<border-style> || \<color>
border	\<border-width> || \<border-style> || \<color>

The notation for the border-top, border-right, border-bottom, border-left, and border properties indicates that one to three values are possible; each value refers to a border-width value, a border-style value, and a border-color value. Figure 7-27 demonstrates the border shorthand properties.

```
div {
    margin: 5px;
    float: left;
    width: 56px;
    height: 56px;
}

div#properties {
    border-top: 1px solid darkkhaki;
    border-right: 1px dashed darkkhaki;
    border-bottom: 1px solid darkkhaki;
    border-left: 1px dashed darkkhaki;
    background: lightyellow;
}
div#border {
    border: 1px dashed darkkhaki;
}
```

Each of the five border shorthand properties accept the border-width, border-style, and border-color. Each side can be specified individually, or all at once with the border property.

Figure 7-27a

The CSS in Figure 7-27a is included in the markup in Figure 7-27b.

```
<!DOCTYPE html PUBLIC "-//W3C//DTD XHTML 1.0 Strict//EN"
                      "http://www.w3.org/TR/xhtml1/DTD/xhtml1-strict.dtd">
<html xmlns='http://www.w3.org/1999/xhtml' xml:lang='en'>
    <head>
        <title>
            border-top, border-right, border-bottom, border-left, border
        </title>
        <link rel='stylesheet' type='text/css' href='096977%20fg0727.css' />
    </head>
    <body>
        <div id='properties'></div>
        <div id='border'></div>
    </body>
</html>
```

Figure 7-27b

The CSS in Figure 7-27a and the markup in Figure 7-27b result in the output that you see in Figure 7-27c.

Figure 7-27c

In Figure 7-27, you see two methods for specifying an element's borders using border shorthand properties. The first method that you see uses four individual border shorthand properties, one for each side of the box, `border-top`, `border-right`, `border-bottom`, and `border-left`, and the second method uses the `border` shorthand property, which specifies the border for all four sides of the box at once.

Unlike the `margin` shorthand property, the `border` property may only be used to specify all four sides of the box at once. If you want a different style, or width, or color for the different sides, you'll need to use the individual shorthand properties.

In the following Try It Out you recap what is possible with CSS border properties.

Try It Out   **Applying Borders**

Example 7-2. To review what is possible with the border properties, follow these steps.

1.   Enter the following markup into your text editor:

```
<!DOCTYPE html PUBLIC "-//W3C//DTD XHTML 1.0 Strict//EN"
                 "http://www.w3.org/TR/xhtml1/DTD/xhtml1-strict.dtd">
<html xmlns='http://www.w3.org/1999/xhtml' xml:lang='en'>
    <head>
        <title>border</title>
        <link rel='stylesheet' type='text/css' href='Example_7-2.css' />
    </head>
    <body>
        <p>
            CSS provides a variety of ways for specifying borders.  At a minimum,
            you must specify a border-style.
```

```
        </p>
        <div id='border-style-properties'>
            Lorem ipsum dolor sit amet, consectetuer adipiscing elit.
        </div>
        <p>
            Like the margin properties, the individual border-style properties
            can be combined into a single property.
        </p>
        <div id='border-style'>
            Lorem ipsum dolor sit amet, consectetuer adipiscing elit.
        </div>
        <p>
            When no border-color is specified, the border color is the value of
            the color property.
        </p>
        <div id='color-default'>
            Lorem ipsum dolor sit amet, consectetuer adipiscing elit.
        </div>
        <p>
            The border-width property can take either one of three keywords or a
length
            value.
        </p>
        <div id='border-width'>
            <div id='thin'>thin</div>
            <div id='medium'>medium</div>
            <div id='thick'>thick</div>
        </div>
        <p>
            Four shorthand properties can be used to specify border-width,
            border-style, and border-color in just one property for each
            side of the box.
        </p>
        <div id='shorthand-sides'>
            border-top, border-right, border-bottom, border-left
        </div>
        <p>
            One shorthand property, the border property, can be used to specify
            border-width, border-style, and border-color for all four sides at
            once.
        </p>
        <div id='shorthand'>
            border
        </div>
    </body>
</html>
```

2. Save the preceding markup as `Example_7-2.html`

3. Enter the following style sheet in your text editor:

```
body {
    font: 12px sans-serif;
}
div#border-style-properties {
    border-top-style: solid;
    border-right-style: dashed;
    border-bottom-style: double;
    border-left-style: inset;
}
div#border-style {
    border-style: solid dashed double inset;
}
div#color-default {
    color: crimson;
    border-style: solid dotted;
}
div#border-width {
    overflow: hidden;
}
div#border-width div {
    float: left;
    border-style: solid;
    border-color: red;
    margin: 0 5px;
}
div#thin {
    border-width: thin;
}
div#medium {
    border-width: medium;
}
div#thick {
    border-width: thick;
}
div#shorthand-sides {
    border-top: 1px solid pink;
    border-right: 1px solid crimson;
    border-bottom: 1px solid pink;
    border-left: 1px solid crimson;
    padding: 5px;
}
div#shorthand {
    border: 1px solid crimson;
    padding: 5px;
}
```

4. Save the preceding style sheet as `Example_7-2.css`. After loading Example 7-2 into a browser, you should come up with something that looks like Figure 7-28.

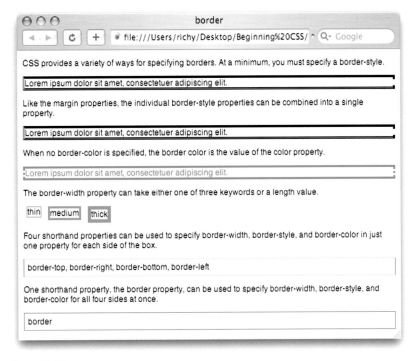

Figure 7-28

How It Works

In Example 7-2, you recapped what was possible with the border properties. You can set an element's border style by four different properties, one for each side, `border-top-style`, `border-right-style`, `border-bottom-style`, and `border-left-style`, or via a shorthand property that lets you set all four sides in the same way as the margin shorthand property, the `border-style` property. The process is the same for `border-width`; you can use the four separate border width properties, `border-top-width`, `border-right-width`, `border-bottom-width`, and `border-left-width`, or the shorthand `border-width` property. Then there are also the similar border-color properties that allow you to set the border color of each side via individual border color properties, `border-top-color`, `border-right-color`, `border-bottom-color`, and `border-left-color`, or the `border-color` shorthand property.

You learned that when there is no border style specified, the default style is none; when there is no width specified; the default width is medium, and when there is no border color specified, the default border color is the value of the color property (in other words, the same as the text color).

You also learned that there are four shorthand properties that allow you to combine `border-width`, `border-style`, and `border-color` into single shorthand properties. These exist for all four sides, `border-top`, `border-right`, `border-bottom`, and `border-left`. The last border shorthand property lets you set all four sides of the box at once, and that's the `border` shorthand property.

In the next section you examine box padding.

Padding

Padding is the space between the content of an element and its borders, as has been mentioned briefly in previous examples. Refer to the diagram in Figure 7-1 to see where padding appears in the box model. The following table shows the various padding properties.

Property	Value
padding	[<length> | <percentage>] {1,4}
padding-top padding-right padding-bottom padding-left	<length> | <percentage>

Like `margin`, `border-width`, `border-style`, and `border-color`, the `padding` property is a shorthand property, meaning that it is a simplified representation of the other `padding` properties, `padding-top`, `padding-right`, `padding-bottom`, and `padding-left`. In the preceding table, the square brackets are used to group the values. In this context, the `padding` property can accept either a length or a percentage value, and can have one to four space-separated values. Figure 7-29 examines the `padding` property.

```
div {
    float: left;
    background: gold;
    margin: 5px;
    width: 250px;
}
div div {
    float: none;
    background: white;
    font: 10px sans-serif;
    color: rgb(200, 200, 200);
    width: auto;
}
div#properties {
    padding-top: 2px;
    padding-right: 4px;
    padding-bottom: 6px;
    padding-left: 8px;
}
div#four-values   {    padding: 2px 4px 6px 8px; }

                 padding-top padding-right padding-bottom  padding-left

div#three-values {    padding: 2px 8px 6px;       }

                 padding-top padding-right padding-bottom
                             padding-left
div#two-values   {    padding: 2px 8px;           }

                 padding-top        padding-right
                 padding-bottom     padding-left
div#one-value    {    padding: 2px;               }

                 padding-top
                 padding-right
                 padding-bottom
                 padding-left
```

As far as its syntax goes, the `padding` property is very similar to the `margin` property. Each side can be specified individually using individual properties, or via the `padding` shorthand property.

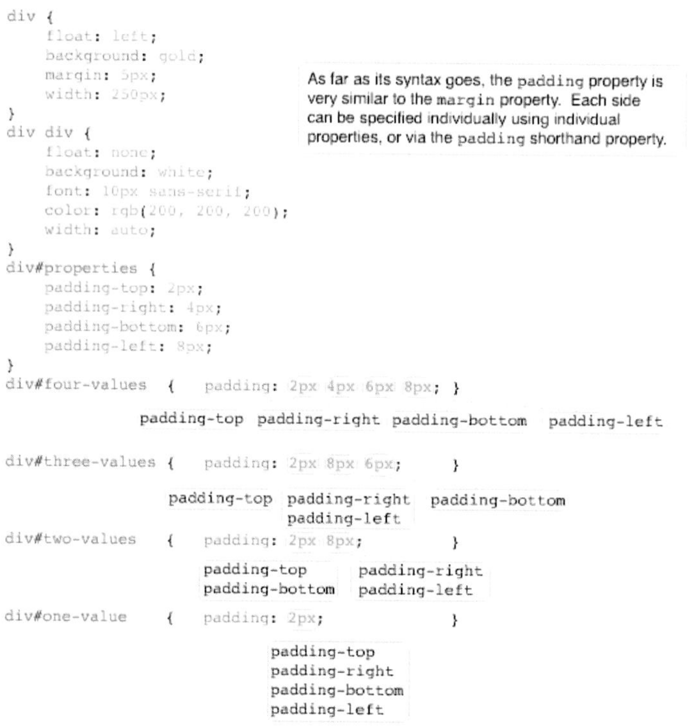

Figure 7-29a

The CSS in Figure 7-29a is combined with the markup in Figure 7-29b.

```
<!DOCTYPE html PUBLIC "-//W3C//DTD XHTML 1.0 Strict//EN"
                      "http://www.w3.org/TR/xhtml1/DTD/xhtml1-strict.dtd">
<html xmlns='http://www.w3.org/1999/xhtml' xml:lang='en'>
    <head>
        <title>padding</title>
        <link rel='stylesheet' type='text/css' href='096977%20fg0729.css' />
    </head>
    <body>
        <div id='properties'>
            <div>
                Lorem ipsum dolor sit amet, consectetuer adipiscing elit.
                Nulla bibendum eros sit amet lectus. Nunc eros massa,
                interdum ut, congue ut, scelerisque quis, tellus.
            </div>
        </div>
        <div id='four-values'>
            <div>
                Lorem ipsum dolor sit amet, consectetuer adipiscing elit.
                Nulla bibendum eros sit amet lectus. Nunc eros massa,
                interdum ut, congue ut, scelerisque quis, tellus.
            </div>
        </div>
        <div id='three-values'>
            <div>
                Lorem ipsum dolor sit amet, consectetuer adipiscing elit.
                Nulla bibendum eros sit amet lectus. Nunc eros massa,
                interdum ut, congue ut, scelerisque quis, tellus.
            </div>
        </div>
        <div id='two-values'>
            <div>
                Lorem ipsum dolor sit amet, consectetuer adipiscing elit.
                Nulla bibendum eros sit amet lectus. Nunc eros massa,
                interdum ut, congue ut, scelerisque quis, tellus.
            </div>
        </div>
        <div id='one-value'>
            <div>
                Lorem ipsum dolor sit amet, consectetuer adipiscing elit.
                Nulla bibendum eros sit amet lectus. Nunc eros massa,
                interdum ut, congue ut, scelerisque quis, tellus.
            </div>
        </div>
    </body>
</html>
```

Figure 7-29b

The markup in Figure 7-29b and the CSS in Figure 7-29a result in the output that you see in
Figure 7-29c.

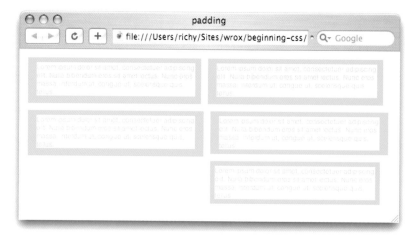

Figure 7-29c

In Figure 7-29, you see that the padding property is similar to the margin property. The main differences with the padding property are as follows:

❑ The padding area is the area between the inside edge of the border and the outer edge of the content.

❑ The auto keyword has no effect with the padding property.

❑ The padding property cannot accept a negative value (the margin property can).

❑ There is no collapsing padding; only margins can collapse.

In the next section, I examine the different length properties supported by CSS.

Setting Dimensions

CSS 1 introduced the width and height properties as part of the CSS box model. CSS 2 expands on those properties, providing minimum and maximum dimensions when variable lengths are involved, as is the case with percentage width and height values.

The following sections examine each of CSS's dimension properties individually.

width

The width property is a pretty simple property; it sets the width of an element. According to the CSS box model diagram presented in Figure 7-1, width is the space measured from inside padding edge to inside padding edge. The following table outlines the width property and its possible values.

Property	Value
Width	<length> | <percentage> | auto
	initial value: auto

The width property accepts a length unit, which is indicated in the preceding table with the <length> notation. In Figure 7-30, you see a simple example of the width property using a length unit.

The CSS in Figure 7-30a is combined with the markup in Figure 7-30b.

```
body {
    margin: 0;
    padding: 0;
    font: 12px sans-serif;
}
div#wrapper {
    border: 1px solid white;
    background: gold;
    width: 280px;
}
div#box {
    margin: 5px;
    border: 5px solid khaki;
    background: yellow;
    padding: 5px;
    width: 250px;
}
div#inner {
    background: white;
    text-align: justify;
}
```

width is the area from inside padding edge to inside padding edge.

Figure 7-30a

Figure 7-30c shows the result of the CSS in Figure 7-30a and the markup in Figure 7-30b.

In Figure 7-30, the <div> with the white background, which contains the Peter Piper copy, has a width of 250 pixels. Width is added in addition to the other box model properties, margin, border, and padding. Figure 7-31 demonstrates how this breaks down using the output that you see in Figure 7-30.

```
<!DOCTYPE html PUBLIC "-//W3C//DTD XHTML 1.0 Strict//EN"
                      "http://www.w3.org/TR/xhtml1/DTD/xhtml1-strict.dtd">
<html xmlns='http://www.w3.org/1999/xhtml' xml:lang='en'>
    <head>
        <title>width</title>
        <link rel='stylesheet' type='text/css' href='096977%20fg0730.css' />
    </head>
    <body>
        <div id='wrapper'>
            <div id='box'>
                <div id='inner'>
                    Peter Piper picked a peck of pickled peppers.
                    Did Peter Piper pick a peck of pickled peppers?
                    If Peter Piper picked a peck of pickled peppers,
                    where's the peck of pickled peppers Peter Piper picked?
                </div>
            </div>
        </div>
    </body>
</html>
```

Figure 7-30b

Figure 7-30c

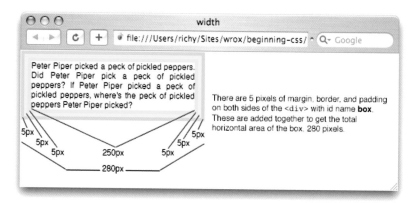

Figure 7-31

When you apply a width to an element, you must also take into account the margin, borders, and padding as part of the overall horizontal area that the element will occupy. In Figure 7-31, you see that the margin, border, padding, and width add up to 20 pixels, which is the width of the wrapper box. In the next section, you see what happens when your margin, border, padding, and width add up to more than the containing element.

In the next section, I talk about the height property.

height

Like the width property, the height property sets the amount of space between the top-inside padding edge and the bottom-inside padding edge. The following table outlines the height property and its possible values.

Property	Value
height	\<length>	\<percentage>	auto
	initial value: auto

The height property causes an element to behave somewhat differently than its HTML height attribute counterpart in standards-compliant browsers. When you explicitly specify a height, the height remains the same regardless of how much text you place inside the element. Figure 7-32 is an example of what happens when there is more content than the height allows.

Figure 7-32a is combined with the tongue twister in Figure 7-32b.

```
body {
    margin: 0;
    padding: 0;
    font: 12px sans-serif;
}
div#wrapper {
    border: 1px solid white;
    background: gold;
    width: 130px;
}
div#box {
    margin: 5px;
    border: 5px solid khaki;
    background: yellow;
    padding: 5px;
    height: 130px;
}
div#inner {
    background: white;
    text-align: justify;
}
```

When there is more content than height allows, the excess content overflows.

Figure 7-32a

Figure 7-32c shows the output of the markup and CSS in Figure 7-32a and Figure 7-32b in various browsers.

```
<!DOCTYPE html PUBLIC "-//W3C//DTD XHTML 1.0 Strict//EN"
                      "http://www.w3.org/TR/xhtml1/DTD/xhtml1-strict.dtd">
<html xmlns='http://www.w3.org/1999/xhtml' xml:lang='en'>
    <head>
        <title>height</title>
        <link rel='stylesheet' type='text/css' href='096977%20fg0732.css' />
    </head>
    <body>
        <div id='wrapper'>
            <div id='box'>
                <div id='inner'>
                    Peter Piper picked a peck of pickled peppers.
                    Did Peter Piper pick a peck of pickled peppers?
                    If Peter Piper picked a peck of pickled peppers,
                    where's the peck of pickled peppers Peter Piper picked?
                </div>
            </div>
        </div>
    </body>
</html>
```

Figure 7-32b

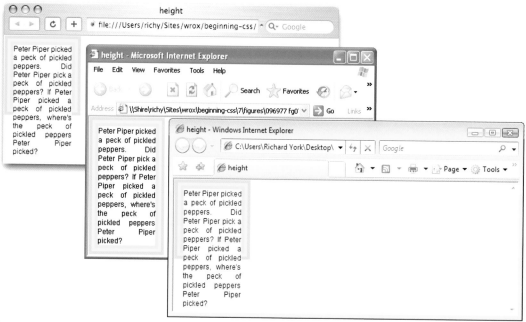

Figure 7-32c

In Figure 7-32, you can see that IE 6 does not correctly interpret CSS dimensions. You can also see that this bug has been fixed in IE 7, because it correctly overflows the excess content as Safari, Firefox, and Opera do. In IE 6, width and height are closer to the definition of the CSS min-width and min-height properties that I talk about later in this chapter.

The next section continues the discussion of dimensions with auto values for width and height.

Auto Values for width and height

By default, width and height properties have an auto value. So, when you do not specify a width or height, the value is the auto keyword. The meaning of the auto keyword changes depending on the type of element that it is applied to. When used on a <div> element, the element spans all the horizontal space available to it and expands vertically to accommodate any content inside of it, including text, images, or other boxes. Elements with this behavior are called *block* elements. Some examples of block elements are <div>, <p>, <h1> through <h6>, <form> and <ul> elements. The example in Figure 7-33 demonstrates auto width for block elements.

```
div {
    padding: 4px;
    background: yellow;
}
```

Block elements expand to fill all the space available to them horizontally by default.

Figure 7-33a

The CSS in Figure 7-33a is combined with the markup in Figure 7-33b.

```
<!DOCTYPE html PUBLIC "-//W3C//DTD XHTML 1.0 Strict//EN"
                      "http://www.w3.org/TR/xhtml1/DTD/xhtml1-strict.dtd">
<html xmlns='http://www.w3.org/1999/xhtml' xml:lang='en'>
    <head>
        <title>width</title>
        <link rel='stylesheet' type='text/css' href='096977%20fg0733.css' />
    </head>
    <body>
        <div>
            Auto width on a block element.
        </div>
    </body>
</html>
```

Figure 7-33b

The output that you see in Figure 7-33c is a result of the CSS in Figure 7-33a and the markup in Figure 7-33b. All three windows pictured display the same document, but at different sizes.

249

Figure 7-33c

In the screenshot in Figure 7-33c, you can see that the width of the `<div>` element adjusts to any changes in the window size. This makes auto width on block elements synonymous with fluid width. The same behavior occurs with other block elements like `<p>` or `<div>`, or headings `<h1>` through `<h6>`. By defini-tion, block elements are to occupy the entire line. When an element takes up all the space available to it horizontally, this method of sizing is called *expand-to-fit*. Auto height on a block element, on the other hand, works a little differently; the element only expands vertically enough to accommodate the content within the element. This method of sizing is known as *shrink-to-fit*. In Figure 7-33, you can see from the yellow background of the `<div>` element that as you add more text, images, or other (X)HTML content, the height of the `<div>` will expand to accommodate that content.

The `auto` value can also have different meanings depending on the type of element you use it with. The `<table>` element is an example of an element where the auto value has different meaning than as say applied to a block element. Similar to height on block elements, `<table>` elements, by default, expand and contract only enough to accommodate the content they contain, but unlike block elements, this siz-ing is applied both horizontally and vertically. This is demonstrated in Figure 7-34.

The CSS in Figure 7-34a is included in the markup in Figure 7-34b.

```
table {
    margin-bottom: 5px;
}
td {
    background: lightyellow;
}
table, td {
    border: 1px solid gold;
}
```

> `<table>` elements expand and contract to accomodate contents. This method of sizing is called *shrink-to-fit*.

Figure 7-34a

```
<!DOCTYPE html PUBLIC "-//W3C//DTD XHTML 1.0 Strict//EN"
                      "http://www.w3.org/TR/xhtml1/DTD/xhtml1-strict.dtd">
<html xmlns='http://www.w3.org/1999/xhtml' xml:lang='en'>
    <head>
        <title>width</title>
        <link rel='stylesheet' type='text/css' href='096977%20fg0734.css' />
    </head>
    <body>
        <table>
            <tbody>
                <tr>
                    <td>
                        Lorem ipsum dolor sit amet, consectetuer adipiscing
                        elit.  Vestibulum tellus orci, dignissim ut,
                        consequat in, consectetuer et, nibh. Donec luctus
                        ante a neque convallis ultricies.
                    </td>
                </tr>
            </tbody>
        </table>
        <table>
            <tbody>
                <tr>
                    <td>
                        Lorem ipsum dolor sit amet, consectetuer adipiscing
                        elit.
                    </td>
                </tr>
            </tbody>
        </table>
        <table>
            <tbody>
                <tr>
                    <td>
                        Lorem ipsum dolor sit amet...
                    </td>
                </tr>
            </tbody>
        </table>
    </body>
</html>
```

Figure 7-34b

In Figure 7-34c, you can see the rendered output of the source code presented in Figure 7-34a and Figure 7-34b. All three windows pictured display the same document, but at different sizes.

Figure 7-34c

In Figure 7-34, you can see that the `<table>` element's size, by default, depends on the content inside of it. Once a `<table>` element has a lot of content, it behaves more like a block element, in that if there is enough content, it will expand to fill up the whole line, then expand vertically as much as necessary to accommodate content.

The `<img />` element is another example of an element where the `auto` keyword has another meaning. When the `auto` keyword is used on images, the `auto` value allows the image to be displayed as is. If the image is 500 pixels by 600 pixels, the `auto` value displays the image as 500 by 600 pixels. In that light, the graphics program that generated the image determines the image's dimensions. When you use `height: auto;` on an image, and you explicitly specify the image's width, the image's height scales in aspect ratio to the image's width, as is demonstrated in Figure 7-35.

The CSS in Figure 7-35a is included in the (X)HTML document in Figure 7-35b.

```
img {
    border: 1px solid black;
    margin: 5px;
}
img#x-aspect-1 {
    width: 200px;
    height: auto;
}
img#x-aspect-2 {
    width: 150px;
    height: auto;
}
img#x-aspect-3 {
    width: 100px;
    height: auto;
}
img#fixed {
    width: 200px;
    height: 200px;
}
img#y-aspect-1 {
    width: auto;
    height: 200px;
}
img#y-aspect-2 {
    width: auto;
    height: 150px;
}
img#y-aspect-3 {
    width: auto;
    height: 100px;
}
```

When applied to an <img /> element, auto value causes the <img /> top to resize while maintaining the aspect ratio, if one width or height value is the auto keyword and the opposite value is an explicit length.

Figure 7-35a

Figure 7-35c shows the output of the CSS in Figure 7-35a and the markup in Figure 7-35b.

In Figure 7-35, you see how the auto keyword works with <img /> elements. By default, whatever dimensions the image was saved with using a graphic editor are the dimensions the <img /> is displayed with. If you include an explicit value for either width or height, and the opposite value is the auto keyword, the image is resized preserving the aspect ratio. In the next section, I talk about percentage measurement.

```
<!DOCTYPE html PUBLIC "-//W3C//DTD XHTML 1.0 Strict//EN"
                      "http://www.w3.org/TR/xhtml1/DTD/xhtml1-strict.dtd">
<html xmlns='http://www.w3.org/1999/xhtml' xml:lang='en'>
    <head>
        <title>auto width and height</title>
        <link rel='stylesheet' type='text/css' href='096977%20fg0735.css' />
    </head>
    <body>
        <div>
            <img src='groucho_marx_and_the_yellow_brick_road.jpg' />
            <img src='groucho_marx_and_the_yellow_brick_road.jpg'
                id='x-aspect-1' />
            <img src='groucho_marx_and_the_yellow_brick_road.jpg'
                id='x-aspect-2' />
            <img src='groucho_marx_and_the_yellow_brick_road.jpg'
                id='x-aspect-3' />
        </div>
        <div>
            <img src='groucho_marx_and_the_yellow_brick_road.jpg'
                id='fixed' />
            <img src='groucho_marx_and_the_yellow_brick_road.jpg'
                id='y-aspect-1' />
            <img src='groucho_marx_and_the_yellow_brick_road.jpg'
                id='y-aspect-2' />
            <img src='groucho_marx_and_the_yellow_brick_road.jpg'
                id='y-aspect-3' />
        </div>
    </body>
</html>
```

Figure 7-35b

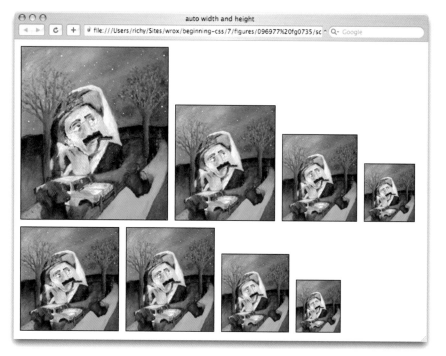

Figure 7-35c

Percentage Measurements

When a percentage measurement is used, the size that the percentage is based on is the parent element of the element the percentage width is applied to. Consider the example in Figure 7-36.

```css
div {
    font: 12px sans-serif;
    border: 1px solid lightblue;
    background: lightsteelblue;
    width: 100%;
    height: 100%;
    padding: 5px;
}
```

Percentage dimensions are derived from the width or height of the element's parent.

Figure 7-36a

The CSS in Figure 7-36a is applied to the markup in Figure 7-36b.

```html
<!DOCTYPE html PUBLIC "-//W3C//DTD XHTML 1.0 Strict//EN"
                      "http://www.w3.org/TR/xhtml1/DTD/xhtml1-strict.dtd">
<html xmlns='http://www.w3.org/1999/xhtml' xml:lang='en'>
    <head>
        <title>percentage measurement</title>
        <link rel='stylesheet' type='text/css' href='096977%20fg0736.css' />
    </head>
    <body>
        <div>
            Lorem ipsum dolor sit amet, consectetuer adipiscing elit.
            Vestibulum tellus orci, dignissim ut, consequat in, consectetuer
            et, nibh. Donec luctus ante a neque convallis ultricies.
            Curabitur ac lorem. Etiam adipiscing, nisi id eleifend feugiat,
            dui lorem tempus lacus, at rutrum lectus ligula quis diam.
        </div>
    </body>
</html>
```

Figure 7-36b

Figure 7-36c shows the rendered output of Figure 7-36a and Figure 7-36b.

The output that you see in Figure 7-36 is probably pretty puzzling to you, in that you more than likely expected the `<div>` element to fill up all the space horizontally and vertically without scroll bars appearing. There is a horizontal scroll bar because of how percentage measurement works; the width of the `<div>` element is made to be the same width as the width of its parent element, the `<body>` element. Now before you take into consideration padding or borders, the `<div>` element already takes up the whole width of the `<body>` element. Once 5 pixels of padding, and 1 pixel of border are added for each side, the `<div>` element becomes 12 pixels bigger than the width of the `<body>` element, causing it to overflow horizontally, and also a horizontal scroll bar to appear. In Figure 7-36, the `<div>` element doesn't stretch at all vertically. That's because the `<body>` and `<html>` elements are block elements, which means that the height of those elements is determined by the amount of content contained within them, and since a percentage height is based on the height of the element's parent, the height of the <div> element becomes the same height as the height of the <body> element. How then can you get fluid height in the same way that you can get fluid width with the auto keyword applied to a block element? The answer involves positioning the element, and since that is off-topic for this chapter, see Chapter 11, "Positioning," for the answer.

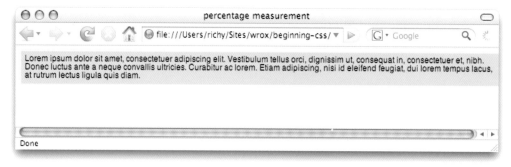

Figure 7-36c

In the next section, I describe what happens to the box model when IE is in quirks mode.

Quirks Mode width and height in Internet Explorer

As I mentioned earlier in this chapter in the section titled "Aligning Elements in IE 6 and IE 7 in Quirks Rendering Mode," IE is a very different browser in quirks rendering mode.

IE in quirks mode is meant to be backward-compatible with the Internet of the past. Having both a standards and a quirks rendering mode lets Microsoft maintain backward compatibility with legacy content created using past methods, while at the same time implementing and supporting W3C standards and moving forward. Microsoft in the past has not always rigidly followed the W3C standards, and one area where Microsoft was at odds with the W3C was in how the box model should be defined. IE up to IE 5.5 used Microsoft's own proprietary box model, which differs from the W3C box model in one very big way: It defined the "width" property as from outside border edge to outside border edge, rather than inside padding edge to inside padding edge as is defined in the W3C box model. In IE 6, Microsoft reconciled the difference by introducing the DOCTYPE switch, thus making two rendering modes, quirks mode and standards mode. When in standards mode, IE uses the W3C box model, but in quirks mode IE uses the Microsoft box model. Introducing two rendering modes has let Microsoft continue to build on IE and make it compliant with the various W3C standards while maintaining backward compatibility with legacy content that relied on that particular "quirk" being present in the IE browsers that came out prior to IE 6.

Figure 7-37 diagrams the differences between the standards box model and the IE box model in quirks rendering mode.

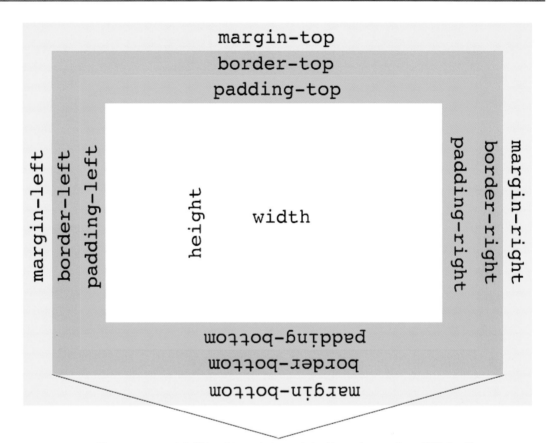

The width property in IE in quirks rendering mode (and in previous versions of IE before there was a quirks rendering mode), is measured from outside border edge to outside border edge. Padding and borders are still available, but these are included within the confines of the measurement specified by the width property.

Figure 7-37

The box-sizing Property

If you are faced with a website that requires IE to be in quirks rendering mode, you have two options for keeping your design consistent between browsers.

The first option is the box-sizing property. The box-sizing property allows you to switch between the standard CSS box model and the IE quirks mode box model. The box-sizing property is outlined in the following table.

Property	Value
box-sizing	content-box | border-box
	initial value: content-box

In Firefox and other Gecko-based browsers, you must add the -moz- *prefix. So it would be* -moz-box-sizing *instead of* box-sizing. -moz-box-sizing *also supports one additional keyword,* padding-box.

The declaration box-sizing: border-box; is provided for Safari and Opera, and the declaration -moz-box-sizing: border-box; is provided for all Gecko-based browsers, Firefox, Netscape, Mozilla SeaMonkey, and so on; thus those browsers use Microsoft's box model instead of the standard W3C box model.

Conditional Comments

The other method that you can use is to alter output for IE instead of altering for other browsers, by using conditional comments to specifically target IE, which is the method that I personally prefer. By targeting the quirk in IE specifically, you can use the standard W3C box model, and not use a property that may or may not be implemented in other lesser-known third party browsers. Conditional comments are a Microsoft-proprietary HTML feature, and they allow you to target various or specific versions of Internet Explorer. Conditional comments were introduced in IE 5.0; Figure 7-38 is an example of conditional comments in action.

The markup in Figure 7-38a results in the output that you see in Figure 7-38b.

```
<!DOCTYPE html PUBLIC "-//W3C//DTD XHTML 1.0 Strict//EN"
                "http://www.w3.org/TR/xhtml1/DTD/xhtml1-strict.dtd">
<html xmlns='http://www.w3.org/1999/xhtml' xml:lang='en'>
    <head>
        <title>Conditional Comments</title>
    </head>
    <body>
        <!--[if lt IE 7]>
            <p>
                This text is only seen by IE 6.0, IE 5.5, and IE 5.0, but not IE
                7.0. Other browsers just ignore this altogether, since it's
                contained in HTML comments.
            </p>
        <![endif]-->
        <!--[if IE 6]>
            <p>
                This text is only seen by IE 6.0.
            </p>
        <![endif]-->
        <!--[if gt IE 6]>
            <p>
                This text is only seen by IE 7.0.
            </p>
        <![endif]-->
    </body>
</html>
```

Figure 7-38a

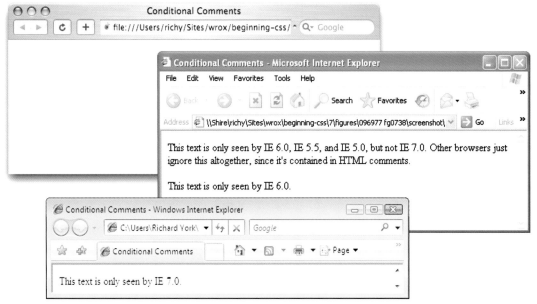

Figure 7-38b

In Figure 7-38, you see how conditional comments can target different versions of IE, and how conditional comments are just ignored by other browsers (you see no output at all in Safari). Conditional comments allow you to provide custom style sheets for Internet Explorer while writing standard CSS for all other browsers. Using conditional comments, you are able to reconcile differences in the box model by providing different width lengths to IE than you would to other browsers.

In the next section, I discuss minimum and maximum dimensions.

Minimum and Maximum Dimensions

The `min-width`, `max-width`, `min-height`, and `max-height` properties define minimum and maximum boundaries when it is necessary to constrain a width or height from expanding or contracting past a certain point. In a variable width design, where you design content to adapt to multiple screen resolutions, it is sometimes helpful to define where you want the document to stop stretching or stop contracting. For instance, if you have designed primarily with an 800 × 600 or 1024 × 768 screen resolution in mind, a user viewing your website at 1600 × 1200 pixels may see the content stretched pretty thin if an `auto` keyword or percentage values are used to define the width. This is where the CSS properties `min-width`, `max-width`, `min-height`, and `max-height` come into play.

min-width

The `min-width` property defines a lower-size constraint on an element. The available values for the `min-width` property are outlined in the following table.

Property	Value
min-width	\<length\> | \<percentage\>
	initial value: 0

IE 6.0 and less do not support the `min-width` *property.*

The `min-width` property defines when an element using an `auto` keyword or percentage width should stop shrinking to fit the user's window. Consider the example in Figure 7-39.

```
p {
    font: 12px sans-serif;
    border: 1px solid steelblue;
    background: lightsteelblue;
    padding: 5px;
    min-width: 500px;
}
```

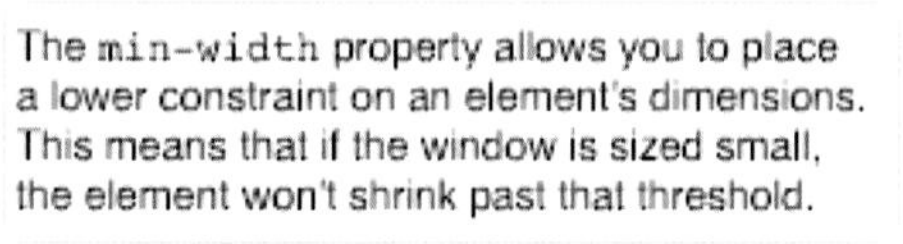

The min-width property allows you to place a lower constraint on an element's dimensions. This means that if the window is sized small, the element won't shrink past that threshold.

Figure 7-39a

The CSS in Figure 7-39a is combined with the markup in Figure 7-39b.

```
<!DOCTYPE html PUBLIC "-//W3C//DTD XHTML 1.0 Strict//EN"
                      "http://www.w3.org/TR/xhtml1/DTD/xhtml1-strict.dtd">
<html xmlns='http://www.w3.org/1999/xhtml' xml:lang='en'>
    <head>
        <title>min-width</title>
        <link rel='stylesheet' type='text/css' href='096977%20fg0739.css' />
    </head>
    <body>
        <p>
            Lorem ipsum dolor sit amet, consectetuer adipiscing elit.
            Vestibulum tellus orci, dignissim ut, consequat in, consectetuer
            et, nibh. Donec luctus ante a neque convallis ultricies.
            Curabitur ac lorem. Etiam adipiscing, nisi id eleifend feugiat,
            dui lorem tempus lacus, at rutrum lectus ligula quis diam.
        </p>
    </body>
</html>
```

Figure 7-39b

Figure 7-39c demonstrates that, if you run this snippet in a browser, when the browser window or containing element becomes smaller than 500 pixels, the \<p\> stops shrinking and a scroll bar appears across the bottom of the browser window.

Figure 7-39c

If the <p> is inside another element, and that element becomes smaller than the <p> element's min-width, the <p> element overflows the edges of that element. But this useful property does not work in IE. In the next section, I describe how to work around the lack of support in IE.

min-width in IE 6 and IE 5.5

IE 6 and IE 5.5 don't support any of the min/max width/height properties, but support for these properties was introduced in IE 7.0. Despite this functionality not being present in older versions of IE, you can work around the problem fairly effortlessly and achieve the same results as having these properties available. This is done in older versions of IE via the combination of two proprietary features, and taking advantage of IE's quirky handling of width and height. In IE 6.0 and earlier, the width and height properties behave more like the standard CSS properties, min-width and min-height. Although they aren't exactly the same, this can be used to get results similar to what you see in other browsers with the standard properties.

The recipe calls for conditional comments, so you can hide the workaround from other browsers, and another Microsoft-proprietary feature called CSS expressions. CSS expressions allow you to place JavaScript within style sheets. Of course, if the client has disabled JavaScript, CSS expressions won't work either, but for most designers this is an acceptable trade-off.

The example that you saw in Figure 7-39 is recreated with IE 6.0 compatibility in Figure 7-40.

The markup from Figure 7-39a is modified to look like the markup that you see in Figure 7-40b.

```
body {
    width: expression(documentElement.clientWidth <= 500? 500 : 'auto');
}
```

In IE, JavaScript expressions can be used to overcome
IE 6's lack of support for the min-width property.

Figure 7-40a

```
<!DOCTYPE html PUBLIC "-//W3C//DTD XHTML 1.0 Strict//EN"
                      "http://www.w3.org/TR/xhtml1/DTD/xhtml1-strict.dtd">
<html xmlns='http://www.w3.org/1999/xhtml' xml:lang='en'>
    <head>
        <title>min-width</title>
        <link rel='stylesheet' type='text/css' href='096977%20fg0740.css' />
        <!--[if IE 6]>
            <link rel='stylesheet' type='text/css'
                  href='096977%20fg0740.ic.css' />
        <![endif]-->
    </head>
    <body>
        <p>
            Lorem ipsum dolor sit amet, consectetuer adipiscing elit.
            Vestibulum tellus orci, dignissim ut, consequat in, consectetuer
            et, nibh. Donec luctus ante a neque convallis ultricies.
            Curabitur ac lorem. Etiam adipiscing, nisi id eleifend feugiat,
            dui lorem tempus lacus, at rutrum lectus ligula quis diam.
        </p>
    </body>
</html>
```

Figure 7-40b

Figure 7-40c is the result of the hack required to emulate the min-width property in IE 6.0.

The scenario outlined in Figure 7-40 only works for IE 6.0, and only if you are working with IE in standards mode. If you also require compatibility with IE 6.0 in quirks mode, IE 5.5, and IE 5.0, the hack is changed to the following:

```
body {
    width: expression(document.body.clientWidth <= 500? 500 : 'auto');
}
```

IE 6.0 in standards mode must have the documentElement.clientWidth as the hack; otherwise it will crash and burn miserably. The hack doesn't have to be applied to the <body> element; it can also be applied to a containing <div>. The hack itself will remain the same; only fill in the numbers that your particular project requires.

The opposite scenario, defining a maximum width, is covered in the next section.

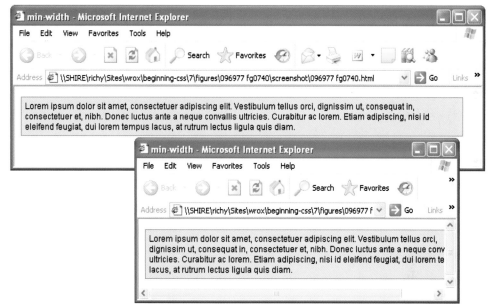

Figure 7-40c

max-width

In contrast to the `min-width` property, the `max-width` property is used to set an upper constraint for width with elements using either an `auto` keyword or percentage measurement for width. The `max-width` property is defined in the following table.

Property	Value
max-width	<length> | <percentage> | none
	initial value: none

As is the case for `min-width`, IE 6.0 does not support the `max-width` property.

The `max-width` property allows you to define a maximum length if the area available to the element becomes larger. An example of the `max-width` property appears in Figure 7-41.

The CSS in Figure 7-41a is combined with the markup that you see in Figure 7-41b.

```
p {
    font: 12px sans-serif;
    border: 1px solid steelblue;
    background: lightsteelblue;
    padding: 5px;
    max-width: 800px;
}
```

The `max-width` property can set an upper constraint on fluid elements so that they stop expanding at the threshold you specify.

Figure 7-41a

```
<!DOCTYPE html PUBLIC "-//W3C//DTD XHTML 1.0 Strict//EN"
                      "http://www.w3.org/TR/xhtml1/DTD/xhtml1-strict.dtd">
<html xmlns='http://www.w3.org/1999/xhtml' xml:lang='en'>
    <head>
        <title>max-width</title>
        <link rel='stylesheet' type='text/css' href='096977%20fg0741.css' />
<!--[if IE 6]>
<style type='text/css'>
    body {
        width: expression(documentElement.clientWidth >= 800? 800 : 'auto');
    }
</style>
<![endif]-->
    </head>
    <body>
        <p>
            Lorem ipsum dolor sit amet, consectetuer adipiscing elit.
            Vestibulum tellus orci, dignissim ut, consequat in, consectetuer
            et, nibh. Donec luctus ante a neque convallis ultricies.
            Curabitur ac lorem. Etiam adipiscing, nisi id eleifend feugiat,
            dui lorem tempus lacus, at rutrum lectus ligula quis diam.
        </p>
    </body>
</html>
```

The max-width hack for IE is the same as the min-width hack; you just check for greater-than or equal-to, instead of less-than or equal-to.

Figure 7-41b

Figure 7-41c shows that the <p> element stops expanding horizontally when it reaches an 800-pixel width.

Figure 7-41c

See the section on `min-width`, *which discusses how to handle hacks for IE 6 in quirks mode, IE 5.5 and IE 5.*

As a block-level element, the `<p>` element expands horizontally, filling all the available space. In this light, it is fluid. On a high-resolution monitor set to 1280 × 1024 pixels, for instance, the content inside of the `<p>` element could potentially get stretched very thin. The minimum and maximum width properties allow an upper and lower limit to be set for the size of an element and allow an author to take advantage of fluid design that adjusts to accommodate the user's environment.

Sometimes, however, you will need both minimum and maximum constraints in IE, and I cover this in the next section.

Hacking Both Minimum and Maximum Widths in IE 6

Hacking both minimum and maximum widths in IE is done using the same technique that I covered for minimum and maximum widths, but combined together. You just do the following:

```
body {
    width: expression(
        documentElement.clientWidth >= 800?
            800
        :
            (documentElement.clientWidth <= 500? 500 : 'auto')
    );
}
```

In this example, 800 is the upper constraint, or `max-width`, and 500 is the lower constraint or `min-width`. All you have to do is replace those numbers with your own values. The same rules apply here as were the case for IE 6 in quirks mode, IE 5.5, and IE 5; in those versions, `documentElement.clientWidth` is replaced with `document.body.clientWidth`. Again, the width declaration can be applied to a container `<div>` as well. If you require the content to be centered, it does not have to be applied to the `<body>` element. In that scenario, only the selector and your minimum and maximum values will change; the rest will remain the same.

CSS also offers identical properties to set upper and lower limits for height.

min-height

If you are using a variable or percentage height, the `min-height` property lets you specify when you want the element to stop shrinking vertically. The following table outlines the possible values for the `min-height` property.

Property	Value
min-height	\<length> | \<percentage> initial value: 0

IE 6 supports the `min-height` *property only when used on* `<td>`, `<th>`, *and* `<tr>` *elements.*

In some layouts it's handy to have a property that can set the minimum height of an element, especially with dynamic templates that can have content of varying lengths. Sometimes there will be very little content, and to keep your template from being broken, you need to define a lower height constraint. This is where the min-height property is useful. Figure 7-42 is a demonstration of the min-height property.

```
p {
    font: 12px sans-serif;
    border: 1px solid steelblue;
    background: lightsteelblue;
    padding: 5px;
    min-height: 50px;
}
```

The min-height property exists for setting a lower height constraint, which is most useful for making consistent templates.

Figure 7-42a

In Figure 7-42b, you see the markup that goes with the CSS in Figure 7-42a. You also see the hack for min-height for IE 6 and earlier.

```
<!DOCTYPE html PUBLIC "-//W3C//DTD XHTML 1.0 Strict//EN"
                      "http://www.w3.org/TR/xhtml1/DTD/xhtml1-strict.dtd">
<html xmlns='http://www.w3.org/1999/xhtml' xml:lang='en'>
    <head>
        <title>min-height</title>
        <link rel='stylesheet' type='text/css' href='096977%20fg0742.css' />
        <!--[if lt IE 7]>
            <style type='text/css'>
                p {
                    height: 50px;
                }
            </style>
        <![endif]-->
    </head>
    <body>
        <p>
            Lorem ipsum dolor sit amet, consectetuer adipiscing elit. In et
            nulla. Vestibulum ante ipsum primis in faucibus orci luctus et
            ultrices posuere cubilia Curae; Maecenas sit amet ligula.
        </p>
        <p>
            Phasellus purus augue, varius eu, semper id, ornare ac, tellus.
        </p>
        <p>
            Etiam bibendum ante et enim. Mauris consectetuer dapibus felis.
            Cras quis lacus. Suspendisse rhoncus felis ut felis. Fusce mollis
            mi in libero. Proin sed ipsum. Vivamus ultrices. In fermentum
            egestas nunc. Mauris nec enim. Donec magna nibh, hendrerit ut,
            euismod id, nonummy eu, mi. Cras porta metus. Cras dictum.
            Curabitur id nisi mattis massa euismod ornare. Sed quam. Aenean
            scelerisque.
        </p>
    </body>
</html>
```

To get the same effect in IE 6 and less, all you have to do is set the height property to the desired minimum height.

Figure 7-42b

In Figure 7-42c, you see the desired effect has been achieved; each <p> element has at least a height of 50 pixels.

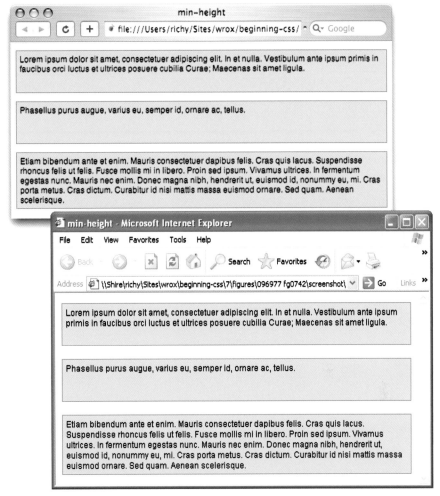

Figure 7-42c

Continuing the discussion on minimum and maximum dimensions, I cover the max-height property next.

max-height

The opposite of the min-height property is the max-height property, which allows the author to tell the browser when an element should stop expanding. It allows an upper height constraint to be specified for the element. The max-height property is outlined in the following table.

Property	Value
max-height	<length> | <percentage> | none
	initial value: none

IE 6 does not support the max-height *property.*

The max-height property does for height what the max-width property does for width. Unfortunately there is no workaround for the max-height property in IE 6, but this property is implemented in IE 7. Figure 7-43 is a demonstration of the max-height property.

```
p {
    font: 12px sans-serif;
    border: 1px solid steelblue;
    background: lightsteelblue;
    padding: 5px;
    max-height: 50px;
}
```

The max-height property exists for setting an upper height constraint.

Figure 7-43a

The CSS in Figure 7-43a is included in the markup in Figure 7-43b.

```
<!DOCTYPE html PUBLIC "-//W3C//DTD XHTML 1.0 Strict//EN"
                      "http://www.w3.org/TR/xhtml1/DTD/xhtml1-strict.dtd">
<html xmlns='http://www.w3.org/1999/xhtml' xml:lang='en'>
    <head>
        <title>max-height</title>
        <link rel='stylesheet' type='text/css' href='096977%20fg0743.css' />
    </head>
    <body>
        <p>
            Lorem ipsum dolor sit amet, consectetuer adipiscing elit. In et
            nulla. Vestibulum ante ipsum primis in faucibus orci luctus et
            ultrices posuere cubilia Curae; Maecenas sit amet ligula.
        </p>
        <p>
            Phasellus purus augue, varius eu, semper id, ornare ac, tellus.
        </p>
        <p>
            Etiam bibendum ante et enim. Mauris consectetuer dapibus felis.
            Cras quis lacus. Suspendisse rhoncus felis ut felis. Fusce mollis
            mi in libero. Proin sed ipsum. Vivamus ultrices. In fermentum
            egestas nunc. Mauris nec enim. Donec magna nibh, hendrerit ut,
            euismod id, nonummy eu, mi. Cras porta metus. Cras dictum.
            Curabitur id nisi mattis massa euismod ornare. Sed quam. Aenean
            scelerisque.
        </p>
    </body>
</html>
```

Figure 7-43b

The output in Figure 7-43c shows that the third paragraph stops growing vertically when the height reaches 50 pixels. If only there were a property that could handle that overflowing text. Wait, there is! Stay tuned to the section on the `overflow` property for information on how to control overflowing text.

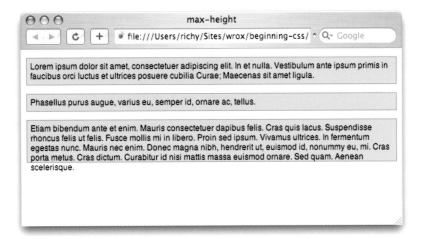

Figure 7-43c

The next section wraps up discussion of dimensions with the `line-height` property.

The line-height property

As I mentioned in Chapter 6, the `line-height` property refers to the height of the line on which each line of text appears. The `line-height` property and its possible values are outlined in the following table.

Property	Value
line-height	normal | <number> | <length> | <percentage>
	initial value: normal

This property allows an explicit length to be defined for each line of text. Consider the CSS in Figure 7-44a and the markup in Figure 7-44b.

```
p {
    font: 12px sans-serif;
    border: 1px solid steelblue;
    background: lightsteelblue;
    padding: 5px;
    line-height: 3em;
}
```

With the `line-height` property, you can adjust the line-height of each line of text.

Figure 7-44a

269

```
<!DOCTYPE html PUBLIC "-//W3C//DTD XHTML 1.0 Strict//EN"
                      "http://www.w3.org/TR/xhtml1/DTD/xhtml1-strict.dtd">
<html xmlns='http://www.w3.org/1999/xhtml' xml:lang='en'>
    <head>
        <title>line-height</title>
        <link rel='stylesheet' type='text/css' href='096977%20fg0744.css' />
    </head>
    <body>
        <p>
            Lorem ipsum dolor sit amet, consectetuer adipiscing elit. In et
            nulla. Vestibulum ante ipsum primis in faucibus orci luctus et
            ultrices posuere cubilia Curae; Maecenas sit amet ligula.
            Phasellus purus augue, varius eu, semper id, ornare ac, tellus.
            Etiam bibendum ante et enim. Mauris consectetuer dapibus felis.
            Cras quis lacus. Suspendisse rhoncus felis ut felis. Fusce mollis
            mi in libero. Proin sed ipsum. Vivamus ultrices. In fermentum
            egestas nunc. Mauris nec enim. Donec magna nibh, hendrerit ut,
            euismod id, nonummy eu, mi. Cras porta metus. Cras dictum.
            Curabitur id nisi mattis massa euismod ornare. Sed quam. Aenean
            scelerisque.
        </p>
    </body>
</html>
```

Figure 7-44b

Figure 7-44c shows that each line of text is contained in a line-height 3em high. This produces the effect of quadruple-spaced text because a 1em font-size is specified.

Figure 7-44c

In the next section I discuss the overflow property.

Overflowing Content

The CSS overflow property exists to manage content that is susceptible to dimensional constraints, where the content could possibly overflow the boundaries of those dimensional constraints. The following table outlines the overflow property and its possible values.

Property	Value
overflow	visible | hidden | scroll | auto
	initial value: visible

The two most common uses of the overflow property are to hide content when more content than space is available, or to apply scroll bars so that the extra content can be accessed. By default, the value of the overflow property is the visible keyword, the effects of which you saw in Figure 7-32c, and will again in Figure 7-45c. These figures show that when the width and height specified are smaller than the content allows, the content overflows the edges of the box containing it. It is possible to control that overflow by causing scroll bars to appear, or the overflowing content to be invisible.

Figure 7-45 demonstrates each of the possible values for the overflow property.

```
p {
    font: 12px sans-serif;
    border: 1px solid gold;
    background: lightyellow;
    padding: 5px;
    width: 100px;
    height: 100px;
    float: left;
    margin: 5px;
}
p#visible {
    overflow: visible;
}
p#auto {
    overflow: auto;
}
p#scroll {
    overflow: scroll;
}
p#hidden {
    overflow: hidden;
}
```

The overflow property is used to control what happens with content that is larger than the element it is contained within.

Figure 7-45a

The CSS in Figure 7-45a is then combined with the markup you see in Figure 7-45b.

```
<!DOCTYPE html PUBLIC "-//W3C//DTD XHTML 1.0 Strict//EN"
                      "http://www.w3.org/TR/xhtml1/DTD/xhtml1-strict.dtd">
<html xmlns='http://www.w3.org/1999/xhtml' xml:lang='en'>
    <head>
        <title>overflow</title>
        <link rel='stylesheet' type='text/css' href='096977%20fg0746.css' />
    </head>
    <body>
        <p id='visible'>
            Peter Piper picked a peck of pickled peppers.
            Did Peter Piper pick a peck of pickled peppers?
            If Peter Piper picked a peck of pickled peppers,
            where's the peck of pickled peppers Peter Piper picked?
        </p>
        <p id='auto'>
            Peter Piper picked a peck of pickled peppers.
            Did Peter Piper pick a peck of pickled peppers?
            If Peter Piper picked a peck of pickled peppers,
            where's the peck of pickled peppers Peter Piper picked?
        </p>
        <p id='scroll'>
            Peter Piper picked a peck of pickled peppers.
            Did Peter Piper pick a peck of pickled peppers?
            If Peter Piper picked a peck of pickled peppers,
            where's the peck of pickled peppers Peter Piper picked?
        </p>
        <p id='hidden'>
            Peter Piper picked a peck of pickled peppers.
            Did Peter Piper pick a peck of pickled peppers?
            If Peter Piper picked a peck of pickled peppers,
            where's the peck of pickled peppers Peter Piper picked?
        </p>
    </body>
</html>
```

Figure 7-45b

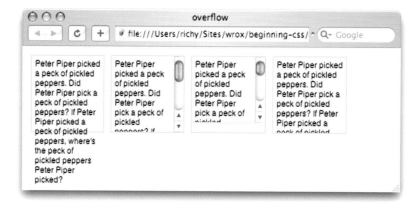

Figure 7-45c

In Figure 7-45, you see what the possible keyword values of the overflow property translate to when applied. The overflowing content can be visible, or the browser can decide if there is overflow to apply scroll bars where necessary, as is the case with the auto keyword. You can force scroll bars to always be visible with the scroll keyword, or you can hide overflow content with the hidden keyword.

CSS 3 overflow-x and overflow-y

The overflow-x and overflow-y properties were originally proprietary to IE, but are now included in a W3C CSS 3 working draft. IE 6, IE 7, and Mozilla Firefox now support the overflow-x and overflow-y properties. Support for these properties is in the next version of Safari, and Opera support is planned.

Property	Value
overflow-x	visible | hidden | scroll | auto
	initial value: visible
overflow-y	visible | hidden | scroll | auto
	initial value: visible

IE 6 and IE 7 only support the overflow-x *and* overflow-y *properties when in standards compliant mode.*

Like the overflow property, overflow-x and overflow-y control overflow content, but they also allow users to control the overflowing content with a scroll bar: only a vertical scroll bar for the overflow-y property, and only a horizontal scroll bar for the overflow-x property. Each property accepts the same values as the overflow property.

Summary

The CSS box model is a set of rules that tells the browser how to handle the width of a box, padding, borders, and margins. The box model offers the designer consistency across multiple platforms and browsers. Margin and padding are essential to a document and prevent the document from rendering in complete chaos. Borders offer more aesthetic possibilities. CSS dimensions offer controls over how wide and high an element can be. Finally, overflow allows the simulation of inline frames and gives you control over content when it is larger than the element containing it.

To recap the material presented in this chapter, you learned the following:

❑　How to apply border widths, border styles, and border colors with the border family of properties

❑　How to apply dimensions to the elements of a document using the width and height family of properties

❑　How to control the line height of text using the line-height property

❑   How to apply padding to a document with the `padding` property

❑   How to apply margins to a document with the `margin` property

❑   How you can use the `overflow` property to manage content in cases where the content of an element is bigger than the element itself

Now that you've had a fairly in-depth exposure to the properties fundamental to CSS design, Chapter 8 discusses CSS buoyancy, a topic involving the `float` and `vertical-align` properties of CSS.

Exercises

1. From left to right, what are the seven box model properties that make up the left, center, and right sides of a box?

2. How do you left-, center-, and right-align a block-level box (using the standard method)?

3. When the `margin` shorthand property has four values, what side of the target element does each value apply margin to, in order?

4. What are the three keyword values of the `border-width` property?

5. If the `border-color` shorthand property has three values, what side of the target element does each value apply to, in order?

6. Name the shorthand properties that encompass the `border-width`, `border-style`, and `border-color` properties.

7. If you target IE 6 in quirks mode and earlier versions of IE, which property would you use to align a box?

8. If the `padding` shorthand property only has two values, what side of the target element does each value apply to, in order?

9. Describe briefly the two situations in which `margin` collapsing occurs?

10. In the following document, which element's `width` is the `<p>` element's `width` based on if it were to be given a percentage `width` value?

```
<!DOCTYPE html PUBLIC "-//W3C//DTD XHTML 1.0 Strict//EN"
                "http://www.w3.org/TR/xhtml1/DTD/xhtml1-strict.dtd">
<html xmlns='http://www.w3.org/1999/xhtml' xml:lang='en'>
    <head>
        <title></title>
    </head>
    <body>
        <p>
            Peter Piper picked a peck of pickled peppers.
            Did Peter Piper pick a peck of pickled peppers?
            If Peter Piper picked a peck of pickled peppers,
            where's the peck of pickled peppers Peter Piper picked?
        </p>
    </body>
</html>
```

11. How do you resize an image while maintaining the aspect ratio?

12. In IE 6 quirks mode and previous versions of IE, what properties of the box model are included in the measurement specified by the `width` property?

13. What is one method of emulating the `min-width` property in IE 6?

14. How is the `min-height` property emulated in IE 6?

15. What browsers do conditional comments apply to?

16. If you wanted both `min-width` and `max-width`, what declaration would you use to bring IE 6 on board?

17. If you wanted to increase the amount of spacing between lines of text, which property would you use?

18. What are the four keywords of the `overflow` property?

CSS Buoyancy: Floating and Vertical Alignment

In Chapter 7, I presented a subset of properties that combine to define a concept known as the CSS box model. In this chapter, I continue introducing new properties, this time focusing on two properties most often misunderstood by users new to CSS design: the float and clear properties. These properties are often misunderstood because of their unique effect on the elements in a document. In this chapter I discuss:

❑   The float property and how it is used to change the flow of elements in a document — for instance, to place text beside an image

❑   The clear property and how this property is used to cancel the effects of the float property

❑   The vertical-align property and how this property is used to control the vertical alignment of text to create subscript or superscript text or control vertical alignment in table cells

The next section begins the discussion of the float property.

The float Property

A simple explanation of the float property is that it is used to put content side by side. In the coming sections, you look in depth at the float property, its idiosyncrasies, and how you can use it to lay out a web page. The following table outlines the float property and its possible values.

Property	Value
float	left | right | none
	Initial value: none

At this point, the float property appears fairly simple. It accepts keyword values of left, right, and none. The effects of the float property are intrinsically tied to the CSS box model. After the float property is applied to an element, regardless of the type of element, that element takes on the behavior of a block element, where its dimensions are defined by width, height, padding, borders, and margins. Before you see some examples of this, Figure 8-1 shows you how the `float` property affects a document's layout.

```css
img {
    width: 200px;
    height: auto;
    float: left;
    margin: 10px;
    border: 1px solid rgb(128, 128, 128);
}
p {
    font: 12px sans-serif;
}
```

Floating causes content to flow around the element the `float` property is applied to.

Figure 8-1a

The CSS in Figure 8-1a is applied to the markup you see in Figure 8-1b.

```html
<!DOCTYPE html PUBLIC "-//W3C//DTD XHTML 1.0 Strict//EN"
                      "http://www.w3.org/TR/xhtml1/DTD/xhtml1-strict.dtd">
<html xmlns='http://www.w3.org/1999/xhtml' xml:lang='en'>
    <head>
        <title>float</title>
        <link rel='stylesheet' type='text/css' href='096977%20fg0801.css' />
    </head>
    <body>
        <img src='antique.jpg' alt='Antique' />
        <p>
            Lorem ipsum dolor sit amet, consectetuer adipiscing elit.  Nunc
            eros leo, molestie eu, laoreet eu, rhoncus suscipit, tortor.
            Fusce interdum, metus eu sagittis mollis, lorem augue fringilla
            leo, at pretium magna tortor sed ligula.  Nulla id nisl. Cras
            interdum velit sit amet lacus. In egestas. Integer aliquet.
            Phasellus sagittis congue dui.  Aenean purus neque, viverra at,
            imperdiet sit amet, dignissim vel, sapien. Suspendisse tristique.
            Fusce nunc.  Pellentesque ultrices magna in leo. Vestibulum
            aliquam quam fermentum sapien. Aenean velit erat, vestibulum sit
            amet, rhoncus a, viverra vitae, lacus. Etiam porttitor, mauris ut
            vulputate egestas, tortor dolor tincidunt leo, non scelerisque
            magna dui vitae urna. Vivamus ut massa. Vestibulum sit amet
            sapien et magna varius auctor. Sed a magna. Pellentesque nonummy
            odio nec metus. Pellentesque habitant morbi tristique senectus et
            netus et malesuada fames ac turpis egestas.
        </p>
        <p>
            Sed non dolor ut tortor imperdiet hendrerit. Etiam malesuada.
            Proin rutrum ligula eu nibh. Maecenas sit amet est. In eros.
            Proin elit lacus, volutpat at, sagittis et, convallis sit amet,
            sapien. Fusce bibendum augue vitae sapien. Morbi feugiat
            venenatis libero. Vestibulum porttitor. Cras neque ante, luctus
            luctus, elementum volutpat, euismod eget, nunc. Praesent ornare.
            Mauris cursus dolor.
        </p>
    </body>
</html>
```

Figure 8-1b

In Figure 8-1c, you can see that the image is floated to the left, meaning that the content in the paragraphs that follow the image floats up to the right of the image.

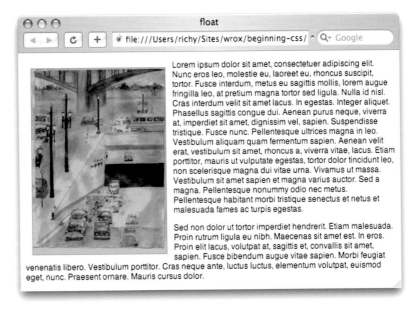

Figure 8-1c

If you were to take away the float property from the example in Figure 8-1, you would get the output that you see in Figure 8-2.

In Figure 8-2, the effects of the `float` property become more obvious — primarily, the `float` property is used to place one element beside one or more other elements. In Figure 8-1, the element being floated was the `<img />` element, and the elements it floated beside were two `<p>` elements.

Figure 8-2

You can also include both left and right floats in a document; this is demonstrated in Figure 8-3.

```
img {
    margin: 10px;
    border: 1px solid rgb(128, 128, 128);
}
img#starfish {
    float: left;
}                                   Left and right floats can be present at the same time.
img#lake {
    float: right;
}
p {
    font: 12px sans-serif;
}
```

Figure 8-3a

The CSS in Figure 8-3a is included in the markup in Figure 8-3b.

```
<!DOCTYPE html PUBLIC "-//W3C//DTD XHTML 1.0 Strict//EN"
                      "http://www.w3.org/TR/xhtml1/DTD/xhtml1-strict.dtd">
<html xmlns='http://www.w3.org/1999/xhtml' xml:lang='en'>
    <head>
        <title>float</title>
        <link rel='stylesheet' type='text/css' href='096977%20fg0803.css' />
    </head>
    <body>
        <img src='starfish.jpg' alt='starfish' id='starfish' />
        <p>
            Lorem ipsum dolor sit amet, consectetuer adipiscing elit.  Nunc
            eros leo, molestie eu, laoreet eu, rhoncus suscipit, tortor.
            Fusce interdum, metus eu sagittis mollis, lorem augue fringilla
            leo, at pretium magna tortor sed ligula.  Nulla id nisl. Cras
            interdum velit sit amet lacus. In egestas. Integer aliquet.
            Phasellus sagittis congue dui.  Aenean purus neque, viverra at,
            imperdiet sit amet, dignissim vel, sapien. Suspendisse tristique.
            <img src='lake.jpg' alt='Lake' id='lake' />
            Fusce nunc.  Pellentesque ultrices magna in leo. Vestibulum
            aliquam quam fermentum sapien. Aenean velit erat, vestibulum sit
            amet, rhoncus a, viverra vitae, lacus. Etiam porttitor, mauris ut
            vulputate egestas, tortor dolor tincidunt leo, non scelerisque
            magna dui vitae urna. Vivamus ut massa. Vestibulum sit amet
            sapien et magna varius auctor. Sed a magna. Pellentesque nonummy
            odio nec metus. Pellentesque habitant morbi tristique senectus et
            netus et malesuada fames ac turpis egestas.
        </p>
        <p>
            Sed non dolor ut tortor imperdiet hendrerit. Etiam malesuada.
            Proin rutrum ligula eu nibh. Maecenas sit amet est. In eros.
            Proin elit lacus, volutpat at, sagittis et, convallis sit amet,
            sapien. Fusce bibendum augue vitae sapien. Morbi feugiat
            venenatis libero. Vestibulum porttitor. Cras neque ante, luctus
            luctus, elementum volutpat, euismod eget, nunc. Praesent ornare.
            Mauris cursus dolor.
        </p>
    </body>
</html>
```

Figure 8-3b

In Figure 8-3c, you can see what happens when there is both a left and right float; the right image floats to the right and allows the content that comes after it to wrap around it. Figure 8-3c shows three images so you can see what happens when the window is made smaller; the browser just reflows the content, and the second float is moved up or down as necessary to make room for the copy.

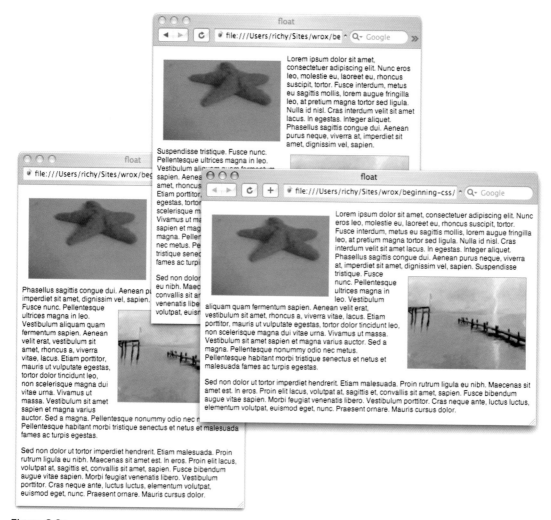

Figure 8-3c

On the surface the concept of floating is pretty simple, and for most things that you set out to accomplish, this is about as complicated as it will get, but there is quite a complex set of rules under the surface of the float property. To understand what happens when an element is floated, you need to know about how the box model is affected, and what happens when certain types of elements are floated. These concepts are explored in the coming sections.

Floating Box Model

Because floated elements are repositioned to allow other content to flow around them, they exhibit unique behavior. This behavior is outlined here:

❑   The margins of floated elements do not collapse, no matter what they are next to.

❑   Only the contents of elements following a floated element are affected by the floated element. That is, the backgrounds, margins, borders, padding, and width (the box model and dimensions) of elements following a floated element are not affected.

❑   A floated element is always treated like a block element.

Each rule is important in determining how floated elements are positioned and rendered. This section examines each rule in depth.

The margins of floated elements never collapse. Consider the diagram in Figure 8-4, which shows how the box model is incorporated when an element has been floated.

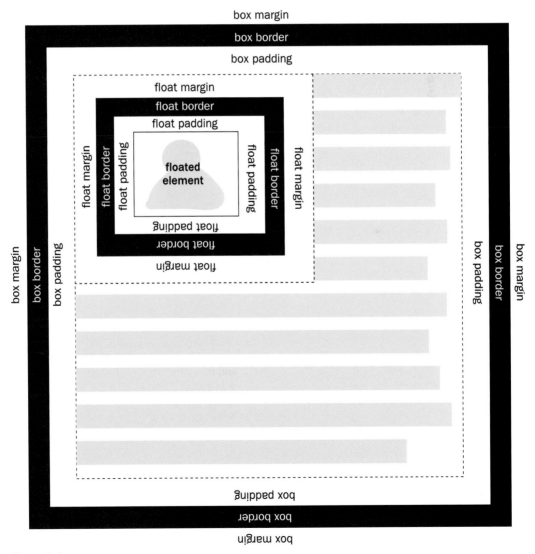

Figure 8-4

When an element is floated, it takes on the behavior of a block element, with one major difference: Its sizing becomes shrink-to-fit horizontally and vertically. That means that if you float a `<div>` element, its dimensions change such that it only expands enough to accommodate the content within it. In Chapter 7, you learned that the default dimensions of a `<div>` element are expand-to-fit horizontally, meaning the `<div>` takes up the whole line, but not so when a `<div>` element is floated. Figure 8-5 is an example of how a `<div>` element changes once floated.

```
img {
    margin: 10px;
    border: 1px solid rgb(128, 128, 128);
}
p {
    font: 12px sans-serif;
}
div#fifty-states {
    text-align: center;
    border: 1px solid rgb(200, 200, 200);
    background: lightyellow;
    margin: 5px;
    float: left;
}
```

When a block element is floated, its default width becomes shrink-to-fit instead of expand-to-fit.

Figure 8-5a

The CSS in Figure 8-5a is included in the markup in Figure 8-5b.

```
<!DOCTYPE html PUBLIC "-//W3C//DTD XHTML 1.0 Strict//EN"
                     "http://www.w3.org/TR/xhtml1/DTD/xhtml1-strict.dtd">
<html xmlns='http://www.w3.org/1999/xhtml' xml:lang='en'>
    <head>
        <title>float</title>
        <link rel='stylesheet' type='text/css' href='096977%20fg0805.css' />
    </head>
    <body>
        <div id='fifty-states'>
            <img src='fifty_states.jpg' alt='fifty states' />
            <p>
                Sed non dolor ut tortor imperdiet hendrerit. Etiam
                malesuada.  Proin rutrum ligula eu nibh.
            </p>
        </div>
        <p>
            Lorem ipsum dolor sit amet, consectetuer adipiscing elit.  Nunc
            eros leo, molestie eu, laoreet eu, rhoncus suscipit, tortor.
            Fusce interdum, metus eu sagittis mollis, lorem augue fringilla
            leo, at pretium magna tortor sed ligula.  Nulla id nisl. Cras
            interdum velit sit amet lacus. In egestas. Integer aliquet.
            Phasellus sagittis congue dui.  Aenean purus neque, viverra at,
            imperdiet sit amet, dignissim vel, sapien. Suspendisse tristique.
            Fusce nunc.  Pellentesque ultrices magna in leo. Vestibulum
            aliquam quam fermentum sapien. Aenean velit erat, vestibulum sit
            amet, rhoncus a, viverra vitae, lacus. Etiam porttitor, mauris ut
            vulputate egestas, tortor dolor tincidunt leo, non scelerisque
            magna dui vitae urna. Vivamus ut massa. Vestibulum sit amet
            sapien et magna varius auctor. Sed a magna. Pellentesque nonummy
            odio nec metus. Pellentesque habitant morbi tristique senectus et
            netus et malesuada fames ac turpis egestas.
        </p>
        <p>
            Sed non dolor ut tortor imperdiet hendrerit. Etiam malesuada.
            Proin rutrum ligula eu nibh. Maecenas sit amet est. In eros.
            Proin elit lacus, volutpat at, sagittis et, convallis sit amet,
            sapien. Fusce bibendum augue vitae sapien. Morbi feugiat
            venenatis libero. Vestibulum porttitor. Cras neque ante, luctus
            luctus, elementum volutpat, euismod eget, nunc. Praesent ornare.
            Mauris cursus dolor.
        </p>
    </body>
</html>
```

Figure 8-5b

In Figure 8-5c, you see what happens before the `<div>` with id name `fifty-states` receives the `float: left;` declaration. You can see that the `<div>` is normal at this point; it expands to fill the whole line.

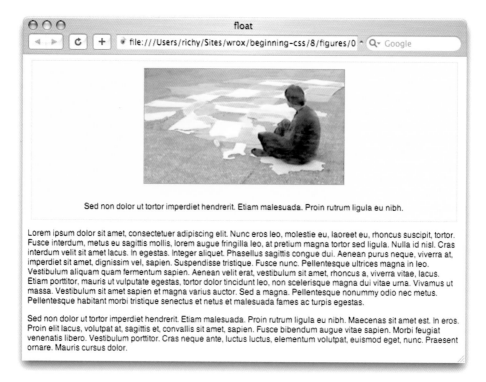

Figure 8-5c

In Figure 8-5d, you see what happens after the `<div>` with id name `fifty-states` receives the `float: left;` declaration; its width has changed. Now the `<div>` element only expands enough horizontally to accommodate the content inside of it.

Figure 8-5d

In Figure 8-5 you see what happens when a block element is floated, but what about an inline element, such as the `<span>` element, or the `<a>` element? This is demonstrated in Figure 8-6.

```
img {
    margin: 10px;
    border: 1px solid rgb(128, 128, 128);
}
p {
    font: 12px sans-serif;
}
span#sailboat {
    text-align: center;
    border: 1px solid rgb(200, 200, 200);
    background: rgb(244, 244, 244);
    margin: 5px;
    float: right;
}
```

When an inline element is floated, it becomes a shrint-to-fit block element.

Figure 8-6a

The CSS in Figure 8-6a is included in the XHTML markup that you see in Figure 8-6b.

```
<!DOCTYPE html PUBLIC "-//W3C//DTD XHTML 1.0 Strict//EN"
                      "http://www.w3.org/TR/xhtml1/DTD/xhtml1-strict.dtd">
<html xmlns='http://www.w3.org/1999/xhtml' xml:lang='en'>
    <head>
        <title>float</title>
        <link rel='stylesheet' type='text/css' href='096977%20fg0806.css' />
    </head>
    <body>
        <p>
            <span id='sailboat'>
                <img src='desert_sailboat.jpg' alt='desert sailboat' />
                <br />
                Fusce bibendum augue vitae sapien. Morbi feugiat
                venenatis libero.
            </span>
            Lorem ipsum dolor sit amet, consectetuer adipiscing elit.  Nunc
            eros leo, molestie eu, laoreet eu, rhoncus suscipit, tortor.
            Fusce interdum, metus eu sagittis mollis, lorem augue fringilla
            leo, at pretium magna tortor sed ligula.  Nulla id nisl. Cras
            interdum velit sit amet lacus. In egestas. Integer aliquet.
            Phasellus sagittis congue dui.  Aenean purus neque, viverra at,
            imperdiet sit amet, dignissim vel, sapien. Suspendisse tristique.
            Fusce nunc.  Pellentesque ultrices magna in leo. Vestibulum
            aliquam quam fermentum sapien. Aenean velit erat, vestibulum sit
            amet, rhoncus a, viverra vitae, lacus. Etiam porttitor, mauris ut
            vulputate egestas, tortor dolor tincidunt leo, non scelerisque
            magna dui vitae urna. Vivamus ut massa. Vestibulum sit amet
            sapien et magna varius auctor. Sed a magna. Pellentesque nonummy
            odio nec metus. Pellentesque habitant morbi tristique senectus et
            netus et malesuada fames ac turpis egestas.
        </p>
        <p>
            Sed non dolor ut tortor imperdiet hendrerit. Etiam malesuada.
            Proin rutrum ligula eu nibh. Maecenas sit amet est. In eros.
            Proin elit lacus, volutpat at, sagittis et, convallis sit amet,
            sapien. Fusce bibendum augue vitae sapien. Morbi feugiat
            venenatis libero. Vestibulum porttitor. Cras neque ante, luctus
            luctus, elementum volutpat, euismod eget, nunc. Praesent ornare.
            Mauris cursus dolor.
        </p>
    </body>
</html>
```

Figure 8-6b

In Figure 8-6c, you see what happens prior to applying the `float: right;` declaration to the `<span>` element with the id name `sailboat`.

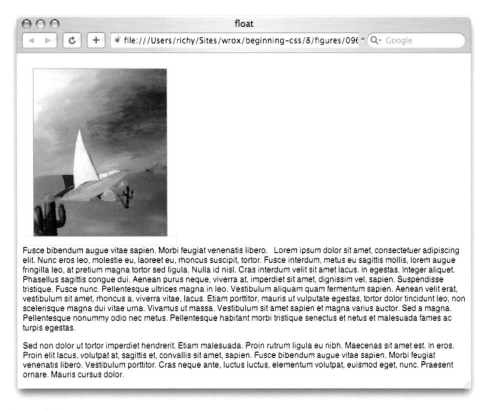

Figure 8-6c

In Figure 8-6d, you see that after applying the `float: right;` declaration to the `<span>` element with id name `sailboat`. The `<span>` element becomes a block element with shrink-to-fit width and height. The `width` and `height` properties are not applicable to inline elements typically; in this situation, if you were to apply width or height to the `<span>` as a floated element, it would work, since it is now a block element.

Figure 8-6d

Now that you've had an overview of the `float` property, the following Try It Out is a recap of what is possible with the `float` property.

Try It Out   Applying the float Property

Example 8-1. To review what's possible with the `float` property, follow these steps.

1.   Enter the following markup in your text editor:

```
<!DOCTYPE html PUBLIC "-//W3C//DTD XHTML 1.0 Strict//EN"
                      "http://www.w3.org/TR/xhtml1/DTD/xhtml1-strict.dtd">
<html xmlns='http://www.w3.org/1999/xhtml' xml:lang='en'>
    <head>
        <title>float</title>
        <link rel='stylesheet' type='text/css' href='Example_8-1.css' />
    </head>
    <body>
        <img src='sun.png' alt='people' id='left' />
        <img src='sun.png' alt='people' id='right' />
        <p>
```

```
        The float property is used to force content to wrap around
        another element.  Elements can be floated to the right
        or the left.
    </p>
    <p class='block'>
        When a block level element is floated, its sizing changes
        from expand-to-fit, to shrink-to-fit, and is no longer
        subject to margin collapsing.
    </p>
    <p>
        When an inline element is floated, it becomes a
        <span id='inline'>
            block-level element with shrink-to-fit sizing.
        </span>
    </p>
 </body>
</html>
```

2. Save the preceding as `Example_8-1.html`.

3. Key in the following CSS in a new document in your text editor:

```
p.block {
    float: left;
    margin: 5px;
    background: lightyellow;
    border: 1px solid khaki;
    width: 150px;
    height: 150px;
    padding: 5px;
}
span#inline {
    float: left;
    background: khaki;
    border: 1px solid gold;
    padding: 5px;
    margin: 5px;
}
img {
    border: 1px solid rgb(244, 244, 244);
    margin: 5px;
}
img#left {
    float: left;
}
img#right {
    float: right;
}
```

4. Save the preceding style sheet as `Example_8-1.css`. The preceding markup and style sheet result in the output that you see in Figure 8-7.

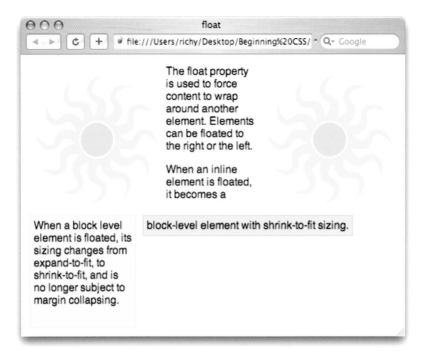

The float property is used to force content to wrap around another element. Elements can be floated to the right or the left.

When an inline element is floated, it becomes a

When a block level element is floated, its sizing changes from expand-to-fit, to shrink-to-fit, and is no longer subject to margin collapsing.

block-level element with shrink-to-fit sizing.

Figure 8-7

How It Works

In Example 8-1, you reviewed three major points about the `float` property: floated elements cause the copy, text, and other elements that follow them to float up beside the floated element. By applying either the `float: right;` or `float: left;` declarations, you can have content that wraps around the left or right of an element, as was the case with the `sun.png` images.

When you float an element, the rules that determine the floated element's size are changed from the default. Floated elements always use the shrink-to-fit sizing, even if the element was originally an inline or a block-level element.

In the next section I present a property that allows you to control floated elements, the `clear` property.

The clear Property

In this section, I discuss a property intrinsically related to the `float` property: the `clear` property. The `clear` property is used to control floating content. The following table outlines the `clear` property and its possible values.

Property	Value
clear	none | left | right | both
	Initial value: none

The simplest explanation for the `clear` property is that it is used to cancel the effects of one or more floated elements. An example of its use can be observed in Figure 8-8.

```
img {
    margin: 10px;
    border: 1px solid rgb(128, 128, 128);
    float: left;
}
img#mercedes-benz {
    clear: left;
}
p {
    font: 12px sans-serif;
}
```

The `clear` property's only purpose is to clear or cancel the effects of the `float` property.

Figure 8-8a

The CSS in Figure 8-8a is combined with the markup in Figure 8-8b.

```
<!DOCTYPE html PUBLIC "-//W3C//DTD XHTML 1.0 Strict//EN"
                      "http://www.w3.org/TR/xhtml1/DTD/xhtml1-strict.dtd">
<html xmlns='http://www.w3.org/1999/xhtml' xml:lang='en'>
    <head>
        <title>float</title>
        <link rel='stylesheet' type='text/css' href='096977%20fg0808.css' />
    </head>
    <body>
        <img src='john_lennon.jpg' alt='john lennon' id='john-lennon' />
        <p>
            Lorem ipsum dolor sit amet, consectetuer adipiscing elit.  Nunc
            eros leo, molestie eu, laoreet eu, rhoncus suscipit, tortor.
            Fusce interdum, metus eu sagittis mollis, lorem augue fringilla
            leo, at pretium magna tortor sed ligula.  Nulla id nisl. Cras
            interdum velit sit amet lacus. In egestas. Integer aliquet.
            Phasellus sagittis congue dui.  Aenean purus neque, viverra at,
            imperdiet sit amet, dignissim vel, sapien. Suspendisse tristique.
            Fusce nunc.  Pellentesque ultrices magna in leo. Vestibulum
            aliquam quam fermentum sapien. Aenean velit erat, vestibulum sit
            amet, rhoncus a, viverra vitae, lacus. Etiam porttitor, mauris ut
            vulputate egestas, tortor dolor tincidunt leo, non scelerisque
            magna dui vitae urna. Vivamus ut massa. Vestibulum sit amet
            sapien et magna varius auctor. Sed a magna. Pellentesque nonummy
            odio nec metus. Pellentesque habitant morbi tristique senectus et
            netus et malesuada fames ac turpis egestas.
        </p>
        <img src='mercedes_benz.jpg' alt='mercedes benz'
             id='mercedes-benz' />
        <p>
            Sed non dolor ut tortor imperdiet hendrerit. Etiam malesuada.
            Proin rutrum ligula eu nibh. Maecenas sit amet est. In eros.
            Proin elit lacus, volutpat at, sagittis et, convallis sit amet,
            sapien. Fusce bibendum augue vitae sapien. Morbi feugiat
            venenatis libero. Vestibulum porttitor. Cras neque ante, luctus
            luctus, elementum volutpat, euismod eget, nunc. Praesent ornare.
            Mauris cursus dolor.
        </p>
        <p>
            Vestibulum ante ipsum primis in faucibus orci luctus et ultrices
            posuere cubilia Curae; Curabitur vitae neque sed nisi luctus
            accumsan. Nulla tincidunt, risus sed sodales molestie, sem eros
            luctus tellus, ut tempus elit dolor quis mauris. Donec pharetra
            sollicitudin turpis. Vivamus fermentum interdum enim. Proin
            sollicitudin eros at neque. Nullam vel turpis ac risus interdum
            ultrices. Cras sit amet diam in arcu ultrices rhoncus. Integer id
            sapien. Fusce adipiscing. Donec lectus tortor, molestie a, porta
            at, tristique sed, enim. Aliquam a lorem a nisl fringilla porta.
            Ut aliquet arcu nec arcu. Sed in elit et pede viverra tempus.
            Duis nisi est, posuere sit amet, venenatis eu, faucibus nec,
            velit.  Vestibulum malesuada tristique urna. Fusce ut est. Sed
            adipiscing nunc sed mi. Vivamus velit nibh, viverra et, cursus
            et, commodo nec, metus. Sed bibendum est in odio.
        </p>
    </body>
</html>
```

Figure 8-8b

In Figure 8-8c, you see what happens before the `clear: left;` declaration is applied to the `<img />` element with the id name `mercedes-benz`. The `mercedes-benz` drawing has floated up beside the drawing of John Lennon. This is where the `clear` property can help; it can cancel the effects of a `float` on the element that it is applied to.

Figure 8-8c

In Figure 8-8d, you see the results of the application of the `clear: left;` declaration on the `<img />` element with the id name `mercedes-benz`. The effects of the `float` applied to the drawing of John Lennon has been canceled, and the image is dropped down below the drawing of John Lennon. However, because the `float: left;` declaration is also applied to the `mercedes-benz` image (since it is applied to all images via the `img` selector), the text still wraps around it.

So the `clear` property is used to control what happens when elements are floated. When you use the `clear` property, you can cancel a `float` on a particular element.

Figure 8-8d

In the following Try It Out, you recap the `clear` property.

Try It Out   Applying the clear Property

Example 8-2. To review the `clear` property, follow these steps.

1. Enter the following markup in your text editor:

```
<!DOCTYPE html PUBLIC "-//W3C//DTD XHTML 1.0 Strict//EN"
                  "http://www.w3.org/TR/xhtml1/DTD/xhtml1-strict.dtd">
<html xmlns='http://www.w3.org/1999/xhtml' xml:lang='en'>
    <head>
        <title>clear</title>
        <link rel='stylesheet' type='text/css' href='Example_8-2.css' />
    </head>
    <body>
        <img src='sun.png' alt='people' id='left' />
        <img src='sun.png' alt='people' id='right' />
        <p>
            The clear property cancels the effects of the
```

```
                    float property, and can prevent wrapping from
                    taking place.
            </p>
        </body>
    </html>
```

2. Save the preceding document as `Example_8-2.html`.

3. Enter the following style sheet in a new document in your text editor:

```
img#left {
    float: left;
}
img#right {
    float: right;
}
p {
    clear: both;
    margin: 20px 0 0 0;
    font: 12px sans-serif;
    border: 1px solid rgb(200, 200, 200);
    background: rgb(244, 244, 244);
    padding: 5px;
}
```

4. Save the CSS that you just keyed in as `Example_8-2.css`. The markup and CSS of Example 8-2 result in the rendered output that you see in Figure 8-9.

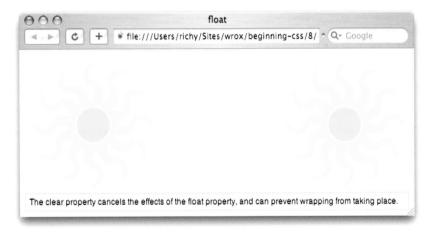

Figure 8-9

How It Works

In Example 8-2, you tried the `clear` property for yourself and observed how the `clear` property is used to cancel the effects of the `float` property on the element that it is applied to.

In the next section I look at some float bugs in IE 6.

Float Bugs in IE 6

The following section takes a look at float bugs that arise in IE 6 and a few of the techniques you can use to work around these bugs. The bugs that I discuss here are as follows:

❑ **Peek-a-boo bug:** As the name implies, this bug involves the use of floats where certain content on a page disappears and occasionally reappears.

❑ **Guillotine bug:** This is another bug that comes up in IE when using floats, where content is cut in half.

❑ **Three-pixel jog:** This bug causes 3 pixels of space to mysteriously appear when using floats in IE.

❑ **Double-margin bug:** This bug causes the left or right margins of a floated box to double when using floats in IE.

Even though the following bugs are a problem in IE 6, all of them have been fixed in IE 7.

The Peek-A-Boo Bug

The peek-a-boo bug can come up in several different contexts — in fact, in far too many to list here. It involves content that disappears and reappears seemingly at random (hence its aptly applied name). The example in Figure 8-10 demonstrates the peek-a-boo bug.

```css
body {
    font: 16px sans-serif;
}
div#container {
    border: 1px solid rgb(200, 200, 200);
    margin: 0 20px;
    background: rgb(234, 234, 234);
    padding: 5px;
}
a:hover {
    background: crimson;
    color: white;
}
div#float {
    text-align: center;
    float: left;
    width: 150px;
    height: 150px;
    border: 1px solid rgb(200, 200, 200);
    background: rgb(234, 234, 234);
}
div.content {
    background: yellow;
    border: 1px solid rgb(200, 200, 200);
}
div#clear {
    border: 1px solid rgb(200, 200, 200);
    background: orange;
    clear: both;
}
```

Figure 8-10a

The CSS in Figure 8-10a is combined with the markup in Figure 8-10b.

```
<!DOCTYPE html PUBLIC "-//W3C//DTD XHTML 1.0 Strict//EN"
                      "http://www.w3.org/TR/xhtml1/DTD/xhtml1-strict.dtd">
<html xmlns='http://www.w3.org/1999/xhtml' xml:lang='en'>
    <head>
        <title>peekaboo</title>
        <link rel='stylesheet' type='text/css' href='096977%20fg0810.css' />
    </head>
    <body>
        <div id='container'>
            <div id='float'>
                Float text. <a href='#'>Link text</a>.
            </div>
                Content text. <a href='#'>Link text</a>.
            <div class='content'>
                Content text. <a href='#'>Link text</a>.
            </div>
                Content text. <a href='#'>Link text</a>.
            <div class='content'>
                Content text. <a href='#'>Link text</a>.
            </div>
                Content text. <a href='#'>Link text</a>.
            <div class='content'>
                Content text. <a href='#'>Link text</a>.
            </div>
                Content text. <a href='#'>Link text</a>.
            <div id='clear'>
                Clear text. <a href='#'>Link text</a>.
            </div>
            <div>
                Another div.
            </div>
        </div>
    </body>
</html>
```

Figure 8-10b

Figure 8-10c shows that when this document is loaded into IE 6, none of the content beside the floated element is visible until you hover your mouse over a link. Hovering causes the lost content to reappear. If you hover your mouse cursor over the links that have reappeared, you find some of the content disappears again.

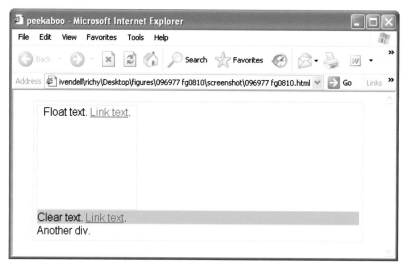

Figure 8-10c

Three properties present in the style sheet trigger this bug:

❑ Floating an element by applying a `float: left;` declaration (`float: right;` also triggers the bug).

❑ Including a background on the containing element. In this example, this is the `background: rgb(234, 234, 234);` declaration.

❑ Including a clear on an element following the float, where the margins of the clearing element come into contact with the floating element.

So, with an overview of what causes the peek-a-boo bug and what it is, what do you do to work around the bug? You have more than one option:

❑ Apply a `position: relative;` declaration to the containing element and floating element.

❑ Prevent the margins of the clearing element from coming into contact with the floating element.

❑ Avoid applying a background to the containing element.

❑ Apply the declaration `zoom: 1;` to the containing element.

❑ Apply the declaration `display: inline-block;` to the containing element.

❑ Apply a fixed width to the containing element.

The next section continues the discussion of Internet Explorer bugs with the guillotine bug.

The Guillotine Bug

The guillotine bug is another aptly named bug where only part of the content disappears. The guillotine bug is demonstrated in the documents in Figure 8-11.

The CSS in Figure 8-11a is combined with the markup in Figure 8-11b.

```
div#container {
    font: 16px sans-serif;
    border: 1px solid black;
    margin: 0 20px;
    background: yellow;
}
a:hover {
    background: orange;
}
div#float {
    background: gold;
    float: left;
    border: 1px solid black;
    width: 150px;
    height: 150px;
    margin: 5px;
}
ul {
    margin: 0;
    list-style: none;
}
```

Figure 8-11a

```
<!DOCTYPE html PUBLIC "-//W3C//DTD XHTML 1.0 Strict//EN"
              "http://www.w3.org/TR/xhtml1/DTD/xhtml1-strict.dtd">
<html xmlns='http://www.w3.org/1999/xhtml' xml:lang='en'>
    <head>
        <title>guillotine</title>
        <link rel='stylesheet' type='text/css' href='096977%20fg0811.css' />
    </head>
    <body>
        <div id='container'>
            <div id='float'>
                <p>
                    Float text. <a href='#'>Content on</a>.
                    Float text. Float text. Float text. Float text.
                    Float text. Float text. Float text. Float text.
                </p>
                <p>
                    This text is chopped off!  This text is chopped off!
                    This text is chopped off!  This text is chopped off!
                </p>
            </div>
            <ul>
                <li><a href='#'>Content on.</a></li>
                <li><a href='#'>Content on.</a></li>
                <li><a href='#'>Content off.</a></li>
                <li><a href='#'>Content off.</a></li>
                <li><a href='#'>Content off.</a></li>
            </ul>
        </div>
    </body>
</html>
```

Figure 8-11b

After you load the preceding in Internet Explorer, when you hover your mouse cursor over the Content Off links, part of the content inside the floating element is chopped off! You can see this in the output in Figure 8-11c.

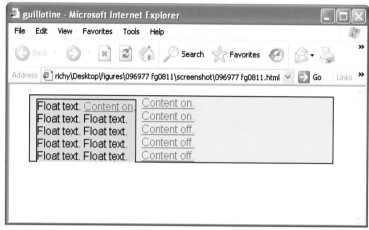

Figure 8-11c

The guillotine bug occurs when the following conditions are present:

❏ IE is in standards-compliant rendering mode.

❏ An element is floated inside of a container element.

❏ Links exist inside the container element in non-floated content that appears after the float.

❏ A :hover pseudo-class is applied to <a> elements that change certain properties.

The guillotine bug is yet another bizarre IE rendering bug. The fix is not nearly as elegant as that for the peek-a-boo bug. To fix the guillotine bug, a clearing element must appear after the containing element. The best method to apply this clearing element without affecting the original design is to apply the following rule to the clearing element:

```
div#clearing {
    clear: both;
    visibility: hidden;
}
```

Then in the markup, add the clearing element:

```
                <li><a href='#'>Content off.</a></li>
            </ul>
        </div>
        <div id='clearing'></div>
    </body>
</html>
```

After you apply this rule and markup, the guillotine bug is corrected without any effects on the intended design. The visibility: hidden; declaration is similar to the display: none; declaration (see Chapter 13 and Chapter 14). The key difference is that an element with display: none; is not rendered and does not appear in a document, whereas an element with visibility: hidden; is rendered, does appear in the document, but is invisible. The easiest way to distinguish between the two is that the display property with a none keyword makes it seem an element doesn't exist at all. If you use the display: none; declaration, properties are not applied and the element takes up no space. If you use visibility: hidden; instead with this declaration, the element still exists; properties are applied, and the dimensions of the element are still honored, even though the element is invisible.

The nest section continues the discussion of IE 6 float bugs with the three-pixel jog.

The Three-Pixel Jog

The next Internet Explorer rendering bug, which also involves floated elements, is called the three-pixel jog. As the name implies, this bug causes 3 pixels of space to appear between text inside an element that follows a floated element and the inner border of that element. This bug is demonstrated by the documents in Figure 8-12.

```
div#container {
    font: 16px sans-serif;
    margin: 0 20px;
    background: yellow;
    width: 300px;
}
div#float {
    background: rgb(234, 234, 234);
    float: left;
    border: 1px solid black;
    width: 75px;
    height: 50px;
}
p {
    margin-left: 76px;
    border: 1px solid black;
}
```

Figure 8-12a

The CSS in Figure 8-12a is combined with the markup in Figure 8-12b.

Figure 8-12c shows the subtle effects of the three-pixel jog. If you look closely in the screenshot, you can see that the first three lines of the paragraph are 3 pixels farther to the right than the two lines that follow, which corresponds directly to the height of the floated element.

```
<!DOCTYPE html PUBLIC "-//W3C//DTD XHTML 1.0 Strict//EN"
                      "http://www.w3.org/TR/xhtml1/DTD/xhtml1-strict.dtd">
<html xmlns='http://www.w3.org/1999/xhtml' xml:lang='en'>
    <head>
        <title>three-pixel jog</title>
        <link rel='stylesheet' type='text/css' href='096977%20fg0812.css' />
    </head>
    <body>
        <div id='container'>
            <div id='float'>
                Float text.
            </div>
            <p>
                Paragraph text. Paragraph text. Paragraph text.
                Paragraph text. Paragraph text. Paragraph text.
                Paragraph text. Paragraph text. Paragraph text.
            </p>
        </div>
    </body>
</html>
```

Figure 8-12b

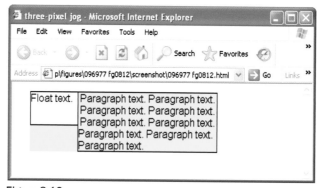

Figure 8-12c

The three-pixel jog doesn't look like much of a big deal, but it can be — especially if a design must be the same, pixel for pixel, in all browsers. The three-pixel jog can be corrected by applying either a width or height (other than auto) to the element that follows the float. Because an explicit width or height is not always desirable, a few methods target IE 6 and less specifically. The first method uses conditional comments like those you saw in Chapter 7.

```
<!--[if lt IE 7]>
<style type='text/css'>
    p {
        height: 1px;
    }
</style>
<![endif]-->
```

This is a very clean, acceptable method to target IE 6 for Windows explicitly, and because IE 6 and earlier versions have incorrect support for the `height` property, the content isn't adversely affected by including this declaration. Other browsers won't be so forgiving, however, so this solution must be applied only to Internet Explorer to avoid complications. The next section continues discussion of Internet Explorer rendering bugs with the double-margin bug.

The Double-Margin Bug

Here's yet another Internet Explorer rendering bug involving floated elements. The double-margin bug is demonstrated in the documents in Figure 8-13.

```css
div#container {
    margin: 0 20px;
    background: yellow;
    width: 300px;
    font: 16px sans-serif;
}
div#float {
    margin-left: 50px;
    background: rgb(234, 234, 234);
    float: left;
    border: 1px solid black;
    width: 75px;
    height: 50px;
}
```

Figure 8-13a

The CSS in Figure 8-13a is combined with the markup in Figure 8-13b.

```html
<!DOCTYPE html PUBLIC "-//W3C//DTD XHTML 1.0 Strict//EN"
                      "http://www.w3.org/TR/xhtml1/DTD/xhtml1-strict.dtd">
<html xmlns='http://www.w3.org/1999/xhtml' xml:lang='en'>
    <head>
        <title>double margin</title>
        <link rel='stylesheet' type='text/css' href='096977%20fg0813.css' />
    </head>
    <body>
        <div id='container'>
            <div id='float'>
                Float text.
            </div>
        </div>
    </body>
</html>
```

Figure 8-13b

Figure 8-13c shows the double-margin bug in action.

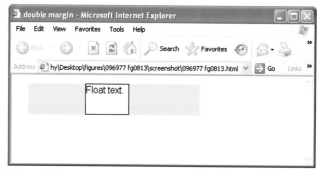

Figure 8-13c

Three ingredients are required to reproduce this bug:

❑ A containing element

❑ A floated element inside the containing element

❑ A left margin specified on the floated element

When these ingredients are present, the left margin of the floated element doubles, so Figure 8-13c shows the floated element with 100 pixels of left margin instead of only 50, as is specified in the style sheet. The fix for this bug is very simple. All you need to do is apply a `display: inline;` declaration to the floated element. If you recall from earlier in this chapter, all floated elements are always block elements. Using the `display: inline;` declaration somehow tricks IE 6 into correct behavior. Be sure to test this fix with different browsers to ensure that unexpected side effects are not encountered. As is the case with the three-pixel jog, you can target IE 6 specifically by including this declaration within a rule inside of a style sheet that resides in conditional comments.

The vertical-align Property

The `vertical-align` property is used primarily in two contexts. In one context, it is used to vertically align text appearing within the lines of a paragraph. One example of this creates subscript or superscript text. The `vertical-align` property may also be used to align the content appearing inside a table cell. The following table outlines the `vertical-align` property and its possible values.

Property	Value
vertical-align	baseline | sub | super | top | text-top | middle | bottom | text-bottom | <percentage> | <length>
	Initial value: baseline

The `vertical-align` property applies exclusively to inline elements, such as `<img/>` and `<span>`. It has different meaning when applied to table cells. I discuss its use in cells in an upcoming section. In the next section, however, I look at how to format subscript text with the `vertical-align` property.

Subscript and Superscript Text

Within a paragraph, you may need several different types of styles that are only applied to snippets of the text, such as bold or italic fonts. Subscript text is an example of styles that often apply only to a selection of text, rather than to a whole paragraph. *Subscript* text is text that appears slightly smaller than the text surrounding it and slightly lower than the baseline of the surrounding text. The *baseline* is the invisible line created for each line of text against which the bottom of each letter is aligned. In other words, the baseline is the line that letters "sit" on. *Superscript* text, on the other hand, is text raised above the baseline and that appears slightly smaller than the surrounding text. Figure 8-14 is a demonstration of subscript and superscript text.

```
p {
    font: 12px sans-serif;
    margin: 25px 0;
}
span#sub {
    vertical-align: sub;
}
span#super {
    vertical-align: super;
}
```

The sub keyword is used for subscript text, and the super keyword is used for superscript text, which causes text to lower and raise from the baseline, respectively.

Figure 8-14a

The CSS in Figure 8-14a is included in the markup document that you see in Figure 8-14b.

```
<!DOCTYPE html PUBLIC "-//W3C//DTD XHTML 1.0 Strict//EN"
                      "http://www.w3.org/TR/xhtml1/DTD/xhtml1-strict.dtd">
<html xmlns='http://www.w3.org/1999/xhtml' xml:lang='en'>
    <head>
        <title>vertical-align</title>
        <link rel='stylesheet' type='text/css' href='096977%20fg0814.css' />
    </head>
    <body>
        <p>
            Subscript text is <span id='sub'>lowered</span>
        </p>
        <p>
            Superscript text is <span id='super'>raised</span>
        </p>
    </body>
</html>
```

Figure 8-14b

The rendered output of the source code appears in Figure 8-14c.

Figure 8-14c

Figure 8-14 shows that the content of the <span> element of the first paragraph appears lower than that of the rest of the line, which is a result of applying the vertical-align: sub; declaration. The figure also shows that the <span> element of the second paragraph appears slightly higher, which is a result of the vertical-align: super; declaration.

The next section continues the discussion of the vertical-align property with top, middle, and bottom vertical alignment text.

The top, middle, and bottom Keywords

The top, middle, and bottom keywords are used to control vertical alignment of selections of text that are slightly smaller than the surrounding text. The top keyword is demonstrated in Figure 8-15.

```
p {
    font: 12px sans-serif;
}
p#control {
    font-size: 100px;
    margin: 5px 0;
}
p#control span {
    border: 1px solid rgb(200, 200, 200);
    background: rgb(244, 244, 244);
}
p#control span span {
    vertical-align: top;
    font-size: 20px;
    background: white;
    border: 1px solid black;
}
```

The top keyword aligns the inline box to the top of the line box.

Figure 8-15a

Combine the style sheet in Figure 8-15a with the markup in Figure 8-15b.

```
<!DOCTYPE html PUBLIC "-//W3C//DTD XHTML 1.0 Strict//EN"
                      "http://www.w3.org/TR/xhtml1/DTD/xhtml1-strict.dtd">
<html xmlns='http://www.w3.org/1999/xhtml' xml:lang='en'>
    <head>
        <title>vertical-align</title>
        <link rel='stylesheet' type='text/css' href='096977%20fg0815.css' />
    </head>
    <body>
        <p>
            Aa Bb Cc Dd Ee Ff Gg Hh Ii Jj Kk Ll Mm
        </p>
        <p id='control'>
            <span>Nn Oo Pp <span>Top</span></span>
        </p>
        <p>
            Qq Rr Ss Tt Uu Vv Ww Xx Yy Zz
        </p>
    </body>
</html>
```
Figure 8-15b

This source code results in the output depicted in Figure 8-15c.

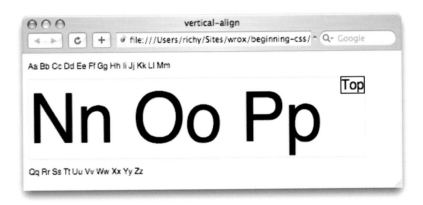

Figure 8-15c

In Figure 8-15c, you see that the <span> element with the contents Top is aligned to the top of the line box. Figure 8-16 demonstrates the middle keyword.

In Figure 8-16, you can see that the `middle` keyword lines the inline box up relative to the center point of the lowercase letters on the line.

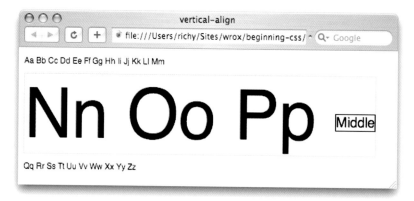

Figure 8-16

Figure 8-17 demonstrates the `bottom` keyword.

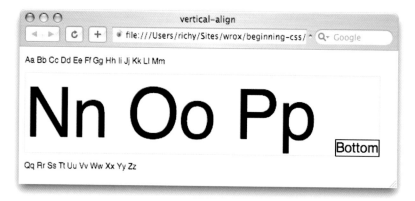

Figure 8-17

In Figure 8-17, you can see that the inline box is aligned with the bottom of the line box. In the next section, I discuss the `text-top` and `text-bottom` keywords.

The text-top and text-bottom Keywords

Like the `top`, `middle`, and `bottom` values, the `text-top` and `text-bottom` keywords raise or lower a subset of text. The difference in the `text-top` keyword as opposed to the `top` keyword is that the `text-top` keyword causes alignment to happen with respect to the tallest character of the font of the surrounding text, for instance the lowercase letters *t, l, f,* or the uppercase letters. Likewise the `text-bottom` keyword aligns with respect to the lowest character, for instance the letters *p, y,* or *g,* which drop below the baseline. The `text-top` and `text-bottom` keyword values produce output similar to that produced by the `top` and `bottom` keywords. The most important difference between `top` and `text-top` is that `top` causes the border of the inline box to align with the top border of the line containing that inline box, whereas `text-top` aligns with respect to the tallest character in the font.

The next section discusses percentage and length values as applied to the `vertical-align` property.

Percentage and Length Value

If the selection of keywords I presented in the previous sections weren't enough for you, the `vertical-align` property also allows percentage and length values to be applied. Figure 8-18 demonstrates the `vertical-align` property with a value of 300%.

Figure 8-18

Percentage values with the `vertical-align` property are based on the `line-height` of the element the percentage value is applied to. If you remember back to Figure 8-15b, which shows the markup structure of this document, the `<span>` element that contains the text 300% has a `line-height` of 23 pixels. If you recall, I didn't give the `<span>` element an explicit `line-height`; I determined the `line-height` by including the `line-height` property and increasing or decreasing the value until I achieved the same results that you see in Figure 8-18. To calculate the pixel value of 300%, I take the `line-height`, 23, and multiply it by 3, to get 69, so the pixel value of 300% in Figure 8-18 is 69px. The default line height differs from browser to browser and between different font sizes, so your own results may vary.

Figure 8-19 demonstrates the `vertical-align` property with a length of 69 pixels, which should be identical to what you see in Figure 8-18, concerning the placement of the box.

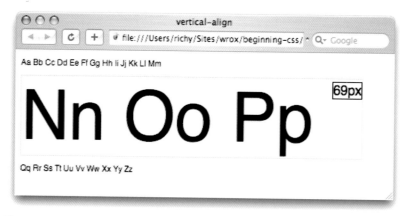

Figure 8-19

Vertically Aligning the Contents of Table Cells

The `vertical-align` property has completely different meaning when it is applied to table cells. When applied to table cells, only the `baseline`, `top`, `middle`, and `bottom` keywords are applicable, and the `vertical-align` property is used to align the entire contents of the cell. This is demonstrated in Figure 8-20.

```
td {
    font: 12px sans-serif;
    border: 1px solid black;
    padding: 5px;
    width: 100%;
}
td#baseline {
    font-size: 50px;
    vertical-align: baseline;
}
td#baseline-copy {
    vertical-align: baseline;
}
td#top {
    vertical-align: top;
}
td#middle {
    vertical-align: middle;
}
td#bottom {
    vertical-align: bottom;
}
```

The `baseline`, `top`, `middle`, and `bottom` keywords of the `vertical-align` property have different meanings when applied to table cells.

Figure 8-20a

Apply the style sheet in Figure 8-20a to the markup in Figure 8-20b.

```
<!DOCTYPE html PUBLIC "-//W3C//DTD XHTML 1.0 Strict//EN"
                     "http://www.w3.org/TR/xhtml1/DTD/xhtml1-strict.dtd">
<html xmlns='http://www.w3.org/1999/xhtml' xml:lang='en'>
    <head>
        <title>vertical-align</title>
        <link rel='stylesheet' type='text/css' href='096977%20fg0820.css' />
    </head>
    <body>
        <table>
            <tbody>
                <tr>
                    <td id='baseline-copy'>
                        Lorem ipsum dolor sit amet, consectetuer adipiscing
                        elit. Proin mauris nisl, tincidunt ut, aliquam nec,
                        ultrices id, sapien. Proin quis urna. Class aptent
                        taciti sociosqu ad litora torquent per conubia
                        nostra, per inceptos hymenaeos.
                    </td>
                    <td id='baseline'>Baseline</td>
                    <td id='top'>Top</td>
                    <td id='middle'>Middle</td>
                    <td id='bottom'>Bottom</td>
                </tr>
            </tbody>
        </table>
    </body>
</html>
```

Figure 8-20b

Figure 8-20c shows the output from this example.

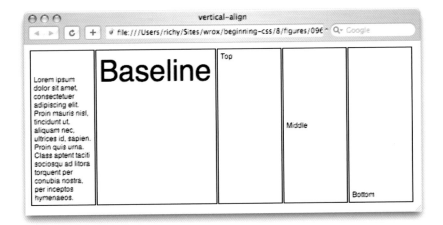

Figure 8-20c

The preceding example is a demonstration of the four `vertical-align` properties that are applicable to table cells: `baseline`, `top`, `middle`, and `bottom`. The first two cells are aligned to the `baseline`. The `baseline` of a table cell is determined by the `baseline` of the table row. The `baseline` of the table row is determined by taking the `baseline` of the first line of each `baseline`-aligned table cell in that row. The one with the largest font, or other inline content, such as an image, determines the `baseline` of the row, which each table cell is aligned against.

In short, this complicated summary of baselining results in the line *Lorem ipsum* in the first table cell in Figure 8-16c having the same `baseline` as the word *Baseline* that appears in the second cell. In this case, the font size of *Baseline* determines where the `baseline` of the table row is.

The third cell is top-aligned, which means the content begins at the top of the cell and flows on downward from there. The fourth cell is middle-aligned, which means that the height of the content is measured to determine the middle point of the content, and then that midpoint is aligned with the midpoint of the cell. Finally, the fifth cell is bottom-aligned, which means that the bottom-most point of the content in the cell is aligned with the bottom of the cell.

Although you might expect the `vertical-align` property to apply to all elements — to block elements, for example, in the same way it is applied to table cells — this isn't the case. The `vertical-align` property is applicable only to inline elements and table cell elements, `<td>` and `<th>`.

The following Try It Out is a recap of the `vertical-align` property.

Try It Out   Applying the vertical-align Property

Example 8-3. To review the vertical-align property, follow these steps.

1.   Enter the following XHTML in your text editor:

```
<!DOCTYPE html PUBLIC "-//W3C//DTD XHTML 1.0 Strict//EN"
                      "http://www.w3.org/TR/xhtml1/DTD/xhtml1-strict.dtd">
<html xmlns='http://www.w3.org/1999/xhtml' xml:lang='en'>
    <head>
        <title>vertical-align</title>
        <link rel='stylesheet' type='text/css' href='Example_8-3.css' />
    </head>
    <body>
        <p>
            The vertical-align property is used in two scenarios: to
            vertically align inline elements with respect to the line
            box, and to vertically align the contents of table cells.
        </p>
        <p>
            When vertically aligning inline elements within a line box,
            the vertical-align property can be used with the keywords
            top, middle, bottom, text-top, text-bottom.
        </p>
        <p>
            <span class='line'>
```

```
            Gg
            <span id='top'>Top</span>
            <span id='middle'>Middle</span>
            <span id='bottom'>Bottom</span>
            <span id='text-top'>Text Top</span>
            <span id='text-bottom'>Text Bottom</span>
        </span>
    </p>
    <p>
        The top and bottom keywords align to the top and bottom of
        the line-box respectively.  The middle keyword aligns to the
        center point of the highest lowercase letter.  The text-top
        and text-bottom keyword align to the tallest and lowest character,
        respectively.
    </p>
    <p>
        The vertical-align property can also accept either a
        percentage or length value.  The percentage value is a
        percentage of the line-height value; the length is offset
        from the bottom of the line-height.
    </p>
    <p>
        <span class='line'>
            Gg
            <span id='percentage'>200%</span>
            <span id='length'>46px</span>
        </span>
    </p>
    <p>
        Finally, when applied to table cells, the baseline, top, middle,
        and bottom keywords have different meanings.
    </p>
    <table>
        <tbody>
            <tr>
                <td id='baseline-copy'>
                    This copy aligns with the bottom of the tallest content
                    in the first row of the table.
                </td>
                <td id='baseline'>Baseline</td>
                <td id='td-top'>Top</td>
                <td id='td-middle'>Middle</td>
                <td id='td-bottom'>Bottom</td>
            </tr>
        </tbody>
    </table>
</body>
</html>
```

2. Save the preceding XHTML document as `Example_8-3.html`.

3. Type the following style sheet in your text editor:

```
p {
    font: 12px sans-serif;
}
span.line {
    border: 1px solid rgb(200, 200, 200);
    background: rgb(244, 244, 244);
    font-size: 100px;
}
span.line span {
    vertical-align: 300%;
    font-size: 20px;
    background: white;
    border: 1px solid black;
}
span#top {
    vertical-align: top;
}
span#middle {
    vertical-align: middle;
}
span#bottom {
    vertical-align: bottom;
}
span#text-top {
    vertical-align: text-top;
}
span#text-bottom {
    vertical-align: text-bottom;
}
span#percentage {
    vertical-align: 200%;
}
span#length {
    vertical-align: 46px;
}
td {
    padding: 5px;
    width: 100px;
    border: 1px solid black;
}
td#baseline-copy {
    vertical-align: baseline;
}
td#baseline {
    font-size: 50px;
    vertical-align: baseline;
}
td#td-top {
    vertical-align: top;
}
```

```
td#td-middle {
    vertical-align: middle;
}
td#td-bottom {
    vertical-align: bottom;
}
```

4. Save the preceding style sheet as `Example_8-3.css`. The preceding source code results in the output that you see in Figure 8-21.

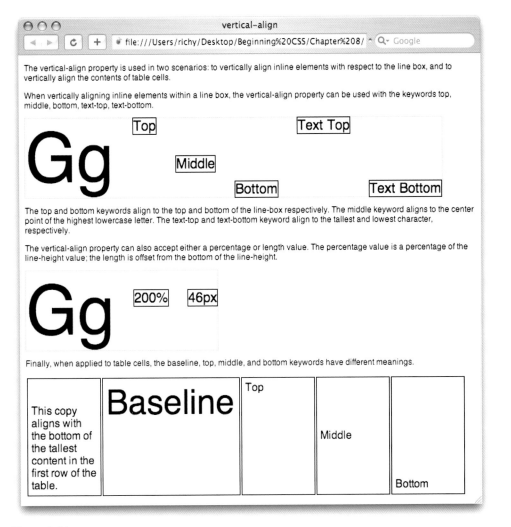

Figure 8-21

How It Works

In Example 8-3, you reviewed the more complicated portions of the vertical-align property. You set up text cases for each of the keywords, save the sub and super keywords, which are used to apply subscript and superscript text styling, respectively.

First were the top, middle, bottom, text-top, and text-bottom keywords. You see that with this example that there really is no discernable difference between the text-top and text-bottom keywords; most browsers simply map these to the top and bottom keywords. You set up a line to test each keyword where the font is 100 pixels, and each line has a border and background so that you can easily see the dimensions of the line box. The top and text-top, and the bottom and text-bottom keywords align to the top and bottom of the line box, respectively. The middle keyword aligns to the center point of the lowercase letter.

In the next test case you set up a line for testing the vertical-align property with a percentage and a length value. The percentage value is based on the height of the line; in this case the line height is 23 pixels, you verify this by the next example, which gives the vertical-align property a length value of 46 pixels, which is offset from the bottom of the line box, just like the percentage.

In the last test, you set up a table for the four values of the vertical-align property that have special value when applied to a table. The first line of the first cell is aligned to the bottom of the word "Baseline" that appears in the second cell. When table cells are aligned to the baseline, each cell is aligned to the bottom of the largest content that appears in the first row of the table. In the last three cells, the contents of each cell are aligned to the top, middle, and bottom.

Summary

This chapter focused on three key areas of CSS design. In this chapter you learned the following:

❑   The float property is a seemingly complex property that has a unique place in CSS design. The float property is used for layout—for instance, to include content in the flow of paragraph text in such a way that text wraps around the floated element.

❑   The clear property is used to control the effects of the float property in situations where you don't want all the content following a floated element to float beside it.

❑   The vertical-align property is used to vertically align inline elements such as the <span> element or the <img/> element relative to the line containing those inline elements; this property can be used, for instance, to create subscript or superscript text.

❑   The vertical-align property may also be applied to table cells to control vertical alignment of the content within table cells. If the vertical-align property is applied to table cells, only a subset of properties are applicable. These include the baseline, top, middle, and bottom properties. The behavior of these properties is completely different when applied to table cells as opposed to normal inline content.

Chapter 9 discusses how to control the styling of list elements with CSS.

Exercises

1. When an element is floated, what rule governs its dimensions?

2. What happens when an inline element, such as a `<span>` element, is floated?

3. What are the three keywords of the `float` property?

4. If an element is floated to the right, and you don't want the following element to wrap around it, what declaration would you apply to that element?

5. What declarations would you use to create subscript and superscript text?

6. When vertically aligning an inline element to the `middle`, how is the element positioned on the line?

7. What is the difference between the `text-top` and `top` keywords of the `vertical-align` property?

8. If you are aligning table cells to the baseline, what determines the baseline?

List Properties

In Chapter 8, you saw how the `float` and `clear` properties are used to control the flow of content in a web document. In this chapter, I look at properties used to control the styling of list elements. I cover the following:

❏ The `list-style-type` property and how it's used to present different types of lists through a variety of marker styles for bulleted lists and numbered lists

❏ The `list-style-image` property and how it's used to provide a custom marker for each list item

❏ The `list-style-position` property and how it's used to control the positioning of list item markers

Like the CSS properties I covered in previous chapters, the CSS list properties give you complete control over the way you present and style list items.

The list-style-type Property

You use the `list-style-type` property to change the presentation of bulleted and numbered lists. For example, you can change an ordered list to a list using Roman numerals for markers, or you can change a bulleted list to one using squares instead of circles for markers. The following table outlines the `list-style-type` property and its possible values (as of CSS 2.1).

Property	Value
list-style-type	disc | circle | square | decimal | decimal-leading-zero | lower-roman | upper-roman | lower-greek | lower-latin | upper-latin | armenian | georgian | none Initial value: disc

IE 6 and IE 7 support only CSS 1 keyword values: disc | circle | square | decimal | lower-roman | upper-roman | lower-alpha | upper-alpha | none.

Naturally, the default list type used also depends on whether <ol> or <ul> list elements are used to structure the list. A variety of keywords allows for a variety of presentational styles.

Styling Unordered Lists

Figure 9-1a demonstrates what's possible with unordered lists (lists made with the <ul> element). There's a possibility of four different styles: disc, circle, square, and none.

```
li#disc {
    list-style-type: disc;
}
li#circle {
    list-style-type: circle;
}
li#square {
    list-style-type: square;
}
li#none {
    list-style-type: none;
}
ul#square {
    list-style-type: square;
}
```

The list-style-type property is applied to either <li> or <ul> elements. It's used to change the style of the marker before list items.

Figure 9-1a

The style sheet in Figure 9-1a is combined with the markup in Figure 9-1b.

Figure 9-1c shows the results of the code in Figure 9-1a and Figure 9-1b.

As you can see from the code in Figure 9-1a and Figure 9-1b, and the output in Figure 9-1c, unordered lists can have four different styles, disc, circle, square, and none.

```
<!DOCTYPE html PUBLIC "-//W3C//DTD XHTML 1.0 Strict//EN"
                      "http://www.w3.org/TR/xhtml1/DTD/xhtml1-strict.dtd">
<html xmlns='http://www.w3.org/1999/xhtml' xml:lang='en'>
    <head>
        <title>list-style-type</title>
        <link rel='stylesheet' type='text/css' href='096977%20fg0901.css' />
    </head>
    <body>
        <ul>
            <li id='disc'>
                This list item has a disc marker.
                <ul>
                    <li>Child markers don't inherit the parent's style.</li>
                </ul>
            </li>
            <li id='circle'>This list item has a circle marker.</li>
            <li id='square'>This list item has a square marker.</li>
            <li id='none'>
                This list item has no marker.
                <ul id='square'>
                    <li>
                        List styles can be applied to &lt;ul&gt; elements
                        too.
                    </li>
                </ul>
            </li>
        </ul>
    </body>
</html>
```

Figure 9-1b

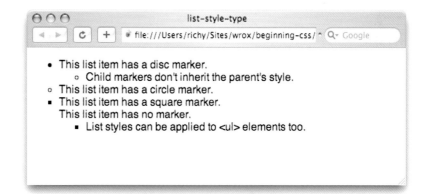

Figure 9-1c

In the next section you see how to style ordered lists.

Styling Ordered Lists

Ordered lists can be styled using a variety of different lettering and numbering conventions. The following series of figures demonstrates what each style looks like in the most popular browsers of the Mac and Windows platforms.

Figure 9-2a shows what each keyword looks like in Safari, Firefox, and Opera on Mac OS X Tiger.

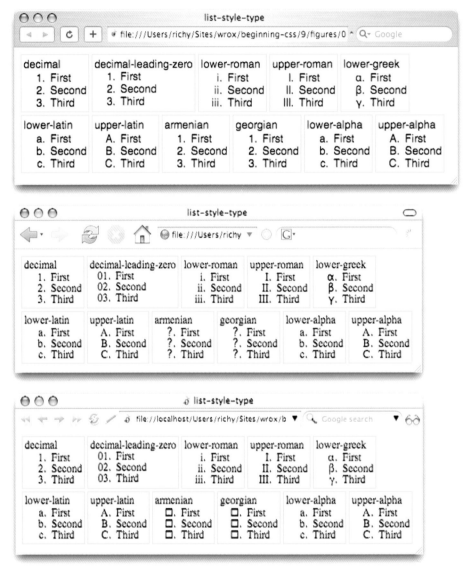

Figure 9-2a

In Figure 9-2a, you can see that three of the keyword values have no effect in Safari: `decimal-leading-zero`, `armenian`, and `georgian` are not supported by Safari. Also in Figure 9-2a, you see that the `armenian` and `georgian` keyword values are not supported by Firefox or Opera for Mac OS X. Figure 9-2b shows the various keywords in browsers on Windows XP.

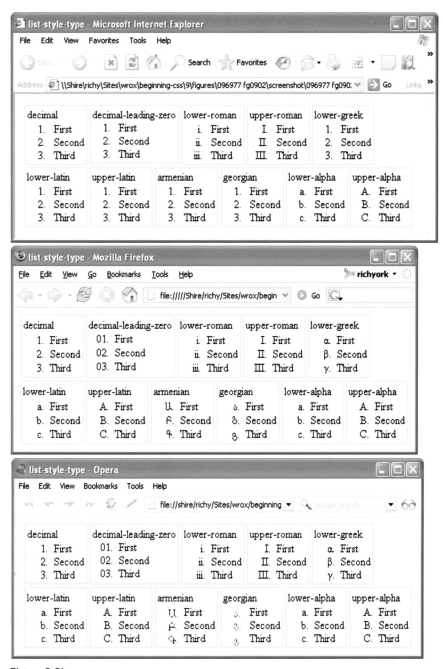

Figure 9-2b

In Figure 9-2b, you see that IE 6 does not support the keywords `decimal-leading-zero`, `lower-greek`, `lower-latin`, `upper-latin`, `armenian`, or `georgian`. Firefox and Opera on Windows support all of the demonstrated keywords. Figure 9-2c demonstrates each keyword in IE 7 on Windows Vista.

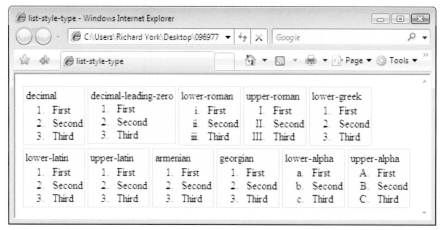

Figure 9-2c

In Figure 9-2c, you can see that nothing has changed with respect to `list-style-type` keyword support in IE 7.

Try It Out   Applying the list-style-type Property

Example 9-1. To apply the list-style-type property, follow these steps.

1.   Enter the following markup into your text editor:

```
<!DOCTYPE html PUBLIC "-//W3C//DTD XHTML 1.0 Strict//EN"
                    "http://www.w3.org/TR/xhtml1/DTD/xhtml1-strict.dtd">
<html xmlns='http://www.w3.org/1999/xhtml' xml:lang='en'>
    <head>
        <title>list-style-type</title>
        <link rel='stylesheet' type='text/css' href='Example_9-1.css' />
    </head>
    <body>
        <p>
            The list-style-type allows you to make use of a variety of
            different markers for list items.  For unordered lists,
            there are three: disc, square, and circle.
        </p>
        <ul>
            <li id='disc' class='safe'>disc</li>
```

```
            <li id='square' class='safe'>square</li>
            <li id='circle' class='safe'>circle</li>
        </ul>
        <p>
            For ordered lists, there are eleven different styles of marker:
        </p>
        <ol>
            <li id='decimal' class='safe'>decimal</li>
            <li id='decimal-leading-zero'>decimal-leading-zero</li>
            <li id='lower-roman' class='safe'>lower-roman</li>
            <li id='upper-roman' class='safe'>upper-roman</li>
            <li id='lower-greek'>lower-greek</li>
            <li id='lower-latin'>lower-latin</li>
            <li id='upper-latin'>upper-latin</li>
            <li id='armenian'>armenian</li>
            <li id='georgian'>georgian</li>
            <li id='upper-alpha' class='safe'>upper-alpha</li>
            <li id='lower-alpha' class='safe'>lower-alpha</li>
        </ol>
        <p>
            Markers that are known to have the most compatibility in all
            browsers are marked with a background of mistyrose.
        </p>
        <p>
            The marker can be removed from either ordered or unordered lists with
            the none keyword.
        </p>
        <ul class='none'>
            <li class='safe'>No marker</li>
        </ul>
        <ol class='none'>
            <li class='safe'>No marker</li>
        </ol>
    </body>
</html>
```

2. Save the preceding markup as `Example_9-1.html`.

3. Enter the following style sheet into your text editor:

```
li#decimal {
    list-style-type: decimal;
}
li#square {
    list-style-type: square;
}
li#circle {
    list-style-type: circle;
}
```

```
.none {
    list-style-type: none;
}
li#decimal {
    list-style-type: decimal;
}
li#decimal-leading-zero {
    list-style-type: decimal-leading-zero;
}
li#lower-roman {
    list-style-type: lower-roman;
}
li#upper-roman {
    list-style-type: upper-roman;
}
li#lower-greek {
    list-style-type: lower-greek;
}
li#lower-latin {
    list-style-type: lower-latin;
}
li#upper-latin {
    list-style-type: upper-latin;
}
li#armenian {
    list-style-type: armenian;
}
li#georgian {
    list-style-type: georgian;
}
li#lower-alpha {
    list-style-type: lower-alpha;
}
li#upper-alpha {
    list-style-type: upper-alpha;
}
li.safe {
    background: mistyrose;
}
```

4. Save the preceding style sheet as `Example_9-1.css`. Since Firefox for Windows has better support for the `list-style-type` keywords than other browsers, load up the example in Firefox for Windows to get the output in Figure 9-3.

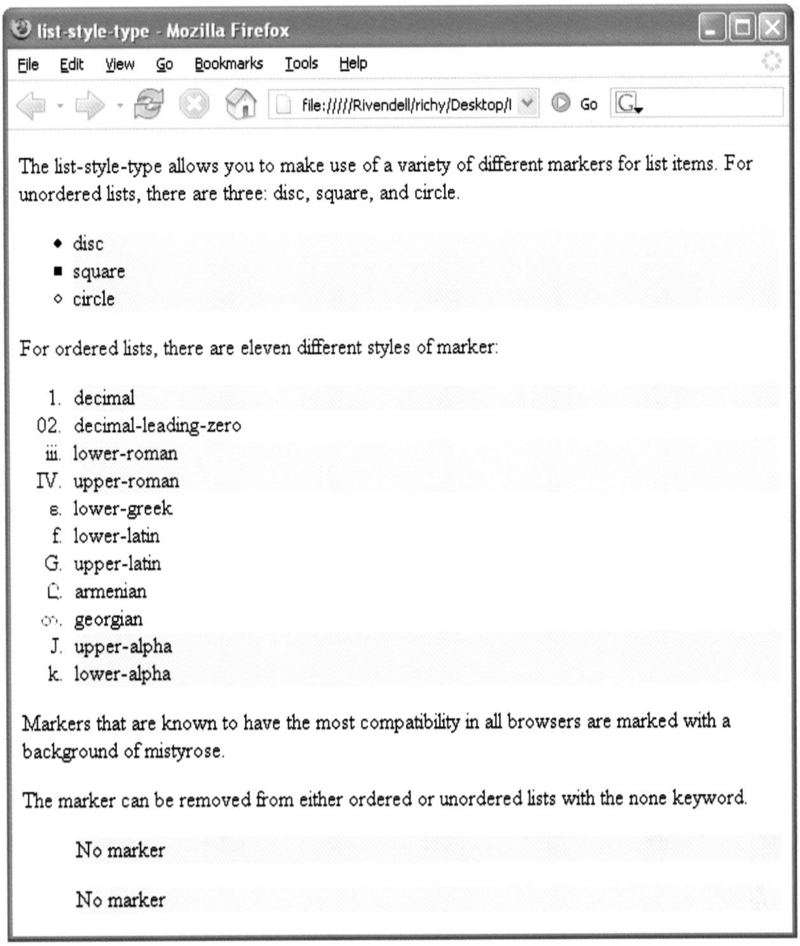
list-style-type - Mozilla Firefox
File Edit View Go Bookmarks Tools Help
file:////Rivendell/richy/Desktop/l
Go
The list-style-type allows you to make use of a variety of different markers for list items. For unordered lists, there are three: disc, square, and circle.
disc
square
circle
For ordered lists, there are eleven different styles of marker:
1. decimal
02. decimal-leading-zero
iii. lower-roman
IV. upper-roman
ε. lower-greek
f. lower-latin
G. upper-latin
armenian
georgian
J. upper-alpha
k. lower-alpha
Markers that are known to have the most compatibility in all browsers are marked with a background of mistyrose.
The marker can be removed from either ordered or unordered lists with the none keyword.
No marker
No marker

Figure 9-3

How It Works

In Example 9-1 you recapped each of the keyword properties that are allowed by the `list-style-type` keyword. Since some keywords pose compatibility problems, you're better off sticking with the ones that have the best browser support. Those keywords are `disc`, `square`, `circle`, `decimal`, `lower-roman`, `upper-roman`, `upper-alpha`, `lower-alpha`, and `none`.

In the next section, I discuss the `list-style-image` property.

The list-style-image Property

Like the `list-style-type` property, you can use the `list-style-image` property to change the marker used for list items. The `list-style-image` property is most suited for custom bulleted lists. The following table outlines the `list-style-image` property and its possible values.

Property	Value
list-style-image	\<uri> | none Initial value: none

The `list-style-image` property is quite straightforward; it accepts a file path to the image, which is denoted in the preceding table by the \<uri> notation. In Figure 9-4, you see a simple example of the `list-style-image` property in action. In Figure 9-4a, you see the CSS required to make a custom list marker.

```
li {
    list-style-image: url('arrow.png');
}
li#other {
    list-style-image: url('arrow2.png');
}
```

To provide a custom list marker, simply provide the URL to the image within the `url()` syntax.

Figure 9-4a

The CSS in Figure 9-4a is combined with the markup in Figure 9-4b.

```
<!DOCTYPE html PUBLIC "-//W3C//DTD XHTML 1.0 Strict//EN"
                      "http://www.w3.org/TR/xhtml1/DTD/xhtml1-strict.dtd">
<html xmlns='http://www.w3.org/1999/xhtml' xml:lang='en'>
    <head>
        <title>list-style-image</title>
        <link rel='stylesheet' type='text/css' href='096977%20fg0904.css' />
    </head>
    <body>
        <ul>
            <li>List markers can be customized!</li>
            <li>You can use any image you like.</li>
            <li id='other'>
                Size and position, however, cannot be controlled.
            </li>
        </ul>
    </body>
</html>
```

Figure 9-4b

The CSS in Figure 9-4a and the markup in Figure 9-4b result in the output in Figure 9-4c.

Figure 9-4c

As you can see in Figure 9-4c, the arrow.png and arrow2.png icons have replaced the list bullets.

In the next section, I discuss the list-style-position property, which enables you to control the placement of list markers.

The list-style-position Property

You can use the list-style-position property to control the placement of list item markers and whether the list item marker appears on the inside of the list item element or outside of it. Where the list marker is placed is only obvious when the <li> element has a border. The following table outlines the list-style-position property and its possible values.

Property	Value
list-style-position	inside | outside
	Initial value: outside

You can highlight the effects of the list-style-position property. Figure 9-5 demonstrates what the list-style-position property does, beginning with the CSS in Figure 9-5a.

The CSS in Figure 9-5 is combined with the markup in Figure 9-5b.

This results in the output shown in Figure 9-5c.

```
li li {
    background: mistyrose;
}
ul#inside {
    list-style-position: inside;
}
ul#outside {
    list-style-position: outside;
}
```

> The list-style-position property controls whether list markers appear inside of a list's borders or outside of it.

Figure 9-5a

```
<!DOCTYPE html PUBLIC "-//W3C//DTD XHTML 1.0 Strict//EN"
                "http://www.w3.org/TR/xhtml1/DTD/xhtml1-strict.dtd">
<html xmlns='http://www.w3.org/1999/xhtml' xml:lang='en'>
    <head>
        <title>list-style-position</title>
        <link rel='stylesheet' type='text/css' href='096977%20fg0905.css' />
    </head>
    <body>
        <ul>
            <li>The markers for these list items are on the inside.
                <ul id='inside'>
                    <li>One</li>
                    <li>Two</li>
                </ul>
            </li>
            <li>The markers for these list items are on the outside.
                <ul id='outside'>
                    <li>One</li>
                    <li>Two</li>
                </ul>
            </li>
        </ul>
    </body>
</html>
```

Figure 9-5b

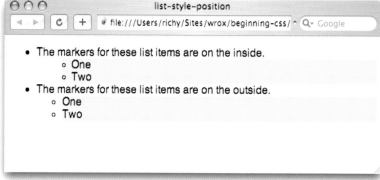

Figure 9-5c

In Figure 9-5, you can see that the `list-style-position` property is used to control whether the list marker appears on the inside of the `<li>` element's borders or on the outside.

The next section wraps up the discussion of CSS list properties with the `list-style` shorthand property. Using this property, you can combine several properties into one.

The list-style shorthand Property

Like the shorthand properties I presented in previous chapters, the `list-style` shorthand property allows multiple properties to be combined into one property. The following table outlines the `list-style` shorthand property and the possible values it allows.

Property	Value
list-style	<'list-style-type'> || <'list-style-position'> || <'list-style-image'>
	Initial value: n/a

The `list-style` property enables you to specify from one to three values, with each value corresponding to the list style properties I have discussed throughout this chapter: `list-style-type`, `list-style-image`, and `list-style-position`. Figure 9-6 is a demonstration of what is possible with the `list-style` property.

The CSS in Figure 9-6a is combined with the markup in Figure 9-6b.

```
li {
    background: mistyrose;
}
li#arrow {
    list-style: square url('arrow.png') outside;
}
li#arrow-inside {
    list-style: url('arrow.png') inside;
}
li#marker-inside {
    list-style: square inside;
}
li#marker-image {
    list-style: square url('arrow.png');
}
li#arrow-only {
    list-style: url('arrow.png');
}
li#marker {
    list-style: circle;
}
li#position {
    list-style: inside;
}
```

The `list-style` property is a shorthand property that combines the `list-style-type`, `list-style-image`, and `list-style-position` properties into just one property.

Figure 9-6a

```
<!DOCTYPE html PUBLIC "-//W3C//DTD XHTML 1.0 Strict//EN"
                      "http://www.w3.org/TR/xhtml1/DTD/xhtml1-strict.dtd">
<html xmlns='http://www.w3.org/1999/xhtml' xml:lang='en'>
    <head>
        <title>list-style</title>
        <link rel='stylesheet' type='text/css' href='096977%20fg0906.css' />
    </head>
    <body>
        <ul>
            <li id='arrow'>
                All three styles can be provided.
            </li>
            <li id='arrow-inside'>
                The image and the position.
            </li>
            <li id='marker-inside'>
                The marker and the position.
            </li>
            <li id='marker-image'>
                The marker and the image.
            </li>
            <li id='arrow-only'>
                Just the image.
            </li>
            <li id='marker'>
                Just the marker.
            </li>
            <li id='position'>
                Just the position.
            </li>
        </ul>
    </body>
</html>
```

Figure 9-6b

The CSS in Figure 9-6a and the markup in Figure 9-6b results in the output in Figure 9-6c.

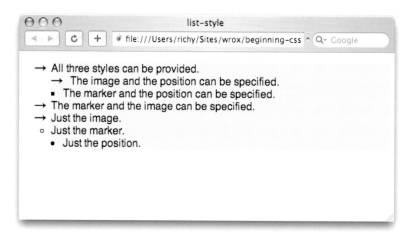

Figure 9-6c

In Figure 9-6, you can see that all three list style properties, list-style-type, list-style-image, and list-style-position can be all consolidated into a single list-style property, which allows any combination of the three styles to be present.

Try It Out   **Applying the list-style Property**

Example 9-2. To try out the list-style property, follow these steps.

1.   Enter the following markup into your text editor:

```
<!DOCTYPE html PUBLIC "-//W3C//DTD XHTML 1.0 Strict//EN"
                      "http://www.w3.org/TR/xhtml1/DTD/xhtml1-strict.dtd">
<html xmlns='http://www.w3.org/1999/xhtml' xml:lang='en'>
    <head>
        <title>list-style</title>
        <link rel='stylesheet' type='text/css' href='Example_9-2.css' />
    </head>
    <body>
        <p>
            The list-style property allows you to combine three separate
            properties, list-style-type, list-style-image, and
            list-style-position, into one single property; any combination of
            those three separate properties can be present.
        </p>
        <ul>
            <li id='marker'>You can specify only a marker.</li>
            <li id='position'>You can specify only the position.</li>
            <li id='image'>You can specify only a marker image.</li>
            <li id='marker-position'>
                The marker and the position can be specified.
            </li>
            <li id='marker-image'>
                The marker and the image can be specified.
            </li>
            <li id='image-position'>
                The image and the position can be specified.
            </li>
            <li id='all-three'>
                Or you can specify all three styles.
            </li>
        </ul>
    </body>
</html>
```

2.   Save the preceding markup as Example_9-2.html.

3.   Enter the following CSS into your text editor:

```
li {
    background: lightyellow;
    border: 1px solid gold;
    padding: 5px;
    margin: 2px;
}
```

```
li#marker {
    list-style: square;
}
li#position {
    list-style: inside;
}
li#image {
    list-style: url('arrow.png');
}
li#marker-position {
    list-style: square inside;
}
li#marker-image {
    list-style: square url('arrow.png');
}
li#image-position {
    list-style: url('arrow.png') inside;
}
li#all-three {
    list-style: square url('arrow.png') inside;
}
```

4. Save the preceding CSS as `Example_9-2.css`. The preceding CSS and markup result in the output in Figure 9-7.

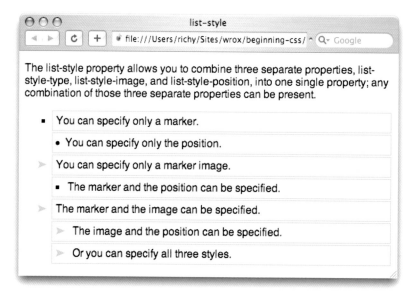

Figure 9-7

How It Works

The list-style property exists as a shortcut for specifying list styles. In fact, its existence pretty much negates the need to ever use the individual list-style-type, list-style-image, and list-style-position properties, since it facilitates all of the functionality of the three individual properties in just one, shorter property.

In Example 9-2, you recapped what's possible with the list-style property by writing out an example that implements every possible combination of the list-style-type, list-style-image, and list-style-position properties.

Summary

The CSS list properties provide complete control over how list elements are presented. To recap, in this chapter you learned the following:

❑   A variety of predefined options are available for the display of list item markers using the list-style-type property.

❑   The list-style-image property may be used to provide a custom image as the list item marker.

❑   The list-style-position property dictates whether the markers appear inside the list item element or outside of it.

❑   The list-style property provides a shortcut syntax where all three list style properties may be referenced at once.

In Chapter 10, I explore the properties that CSS provides for control over the presentation of backgrounds.

Exercises

1.   Name which keywords of the list-style-type property are not supported by IE 6?

2.   What list-style-type keywords are supported by IE 7?

3.   What properties does the list-style property render utterly and completely useless?

4.   Can size and position be controlled with the list-style-image property? If so, how?

Backgrounds

In Chapter 9, you learned how CSS lists are styled. In this chapter, I explore the CSS background properties and see how these provide control over the presentation of the background. In this chapter, I discuss the following:

❑   How to use the `background-color` property to set a background color

❑   How to use the `background-image` property to specify a background image

❑   How to use the `background-repeat` property to control background tiling

❑   How to use the `background-position` property to control how the background is positioned

❑   How to use the `background-attachment` property to control whether the background scrolls with the page or remains fixed in place with respect to the view port

❑   How to use the `background` shorthand property to combine all the separate background properties into a single property

Backgrounds play a large role in CSS design and are often the bread and butter of the overall aesthetic presentation of a web page. This chapter begins the discussion of background properties by exploring the `background-color` property.

The background-color Property

The `background-color` property is used to specify a solid background color. The following table shows the possible values for the `background-color` property.

Property	Value
background-color	<color> | transparent
	Initial value: transparent

The `background-color` property allows any of the color values supported by CSS, such as a color keyword, an RGB value, or a hexadecimal, or short hexadecimal value. It may also be given the `transparent` keyword, which indicates that no color should be used. Consider the example in Figure 10-1.

```
body {
    background-color: yellow;
}
div {
    width: 50px;
    height: 50px;
    border: 1px solid rgb(128, 128, 128);
    margin: 5px;
    float: left;
}
div#one {
    background-color: pink;
}
div#two {
    background-color: rgb(200, 0, 0);
}
div#three {
    background-color: #ffffff;
}
div#four {
    background-color: #000;
}
div#five {
    background-color: transparent;
}
```

The background property can accept any color value, be it a color keyword, RGB value, hexadecimal, or short hexadecimal color value. In addition to these, it supports one additional option, transparent.

Figure 10-1a

The CSS in Figure 10-1a is combined with the markup in Figure 10-1b.

```
<!DOCTYPE html PUBLIC "-//W3C//DTD XHTML 1.0 Strict//EN"
                      "http://www.w3.org/TR/xhtml1/DTD/xhtml1-strict.dtd">
<html xmlns='http://www.w3.org/1999/xhtml' xml:lang='en'>
    <head>
        <title>background-color</title>
        <link rel='stylesheet' type='text/css' href='096977%20fg1001.css' />
    </head>
    <body>
        <div id='one'></div>
        <div id='two'></div>
        <div id='three'></div>
        <div id='four'></div>
        <div id='five'></div>
    </body>
</html>
```

Figure 10-1b

The CSS in Figure 10-1a and the markup in Figure 10-1b result in the output you see in Figure 10-1c.

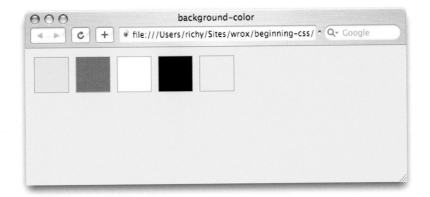

Figure 10-1c

In Figure 10-1, you see a few different methods of specifying a background color via CSS. The `background-color` property takes a color value, which as you saw in Chapter 2, can be a color keyword, like `pink`, an RGB value like `rgb(200, 0, 0)`, a hexadecimal color value such as `#ffffff`, or a short hexadecimal color like `#000`. The `background-color` property also supports one additional color keyword not supported by most other color properties, `transparent`. The `transparent` keyword is also supported by the `border-color` property, but not by IE, as you saw in Chapter 7.

The following exercise applies the `background-color` property to a style sheet.

Try It Out   Applying a Background Color

Example 10-1. To apply the `background-color` property, follow these steps.

1. Enter the following HTML document:

```
<!DOCTYPE html PUBLIC "-//W3C//DTD XHTML 1.0 Strict//EN"
                "http://www.w3.org/TR/xhtml1/DTD/xhtml1-strict.dtd">
<html xmlns='http://www.w3.org/1999/xhtml' xml:lang='en'>
    <head>
        <title>background-color</title>
        <link rel='stylesheet' type='text/css' href='Example_10-1.css' />
    </head>
    <body>
        <p>
            The background-color property accepts a color value.  The
            color value can be a <span id='keyword'>color keyword</span>,
            an <span id='rgb'>RGB value</span>, a
            <span id='hexadecimal'>hexadecimal value</span> or a
            <span id='short-hex'>short hexadecimal</span> value or,
            additionally, the value can be the
            <span id='transparent'>transparent</span> keyword, which
            is also the default value.
        </p>
    </body>
</html>
```

2. Save the preceding as `Example_10-1.html`.

3. Enter the following style sheet:

```css
body {
    background-color: pink;
    line-height: 32px;
}
span {
    border: 1px solid rgb(0, 0, 0);
}
span#keyword {
    background-color: yellow;
}
span#rgb {
    background-color: rgb(200, 0, 0);
    color: #fff;
}
span#hexadecimal {
    background-color: #000000;
    color: #ffffff;
}
span#short-hex {
    background-color: #fff;
    color: #000;
}
span#transparent {
    background-color: transparent;
}
```

4. Save the preceding document as `Example_10-1.css`. The rendered output of Example 10-1 should look like the screenshot you see in Figure 10-2.

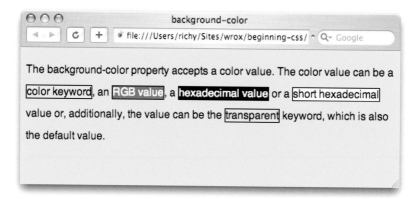

Figure 10-2

How It Works

In Example 10-1, you created an example for the `background-color` property that makes use of all the various color values supported by it. In Example 10-1, you can also see that the `background-color` property is applicable to either inline elements or block-level elements. In fact, the `background-color` property can be applied to just about every HTML element there is, save for the `<col />` element, which is used in the layout of HTML tables.

In the next section I discuss the `background-image` property.

The background-image Property

As you probably guessed, the `background-image` property enables you to provide an image for the background. The following table outlines the possible values available for the `background-image` property.

Property	Value
background-image	<uri> | none
	Initial value: none

Like the `list-style-image` property that I discussed in Chapter 9, the `background-image` property allows you to reference a URL, which is indicated by the `<uri>` notation in the preceding table, or a keyword of none. When you specify a background image, by default the image tiles across the entire area available to it. You can see an example of this in Figure 10-3.

```
body {
    background-image: url('sun.png');
}
```

The image sun.png is specified using the url() syntax

By default, the image is tiled vertically and horizontally.

Figure 10-3a

The CSS in Figure 10-3a is combined with the markup in Figure 10-3b.

```
<!DOCTYPE html PUBLIC "-//W3C//DTD XHTML 1.0 Strict//EN"
                      "http://www.w3.org/TR/xhtml1/DTD/xhtml1-strict.dtd">
<html xmlns='http://www.w3.org/1999/xhtml' xml:lang='en'>
    <head>
        <title>background-image</title>
        <link rel='stylesheet' type='text/css' href='096977%20fg1003.css' />
    </head>
    <body>
    </body>
</html>
```

Figure 10-3b

The CSS in Figure 10-3a and the markup in Figure 10-3b result in the output you see in Figure 10-3c.

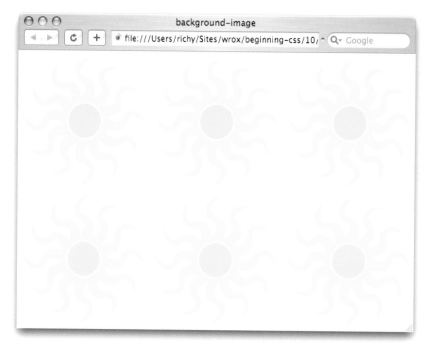

Figure 10-3c

In Figure 10-3, you see the background-image property applied to the <body> element; by default it tiles both horizontally (along the x-axis) and vertically (along the y-axis). You'll see how to control tiling in the next section with the background-repeat property.

In the following Try It Out, you try the background-image property for yourself. The images and source code for this and all the other examples in this book can be found online at www.wrox.com.

Try It Out   **Applying a Background Image**

Example 10-2. In the following steps, you apply background images to a web page.

1. Enter the following (X)HTML document into your text editor:

```
<!DOCTYPE html PUBLIC "-//W3C//DTD XHTML 1.0 Strict//EN"
                "http://www.w3.org/TR/xhtml1/DTD/xhtml1-strict.dtd">
<html xmlns='http://www.w3.org/1999/xhtml' xml:lang='en'>
    <head>
        <title>background-image</title>
        <link rel='stylesheet' type='text/css' href='Example_10-2.css' />
    </head>
    <body>
        <p>
            The background-image property uses the url() syntax to specify
            a background-image.  The image is tiled along the x-axis and
            the y-axis.
        </p>
    </body>
</html>
```

2. Save the preceding document as `Example_10-2.html`.

3. Enter the following CSS in your text editor:

```
body {
    background-image: url('pattern.png');
}
p {
    background-color: #fff;
    padding: 3px;
    margin: 3px;
    border: 1px solid rgb(244, 244, 244);
    width: 200px;
    margin: auto;
}
```

4. Save the preceding document as `Example_10-2.css`. The output of Example 10-2 can be seen in Figure 10-4.

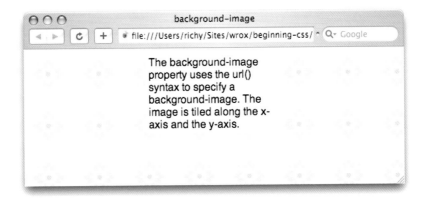

Figure 10-4

How It Works

In Example 10-2, you applied an image to the `<body>` element, `pattern.png`, which was then tiled horizontally along the x-axis, and vertically along the y-axis for the whole of the document as you can see in Figure 10-4, where you have the lovely beginnings of a toilet paper homepage. *Don't squeeze the Safari!*

As you saw with the `background-image` property, the image is tiled by default. In the next section, I describe how to control tiling with the `background-repeat` property.

The background-repeat Property

The `background-repeat` property is used to control how an image is tiled, or if it is tiled at all. The following table shows the possible values for the `background-repeat` property.

Property	Value
background-repeat	repeat | repeat-x | repeat-y | no-repeat
	Initial value: repeat

As you saw in the last section, by default, a background is tiled vertically and horizontally. The `background-repeat` property offers control over this. For instance, you can limit the tiling of a background image to the x-axis by supplying the `repeat-x` keyword value to the `background-repeat` property. Figure 10-5 demonstrates the various keywords of the `background-repeat` property.

```
div {
    width: 200px;
    height: 200px;
    margin: 5px;
    float: left;
    background-image: url('pattern.png');
    background-color: lightyellow;
    border: 1px solid rgb(223, 223, 200);
    padding: 2px;
}
div#repeat {
    background-repeat: repeat;
}
div#repeat-x {
    background-repeat: repeat-x;
}
div#repeat-y {
    background-repeat: repeat-y;
}
div#no-repeat {
    background-repeat: no-repeat;
}
```

As you would expect, the `background-repeat` property provides you with control over how the background is tiled. Tiling can be limited to x-axis or the y-axis with the `repeat-x` and `repeat-y` keywords, respectively, or tiling can be turned off with the `no-repeat` keyword.

Figure 10-5a

The CSS in Figure 10-5a is combined with the markup in Figure 10-5b.

```
<!DOCTYPE html PUBLIC "-//W3C//DTD XHTML 1.0 Strict//EN"
                      "http://www.w3.org/TR/xhtml1/DTD/xhtml1-strict.dtd">
<html xmlns='http://www.w3.org/1999/xhtml' xml:lang='en'>
    <head>
        <title>background-repeat</title>
        <link rel='stylesheet' type='text/css' href='096977%20fg1005.css' />
    </head>
    <body>
        <div id='repeat'></div>
        <div id='repeat-x'></div>
        <div id='repeat-y'></div>
        <div id='no-repeat'></div>
    </body>
</html>
```

Figure 10-5b

The CSS in Figure 10-5a and the markup in Figure 10-5b result in the output you see in Figure 10-5c.

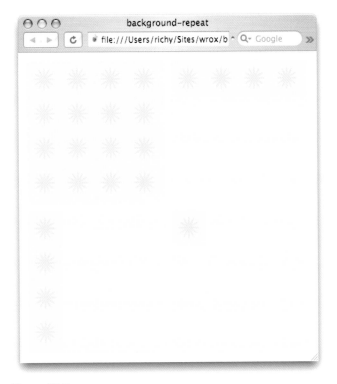

Figure 10-5c

In Figure 10-5, you see a demonstration of each of the keywords of the `background-repeat` property; repeat is the default value, and images are repeated along both the x-axis and y-axis. The `repeat-x` keyword limits tiling to the x-axis, and the `repeat-y` keyword limits tiling to the y-axis. The `no-repeat` keyword turns off tiling altogether.

Try It Out   **Controlling Background Repetition**

Example 10-3. In the following steps you can see the effects of the `background-repeat` property.

1.   Enter the following markup into your text editor:

```
<!DOCTYPE html PUBLIC "-//W3C//DTD XHTML 1.0 Strict//EN"
                    "http://www.w3.org/TR/xhtml1/DTD/xhtml1-strict.dtd">
<html xmlns='http://www.w3.org/1999/xhtml' xml:lang='en'>
    <head>
        <title>background-repeat</title>
        <link rel='stylesheet' type='text/css' href='Example_10-3.css' />
    </head>
    <body>
        <p>
            The background-repeat property controls repetition.  The default
            value is repeat, which causes the background image to be tiled
            along both the x-axis and y-axis.
        </p>
        <div id='repeat'>
        </div>
        <p>
            The repeat-x keyword forces repetition along only the x-axis.
        </p>
        <div id='repeat-x'>
        </div>
        <p>
            The repeat-y keyword forces repetition along only the y-axis.
        </p>
        <div id='repeat-y'>
        </div>
        <p>
            Finally, no-repeat, causes there to be no repetition along
            either axis, and the background image to be included but once.
        </p>
        <div id='no-repeat'>
        </div>
    </body>
</html>
```

2.   Save the preceding markup as `Example_10-3.html`.

3.   Enter the following CSS into your text editor:

```
p {
    background: lightyellow;
    padding: 3px;
}
div {
    height: 81px;
    margin: 10px 0;
```

```
        background-image: url('note.png');
    }
    div#repeat {
        background-repeat: repeat;
    }
    div#repeat-x {
        background-repeat: repeat-x;
    }
    div#repeat-y {
        background-repeat: repeat-y;
    }
    div#no-repeat {
        background-repeat: no-repeat;
    }
```

4. Save the preceding CSS as `Example_10-3.css`. The output from the code in Example 10-3 is shown in Figure 10-6.

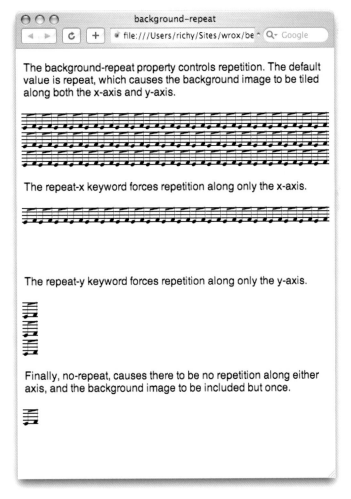

Figure 10-6

How It Works

In Example 10-3, you deploy all possible keyword values of the background-repeat property. You begin with an example of repeat, the default value, which tiles the background image along both the x-axis and y-axis. Then you include the repeat-x keyword, which limits the background image to repetition along the x-axis. The repeat-y keyword, naturally, limits the background image to repetition along the y-axis. Finally, the no-repeat keyword stops repetition all together.

In the next section, I discuss the background-position property.

The background-position Property

The background-position property, as its name implies, allows you to control the placement of the background. The following table shows the possible values for the background-position property.

Property	Value
background-position	[<percentage> | <length>]{1,2} | [[top | center | bottom] | | [left | center | right]]
	Initial value: 0% 0%

At first glance, this property looks a little complicated; in truth, it isn't all that complex. The notation boils down to this: The property allows one or two values that express the position of the background. Square brackets are used to group the possible values. The following is the first subgrouping of values within the first grouping:

```
[<percentage> | <length> ]{1,2}
```

The first grouping indicates that the value may be a percentage or length value. Either one or two values may be provided. The second subgrouping is preceded by a vertical bar, which indicates another possibility for the value:

```
| [ [top | center | bottom] || [left | center | right] ]
```

The second grouping indicates that either one or two keyword values may be provided. If two values are provided, it may be any keyword from the first grouping combined with any of the keywords from the second grouping. In addition, any of the keyword values can be mixed with either a <length> or <percentage> value.

Figure 10-7 demonstrates some possible values for the background-position property.

```
div {
    width: 100px;
    height: 100px;
    border: 1px solid rgb(128, 128, 128);
    margin: 4px;
    float: left;
    background-image: url('cat.png');
    background-repeat: no-repeat;
    font: 12px sans-serif;
}
div#length          {background-position: 10px 10px;     }
div#percentage      {background-position: 10% 10%;        }
div#top-left        {background-position: top left;       }
div#top-center      {background-position: top center;     }
div#top-right       {background-position: top right;      }
div#right-center    {background-position: right center;   }
div#bottom-right    {background-position: bottom right;   }
div#bottom-center   {background-position: bottom center;  }
div#bottom-left     {background-position: bottom left;    }
div#left-center     {background-position: left center;    }
div#center-center   {background-position: center center;  }
```

The background-position property can take a length value, a percentage value, or any combination of the three keywords, top, bottom, center and the three keywords, left, right, center.

Figure 10-7a

The CSS in Figure 10-7a is combined with the markup in Figure 10-7b.

```
<!DOCTYPE html PUBLIC "-//W3C//DTD XHTML 1.0 Strict//EN"
                      "http://www.w3.org/TR/xhtml1/DTD/xhtml1-strict.dtd">
<html xmlns='http://www.w3.org/1999/xhtml' xml:lang='en'>
    <head>
        <title>background-position</title>
        <link rel='stylesheet' type='text/css' href='096977%20fg1007.css' />
    </head>
    <body>
        <div id='length'>10px, 10px</div>
        <div id='percentage'>10%, 10%</div>
        <div id='top-left'>top, left</div>
        <div id='top-center'>top, center</div>
        <div id='top-right'>top, right</div>
        <div id='right-center'>right, center</div>
        <div id='bottom-right'>bottom, right</div>
        <div id='bottom-center'>bottom, center</div>
        <div id='bottom-left'>bottom, left</div>
        <div id='left-center'>left, center</div>
        <div id='center-center'>center, center</div>
    </body>
</html>
```

Figure 10-7b

The CSS in Figure 10-7a and the markup in Figure 10-7b result in the output you see in Figure 10-7c.

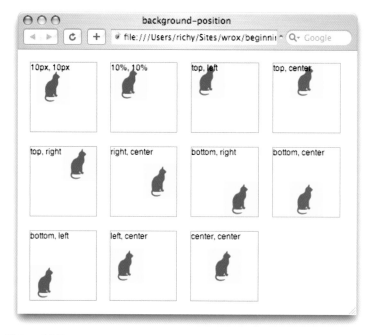

Figure 10-7c

In Figure 10-7, you see what the `background-position` property with two values looks like. This figure shows what happens when both values are of the same ilk, that is to say: both length values, or both percentage values, or both keyword values.

Mixing Different Kinds of Position Values

What happens when you mix length with percentage, or percentage with a keyword? This question is answered by the example in Figure 10-8.

```
div {
    width: 100px;
    height: 100px;
    border: 1px solid rgb(128, 128, 128);
    margin: 4px;
    float: left;
    background-image: url('tree.png');
    background-repeat: no-repeat;
    font: 12px sans-serif;
}
div#keyword-length      {background-position: top 10px;  }
div#length-keyword      {background-position: 10px top;  }
div#keyword-percentage  {background-position: center 50%;}
div#percentage-keyword  {background-position: 50% center;}
div#percentage-length   {background-position: 50% 10px;  }
div#length-percentage   {background-position: 10px 50%;  }
```

You can mix and match any type of measurement.

Figure 10-8a

352

> Per the CSS 2.1 specification, when keywords are mixed with nonkeyword values,
> the first value must be left or right, if left or right is used, and the second value must
> be top or bottom, if top or bottom is used. Some technically invalid declarations
> appear in Figure 10-8a for proof-of-concept.

The CSS in Figure 10-8a is combined with the markup in Figure 10-8b.

```
<!DOCTYPE html PUBLIC "-//W3C//DTD XHTML 1.0 Strict//EN"
                      "http://www.w3.org/TR/xhtml1/DTD/xhtml1-strict.dtd">
<html xmlns='http://www.w3.org/1999/xhtml' xml:lang='en'>
    <head>
        <title>background-position</title>
        <link rel='stylesheet' type='text/css' href='096977%20fg1008.css' />
    </head>
    <body>
        <div id='keyword-length'>top, 10px</div>
        <div id='length-keyword'>10px, top</div>
        <div id='keyword-percentage'>center, 50%</div>
        <div id='percentage-keyword'>50%, center</div>
        <div id='percentage-length'>50%, 10px</div>
        <div id='length-percentage'>10px, 50%</div>
    </body>
</html>
```

Figure 10-8b

The CSS and markup in Figure 10-8a and Figure 10-8b are combined to get the rendered output you see in Figure 10-8c.

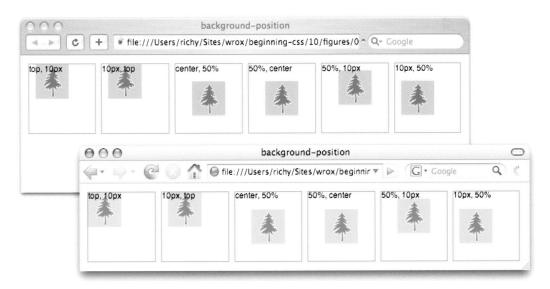

Figure 10-8c

353

In Figure 10-8, you see the combination of each different type of value for the background-position property. You'll note the difference in the rendering of the first box between Safari and Firefox. Firefox rejects the background position of the first box entirely because the top keyword appears first, rather than second as required by the CSS 2.1 specification. Safari tolerates the ordering being different.

Tiling and Position

What happens when the background is tiled and a position is set? You see an example of positioning a tiled background with a length measurement in Figure 10-9.

```
div {
    width: 100px;
    height: 100px;
    border: 1px solid rgb(128, 128, 128);
    margin: 4px;
    float: left;
    background-image: url('star.png');
}
div#repeat {
    background-position: 10px 10px;
}
div#repeat-single {
    background-position: 10px;
}
div#repeat-x-control {
    background-repeat: repeat-x;
}
div#repeat-x {
    background-position: 10px 10px;
    background-repeat: repeat-x;
}
div#repeat-x-single {
    background-position: 10px;
    background-repeat: repeat-x;
}
div#repeat-y-control {
    background-repeat: repeat-y;
}
div#repeat-y {
    background-position: 10px 10px;
    background-repeat: repeat-y;
}
div#repeat-y-single {
    background-position: 10px;
    background-repeat: repeat-y;
}
br {
    clear: both;
}
```

When both axes are tiled, the position specified adjusts when tiling of the image begins.

When just one axis is tiled, the position specified adjusts the offset of the tiled axis. The top position of the x-axis, for example, adjusts where the x-axis is drawn, but the left position adjusts where the tiling of the image begins.

Figure 10-9a

The CSS in Figure 10-9a is combined with the markup in Figure 10-9b.

```
<!DOCTYPE html PUBLIC "-//W3C//DTD XHTML 1.0 Strict//EN"
                      "http://www.w3.org/TR/xhtml1/DTD/xhtml1-strict.dtd">
<html xmlns='http://www.w3.org/1999/xhtml' xml:lang='en'>
    <head>
        <title>background-position</title>
        <link rel='stylesheet' type='text/css' href='096977%20fg1009.css' />
    </head>
    <body>
        <div id='repeat-control'></div>
        <div id='repeat'></div>
        <div id='repeat-single'></div>
        <br />
        <div id='repeat-x-control'></div>
        <div id='repeat-x'></div>
        <div id='repeat-x-single'></div>
        <br />
        <div id='repeat-y-control'></div>
        <div id='repeat-y'></div>
        <div id='repeat-y-single'></div>
    </body>
</html>
```

Figure 10-9b

The CSS in Figure 10-9a and the markup in Figure 10-9b produce the output you see in Figure 10-9c.

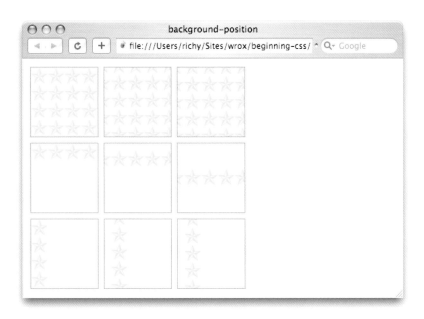

Figure 10-9c

In Figure 10-9, you see how specifying a background position affects the tiling of a background image. When both axes are tiled, the position that you specify determines where the image tiling begins.

Specifying `background-position: 10px 10px;` causes the tiling to begin with the first ten pixels of the image clipped. When the same declaration is applied to an element with `background-repeat: repeat-x;`, you can see that the tiling of the image also begins with the first ten pixels of the image clipped for the value of the left position. The value of the top position causes the axis of tiled images to be offset ten pixels from the top border.

Just for the sake of completeness, what happens when keywords are used instead of lengths to position a tiled image? The answer is found in Figure 10-10.

```
div {
    width: 100px;
    height: 100px;
    border: 1px solid rgb(223, 223, 200);
    margin: 4px;
    float: left;
    background-image: url('star.png');
}
div#repeat {
    background-position: center center;
}
div#repeat-single {
    background-position: center;
}
div#repeat-x-control {
    background-repeat: repeat-x;
}
div#repeat-x {
    background-position: center center;
    background-repeat: repeat-x;
}
div#repeat-x-single {
    background-position: center;
    background-repeat: repeat-x;
}
div#repeat-y-control {
    background-repeat: repeat-y;
}
div#repeat-y {
    background-position: center center;
    background-repeat: repeat-y;
}
div#repeat-y-single {
    background-position: center;
    background-repeat: repeat-y;
}
br {
    clear: both;
}
```

When both axes are tiled, the position specified adjusts when tiling of the image begins.

When just one axis is tiled, the position specified adjusts the offset of the tiled axis. The top position of the x-axis, for example, adjusts where the x-axis is drawn, but the left position adjusts where the tiling of the image begins

Figure 10-10a

The CSS in Figure 10-10a is combined with the markup in Figure 10-10b.

```
<!DOCTYPE html PUBLIC "-//W3C//DTD XHTML 1.0 Strict//EN"
                "http://www.w3.org/TR/xhtml1/DTD/xhtml1-strict.dtd">
<html xmlns='http://www.w3.org/1999/xhtml' xml:lang='en'>
    <head>
        <title>background-position</title>
        <link rel='stylesheet' type='text/css' href='096977%20fg1010.css' />
    </head>
    <body>
        <div id='repeat-control'></div>
        <div id='repeat'></div>
        <div id='repeat-single'></div>
        <br />
        <div id='repeat-x-control'></div>
        <div id='repeat-x'></div>
        <div id='repeat-x-single'></div>
        <br />
        <div id='repeat-y-control'></div>
        <div id='repeat-y'></div>
        <div id='repeat-y-single'></div>
    </body>
</html>
```

Figure 10-10b

The result of the CSS in Figure 10-10a and the markup in Figure 10-10b is seen in Figure 10-10c.

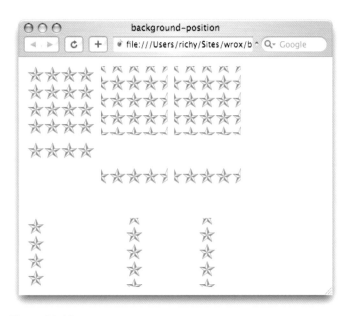

Figure 10-10c

In Figure 10-10 you used the center keyword instead of a length measurement. When the tiling is along the x-axis, one center keyword centers the tiled images along the y-axis, and the other center keyword causes the tiling of each image to begin with the center of the image, rather than the left border of the image. This result is the same in every browser.

Try It Out   **Controlling the Background's Position**

Example 10-4. The following steps recap how you can use the `background-position` property in a web page.

1.   Enter the following HTML document into your text editor:

```
<!DOCTYPE html PUBLIC "-//W3C//DTD XHTML 1.0 Strict//EN"
                      "http://www.w3.org/TR/xhtml1/DTD/xhtml1-strict.dtd">
<html xmlns='http://www.w3.org/1999/xhtml' xml:lang='en'>
    <head>
        <title>background-position</title>
        <link rel='stylesheet' type='text/css' href='Example_10-4.css' />
    </head>
    <body>
        <p>
            The background-position property allows you to specify a
            position using one of three primary methods, by length,
            by percentage, or by keyword.
        </p>
        <div id='length'>
        </div>
        <div id='percentage'>
        </div>
        <div id='keyword'>
        </div>
        <p>
            You can mix and match different types of positions.
        </p>
        <div id='length-percentage'>
        </div>
        <div id='percentage-keyword'>
        </div>
        <div id='length-keyword'>
        </div>
        <p>
            When positioning a tiled image, the position can adjust where
            tiling of the image begins with respect to the image itself, or
            the position of the axis of tiled images.
        </p>
        <div id='tiled'>
        </div>
        <div id='x-tiled'>
        </div>
        <div id='y-tiled'>
        </div>
    </body>
</html>
```

2.   Save the HTML document as `Example_10-4.html`.

3. Enter the following CSS in your text editor:

```
body {
    font: 12px sans-serif;
}-
p {
    background: yellow;
    padding: 3px;
    clear: left;
}
div {
    height: 81px;
    width: 81px;
    margin: 20px;
    background-image: url('fish.png');
    background-repeat: no-repeat;
    float: left;
    border: 1px solid rgb(128, 128, 128);
}
div#length {
    background-position: 10px 10px;
}
div#percentage {
    background-position: 60% 60%;
}
div#keyword {
    background-position: center center;
}
div#length-percentage {
    background-position: 80% 10px;
}
div#percentage-keyword {
    background-position: center 100%;
}
div#length-keyword {
    background-position: center 10px;
}
div#tiled {
    background-repeat: repeat;
    background-position: center center;
}
div#x-tiled {
    background-repeat: repeat-x;
    background-position: center center;
}
div#y-tiled {
    background-repeat: repeat-y;
    background-position: center center;
}
```

4. Save the CSS document as `Example_10-4.css`. The source code in Example 10-4 renders something like what you see in Figure 10-11.

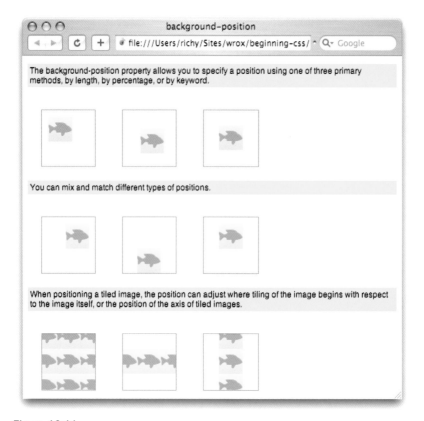

Figure 10-11

How It Works

In Example 10-4, you recapped the different ways that a background image can be positioned with the background-position property. You can choose one of three different methods of positioning, keyword, length, or percentage, and any one of those will get the job done. You can also mix different methods, such as percentage with a keyword, or length with a keyword, and the browser can handle that. You can also use the background-position property to adjust the position of a tiled background image, be it the axis of tiled images, or where tiling of the image begins.

In the next section, I describe how to control the background-position when the page is scrolled with the background-attachment property.

The background-attachment Property

You can use the background-attachment property to control whether a background image scrolls with the content of a web page (when scroll bars are activated because that content is larger than the browser window). The following table outlines the possible values for the background-attachment property.

Property	Value
background-attachment	scroll | fixed
	Initial value: scroll

IE 6 supports the `fixed` *keyword only if applied to the* `<body>` *element; IE 7, Firefox, Opera, and Safari support the* `fixed` *keyword as applied to any element.*

The `background-attachment` property provides one very cool effect. By default, the background image scrolls with the content of the web page; this is the behavior of the `background-attachment: scroll;` declaration. If the `fixed` keyword is provided and the browser in question supports it, the background image remains fixed in place while the page scrolls. Figure 10-12 shows an example of this scenario.

```
body, p {
    background-color: #fff;
    background-image: url('palms.png');
    background-position: right bottom;
    background-repeat: no-repeat;
    background-attachment: fixed;
}
p {
    border: 1px solid rgb(200, 200, 200);
    background-image: url('palms2.png');
    margin: 10px 10px 10px auto;
    width: 200px;
    padding: 20px;
}
```

Fixed background images always have the same point of reference for positioning, the document `<body>`, no matter what element the background is applied to. This makes for cool effects that give the illusion of transparency.

The two images here are identical in size, and content, only the coloring of `palms2.jpg` has been adjusted.

Figure 10-12a

The CSS in Figure 10-12a is combined with the markup in Figure 10-12b.

The CSS in Figure 10-12a and the markup in Figure 10-12b result in the output you see in Figure 10-12c. Keep in mind that two separate images come together to create the illusion of transparency.

```
<!DOCTYPE html PUBLIC "-//W3C//DTD XHTML 1.0 Strict//EN"
                      "http://www.w3.org/TR/xhtml1/DTD/xhtml1-strict.dtd">
<html xmlns='http://www.w3.org/1999/xhtml' xml:lang='en'>
    <head>
        <title>background-attachment</title>
        <link rel='stylesheet' type='text/css' href='096977%20fg1012.css' />
    </head>
    <body>
        <p>
            Lorem ipsum dolor sit amet, consectetuer adipiscing elit. Sed
            vitae augue. Vivamus viverra libero in pede. Nam nisl ipsum,
            eleifend aliquet, laoreet vel, aliquet non, urna. Duis eget velit
            sed metus tincidunt viverra. Nulla imperdiet ligula nec velit.
            Vivamus augue pede, pharetra ac, dictum quis, aliquet at, ante.
            Aliquam vehicula arcu a ligula.  Mauris accumsan nunc at tortor.
            Aenean vitae eros. Maecenas rutrum risus id metus. Duis ac leo.
            Phasellus sit amet diam. Sed semper, purus ut commodo interdum,
            mi tortor ullamcorper turpis, quis porta pede ante vitae erat.
            Integer imperdiet tempus purus. Aliquam erat volutpat.  Aliquam
            eget magna. Nunc rhoncus mi vitae velit. Proin tempus tellus
            non orci. Nulla nec tortor.
        </p>
    </body>
</html>
```

Figure 10-12b

Figure 10-12c

In Figure 10-12, you see one of the primary effects of the background-attachment property. When the fixed keyword is provided, the background image's position is set offset relative to the <body> element, no matter what element the background image is applied to. The other effect the fixed keyword creates is the background image stays fixed in place as the document content is scrolled. If you make the window smaller and adjust the position of the scroll bar, you can see the effect shown in Figure 10-13.

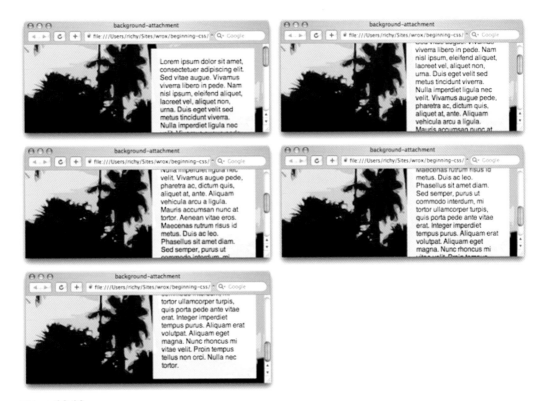

Figure 10-13

In Figure 10-13, you can see that as the page is scrolled both background images remain fixed in place, providing the illusion of transparency — scrolling the page makes it as though I've just applied some kind of filter or transparency to the <p> element. I've done neither. Because the images are positioned in exactly the same spot, you can make small adjustments to one of the images to provide the illusion of transparency. In IE 6, only the image applied to the <body> element remains fixed in place. The background image applied to the <p> element does not, since IE 6 does not support fixed background images on any element other than the <body> element.

The following Try It Out recaps the `background-attachment` property.

Fixing the Background in Place

Example 10-5. To recap the `background-attachment` property, follow these steps.

1. Enter the following HTML document in your text editor:

```
<!DOCTYPE html PUBLIC "-//W3C//DTD XHTML 1.0 Strict//EN"
                "http://www.w3.org/TR/xhtml1/DTD/xhtml1-strict.dtd">
<html xmlns='http://www.w3.org/1999/xhtml' xml:lang='en'>
    <head>
        <title>background-attachment</title>
        <link rel='stylesheet' type='text/css' href='Example_10-5.css' />
    </head>
    <body>
        <p>
            The background-attachment property provides two effects.
            First it positions the background image relative to the
            &lt;body&gt; element. Second it forces the background
            image to remain fixed in place when the document is
            scrolled.
        </p>
    </body>
</html>
```

2. Save the preceding HTML document as `Example_10-5.html`.

3. Enter the following CSS document in your text editor:

```
body, p {
    background-color: #fff;
    background-attachment: fixed;
    background-image: url('palms.jpg');
    background-position: right bottom;
    background-repeat: no-repeat;
}
p {
    width: 400px;
    margin: 20px auto;
    padding: 20px;
    border: 1px solid rgb(200, 200, 200);
    background-image: url('palms2.jpg');
    height: 400px;
}
```

4. Save the preceding CSS document as `Example_10-5.css`. The code from Example 10-5 should look something like the screenshot you see in Figure 10-14.

The background-attachment property provides two effects. First it positions the background image relative to the <body> element. Second it forces the background image to remain fixed in place when the document is scrolled.

Figure 10-14

How It Works

In Example 10-5, you recapped the background-attachment property with another brief demonstration of what it does. Using the background-attachment property, you can position images relative to the <body> element, even if they are applied to <p> elements or <div> elements or <td> elements. When the background-attachment: fixed; declaration is provided, the background image is always positioned relative to the <body> element, regardless of what element the background image is applied to. The background image also remains fixed in place as the content within the document is scrolled. One use for this effect is to provide effects that mimic and give the illusion of transparency.

In the next section, I describe how to simplify the plethora of separate background properties into just one property using the background shorthand property.

The background shorthand Property

Like the shorthand properties I introduced in previous chapters, the background property combines each of the individual background properties into a single property. The following table outlines the values allowed by the background property.

Property	Value
background	<'background-color'> || <'background-image'> || <'background-repeat'> || <'background-attachment'> || <'background-position'> Initial value: n/a

With the `background` property, you can specify anywhere from one to five separate background properties. An example of how the background property combines different background properties appears in Figure 10-15.

```
body {
    background-color: white;
    background-image: url('palms.png');
    background-repeat: no-repeat;
    background-attachment: fixed;
    background-position: bottom center;
}
```

The background shorthand property combines these five separate properties into a single property. All five properties can be present, just one, or any combination.

```
body {
    background: white url('palms.png') no-repeat fixed bottom center;
}
```
Figure 10-15a

The CSS in Figure 10-15a is combined with the markup in Figure 10-15b.

```
<!DOCTYPE html PUBLIC "-//W3C//DTD XHTML 1.0 Strict//EN"
                "http://www.w3.org/TR/xhtml1/DTD/xhtml1-strict.dtd">
<html xmlns='http://www.w3.org/1999/xhtml' xml:lang='en'>
    <head>
        <title>background</title>
        <link rel='stylesheet' type='text/css' href='096977%20fg10155.css' />
    </head>
    <body>
    </body>
</html>
```
Figure 10-15b

The source code in Figures 10-15a and 10-15b result in the output you see in Figure 10-15c

In Figure 10-15, you see how to use the `background` shorthand property to combine the five separate background properties, `background-color`, `background-image`, `background-repeat`, `background-attachment`, and `background-position` into just one single `background` property. Using the `background` property, you can include all five properties, or any combination of the other properties, in any order.

Figure 10-15c

The following Try It Out recaps the `background` shorthand property.

Try It Out   Applying the Background Shorthand Property

Example 10-6. To see how individual background properties can be rewritten using the `background` property, follow these steps.

1.   Enter the following HTML document into your text editor:

```
<!DOCTYPE html PUBLIC "-//W3C//DTD XHTML 1.0 Strict//EN"
                      "http://www.w3.org/TR/xhtml1/DTD/xhtml1-strict.dtd">
<html xmlns='http://www.w3.org/1999/xhtml' xml:lang='en'>
    <head>
        <title>background</title>
        <link rel='stylesheet' type='text/css' href='Example_10-6.css' />
    </head>
    <body>
        <p>
            The background shorthand property provides for specifying all
            five separate background properties in one single property.
        </p>
```

```
        <p>
            You can specify all five background properties.
        </p>
        <div id='background'>
        </div>
        <p>
            You can also specify just one property or any combination of
            each of the five separate background properties.
        </p>
        <div id='background-color'>
        </div>
        <div id='background-image-position'>
        </div>
        <div id='background-image-repeat'>
        </div>
        <div id='background-image-repeat-attachment'>
        </div>
    </body>
</html>
```

2. Save the preceding document as `Example_10-6.html`.

3. Enter the following CSS document in your text editor:

```
p {
    clear: left;
}
div {
    border: 1px solid yellow;
    width: 100px;
    height: 100px;
    margin: 10px;
    float: left;
}
div#background {
    background: white url('pattern.png') no-repeat scroll center center;
}
div#background-color {
    background: yellow;
}
div#background-image-position {
    background: white url('pattern.png') center center;
}
div#background-image-repeat {
    background: url('pattern.png') repeat-x;
}
div#background-image-repeat-attachment {
    background: url('pattern.png') repeat-y scroll;
}
```

4. Save the preceding document as `Example_10-6.css`. The result of the source code in Example 10-6 should look something like the screenshot that you see in Figure 10-16.

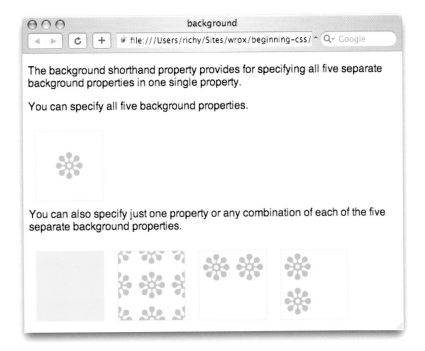

Figure 10-16

How It Works

In Example 10-6, you recapped how the `background` property is used to simplify setting element backgrounds via its ability to specify one to five of the separate background properties: `background-color`, `background-image`, `background-repeat`, `background-attachment`, and `background-position`. All five properties can be specified, or just one property can be specified, or any combination of the five. Typically, when only one property is specified, it's the `background-color` or the `background-image`, and when more than one property is specified, typically a `background-image` is specified, since you can't modify the position, the tiling or whether or not the image scrolls without, you guessed it, a background image.

Summary

The CSS background properties provide a fine-grained control over the presentation of backgrounds in a web document, which allows interesting aesthetic possibilities. To recap, in this chapter you learned the following:

❑   You can specify a solid background color by using the `background-color` property.

❑   You can use the `background-image` property to provide a background image that tiles all the space available to it by default.

❑ You can use the `background-repeat` property to control the tiling of background images. This can be limited to the x-axis or the y-axis, or you can use the `no-repeat` keyword to prevent the background image from tiling.

❑ You can use the `background-position` property to position the background image.

❑ You can use the `background-attachment` property to control whether a background image scrolls with a page or remains fixed in place. If the image is fixed in place, it becomes positioned relative to the browser window itself instead of the element it is applied to.

❑ You can use the `background` shorthand property to put the control of all five properties into one property.

Chapter 11 discusses the properties that CSS provides to position elements. In this, the most important chapter of the book, you'll learn how to layer content, and how to apply layering in practical ways, for example, how to do the much-coveted multicolumn layout.

Exercises

1. What are two properties that you can use to specify a background color in a web page?

2. What are different color values that you can use for a background color?

3. What declaration causes a background image to be tiled only along the x-axis?

4. What keyword value can you use to turn off tiling of a background image?

5. What are the three methods of positioning a background image?

6. If you wanted to offset an image ten pixels from the left and ten pixels from the top, what declaration would you use?

7. Can the different methods of positioning a background image be mixed with one another?

8. If you wanted a background image to scroll with the document, what declaration would you use?

9. When a background image is said to be "fixed," what (X)HTML element does the background image position relative to?

10. What is the only element that IE 6 supports "fixed" backgrounds on?

11. Write a declaration that contains all five background properties in one.

Positioning

This chapter examines the various properties that CSS provides to position elements in a document. *Positioning* can be thought of as layering, in that the various elements of a page can be layered on top of others and given specific places to appear in the browser's window. In this chapter I discuss:

❑ The `position` property and the four types of positioning that CSS has to offer: `static`, `relative`, `absolute`, and `fixed`

❑ The offset properties `top`, `right`, `bottom`, and `left`, and how these are used to deliver an element to a specific position in a web document

❑ The `z-index` property and how this property is used to layer the elements of a document

❑ Some practical applications of positioning, such as multicolumn layouts and vertically centering a positioned element

Positioning makes CSS a very powerful presentational language, and further enhances its flexibility. Like floating elements, positioning offers some unique characteristics that allow behavior you might not always expect. This chapter begins the discussion of positioning with none other than the `position` property.

Introduction to Positioning

The `position` property is used to give elements different types of positioning. Positioning, gives you the ability to, with precision, dictate where in a document you want an element to appear. You can choose whether an element appears relative to another element, or relative to the browser window. You can layer elements one on top of another.

The following table outlines the `position` property and its possible values, and the four offset properties, `top`, `right`, `bottom`, and `left`, and their possible values.

Property	Value
position	static | relative | absolute | fixed Initial value: static
top	\<length> | \<percentage> | auto Initial value: auto
right	\<length> | \<percentage> | auto Initial value: auto
bottom	\<length> | \<percentage> | auto Initial value: auto
left	\<length> | \<percentage> | auto Initial value: auto

Positioning gives you a fantastic amount of control and increases the possibilities for the layout of a document, since you can specifically say where you want an element to appear, in addition to layering elements one on top of another.

In the next section, I begin the discussion of positioning with absolute positioning.

Absolute Positioning

Absolute positioning allows you to render an element to a particular place in a document. The only way to grasp this concept is to see a demonstration of it in action. Figure 11-1 shows a document that we'll apply absolute positioning to.

The CSS in Figure 11-1a is combined with the markup in Figure 11-1b.

```
body {
    background: lightyellow;
    font: 12px sans-serif;
}
div {
    width: 100px;
    height: 100px;
    border: 1px solid rgb(200, 200, 200);
}
div#one {
    background: pink;
}
div#two {
    background: lightblue;
}
div#three {
    background: yellowgreen;
}
div#four {
    background: orange;
}
```

By default, elements are positioned statically, which means they just appear one after another in the document.

The majority of examples that you've seen so far are examples of static positioning.

Figure 11-1a

```
<!DOCTYPE html PUBLIC "-//W3C//DTD XHTML 1.0 Strict//EN"
                "http://www.w3.org/TR/xhtml1/DTD/xhtml1-strict.dtd">
<html xmlns='http://www.w3.org/1999/xhtml' xml:lang='en'>
    <head>
        <title>positioning</title>
        <link rel='stylesheet' type='text/css' href='096977%20fg1101.css' />
    </head>
    <body>
        <p>
            Lorem ipsum dolor sit amet, consectetuer adipiscing elit. Sed
            sit amet sem quis orci malesuada facilisis. Nulla dictum
            malesuada magna. Quisque ac est et nibh porta nonummy. Cras pede
            tortor, lacinia et, eleifend quis, consequat vel, odio. Proin
            urna mi, facilisis et, consequat eu, scelerisque vel, lacus. Nunc
            turpis. Vestibulum sed felis.
        </p>
        <div id='one'></div>
        <div id='two'></div>
        <div id='three'></div>
        <div id='four'></div>
    </body>
</html>
```

Figure 11-1b

The CSS in Figure 11-1a and the markup in Figure 11-1b results in the output that you see in Figure 11-1c.

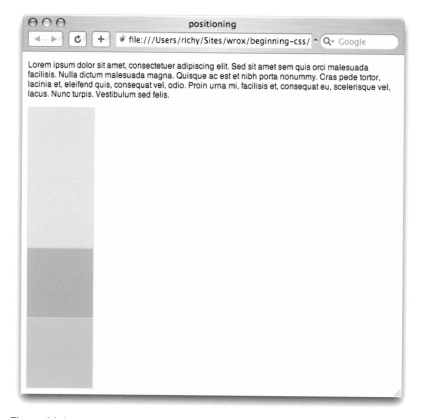

Figure 11-1c

In Figure 11-1, you see what the document looks like before any kind of positioning is applied. Each <div> element in the example appears one after another from top to bottom. This is static positioning. In Figure 11-2, you can see how absolute positioning works.

```
body {
    background: lightyellow;
    font: 12px sans-serif;
}
div {
    width: 100px;
    height: 100px;
    border: 1px solid rgb(200, 200, 200);
    /* Moz proprietary opacity property */
    -moz-opacity: 0.7;
    /* Microsoft proprietary filter property (for opacity) */
    filter: progid:DXImageTransform.Microsoft.Alpha(opacity=70);
    /* CSS 3 opacity property */
    opacity: 0.7;
}
div#one {
    background: pink;
    position: absolute;
    top: 0;
    left: 0;
}
div#two {
    background: lightblue;
    position: absolute;
    top: 0;
    right: 0;
}
div#three {
    background: yellowgreen;
    position: absolute;
    bottom: 0;
    left: 0;
}
div#four {
    background: orange;
    position: absolute;
    bottom: 0;
    right: 0;
}
```

Absolute positioning is used to position an element in a specific place in a document. The offset keywords accept a length value, or a percentage value, and are used to fine-tune the element's position.

Figure 11-2a

The CSS in Figure 11-2a is combined with the markup in Figure 11-2b to get the output that you see in Figure 11-2c.

```
<!DOCTYPE html PUBLIC "-//W3C//DTD XHTML 1.0 Strict//EN"
                      "http://www.w3.org/TR/xhtml1/DTD/xhtml1-strict.dtd">
<html xmlns='http://www.w3.org/1999/xhtml' xml:lang='en'>
    <head>
        <title>positioning</title>
        <link rel='stylesheet' type='text/css' href='096977%20fg1101.css' />
    </head>
    <body>
      __<p>
            Lorem ipsum dolor sit amet, consectetuer adipiscing elit. Sed
            sit amet sem quis orci malesuada facilisis. Nulla dictum
            malesuada magna. Quisque ac est et nibh porta nonummy. Cras pede
            tortor, lacinia et, eleifend quis, consequat vel, odio. Proin
            urna mi, facilisis et, consequat eu, scelerisque vel, lacus. Nunc
            turpis. Vestibulum sed felis.
        </p>
        <div id='one'></div>
        <div id='two'></div>
        <div id='three'></div>
        <div id='four'></div>
    </body>
</html>
```

Figure 11-2b

Figure 11-2c

In Figure 11-2c, you can see that the four `<div>` elements are positioned in specific places in the document. The declaration `position: absolute;` causes the element to leave the normal flow of the document and become layered along an invisible z-axis. The position of each element is controlled by the four offset keywords, `top`, `right`, `bottom`, and `left`.

You also see in Figure 11-2a that I've used a few properties that you haven't seen before. These are the opacity, `-moz-opacity`, and filter properties. These are all used for the same thing: to make the positioned `<div>` elements semitransparent so that you can see what's underneath each `<div>`. I use three properties for the best cross-browser compatibility. Firefox prior to Firefox 1.5, Netscape, and the Mozilla SeaMonkey browser suite all used the `-moz-opacity` property for transparency. Firefox 1.5 and later, Safari, and Opera 9 all support the official CSS 3 `opacity` property. Both `-moz-opacity` and the CSS 3 `opacity` property take a floating-point value between 0 and 1, with 0 being fully transparent and 1 being fully opaque. For example, the value 0.5 would be half transparent and half opaque. The `filter` property, if you hadn't already guessed by its value, is proprietary to Microsoft and works in IE 5.5 and later. Although its syntax is quite a bit more verbose, it provides an identical effect to the CSS 3 `opacity` property supported by other browsers. Instead of a floating-point value between 0 and 1, it takes a percentage value between 0 and 100, where 100 is fully opaque, and 0 is fully transparent.

You'll notice in the simple example that I provide that the boxes are positioned relative to the viewport. This is made clearer by adding more copy to the document to make it scroll. In Figure 11-3a, you can see that each `<div>` element is positioned relative to the browser's viewport, that is, the initial visible area of the document.

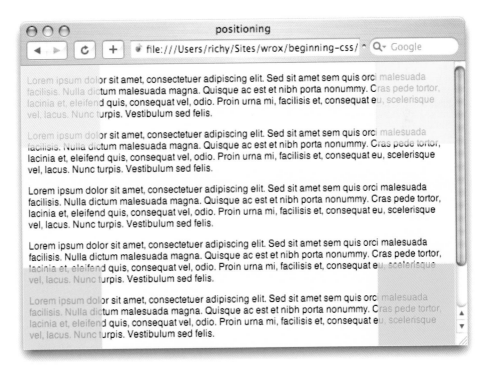

Figure 11-3a

In Figure 11-3b, you can see that when you scroll down, the boxes stay where they were initially positioned when the page was loaded up.

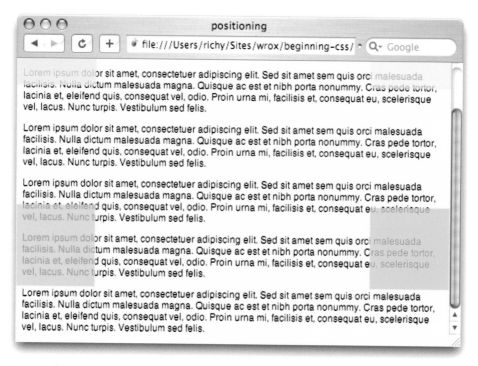

Figure 11-3b

You can modify what element is used as the point of reference for absolutely positioned elements. The rules are pretty simple: If an absolutely positioned element is contained within another element that has a position other than static, then that element is used as the point of reference for positioned elements. One common way to change the point of reference for positioned elements is to give the containing element a "relative" position, and that is the topic of the next section.

Try It Out   A Recap of Absolute Positioning

Example 11-1. To review the concepts of absolute positioning that you learned in this section, follow these steps.

1.   Enter the following XHTML document in your text editor:

```
<!DOCTYPE html PUBLIC "-//W3C//DTD XHTML 1.0 Strict//EN"
                "http://www.w3.org/TR/xhtml1/DTD/xhtml1-strict.dtd">
<html xmlns='http://www.w3.org/1999/xhtml' xml:lang='en'>
    <head>
        <title>Absolute Positioning</title>
        <link rel='stylesheet' type='text/css' href='Example_11-1.css' />
    </head>
    <body>
```

```
        <p>
            Elements that are absolutely positioned are positioned, by default,
            relative to the browser's viewport.  This is done using the
            position property.  The position property is used in conjunction
            with four offset properties, which are used to control where on
            the screen an absolutely positioned element is placed.
        </p>
        <div id='top-left'>
            Top, Left
        </div>
        <div id='top-right'>
            Top, Right
        </div>
        <div id='bottom-left'>
            Bottom, Left
        </div>
        <div id='bottom-right'>
            Bottom, Right
        </div>
    </body>
</html>
```

2. Save the preceding document as `Example_11-1.html`.

3. Enter the following CSS in your text editor:

```
body {
    background: yellowgreen;
}
p {
    margin: 10px 110px;
}
div {
    position: absolute;
    background: yellow;
    padding: 5px;
    width: 100px;
    height: 100px;
}
div#top-left {
    top: 0;
    left: 0;
    border-right: 1px solid black;
    border-bottom: 1px solid black;
}
div#top-right {
    top: 0;
    right: 0;
    border-left: 1px solid black;
    border-bottom: 1px solid black;
}
div#bottom-left {
    bottom: 0;
    left: 0;
```

```
        border-right: 1px solid black;
        border-top: 1px solid black;
    }
div#bottom-right {
        bottom: 0;
        right: 0;
        border-left: 1px solid black;
        border-top: 1px solid black;
    }
```

4. Save the preceding document as `Example_11-1.css`. The preceding source results in the output in Figure 11-4.

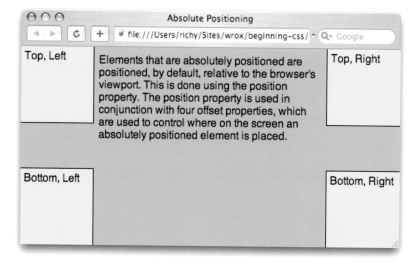

Figure 11-4

How It Works

In Example 11-1, you saw a brief recap of the concepts presented so far. Elements that are absolutely positioned are delivered to a specific place onscreen, more specifically, to a specific place in the browser's viewport, which is the visible area of the rendered document. In Example 11-1, you placed four <div> elements at the four corners of the browser's viewport by absolutely positioning each <div> element with the `position: absolute;` declaration, and then specifically positioning each one with various combinations of the four offset properties. For example, the declarations `top: 0;` and `left: 0;` places the <div> element with the id name *top-left* to the top left corner of the viewport. Then you repeated the process for each of the other three <div> elements, positioning them in each of the three other corresponding corners of the browser's viewport. Later in this chapter you will observe some more practical uses for absolute positioning with various multicolumn layouts.

In the next section, I introduce a concept that goes hand-in-hand with absolute positioning because it enables you to control the context used when an element is positioned, and that is relative positioning.

Relative Positioning

Relative positioning is very similar to static positioning; elements to which relative positioning is applied do not leave the document flow. There are three differences between relative positioning and static positioning:

1. Elements with a relative position can be used as a point of reference for elements nested within them that are absolutely positioned.

2. The position of a relatively positioned element can be adjusted using the offset properties.

3. A relatively positioned element can have a position on the (invisible) z-axis (more on this later in this chapter).

To observe how a relatively positioned element can be used as a point of reference for absolutely positioned descendant elements, take a look at Figure 11-5.

As always, the CSS in Figure 11-5a is combined with the markup in Figure 11-5b to produce the output that you see in Figure 11-5c.

```
body {
    background: lightyellow;
    font: 12px sans-serif;
}
div#container {
    position: relative;
    width: 300px;
    height: 300px;
    margin: auto;
}
div {
    width: 100px;
    height: 100px;
    border: 1px solid rgb(200, 200, 200);
    position: absolute;
}
div#one {
    background: pink;
    top: 0;
    left: 0;
}
div#two {
    background: lightblue;
    top: 0;
    right: 0;
}
div#three {
    background: yellowgreen;
    bottom: 0;
    left: 0;
}
div#four {
    background: orange;
    bottom: 0;
    right: 0;
}
```

One use of relative positioning is to change the point of reference used for absolutely positioned descendants. The element in which relative positioning is applied remains in the document flow.

Figure 11-5a

```
<!DOCTYPE html PUBLIC "-//W3C//DTD XHTML 1.0 Strict//EN"
                      "http://www.w3.org/TR/xhtml1/DTD/xhtml1-strict.dtd">
<html xmlns='http://www.w3.org/1999/xhtml' xml:lang='en'>
    <head>
        <title>positioning</title>
        <link rel='stylesheet' type='text/css' href='096977%20fg1105.css' />
    </head>
    <body>
        <p>
            Lorem ipsum dolor sit amet, consectetuer adipiscing elit. Sed
            sit amet sem quis orci malesuada facilisis. Nulla dictum
            malesuada magna. Quisque ac est et nibh porta nonummy. Cras pede
            tortor, lacinia et, eleifend quis, consequat vel, odio. Proin
            urna mi, facilisis et, consequat eu, scelerisque vel, lacus. Nunc
            turpis. Vestibulum sed felis.
        </p>
        <div id='container'>
            <div id='one'></div>
            <div id='two'></div>
            <div id='three'></div>
            <div id='four'></div>
        </div>
    </body>
</html>
```

Figure 11-5b

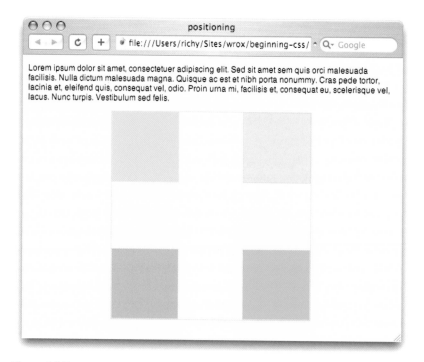

Figure 11-5c

In Figure 11-5c, you can see that the position of each <div> element has changed. By nesting them inside a descendant of a <div> element that has a relative position, each <div> is positioned relative to the <div> element with an id name of *container*.

What happens if the <div> element with id name *container* has a static position? The output is shown in Figure 11-6.

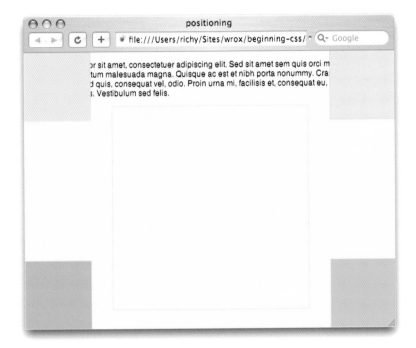

Figure 11-6

In Figure 11-6, you see that the point of reference for positioning is determined by which element in the positioned element's ancestry has a position other than static (absolute, relative, or fixed). If there aren't any elements with a position other than static, the element is positioned relative to the browser's viewport.

> **When no position is defined for any of an element's ancestral lineage (parent, grandparent, and so on), all elements are positioned relative to the browser's viewport by default. If an element does have a relative, absolute, or fixed position and is the ancestor of an element with absolute positioning, that element is used as the point of reference for the absolutely positioned element.**

Applying Offset Positioning to Relatively Positioned Elements

The position of elements with relative positioning can be adjusted using combinations of the four offset properties, top, right, bottom, and left. For example, the top and left properties can be used to adjust the position of a relatively positioned element. This works similarly to the margin property that you saw in Chapter 7. An example appears in Figure 11-7.

```
body {
    background: lightyellow;
    font: 12px sans-serif;
    margin: 50px;
    border: 1px solid rgb(200, 200, 200);
    padding: 0;
}
p {
    background: pink;
    border: 1px solid rgb(200, 200, 200);
    padding: 5px;
}
p#margin {
    margin: 25px 0 0 25px;
}
p#relative {
    background: lightblue;
    position: relative;
    top: 25px;
    left: 25px;
    margin: 0;
}
```

The four offset properties can be used to modify the position of relatively positioned elements.

Figure 11-7a

The CSS in Figure 11-7a is included in the markup in Figure 11-7b.

```
<!DOCTYPE html PUBLIC "-//W3C//DTD XHTML 1.0 Strict//EN"
                      "http://www.w3.org/TR/xhtml1/DTD/xhtml1-strict.dtd">
<html xmlns='http://www.w3.org/1999/xhtml' xml:lang='en'>
    <head>
        <title>positioning</title>
        <link rel='stylesheet' type='text/css' href='096977%20fg1107.css' />
    </head>
    <body>
        <p id='margin'>
            Lorem ipsum dolor sit amet, consectetuer adipiscing elit. Donec eu
            massa. Phasellus est eros, malesuada vel, tempus quis, pharetra at,
            lacus. Ut sit amet libero. Aliquam erat volutpat. Morbi erat. Nunc
            et purus vitae tortor sodales auctor. Nulla molestie. Pellentesque
            ante mauris, tristique ac, placerat sit amet, placerat nec, ante.
            Vestibulum interdum. Donec vitae tellus. Aliquam erat volutpat.
            Aenean dictum dolor ut sem.
        </p>
        <p id='relative'>
            Ut commodo. Sed non nisi at leo aliquet lobortis. Donec a elit vel
            nulla pharetra dignissim. Lorem ipsum dolor sit amet, consectetuer
            adipiscing elit. Aliquam cursus tortor eget diam. Pellentesque
            pellentesque turpis sed erat. Duis non libero vel metus
            sollicitudin aliquet. Aenean neque. Nunc eget quam a mauris
            vulputate laoreet. Mauris dictum, eros venenatis fringilla
            vehicula, tortor augue dignissim ante, id imperdiet risus sapien
            at odio. Praesent ligula magna, nonummy vitae, facilisis at,
            fermentum non, diam. Integer sit amet ligula quis lectus bibendum
            porta. Aliquam neque ipsum, aliquet et, semper vel, blandit ac,
            massa. Etiam porttitor justo id arcu. Ut ante lacus, rutrum id,
            vehicula non, faucibus in, lorem. Integer eu ante ut mauris
            rhoncus molestie. Aenean ut est et lectus tempor pharetra. Fusce
            sed nibh. Class aptent taciti sociosqu ad litora torquent per
            conubia nostra, per inceptos hymenaeos.
        </p>
    </body>
</html>
```

Figure 11-7b

In Figure 11-7c, you see what happens when the offset properties top and left are applied to a relatively positioned <p> element, as opposed to margin with the same values applied to another <p> element.

In Figure 11-7c, you see that relatively positioned elements can be layered. In the example, the top and left properties each have a value of 25px, which results in the <p> element with an id name of *relative* being layered over the border of the <body> element. You also see how this differs from margin — the top <p> element with an id name of *margin* — is given a top and left margin of 25px. The top element's width is adjusted to accommodate the 25px of margin, but the bottom element width is not adjusted to accommodate the 25px that it is offset from the top and left.

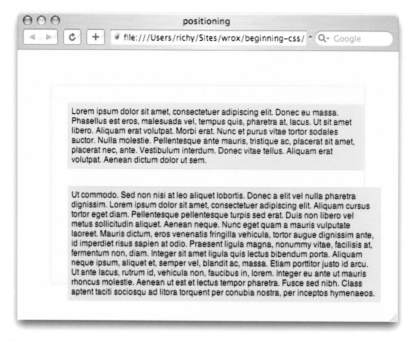

Figure 11-7c

A recap of relative positioning:

- ❑ Relative positioning is just like static positioning, in that the elements remain in the normal document flow, but that's where the similarities end.

- ❑ Relatively positioned elements can be used as a point of reference for absolutely positioned elements.

- ❑ Relatively positioned elements can accept combinations of the four offset properties, `top` and `left`, `top` and `right`, `bottom` and `left`, and `bottom` and `right`. The browser will ignore combinations of the offset properties beyond those mentioned here. For example, you can't combine the `top` and `bottom` offset properties on the same relatively positioned element.

- ❑ Relatively positioned content can be stacked and layered along the z-axis (more on this later in this chapter).

In the next section I cover fixed positioning.

Try It Out   **Applying Relative Positioning**

Example 11-2. To review the concept of relative positioning, follow these steps.

1. Enter the following XHTML document in your text editor:

```
<!DOCTYPE html PUBLIC "-//W3C//DTD XHTML 1.0 Strict//EN"
                    "http://www.w3.org/TR/xhtml1/DTD/xhtml1-strict.dtd">
<html xmlns='http://www.w3.org/1999/xhtml' xml:lang='en'>
    <head>
        <title>Relative Positioning</title>
        <link rel='stylesheet' type='text/css' href='Example_11-2.css' />
    </head>
    <body>
        <p>
            Relative positioning has two primary purposes in web design.
            The first purpose is to create a point of reference for an
            absolutely positioned element.  When an element with absolute
            positioning is nested within an element with relative positioning,
            the absolutely positioned element is positioned in context to
            the dimensions of the relatively positioned element.
        </p>
        <div id='relative'>
            <p>
                Relative positioning is a lot like static positioning; elements
                don't appear to leave the flow of the document.
            </p>
            <p id='bottom-right'>
                This element is positioned to the bottom right of the
                relatively positioned element.
            </p>
        </div>
        <p>
            The four offset properties can also be applied to relatively
            positioned elements, which can be used to modify the position
            of an element.
        </p>
        <div>
            <p id='offset'>
                This element is offset from its original position.
            </p>
        </div>
    </body>
</html>
```

2. Save the preceding document as `Example_11-2.html`.

3. Enter the following CSS in your text editor:

```
body {
    font: 12px sans-serif;
}
div {
    background: yellow;
    border: 1px solid black;
    margin: 0 20px;
}
div#relative {
    position: relative;
    height: 200px;
```

```
}
p {
    padding: 5px;
}
p#bottom-right {
    margin: 0;
    background: gold;
    border: 1px solid crimson;
    height: 50px;
    width: 200px;
    position: absolute;
    bottom: 5px;
    right: 5px;
}
p#offset {
    margin: 0;
    background: pink;
    border: 1px solid crimson;
    position: relative;
    top: 10px;
    left: 10px;
}
```

4. Save the preceding document as `Example_11-2.css`. The preceding source code results in the rendered output that you see in Figure 11-8.

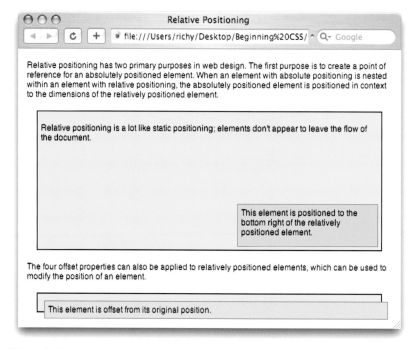

Figure 11-8

How It Works

In Example 11-2, you reviewed two concepts used for positioning an element relatively: the first using an element as a point of reference for positioning absolutely positioned elements, and the second, using the four offset properties to adjust the position of a relatively positioned element.

To create a point-of-reference, you made a `<div>` element, with an id name of *relative*, which had one absolutely positioned child `<p>` element with an id name of *bottom-right*. The `<p>` element with the id name *bottom-right* is given an absolute position, and the declarations `bottom: 5px;` and `right: 5px;`. As you see in the rendered output in Figure 11-8, this causes the element to be positioned to the bottom and right of the `<div>` element with id name *relative*. If the `position: relative;` declaration were to be removed from the `<div>` element with id name *relative*, the *bottom-right* `<p>` element would be positioned relative to the viewport, as you saw in Figure 11-6.

The second concept at play in Example 11-2 is using offset properties to adjust the position of a relatively positioned element. The `<p>` element with id name *offset* is given the `position: relative;` declaration, and the declarations `top: 10px;` and `left: 10px;`, which caused its position to be modified from the top by 10 pixels, from its original position, which is where it would have been if it were a statically positioned element, and to the left 10 pixels. This causes it to overlap its parent `<div>` element. If these properties were not present, you would not see any of the parent `<div>` element's yellow background, since the `<p>` element would have completely blocked it out.

In the next section, I continue the concept of positioning with fixed positioning, which is similar to absolute positioning, in that the element leaves the normal flow of the document, but unlike absolute positioning, the context of a fixed positioned element cannot be altered by nesting the element in a relatively positioned element or another absolutely positioned element. Fixed position elements are always positioned relative to the browser's viewport, and remain in that position, even if the document is scrolled.

Fixed Positioning

Fixed positioning is used to make an element remain in the same fixed position, even if the document is being scrolled. Alas, IE 6 does not support fixed positioning, so the example that follows will not work in IE 6. All is not lost however; there is a well-known workaround for IE 6's lack of support for fixed positioning, which is covered in the next section.

Elements with a fixed position are always positioned relative to the viewport, regardless of whether it is contained in an element with relative or absolute positioning applied. An example of fixed positioning appears in Figure 11-9.

```
body {
    background: lightyellow;
    font: 12px sans-serif;
}
p {
    line-height: 2em;
    margin: 10px 110px;
}
div {
    width: 100px;
    height: 100px;
    border: 1px solid rgb(200, 200, 200);
    position: fixed;
}
div#one {
    background: pink;
    top: 0;
    left: 0;
}
div#two {
    background: lightblue;
    top: 0;
    right: 0;
}
div#three {
    background: yellowgreen;
    bottom: 0;
    left: 0;
}
div#four {
    background: orange;
    bottom: 0;
    right: 0;
}
```

Fixed positioning causes an element to remain fixed in place while the rest of the document is scrolled.

Figure 11-9a

The CSS in Figure 11-9a is included in the markup that appears in Figure 11-9b.

```
<!DOCTYPE html PUBLIC "-//W3C//DTD XHTML 1.0 Strict//EN"
                      "http://www.w3.org/TR/xhtml1/DTD/xhtml1-strict.dtd">
<html xmlns='http://www.w3.org/1999/xhtml' xml:lang='en'>
    <head>
        <title>positioning</title>
        <link rel='stylesheet' type='text/css' href='096977%20fg1109.css' />
    </head>
    <body>
        <p>
            Lorem ipsum dolor sit amet, consectetuer adipiscing elit. Donec eu
            massa. Phasellus est eros, malesuada vel, tempus quis, pharetra at,
            lacus. Ut sit amet libero. Aliquam erat volutpat. Morbi erat. Nunc
            et purus vitae tortor sodales auctor. Nulla molestie. Pellentesque
            ante mauris, tristique ac, placerat sit amet, placerat nec, ante.
            Vestibulum interdum. Donec vitae tellus. Aliquam erat volutpat.
            Aenean dictum dolor ut sem.
        </p>
        <p>
            Ut commodo. Sed non nisi at leo aliquet lobortis. Donec a elit vel
            nulla pharetra dignissim. Lorem ipsum dolor sit amet, consectetuer
            adipiscing elit. Aliquam cursus tortor eget diam. Pellentesque
            pellentesque turpis sed erat. Duis non libero vel metus
            sollicitudin aliquet. Aenean neque. Nunc eget quam a mauris
            vulputate laoreet. Mauris dictum, eros venenatis fringilla
            vehicula, tortor augue dignissim ante, id imperdiet risus sapien
            at odio. Praesent ligula magna, nonummy vitae, facilisis at,
            fermentum non, diam. Integer sit amet ligula quis lectus bibendum
            porta. Aliquam neque ipsum, aliquet et, semper vel, blandit ac,
            massa. Etiam porttitor justo id arcu. Ut ante lacus, rutrum id,
            vehicula non, faucibus in, lorem. Integer eu ante ut mauris
            rhoncus molestie. Aenean ut est et lectus tempor pharetra. Fusce
            sed nibh. Class aptent taciti sociosqu ad litora torquent per
            conubia nostra, per inceptos hymenaeos.
        </p>
        <div id='one'></div>
        <div id='two'></div>
        <div id='three'></div>
        <div id='four'></div>
    </body>
</html>
```

Figure 11-9b

In Figure 11-9c, you see how fixed positioning is different from the example of absolute positioning that you saw in Figure 11-2c and Figure 11-3c. The same document is shown three times with the scroll bar in different positions to illustrate how the <div> elements with id names *one*, *two*, *three*, and *four* remain fixed in place as the document is scrolled.

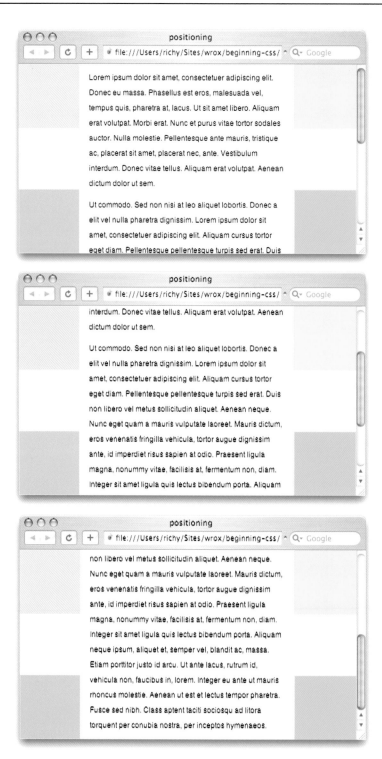

Figure 11-9c

Fixed positioning keeps the elements snapped into their positions, which is always determined relative to the viewport, as the document is scrolled. This type of positioning can be used for things such as side columns, headings, footers, or watermarks that remain in place as the document is scrolled. In the next section, you see some workarounds for IE 6 for its lack of support for fixed positioning.

In the following sections, I discuss two different methods of achieving fixed positioning without actually using CSS fixed positioning. The first method applies to IE exclusively, and it entails emulating fixed positioning in IE 6 with JavaScript and proprietary CSS features. The second method I present is applicable to all browsers, even those with proper support for fixed positioning, and is useful beyond fixing up IE's lack of support, and can be used for web page layouts in general, in all browsers.

Emulating Fixed Positioning

A well-known and annoying limitation of IE 6 is that it does not support fixed positioning. Not to be left without this useful feature, some developers have gone to great lengths to find alternative methods that produce the same results.

I first read about the following IE 6 fixed positioning hacks on Anne van Kesteren's blog at `http://annevankesteren.nl/test/examples/ie/position-fixed.html`. Therefore, the following workarounds are derivative of the ones collected by Anne and others as documented in his blog.

This first technique involves reproducing the same effects you would get if the declaration `position: fixed;` were supported in IE 6. For this technique, you'll need Microsoft's proprietary `expression()` feature, which allows you to use JavaScript within a style sheet, which you first saw in Chapter 7, where it helped you to overcome IE 6's lack of support for the min/max width/height properties. The first example demonstrates `position: fixed;` with `top: 0;` and `left: 0;` as the offset properties, and works when IE 6 is in standards-compliant rendering mode (see Chapter 7).

Emulation of fixed positioning is demonstrated in Figure 11-10.

The style sheets in Figures 11-10a and 11-10b are included in the markup that you see in Figure 11-10c.

```
body {
    background: lightyellow;
    font: 12px sans-serif;
}
p {
    line-height: 2em;
    margin: 10px 10px 10px 110px;
}
div {
    width: 100px;
    height: 100px;
    border: 1px solid rgb(200, 200, 200);
    background: pink;
    position: fixed;
    top: 0;
    left: 0;
}
```

The main style sheet is set up like normal for the browsers that do support fixed positioning.

Figure 11-10a

```
body {
    background: lightyellow url('http://') fixed;
}
div {
    position: absolute;
    top: expression(eval(documentElement.scrollTop));
}
```

> expression() is used to reference the position of the scroll bar with JavaScript. eval() is used to force IE to continuously reevaluate the position of the scrollbar.

Figure 11-10b

```
<!DOCTYPE html PUBLIC "-//W3C//DTD XHTML 1.0 Strict//EN"
                "http://www.w3.org/TR/xhtml1/DTD/xhtml1-strict.dtd">
<html xmlns='http://www.w3.org/1999/xhtml' xml:lang='en'>
    <head>
        <title>positioning</title>
        <link rel='stylesheet' type='text/css' href='096977%20fg1110.css' />
        <!--[if lt IE 7]>
        <link rel='stylesheet' type='text/css' href='096977%20fg1110.ie.css' />
        <![endif]-->
    </head>
    <body>
        <p>
            Lorem ipsum dolor sit amet, consectetuer adipiscing elit. Donec eu
            massa. Phasellus est eros, malesuada vel, tempus quis, pharetra at,
            lacus. Ut sit amet libero. Aliquam erat volutpat. Morbi erat. Nunc
            et purus vitae tortor sodales auctor. Nulla molestie. Pellentesque
            ante mauris, tristique ac, placerat sit amet, placerat nec, ante.
            Vestibulum interdum. Donec vitae tellus. Aliquam erat volutpat.
            Aenean dictum dolor ut sem.
        </p>
        <p>
            Ut commodo. Sed non nisi at leo aliquet lobortis. Donec a elit vel
            nulla pharetra dignissim. Lorem ipsum dolor sit amet, consectetuer
            adipiscing elit. Aliquam cursus tortor eget diam. Pellentesque
            pellentesque turpis sed erat. Duis non libero vel metus
            sollicitudin aliquet. Aenean neque. Nunc eget quam a mauris
            vulputate laoreet. Mauris dictum, eros venenatis fringilla
            vehicula, tortor augue dignissim ante, id imperdiet risus sapien
            at odio. Praesent ligula magna, nonummy vitae, facilisis at,
            fermentum non, diam. Integer sit amet ligula quis lectus bibendum
            porta. Aliquam neque ipsum, aliquet et, semper vel, blandit ac,
            massa. Etiam porttitor justo id arcu. Ut ante lacus, rutrum id,
            vehicula non, faucibus in, lorem. Integer eu ante ut mauris
            rhoncus molestie. Aenean ut est et lectus tempor pharetra. Fusce
            sed nibh. Class aptent taciti sociosqu ad litora torquent per
            conubia nostra, per inceptos hymenaeos.
        </p>
        <div></div>
    </body>
</html>
```

Figure 11-10c

You get the output that you see in Figure 11-10d, an element that acts as though the `position: fixed;` declaration is applied in IE 6.

This source code in Figure 11-11 results in the output that you see in Figure 11-11d.

394

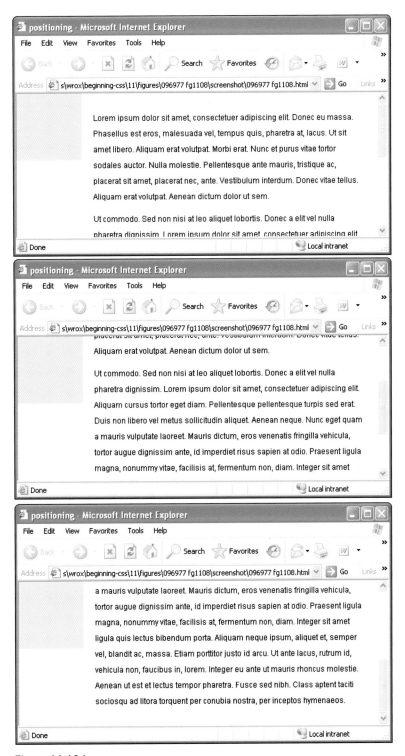

Figure 11-10d

There are a few things to keep in mind about this effect:

❑ You must specify a "fixed" background image. The image doesn't have to exist; you can just include `http://` as the background image, as I have. If you are using this effect in an SSL encrypted web page, be sure to make that `https://`, or you'll see SSL errors in IE. Without this essential hack, the element that you want to give a fixed position to will flicker as the page scrolls.

❑ This effect does not work in IE 6 or IE 7 in quirks mode, or IE 5.5. To get a compatible hack for IE 6 and IE 7 in quirks mode and IE 5.5, just change the declaration for the `top` property to:

```
top: expression(eval(document.body.scrollTop));
```

❑ This effect does not work if JavaScript is disabled.

❑ The effect emulates `top: 0;`. To get a pixel value other than zero, use something like the following declaration:

```
top: expression(eval(documentElement.scrollTop) + 5);
```

Just replace 5 with the pixel value you want.

❑ You specify the `left` or `right` properties as you normally would.

What if you're looking for `bottom: 0;`, instead of `top: 0;` with a fixed position element? An example of this appears in Figure 11-11. Figure 11-11a begins with the style sheet that you give to all browsers.

```
body {
    background: lightyellow;
    font: 12px sans-serif;
}
p {
    line-height: 2em;
    margin: 10px 10px 10px 110px;
}
div {
    width: 100px;
    height: 100px;
    border: 1px solid rgb(200, 200, 200);
    background: pink;
    position: fixed;
    bottom: 0;
    left: 0;
}
```

Figure 11-11a

The main style sheet in Figure 11-11a is followed by the IE 6 style sheet that appears in Figure 11-11b. As you see in Figure 11-11b, slightly more complicated trickery is required to emulate `bottom: 0;`. You have to subtract two pixels from the value; otherwise when the user scrolls to the bottom in IE 6, it will continue scrolling infinitely.

The style sheets in Figure 11-11a and Figure 11-11b are included in the markup document that you see in Figure 11-11c.

```
body {
    background: lightyellow url('http://') fixed;
}
div {
    position: absolute;
    bottom: auto;
    top: expression(
      (documentElement.scrollTop + documentElement.clientHeight - this.clientHeight) - 2
    );
}
```

In IE, you fix position an element to the bottom via the top. You take the position of the scroll bar and add that to the height of the viewport, then subtract the height of the element. This isn't precise, however, and you have to adjust the result by two pixels.

Figure 11-11b

```
<!DOCTYPE html PUBLIC "-//W3C//DTD XHTML 1.0 Strict//EN"
                "http://www.w3.org/TR/xhtml1/DTD/xhtml1-strict.dtd">
<html xmlns='http://www.w3.org/1999/xhtml' xml:lang='en'>
    <head>
        <title>positioning</title>
        <link rel='stylesheet' type='text/css' href='096977%20fg1111.css' />
        <!--[if lt IE 7]>
        <link rel='stylesheet' type='text/css' href='096977%20fg1111.ie.css' />
        <![endif]-->
    </head>
    <body>
        <p>
            Lorem ipsum dolor sit amet, consectetuer adipiscing elit. Donec eu
            massa. Phasellus est eros, malesuada vel, tempus quis, pharetra at,
            lacus. Ut sit amet libero. Aliquam erat volutpat. Morbi erat. Nunc
            et purus vitae tortor sodales auctor. Nulla molestie. Pellentesque
            ante mauris, tristique ac, placerat sit amet, placerat nec, ante.
            Vestibulum interdum. Donec vitae tellus. Aliquam erat volutpat.
            Aenean dictum dolor ut sem.
        </p>
        <p>
            Ut commodo. Sed non nisi at leo aliquet lobortis. Donec a elit vel
            nulla pharetra dignissim. Lorem ipsum dolor sit amet, consectetuer
            adipiscing elit. Aliquam cursus tortor eget diam. Pellentesque
            pellentesque turpis sed erat. Duis non libero vel metus
            sollicitudin aliquet. Aenean neque. Nunc eget quam a mauris
            vulputate laoreet. Mauris dictum, eros venenatis fringilla
            vehicula, tortor augue dignissim ante, id imperdiet risus sapien
            at odio. Praesent ligula magna, nonummy vitae, facilisis at,
            fermentum non, diam. Integer sit amet ligula quis lectus bibendum
            porta. Aliquam neque ipsum, aliquet et, semper vel, blandit ac,
            massa. Etiam porttitor justo id arcu. Ut ante lacus, rutrum id,
            vehicula non, faucibus in, lorem. Integer eu ante ut mauris
            rhoncus molestie. Aenean ut est et lectus tempor pharetra. Fusce
            sed nibh. Class aptent taciti sociosqu ad litora torquent per
            conubia nostra, per inceptos hymenaeos.
        </p>
        <div></div>
    </body>
</html>
```

Figure 11-11c

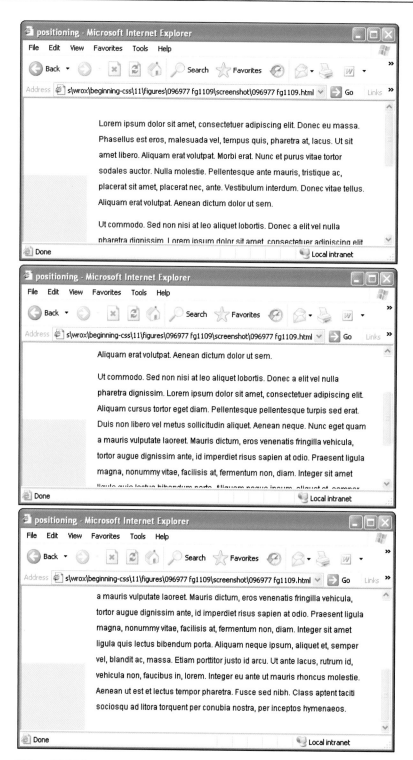

Figure 11-11d

Emulating `position: fixed;` with `bottom: 0;` is similar to the process required for `top: 0;`, and it is therefore subject to the same limitations. Again, to create this effect in IE 6 and IE 7 in quirks mode, and IE 5.5, just replace `documentElement` with `document.body`. For emulating the `bottom` property with a value other than 0, take the value, add 2 to it, and replace where 2 is being subtracted with your new value. For example, to emulate `bottom: 5px;`, you'd do the following:

```
top: expression(
  (documentElement.scrollTop + documentElement.clientHeight - this.clientHeight) - 7
);
```

I use the value 7 in the preceding example, because at least 2 pixels must always be subtracted, so, 2 + 5 = 7. In the next section, I explore how you create the illusion of fixed positioning to workaround the lack of support for fixed positioning in IE 6.

Try It Out   A Review of Fixed Positioning

Example 11-3. To recap the concept of fixed positioning, follow these steps.

1.   Enter the following XHTML document in your text editor:

```
<!DOCTYPE html PUBLIC "-//W3C//DTD XHTML 1.0 Strict//EN"
                "http://www.w3.org/TR/xhtml1/DTD/xhtml1-strict.dtd">
<html xmlns='http://www.w3.org/1999/xhtml' xml:lang='en'>
    <head>
        <title>Fixed Positioning</title>
        <link rel='stylesheet' type='text/css' href='Example_11-3.css' />
        <!--[if lt IE 7]>
        <link rel='stylesheet' type='text/css' href='Example_11-3.ie.css' />
        <![endif]-->
    </head>
    <body>
        <div id='fixed-top'>
        </div>
        <div id='fixed-bottom'>
        </div>
        <p>
            The concept of fixed positioning is pretty straightforward.
            Elements with a fixed position stay in place, even when a document
            is scrolled.  Elements with a fixed position are always positioned
            relative to the browser's viewport, no matter where they appear
            in a document's structure.
        </p>
        <p>
            IE 6 and IE 7 in quirks mode do not support fixed positioning, even
            though IE 7 in standards mode does support fixed positioning.  Some
            tricks are employed to make the document work in IE 6, in standards
            mode.
        </p>
        <p>
            Even though fixed positioning technically allows an element to be
            placed anywhere in the document's structure, the IE hacks that I
            present here require that fixed position elements always be immediate
            children of the &lt;body&gt; element.
        </p>
```

```
            <p id='long'>
                This element is used to make the document longer, so that scroll bars
                are invoked.
            </p>
        </body>
    </html>
```

2. Save the preceding document as `Example_11-3.html`.

3. Enter the following CSS in your text editor:

```
body {
    font: 12px sans-serif;
    background: lightyellow;
}
p {
    padding: 5px;
    margin-left: 110px;
}
p#long {
    height: 400px;
}
div {
    position: fixed;
    background: gold;
    border: 1px solid black;
    width: 100px;
    height: 100px;
}
div#fixed-top {
    top: 5px;
    left: 5px;
}
div#fixed-bottom {
    bottom: 5px;
    left: 5px;
}
```

4. Save the preceding CSS document as `Example_11-3.css`.

5. Enter the following style sheet for IE 6 in your text editor:

```
body {
    background: lightyellow url('http://') fixed;
}
div#fixed-top {
    position: absolute;
    top: expression(eval(documentElement.scrollTop) + 5);
}
div#fixed-bottom {
    position: absolute;
    bottom: auto;
    top: expression((documentElement.scrollTop +
                        documentElement.clientHeight - this.clientHeight) - 7);
}
```

6. Save the preceding document as `Example_11-3.ie.css`. The preceding source code results in the rendered output that you see in Figure 11-12.

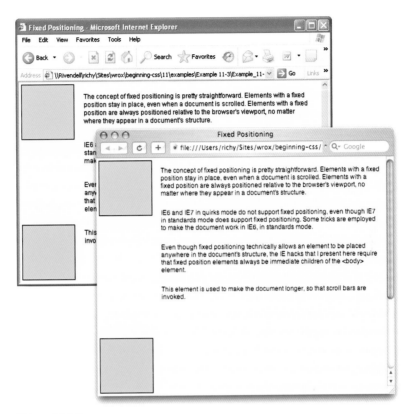

Figure 11-12

How It Works

In Example 11-3 you see the tools required for making cross-browser, fixed-position elements. These elements stay fixed in place even when the content is scrolled. For most browsers, Safari, Firefox, IE 7 in standards mode, and Opera, this is done using standard CSS 2. You apply the declaration `position: fixed;` to an element in tandem with offset properties, which provide the position of the element. In Example 11-3, you made two examples: one fixed-position element that's positioned to the top and left of the browser's viewport, and one fixed-position element that's positioned to the left and bottom of the browser's viewport.

To make this work in IE 6, you supplied a Microsoft-proprietary conditional comment style sheet, which uses dynamic expressions and a tiny snippet of JavaScript. The JavaScript that you keyed in dynamically updates the position of the pseudo-fixed position elements. For the fixed position element that's positioned to the top and left, you supply the declaration `position: absolute;`, since IE 6 doesn't recognize `position: fixed;`, and in the dynamic expression, you evaluate the position of the viewport's scroll bar with the JavaScript `eval(documentElement.scrollTop)`. This causes the element to remain fixed in place as the document is scrolled. But you need one more hack to make it function as fluid as `position: fixed;` does on other browsers; you must give the `<body>` element a fixed background image. As you saw in Example 11-3, the background image doesn't even have to exist. The application of this hack causes IE 6 to render the fixed position element smoothly as the document is scrolled, rather than jerky. To get the same result as `top: 5px;` you also have to add 5 to the result of the evaluation, which gives you the following CSS:

```
top: expression(eval(documentElement.scrollTop) + 5);
```

To fix position an element to the bottom and left of the viewport in IE 6, you see a little more involved script. The element is again absolutely positioned, but instead of positioning from the bottom, as you might expect, the element is positioned from the top. To do this, you reset the `bottom` property to its default value, `bottom: auto;`. To get the element on the bottom, you get the position of the scroll bar, the height of the viewport, then subtract the height of the element that's being fixed positioned, which results in the same output as `position: fixed;`, with the declaration `bottom: 5px;` and `left: 5px;`.

```
top: expression((documentElement.scrollTop +
                 documentElement.clientHeight - this.clientHeight) - 7);
```

In the next section, I discuss how to create the illusion of fixed positioning using only absolute positioning.

Creating the Illusion of Fixed Positioning

The other way to get around IE 6, IE 5.5, and IE 7 quirks mode lack of support for fixed positioning is to just not use it at all, and use the principles of absolute positioning to your advantage. The following sections describe how to do the following:

❑ Make a fixed header

❑ Make a fixed footer

❑ Make fixed side columns

All are with support for IE 6, and all are the usual suspects, Safari, Firefox, Opera, and so on. I begin with a discussion of how to stretch content by using offset properties in pairs.

Stretching Content by Using Offset Properties in Pairs

One fundamental concept that is essential to making the fixed header, footer, and side columns techniques work has to do with how absolutely positioned elements handle sizing. In Chapter 7, you learned that block elements have a width that is expand-to-fit by default. Block elements such as `<h1>`, `<div>`, `<p>`, and so on, expand to fill the space available to them horizontally, and expand vertically in the shrink-to-fit fashion, that is, only enough to accommodate the content contained within them. When elements are positioned absolutely, they all take on the shrink-to-fit sizing behavior, for both width and height. An example of this appears in Figure 11-13.

```
body {
    background: lightyellow;
    font: 12px sans-serif;
    margin: 0;
    padding: 0;
}
p {
    background: yellowgreen;
    border: 1px solid green;
    padding: 5px;
    margin: 5px;
}
p#absolute {
    position: absolute;
    bottom: 0;
    left: 0;
}
```

Absolutely and fixed positioned elements use shrink-to-fit sizing.

Figure 11-13a

The main style sheet in Figure 11-13a contains two demonstrations of sizing: a statically positioned <p> element, and an absolutely positioned <p> element. As you'll see in Figure 11-13c, positioning an element absolutely causes it to use a different method of sizing, shrink-to-fit. The main style sheet in Figure 11-13a is included in the markup that you see in Figure 11-13b to create the rendered output in Figure 11-13c.

```
<!DOCTYPE html PUBLIC "-//W3C//DTD XHTML 1.0 Strict//EN"
                      "http://www.w3.org/TR/xhtml1/DTD/xhtml1-strict.dtd">
<html xmlns='http://www.w3.org/1999/xhtml' xml:lang='en'>
    <head>
        <title>positioning and sizing</title>
        <link rel='stylesheet' type='text/css' href='096977%20fg1110.css' />
    </head>
    <body>
        <p>
            Lorem ipsum dolor sit amet, consectetuer adipiscing elit. Donec eu
            massa.
        </p>
        <p id='absolute'>
            Lorem ipsum dolor sit amet, consectetuer adipiscing elit. Donec eu
            massa.
        </p>
    </body>
</html>
```

Figure 11-13b

In Figure 11-13c, you see that the two <p> elements have different dimensions. The statically positioned one takes up all the horizontal area that's available to it, and the absolutely positioned <p> element only expands enough to accommodate the content that it contains.

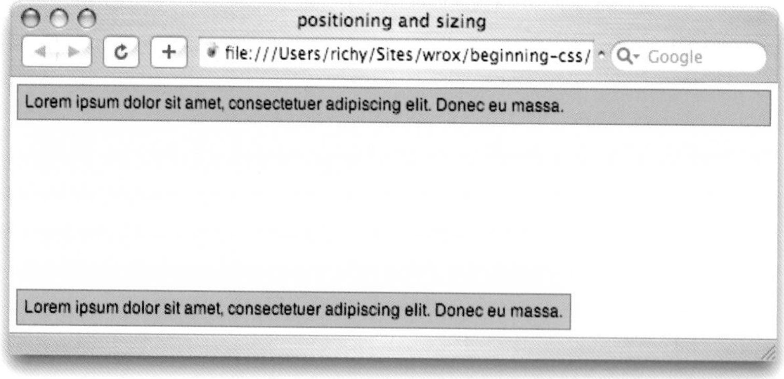

Figure 11-13c

To use absolute positioning to emulate fixed positioning for a header, you need a way to make an absolutely positioned element use the other method of sizing, expand-to-fit. The CSS specification just so happens to support just such a feature, and specifying opposing offset properties on the same absolutely positioned element does it. For example, to stretch content horizontally for the entire width available to it, you specify both the `left` and `right` offset properties to imply width. Or if you want to stretch an element vertically for all the space available to it, you specify both the `top` and `bottom` offset properties to imply height. The term *imply* is used here because you don't actually specify `width` or `height`. Dimensions are implied because you expect specifying both the `left` and `right` offset properties on the same absolutely or fixed positioned element to stretch the element.

If you want both horizontal and vertical fluidity on an absolutely positioned element, you specify all four offset properties on the same element. Unfortunately IE 7 in quirks rendering mode, IE 6, and earlier do not support this useful feature (IE 7 in standards mode does support this feature), but as is the case with most problems with IE, there is a relatively painless workaround, which you observe later in this chapter.

An example of horizontally stretching an absolutely positioned element appears in Figure 11-14.

```
body {
    background: lightyellow;
    font: 12px sans-serif;
    margin: 0;
    padding: 0;
}
p {
    background: yellowgreen;
    border: 1px solid green;
    padding: 5px;
    margin: 5px;
}
p#absolute {
    position: absolute;
    bottom: 0;
    left: 0;
    right: 0;
}
```

Specifying both the `left` and `right` offset properties on the same element implies width.

Figure 11-14a

In Figure 11-14a, you see the main style sheet, and within it you see an example strikingly similar to the one you saw in the source code and screenshot that make up Figure 11-13. That is to say, you have a statically positioned <p> element, and an absolutely positioned <p> element. This time the absolutely positioned <p> element will wind up having the same dimensions as the statically positioned <p> element, and this is done by specifying left: 0; and right: 0; on that element to make it stretch horizontally, for all the space available to it, the same way that the statically positioned <p> element is sized as a normal block-level element. The main style sheet in Figure 11-14a is included in the markup that you see in Figure 11-14b.

```
<!DOCTYPE html PUBLIC "-//W3C//DTD XHTML 1.0 Strict//EN"
                "http://www.w3.org/TR/xhtml1/DTD/xhtml1-strict.dtd">
<html xmlns='http://www.w3.org/1999/xhtml' xml:lang='en'>
    <head>
        <title>horizontally stretching content</title>
        <link rel='stylesheet' type='text/css' href='096977%20fg1114.css' />
    </head>
    <body>
        <p>
            Lorem ipsum dolor sit amet, consectetuer adipiscing elit.
        </p>
        <p id='absolute'>
            Lorem ipsum dolor sit amet, consectetuer adipiscing elit.
        </p>
    </body>
</html>
```

Figure 11-14b

In Figure 11-14c, the screenshot shows that the statically positioned <p> element and the absolutely positioned <p> element now have the same width. You'll see the same results in IE 7, but as I mentioned earlier, IE 6 has other plans, which you see a workaround for later in this chapter.

Figure 11-14c

In Figure 11-14c, the concept of horizontally stretching an absolutely positioned element via specifying both the `left` and `right` properties is made clear, but this example begs the question, why can't you just specify the width as 100 percent? That's a good question, and a common misconception made by beginners. The answer to this question is, when you have any block element, absolutely positioned or not, and you apply padding, borders, or margin to it, and then give it a width of 100 percent on top of those properties, you won't end up with the results that you expect. This has to do with how percentage measurement works. If you recall from Chapter 7, a percentage width is determined by the width of an element's parent. So if the parent element has a width of 700 pixels, for example, your element with 100 percent width will also have a width of 700 pixels, and then the lengths for margin, borders, and padding are applied on top of that width, and your element overflows the boundaries of its parent. If the parent element is the `<body>` element, and the 700 pixels measurement happens to be the width of the browser's viewport, you'll wind up with your element with 100 percent width causing horizontal scroll bars, because it is too big to fit in that 700-pixel width. By stretching elements with opposing offset properties, the resulting width is whatever is left over after margin, borders, and padding are already applied, thus avoiding scroll bars.

Still not clear on how percentage width works? Try a small experiment for testing percentage width. Take the source code from Figure 11-14a and Figure 11-14b (you can get the source code for all of this book's examples with the book's source code download from www.wrox.com), and try applying a width of 100 percent to the absolutely positioned `<div>`. Compare the resulting output with what you see in Figure 11-14c. Notice any differences?

Conversely, Figure 11-15 demonstrates how to stretch an element vertically by specifying both the `top` and `bottom` offset properties.

```
body {
    background: lightyellow;
    font: 12px sans-serif;
    margin: 0;
    padding: 0;
}
p {
    background: yellowgreen;
    border: 1px solid green;
    padding: 5px;
    margin: 5px;
}
p#absolute {
    position: absolute;
    top: 0;
    right: 0;
    bottom: 0;
}
```

Specifying both the `top` and `bottom` offset properties on the same element implies height.

Figure 11-15a

In the main style sheet that you see in Figure 11-15a, the absolutely positioned `<p>` element now has both the `top` and `bottom` properties set as `top: 0;` and `bottom: 0;`, which will cause the `<p>` element to be stretched vertically for the height of the browser's viewport.

In Figure 11-15c, you observe that the absolutely positioned `<p>` element is stretched vertically for the height of the browser's viewport.

```
<!DOCTYPE html PUBLIC "-//W3C//DTD XHTML 1.0 Strict//EN"
                "http://www.w3.org/TR/xhtml1/DTD/xhtml1-strict.dtd">
<html xmlns='http://www.w3.org/1999/xhtml' xml:lang='en'>
    <head>
        <title>vertically stretching content</title>
        <link rel='stylesheet' type='text/css' href='096977%20fg1l15.css' />
    </head>
    <body>
        <p>
            Lorem ipsum dolor sit amet, consectetuer adipiscing elit.
        </p>
        <p id='absolute'>
            Lorem ipsum dolor sit amet, consectetuer adipiscing elit.
        </p>
    </body>
</html>
```

Figure 11-15b

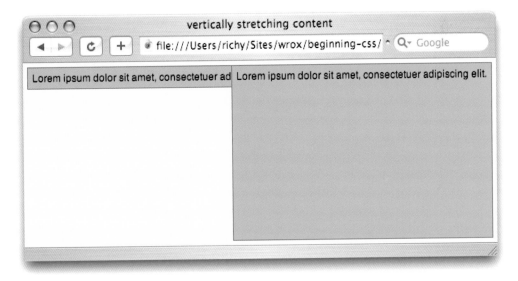

Figure 11-15c

Figure 11-16 demonstrates both horizontal and vertical fluidity on the same element via specification of all four offset properties.

In the main style sheet that appears in Figure 11-16a, the absolutely positioned <p> element now has all four offset properties set, which causes the <p> element to be stretched both horizontally and vertically.

The CSS from Figure 11-16a is included in the markup that you see in Figure 11-16b.

In Figure 11-16c, you see that the <p> element is stretched both vertically and horizontally, taking up the whole browser window.

```
body {
    background: lightyellow;
    font: 12px sans-serif;
    margin: 0;
    padding: 0;
}
p {
    background: pink;
    border: 1px solid red;
    padding: 5px;
    margin: 5px;
    position: absolute;
    top: 0;
    right: 0;           Specifying opposing offset properties on the
    bottom: 0;          same element implies dimensions.
    left: 0;
}
```

Figure 11-16a

```
<!DOCTYPE html PUBLIC "-//W3C//DTD XHTML 1.0 Strict//EN"
                    "http://www.w3.org/TR/xhtml1/DTD/xhtml1-strict.dtd">
<html xmlns='http://www.w3.org/1999/xhtml' xml:lang='en'>
    <head>
        <title>stretching content</title>
        <link rel='stylesheet' type='text/css' href='096977%20fg1116.css' />
    </head>
    <body>
        <p>
            Lorem ipsum dolor sit amet, consectetuer adipiscing elit.
        </p>
    </body>
</html>
```

Figure 11-16b

Figure 11-16c

The screenshot shows how both horizontal and vertical fluidity is achieved through specifying `top`, `right`, `bottom`, and `left` on the same element. At this point you may be asking yourself, does the value of the offset property have to be zero? No, it does not. You can use any value you like, a value larger than zero will simply modify where the element is positioned and decrease its dimensions.

Try It Out   **Implying Dimensions by Opposing Offset Properties**

Example 11-4. To recap the concepts at play with implying dimensions via opposing offset properties, follow these steps.

1.   Enter the following XHTML document in your text editor:

```
<!DOCTYPE html PUBLIC "-//W3C//DTD XHTML 1.0 Strict//EN"
                "http://www.w3.org/TR/xhtml1/DTD/xhtml1-strict.dtd">
<html xmlns='http://www.w3.org/1999/xhtml' xml:lang='en'>
    <head>
        <title>Opposing Offset Properties</title>
        <link rel='stylesheet' type='text/css' href='Example_11-4.css' />
    </head>
    <body>
        <div id='offset-four'>
            <p id='offset-x'>
                When the left and right offset properties are applied to the same
                element, width is implied.
            </p>
            <p id='offset-y'>
                When the top and bottom offset properties are applied to the same
                element, height is implied.
            </p>
            <p id='offset-four-copy'>
                When all four offset properties are specified on the same element
                both width and height are implied.
            </p>
        </div>
    </body>
</html>
```

2.   Save the preceding document as `Example_11-4.html`.

3.   Enter the following CSS in your text editor:

```
body {
    font: 12px sans-serif;
    background: lightyellow;
}
div#offset-four {
    background: yellow;
    border: 1px solid rgb(128, 128, 128);
    position: absolute;
    top: 20px;
    right: 20px;
    bottom: 20px;
    left: 20px;
}
p {
    margin: 0;
```

409

```
    padding: 5px;
    border: 1px solid black;
}
p#offset-x {
    position: absolute;
    bottom: 5px;
    left: 5px;
    right: 123px;
    background: gold;
}
p#offset-y {
    position: absolute;
    top: 5px;
    right: 5px;
    bottom: 5px;
    width: 100px;
    background: khaki;
}
p#offset-four-copy {
    border: none;
    margin-right: 123px;
}
```

4. Save the preceding document as `Example_11-14.css`. When viewed in IE 7, Safari, Opera, or Firefox, you should see output like that in Figure 11-17. Bear in mind that this example does not work in IE 6, but you see a workaround for this lack of support in the coming sections.

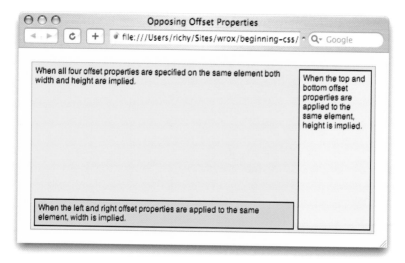

Figure 11-17

How It Works

In Example 11-4, you see three different examples of using opposing offset properties to imply width or height, or both. The first example is a <p> element with id name *offset-x*. It is positioned relative to the <div> element with id name *offset-four*, and it is positioned relative to this element rather than the viewport, since the *offset-four* <div> element is positioned absolutely. To get the *offset-x* <p> element to span the bottom of the *offset-four* <div> element, you supplied to it both the left and right offset properties. In this example, you also see that the value can be any measurement you like. In this case, you offset from the left, 5 pixels, and from the right 123 pixels, which causes the element to be stretched along the bottom of the *offset-four* <div> element.

The second example that you see in Example 11-4 of using opposing offset properties is with the <p> element with id name *offset-y*. It is offset from the right 5 pixels, from the top 5 pixels, and from the bottom 5 pixels. Since it is offset from both the top and bottom by five pixels, height is implied, and the <p> element spans the whole height of the *offset-four* <div> element.

The third and last example that you see in Example 11-4 of using offset properties to imply dimensions is in the <div> element with id name *offset-four*. It is offset from all four sides by 20 pixels, which causes it to be stretched both horizontally and vertically relative to the browser's viewport.

This concept of stretching elements via absolute positioning is also an essential ingredient in the multi-column layouts that I present later in this chapter. In the next section, I discuss how to make a fixed header without fixed positioning.

A Fixed Heading

A fixed heading is pretty easy to pull off, without support for fixed positioning. You simply use absolute positioning to make a fixed heading, and a second container element that is also absolutely positioned, that invokes scroll bars using the overflow property that you saw in Chapter 7. Making a fixed heading is demonstrated in Figure 11-18.

In Figure 11-18a, you see the main style sheet that all browsers will see. The <h1> element is acting as your fixed heading for this example, and the document's content is going to be kept inside the <div> element with id name *container*. Both the <h1> element and the container <div> element are given an absolute position, so that their place on the screen can be dictated with fine precision. For the heading, you take the <h1> element and stretch it horizontally by specifying both the left and right offset properties with a value of zero. This will cause the absolutely positioned <h1> element to act like a statically positioned <h1> element, and take up all the space available to it horizontally. Could you just use a statically positioned <h1> element and get the same result? You can. It is not essential that the <h1> element be absolutely positioned; it's just another means to the same end, and a fine example of how web designers sometimes forget fundamental design concepts when designing a page, and actually end up over-engineering a design. The rule for the <h1> element could be rewritten as follows:

```
h1 {
    height: 20px;
    font-weight: normal;
    font-size: 18px;
    border-bottom: 1px solid rgb(200, 200, 200);
    background: white;
    margin: 0;
    padding: 5px;
}
```

The preceding rule produces the same result. I've included the over-engineered version to demonstrate how unnecessary properties can creep in unexpectedly. While it doesn't have to be positioned, I'm going to leave it that way merely for consistency with the other elements on the page, but bear in mind, it doesn't have to be that way.

```
body {
    background: lightyellow;
    font: 12px sans-serif;
    margin: 0;
    padding: 0;
}
h1 {
    position: absolute;
    top: 0;
    right: 0;
    left: 0;
    height: 20px;
    font-weight: normal;
    font-size: 18px;
    border-bottom: 1px solid rgb(200, 200, 200);
    background: white;
    margin: 0;
    padding: 5px;
}
div#container {
    position: absolute;
    top: 31px;
    right: 0;
    bottom: 0;
    left: 0;
    overflow: auto;
    padding: 0 10px;
    line-height: 2em;
}
```

Figure 11-18a

For IE 6 to properly stretch the absolutely positioned elements, it needs a bit of help. The workarounds appear in Figure 11-18b.

```
h1 {
    width: expression(documentElement.offsetWidth);
}
div#container {
    top: 32px;
    width: expression(documentElement.offsetWidth - 21);
    height: expression(documentElement.offsetHeight - 35);
}
```

Figure 11-18b

The CSS in Figure 11-18b is included because IE 6 does not support stretching an element via specifying opposing offset properties on the same element. As you've seen in earlier examples in this Chapter, and in Chapter 7, a dynamic expression is used to emulate the effect of opposing offset properties in IE 6. You simply include the dynamic expression feature, which references a small snippet of JavaScript. documentElement refers to the <html> element, and offsetHeight is a property that is used to get the <html> element's, well, offset height, which for you and me means the height of the browser's viewport. Remember, if you use a Document Type Declaration that causes IE 6 or IE 7 to render in quirks mode, this trick won't work. If you face this situation, you'll want to use `document.body.offsetHeight` instead of `documentElement.offsetHeight`. See Chapter 7 for more information on quirks rendering mode versus standard rendering mode (nearly all of the examples in this book invoke standards rendering mode).

The CSS in Figure 11-18a and Figure 11-18b are included in the markup that you see in Figure 11-18c.

```
<!DOCTYPE html PUBLIC "-//W3C//DTD XHTML 1.0 Strict//EN"
                      "http://www.w3.org/TR/xhtml1/DTD/xhtml1-strict.dtd">
<html xmlns='http://www.w3.org/1999/xhtml' xml:lang='en'>
    <head>
        <title>positioning</title>
        <link rel='stylesheet' type='text/css' href='096977%20fg1118.css' />
        <!--[if lt IE 7]>
        <link rel='stylesheet' type='text/css' href='096977%20fg1118.ie.css' />
        <![endif]-->
        <!--[if lte IE 7]>
        <style type='text/css'>
            html {
                overflow: hidden;
            }
        </style>
        <![endif]-->
    </head>
    <body>
        <h1>A Fixed Heading</h1>
        <div id='container'>
            <p>
                Lorem ipsum dolor sit amet, consectetuer adipiscing elit. Donec eu
                massa. Phasellus est eros, malesuada vel, tempus quis, pharetra at,
                lacus. Ut sit amet libero. Aliquam erat volutpat. Morbi erat. Nunc
                et purus vitae tortor sodales auctor. Nulla molestie. Pellentesque
                ante mauris, tristique ac, placerat sit amet, placerat nec, ante.
                Vestibulum interdum. Donec vitae tellus. Aliquam erat volutpat.
                Aenean dictum dolor ut sem.
            </p>
            <p>
                Ut commodo. Sed non nisi at leo aliquet lobortis. Donec a elit vel
                nulla pharetra dignissim. Lorem ipsum dolor sit amet, consectetuer
                adipiscing elit. Aliquam cursus tortor eget diam. Pellentesque
                pellentesque turpis sed erat. Duis non libero vel metus
                sollicitudin aliquet. Aenean neque. Nunc eget quam a mauris
                vulputate laoreet. Mauris dictum, eros venenatis fringilla
                vehicula, tortor augue dignissim ante, id imperdiet risus sapien
                at odio. Praesent ligula magna, nonummy vitae, facilisis at,
                fermentum non, diam. Integer sit amet ligula quis lectus bibendum
                porta. Aliquam neque ipsum, aliquet et, semper vel, blandit ac,
                massa. Etiam porttitor justo id arcu. Ut ante lacus, rutrum id,
                vehicula non, faucibus in, lorem. Integer eu ante ut mauris
                rhoncus molestie. Aenean ut est et lectus tempor pharetra. Fusce
                sed nibh. Class aptent taciti sociosqu ad litora torquent per
                conubia nostra, per inceptos hymenaeos.
            </p>
        </div>
    </body>
</html>
```

Figure 11-18c

IE 6 and IE 7 continue to show a scroll bar for the whole window, even though it isn't needed. You apply the `overflow: hidden;` declaration to the `<html>` element to get rid of the scroll bar via Microsoft's conditional comments that target IE 7 and earlier versions. Now the redundant scroll bar is no more.

The source code in Figure 11-18 a, b, and c gives you a layout that works well between the different browsers, as you see in the screenshot that appears in Figure 11-18d.

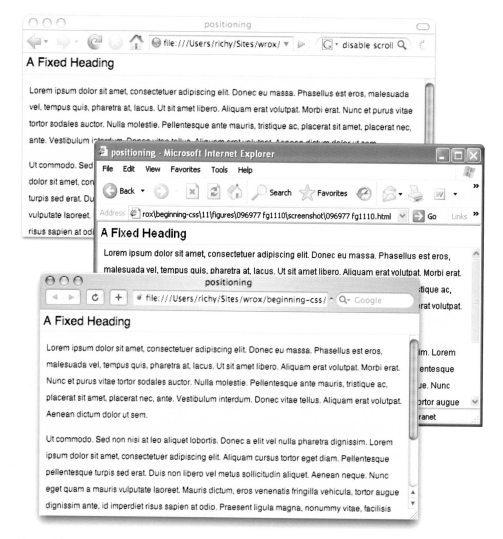

Figure 11-18d

In Figure 11-18d, you can see that the heading stays in place whenever the content is scrolled. You could just as easily replace the `<h1>` with a `<div>` there and include additional content that stays fixed in place at the top of the page. But how do you do a fixed footer? This is covered in the next section.

A Fixed Footer

For a fixed footer, the idea is pretty much the same as you saw for making a fixed heading, but everything's reversed to the bottom. A demonstration of how to do a fixed footer appears in Figure 11-19.

```css
body {
    background: lightyellow;
    font: 12px sans-serif;
    margin: 0;
    padding: 0;
}
div#container {
    position: absolute;
    top: 0;
    right: 0;
    bottom: 31px;
    left: 0;
    overflow: auto;
    padding: 0 10px;
    line-height: 2em;
}
div#footer {
    position: absolute;
    bottom: 0;
    right: 0;
    left: 0;
    height: 20px;
    font-weight: normal;
    font-size: 14px;
    text-align: center;
    border-top: 1px solid rgb(200, 200, 200);
    background: white;
    margin: 0;
    padding: 5px;
}
div#footer p {
    margin: 0;
}
```

Figure 11-19a

Then as was the case with the fixed heading example in the last section, another style sheet targeting IE 6 is made with adjustments to facilitate a fixed footer rather than a heading. The technique can have several approaches, but the principle is that either the top or the bottom offset property can be set, and the height of the container element must be adjusted in relation to the height of the viewport, and the height of the footer. The IE 6 style sheet appears in Figure 11-19b.

```css
div#footer {
    width: expression(documentElement.offsetWidth);
}
div#container {
    top: auto;
    bottom: 30px;
    width: expression(documentElement.offsetWidth - 21);
    height: expression(documentElement.offsetHeight - 35);
}
```

Figure 11-19b

Again, the scroll bar for the viewport that is present by default must be turned off in IE 6 and IE 7, just as it was for the fixed heading example in the previous section. The CSS from Figure 11-19a and Figure 11-19b are included in the markup that appears in Figure 11-19c.

```
<!DOCTYPE html PUBLIC "-//W3C//DTD XHTML 1.0 Strict//EN"
                      "http://www.w3.org/TR/xhtml1/DTD/xhtml1-strict.dtd">
<html xmlns='http://www.w3.org/1999/xhtml' xml:lang='en'>
    <head>
        <title>positioning</title>
        <link rel='stylesheet' type='text/css' href='096977%20fg1119.css' />
        <!--[if lt IE 7]>
        <link rel='stylesheet' type='text/css' href='096977%20fg1119.ie.css' />
        <![endif]-->
        <!--[if lte IE 7]>
        <style type='text/css'>
            html {
                overflow: hidden;
            }
        </style>
        <![endif]-->
    </head>
    <body>
        <div id='container'>
            <p>
                Lorem ipsum dolor sit amet, consectetuer adipiscing elit. Donec eu
                massa. Phasellus est eros, malesuada vel, tempus quis, pharetra at,
                lacus. Ut sit amet libero. Aliquam erat volutpat. Morbi erat. Nunc
                et purus vitae tortor sodales auctor. Nulla molestie. Pellentesque
                ante mauris, tristique ac, placerat sit amet, placerat nec, ante.
                Vestibulum interdum. Donec vitae tellus. Aliquam erat volutpat.
                Aenean dictum dolor ut sem.
            </p>
            <p>
                Ut commodo. Sed non nisi at leo aliquet lobortis. Donec a elit vel
                nulla pharetra dignissim. Lorem ipsum dolor sit amet, consectetuer
                adipiscing elit. Aliquam cursus tortor eget diam. Pellentesque
                pellentesque turpis sed erat. Duis non libero vel metus
                sollicitudin aliquet. Aenean neque. Nunc eget quam a mauris
                vulputate laoreet. Mauris dictum, eros venenatis fringilla
                vehicula, tortor augue dignissim ante, id imperdiet risus sapien
                at odio. Praesent ligula magna, nonummy vitae, facilisis at,
                fermentum non, diam. Integer sit amet ligula quis lectus bibendum
                porta. Aliquam neque ipsum, aliquet et, semper vel, blandit ac,
                massa. Etiam porttitor justo id arcu. Ut ante lacus, rutrum id,
                vehicula non, faucibus in, lorem. Integer eu ante ut mauris
                rhoncus molestie. Aenean ut est et lectus tempor pharetra. Fusce
                sed nibh. Class aptent taciti sociosqu ad litora torquent per
                conubia nostra, per inceptos hymenaeos.
            </p>
        </div>
        <div id='footer'>
            <p>
                A fixed footer.
            </p>
        </div>
    </body>
</html>
```

Figure 11-19c

The result of the source code appears in Figure 11-19d, where you see a fixed footer that works on a variety of browsers and platforms.

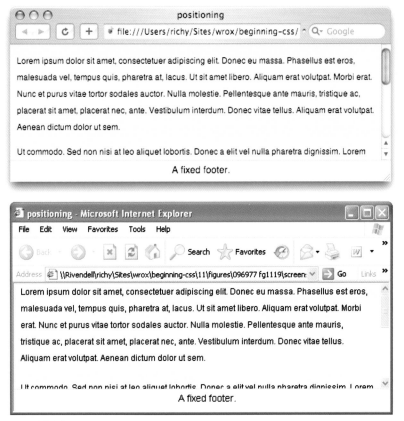

Figure 11-19d

In Figure 11-19d, `top` has become `bottom`, and the heading becomes the footer. The same concepts are at play here as you saw for the fixed heading. So naturally, it ought to be easy to combine the two now in one example. The next section describes how to do both.

A Fixed Heading and a Fixed Footer

The concepts of the previous two sections are now married into one example, which is demonstrated in the source code and screenshots shown in Figure 11-20. In Figure 11-20a, you see the styles from the fixed heading and the fixed footer examples have been merged into one style sheet.

Again, in Figure 11-20b, you see the IE 6 style sheet, which now contains styles that facilitate both a fixed heading and a fixed footer.

```
body {
    background: lightyellow;
    font: 12px sans-serif;
    margin: 0;
    padding: 0;
}
h1 {
    position: absolute;
    top: 0;
    right: 0;
    left: 0;
    height: 20px;
    font-weight: normal;
    font-size: 18px;
    border-bottom: 1px solid rgb(200, 200, 200);
    background: white;
    margin: 0;
    padding: 5px;
}
div#container {
    position: absolute;
    top: 31px;
    right: 0;
    bottom: 31px;
    left: 0;
    overflow: auto;
    padding: 0 10px;
    line-height: 2em;
}
div#footer {
    position: absolute;
    bottom: 0;
    right: 0;
    left: 0;
    height: 20px;
    font-weight: normal;
    font-size: 14px;
    text-align: center;
    border-top: 1px solid rgb(200, 200, 200);
    background: white;
    margin: 0;
    padding: 5px;
}
div#footer p {
    margin: 0;
}
```

Figure 11-20a

```
h1, div#footer {
    width: expression(documentElement.offsetWidth);
}
div#container {
    top: 32px;
    width: expression(documentElement.offsetWidth - 21);
    height: expression(documentElement.offsetHeight - 65);
}
```

Figure 11-20b

Then the styles from Figure 11-20a and Figure 11-20b are included in Figure 11-20c.

```
<!DOCTYPE html PUBLIC "-//W3C//DTD XHTML 1.0 Strict//EN"
                      "http://www.w3.org/TR/xhtml1/DTD/xhtml1-strict.dtd">
<html xmlns='http://www.w3.org/1999/xhtml' xml:lang='en'>
    <head>
        <title>positioning</title>
        <link rel='stylesheet' type='text/css' href='096977%20fg1120.css' />
        <!--[if lt IE 7]>
        <link rel='stylesheet' type='text/css' href='096977%20fg1120.ie.css' />
        <![endif]-->
        <!--[if lte IE 7]>
        <style type='text/css'>
            html {
                overflow: hidden;
            }
        </style>
        <![endif]-->
    </head>
    <body>
        <h1>A Fixed Heading</h1>
        <div id='container'>
            <p>
                Lorem ipsum dolor sit amet, consectetuer adipiscing elit. Donec eu
                massa. Phasellus est eros, malesuada vel, tempus quis, pharetra at,
                lacus. Ut sit amet libero. Aliquam erat volutpat. Morbi erat. Nunc
                et purus vitae tortor sodales auctor. Nulla molestie. Pellentesque
                ante mauris, tristique ac, placerat sit amet, placerat nec, ante.
                Vestibulum interdum. Donec vitae tellus. Aliquam erat volutpat.
                Aenean dictum dolor ut sem.
            </p>
            <p>
                Ut commodo. Sed non nisi at leo aliquet lobortis. Donec a elit vel
                nulla pharetra dignissim. Lorem ipsum dolor sit amet, consectetuer
                adipiscing elit. Aliquam cursus tortor eget diam. Pellentesque
                pellentesque turpis sed erat. Duis non libero vel metus
                sollicitudin aliquet. Aenean neque. Nunc eget quam a mauris
                vulputate laoreet. Mauris dictum, eros venenatis fringilla
                vehicula, tortor augue dignissim ante, id imperdiet risus sapien
                at odio. Praesent ligula magna, nonummy vitae, facilisis at,
                fermentum non, diam. Integer sit amet ligula quis lectus bibendum
                porta. Aliquam neque ipsum, aliquet et, semper vel, blandit ac,
                massa. Etiam porttitor justo id arcu. Ut ante lacus, rutrum id,
                vehicula non, faucibus in, lorem. Integer eu ante ut mauris
                rhoncus molestie. Aenean ut est et lectus tempor pharetra. Fusce
                sed nibh. Class aptent taciti sociosqu ad litora torquent per
                conubia nostra, per inceptos hymenaeos.
            </p>
        </div>
        <div id='footer'>
            <p>
                A fixed footer.
            </p>
        </div>
    </body>
</html>
```

Figure 11-20c

You see the result of the merged fixed heading and fixed footer examples in Figure 11-20d.

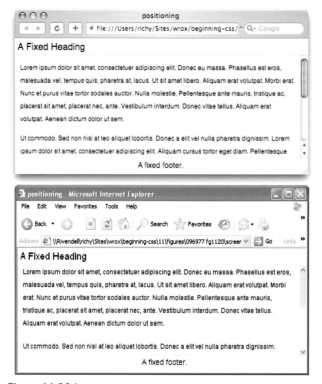

Figure 11-20d

In Figure 11-20d, you can see that with just a few tweaks, you can have both a fixed heading and a fixed footer in your document. In the next section, I continue this style of layout with fixed side columns instead of a fixed heading or a fixed footer.

Fixed Side Columns

The ideas at play for making fixed side columns are along the same lines that you've observed in the previous three sections. With just a few modifications, you can have fixed side columns instead of fixed heading or a fixed footer. The source code and screenshots are in the collection of figures that together make up Figure 11-21. You begin with the main style sheet that's presented in Figure 11-21a.

```css
body {
    background: lightyellow;
    font: 12px sans-serif;
    margin: 0;
    padding: 0;
}
div#left,
div#right {
    position: absolute;
    top: 0;
    bottom: 0;
    width: 200px;
    background: white;
    padding: 5px;
}
div#left {
    left: 0;
    border-right: 1px solid rgb(200, 200, 200);
}
div#right {
    right: 0;
    border-left: 1px solid rgb(200, 200, 200);
}
div#container {
    position: absolute;
    top: 0;
    right: 211px;
    bottom: 0;
    left: 211px;
    overflow: auto;
    padding: 0 10px;
    line-height: 2em;
}
```

Figure 11-21a

In Figure 11-21a, you see that instead of an `<h1>` element for the heading, and a `<div>` with an id name of *footer* for the footer, you have two `<div>` elements with id names *left* and *right*. Common style sheet declarations that both the *left* and *right* `<div>` elements share are grouped together, and additional rules appear for declarations that are unique to each. Again, the concept of absolute positioning is to create elements that remain fixed in place when the `<div>` element with id name *container* is scrolled. Like the examples that you saw for the fixed heading and the fixed footer, you use opposing offset properties to stretch each of the absolutely positioned elements vertically, which is done by specifying both the `top` and `bottom` offset properties on all three absolutely positioned elements to imply height. You must also alter the container `<div>` element so that there is enough room for the side columns; otherwise the side columns would simply overlap that container `<div>` element. You do this by setting the left and right offset properties to 211 pixels. This figure is arrived at by taking the width of the left `<div>`, for example, plus its left padding, plus its right padding, plus one pixel of border, which together add up to 211 pixels. The remaining styles present in the style sheet aren't really important, since they're really just cosmetic and don't effect the overall concept of making fixed side columns.

Of course, as you saw in previous examples, specifying opposing offset properties to stretch an element doesn't work in IE 6. You correct this deformity by supplying IE 6 a style sheet all its own, as you did in previous examples. This style sheet appears in Figure 11-21b.

```
div#left,
div#right {
    height: expression(documentElement.offsetHeight);
}
div#container {
    left: 211px;
    width: expression(documentElement.offsetWidth - 446);
    height: expression(documentElement.offsetHeight);
}
```

Figure 11-21b

The IE 6 style sheet makes similar adjustments as you've seen in previous examples. The two `<div>` elements with id names *left* and *right* are stretched for the whole height of the browser's viewport via a dynamic expression that calls a small snippet of JavaScript, which provides the height of the `documentElement`, or the `<html>` element, via its `offsetHeight` property. Remember, this technique does not work in IE 6 or IE 7 when those browsers are in quirks rendering mode, nor older versions of IE prior to version 6, and must be replaced with `document.body.offsetHeight`, instead of `documentElement.offsetHeight`. The style sheets that you saw in Figure 11-21a and Figure 11-21b are included in the markup that you see in Figure 11-21c.

```
<!DOCTYPE html PUBLIC "-//W3C//DTD XHTML 1.0 Strict//EN"
                      "http://www.w3.org/TR/xhtml1/DTD/xhtml1-strict.dtd">
<html xmlns='http://www.w3.org/1999/xhtml' xml:lang='en'>
    <head>
        <title>positioning</title>
        <link rel='stylesheet' type='text/css' href='096977%20fg1121.css' />
        <!--[if lt IE 7]>
        <link rel='stylesheet' type='text/css' href='096977%20fg1121.ie.css' />
        <![endif]-->
        <!--[if lte IE 7]>
        <style type='text/css'>
            html {
                overflow: hidden;
            }
        </style>
        <![endif]-->
    </head>
    <body>
        <div id='left'>
            Left side column.
        </div>
        <div id='right'>
            Right side column.
        </div>
        <div id='container'>
            <p>
                Lorem ipsum dolor sit amet, consectetuer adipiscing elit. Donec eu
                massa. Phasellus est eros, malesuada vel, tempus quis, pharetra at,
                lacus. Ut sit amet libero. Aliquam erat volutpat. Morbi erat. Nunc
                et purus vitae tortor sodales auctor. Nulla molestie. Pellentesque
                ante mauris, tristique ac, placerat sit amet, placerat nec, ante.
                Vestibulum interdum. Donec vitae tellus. Aliquam erat volutpat.
                Aenean dictum dolor ut sem.
            </p>
            <p>
                Ut commodo. Sed non nisi at leo aliquet lobortis. Donec a elit vel
                nulla pharetra dignissim. Lorem ipsum dolor sit amet, consectetuer
                adipiscing elit. Aliquam cursus tortor eget diam. Pellentesque
                pellentesque turpis sed erat. Duis non libero vel metus
                sollicitudin aliquet. Aenean neque. Nunc eget quam a mauris
                vulputate laoreet. Mauris dictum, eros venenatis fringilla
                vehicula, tortor augue dignissim ante, id imperdiet risus sapien
                at odio. Praesent ligula magna, nonummy vitae, facilisis at,
                fermentum non, diam. Integer sit amet ligula quis lectus bibendum
                porta. Aliquam neque ipsum, aliquet et, semper vel, blandit ac,
                massa. Etiam porttitor justo id arcu. Ut ante lacus, rutrum id,
                vehicula non, faucibus in, lorem. Integer eu ante ut mauris
                rhoncus molestie. Aenean ut est et lectus tempor pharetra. Fusce
                sed nibh. Class aptent taciti sociosqu ad litora torquent per
                conubia nostra, per inceptos hymenaeos.
            </p>
        </div>
    </body>
</html>
```

Figure 11-21c

Again in Figure 11-21c, the redundant scroll bar that IE 6 and IE 7 include is nullified with the `overflow: hidden;` declaration. Now IE 6, IE 7, Safari, Firefox, and Opera all produce the same results. The output from IE 6 as well as Safari appears in Figure 11-21d.

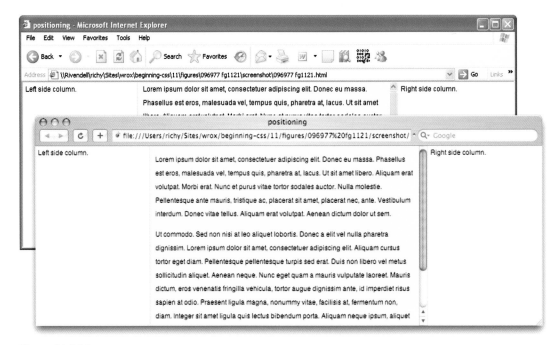

Figure 11-21d

And to wind down the examples of fixed headings and footers and side columns, the next section demonstrates all of them together in the same document.

A Fixed Heading, Footer, and Side Columns

In this example, you put together the examples of the previous two sections to get a document with a fixed heading, footer, and side columns. You begin with the style sheet shown in Figure 11-22a.

```css
body {
    background: lightyellow;
    font: 12px sans-serif;
    margin: 0;
    padding: 0;
}
h1,
div#footer {
    position: absolute;
    right: 0;
    left: 0;
    background: white;
    margin: 0;
    padding: 5px;
    height: 20px;
}
div#footer {
    bottom: 0;
    font-size: 14px;
    text-align: center;
    border-top: 1px solid rgb(200, 200, 200);
}
h1 {
    top: 0;
    font-weight: normal;
    font-size: 18px;
    border-bottom: 1px solid rgb(200, 200, 200);
}
div#left,
div#right {
    position: absolute;
    top: 31px;
    bottom: 31px;
    width: 200px;
    background: white;
    padding: 5px;
}
div#left {
    left: 0;
    border-right: 1px solid rgb(200, 200, 200);
}
div#right {
    right: 0;
    border-left: 1px solid rgb(200, 200, 200);
}
div#container {
    position: absolute;
    top: 31px;
    right: 211px;
    bottom: 31px;
    left: 211px;
    overflow: auto;
    padding: 0 10px;
    line-height: 2em;
}
div#footer p {
    margin: 0;
}
```

Figure 11-22a

No surprises here. The main style sheet in Figure 11-22a makes adjustments to the *container* <div> element to accommodate both a heading and a footer and side columns. You'll note that the *container* <div> element is offset from the top and bottom respective to the collective height of the heading and the footer, that is to say, the height property, plus top and bottom margin, border, and padding, and from the left and right relative to the collective width of the left and right side columns, which is the width property plus left and right margin, border, and padding. The side columns are also adjusted from the top and bottom with respect to the collective height of the footer and the heading. With the exception of these minor tweaks, the concept is basically the same as you've seen in previous sections. In Figure 11-22b, you see the IE 6 style sheet that's required to bring IE 6 on par with the output seen in other browsers.

```
h1,
div#footer {
    width: expression(documentElement.offsetWidth);
}
div#left,
div#right {
    height: expression(documentElement.offsetHeight - 65);
}
div#container {
    top: 32px;
    left: 211px;
    width: expression(documentElement.offsetWidth - 446);
    height: expression(documentElement.offsetHeight - 65);
}
```

Figure 11-22b

In the IE 6 style sheet that you see in Figure 11-22b, you again see a marriage of the concepts that you've observed in previous sections, only now you see measurements that accommodate both side columns, a heading, and a footer. The style sheets in Figure 11-22a and Figure 11-22b are included in the markup that you see in Figure 11-22c.

```
<!DOCTYPE html PUBLIC "-//W3C//DTD XHTML 1.0 Strict//EN"
                 "http://www.w3.org/TR/xhtml1/DTD/xhtml1-strict.dtd">
<html xmlns='http://www.w3.org/1999/xhtml' xml:lang='en'>
    <head>
        <title>positioning</title>
        <link rel='stylesheet' type='text/css' href='096977%20fg1122.css' />
        <!--[if IE 7]>
        <link rel='stylesheet' type='text/css' href='096977%20fg1122.ie.css' />
        <![endif]-->
        <!--[if lte IE 7]>
        <style type='text/css'>
            html {
                overflow-y: hidden;
            }
        </style>
        <![endif]-->
    </head>
    <body>
        <h1>A Fixed Heading</h1>
        <div id='left'>
            Left side column.
        </div>
        <div id='right'>
            Right side column.
        </div>
        <div id='container'>
            <p>
                Lorem ipsum dolor sit amet, consectetuer adipiscing elit. Donec eu
                massa. Phasellus est eros, malesuada vel, tempus quis, pharetra at,
                lacus. Ut sit amet libero. Aliquam erat volutpat. Morbi erat. Nunc
                et purus vitae tortor sodales auctor. Nulla molestie. Pellentesque
                ante mauris, tristique ac, placerat sit amet, placerat nec, ante.
                Vestibulum interdum. Donec vitae tellus. Aliquam erat volutpat.
                Aenean dictum dolor ut sem.
            </p>
            <p>
                Ut commodo. Sed non nisi at leo aliquet lobortis. Donec a elit vel
                nulla pharetra dignissim. Lorem ipsum dolor sit amet, consectetuer
                adipiscing elit. Aliquam cursus tortor eget diam. Pellentesque
                pellentesque turpis sed erat. Duis non libero vel metus
                sollicitudin aliquet. Aenean neque. Nunc eget quam a mauris
                vulputate laoreet. Mauris dictum, eros venenatis fringilla
                vehicula, tortor augue dignissim ante, id imperdiet risus sapien
                at odio. Praesent ligula magna, nonummy vitae, facilisis at,
                fermentum non, diam. Integer sit amet ligula quis lectus bibendum
                porta. Aliquam neque ipsum, aliquet et, semper vel, blandit ac,
                massa. Etiam porttitor justo id arcu. Ut ante lacus, rutrum id,
                vehicula non, faucibus in, lorem. Integer eu ante ut mauris
                rhoncus molestie. Aenean ut est et lectus tempor pharetra. Fusce
                sed nibh. Class aptent taciti sociosqu ad litora torquent per
                conubia nostra, per inceptos hymenaeos.
            </p>
        </div>
        <div id='footer'>
            <p>
                A fixed footer.
            </p>
        </div>
    </body>
</html>
```

Figure 11-22c

The output that you see in Figure 11-22d is what results from the source code in Figure 11-22a, Figure 11-22b, and Figure 11-22c.

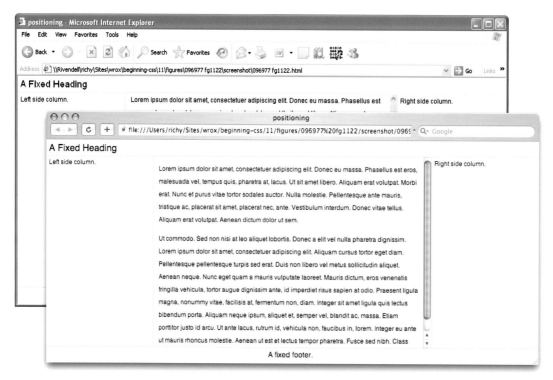

Figure 11-22d

In the next section, I discuss how you can control layering of positioned elements with the `z-index` property.

The z-axis and the z-index Property

The `z-index` property is used to control layering of positioned elements along an invisible z-axis, which you might imagine as an invisible line coming out of the computer screen. The following table outlines the `z-index` property and its possible values.

Property	Value
z-index	auto | <integer>
	Initial value: auto

The z-index property controls elements' position on along the invisible z-axis, if those elements are positioned relative, absolute, or fixed. The concept of the z-axis is used to create dynamic applications like pop-up menus. The z-index property is demonstrated in Figure 11-23.

```css
body {
    background: lightyellow;
}
div {
    position: absolute;
    width: 100px;
    height: 100px;
    border: 1px solid rgb(200, 200, 200);
    /* Moz proprietary opacity property */
    -moz-opacity: 0.7;
    /* Microsoft proprietary filter property */
    filter: progid:DXImageTransform.Microsoft.Alpha(opacity=70);
    /* CSS 3 opacity property */
    opacity: 0.7;
    z-index: auto;
}
div#one {
    background: pink;
    top: 10px;
    left: 10px;
}
div#two {
    background: lightblue;
    top: 20px;
    left: 20px;
}
div#three {
    background: yellowgreen;
    top: 30px;
    left: 30px;
}
div#four {
    background: orange;
    top: 40px;
    left: 40px;
}
```

Figure 11-23a

In the main style sheet in Figure 11-23a, four <div> elements are absolutely positioned to the top and left; each is increasingly positioned 10 pixels more from the top and left from the last so that they are overlapping, but each of the overlapped elements are still visible. For all of the <div> elements, the declaration z-index: auto; is supplied, although since this is the default value of the z-index property, it does not have to be provided at all. The style sheet in Figure 11-23a is included in the markup in Figure 11-23b.

```
<!DOCTYPE html PUBLIC "-//W3C//DTD XHTML 1.0 Strict//EN"
                       "http://www.w3.org/TR/xhtml1/DTD/xhtml1-strict.dtd">
<html xmlns='http://www.w3.org/1999/xhtml' xml:lang='en'>
    <head>
        <title>z-index</title>
        <link rel='stylesheet' type='text/css' href='096977%20fg1123.css' />
    </head>
    <body>
        <div id='one'></div>
        <div id='two'></div>
        <div id='three'></div>
        <div id='four'></div>
    </body>
</html>
```

Figure 11-23b

In Figure 11-23c, you see how the z-index property with an auto value works. Each additional element in the document that is positioned absolutely has a higher z-index value than the last, so the <div> element with an id name of *one* is positioned at z-index: 1; on up to four.

Figure 11-23c

In the next section, you see how to control the behavior of the z-index property with an integer value.

The z-index Property with an Integer Value

To control the layering of elements in a document, all you need to do is supply an integer value to the z-index property. In Figure 11-24, you see the layering of each of the positioned elements is reversed from what you saw in Figure 11-23c.

```
body {
    background: lightyellow;
}
div {
    position: absolute;
    width: 100px;
    height: 100px;
    border: 1px solid rgb(200, 200, 200);
    /* Moz proprietary opacity property */
    -moz-opacity: 0.7;
    /* Microsoft proprietary filter property */
    filter: progid:DXImageTransform.Microsoft.Alpha(opacity=70);
    /* CSS 3 opacity property */
    opacity: 0.7;
}
div#one {
    background: pink;
    top: 10px;
    left: 10px;
    z-index: 4;
}
div#two {
    background: lightblue;
    top: 20px;
    left: 20px;
    z-index: 3;
}
div#three {
    background: yellowgreen;
    top: 30px;
    left: 30px;
    z-index: 2;
}
div#four {
    background: orange;
    top: 40px;
    left: 40px;
    z-index: 1;
}
```

Figure 11-24a

In the main style sheet that you see in Figure 11-24a, you explicitly set the z-index of each of the four <div> elements present in the document, giving the <div> element with id name *one* the highest z-index and the <div> element with id name *four* the lowest z-index. The style sheet in Figure 11-24a is included in the markup that you see in Figure 11-24b.

```
<!DOCTYPE html PUBLIC "-//W3C//DTD XHTML 1.0 Strict//EN"
                      "http://www.w3.org/TR/xhtml1/DTD/xhtml1-strict.dtd">
<html xmlns='http://www.w3.org/1999/xhtml' xml:lang='en'>
    <head>
        <title>z-index</title>
        <link rel='stylesheet' type='text/css' href='096977%20fg1124.css' />
    </head>
    <body>
        <div id='one'></div>
        <div id='two'></div>
        <div id='three'></div>
        <div id='four'></div>
    </body>
</html>
```

Figure 11-24b

In Figure 11-24c, you can see that the layering of the <div> elements is reversed from what you saw in Figure 11-23c. The <div> element with id name *one* is now on top, and the <div> element with id name *four* is now on the bottom.

Figure 11-24c

Although I presented the z-index in Figure 11-24a with z-index values that ascend from one to four, you don't have to keep the values sequential. You can have any z-index value you like, 1,000, even 10,000, if you deem it appropriate. The browser will sort the highest z-index value as being on top, and the lowest on the bottom where elements are layered one on top of another.

Layering Nested Elements

Nested elements take on a different behavior where the z-index property is concerned. Nested elements behave like z-index is set to auto, and the integer value is ignored. Take for example the code presented in Figure 11-25.

In the main style sheet, you see something similar to what you saw in Figure 11-24a, with the exception that all four <div> elements are offset from the top and left ten pixels. This is done since the elements are now nested one inside of each other, as you can see in the markup in Figure 11-25b.

```css
body {
    background: lightyellow;
}
div {
    position: absolute;
    width: 100px;
    height: 100px;
    border: 1px solid rgb(200, 200, 200);
    /* Moz proprietary opacity property */
    -moz-opacity: 0.7;
    /* Microsoft proprietary filter property */
    filter: progid:DXImageTransform.Microsoft.Alpha(opacity=70);
    /* CSS 3 opacity property */
    opacity: 0.7;
    top: 10px;
    left: 10px;
}
div#one {
    background: pink;
    z-index: 4;
}
div#two {
    background: lightblue;
    z-index: 3;
}
div#three {
    background: yellowgreen;
    z-index: 2;
}
div#four {
    background: orange;
    z-index: 1;
}
```

Figure 11-25a

```
<!DOCTYPE html PUBLIC "-//W3C//DTD XHTML 1.0 Strict//EN"
                       "http://www.w3.org/TR/xhtml1/DTD/xhtml1-strict.dtd">
<html xmlns='http://www.w3.org/1999/xhtml' xml:lang='en'>
    <head>
        <title>z-index</title>
        <link rel='stylesheet' type='text/css' href='096977%20fg1125.css' />
    </head>
    <body>
        <div id='one'>
            <div id='two'>
                <div id='three'>
                    <div id='four'>
                    </div>
                </div>
            </div>
        </div>
    </body>
</html>
```

Figure 11-25b

In Figure 11-25c, you find that the z-index is being ignored; the `<div>` element with id name *one* is still on the bottom. This fulfills the rule that an element's descendents cannot have a higher `z-index` than it does.

Figure 11-25c

The IE 6/IE 7 z-index Bug

IE 6 and IE 7 support the `z-index` property just fine, but both browsers have trouble with the `z-index` property in certain situations. It doesn't take a vary complex design to invoke these bugs either, so anyone looking to utilize positioning in a layout should be aware of how to spot and crush these bugs. In the following source, you actually see two IE 6/IE 7 bugs. The first bug has to do with `z-index` stacking, and the other has to do with spacing between `<li>` elements. The example in Figure 11-26 demonstrates these bugs.

```
body {
    background: lightyellow;
}
ul {
    list-style: none;
    width: 200px;
}
li {
    background: pink;
    border: 1px solid red;
    margin: 2px;
    position: relative;
    width: 200px;
    height: 20px;
}
div {
    background: lightblue;
    border: 1px solid blue;
    position: absolute;
    z-index: 2;
    top: 2px;
    left: 150px;
    height: 100px;
    width: 200px;
}
```

Figure 11-26a

In the main style sheet you see that I've set up a list, where the <li> elements are relatively positioned, and the <div> element is absolutely positioned. The style sheet in Figure 11-26a is included in Figure 11-26b.

```
<!DOCTYPE html PUBLIC "-//W3C//DTD XHTML 1.0 Strict//EN"
                      "http://www.w3.org/TR/xhtml1/DTD/xhtml1-strict.dtd">
<html xmlns='http://www.w3.org/1999/xhtml' xml:lang='en'>
    <head>
        <title>z-index</title>
        <link rel='stylesheet' type='text/css' href='096977%20fg1126.css' />
    </head>
    <body>
        <ul>
            <li>
                <div></div>
            </li>
            <li></li>
            <li></li>
            <li></li>
        </ul>
    </body>
</html>
```

Figure 11-26b

In Figure 11-26c, the problem becomes clear. In IE the absolutely positioned <div> element is positioned correctly where its parent <li> element is concerned, but incorrectly where the additional <li> elements are concerned. IE also has a list bug, where if an absolutely positioned element appears in an <li> element, additional space is included above or below the <li> element. Luckily, both of these problems have a fix, but they aren't pretty.

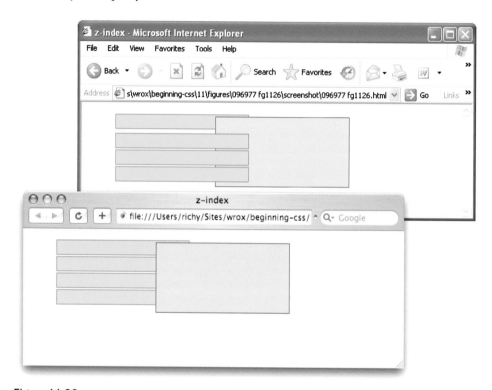

Figure 11-26c

To correct the z-index bug that you see in Figure 11-26, you have to manually z-index all of the elements involved. That is to say, beginning with the first <li> element, assign each a z-index in decreasing order. So the first <li> element would be four, the second <li> element would be three, and so on to the last <li> element. This is demonstrated in Figure 11-27. There are no changes in the main style sheet from the CSS that you saw in Figure 11-26a, so you begin with the markup in Figure 11-27a.

In Figure 11-27a, you see that I've applied this fix inline, since I didn't believe that it would be any better to create a unique id for each <li> element, and then apply each z-index in the external style sheet. You'll see that the <div> element doesn't need a z-index at all. Since it is a nested element, it has a higher z-index than its parent, and the z-index problem that you see here is with the z-index of each <li> element, rather than the <div> element.

```
<!DOCTYPE html PUBLIC "-//W3C//DTD XHTML 1.0 Strict//EN"
                      "http://www.w3.org/TR/xhtml1/DTD/xhtml1-strict.dtd">
<html xmlns='http://www.w3.org/1999/xhtml' xml:lang='en'>
    <head>
        <title>z-index</title>
        <link rel='stylesheet' type='text/css' href='096977%20fg1127.css' />
    </head>
    <body>
        <ul>
            <li style='z-index: 4;'>
                <div></div>
            </li>
            <li style='z-index: 3;'></li>
            <li style='z-index: 2;'></li>
            <li style='z-index: 1;'></li>
        </ul>
    </body>
</html>
```

Figure 11-27a

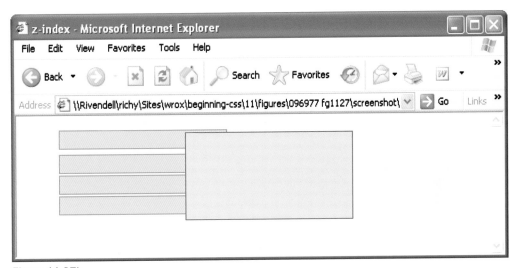

Figure 11-27b

As for the <li> spacing bug, there is only one known fix: to make the <li> element an inline element with the declaration display: inline;. Since this would have adverse effects for other browsers, you need to apply the fix to IE only (via conditional comments), and to avoid the content collapsing, you need to nest a block-level element inside each <li> element, like this: <li><div></div></li>. The nested <div> element prevents the content from collapsing, as would be the case if the <li> elements were inline elements.

Try It Out   **The z-index Property**

Example 11-5. To review the `z-index` property, follow these steps.

1. Enter the following XHTML in your text editor:

```
<!DOCTYPE html PUBLIC "-//W3C//DTD XHTML 1.0 Strict//EN"
                "http://www.w3.org/TR/xhtml1/DTD/xhtml1-strict.dtd">
<html xmlns='http://www.w3.org/1999/xhtml' xml:lang='en'>
    <head>
        <title>The z-index</title>
        <link rel='stylesheet' type='text/css' href='Example_11-5.css' />
    </head>
    <body>
        <div class='slide'>
            <p>
                The z-index property controls how elements are layered along an
                invisible z-axis.  By default, elements are layered automatically.
                The first instance of an absolutely positioned element results in
                a z-index value of one, and with each subsequent element, the
                z-index is increased.
            </p>
            <div class='container'>
                <div class='zauto zone'></div>
                <div class='zauto ztwo'></div>
                <div class='zauto zthree'></div>
                <div class='zauto zfour'></div>
            </div>
        </div>
        <div class='slide'>
            <p>
                You can control the z-index explicitly, however, by providing an
                integer value to the z-index property.
            </p>
            <div class='container'>
                <div class='zauto zone' id='five'></div>
                <div class='zauto ztwo' id='six'></div>
                <div class='zauto zthree' id='seven'></div>
                <div class='zauto zfour' id='eight'></div>
            </div>
        </div>
        <div class='slide'>
            <p>
                Nested elements handle the z-index property differently. Descendant
                elements must always have a z-index higher than that of their
                parent.
            </p>
            <div class='container' id='nested'>
                <div class='zauto zone' id='nine'>
                    <div class='zauto ztwo' id='ten'>
                        <div class='zauto zthree' id='eleven'>
                            <div class='zauto zfour' id='twelve'></div>
                        </div>
                    </div>
                </div>
```

```
            </div>
        </div>
    </body>
</html>
```

2. Save the preceding XHTML source code as `Example_11-5.html`.

3. Enter the following style sheet in your text editor:

```
body {
    font: 12px sans-serif;
    background: lightyellow;
}
div.container {
    height: 132px;
    position: relative;
}
div.zauto {
    position: absolute;
    border: 1px solid black;
    width: 100px;
    height: 100px;
}
div.zone {
    background: purple;
    top: 0;
    left: 0;
}
div.ztwo {
    background: orange;
    top: 10px;
    left: 10px;
}
div.zthree {
    background: magenta;
    top: 20px;
    left: 20px;
}
div.zfour {
    background: yellow;
    top: 30px;
    left: 30px;
}
div#five,
div#nine {
    z-index: 4;
}
div#six,
div#ten {
    z-index: 3;
}
div#seven,
div#eleven {
    z-index: 2;
```

```
}
div#eight,
div#twelve {
    z-index: 1;
}
div#nested div {
    top: 10px;
    left: 10px;
}
div.slide {
    float: left;
    padding: 5px;
    width: 200px;
    border: 1px solid rgb(200, 200, 200);
    background: white;
    margin: 5px;
    height: 400px;
}
```

4. Save the preceding style sheet as `Example_11-5.css`. When you run the preceding source code in your browser, you should see output like that in Figure 11-28.

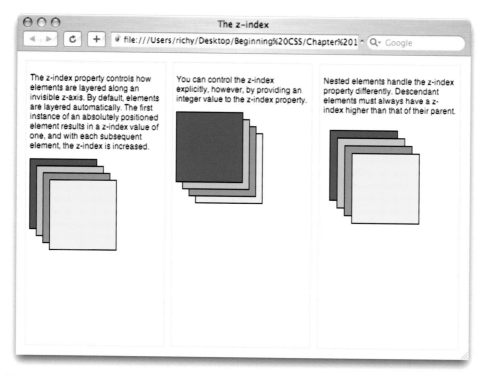

Figure 11-28

How It Works

In Example 11-5, you saw three fundamental concepts to the z-index property. In the first example, you saw how when there is no explicit z-index defined, it is defined automatically, and each subsequent element is positioned higher than the last one.

Then, in the second example, you gave each of the elements an explicit z-index; starting with the <div> element with the id name *five* through the <div> element with id name *eight*. The <div> element with id name *five* is positioned highest in this stack, since it has a z-index of 4, then each subsequent <div> element is stacked lower, all the way to the <div> element with id name *eight*, which has a z-index of 1.

In the third example, you see how the z-index is ignored when it is placed on descendant elements, since descendant elements must always have a higher z-index than that of their parents and ancestors.

In the next section I demonstrate how to apply positioning to some real-world examples, such as vertically aligning content and multicolumn layouts.

Other Ways to Apply Positioning

Positioning is a powerful tool that enables you to create applications in web-based layouts from the simple to the very complex. In the following sections I examine a couple of practical applications of positioning in website design, starting with vertically and horizontally aligning content.

Horizontally and Vertically Aligning Positioned Content

The following technique is used to horizontally and vertically center content in a web browser, although, it could be easily adapted for other alignment scenarios. The technique is demonstrated in Figure 11-29.

In the main style sheet in Figure 11-29a, you see two fundamental concepts coming together. The <div> element with id name *dialogue* is positioned absolutely, and then offset from the top and the left by 50 percent. This is one of the few places where percentage measurement is actually useful. Then the top and left margins of the <div> with id name *dialogue* are adjusted in the negative by exactly half of the element's collective width and collective height. So the top margin is set to a negative number that is exactly half of the sum of the top and bottom border-width, padding, and height values. In this case that number is 112, so half of 112 is 56. Then the left margin is adjusted in the negative by exactly half of the element's collective width, or the left and right border-width, padding, and width values, which comes to the sum of 212, half of which is 106.

The style sheet in Figure 11-29a is included in the markup in Figure 11-29b.

Once the source code in Figure 11-29a and Figure 11-29b is rendered in a browser, you get output like that in Figure 11-29c.

```
body {
    background: lightyellow;
    font: 16px sans-serif;
}
div#dialogue {
    position: absolute;
    width: 200px;
    height: 100px;
    background: yellow;
    border: 1px solid gold;
    top: 50%;
    left: 50%;
    margin: -56px 0 0 -106px;
    padding: 5px;
}
p {
    margin: 0;
}
```

Figure 11-29a

```
<!DOCTYPE html PUBLIC "-//W3C//DTD XHTML 1.0 Strict//EN"
                "http://www.w3.org/TR/xhtml1/DTD/xhtml1-strict.dtd">
<html xmlns='http://www.w3.org/1999/xhtml' xml:lang='en'>
    <head>
        <title>Vertical and Horizontal Alignment</title>
        <link rel='stylesheet' type='text/css' href='096977%20fg1129.css' />
    </head>
    <body>
        <div id='dialogue'>
            <p>
                The dialogue &lt;div&gt; element is aligned vertically and
                horizontally, no matter what the size of the browser
                window.
            </p>
        </div>
    </body>
</html>
```

Figure 11-29b

In Figure 11-29c, you see that the <div> element with id name dialogue is centered both vertically and horizontally in the browser window. Having seen this technique, you might wonder if this can be achieved with variable width or variable height content, that is to say, have a <div> with id name *dialogue* that doesn't have a fixed width or height. And the answer is no, the element this technique is applied to must have a fixed width and height for this technique to succeed. For the overwhelming majority of cases, however, this isn't a problem. You can always overflow content, and provide scroll bars if necessary with the overflow property.

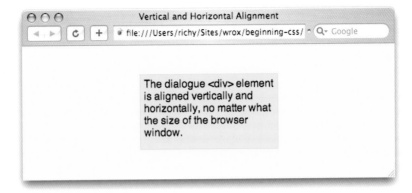

Figure 11-29c

With this technique, you can create dialogues for your users that pop up layered over other content, for example, as shown in Figure 11-30.

You can make the <div> with id name *dialogue* a fixed position element, and you'll have a dialogue that stays in place as the user scrolls. This technique is typically coupled with JavaScript to create pop-up dialogues, and those despised pop-up advertisements that come floating onto the screen from nowhere. Unfortunately, pop-ups like this have many, many legitimate uses, too, so browsers are unable to block them.

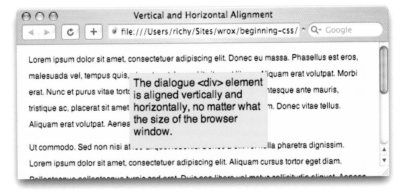

Figure 11-30

In the next section I discuss multicolumn layouts.

Multicolumn Layout

Multicolumn layouts are the crown jewel of web design. Multicolumn web design is pretty ubiquitous and, thankfully, they're easy to crank out too. Earlier in this chapter I demonstrated how to make fixed side columns, and fixed headers and footers. The techniques I discuss in this section are very similar. In fact, you'll see some familiar techniques from those earlier examples at play in the ones that follow, with the difference being that these designs feature no "fixed" position elements, and are designed to be scalable.

A challenge of web page design in making pages that work on a variety of platforms, operating systems, and viewing environments is that different environments hold different challenges. One challenge in particular is creating fluid designs that function on a variety of screen resolutions. A typical goal today is to design for a minimum, 800×600 screen resolution, and scale up if the resolution is higher. Thankfully, the number of people still using an 800×600 screen resolution is diminishing all the time; you can expect to see about 10 percent of your audience using this screen resolution, and less than a fraction of a percent are using a lower screen resolution, with the majority of people at 1024×768 or greater. The designs that I present here scale down to 800×600 as the lowest screen resolution threshold, and up to 1024×768 as an upper viewing threshold. In Chapter 7, you saw that the `min-width` and `max-width` properties are used to define thresholds like this.

So without further ado, the first example of a multicolumn layout that I demonstrate is a simple two-column design. This is demonstrated in Figure 11-31.

In the main style sheet in Figure 11-31a, you see that the `<div>` element with id name *container* contains some groundwork for the multicolumn design. As the id name implies, the *container* `<div>` element contains the elements that will come together to create the two-column layout. It is given a relative position, so that the absolutely positioned *left* column `<div>` positions relative to it. It has a lower width threshold of 600 pixels, and an upper threshold of 1,000 pixels, so that the design can scale up and down, as necessary, to accommodate changes to the window size, or the user's screen resolution. The element that holds the document's content is the `<div>` element with id name *content*. It is given a left margin equal to the left column `<div>` element's collective width, which includes the sum of that element's left and right margin, border, padding, and width. Thus, the framework for a two-column layout is made. In Figure 11-31b, you see a style sheet that targets IE 6 and less.

In Figure 11-31b, you'll recognize the dynamic expressions from both Chapter 7 and earlier in this chapter. To emulate the `min-width` and `max-width` properties, you apply a dynamic expression to the container `<div>` element. When the width of the browser's viewport is greater than 1,000, the width of the container `<div>` element is set to 1000; when it's less than 1,000, but greater than 600, the width of the container element is set to `auto`; and when the browser's viewport is smaller than 600 pixels, the width is set to 600 pixels. The second hack present emulates setting opposing offset properties to imply height for the left column. The style sheets in Figure 11-31a and Figure 11-31b are included in the markup in Figure 11-31c.

```
body {
    background: lightyellow;
    font: 12px sans-serif;
    margin: 0;
    padding: 0;
}
div#container {
    border: 1px solid black;
    min-width: 600px;
    max-width: 1000px;
    position: relative;
    margin: 10px;
}
div#left {
    position: absolute;
    top: 0;
    bottom: 0;
    left: 0;
    width: 200px;
    background: rgb(234, 234, 234);
    padding: 5px;
    border-right: 1px solid black;
}
div#content {
    margin-left: 211px;
    background: white;
    border: 1px solid white;
    padding: 10px;
}
```

Figure 11-31a

```
div#container {
    width: expression(
        documentElement.clientWidth >= 1000?
            1000
        :
            (documentElement.clientWidth <= 600? 600 : 'auto')
    );
}
div#left {
    top: 1px;
    height: expression(
        document.getElementById('container').offsetHeight - 12
    );
}
```

Figure 11-31b

```
<!DOCTYPE html PUBLIC "-//W3C//DTD XHTML 1.0 Strict//EN"
                      "http://www.w3.org/TR/xhtml1/DTD/xhtml1-strict.dtd">
<html xmlns='http://www.w3.org/1999/xhtml' xml:lang='en'>
    <head>
        <title>Multi-column Layout</title>
        <link rel='stylesheet' type='text/css' href='096977%20fgl131.css' />
        <!--[if lt IE 7]>
        <link rel='stylesheet' type='text/css' href='096977%20fgl131.ie.css' />
        <![endif]-->
    </head>
    <body>
        <div id='container'>
            <div id='left'>
                Left side column.
            </div>
            <div id='content'>
                <h4>Lorem Ipsum</h4>
                <p>
                    Lorem ipsum dolor sit amet, consectetuer adipiscing elit.
                    Donec eu massa. Phasellus est eros, malesuada vel, tempus quis,
                    pharetra at, lacus. Ut sit amet libero. Aliquam erat volutpat.
                    Morbi erat. Nunc et purus vitae tortor sodales auctor. Nulla
                    molestie. Pellentesque ante mauris, tristique ac, placerat sit
                    amet, placerat nec, ante. Vestibulum interdum. Donec vitae
                    tellus. Aliquam erat volutpat. Aenean dictum dolor ut sem.
                </p>
                <p>
                    Ut commodo. Sed non nisi at leo aliquet lobortis. Donec a elit
                    vel nulla pharetra dignissim. Lorem ipsum dolor sit amet,
                    consectetuer adipiscing elit. Aliquam cursus tortor eget diam.
                    Pellentesque pellentesque turpis sed erat. Duis non libero vel
                    metus sollicitudin aliquet. Aenean neque. Nunc eget quam a
                    mauris vulputate laoreet. Mauris dictum, eros venenatis
                    fringilla vehicula, tortor augue dignissim ante, id imperdiet
                    risus sapien at odio. Praesent ligula magna, nonummy vitae,
                    facilisis at, fermentum non, diam. Integer sit amet ligula quis
                    lectus bibendum porta. Aliquam neque ipsum, aliquet et, semper
                    vel, blandit ac, massa. Etiam porttitor justo id arcu. Ut ante
                    lacus, rutrum id, vehicula non, faucibus in, lorem. Integer eu
                    ante ut mauris rhoncus molestie. Aenean ut est et lectus tempor
                    pharetra. Fusce sed nibh. Class aptent taciti sociosqu ad litora
                    torquent per conubia nostra, per inceptos hymenaeos.
                </p>
            </div>
        </div>
    </body>
</html>
```

Figure 11-31c

Figure 11-31d shows a simple two-column layout that works in a variety of browsers.

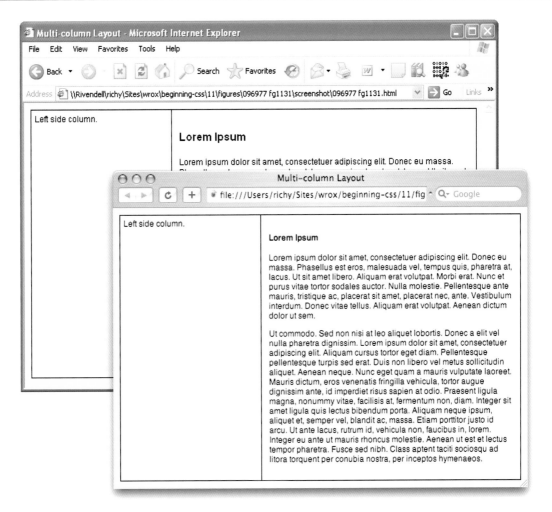

Figure 11-31d

The technique presented in Figure 11-31 puts together concepts from Chapter 7, and concepts that you've see throughout this chapter, but why stop with just a two-column layout? In the next section, I present how to add a heading and a footer to the two-column layout.

Multicolumn Layout with a Heading and Footer

Adding a heading and footer to the multicolumn layout is pretty straightforward; you simply have to make room with the left column, and everything else falls into place. Figure 11-32 demonstrates how to alter the multicolumn layout to accommodate a heading and footer.

```
body {
    background: lightyellow;
    font: 12px sans-serif;
    margin: 0;
    padding: 0 20px;
}
div#heading,
div#container,
div#footer {
    border: 1px solid black;
    max-width: 1000px;
    min-width: 600px;
    background: rgb(244, 244, 244);
}
div#container {
    position: relative;
    margin: 0 auto;
}
div#heading {
    margin: 10px auto -1px auto;
}
div#heading h1 {
    margin: 5px;
}
div#left {
    position: absolute;
    top: 0;
    bottom: 0;
    left: 0;
    width: 200px;
    background: rgb(234, 234, 234);
    padding: 5px;
    border-right: 1px solid black;
}
div#content {
    margin-left: 211px;
    background: white;
    border: 1px solid white;
    padding: 10px;
}
div#footer {
    margin: -1px auto 10px auto;
}
div#footer p {
    margin: 5px;
}
```

Figure 11-32a

The main style sheet in Figure 11-32a is followed by the IE 6 style sheet that you see in Figure 11-32b.

```
div#heading,
div#container,
div#footer {
    width: expression(
        documentElement.clientWidth >= 1000?
            1000
        :
            (documentElement.clientWidth <= 600? 600 : 'auto')
    );
    height: 1px;
}
div#left {
    height: expression(
        document.getElementById('container').offsetHeight - 12
    );
}
```

Figure 11-32b

The style sheets in Figure 11-32a and the style sheet in Figure 11-32b are included in the markup in Figure 11-32c.

Figure 11-32d shows a flexible, two-column design that includes a heading and footer.

There are a few important concepts at play that you need to be aware of in this example. First, have a look at the styles for the heading and the footer; each contains an element that has margin applied. The heading has an <h1> element nested with 5 pixels of margin applied, and the footer has a <p> element nested within it with 5 pixels of margin applied. The heading and the footer both have a one-pixel, solid, black border around each. This is done for more than mere aesthetic reasons; without the border you have the margin of the nested element collapsing with the margin of its parent element. If you recall from Chapter 7, margin collapsing happens whenever the top or bottom margin of one element comes into contact with the top or bottom margin of a parent, or adjacent element. In this example, to prevent margin collapsing from taking place, you need to apply a border to the parent elements, which are the <div> elements with id names *heading* and *footer*. If you remove the border, do so remembering to take margin collapsing into account.

The heading and the footer are also included outside of the container <div> element; you do this to accommodate content in each of these that is of variable height. If the heading and footer were to be placed inside of the container <div> element, you would have to give each a fixed height, and adjust the top and bottom properties of the left column <div> with respect to the collective height of the heading and the footer.

```
<!DOCTYPE html PUBLIC "-//W3C//DTD XHTML 1.0 Strict//EN"
                "http://www.w3.org/TR/xhtml1/DTD/xhtml1-strict.dtd">
<html xmlns='http://www.w3.org/1999/xhtml' xml:lang='en'>
    <head>
        <title>Multi-column Layout</title>
        <link rel='stylesheet' type='text/css' href='096977%20fg1132.css' />
        <!--[if lt IE 7]>
        <link rel='stylesheet' type='text/css' href='096977%20fg1132.ie.css' />
        <![endif]-->
    </head>
    <body>
        <div id='heading'>
            <h1>Heading</h1>
        </div>
        <div id='container'>
            <div id='left'>
                Left side column.
            </div>
            <div id='content'>
                <h4>Lorem Ipsum</h4>
                <p>
                    Lorem ipsum dolor sit amet, consectetuer adipiscing elit.
                    Donec eu massa. Phasellus est eros, malesuada vel, tempus quis,
                    pharetra at, lacus. Ut sit amet libero. Aliquam erat volutpat.
                    Morbi erat. Nunc et purus vitae tortor sodales auctor. Nulla
                    molestie. Pellentesque ante mauris, tristique ac, placerat sit
                    amet, placerat nec, ante. Vestibulum interdum. Donec vitae
                    tellus. Aliquam erat volutpat. Aenean dictum dolor ut sem.
                </p>
                <p>
                    Ut commodo. Sed non nisi at leo aliquet lobortis. Donec a elit
                    vel nulla pharetra dignissim. Lorem ipsum dolor sit amet,
                    consectetuer adipiscing elit. Aliquam cursus tortor eget diam.
                    Pellentesque pellentesque turpis sed erat. Duis non libero vel
                    metus sollicitudin aliquet. Aenean neque. Nunc eget quam a
                    mauris vulputate laoreet. Mauris dictum, eros venenatis
                    fringilla vehicula, tortor augue dignissim ante, id imperdiet
                    risus sapien at odio. Praesent ligula magna, nonummy vitae,
                    facilisis at, fermentum non, diam. Integer sit amet ligula quis
                    lectus bibendum porta. Aliquam neque ipsum, aliquet et, semper
                    vel, blandit ac, massa. Etiam porttitor justo id arcu. Ut ante
                    lacus, rutrum id, vehicula non, faucibus in, lorem. Integer eu
                    ante ut mauris rhoncus molestie. Aenean ut est et lectus tempor
                    pharetra. Fusce sed nibh. Class aptent taciti sociosqu ad litora
                    torquent per conubia nostra, per inceptos hymenaeos.
                </p>
            </div>
        </div>
        <div id='footer'>
            <p>
                Lorem ipsum dolor sit amet, consectetuer adipiscing elit. Donec eu
                massa. Phasellus est eros, malesuada vel, tempus quis, pharetra at,
                lacus.
            </p>
        </div>
    </body>
</html>
```

Figure 11-32c

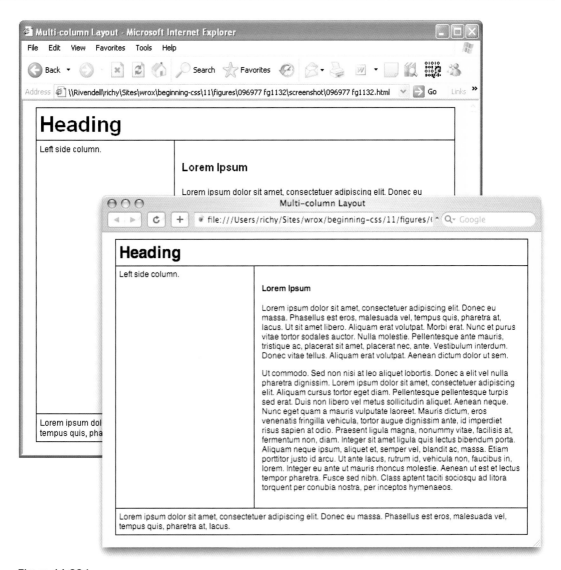

Figure 11-32d

In the IE style sheet, you'll see one odd declaration, `height: 1px;`. You'll also note that the height of the heading, footer, and container `<div>` elements is not one pixel in IE 6. This is a hack! In the web design community, this hack is a variation of a famous hack known as the "Holly Hack." Big John and Holly Gergevin of `positioniseverything.net` originally devised the Holly Hack. The Holly Hack is used to correct certain layout calculation errors that can come up in IE 6 and IE 7. In this case, the left column `<div>` element was not positioning correctly; the values of `top` and `left` were inconsistent with other browsers. When you encounter this, it is usually a case where the Holly Hack is appropriate. To fix a layout bug in IE, you need to apply the Holly Hack to each parent of the element with wacky positioning until its layout corrects. Since explaining the Holly Hack requires a complicated discussion about the internals of IE 6, I avoid going deeper into the topic than what I've explained here. If you'd like to learn more about the Holly Hack, and the concepts at play there, have a look at http://www.satzansatz.de/cssd/onhavinglayout.html.

Summary

In this chapter, you saw the power of positioning in web design. Positioning offers web designers solutions to challenges both simple and complex. In this chapter, you learned the following:

❑ Absolute positioned elements are positioned relative to the viewport, by default.

❑ Relative positioning allows you to change the point of reference used for absolute positioning.

❑ The four offset properties can be used on relatively positioned content to adjust its position with respect to its static origin.

❑ Fixed position elements remain in the same place when a document is scrolled, and fixed position elements are always positioned relative to the viewport.

❑ IE 6 doesn't support fixed positioning, but you can use dynamic expressions and JavaScript to work around the lack of support.

❑ Specifying opposing offset properties on the same element is used to imply dimensions, which is used to get positioned elements that are stretched with fluidity.

❑ You can create the illusion of fixed positioning with absolute positioning, a technique that's often used to create frame-like designs without the frames.

❑ The way in which positioned elements are layered can be controlled with the z-index property, which accepts an integer value.

❑ By default, elements are stacked in ascending order.

❑ Nested elements can't have a higher z-index than their parent.

❑ You can center content vertically and horizontally using positioning, and some tricks with the margin property.

❑ Absolute positioning is key in making multicolumn designs.

Exercises

1. What is the default value of the top, right, bottom, and left properties?

2. What are offset properties used for?

3. If the <body> element has a sole child that is positioned absolutely, what point of reference is used for its positioning?

4. If the <body> element has a sole child that is positioned relatively, with an id name of *relative-element*, and that relatively positioned element has a child that is absolutely positioned, what point of reference is used for the absolutely positioned element?

5. If the element from Exercise 4, *relative-element*, has a fixed position child, what point of reference is used for its positioning?

6. Write a rule that you would use to make an element with the following standard CSS work in IE 6 in standards rendering mode.

```
div#element {
    position: fixed;
    top: 0;
    left: 0;
}
```

7. To make fixed position elements compatible with IE 6, what element must you always place fixed position elements inside of?

8. Write a rule that you would use to make an element with the following standard CSS work in IE 6 and IE 7 in quirks rendering mode.

```
div#element {
    position: fixed;
    bottom: 0;
    left: 0;
}
```

9. The following rule refers to an element that you want to take up all of the space available to it vertically, and positioned to the left. Fill in the blanks.

```
div#column {
    position: absolute;
    _____: 0;
    _____: 0;
    _____: 0;
    padding: 10px;
     border: 1px solid black;
}
```

10. You have five elements that are all absolutely positioned siblings, but no z-index is specified for any of them. Name the stacking order that the browser will use for those elements' z-index property. Provide the z-index declaration for each element, in order.

11. How do you fix the z-index bug in IE 6 and IE 7?

Tables

In Chapter 11, I introduced positioning. In this chapter, I discuss some odds and ends related to styling (X)HTML <table> elements and the controls that CSS provides for flexibility.

Tables are primarily a method to show the relationship between data, much as a spreadsheet application does. As I explore some acceptable uses of tables in this chapter, I discuss:

❑ The optional table elements that can make it easier to style a table and that make the structure more intuitive

❑ Controlling placement of the table caption

❑ Controlling the layout of the table

❑ Controlling the spacing between table cells

Tables can be complex creatures in (X)HTML. If used properly, they allow information to be presented in a neat, organized, and consistent manner. Put simply, data that needs to show relation and logic should be placed into tables. The discussion presented in this chapter also plays heavily into the discussion about styling XML in Chapter 14. The examples presented in Chapter 14 are identical to those presented in this chapter with one very important difference: They're written in XML.

Tables have several optional elements that may be used to further enhance the structure and presentation of a table. This is where I start the discussion.

Optional Table Elements

The <table> element has several optional elements that can be used to enhance the presentation of a table, including captions, columns, headings, and footers. Take a look at a <table> element that makes use of all these optional elements. When I get into the discussion of styling tables, beginning with the section "Table Captions and the caption-side Property," you'll need to understand what is possible in a table. I also present CSS 2 properties that are table-specific, allowing more control over table presentation. The markup in Figure 12-1 shows a table complete with all the optional bells and whistles.

```
<!DOCTYPE html PUBLIC "-//W3C//DTD XHTML 1.0 Strict//EN"
                "http://www.w3.org/TR/xhtml1/DTD/xhtml1-strict.dtd">
<html xmlns='http://www.w3.org/1999/xhtml' xml:lang='en'>
    <head>
        <title>Tables</title>
    </head>
    <body>
        <table>
            <caption>
                Table: My favorite records.
            </caption>
            <colgroup>
                <col id='album' />
                <col id='artist' />
                <col id='released' />
            </colgroup>
            <thead>
                <tr>
                    <th> album          </th>
                    <th> artist         </th>
                    <th> released       </th>
                </tr>
            </thead>
            <tbody>
                <tr>
                    <td> Rubber Soul    </td>
                    <td> The Beatles    </td>
                    <td> 1965           </td>
                </tr>
                <tr>
                    <td> Brown Eyed Girl </td>
                    <td> Van Morrison    </td>
                    <td> 1967            </td>
                </tr>
                <tr>
                    <td> Mellon Collie and the Infinite Sadness </td>
                    <td> The Smashing Pumpkins                   </td>
                    <td> 1995                                    </td>
                </tr>
            </tbody>
            <tfoot>
                <tr>
                    <td> album          </td>
                    <td> artist         </td>
                    <td> released       </td>
                </tr>
            </tfoot>
        </table>
    </body>
</html>
```

The `<caption>` element holds the name of the table, or some other notes about its purpose.

`<col />` elements are used to control certain properties about each table column; most commonly this is used to control the width of each column.

The `<thead>` element designates the table headers. If you are printing a long table, the contents of the `<thead>` element are repeated at the top of every printed page.

The `<th>` element is just like the `<td>` element, except its contents are made bold and centered by default.

The `<tfoot>` element is like the `<thead>` element. When you're printing a long table, the contents of thed `<tfoot>` element are repeated at the bottom of each page.

Figure 12-1

In Figure 12-1, you can see that (X)HTML tables support many additional, optional elements.

❑ The `<caption>` element is used to provide the table with a caption or the name of the table.

❑ The `<colgroup>` element is used to enclose each of the table `<col />` elements.

- ❏ `<col />` elements are used to control certain properties about each table column, the most common being the column width.

- ❏ The `<thead>` element encloses information about column headers. If you print a table that spans more than one page, the information in the `<thead>` element is repeated at the top of each page.

- ❏ The `<tbody>` element contains the main table data.

- ❏ The `<tfoot>` element is similar to the `<thead>` element. When you print a table that spans more than one page, the information in the `<tfoot>` element is repeated at the bottom of each page.

In the coming sections, you learn more about what properties CSS offers for tweaking the visual presentation of (X)HTML tables.

Table Captions and the caption-side Property

Captions are presented in the `<caption>` element. By default, these are rendered above the table in the document. You use the `caption-side` property to control the placement of the table caption.

The following table shows the `caption-side` property and its possible values.

Property	Value
caption-side	top | bottom
	Initial value: top

Although IE 6 and IE 7 support the `<caption>` *element for tables, neither IE 6 nor IE 7 supports the CSS* `caption-side` *property.*

Using the `caption-side` property, you can control whether the caption appears above or below the table. Figure 12-2 is a demonstration of the `caption-side` property.

```
body {
    font-family: sans-serif;
}
table {
    border: 1px solid rgb(200, 200, 200);
    caption-side: bottom;
}
th {
    background: lightyellow;
}
th, td {
    border: 1px solid rgb(200, 200, 200);
    padding: 5px;
}
```

The `caption-side` property controls whether the table caption appears above or below the `<table>`.

Figure 12-2a

The CSS in Figure 12-2a is included in the markup in Figure 12-2b.

```
<!DOCTYPE html PUBLIC "-//W3C//DTD XHTML 1.0 Strict//EN"
                      "http://www.w3.org/TR/xhtml1/DTD/xhtml1-strict.dtd">
<html xmlns='http://www.w3.org/1999/xhtml' xml:lang='en'>
    <head>
        <title>caption-side</title>
        <link rel='stylesheet' type='text/css' href='096977%20fg1202.css' />
    </head>
    <body>
        <table>
            <caption>
                Table: My favorite records.
            </caption>
            <colgroup>
                <col id='album' />
                <col id='artist' />
                <col id='released' />
            </colgroup>
            <thead>
                <tr>
                    <th> album           </th>
                    <th> artist          </th>
                    <th> released        </th>
                </tr>
            </thead>
            <tbody>
                <tr>
                    <td> Rubber Soul      </td>
                    <td> The Beatles      </td>
                    <td> 1965             </td>
                </tr>
                <tr>
                    <td> Brown Eyed Girl  </td>
                    <td> Van Morrison     </td>
                    <td> 1967             </td>
                </tr>
                <tr>
                    <td> Mellon Collie and the Infinite Sadness </td>
                    <td> The Smashing Pumpkins                   </td>
                    <td> 1995                                    </td>
                </tr>
            </tbody>
        </table>
    </body>
</html>
```

Figure 12-2b

In Figure 12-2c, you see how the caption-side property works in the browsers that support it. In Safari and Firefox, the table caption appears beneath the table, but in IE 6 and IE 7, neither of which support the caption-side property, the table caption appears above the table (which is the default position of the caption).

In the next section, I continue the discussion of tables with what styles are allowed on table columns.

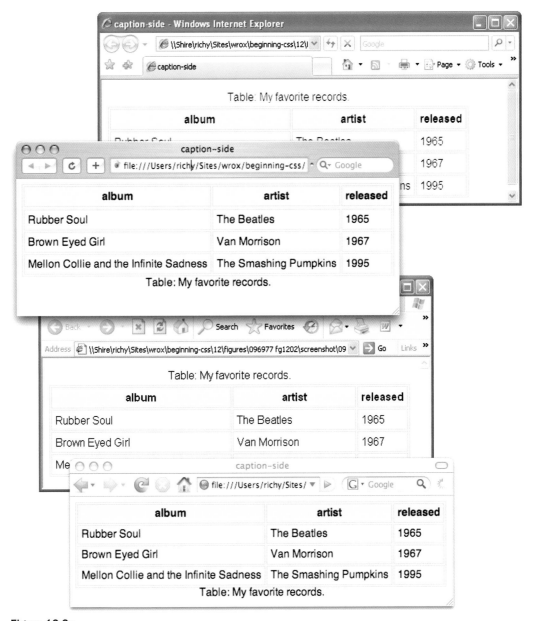

Figure 12-2c

Table Columns

In HTML/XHTML, the `<colgroup>` and `<col>` elements allow the vertical columns of a table to be controlled. This is useful for controlling the width of a column of data or other aspects of presentation, such as background color or text color.

By using these elements, you can span more than one column or have one column defined for each actual column, as in the following example:

```
<table>
    <colgroup>
        <col span='2' />
        <col />
    </colgroup>
    <tbody>
        <tr>
            <td> column 1 </td>
            <td> column 2 </td>
            <td> column 3 </td>
        </tr>
    </tbody>
</table>
```

<col span='2' /> controls the presentation of the <td> elements containing the text of column 1 and column 2, the first two columns of the table. The last <col /> element (without the span attribute) controls the presentation of column 3, contained in the last <td> element.

Using CSS, I can continue the example containing my favorite records. This example shows a column defined for each actual column of data, or in other words, each <td> element appearing in a row. In the example in Figure 12-3, a column is defined for each cell, and each row has three cells; consequently, there are three columns. In Figure 12-3, you see what styles are allowed on the <col /> element.

The CSS in Figure 12-3a is included in the markup in Figure 12-3b.

```
body {
    font-family: sans-serif;
}
table {
    border: 1px solid rgb(200, 200, 200);
    caption-side: bottom;
    width: 100%;
}
th {
    background: lightyellow;
}
th, td {
    border: 1px solid rgb(200, 200, 200);
    padding: 5px;
}
col#album {
    width: 200px;
    background: rgb(244, 244, 244);
    color: crimson;
}
col#released {
    width: 1%;
    background: rgb(244, 244, 244);
}
```

The <col /> is most commonly used to control column width, since this is the most supported CSS feature.

Figure 12-3a

Figure 12-3c shows what you get when the markup is loaded into a browser. You can see in Figure 12-3c that Safari supports no CSS on the (X)HTML <col /> element. IE 6 (and IE 7) support the width, background, and color properties on the <col /> element. Mozilla Firefox supports the width and background properties.

```
<!DOCTYPE html PUBLIC "-//W3C//DTD XHTML 1.0 Strict//EN"
                "http://www.w3.org/TR/xhtml1/DTD/xhtml1-strict.dtd">
<html xmlns='http://www.w3.org/1999/xhtml' xml:lang='en'>
    <head>
        <title>columns</title>
        <link rel='stylesheet' type='text/css' href='096977%20fg1203.css' />
    </head>
    <body>
        <table>
            <caption>
                Table: My favorite records.
            </caption>
            <colgroup>
                <col id='album' />
                <col id='artist' />
                <col id='released' />
            </colgroup>
            <thead>
                <tr>
                    <th> album          </th>
                    <th> artist         </th>
                    <th> released       </th>
                </tr>
            </thead>
            <tbody>
                <tr>
                    <td> Rubber Soul     </td>
                    <td> The Beatles     </td>
                    <td> 1965            </td>
                </tr>
                <tr>
                    <td> Brown Eyed Girl </td>
                    <td> Van Morrison    </td>
                    <td> 1967            </td>
                </tr>
                <tr>
                    <td> Mellon Collie and the Infinite Sadness </td>
                    <td> The Smashing Pumpkins                   </td>
                    <td> 1995                                    </td>
                </tr>
            </tbody>
        </table>
    </body>
</html>
```

Figure 12-3b

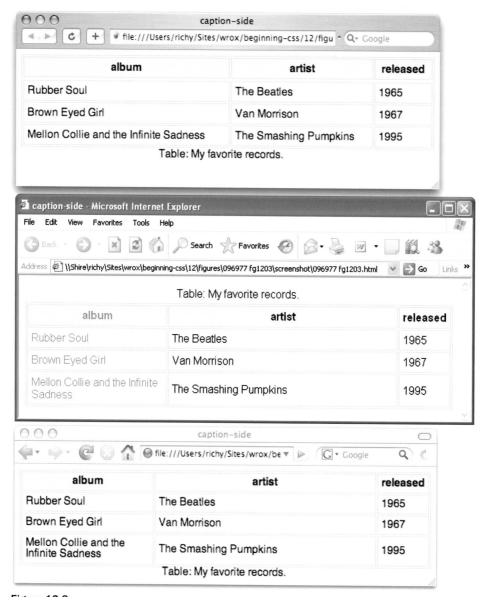

Figure 12-3c

In the following Try It Out, I show how all the extra bells and whistles available for `<table>` elements work in a real-world project and how these elements help you take advantage of CSS. This Try It Out demonstrates placing a recipe in a table. I'm also adding a little eye candy here with CSS background images to enhance the look and feel of the document. This example is also important in Chapter 14, where I show you how it can be ported to XML and styled with CSS as an XML document.

Try It Out   **Applying Tables to a Real Project**

Example 12-1. In the following steps, you apply tables to a real-world project.

1.   Type the following XHTML markup into your text editor:

```
<!DOCTYPE html PUBLIC "-//W3C//DTD XHTML 1.0 Strict//EN"
                "http://www.w3.org/TR/xhtml1/DTD/xhtml1-strict.dtd">
<html xmlns='http://www.w3.org/1999/xhtml' xml:lang='en'>
    <head>
        <title>Spicy Thai Peanut Sauce</title>
        <link rel='stylesheet' type='text/css' href='Example_12-1.css' />
    </head>
    <body>
        <table class='recipe'>
            <caption>
                Spicy Thai Peanut Sauce
            </caption>
            <colgroup>
                <col/>
                <col/>
                <col/>
                <col/>
            </colgroup>
            <thead>
                <tr>
                    <th> quantity    </th>
                    <th> measurement </th>
                    <th> product     </th>
                    <th> instructions </th>
                </tr>
            </thead>
            <tbody>
                <tr>
                    <td> &frac12;        </td>
                    <td> CUPS            </td>
                    <td> Peanut Oil      </td>
                    <td></td>
                </tr>
                <tr>
                    <td> 12              </td>
                    <td> Each            </td>
                    <td> Serrano Peppers </td>
                    <td> Sliced          </td>
                </tr>
                <tr>
                    <td> 16              </td>
                    <td> Each            </td>
                    <td> Garlic Cloves   </td>
                    <td> Minced          </td>
                </tr>
                <tr>
                    <td> 2               </td>
```

```
                    <td> CUPS            </td>
                    <td> Peanut Butter   </td>
                    <td></td>
          </tr>
          <tr>
                    <td> 1               </td>
                    <td> CUPS            </td>
                    <td> Soy Sauce       </td>
                    <td></td>
          </tr>
          <tr>
                    <td> &frac12;        </td>
                    <td> CUPS            </td>
                    <td> Lime Juice      </td>
                    <td></td>
          </tr>
          <tr>
                    <td> 4               </td>
                    <td> TABLESPOONS     </td>
                    <td> Sesame Oil      </td>
                    <td></td>
          </tr>
          <tr>
                    <td> 4               </td>
                    <td> CUPS            </td>
                    <td> Coconut Milk    </td>
                    <td></td>
          </tr>
          <tr>
                    <td> &frac12;        </td>
                    <td> CUPS            </td>
                    <td> Honey           </td>
                    <td></td>
          </tr>
          <tr>
                    <td> &frac12;        </td>
                    <td> CUPS            </td>
                    <td> Brown Sugar     </td>
                    <td></td>
          </tr>
    </tbody>
    <tfoot>
          <tr>
                <td colspan='4'>
                    <ul>
                        <li>
                            Saut&eacute; sliced serranos and garlic in peanut
                            oil till lightly browned.
                        </li>
                        <li>
                            Add all other ingredients and stir till dissolved.
                        </li>
                        <li>
                            Simmer for 5 minutes.
                        </li>
                        <li>
```

```
                                    Pur&eacute;e all in blender.
                                </li>
                            </ul>
                            <p>
                                Saut&eacute; your favorite vegetables; onions,
                                mushrooms, green peppers, and squash work best.

Sprinkle

                                with allspice, salt, and pepper. Optionally add walnuts
                                or pine nuts. Add browned chicken or tofu and glaze
                                with sauce. Serve with jasmine rice.
                            </p>
                        </td>
                    </tr>
                </tfoot>
            </table>
        </body>
    </html>
```

2. Save the file as `Example_12-1.html`.

3. Write the following CSS into your text editor in a separate document:

```css
html {
    background: #fff url('fruit_veg_web.jpg') no-repeat fixed center center;
}
body {
    font-family: monospace;
    padding: 10px;
    margin: 10px;
    /* Moz proprietary opacity property */
    -moz-opacity: 0.7;
    /* Microsoft proprietary filter property */
    filter: progid:DXImageTransform.Microsoft.Alpha(opacity=70);
    /* CSS 3 opacity property */
    opacity: 0.7;
    background: url('cross_hatch.jpg') repeat;
}
table.recipe {
    width: 100%;
    margin-bottom: 5px;
}
caption {
    text-align: left;
    margin-bottom: 5px;
    text-transform: lowercase;
    font-size: 160%;
    padding: 5px;
    letter-spacing: 10px;
    font-weight: bold;
}
table.recipe thead th {
    font-weight: bold;
    font-size: 150%;
    color: black;
}
table.recipe thead th, table.recipe tbody td {
```

```
        padding: 5px;
        text-transform: lowercase;
    }
    table.recipe tbody td, table.recipe tfoot td {
        font-size: 130%;
    }
    table.recipe tfoot td {
        padding: 5px;
    }
    table.recipe tfoot td p {
        padding: 5px;
    }
    li {
        margin-left: 30px;
        padding-left: 30px;
    }
```

4. Save the file as `Example_12-1.css`. This results in the output shown in Figure 12-4.

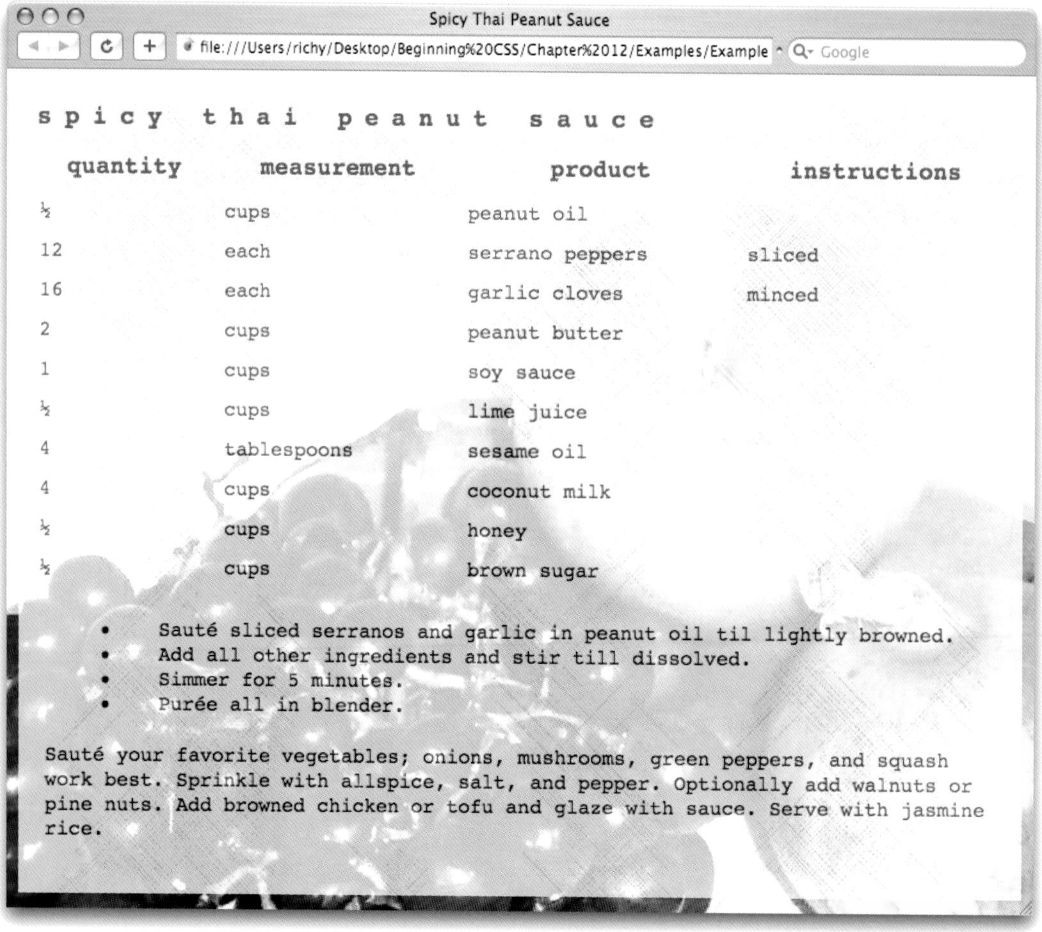

Figure 12-4

How It Works

This example is a lot to digest. Take a look at each part of it in detail to see how it comes together. First, explore the markup of the document. I have included a `<caption>` element inside the table to house the name of the recipe:

```
<table class='recipe'>
    <caption>
        Spicy Thai Peanut Sauce
    </caption>
    <colgroup>
        <col/>
        <col/>
```

I could just as easily have put the name of the recipe in a heading element like `<h1>` and placed it outside the table. I chose the caption so the name of the recipe is bound to the table of ingredients. Later, if I choose to, I can include the name of the website or a logo above the table of ingredients. Next, I've added `<colgroup>` and `<col/>` elements. These can be used to control the layout of each column, although I haven't chosen to take advantage of this capability yet. Although you can use these elements, they are not absolutely necessary. I can leave them out, causing no impact on the table's final rendered layout. Next, I added the table headings, placed inside `<thead>` elements, and I used `<th>` instead of `<td>` to house the contents of each cell:

```
        <col/>
        <col/>
    </colgroup>
    <thead>
        <tr>
            <th> quantity      </th>
            <th> measurement   </th>
            <th> product       </th>
            <th> instructions </th>
        </tr>
    </thead>
    <tbody>
```

I added the `<tbody>` element to house the contents of the recipe itself, and near the bottom of the recipe I listed the instructions in an unordered list (`<ul>`) element. I placed final suggestions in a paragraph at the bottom of the document.

Look more closely at how the CSS comes together with the markup to produce the final rendered output in Figure 12-4. The first rule styles the `<body>` element, and there's quite a bit going on here:

```
body {
    font-family: monospace;
    padding: 10px;
    margin: 10px;
    /* Moz proprietary opacity property */
    -moz-opacity: 0.7;
    /* Microsoft proprietary filter property */
    filter:progid:DXImageTransform.Microsoft.Alpha(opacity=70);
    /* CSS 3 opacity property */
    opacity: 0.7;
    background: url('cross_hatch.jpg') repeat;
}
```

First things first: The <body> element is given a monospace font face, and 10 pixels of margin and 10 pixels of padding. I do both here because some browsers have a default margin, and others have default padding; by setting both values, you get cross-browser consistency.

The next three declarations all deal with opacity. At the time of this writing, the opacity property is an official part of CSS 3. Before the CSS 3 implementation, each browser had its own way of handling opacity, with the exception of Opera, which prior to version 9, did not support opacity, and as of version 9 supports the CSS 3 opacity property. The Mozilla proprietary CSS opacity property is -moz-opacity. Microsoft has a completely different method for specifying opacity: It's handled through a proprietary filter property, but despite its verbose syntax, it produces the same results as the standard CSS 3 opacity property that other browsers support. The use of these opacity properties produces an aesthetically pleasing transparency effect that allows the background specified for the <html> element in this rule to bleed through:

```
html {
    background: #fff url('fruit_veg_web.jpg') no-repeat fixed center center;
}
```

For the <body> element, I've applied a background that uses a cross-hatching effect. The backgrounds I've chosen for this document are purely aesthetic. The image 'fruit_veg_web.jpg' is quite large in size, over 100KB. On first download, this image takes a while to load on a low-bandwidth connection. However, with browser caching, the technique that saves a local copy of all the documents and components of the web page, the bite caused by this large file is limited to the first visit. As visitors view subsequent pages with the same background, the browser remembers that this file is the same one requested from the page before and simply displays that local copy instead of requesting it again from the server.

The next rule on the style sheet is the <table> containing the Spicy Thai Peanut Sauce recipe:

```
table.recipe {
    width: 100%;
    margin-bottom: 5px;
}
```

Here the table is told to take up 100% of the available space horizontally. Because it resides inside of the <body> element, the amount of free space is what's available inside of that element. A margin is applied to the bottom of the table to provide more spacing from the end of the <table> and the start of the <ul>. The caption, containing the name of the recipe, renders above the table by default. Therefore, the table appears in Figure 12-4 just as if you had written the following:

```
table.recipe {
    caption-side: top;
    width: 100%;
    margin-bottom: 5px;
}
```

If I wanted the caption to appear below the table, after the data contained in the <table> element, I would have included caption-side: bottom; instead. For this example, it made more sense for the caption to appear above the table because it contains the name of the recipe.

The next group of style sheet rules style the cells of the table:

```
table.recipe thead th {
    font-weight: bold;
    font-size: 150%;
    color: black;
}
table.recipe thead th, table.recipe tbody td {
    padding: 5px;
    text-transform: lowercase;
}
table.recipe tbody td, table.recipe tfoot td {
    font-size: 130%;
}
table.recipe tfoot td {
    padding: 5px;
}
```

For the cells of the table, I have chosen to take advantage of grouping elements to differentiate the styles for table headings (<thead> element), the body of the table (<tbody> element), and the footer of the table (<tfoot> element). This approach allows me to apply style to the table without adding additional id or class attributes. I use the descendant selector here to ensure that styles are applied only to tables containing the recipe class name. This allows me to include more than one recipe per page or possibly introduce other tables of data without affecting the styles for those tables. Again, the descendant selector works by looking at the element's ancestry. For instance, table.recipe thead th says to look first for a <table> that contains a recipe class name; then look for a <thead> element inside that table; look for a <th> element inside the <thead> element; and finally, apply the declarations contained inside the rule.

Now that you have seen the various elements available for use in a <table> element, the following section explores how you control table width with the table-layout property.

Controlling Table Width with the table-layout Property

The following table outlines the table-layout property and its possible values.

Property	Value
table-layout	auto | fixed
	Initial value: auto

As you learned in Chapter 7, by default, a table expands and contracts to accommodate the data contained inside. As data fills the table, it continues to expand as long as there is space. When you look at them this way, tables are inherently fluid.

```
table {
    border: thin solid black;
}
```

This rule is the same as saying:

```
table {
    border: thin solid black;
    table-layout: auto;
}
```

The `table-layout: auto;` declaration is the default behavior of a table.

By default, the table expands only enough for the content that it contains, and this is the same as `table-layout: auto;`. Sometimes, however, it is necessary to force a table into a fixed width for both the table and the cells. Figure 12-5 is a demonstration of what happens when you specify a fixed width for the table.

```
body {
    font-family: sans-serif;
}
table {
    border: 1px solid rgb(200, 200, 200);
    caption-side: bottom;
    width: 200px;
}
th {
    background: lightyellow;
}
th, td {
    border: 1px solid rgb(200, 200, 200);
    padding: 5px;
}
div#control {
    width: 200px;
    background: crimson;
    color: white;
    text-align: center;
    font-family: monospace;
    margin-bottom: 5px;
    padding: 3px 0;
}
```

Tables do not honor explicit widths, with tables dimensions are always treated like minimum dimensions. To observe this, <table> and <div> elements are both set to the same width.

Figure 12-5a

To see what a 200-pixel width looks like, Figure 12-5b adds a snippet of markup to the body of the XHTML document showing my favorite records.

This code results in the output depicted in Figure 12-5c.

The table is larger than 200 pixels because the text contained in the cells results in a width larger than 200 pixels. You can use the `table-layout: fixed;` declaration to force the table into a 200-pixel width. You simply add the declaration, like so:

```
table {
    border: 1px solid rgb(200, 200, 200);
    caption-side: bottom;
    width: 200px;
    table-layout: fixed;
}
```

```
<!DOCTYPE html PUBLIC "-//W3C//DTD XHTML 1.0 Stric
                      "http://www.w3.org/TR/xhtml1
<html xmlns='http://www.w3.org/1999/xhtml' xml:lan
    <head>
        <title>table-layout</title>
        <link rel='stylesheet' type='text/css' hre
    </head>
    <body>
        <div id='control'>
            &lt; -- 200 pixels -- &gt;
        </div>
        <table>
            <caption>
                Table: My favorite records.
            </caption>
            <colgroup>
                <col id='album' />
                <col id='artist' />
                <col id='released' />
            </colgroup>
            <thead>
                <tr>
                    <th> album        </th>
                    <th> artist       </th>
                    <th> released     </th>
                </tr>
            </thead>
            <tbody>
                <tr>
                    <td> Rubber Soul      </td>
                    <td> The Beatles      </td>
                    <td> 1965             </td>
                </tr>
                <tr>
                    <td> Brown Eyed Girl  </td>
                    <td> Van Morrison     </td>
                    <td> 1967             </td>
                </tr>
                <tr>
                    <td> Mellon Collie and the Inf
                    <td> The Smashing Pumpkins
                    <td> 1995
                </tr>
            </tbody>
        </table>
    </body>
</html>
```

Figure 12-5b

Figure 12-5c

Once you've added the `table-layout: fixed;` declaration, you get the output that you see in Figure 12-6.

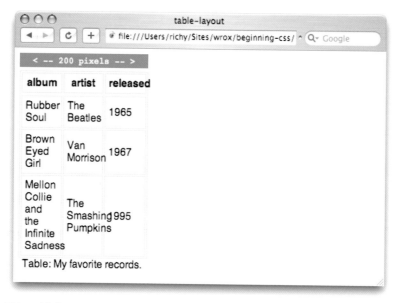

Figure 12-6

The table is forced to maintain its width of 200 pixels, regardless of how much data is contained in its table cells. If the content inside the cells results in a width larger than 200 pixels, the content overflows. The clipped content is not visible when the document is viewed using IE 6 and IE 7, which is what is supposed to happen. As you see in Figure 12-6, however, the clipped content is visible in Safari, and the same is seen when the document is viewed in Firefox or Opera. You can correct this by adding the following rule:

```
th, td {
    overflow: hidden;
}
```

The result is shown in Figure 12-7.

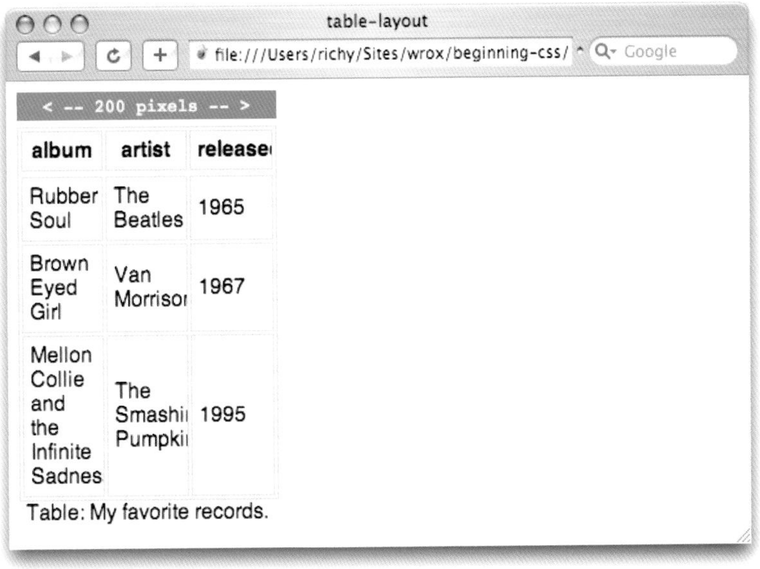

Figure 12-7

This is what the output is supposed to look like according to the `table-layout` property as it appears in the CSS 2 standard, and as supported by IE and Opera. In contrast, as you saw in Chapter 7, the `overflow` property may also be used to add scroll bars so that the clipped content can be viewed.

The `table-layout: fixed;` declaration goes by the width defined for the `<table>` element. In this example, the width is 200 pixels, so the table is forced into having a 200-pixel width. If a width isn't defined for the `<table>` element, it goes by the width for each `<col>` element. If no width is defined there, it goes by the width for the `<td>` elements in the first row of the table.

By default, tables are rendered with `table-layout: auto;`, which in essence means that the table can expand and contract to accommodate the data contained in its cells. What happens if a percentage width is specified for the table? When the table has a percentage width, each cell is given an equal width that expands and contracts, depending on the space available to it. If the content of the cell is larger than the width, however, the content is clipped, just as it was with a fixed width. The rule for the table is changed to `width: 100%;` from `width: 200px;`, as seen in the following example:

```
table {
    border: 1px solid rgb(200, 200, 200);
    caption-side: bottom;
    width: 100%;
    table-layout: fixed;
}
```

The result is shown in Figure 12-8.

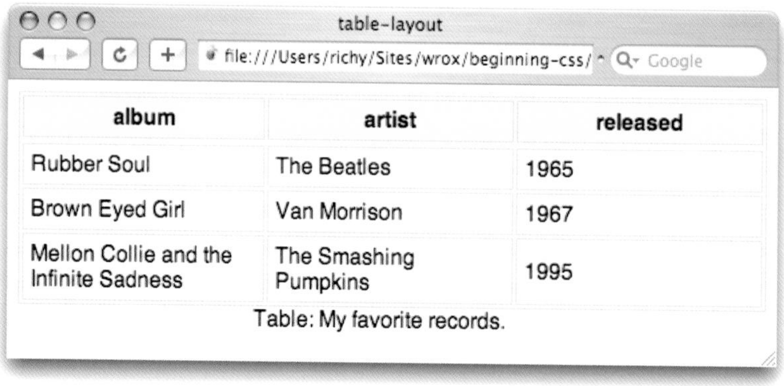
table-layout
file:///Users/richy/Sites/wrox/beginning-css/
Google
album
artist
released
Rubber Soul
The Beatles
1965
Brown Eyed Girl
Van Morrison
1967
Mellon Collie and the Infinite Sadness
The Smashing Pumpkins
1995
Table: My favorite records.

Figure 12-8

Each cell is spaced evenly. When the browser window is resized, the table gets smaller. As it gets smaller and the content of the cells become larger than the cell, the content gets clipped as it did in Figure 12-7.

Now that I've presented what the `table-layout` property does, I want to demonstrate the results of this property when it's applied to the Spicy Thai Peanut Sauce recipe table. Before I apply the `table-layout` property, however, I first need to apply a temporary rule that adds a border to each cell so that you can see the effect of the `table-layout` property. In the following Try It Out, you add this rule to the style sheet.

Try It Out Highlighting Cell Widths

Example 12-2. The following steps show you how to add a rule that applies a border to each cell.

1. Open `Example_12-1.css` and add the following rule to the style sheet:

```
th, td {
    border: 1px solid crimson;
}
```

2. Save the file as `Example_12-2.css`.

3. Make the following changes to `Example_16-1.html` to reference the new style sheet:

```
<!DOCTYPE html PUBLIC "-//W3C//DTD XHTML 1.0 Strict//EN"
                      "http://www.w3.org/TR/xhtml1/DTD/xhtml1-strict.dtd">
<html xmlns='http://www.w3.org/1999/xhtml' xml:lang='en'>
    <head>
        <title>Spicy Thai Peanut Sauce</title>
        <link rel='stylesheet' type='text/css' href='Example_12-2.css' />
    </head>
    <body>
        <table class='recipe'>
            <caption>
                Spicy Thai Peanut Sauce
            </caption>
```

4. Save the file as `Example_12-2.html`. The result is depicted in Figure 12-9.

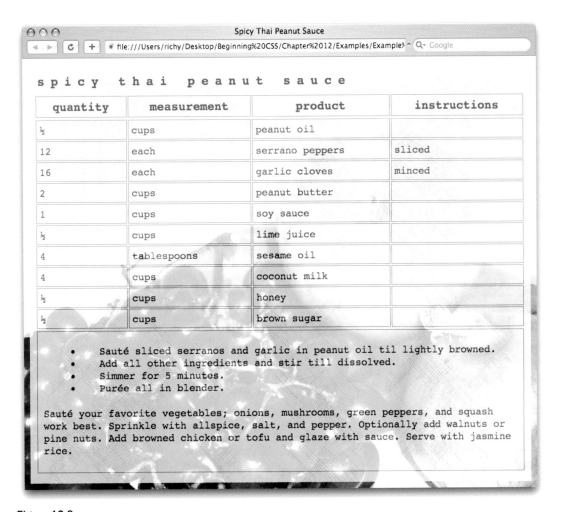

Figure 12-9

How It Works

The borders highlight the fact that the cells of the table are uneven. Each column has a different width depending on the contents of the cells of that column; by default, a table expands just enough to accommodate its content. This table has a 100% width, which only alters that behavior slightly. The columns still expand and contract depending only on how much content is in each cell. The more content a cell is given, the more its column width expands.

Temporary style rules like this are often helpful in highlighting the effects of rendering that are difficult to see. Keeping the highlighted borders, examine the following Try It Out to see what this example looks like when the `table-layout: fixed;` declaration is applied.

Try It Out   **Applying the table-layout Property**

Example 12-3. In the following steps, you apply the `table-layout: fixed;` property.

1. Open `Example_12-2.css` and add the highlighted declaration to the style sheet:

```
table.recipe {
    width: 100%;
    margin-bottom: 5px;
    table-layout: fixed;
}
```

2. Save the file as `Example_12-3.css`.

3. Make the following changes to modify `Example_12-2.html` so that it references the new style sheet:

```
<!DOCTYPE html PUBLIC "-//W3C//DTD XHTML 1.0 Strict//EN"
                      "http://www.w3.org/TR/xhtml1/DTD/xhtml1-strict.dtd">
<html xmlns='http://www.w3.org/1999/xhtml' xml:lang='en'>
    <head>
        <title>Spicy Thai Peanut Sauce</title>
        <link rel='stylesheet' type='text/css' href='Example_12-3.css' />
    </head>
    <body>
        <table class='recipe'>
            <caption>
                Spicy Thai Peanut Sauce
            </caption>
```

4. Save the file as `Example_12-3.html`. The result is shown in Figure 12-10.

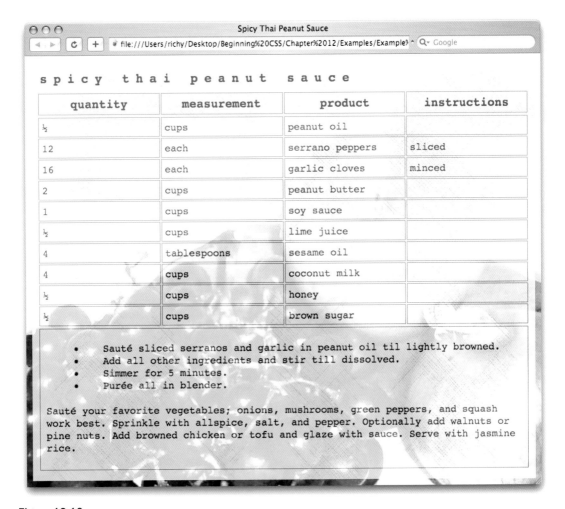

Figure 12-10

How It Works

The addition of the `table-layout: fixed;` declaration gives the table a very clean, organized look. All the columns have equal, consistent widths. With this particular design, the table fills the area available inside the `<body>` element because it has a width of 100%.

The `table-layout: fixed;` declaration allows a table's layout to be more consistent by forcing a table to honor the value contained in the `width` property. The `width` property may be applied to the `<table>` element, to the `<col/>` elements inside the table, or to the cells.

Now that I've thoroughly explored the `table-layout` property, in the following sections I examine the other CSS properties that exist for controlling table layout.

Removing Cell Spacing with the border-collapse Property

The following table outlines the `border-collapse` property and its possible values.

Property	Value
border-collapse	collapse | separate
	Initial value: separate

Tables, by default, include some spacing between each of the cells appearing in the table. In this chapter, you've observed this in each of the "My Favorite Records" examples. In HTML, this was controlled with the `cellspacing` attribute. CSS 2 replaces this attribute with the `border-collapse` property and the `border-spacing` property. By default, the `border-collapse` property has a value of `separate`. If you set the value to `collapse`, you remove the spacing between each cell. When you use the "My Favorite Records" table example again, this is what the rule looks like with the `border-collapse: collapse;` declaration applied.

```
table {
    border: 1px solid rgb(200, 200, 200);
    caption-side: bottom;
    width: 100%;
    table-layout: fixed;
    border-collapse: collapse;
}
```

If you apply the `collapse` value, all the cells are squeezed tightly together. Figure 12-11 shows what happens.

Figure 12-11

The `border-collapse: collapse;` *property is currently the best way to remove all spacing from between cells, because this property is supported by IE 6, IE 7, Firefox, Opera, and Safari.*

The next section talks about how you can control spacing between table cells with greater precision with the `border-spacing` property.

The border-spacing Property

The following table outlines the `border-spacing` property and its possible values.

Property	Value
border-spacing	\<length\> \<length\>? Initial value: 0

IE 6 and IE 7 do not support the `border-spacing` *property.*

To control the spacing between cells, the `border-spacing` property was added in CSS 2. The `border-spacing` property allows more control over cell spacing than `border-collapse` because it allows the length to be specified.

If, as in the following example, you provide a single length value of 15px, 15 pixels of space are added between each cell, both vertically and horizontally:

```
table {
    border: 1px solid rgb(200, 200, 200);
    caption-side: bottom;
    width: 100%;
    table-layout: fixed;
    border-spacing: 15px;
}
```

The result is shown in Figure 12-12. You can see that IE 6 does not support the `border-spacing` property (nor does IE 7, for that matter). Firefox, Opera, and Safari do support this property.

The `border-spacing` property has the following syntax:

```
border-spacing: <vertical spacing length> <horizontal spacing length>;
```

If the optional second value is present, this property allows the vertical and horizontal spacing to be specified. The following snippet results in 15 pixels of space between the top and bottom of each cell:

```
table {
    border: 1px solid rgb(200, 200, 200);
    caption-side: bottom;
    width: 100%;
    table-layout: fixed;
    border-spacing: 0 15px;
}
```

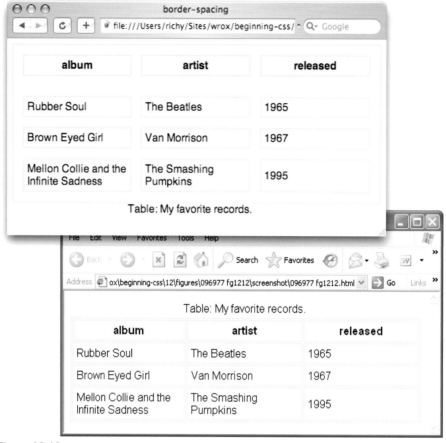

Figure 12-12

The result is shown in Figure 12-13.

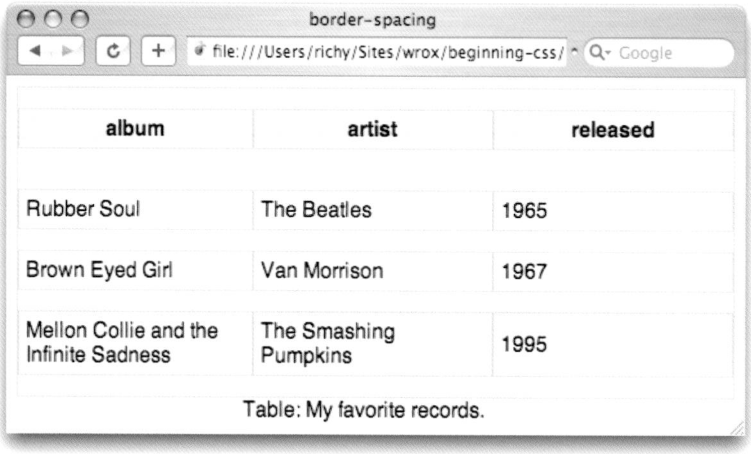

Figure 12-13

Whereas, if I flip the values around, as in the following:

```
table {
    border: 1px solid rgb(200, 200, 200);
    caption-side: bottom;
    width: 100%;
    table-layout: fixed;
    border-spacing: 15px 0;
}
```

I get 15 pixels of space between the left and right edges of each cell. The result is shown in Figure 12-14.

Figure 12-14

Now that I've shown you how to control the spacing between cells, you can apply this knowledge to the Spicy Thai Peanut Sauce recipe table. The following Try It Out demonstrates a practical use of the `border-collapse` property in action.

Try It Out   Applying Cell Spacing

Example 12-4. The following steps show how to work with cell spacing.

1.   Open `Example_12-3.css` and make the following modifications to the file:

```
table.recipe {
    width: 100%;
    margin-bottom: 5px;
    table-layout: fixed;
    border-collapse: collapse;
}
```

2.   Save the file as `Example_12-4.css`.

3.   Update the markup in `Example_12-3.html` to reflect the new style sheet:

```
<!DOCTYPE html PUBLIC "-//W3C//DTD XHTML 1.0 Strict//EN"
                    "http://www.w3.org/TR/xhtml1/DTD/xhtml1-strict.dtd">
<html xmlns='http://www.w3.org/1999/xhtml' xml:lang='en'>
```

```
<head>
    <title>Spicy Thai Peanut Sauce</title>
    <link rel='stylesheet' type='text/css' href='Example_12-4.css' />
</head>
<body>
    <table class='recipe'>
        <caption>
            Spicy Thai Peanut Sauce
        </caption>
```

4. Save the file as `Example_12-4.html`. The result of these changes is shown in Figure 12-15.

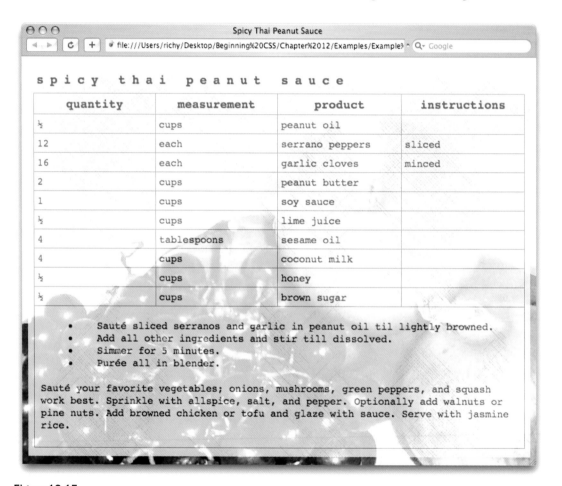

Figure 12-15

How It Works

As you can see in the output, the addition of `border-collapse: collapse;` fine-tunes the design for the Spicy Thai Peanut Sauce recipe table. Removing the extra space between the cells tightens up the design.

At this point, I can remove the temporary borders that I included to make the cell edges obvious:

```
th, td {
    border: 1px solid crimson;
}
```

With this rule removed, the page looks like what's shown in Figure 12-16.

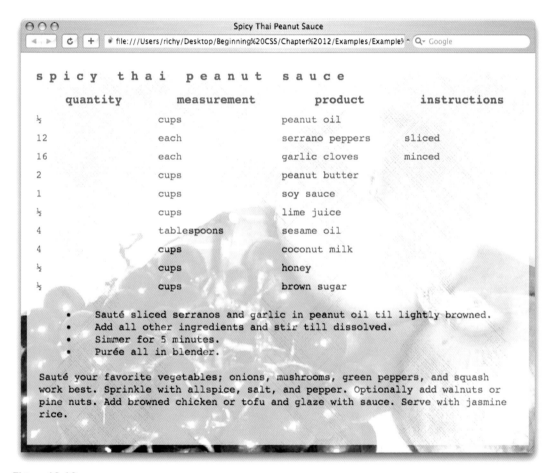

Figure 12-16

The final product shown in Figure 12-16, with the temporary border removed, is saved in the source code files for download at www.wrox.com. After downloading the entire folder structure, you can find the files, Example_12-5.html and Example_12-5.css, under Chapter 12/Try It Out.

Summary

In this chapter, I showed you what is possible with HTML/XHTML tables. Here is what I covered:

❑ Tables have a lot of optional elements that make the structure easier to style. These include columns, heading groupings, body groupings, and footer groupings.

❑ You control the placement of a table's caption by using the `caption-side` property.

❑ You control a table's layout by using the `table-layout` property. With this property, it is possible to force a table into a certain width.

❑ You can remove the spacing between table cells by using the `border-collapse` property.

❑ You can adjust the spacing between table cells by using the `border-spacing` property.

In the next chapter, I discuss what CSS offers for styling content printing.

Later on, in Chapter 14, I begin discussing how to style an XML document. As I mentioned earlier in this chapter, Chapter 14 relies heavily on the content presented in this chapter because it shows you how to create the examples presented in this chapter with XML and CSS.

Exercises

1. Which of the properties discussed in this chapter do not work in IE 6 and IE 7?

2. Describe what the `table-layout: fixed;` declaration does.

3. When sizing using the `table-layout: fixed;` declaration, how does the browser determine the width of table columns?

4. What purpose does the optional `<thead>` element serve?

5. What element would you use if you wanted table column headers that are styled bold and centered?

6. In what containing element does the main table data appear?

7. What browser does not support applying width to table columns? (At the time of this writing, of course.)

Part III

Advanced CSS and Alternative Media

13

Styling for Print

You can use a specific style sheet to style content for print. In Chapter 2, you saw the differences between length units used for a computer screen and length units used for print. This is one of the key reasons that separate style sheets for print exist. Specifying measurements designated for computer screens, such as pixel units, can potentially be inconsistent in printed documents, whereas real-world, absolute length units, such as inches, centimeters, points, and so on are ideally suited for print.

A style sheet written explicitly for print enables developers to exclude irrelevant portions of a web document from the printed version. For example, no document navigation is required in a printed version. Additionally, because color documents have some expense associated with them, depending on the type of printer and what type of ink or toner the printer uses, it is also often better to exclude background images or other aspects of the design that result in greater consumption of expensive ink or toner. For these reasons, print versions of web documents are often simplified to simple black and white productions of the original document. Only foreground images relevant to the document are retained. In fact browsers, by default, strip out all background images and color; to print these, the user must specifically enable them before printing.

CSS 2 provides several properties for controlling the presentation of paged media, although at the time of this writing a sparse selection of those properties is actually implemented in current browsers. CSS 2 properties control such things as where page breaks occur, the size of the page margins, and the size of the page itself. In this area, Opera boasts the best support for the CSS 2 paged media properties; I focus on only the features that have the best support.

Applying Styles Based on Media

In order to print in CSS, you need a way of differentiating styles intended for print from styles intended for the computer screen. CSS can apply to a variety of documents, not just (X)HTML, and CSS can be used on a variety of different devices and media.

To target different media, you use the media attribute, which is applied to the `<link />` element, or the `<style>` element. Or, from within a style sheet, you can target different media using @media rules. You see examples of these later in this section. First, let's examine the different types of media that CSS can theoretically be applied to. The different types of media are outlined in the following table.

Media	Purpose
all	Suitable for all devices.
braille	Intended for Braille tactical feedback devices.
embossed	Intended for paged Braille printers.
handheld	Intended for handheld devices.
print	Intended for presentation to a printer (in a browser, use print preview to view the print style sheet).
projection	Intended for projected presentations.
screen	Intended for presentation on a color computer screen.
speech | aural	Intended for presentation to a speech synthesizer (called aural in CSS 2 and speech in CSS 2.1).
tty	Intended for media using a fixed-pitch character grid (such as teletypes, terminals, or portable devices with limited display capabilities).
tv	Intended for television (low resolution, low color, limited scrollability).

PC and Mac browsers recognize only screen, print, and all values.

As you can see in the preceding table, CSS can target a wide variety of media types. For the purposes of the discussion presented in this chapter, you need only be concerned with the screen, print, and all media. Each medium can be supplied as a value to the media attribute. For example, if you wanted a style sheet to apply only to styles presented in a PC or Mac browser, you would add the attribute media="screen" to either the `<link />` or `<style>` elements. A demonstration appears in Figure 13-1.

```
p {
    width: 200px;
    height: 200px;
    padding: 10px;
    margin: 10px;
    border: 1px solid gold;
    background: yellow;
    font: 12px sans-serif;
}
```

Figure 13-1a

In Figure 13-1a, you see that some basic styles have been applied to the `<p>` element, nothing fancy, or really of particular interest. The style sheet in Figure 13-1a is included in the markup that you see in Figure 13-1b.

In Figure 13-1b, you see one new addition, the `media='screen'` attribute, is applied to the `<link />` element, which tells the browser that the styles are intended for onscreen display only.

```
<!DOCTYPE html PUBLIC "-//W3C//DTD XHTML 1.0 Strict//EN"
                      "http://www.w3.org/TR/xhtml1/DTD/xhtml1-strict.dtd">
<html xmlns='http://www.w3.org/1999/xhtml' xml:lang='en'>
    <head>
        <title>print</title>
        <link rel='stylesheet'
            type='text/css'
            media='screen'
            href='096977%20fg1301.css' />
    </head>
    <body>
        <p>
            Lorem ipsum dolor sit amet, consectetuer adipiscing elit. Donec eu
            massa. Phasellus est eros, malesuada vel, tempus quis, pharetra at,
            lacus. Ut sit amet libero. Aliquam erat volutpat. Morbi erat. Nunc
            et purus vitae tortor sodales auctor. Nulla molestie. Pellentesque
            ante mauris, tristique ac, placerat sit amet, placerat nec, ante.
            Vestibulum interdum. Donec vitae tellus. Aliquam erat volutpat.
            Aenean dictum dolor ut sem.
        </p>
    </body>
</html>
```

Figure 13-1b

In Figure 13-1c, you don't notice anything extraordinary; you see a `<p>` element with the styles applied as you would expect. The effects of the addition of the `media='screen'` attribute become noticeable when you go to print the document. Figure 13-1d shows what the print preview looks like.

Figure 13-1c

Figure 13-1d

In Figure 13-1d, you see what's happened here—since the styles only apply to onscreen display, they aren't applied to the print version of the document. If you would have included media='all', the styles would be present in the printed version. Or, you could create a style sheet that applies to print exclusively, by using the media='print' attribute. In the next section I discuss the @media rule, which allows you to make medium-based distinctions from within the style sheet.

The @media Rule

The @media rule is used within a style sheet to enclose rules where you can make style sheet adjustments based on medium. A demonstration of the @media rule appears in Figure 13-2.

```
@media screen {
    p {
        width: 200px;
        height: 200px;
        padding: 10px;
        margin: 10px;
        border: 1px solid gold;
        background: yellow;
        overflow: auto;
        font: 12px sans-serif;
    }
}
@media print {
    p {
        width: 2in;
        padding: 0.25in;
        border: 1pt solid black;
        text-align: justify;
    }
}
```

Figure 13-2a

In Figure 13-2a, in the external style sheet, you see that new syntax is enclosing the two rules that refer to the <p> element; these are the @media rules. The top @media rule applies to onscreen display of <p> elements, and the bottom @media rule applies to print display of <p> elements. You'll also note that the measurements for each <p> element also differ based on medium. If you recall from Chapter 2, real-world lengths such as centimeters, inches, and so forth, work better in print, whereas onscreen layout works better with screen-based measurements such as pixels. The style sheet in Figure 13-2a is included in the markup in Figure 13-2b.

```
<!DOCTYPE html PUBLIC "-//W3C//DTD XHTML 1.0 Strict//EN"
                      "http://www.w3.org/TR/xhtml1/DTD/xhtml1-strict.dtd">
<html xmlns='http://www.w3.org/1999/xhtml' xml:lang='en'>
    <head>
        <title>print</title>
        <link rel='stylesheet' type='text/css' href='096977%20fg1302.css' />
    </head>
    <body>
        <p>
            Lorem ipsum dolor sit amet, consectetuer adipiscing elit. Donec eu
            massa. Phasellus est eros, malesuada vel, tempus quis, pharetra at,
            lacus. Ut sit amet libero. Aliquam erat volutpat. Morbi erat. Nunc
            et purus vitae tortor sodales auctor. Nulla molestie. Pellentesque
            ante mauris, tristique ac, placerat sit amet, placerat nec, ante.
            Vestibulum interdum. Donec vitae tellus. Aliquam erat volutpat.
            Aenean dictum dolor ut sem.
        </p>
    </body>
</html>
```

Figure 13-2b

The code in Figure 13-2a and Figure 13-2b result in the output that you see in Figure 13-2c.

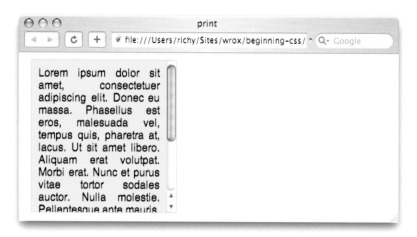

Figure 13-2c

In Figure 13-2c, you see the result of the onscreen styles presented in the first rule. Figure 13-2d shows the result of the print styles.

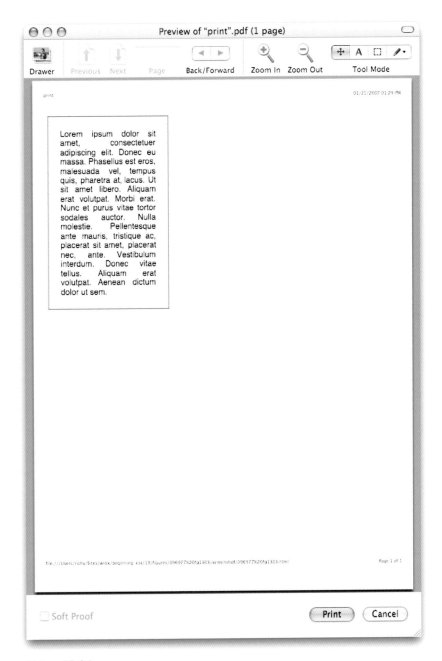

Figure 13-2d

In the following Try It Out, you review the media attribute and @media rules.

Try It Out   **Making Style Sheets for Specific Media**

Example 13-1. To review the `media` attribute and `@media` rules, follow these steps.

1. Enter the following XHTML document in your text editor:

```
<!DOCTYPE html PUBLIC "-//W3C//DTD XHTML 1.0 Strict//EN"
                      "http://www.w3.org/TR/xhtml1/DTD/xhtml1-strict.dtd">
<html xmlns='http://www.w3.org/1999/xhtml' xml:lang='en'>
    <head>
      <title>media</title>
      <link rel='stylesheet' type='text/css' href='Example_13-1.css' media='all' />
    </head>
    <body>
        <p id='screen'>
            The media attribute lets you control what styles are applied to which
            media.  PC and Mac browsers use the values print, all, and screen,
            but there are many more media types than these.
        </p>
        <p id='print'>
            The @media rule can also be used to control styles based on medium,
            but it can do so directly from the style sheet, with no need for HTML.
        </p>
        <p>
            The @media rule simply wraps the rules that are to be applied to a
            particular medium.
        </p>
    </body>
</html>
```

2. Save the preceding document as `Example_13-1.html`.

3. Enter the following style sheet in your text editor:

```
p {
    font: 12px sans-serif;
    background: yellow;
    padding: 10px;
}
@media screen {
    p#print {
        display: none;
    }
    p#screen {
        border: 10px solid gold;
    }
}
@media print {
    p {
        padding: 0.05in;
    }
    p#print {
        border: 10pt solid gold;
    }
    p#screen {
```

```
        display: none;
    }
}
```

4. Save the preceding document as `Example_13-1.css`. Figure 13-3 shows the rendered output in Safari, and the print preview.

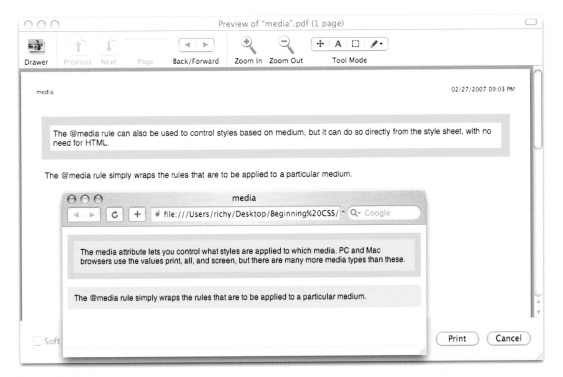

Figure 13-3

How It Works

In Example 13-1, you made use of the `media` attribute and the `@media` rule. In the XHTML document, you included an external style sheet via the `<link />` element, and on the `<link />` element you included the attribute `media='all'`, which tells the browser that the style sheet applies to all media. Insofar as your PC or Mac browser is concerned, that means the styles apply to both print and screen media.

Within the style sheet, you see the style sheet divided into three parts: portions that apply to all media, rules that apply only to screen, and rules that apply only to print. Let's look at the first rule in the style sheet.

```
p {
    font: 12px sans-serif;
    background: yellow;
    padding: 10px;
}
```

In this rule you see a font specified in pixels, and a background color, and padding applied to all <p> elements. You'll note that in the print preview in Figure 13-3, you don't see any background colors, and that the text is still readable, even though it is specified in pixels. Browsers don't print background colors or images, by default. There are no workarounds for this limitation of printing from a browser, except for what controls the browser provides to the end user. Safari doesn't offer the option of printing background colors or images, nor does Firefox or Opera on the Mac. In IE 6 and IE 7, you can enable the printing of background colors and images from Internet Options ⇨ Tools ⇨ Advanced, scroll down to the "Printing" heading under "Settings," and then check the box "Print background colors and images." In Firefox on Windows, you can print background colors and images by going to File ⇨ Page Setup and checking the box labeled "Print Background (colors & images) ." In Opera on Windows, go to File ⇨ Print Options and check the box labeled "Print page background."

Next in the style sheet is a collection of rules that apply to the screen exclusively. The <p> element with id name *print* is hidden from the screen by setting the value of the display property to none, and the <p> element with id name screen is given a 10-pixel, solid, gold border. You learn more about the display property in Chapter 14.

```
@media screen {
    p#print {
        display: none;
    }
    p#screen {
        border: 10px solid gold;
    }
}
```

Then, following the collection of rules that apply to the screen is a collection of rules that apply to print.

```
@media print {
    p {
        padding: 0.05in;
    }
    p#print {
        border: 10pt solid gold;
    }
    p#screen {
        display: none;
    }
}
```

In the second collection of rules, the padding around each <p> element is set to 0.05in, the border is set to 10pt, and the <p> element with id name screen is set to not display, with the display: none; declaration.

In the next section, I describe how to control page breaks in printed content.

Controlling Page Breaks

Two print properties, or paged media properties as it is referred to by the W3C, that all popular browsers have in common are `page-break-before` and `page-break-after`. These properties are outlined in the following table.

Property	Value
page-break-before	auto | always | avoid | left | right Initial value: auto
page-break-after	auto | always | avoid | left | right Initial value: auto

The `page-break-before` and `page-break-after` properties control where page breaks are made. Unfortunately, even though different browsers offer support for these two properties, they do not support all the values that CSS 2 allows. Firefox, Safari, IE 6, and IE 7 support only the keywords `always` and `auto`. Opera supports all of the keywords.

The `page-break-before` and `page-break-after` properties dictate where a page break should be made depending on where an element appears in a document. A demonstration of `page-break-before` is shown in Figure 13-4.

```
p {
    font: 16px sans-serif;
    border: 1px solid black;
    padding: 10px;
    margin: 10px;
}
@media print {
    p {
        font: 12pt sans-serif;
        border: 1pt solid black;
        padding: 0.05in;
        margin: 0.05in;
    }
    p#before {
        page-break-before: always;
    }
}
```

Figure 13-4a

In the style sheet that you see in Figure 13-4a, you see some styles that apply to all media (the first rule), and styles that apply to print, exclusively. You are setting basically the same styles for onscreen and print, but you are applying screen-specific measurements for the screen, and print-specific measurements for print. Then, you apply the declaration `page-break-before: always;` to the <p> element with id name *before*. The styles in Figure 13-4a are applied to the markup in Figure 13-4b.

The code in Figure 13-4a and Figure 13-4b result in the output that you see in Figure 13-4c.

```
<!DOCTYPE html PUBLIC "-//W3C//DTD XHTML 1.0 Strict//EN"
                      "http://www.w3.org/TR/xhtml1/DTD/xhtml1-strict.dtd">
<html xmlns='http://www.w3.org/1999/xhtml' xml:lang='en'>
    <head>
        <title>print</title>
        <link rel='stylesheet' type='text/css' href='096977%20fg1304.css' />
    </head>
    <body>
        <p>
            Lorem ipsum dolor sit amet, consectetuer adipiscing elit. Donec eu
            massa. Phasellus est eros, malesuada vel, tempus quis, pharetra at,
            lacus. Ut sit amet libero. Aliquam erat volutpat. Morbi erat. Nunc
            et purus vitae tortor sodales auctor. Nulla molestie. Pellentesque
            ante mauris, tristique ac, placerat sit amet, placerat nec, ante.
            Vestibulum interdum. Donec vitae tellus. Aliquam erat volutpat.
            Aenean dictum dolor ut sem.
        </p>
        <p id='before'>
            Ut commodo. Sed non nisi at leo aliquet lobortis. Donec a elit vel
            nulla pharetra dignissim. Lorem ipsum dolor sit amet, consectetuer
            adipiscing elit. Aliquam cursus tortor eget diam. Pellentesque
            pellentesque turpis sed erat. Duis non libero vel metus
            sollicitudin aliquet. Aenean neque. Nunc eget quam a mauris
            vulputate laoreet. Mauris dictum, eros venenatis fringilla
            vehicula, tortor augue dignissim ante, id imperdiet risus sapien
            at odio. Praesent ligula magna, nonummy vitae, facilisis at,
            fermentum non, diam. Integer sit amet ligula quis lectus bibendum
            porta. Aliquam neque ipsum, aliquet et, semper vel, blandit ac,
            massa. Etiam porttitor justo id arcu. Ut ante lacus, rutrum id,
            vehicula non, faucibus in, lorem. Integer eu ante ut mauris
            rhoncus molestie. Aenean ut est et lectus tempor pharetra. Fusce
            sed nibh. Class aptent taciti sociosqu ad litora torquent per
            conubia nostra, per inceptos hymenaeos.
        </p>
    </body>
</html>
```

Figure 13-4b

When you preview the printed version of the document, you get output similar to what you see in Figure 13-4d. A page break appears before the <p> element with id name *before*.

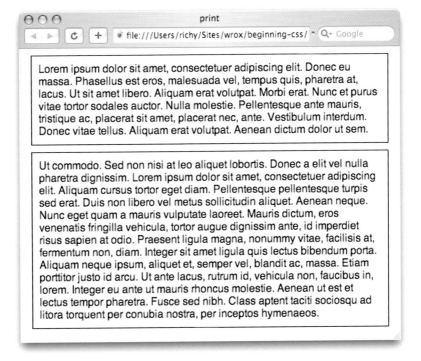

Figure 13-4c

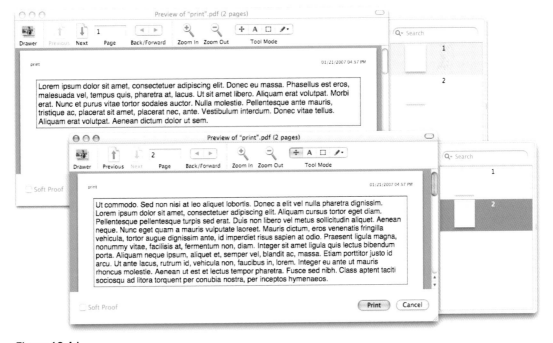

Figure 13-4d

As you can surmise from the example in Figure 13-4c, the `page-break-after` property works the same way as `page-break-before`, but it forces a page break after an element.

> The print properties that CSS provides should be used in situations where you have control over the actual printing of a document (size of the paper and the printer settings), such as in a corporate intranet application. For a public website, you should provide a print version of the document that exhibits as much flexibility as possible.

Summary

Style sheets can be made specifically for onscreen display, or for print, or for both.

❑ For print, you should consider the cost of ink. Because ink and toner are expensive, avoiding high color designs is considered best practice in the formulation of print style sheets.

❑ The print properties that CSS provides should not be used unless you have control over the actual printing of the document.

In Chapter 14, I take a look at the properties that CSS provides for styling XML data.

Exercises

1. Which media values apply to PC and Mac browsers?

2. Write the opening tag for the `<style>` element, targeting the styles to print.

3. What does the `page-break-before` property do?

4. Write a sample style sheet that includes three rules; the first rule applies to all media types, the second rule applies to onscreen layout, and the third applies to print.

XML

In Chapter 12, I demonstrated the various options available to structure and style tables. In this chapter, I discuss how CSS can be combined with XML to style XML documents. This chapter covers the following:

- ❑ What XML is
- ❑ How to create an XML document structure suitable for presentation
- ❑ The XML declaration
- ❑ The CSS `display` property
- ❑ Displaying block-level boxes with XML and CSS
- ❑ Displaying inline-level boxes with XML and CSS
- ❑ Recreating the structure, layout, and behavior of HTML tables using XML and CSS

XML is a robust and flexible markup language. Its uses extend to desktop applications such as spreadsheets and music jukebox software. It is also used heavily on the Internet for a plethora of applications. Many people see XML as the web language of tomorrow, one that will eventually replace HTML as the mainstream markup language of choice for building websites. In the following sections, you look further into XML.

> In this chapter I assume that you have a basic familiarity with XHTML. If you'd like to learn more about XHTML, try *Beginning Web Programming with HTML, XHTML, and CSS* by Jon Duckett (Wrox Press, 2004). For more information about XML, try *Beginning XML, Third Edition*, by David Hunter et al. (Wrox Press, 2004).

Crash Course in XML

XML documents have many uses. For example, an XML document can be used to store data (like a database) because in an XML document you invent the tags and attributes. You have the advantage of creating tags in an XML document that describe the data they contain. Because you have the freedom to create elements and attributes as you wish, the data contained in the document can be organized much more efficiently and semantically than by using HTML alone. Your ability to invent elements and attributes makes using XML advantageous in another way: It creates a document structure that makes sense to both humans and computers. Placing a recipe between `<recipe>` tags makes much more sense than using the various elements of HTML and XHTML. Placing a recipe between `<recipe>` tags also makes it easier for a web developer to design a search that looks for pages that contain only recipes. He or she can also share or transport those recipes to a variety of applications, such as spreadsheet programs and word processors, or by syndication to thousands or even millions of websites worldwide. XML's most impressive benefit is that it can be used for a variety of applications, not just for display on a web page.

> *The use of XML to syndicate data is typically called Really Simple Syndication (RSS), a specification that uses the XML language to describe syndicated data. RSS is in use today by thousands (perhaps even millions) of websites, and this is just one of the many uses of XML.*

XML can also be used to present data on the web as an HTML or XHTML document does. This isn't, however, the most common use of XML; in fact, the world's most popular browser, Internet Explorer 6, offers only mediocre support for XML display using CSS. Mozilla, Opera, and Safari, in contrast, have excellent support for the CSS required to display an XML document, and the examples in this chapter display very well if viewed in one of these browsers. Note that CSS is not the only solution in the works for displaying XML in a browser. Another solution is the Extensible Stylesheet Language (XSL), a style-sheet language designed specifically for XML.

> *XSL isn't a replacement for CSS in XML documents; XSL is a more complicated style-sheet language that uses XML syntax. XSL is capable of much more than CSS. For instance, XSL is capable of completely transforming documents. Both languages have advantages for particular tasks and may both be utilized to present XML documents.*

For the sake of staying on topic and simplicity, I cover styling XML using only CSS with what's available in today's browsers.

XML most closely resembles HTML; however, the angle bracket is about the only thing the two languages have in common. Let's take a look at XML document structure.

❑ XML must be well formed; all elements must have both an opening and a closing tag, and all attribute values must be enclosed with quotations. All elements must be properly nested, that is, you can't have `<recipe><ingredient></recipe></ingredient>`, it must be `<recipe><ingredient></ingredient></recipe>`.

❑ XML documents can contain only one root element.

❑ XML is case-sensitive.

Figure 14-1a is a brief example of an XML document.

```
<?xml version="1.0"?>
<page>
    <books>
        <book favorite="true">
            The Alchemist <cover art="alchemist.jpg"/>
        </book>
        <book>Dante's Inferno</book>
    </books>
</page>
```

Figure 14-1a

When you view this in a browser, IE 6 and Firefox display a tree of the XML source code as shown in Figure 14-1b. Safari doesn't show the source elements; it just shows the data.

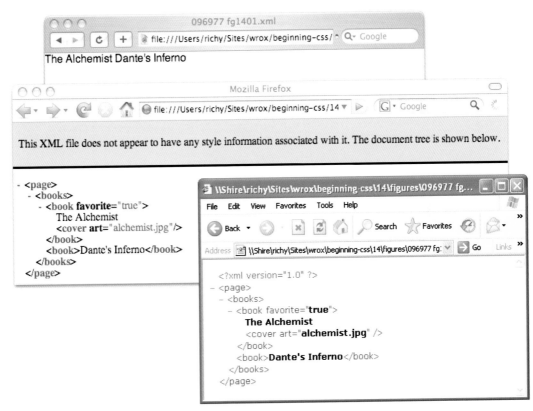

Figure 14-1b

XML is said to be well formed when the document contains an XML declaration — the `<?xml version="1.0"?>` in this example — and all tags have both an opening and closing tag, any attributes in the document are all enclosed in quotes, and only one root element exists. In this example, the root element is `<page>`. I cover the XML declaration in more detail later in this chapter. As with XHTML, you can use the shortcut syntax to close a tag, as shown in the `<cover/>` element in this example.

> **The XML declaration is technically optional, but experts agree that it is considered best practice to include it. The reasoning behind this is outside of the scope of this book; just keep in mind that it's better to have it.**

Next, an XML document can only contain one root element. The root element in this example is the `<page>` element; in HTML and XHTML the root element is the `<html>` element. Therefore, the following is not a valid XML document because it contains two root elements.

```
<?xml version="1.0"?>
<library>
    <books>
        <book>The Alchemist <favorite/></book>
        <book>Dante's Inferno</book>
    </books>
</library>
<library>
    <books>
        <book>The Stand <favorite/></book>
        <book>The Poet</book>
    </books>
</library>
```

Figure 14-2a

If an XML document is not well formed, the browser refuses to display it and instead displays some error text indicating what went awry. This error text is depicted in Figure 14-2b.

You can use this error text to correct the document, after which the browser displays the XML document tree like that shown in Figure 14-1.

Finally, XML is case-sensitive. So `<PAGE>` and `<page>` are two different tags in XML.

As you've just seen here, XML's markup structure can describe the data it contains. This is a benefit of XML, but not a requirement. In the following section, I discuss creating an XML schema that you can use to structure the data contained in an XML document.

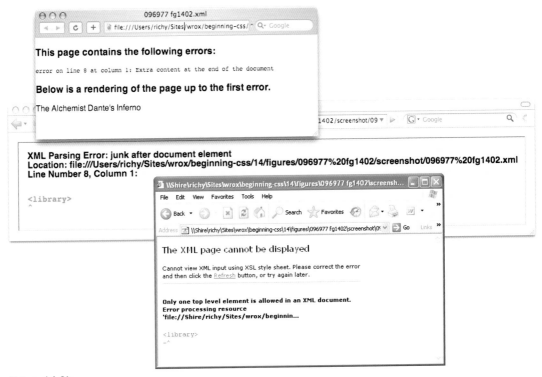

Figure 14-2b

Creating an XML Schema

The term *schema* refers to the structure and naming of XML elements that work together to produce a well-formed XML document. In this context, you are going to define your own XML elements, so having a schema means that you are going to decide on what element names and attributes that you will use in your XML document. Typically your XML schema reflects the data that you want in your XML document. If your XML document is a recipe, you want to define the different elements that will be included to describe recipe data, and that naming convention will be your schema. For example, you might opt to create an element named <measurement> that includes all measurement data, and you might define an element named <ingredient> that includes ingredient data. These and all the other elements that you create come together to make up your schema.

Some requirements that you have to consider are the following:

❏ Defining a page structure that resembles tabular data or list data, such as HTML/XHTML `<table>`, `<tr>`, and `<td>` elements and list elements such as `<ul>` and `<li>`.

❏ Determining which elements are block-level elements (like the `<div>` element in HTML/XHTML) and which are inline-level elements (like `<span>`).

This schema business really isn't difficult. Take a look at how the "My Favorite Records" example from Chapter 12 is written as an XML document.

```
<favorites>
    <title>
        Table: My favorite records.
    </title>
    <cols>
        <album/>
        <artist/>
        <released/>
    </cols>
    <headings>
        <record>
            <album>    album        </album>
            <artist>   artist       </artist>
            <released> released      </released>
        </record>
    </headings>
    <records>
        <record>
            <album>    Rubber Soul   </album>
            <artist>   The Beatles   </artist>
            <released> 1965          </released>
        </record>
        <record>
            <album>    Brown Eyed Girl </album>
            <artist>   Van Morrison    </artist>
            <released> 1967            </released>
        </record>
        <record>
            <album>    Mellon Collie and the Infinite Sadness </album>
            <artist>   The Smashing Pumpkins                  </artist>
            <released> 1995                                   </released>
        </record>
    </records>
    <footers>
        <record>
            <album>    album        </album>
            <artist>   artist       </artist>
            <released> released     </released>
        </record>
    </footers>
</favorites>
```

This is the entire XML document. In this version of the document, the XML tags that structure the data also describe the data contained in the document. Instead of the `<table>` element, there is the `<favorites>` element; instead of the `<caption>` element, the `<title>` element is used. Instead of the `<colgroup>` element, the `<cols>` element is used to group the columns, and the columns themselves are named for what type of columns they are: `<album/>`, `<artist/>`, and `<released/>` instead of `<col />`. `<headings>` replaces the `<thead>` element, and `<record>` replaces the `<tr>` element. `<album>`, `<artist>`, and `<released>` are used here as cells, replacing the `<th>` and `<td>` elements. You can use the same names for the cells as for columns here because CSS offers options to distinguish between the two. Likewise, the rest of the table elements in Chapter 12 in the "My Favorite Records" example are also represented here with an XML counterpart. Finally, unlike the example in Chapter 12, the XML document here is complete — you don't add `<html>` or `<body>` elements. However, before the XML version of the "My Favorite Records" example is complete, it needs two more things: an XML declaration and an XML `stylesheet` declaration, both of which I add later in this chapter.

Now that you've seen an example of converting an HTML document to an XML document, the following Try It Out presents the Spicy Thai Peanut Sauce recipe that you saw in Chapter 12. Here the recipe is reformatted as an XML document.

Try It Out   Creating an XML Schema

Example 14-1. In the following steps, you create an XML version of Spicy Thai Peanut Sauce recipe in Chapter 12.

1. Enter the following XML into your text editor:

```
<page>
    <recipe>
        <ingredients>
            <title>
                Spicy Thai Peanut Sauce
            </title>
            <columns>
                <quantity/>
                <measurement/>
                <product/>
                <instructions/>
            </columns>
            <headings>
                <heading>
                    <quantity>        quantity        </quantity>
                    <measurement>     measurement     </measurement>
                    <product>         product         </product>
                    <instructions>    instructions    </instructions>
                </heading>
            </headings>
            <ingredientsbody>
                <ingredient>
                    <quantity>        f¹/₂            </quantity>
                    <measurement>     CUPS            </measurement>
                    <product>         Peanut Oil      </product>
                    <instructions></instructions>
```

```
        </ingredient>
        <ingredient>
            <quantity>        12            </quantity>
            <measurement>     Each          </measurement>
            <product>         Serrano Peppers </product>
            <instructions>    Sliced        </instructions>
        </ingredient>
         <ingredient>
            <quantity>        16            </quantity>
            <measurement>     Each          </measurement>
            <product>         Garlic Cloves </product>
            <instructions>    Minced        </instructions>
        </ingredient>
        <ingredient>
            <quantity>        2             </quantity>
            <measurement>     CUPS          </measurement>
            <product>         Peanut Butter </product>
            <instructions></instructions>
        </ingredient>
        <ingredient>
            <quantity>        1             </quantity>
            <measurement>     CUPS          </measurement>
            <product>         Soy Sauce     </product>
            <instructions></instructions>
        </ingredient>
        <ingredient>
            <quantity>        f¹/₂           </quantity>
            <measurement>     CUPS          </measurement>
            <product>         Lime Juice    </product>
            <instructions></instructions>
        </ingredient>
        <ingredient>
            <quantity>        4             </quantity>
            <measurement>     TABLESPOONS   </measurement>
            <product>         Sesame Oil    </product>
            <instructions></instructions>
        </ingredient>
        <ingredient>
            <quantity>        4             </quantity>
            <measurement>     CUPS          </measurement>
            <product>         Coconut Milk  </product>
            <instructions></instructions>
        </ingredient>
        <ingredient>
            <quantity>        ¹/₂            </quantity>
            <measurement>     CUPS          </measurement>
            <product>         Honey         </product>
            <instructions></instructions>
        </ingredient>
        <ingredient>
            <quantity>        ¹/₂            </quantity>
            <measurement>     CUPS          </measurement>
            <product>         Brown Sugar   </product>
```

```
            <instructions></instructions>
        </ingredient>
      </ingredientsbody>
  </ingredients>
  <directions>
      <direction>
          Sauté sliced serranos and garlic in peanut oil
          till lightly browned.
      </direction>
      <direction>
          Add <really>all</really> other ingredients and stir till
          dissolved.
      </direction>
      <direction>
          Simmer for 5 minutes.
      </direction>
      <direction>
          Purée all in blender.
      </direction>
  </directions>
  <suggestions>
      Sauté your favorite vegetables; onions, mushrooms,
      green peppers, and squash work best. Sprinkle with allspice,
      salt, and pepper. Optionally add walnuts or pine nuts. Add
      browned chicken or tofu and glaze with sauce. Serve with
      jasmine rice.
  </suggestions>
  </recipe>
</page>
```

2. Save the file as `Example_14-1.xml`.

3. Open it in the browser and see what you've created.

You may experience problems with the special characters that appear in this file, such as the fractions "f½" or the "e" with acute accent, or "é." You learn more about this later in this chapter.

How It Works

Nothing fancy here just yet. When viewed in a browser, the code in Example 14-1 simply shows a tree of the XML source file similar to that depicted in Figure 14-1b. The differences here are important because each has an effect on how the document is presented with CSS, and each offers further flexibility in the presentation of the document.

First, the `<page>` tag is added so that the `<recipe>` element can be styled independently. The `<page>` element is to this XML document as the `<html>` element is to an HTML/XHTML document, with one major difference: You can give the `<page>` tag any name you like. If you recall from Chapter 12, I applied a background to the `<html>` element using CSS, which is why I have created a `<page>` element for this example. The `<recipe>` element emulates the behavior of the `<body>` element presented in Chapter 12, and it has the semitransparent crosshatch background that was used there.

Next is the `<ingredients>` element, which contains the recipe's ingredients. All the table elements presented in Chapter 12 are represented here using an XML counterpart with one minor difference: In Chapter 12, I included the directions and suggestions as part of the table footers. When you are using only XML and CSS, this presents a problem. At the time of this writing, you have no way to span multiple columns with the CSS implemented in today's browsers. However, here I can simply move portions of the recipe that span multiple columns outside of the table.

Now that the Spicy Thai Peanut Sauce recipe has a viable XML document structure, let's continue the discussion. In the next section I discuss the XML declaration.

The XML Declaration

Most XML documents contain an XML declaration. If one is included, it's the very first tag in the document, and it looks like this:

```
<?xml version="1.0"?>
```

This declaration announces which version of XML is contained in the document. This is not very complicated, and it isn't required. In an XML document, it simply says, "Hey, I'm an XML document!" When an XML document encounters a browser or any other type of application that is able to read XML documents, the browser or application doesn't have to guess what kind of document is being presented. I say *encounter* in this context because, as I discussed earlier, an XML document is not restricted to web browsers.

XML Declaration Attributes

An XML declaration can contain three attributes, two of which are optional. These are called *pseudo-attributes* because they resemble markup attributes. The first attribute is the `version` attribute (see the previous example). This denotes which version of the XML specification is being referenced. Currently, two versions, 1.0 and 1.1 exist. Version 1.1 was only recently made a candidate recommendation by the W3C. As a candidate recommendation (and not a standard), Version 1.1 is still shiny and new, meaning it isn't yet widely available. For the purpose of this discussion I'll stick with 1.0. Which version I use is moot, because the differences between the two versions do not affect the basic syntactical presentation of XML documents in the examples of this chapter. The features in the XML 1.1 specification affect more complicated uses of XML that are beyond this immediate discussion.

The next attribute is an optional `encoding` attribute:

```
<?xml version="1.0" encoding="ISO-8859-1"?>
```

The `encoding` attribute tells the parser (the program interpreting the XML) about the characters contained in the document, that is to say, the data contained in the document. The value `"ISO-8859-1"` refers to characters common to the Americas and Western Europe. Actually, it's part of an International Standard. The letters ISO stand for *International Standards Organization*; the numbers refer to the ISO document. This can also go by the much simpler name of `"LATIN-1"`, as in the following:

```
<?xml version="1.0" encoding="LATIN-1"?>
```

The inclusion of the `encoding` *attribute is very important because the default encoding value is not* `"LATIN-1"` *but an even smaller set of characters. You must include the proper encoding type in order to have all characters correctly translated to their proper display equivalents.*

The third attribute is the `standalone` attribute, which looks like this:

```
<?xml version="1.0" encoding="LATIN-1" standalone="yes"?>
```

The `standalone` attribute has to do with the inclusion of a Document Type Definition (discussed briefly in Chapter 7). Document Type Definition (DTDs) may also be included in XML documents, but they require the DTD to be custom written because the elements of an XML document can be invented. Creating a Document Type Declaration is beyond the scope of this book, so for the purpose of this discussion the standalone attribute with a value of `"yes"` tells the browser that no Document Type Declaration is accompanying the XML document.

> **An XML declaration should always be included in XML documents because it helps both humans and the computer program that is interpreting the XML to determine what kind of XML appears in the document.**

The pseudo-attributes of an XML declaration must also appear in a particular order: The first attribute must always be the `version` attribute, followed by the optional `encoding` attribute, followed by the optional `standalone` attribute.

The XML stylesheet Declaration

The syntax for including a style sheet in an XML document closely resembles a cross between the XML declaration itself and the `<link>` tag in HTML/XHTML:

```
<?xml-stylesheet type="text/css" href="test.css"?>
```

Like the `<link>` element in an HTML or XHTML document, this references the external style sheet, which styles the XML document. The XML `stylesheet` declaration must appear after the XML declaration. The declaration must appear first in the document and before the document markup itself. By including a style sheet, you gain access to the full range of CSS properties and values in an XML document, just as you gain access in an HTML or XHTML document.

Now that you are familiar with the XML declaration and the `stylesheet` declaration, you can append the syntax to the My Favorite Records example shown in Figure 14-3a.

This results in the output depicted in Figure 14-3b.

I'll be using the My Favorite Records example again later in the chapter, but for now just put it aside.

```xml
<?xml version="1.0" encoding="ISO-8859-1" standalone="yes"?>
<?xml-stylesheet type="text/css" href="096977%20fg1403.css"?>
<favorites>
    <title>
        Table: My favorite records.
    </title>
    <cols>
        <album/>
        <artist/>
        <released/>
    </cols>
    <headings>
        <record>
            <album>      album      </album>
            <artist>     artist     </artist>
            <released>   released   </released>
        </record>
    </headings>
    <records>
        <record>
            <album>      Rubber Soul        </album>
            <artist>     The Beatles        </artist>
            <released>   1965               </released>
        </record>
        <record>
            <album>      Brown Eyed Girl  </album>
            <artist>     Van Morrison       </artist>
            <released>   1967               </released>
        </record>
        <record>
            <album>      Mellon Collie and the Infinite Sadness </album>
            <artist>     The Smashing Pumpkins                  </artist>
            <released>   1995                                   </released>
        </record>
    </records>
    <footers>
        <record>
            <album>      album      </album>
            <artist>     artist     </artist>
            <released>   released   </released>
        </record>
    </footers>
</favorites>
```

Figure 14-3a

Because the stylesheet declaration has been added, even though no actual style sheet is created, the text is run together. You can now include style sheet rules in the external CSS file to format the text of the XML document.

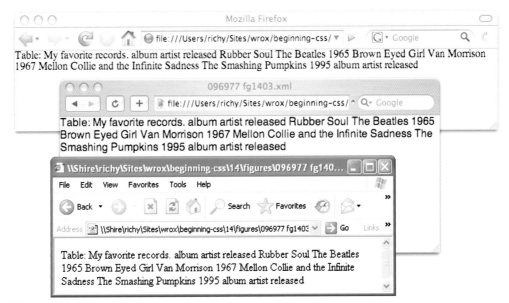

Figure 14-3b

You've just seen what including both the XML declaration and the XML `stylesheet` declaration does to an XML document. In the following Try It Out, you'll update the Spicy Thai Peanut Sauce recipe presented in Example 14-1 so that it has an XML declaration and a reference to an XML style sheet.

Try It Out   Adding an XML Declaration and Style Declaration

Example 14-2. The steps below add an XML declaration and style sheet reference to the Spicy Thai Peanut Sauce recipe document.

1. Open `Example_14-1.xml` and add the following modifications:

```
<?xml version="1.0" encoding="UTF-8" standalone="yes"?>
<?xml-stylesheet type="text/css" href="Example_14-2.css"?>
<page>
    <recipe>
```

2. Save this file as `Example_14-2.xml`

3. Create a blank style sheet and save it as `Example_14-2.css`. This results in the output depicted in Figure 14-4.

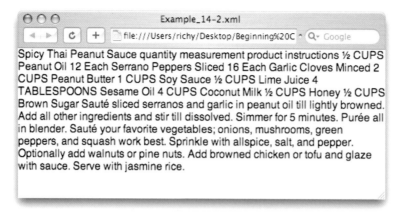

Figure 14-4

How It Works

By referencing a style sheet, you have taken the first step for applying style to an XML document. Now when you view the XML document in a browser, it no longer appears with the tree structure of the XML source code, as it would if you had not specified a style sheet. At this point the document isn't very pretty—it is displayed as one long string of text. This is why the CSS `display` property is essential. It explains to the browser how to display each tag contained in the XML document.

In the XML declaration, you've also included an encoding; here you've used the encoding type, UTF-8, which covers the fraction and the "e" with acute accent characters used in the source file. Without the UTF-8 encoding, your browser may not display these characters properly, since typically, browsers default to UTF-7, which is a small subset of characters. UTF-8 is similar to the LATIN-1 encoding that you saw earlier in this section, but it includes thousands of characters more.

The display Property

Displaying XML documents with CSS requires heavy use of the CSS `display` property, a property that has the capability of defining an element's behavior when it is rendered in a browser. The following table shows the `display` property and its possible values.

Property	Value
display	inline | block | list-item | run-in | inline-block | table | inline-table | table-row-group | table-header-group | table-footer-group | table-row | table-column-group | table-column | table-cell | table-caption | none

The display property can have one of 17 different values (as of CSS 2.1). IE 6 and IE 7 are behind the times in terms of supporting the full list of display value possibilities. Firefox, Opera, and Safari have fantastic support of the CSS 2 display values. Opera, in this case, supports the full set of possible display property values, and Firefox supports most of the possible values, but not all. In the coming sections, I look at each possible value individually, what display mode each triggers when applied to an XML element, and what elements with the same rendering behavior are found in HTML and XHTML.

Styling Inline Elements with display: inline

The display: inline; declaration emulates elements like <span>; that means it causes the target element to behave like an inline-level element, enabling it to appear in the flow of text. In an XML document, it might be necessary to emphasize a word or phrase in the context of the text. This is done by assigning the element a display: inline; declaration in the CSS style sheet. The XML document in Figure 14-5a and the style sheet demonstrate how inline elements are displayed in XML.

```
<?xml version="1.0" encoding="ISO-8859-1" standalone="yes"?>
<?xml-stylesheet type="text/css" href="096977%20fg1405.css"?>
<tonguetwister>
    How much <wood>wood</wood> would a <wood>wood</wood>chuck chuck
    if a <wood>wood</wood>chuck could chuck <wood>wood</wood>?
    A <wood>wood</wood>chuck would chuck all the <wood>wood</wood> a
    <wood>wood</wood>chuck could chuck if a <wood>wood</wood>chuck
    could chuck <wood>wood</wood>.
</tonguetwister>
```

Figure 14-5a

In the CSS style sheet (Figure 14-5b) the <wood> element can be defined to have whatever emphasis you deem appropriate.

```
wood {
    display: inline;
    font-weight: bold;
    color: forestgreen;
}
```

The declaration display: inline; causes the target element to be an inline element. Some examples of inline elements in (X)HTML are <span>, <b>, <i>, <u>, <strong>, and <em>

Figure 14-5b

Now the browser has explicit instructions for displaying any <wood> elements appearing in XML documents. The effects of this are depicted in Figure 14-5c.

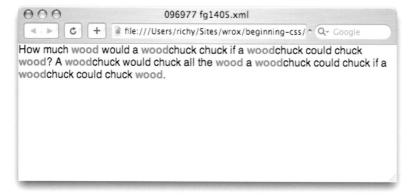

Figure 14-5c

Styling Block Elements with display: block

After looking over the first bit of code in the previous section, naturally I'll bet your next question is, "What about the `<tonguetwister>` element?" The answer is that you can give the browser a variety of explicit instructions for how to display this element. For this example, you can make the `<tonguetwister>` element a block-level element with the `display: block;` declaration. The XML is shown again in Figure 14-6a.

```
<?xml version="1.0" encoding="ISO-8859-1" standalone="yes"?>
<?xml-stylesheet type="text/css" href="096977%20fg1406.css"?>
<tonguetwister>
    How much <wood>wood</wood> would a <wood>wood</wood>chuck chuck
    if a <wood>wood</wood>chuck could chuck <wood>wood</wood>?
    A <wood>wood</wood>chuck would chuck all the <wood>wood</wood> a
    <wood>wood</wood>chuck could chuck if a <wood>wood</wood>chuck
    could chuck <wood>wood</wood>.
</tonguetwister>
```

Figure 14-6a

The CSS in Figure 14-6b is included in the XML document.

```
tonguetwister {
    display: block;
    background: lightyellow;
}
wood {
    display: inline;
    font-weight: bold;
    color: forestgreen;
}
```

The declaration `display: block;` causes the target element to be a block element. Some examples of inline elements in (X)HTML are `<div>`, `<p>`, `<blockquote>`, `<body>`, and `<html>`

Figure 14-6b

This results in the output depicted in Figure 14-6c.

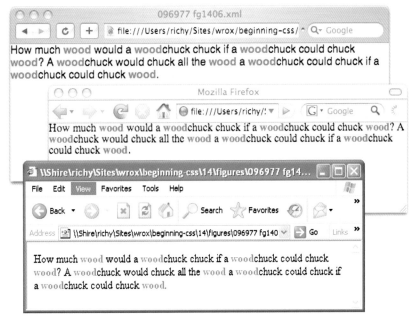

Figure 14-6c

Just as in HTML/XHTML, block-level element default behaviors still apply: The output will automatically span the entire window unless told to do differently, because its default width value is `auto`. With this declaration, the `<tonguetwister>` element emulates the behavior of the `<html>` element found in HTML and XHTML because it is the root element of the document. This is why you see the lightyellow background taking up the whole screen. In fact it's the same thing as writing:

```
<html>
    How much <span>wood</span> would a <span>wood</span>chuck chuck
    if a <span>wood</span>chuck could chuck <span>wood</span>?
    A <span>wood</span>chuck would chuck all the <span>wood</span> a
    <span>wood</span>chuck could chuck if a <span>wood</span>chuck
    could chuck <span>wood</span>.
</html>
```

Styling List Items with display: list-item

The `display: list-item;` declaration causes an element to appear with a default bullet character next to it, as is the case with the `<li>` element in HTML and XHTML. When combined with the `list-style-type` property or `list-style-image` properties (see Chapter 9), the list can be numbered, bulleted, or have a custom image applied. Consider the snip of XML in Figure 14-7a.

```
<?xml version="1.0" encoding="ISO-8859-1" standalone="yes"?>
<?xml-stylesheet type="text/css" href="096977%20fg1407.css"?>
<list>
    <item>Rubber Soul</item>
    <item>Revolver</item>
    <item>Sgt. Pepper's Lonely Hearts Club Band</item>
</list>
```

Figure 14-7a

When combined with the right CSS (Figure 14-7b), this is transformed into a list.

```
list {
    display: block;
    margin-left: 20px;
    list-style: disc;
}
item {
    display: list-item;
}
```

The declaration `display: list-item;` causes the target element to be a `<li>` element.

Figure 14-7b

This results in the output shown in Figure 14-7c.

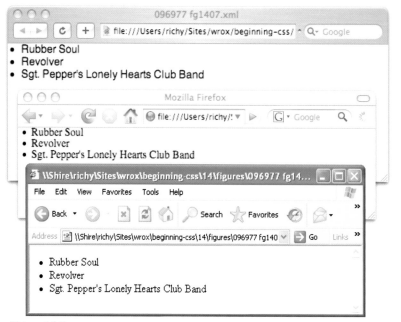

Figure 14-7c

This is the same as writing the following in HTML/XHTML:

```
<ul>
    <li>Rubber Soul</li>
    <li>Sgt. Pepper's Lonely Heart's Club Band</li>
    <li>Revolver</li>
</ul>
```

The `<list>` element is made into a block-level element to emulate the behavior of a `<ul>` HTML element. It's also given some margin on the left side to indent the list. Next, the `list-style: disc;` declaration makes the list into a bulleted list. The `<item>` element is told to be a list-item with the `display: list-item;` declaration. Without the `list-style: disc;` declaration, the list still appears with bullets because a bulleted list is the default behavior of the `display: list-item;` declaration.

Generating Numbered Lists

Creating numbered lists is a more difficult undertaking in XML documents than it is in HTML given current browser limitations. Applying a simple `list-style-type: decimal;` declaration should produce a numbered list, and it does so if you're viewing the output in Safari, Opera, or IE 6. However, a bug in Firefox prevents it from producing a numbered list. When viewed in Firefox, the list appears with all zeros, as seen in Figure 14-8b.

Figure 14-8a shows the required CSS to generate numbered lists.

```
list {
    display: block;
    margin-left: 20px;
    list-style: decimal;
}
item {
    display: list-item;
}
```

As you saw in Chapter 9 for (X)HTML, the `list-style: decimal;` declaration is used to make numbered lists in XML too.

Figure 14-8a

When applied to the same XML as seen in Figure 14-7a, you get the results depicted in Figure 14-8b.

This is the same as writing the following in HTML/XHTML:

```
<ol>
    <li>Rubber Soul</li>
    <li>Sgt. Pepper's Lonely Heart's Club Band</li>
    <li>Revolver</li>
</ol>
```

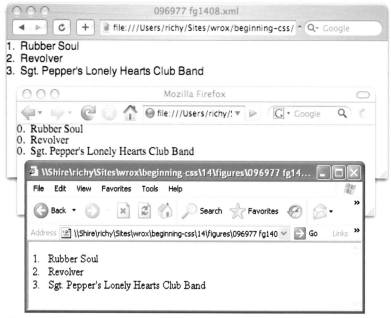

Figure 14-8b

Using the `display` and `list-style` properties allows for emulation of the HTML `<ol>` element.

Now that you have some idea of what is involved with using the `display` property to dictate the behavior of XML elements, the following Try It Out example continues the Spicy Thai Peanut Sauce recipe with the addition of some style sheet rules.

Try It Out   **Applying inline, block, and list Styles**

Example 14-3. Follow these steps to apply `display` property values to the Spicy Thai Peanut Sauce recipe.

1.   Enter the following CSS into your text editor:

```
page {
    display: block;
    width: 100%;
    height: 100%;
    background: #fff url('fruit_veg_web.jpg') no-repeat fixed center center;
}
recipe {
    display: block;
    font-family: monospace;
    padding: 10px;
    margin: 10px;
    /* Moz proprietary opacity property */
    -moz-opacity: 0.7;
```

```
        /* Microsoft proprietary filter property */
        filter:progid:DXImageTransform.Microsoft.Alpha(opacity=70);
        /* CSS 3 opacity property */
        opacity: 0.7;
        background: url('cross_hatch.jpg') repeat;
}
directions, suggestions {
        display: block;
        font-size: 130%;
}
directions {
        list-style-type: disc;
}
direction {
        display: list-item;
}
really {
        display: inline;
        font-weight: bold;
}
```

2. Save the file as `Example_14-3.css`.

3. Modify `Example_14-2.xml` to reference the new CSS file:

```
<?xml version="1.0" encoding="UTF-8" standalone="yes"?>
<?xml-stylesheet type="text/css" href="Example_14-3.css"?>
<page>
    <recipe>
```

4. Save the result as `Example_14-3.xml`. This results in the output depicted in Figure 14-9.

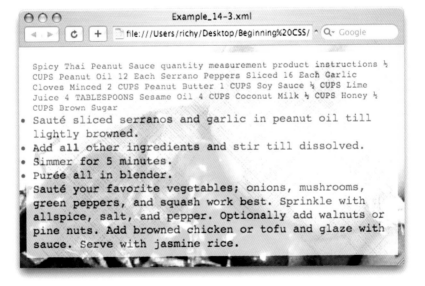

Figure 14-9

How It Works

As you can see after viewing the output in a browser, after you add just a few XML declarations to the XML document, the recipe is beginning to take shape. At this point, the example looks similar when viewed in IE 6, Safari, or Firefox. IE 6 has a bug that prevents the display of the background image; you can overcome this by adding the `width: 100%;` and `height: 100%;` declarations to the <page> element. The recipe renders best in Safari, Opera, and Firefox, which display the document as intended.

Let's go through the example line by line:

```
page {
    display: block;
    width: 100%;
    height: 100%;
    background: #fff url('fruit_veg_web.jpg') no-repeat fixed center center;
}
```

The <page> element is intended to emulate the <html> element in HTML/XHTML. This is defined as a block-level element, and it is given a background image, as it was in Example 12-1 from Chapter 12.

Next is the <recipe> element, which contains all the ingredients and other information for the Spicy Thai Peanut Sauce recipe:

```
recipe {
    display: block;
    font-family: monospace;
    padding: 10px;
    margin: 10px;
    /* Moz proprietary opacity property */
    -moz-opacity: 0.7;
    /* Microsoft proprietary filter property */
    filter:progid:DXImageTransform.Microsoft.Alpha(opacity=70);
    /* CSS 3 opacity property */
    opacity: 0.7;
    background: url('cross_hatch.jpg') repeat;
}
```

Once more, the element is made into a block-level element with the `display: block;` declaration. Here, the same properties are applied to the <recipe> element as were applied to the <body> element in Chapter 12 in Example 12-1. They include the semitransparent effect. In IE 6, you can see that Microsoft's proprietary `filter` property does not work with XML documents.

Next are the <directions> and <suggestions> elements:

```
directions, suggestions {
    display: block;
    font-size: 130%;
}
```

Each of these is made into a block-level element. The <directions> element emulates the HTML/XHTML <ul> element, and the <suggestions> element emulates a plain <div> or <p> element. Because the <directions> element emulates a <ul> element, it is given a list-style-type declaration:

```
directions {
    list-style-type: disc;
}
```

Next, the list items are styled:

```
direction {
    display: list-item;
}
```

The `display: list-item;` declaration lets the `<direction>` element emulate a `<li>` element. Finally, each `<really>` element is told to be an inline-level element with the `display: inline;` declaration:

```
really {
    display: inline;
    font-weight: bold;
}
```

Here the `<really>` element is bold for emphasis.

The `display` property gives an element its behavior, and block-level elements such as `<html>`, `<body>`, `<div>`, and `<ul>` can be emulated using the `display: block;` declaration. Inline-level elements such as `<a>`, `<span>`, `<em>`, `<strong>` can be emulated using the `display: inline;` declaration. List elements (`<li>`) can be emulated using the `display: list-item;` declaration. You now need to style only the table containing the recipe's ingredients. This part of the styling is also taken care of using the `display` property and the table display values.

Table Display Values

The `table` set of display values enables you to emulate HTML tables. With these tools, it's possible to fully recreate the behavior of an HTML table using XML elements. The following table shows the display value and the table element that it emulates.

Display Declaration	Emulated Element
display: table;	`<table>`
display: table-caption;	`<caption>`
display: table-column-group;	`<colgroup>`
display: table-column;	`<col/>`
display: table-header-group;	`<thead>`
display: table-row-group;	`<tbody>`
display: table-row;	`<tr>`
display: table-cell;	`<td>`, `<th>`
display: table-footer-group;	`<tfoot>`

Unfortunately neither IE 6 nor IE 7 supports the table display keywords presented in the preceding table, and currently there is no workaround for the lack of this support, other than to use the values that these browsers do support, such as inline, block, list-item, *and* inline-block.

Each table keyword for the display property has an XHTML/HTML element counterpart. Look at each value individually and how each is applied to an XML document.

Applying display: table

The following example uses *My Favorite Records* XML that you see in Figure 14-10a.

```
<?xml version="1.0" encoding="ISO-8859-1" standalone="yes"?>
<?xml-stylesheet type="text/css" href="096977%20fg1410.css"?>
<favorites>
    <title>
        Table: My favorite records.
    </title>
    <cols>
        <album/>
        <artist/>
        <released/>
    </cols>
    <headings>
        <record>
            <album>    album     </album>
            <artist>   artist    </artist>
            <released> released  </released>
        </record>
    </headings>
    <records>
        <record>
            <album>    Rubber Soul    </album>
            <artist>   The Beatles    </artist>
            <released> 1965           </released>
        </record>
        <record>
            <album>    Brown Eyed Girl </album>
            <artist>   Van Morrison    </artist>
            <released> 1967            </released>
        </record>
        <record>
            <album>    Mellon Collie and the Infinite Sadness </album>
            <artist>   The Smashing Pumpkins                   </artist>
            <released> 1995                                    </released>
        </record>
    </records>
    <footers>
        <record>
            <album>    album     </album>
            <artist>   artist    </artist>
            <released> released  </released>
        </record>
    </footers>
</favorites>
```

Figure 14-10a

The `<favorites>` element emulates an HTML/XHTML `<table>` element when the CSS in Figure 14-10b is applied.

```
favorites {
    display: table;
    font-family: sans-serif;
    border: 1px solid rgb(200, 200, 200);
    border-spacing: 2px;
    margin: 8px;
}
```

The declaration `display: table;` causes the target element to be a `<table>` element.

Figure 14-10b

This is done with the `display: table;` declaration. The `<favorites>` element now behaves just like the `<table>` element found in HTML/XHTML. As I did in Chapter 12, I've also added some other declarations so that the My Favorite Records example here renders identically to the example that you saw in Chapter 12. Additionally, as in HTML/XHTML, other display properties can be applied, such as the `border: 1px solid black;` declaration and `width: 100%;` that I've added to the rule. So far, you get the results seen in Figure 14-10c.

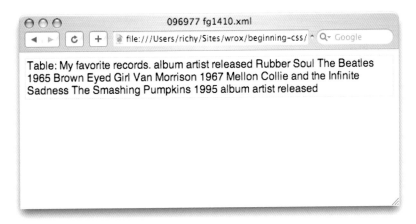

Figure 14-10c

Adding a Caption with display: table-caption

Just as was the case with `display: table;`, the caption can be displayed with the `display: table-caption;` declaration. In the XML source for My Favorite Records, the caption is the `<title>` element. I could have just as easily called it `<caption>`, as it is in XHTML/HTML. However, I have chosen to take advantage of XML's capability that allows me to invent any tag name I like. The CSS in Figure 14-11a is applied to the XML in Figure 14-10a.

The `<title>` element is made to behave like a table caption and now has behavior that is identical to the `<caption>` element found in HTML/XHTML. Figure 14-11b shows the results so far.

```
favorites {
    display: table;
    font-family: sans-serif;
    border: 1px solid rgb(200, 200, 200);
    border-spacing: 2px;
    margin: 8px;
}
title {
    display: table-caption;
}
```

The declaration display: table-caption; causes the target element to be a <caption> element.

Figure 14-11a

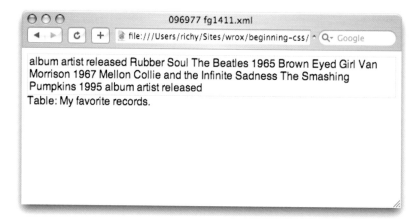

Figure 14-11b

Applying display: table-column-group and display: table-column

Table columns are styled next. In XML, styling is accomplished in the same way as with the table columns example presented earlier in this chapter, except that the elements have to be told they are columns. The CSS in Figure 14-12 is applied to the My Favorite Records XML in Figure 14-10a.

```
favorites {
    display: table;
    font-family: sans-serif;
    border: 1px solid rgb(200, 200, 200);
    border-spacing: 2px;
    margin: 8px;
}
title {
    display: table-caption;
}
cols {
    display: table-column-group;
}
cols album, cols artist, cols released {
    display: table-column;
}
```

The declaration display: table-column-group; causes the target element to be a <colgroup> element, and the declaration display: table-column; makes the target element a <col /> element.

Figure 14-12

The `display: table-column-group;` declaration causes the `<cols>` element to emulate the `<colgroup>` element found in XHTML/HTML; it is used to group the columns. The individual columns are displayed in the same way as the `<col />` element in XHTML/HTML with the `display: table-column;` declaration, which results in no change in the output.

Styling Groupings, Table Rows, and Table Cells

Figure 14-13a shows the remaining declarations required to create the My Favorite Records table.

```
favorites {
    display: table;
    font-family: sans-serif;
    border: 1px solid rgb(200, 200, 200);
    border-spacing: 2px;
    margin: 8px;
}
title {
    display: table-caption;
    text-align: center;
}
cols {
    display: table-column-group;
}
cols album, cols artist, cols released {
    display: table-column;
}
records {
    display: table-row-group;
}
records {
    display: table-row;
}
artist,
album,
released {
    display: table-cell;
    padding: 5px;
    border: 1px solid rgb(200, 200, 200);
}
headings {
    display: table-header-group;
}
footers {
    display: table-footer-group;
}
headings artist,
headings album,
headings released,
footers artist,
footers album,
footers released {
    background: lightyellow;
    text-align: center;
    font-weight: bold;
}
```

The declaration `display: table-row-group;` causes the target element to behave like a `<tbody>` element.

The declaration `display: table-row;` causes the target element to behave like a `<tr>` element.

The declaration `display: table-cell;` causes the target element to behave like a `<td>` element.

The declaration `display: table-header-group;` causes `<headings>` to behave like a `<thead>` element.

The declaration `display: table-footer-group;` causes `<footers>` to behave like a `<tfoot>` element.

Figure 14-13a

527

The CSS in Figure 14-13a is applied to the XML that you saw in Figure 14-10a to get the output in Figure 14-13b.

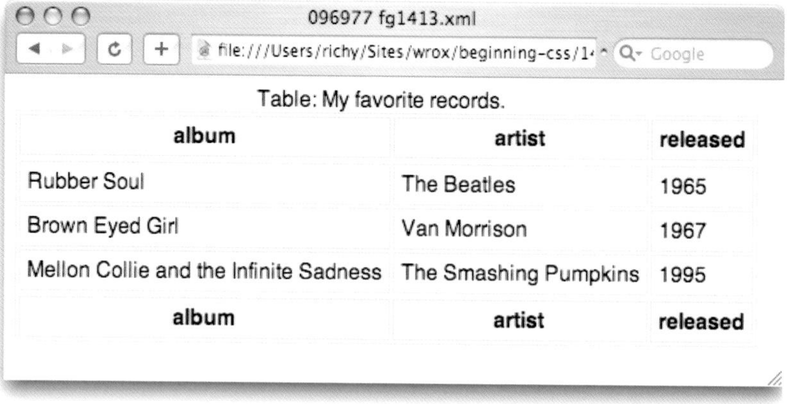

Figure 14-13b

The `<tbody>` element found in HTML and XHTML is emulated with the CSS declaration `display: table-row-group;`, and again this element doesn't offer any changes in presentation other than further distinction in the structure of the document. This rule makes the `<records>` element emulate the `<tbody>` element.

```
records {
    display: table-row-group;
}
```

Now that you've distinguished the different groupings of table data, the next step is to make table rows. This is done with the `display: table-row;` declaration. Here, the purpose is mimicking the behavior of the `<tr>` element:

```
record {
    display: table-row;
}
```

Table cells are styled with the `display: table-cell;` declaration to obtain the behavior of the `<td>` element:

```
artist,
album,
released {
    display: table-cell;
    padding: 5px;
    border: 1px solid rgb(200, 200, 200);
}
```

The next element in the My Favorite Records example is the `<footers>` element. Here, my intention is to emulate the `<tfoot>` element. As was the case with the `<tbody>` element, this offers no change in presentation, but places further distinctions in the structure of the document:

```
headings {
    display: table-header-group;
}
footers {
    display: table-footer-group;
}
headings artist,
headings album,
headings released,
footers artist,
footers album,
footers released {
    background: lightyellow;
    text-align: center;
    font-weight: bold;
}
```

The remaining styles contribute further to giving the XML version of My Favorite Records the same look and feel as the XHTML version.

Now that you have some idea of how tables are styled in XML, you can apply the information to an example with more real-world merit and pizzazz. The following Try It Out continues building on the Spicy Thai Peanut Sauce recipe presented in earlier examples and applies the table set of display values.

Try It Out   Styling XML Tables

Example 14-4. With these steps, you apply table style formatting to the Spicy Thai Peanut Sauce recipe.

1. Open Example_14-3.css and modify the CSS document to reflect the following highlighted changes:

```
page {
    display: block;
    background: #fff url('fruit_veg_web.jpg') no-repeat fixed center center;
    width: 100%;
    height: 100%;
}
recipe {
    display: block;
    font-family: monospace;
    padding: 10px;
    margin: 10px;
    /* Moz proprietary opacity property */
    -moz-opacity: 0.7;
    /* Microsoft proprietary filter property */
    filter:progid:DXImageTransform.Microsoft.Alpha(opacity=70);
    /* CSS 3 opacity property */
    opacity: 0.7;
    background: url('cross_hatch.jpg') repeat;
}
ingredients {
    display: table;
    width: 100%;
    margin-bottom: 5px;
    table-layout: fixed;
```

```
      border-collapse: collapse;
}
title {
    display: table-caption;
    text-align: left;
    margin-bottom: 5px;
    text-transform: lowercase;
    font-size: 160%;
    padding: 5px;
    letter-spacing: 10px;
    font-weight: bold;
}
columns {
    display: table-column-group;
}
columns * {
    display: table-column;
}
headings {
    display: table-header-group;
}
ingredientsbody {
    display: table-row-group;
}
heading, ingredient {
    display: table-row;
}
heading * {
    font-weight: bold;
    font-size: 150%;
    color: black;
    text-align: center;
}
heading *, ingredient * {
    display: table-cell;
    padding: 5px;
    text-transform: lowercase;
}
ingredient * {
    font-size: 130%;
}
directions, suggestions {
    display: block;
    font-size: 130%;
}
directions {
    margin: 17px 0 15px 0;
    padding: 0 0 0 45px;
    list-style-type: disc;
}
suggestions {
    margin: 22px 0 32px 0;
    padding: 0 5px 0 10px;
}
direction {
```

```
    display: list-item;
    margin-left: 30px;
    padding-left: 30px;
}
really {
    display: inline;
    font-weight: bold;
}
```

2. Save the file as `Example_14-4.css`.

3. Modify `Example_14-3.xml` to point to the new CSS document and save as `Example_14-4.xml`. This results in the output depicted in Figure 14-14.

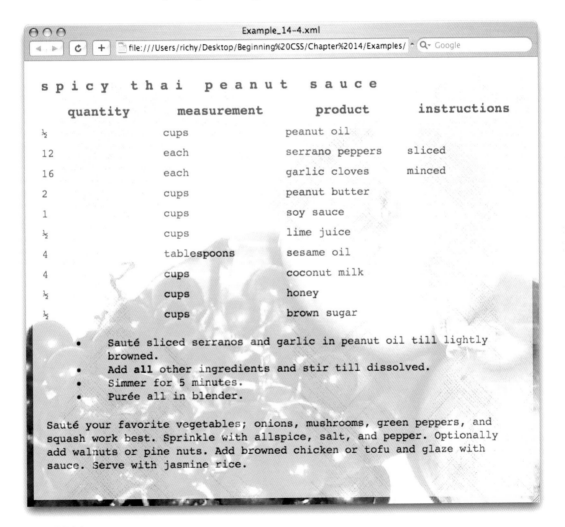

Figure 14-14

How It Works

Here, you applied several rules to style the table portion of the Spicy Thai Peanut Sauce recipe:

```
ingredients {
    display: table;
    width: 100%;
    margin-bottom: 5px;
    table-layout: fixed;
    border-collapse: collapse;
}
```

The <ingredients> element is made into a table here with the display: table; declaration. This essentially makes the <ingredients> element behave the same as the <table> element found in HTML/XHTML. The table display properties that I discussed in Chapter 12 are now available to apply additional formatting. I removed spacing between the cells contained in the table with the border-collapse: collapse; declaration. Next, the <title> element is made into the table caption with the display: table-caption; declaration. This makes the <title> element in this document the same as the <caption> element I discussed in Chapter 12:

```
title {
    display: table-caption;
    text-align: left;
    margin-bottom: 5px;
    text-transform: lowercase;
    font-size: 160%;
    padding: 5px;
    letter-spacing: 10px;
    font-weight: bold;
}
```

The <title> element contains the recipe's title and several styles that are applied to format the text. Next, the column-grouping element <columns> is given its behavior via the display: table-column-group; declaration. The columns are given their behavior via the display: table-column; declaration:

```
columns {
    display: table-column-group;
}
columns * {
    display: table-column;
}
```

At this point in the design, I have chosen to not take advantage of column styling, but I hold these elements in reserve for possible future enhancements to the document. In a real-world application it's perfectly fine to omit elements that have no effect on the document's final presentation; I have included this here simply to demonstrate its possibility.

As for the table headings, the <thead> element is emulated in this document with the <headings> element, and this element is given its style via the display: table-header-group; declaration:

```
headings {
    display: table-header-group;
}
```

The <tbody> element is also represented with the <instructionsbody> element, and this is given its style using the display: table-row-group; declaration:

```
ingredientsbody {
    display: table-row-group;
}
```

So far, nothing other than the <ingredients> and <title> elements contributes to the actual presentation of the document.

Next, table rows are given their behavior:

```
heading, ingredient {
    display: table-row;
}
```

Unlike the columns, heading groupings, and row groupings, table rows are very important for the structure of the document. These keep the cells in their places.

Next the cells in the heading are styled with a bold font, centering, black text, and 150% font size, which, in this case, is 50% larger than the browser's default font size:

```
heading * {
    font-weight: bold;
    font-size: 150%;
    color: black;
    text-align: center;
}
```

The cells inside the <heading> element are selected using two selectors, the descendant selector and the universal selector. The descendant selector is the space between the type selector, heading, and the universal selector, which selects all descendants of the <heading> element. In this example, that is the <quantity> element, the <measurement> element, the <product> element, and the <instructions> element: All these are descendants of the <heading> element. The universal selector is the asterisk. As you learned in Chapter 3, using the universal selector by itself selects all elements. Here the principal is the same. I want to select all children of the <heading> element without calling them by name, so I use heading * as the selector. This selects all the children without having to type each element's name. The cells contained in the <heading> element haven't been made into cells yet. That is handled by the next rule:

```
heading *, ingredient * {
    display: table-cell;
    padding: 5px;
    text-transform: lowercase;
}
```

Here again I've chosen the universal and descendant combination of selectors, which provides me with flexibility should I chose to add additional elements to the recipe in the future. Here I am selecting the children of the <heading> element, as I did for the last rule, and the children of the <ingredient> element, which selects all remaining cells in the table. The cells of the table's body that actually contain the ingredients are styled with the next rule:

```
ingredient * {
    font-size: 130%;
}
```

533

The last additions to the style sheet are put in place so that the XML version of the Spicy Thai Peanut Sauce recipe is a pixel-for-pixel perfect emulation of its HTML cousin:

```
directions {
    margin: 17px 0 15px 0;
    padding: 0 0 0 45px;
    list-style-type: disc;
}
suggestions {
    margin: 22px 0 32px 0;
    padding: 0 5px 0 10px;
}
direction {
    display: list-item;
    margin-left: 30px;
    padding-left: 30px;
}
```

The padding and margin values here were determined using trial and error, switching back and forth between the document presented in Example 12-5 and this example, Example 14-4.

Other Display Values

I have chosen not to cover other display values at this time because browser support for these is incredibly marginal. Opera and Safari 1.2 do support the remaining display values: run-in, inline-block, and inline-table. IE also supports the value inline-block.

I also want to mention that, although I chose to use XML as the vehicle for demonstrating the various display values covered in this chapter, their use is not limited to XML. For clarity in presenting the material, I felt XML was the cleanest and most intuitive approach. It is perfectly acceptable to use the display property and its various values in (X)HTML documents. These values can be applied, conceivably, to any element. For instance:

```
<!DOCTYPE html PUBLIC "-//W3C//DTD XHTML 1.0 Strict//EN"
                "http://www.w3.org/TR/xhtml1/DTD/xhtml1-strict.dtd">
<html xmlns='http://www.w3.org/1999/xhtml' xml:lang='en'>
    <head>
        <title>table display in XHTML</title>
        <style type="text/css">
            html {
                display: table;
                border-spacing: 5px;
            }
            body {
                display: table-row;
            }
            div {
                display: table-cell;
                padding: 5px;
                border: thin solid black;
```

```
            }
        </style>
    </head>
    <body>
        <div> table cell </div>
        <div> table cell </div>
    </body>
</html>
```

This results in the output shown in Figure 14-15.

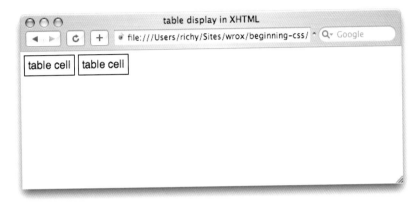

Figure 14-15

Using an HTML document, I have essentially recreated the behavior of tables using as little extra HTML code as is possible. This is a perfectly acceptable use of the `display` property. And I might also add an acceptable use of table-based layouts.

Summary

XML is a flexible, robust markup language with multiple applications. CSS provides powerful control over how an XML document is presented. CSS can emulate any type of HTML/XHTML element. XML declarations provide the browser with important information about the XML document, including the XML version and the encoding. This, in turn, provides information about the characters contained in the document. The display property can be used to create block-level and inline-level boxes as well as the various elements used in tables. In this chapter you learned the following:

❑ What XML is and some of its uses

❑ How to create an XML schema, and the document structure necessary to emulate HTML tables, block-level, inline-level, and list elements

❑ What the XML declaration and the pseudo-attributes inside of it mean

❑ How to style an XML document

- ❑ How to create block-level boxes like the `<div>` element in HTML/XHTML
- ❑ How to create inline-level boxes like the `<span>` element in HTML/XHTML
- ❑ How to style lists in XML
- ❑ How to style tables in XML

Exercises

1. What happens when you load an XML document into a browser that doesn't strictly conform to XML structural requirements?

2. What are the three pseudo-attributes used in the XML declaration? (Hint: The declaration is the `<?xml version="1.0"?>` bit.)

3. What is the syntax that you would use to include CSS in an XML document?

4. Name the keywords of the `display` property that have the best browser support.

5. Name all of the keywords of the `display` property used to emulate (X)HTML table elements (including all optional elements) and their (X)HTML element equivalent. (Hint: `display: table;` = `<table>`)

6. Can the `display` property be used on (X)HTML elements?

7. Which browsers do not support the table keyword values of the `display` property?

8. Which browser displays zeros instead of numbers when making a numbered list in XML?

15

The Cursor Property

CSS provides the cursor property to control the type of cursor displayed for a particular element. The following table outlines the cursor property and its possible values.

Property	Value
Cursor	[<uri> ,]* [auto | crosshair | default | pointer | move | e-resize | ne-resize | nw-resize | n-resize | se-resize | sw-resize | s-resize | w-resize | text | wait | help | progress]
Initial value: auto	
Non-standard extensions to cursor	hand | all-scroll | col-resize | row-resize | no-drop | not-allowed | vertical-text

Safari does not support custom cursors, or non-standard cursor keywords. Opera for the Mac does not support *-resize keywords, or non-standard cursor keywords. Opera for Windows supports *-resize keywords, but not non-standard keywords. Firefox for the Mac does not support the all-scroll keyword, but Firefox for Windows does. IE 6 and IE 7 support all possible options.

The notation in the preceding table shows that the cursor property can accept a reference to a custom cursor with the <uri> notation. The table also shows that you can provide more than one URL by giving a comma-separated list of URLs. Alternatively, you can provide a keyword to change the cursor displayed while the user's mouse pointer is hovering over an element. To demonstrate how the cursor can be changed using a keyword, consider the example in Figure 15-1.

```
div {
    width: 50px;
    height: 50px;
    border: 1px solid rgb(234, 234, 234);
    margin: 5px;
    cursor: wait;
    background: mistyrose;
}
```

The user's mouse cursor can be changed using the cursor property, and one of 23 keywords.

Figure 15-1a

The CSS in Figure 15-1a is combined with the markup in Figure 15-1b.

```
<!DOCTYPE html PUBLIC "-//W3C//DTD XHTML 1.0 Strict//EN"
                      "http://www.w3.org/TR/xhtml1/DTD/xhtml1-strict.dtd">
<html xmlns='http://www.w3.org/1999/xhtml' xml:lang='en'>
    <head>
        <title>cursor</title>
        <link rel='stylesheet' type='text/css' href='096977%20fg1501.css' />
    </head>
    <body>
        <div></div>
    </body>
</html>
```

Figure 15-1b

The CSS in Figure 15-1a and the markup in Figure 15-1b result in the output in Figure 15-1c.

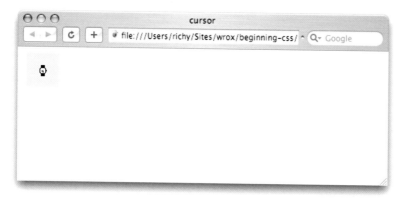

Figure 15-1c

In Figure 15-1, you can see that the cursor for the <div> element becomes a clock with the property and keyword value combination of cursor: wait;. Naturally, the results will differ depending on the browser and operating system.

Cursor Compatibility

To assist you in anticipating the differences in cursors between browsers and operating systems, I've prepared the following table. The cursors in the following table indicate what cursor is used for that browser when the keyword is supported.

Cursor	IE 6 Win XP	IE 7 Vista	Firefox Mac	Firefox Win	Safari	Opera Mac	Opera Win
default							
crosshair							
pointer							
move							
e-resize							
w-resize							
ne-resize							
sw-resize							
n-resize							
s-resize							
nw-resize							
se-resize							
text							
wait							
help							
progress							
hand							
all-scroll							

Table continued on following page

539

Cursor	IE 6 Win XP	IE 7 Vista	Firefox Mac	Firefox Win	Safari	Opera Mac	Opera Win
col-resize				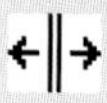			
row-resize							
no-drop							
not-allowed							
vertical-text			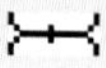				

In the preceding table where a box is empty, the cursor keyword is unsupported by that browser on that platform.

Custom Cursors

Some browsers also support specifying your own custom cursor. You can also provide a custom cursor by referencing the file path to the cursor file, as you can see demonstrated in Figure 15-2a.

```
div {
    width: 50px;
    height: 50px;
    border: 1px solid rgb(234, 234, 234);
    margin: 5px;
    cursor: url('custom_cursor.png'), default;
    background: mistyrose;
}
```

A custom cursor is supplied via the url() syntax. In order for the custom cursor to work, a fallback keyword must be supplied.

Figure 15-2a

The CSS in Figure 15-2a is combined with the markup in Figure 15-2b.

```
<!DOCTYPE html PUBLIC "-//W3C//DTD XHTML 1.0 Strict//EN"
                      "http://www.w3.org/TR/xhtml1/DTD/xhtml1-strict.dtd">
<html xmlns='http://www.w3.org/1999/xhtml' xml:lang='en'>
    <head>
        <title>cursor</title>
        <link rel='stylesheet' type='text/css' href='096977%20fg1502.css' />
        <!--[if ie]>
            <style type='text/css'>
                div {
                    cursor: url('custom_cursor.cur'), default;
                }
            </style>
        <![endif]-->
    </head>
    <body>
        <div></div>
    </body>
</html>
```

> Another custom cursor is supplied for IE, which must be provided a custom cursor in the Windows-proprietary .cur format.

Figure 15-2b

The result is shown in IE 6, IE 7, and Firefox for Windows in Figure 15-2c.

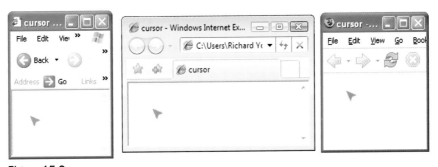

Figure 15-2c

In Figure 15-2c, you can see that IE 6, IE 7, and Mozilla Firefox support custom cursors. I used a PNG image for the custom cursor in Firefox and a Windows-proprietary .cur file for the custom cursor in IE 6 and IE 7. To make custom cursors, you'll need software such as Aha-Soft's ArtCursors software available from http://www.aha-soft.com/. This shareware application for Windows is available for $40 at the time of this writing, and it allows you to make cursor images in the Windows-proprietary .cur format, or animated cursors in the Windows-proprietary .ani format.

In order to provide Firefox with a PNG image, and IE with a .cur image, I employed Microsoft's proprietary conditional comments. As you saw in Chapter 7, by using conditional comments you are able to show IE code that isn't shown to Firefox or any other browser, and thus IE has a .cur image for the cursor, while Firefox retains a PNG image.

Custom cursors are not supported by Safari, Firefox for the Mac, or Opera.

Additional CSS Resources

A multitude of websites exists for CSS how-to, articles, experiments, and other general discussion. A few of the websites that I frequent most and personally recommend are:

- ❑ A List Apart: `http://www.alistapart.com`
- ❑ Position Is Everything: `http://www.positioniseverything.net`
- ❑ Quirks Mode: `http://www.quirksmode.org`
- ❑ CSS Zen Garden: `http://www.csszengarden.com`
- ❑ Eric Meyer's website: `http://www.meyerweb.com`

There are also a few venues that exist to help newcomers and veterans alike through forums and mailing lists. Two that I recommend are:

- ❑ Wrox Programmer to Programmer (P2P): `http://p2p.wrox.com`. Wrox's P2P forums have venues for asking questions about specific Wrox books, like this one, as well as general programming and web development topics, such as (X)HTML, CSS, and JavaScript.
- ❑ CSS Discussion (mailing list): `http://www.css-discuss.org`. The css-discuss mailing list was founded and is maintained today by CSS guru, Eric Meyer.

Beginning CSS, Second Edition Online

Because I ran out of space and couldn't include them in the print edition of this book, an additional chapter appears online at the Wrox website.

- ❑ Chapter 16: Dean Edwards's "IE 7" JavaScript. Dean Edwards's "IE 7" JavaScript enables CSS features that IE 6 doesn't support natively, such as the direct child and next sibling selectors that you saw in Chapter 3. The "IE7" JavaScript is a package that you embed in your web pages to obtain a greater spectrum of CSS support in IE 6.

This chapter, in addition to the book's source code download, is available at the Wrox website via the following URL:

```
http://www.wrox.com/go/beginning_css2e
```

Summary

The CSS cursor property provides control over which mouse cursor is used when the user moves their mouse cursor over an element. To recap, in this chapter you learned that the cursor property may be used to change the cursor displayed to the user, which may be via a predefined list of keywords or by referencing a custom image via a URL, although the latter is only supported (at the time of this writing) by IE 6, IE 7 and Firefox.

Exercises

1. What cursor keywords are supported by Mac Opera?

2. Write the syntax for including a custom cursor in Firefox.

3. Write the syntax for including a custom cursor in IE.

4. What browser(s) supports all cursor keywords?

5. What browser(s) supports all but one of the cursor keywords?

Answers to Exercises

Chapter 2

1. Style sheets are made of what?

A. Rules.

2. What's the difference between when `width: auto;` is applied to a `<table>` as opposed to a `<div>` element?

A. A `<table>` shrinks-to-fit, a `<div>` expands-to-fit.

3. Complete the sequence: Declaration, Property, _____

A. Value.

4. Convert the color RGB(234, 123, 45) to hexadecimal.

A. #EA7B2D.

5. What is the shortened hexadecimal notation of #FFFFFF?

A. #FFF.

6. When does dithering occur?

A. When one or more colors are not supported by the operating system or display device, the operating system will attempt to make the nonsupported color by using one or more colors it does support.

7. If I have a style sheet located at `http://www.example.com/stylesheet.css`, and a web page located at `http://www.example.com/index.html`, what markup would I include in index.html to include `stylesheet.css` via a relative path?

A. <link rel="stylesheet" type="text/css" href="stylesheet.css" />

Chapter 3

1. Does the selector body * apply to <input> elements (assuming an <input> element appears between the <body> and </body> tags)?

A. Yes, the selector applies to all descendants of the <body> element.

2. In the following HTML document, do the selectors li a and li > a refer to the same element(s)? Can those selectors be used interchangeably? What type of selector is each? Which one is better to use and why?

```
<!DOCTYPE html PUBLIC "-//W3C//DTD XHTML 1.0 Strict//EN"
                      "http://www.w3.org/TR/xhtml1/DTD/xhtml1-strict.dtd">
<html xmlns='http://www.w3.org/1999/xhtml' xml:lang='en'>
    <head>
        <title>Dynamic Pseudo-Class Selectors</title>
        <link rel='stylesheet' type='text/css' href='Example_3-9.css' />
    </head>
    <body>
        <h1>Proof-of-Concept: Dynamic Pseudo-Class Selectors</h1>
        <ul>
            <li><a href='http://www.wrox.com/'>Wrox</a></li>
            <li><a href='http://p2p.wrox.com/'>Wrox P2P</a></li>
            <li><a href='http://www.google.com/'>Google</a></li>
            <li><a href='http://www.amazon.com/'>Amazon</a></li>
        </ul>
    </body>
</html>
```

A. a) Yes, both apply to the same <a> elements in that document.

b) Yes.

c) The former is a descendant selector, the latter a direct child selector.

d) The descendant selector is better to use because it is more compatible. IE 6 does not support the direct child selector.

3. Given the HTML document in question 2, does the selector ul + h1 apply? What is the official name of that selector?

A. No, the selector ul + h1 does not apply to the HTML document in question 2. The next sibling selector requires that the target element be the next sibling of the first element in the chain. It does not apply to the previous sibling. The official name of the selector is the Direct Adjacent Sibling Combinator.

4. If you wanted to apply a style based on an HTML attribute's value, what would the selector look like?

A. An attribute value selector looks like element[attribute="value"].

5. If you were to style an element based on the presence of an HTML attribute, what would the selector look like?

A. A basic attribute selector looks like element[attribute]. This selector applies when an attribute is merely present.

6. What special character must you include in an attribute value selector to style an element based on what appears at the beginning of an attribute's value? What does a sample selector using that character look like?

A. The caret character, `element[attribute^="value"]`.

7. How many class names can one element have?

A. As many as you like.

8. What special character must you include in an attribute value selector to style an element based on what appears at the end of an attribute's value? What does a sample selector using that character look like?

A. The dollar sign, `element[attribute$="value"]`.

9. If you wanted to style a link a different color when the user's mouse hovers over it, what might the selector look like?

A. The selector would at minimum look like `a:hover`, though `a.classname:hover`, `a#idname:hover`, and so on, are acceptable answers as well.

Chapter 4

1. In the following style sheet, determine the specificity of each selector.

```
ul#hmenu ul.menu {
    margin: 0;
    padding: 0;
    list-style: none;
    position: absolute;
    top: 35px;
    left: 0;
    width: 100%;
    visibility: hidden;
    text-align: left;
    background: rgb(242, 242, 242);
    border: 1px solid rgb(178, 178, 178);
    border-right: 1px solid rgb(128, 128, 128);
    border-bottom: 1px solid rgb(128, 128, 128);
}
ul#hmenu li li:hover {
    background: rgb(200, 200, 200);
}
ul#hmenu ul.menu ul.menu {
    top: -1px;
    left: 100%;
}
ul#hmenu li#menu-204 ul.menu ul.menu,
ul#hmenu li#menu-848 ul.menu ul.menu ul.menu ul.menu,
ul#hmenu li#menu-990 ul.menu ul.menu {
    left: auto;
    right: 100%;
}
ul#hmenu > li.menu.eas + li.menu.eas ul.menu ul.menu ul.menu ul.menu {
```

```
        right: auto;
        left: 100%;
    }
    li.menu,
    li.menu-highlight {
        position: relative;
    }
    ul.menu li a {
        text-decoration: none;
        color: black;
        font-size: 12px;
        display: block;
        width: 100%;
        height: 100%;
    }
    ul.menu li a span {
        display: block;
        padding: 3px 10px;
    }
    ul.menu span.arrow {
        position: absolute;
        top: 2px;
        right: 10px;
        width: 11px;
        height: 11px;
        background: url('/images/arrow.gif') no-repeat;
    }
```

A.   In the following style sheet, determine the specificity of each selector.

```
ul#hmenu ul.menu
```

> 112

```
ul#hmenu li li:hover
```

> 113

```
ul#hmenu ul.menu ul.menu
```

> 123

```
ul#hmenu li#menu-204 ul.menu ul.menu
```

> 224

```
ul#hmenu li#menu-848 ul.menu ul.menu ul.menu ul.menu
```

> 246

```
ul#hmenu li#menu-990 ul.menu ul.menu
```

> 224

```
ul#hmenu > li.menu.eas + li.menu.eas ul.menu ul.menu ul.menu ul.menu
```

```
    187

li.menu

    11

li.menu-highlight

    11

ul.menu li a

    13

ul.menu li a span

    14

ul.menu span.arrow

    22
```

2. According to the following style sheet, what color is the link?

```
a.context:link {
    color: blue;
}
a.context:visited {
    color: purple;
}
a.context:hover {
    color: green;
}
a.context:active {
    color: red;
}
```

A. It depends on what state the link is in. If the link is unvisited, the link is blue. If the link is visited, it's purple. If the user is hovering their mouse over the link, it's green, and if the user is clicking on the link, it's red.

3. According to the following style sheet, what color is the link?

```
a.context:visited {
    color: purple;
}
a.context:hover {
    color: green;
}
a.context:active {
    color: red;
}
a.context:link {
    color: blue;
}
```

A. The link is blue, regardless of its state, since the `:link` selector appears last and it has the same specificity as the other selectors.

4. According to the following style sheet, what color is the link?

```
a.context:link {
    color: blue;
}
a.context:visited {
    color: purple !important;
}
a.context:hover {
    color: green;
}
a.context:active {
    color: red;
}
```

A. It depends on the state; if the link is unvisited, it's blue. If the link is unvisited and the user is hovering their mouse over the link, it's green. If the link is unvisited and the user is clicking on the link, it's red. If the link is visited, it's purple, regardless of whether the user is hovering over the link or clicking on it.

Chapter 5

1. If you wanted to reduce the spacing between letters, how would it be done? Provide an example declaration.

A. Provide a negative length value to the `letter-spacing` property, such as `letter-spacing: -1px;`

2. How would you produce the output you see in the following figure? Provide the declaration.

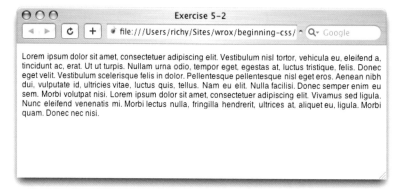

A. `text-align: justify;`

3. When indenting text in a paragraph, how is a percentage value calculated?

A. Providing a percentage value to the `text-indent` property causes the indentation to be calculated based on the width of the parent element of the target element.

4. What are the keywords that CSS offers for changing the case of text within an element?

A. Lowercase, uppercase, and capitalize.

5. If you wanted to preserve line breaks and spacing as formatted in the source code, what would the CSS declaration be?

A. `white-space: pre;`

6. What browsers do not support the annoying `blink` keyword?

A. IE and Safari.

7. If you wanted to put a line over a section of text, rather than underlining it, what property and keyword would you use?

A. `text-decoration: overline;`

Chapter 6

1. Why aren't the values of the `font-weight` property `100` through `900`, `bolder`, and `lighter` used in real-world web design?

A. Because commonly available fonts are either bold or they aren't, and since there is only one variation, bold and normal, the other values aren't used.

2. If "Font A" is supported on Mac OS X, and "Font B" is supported on Windows XP, and "Font C" is supported on Linux, what style would you write so that one of the three would always be used in the absence of one of the others?

A. `font-family: "Font A", "Font B", "Font C";`

3. If you want to make text italic, what are two possible declarations for doing that?

A. `font-style: italic;` and `font-style: oblique;`

4. What's the difference between the `font-variant: small-caps;` and `text-transform: uppercase;` declarations?

A. `font-variant: small-caps;` results in lowercase letters becoming uppercase letters that are scaled slightly smaller than real uppercase letters. `text-transform: uppercase;` makes all letters uppercase of the same size.

5. How could the following rules be better written?

```
p {
    font-family: Arial, sans-serif;
    font-weight: bold;
    font-size: 24px;
    color: crimson;
}
p.copy {
    font-style: italic;
```

```
        font-weight: bold;
        line-height: 2em;
    }
    p#footer {
        font-size: 12px;
        line-height: 2em;
        font-family: Helvetica, Arial, sans-serif;
    }
```

A.

```
    p {
        font: bold 24px Arial, sans-serif;
        color: crimson;
    }
    p.copy {
        font-style: italic;
        font-weight: bold;
        line-height: 2em;
    }
    p#footer {
        font-size: 12px/2em Helvetica, Arial, sans-serif;
    }
```

The second rule, which begins with the selector p.copy had no change, because there is no font-size and no font-family specified in the rule, which are both required for the font shorthand property. Another acceptable approach would be to repeat the font-size and font-family as defined in the first rule, since it applies to all <p> elements. If you repeated the font-size and font-family from the first rule, another acceptable answer would be:

```
    p.copy {
        font: italic bold 24px/2em Arial, sans-serif;
    }
```

6. What's wrong with the following rule?

```
    p {
        font-size: 24;
    }
```

A. It is missing a length unit. Measurements that don't include a length unit are illegal, unless the specification specifically says it is allowed.

7. If you include the declaration font-size: larger; in a style sheet rule, how much larger would the text be?

A. 1.2 times larger.

8. Would the declaration font-size: 75%; make the font size larger or smaller?

A. Smaller. Values under 100% result in a smaller font size, and values larger than 100% result in a larger font size.

Chapter 7

1. From left to right, what are the seven box model properties that make up the left, center, and right sides of a box?

A. `margin-left`, `border-left`, `padding-left`, `width`, `padding-right`, `border-right`, `margin-right`

2. How do you left-, center-, and right-align a block-level box (using the standard method)?

A. To left-align: `margin-right: auto;` or `margin: 0 auto 0 0;`

To center-align: `margin: 0 auto;` or `margin: 0 auto 0 auto;` or `margin-left: auto;` `margin-right: auto;`

To right-align: `margin-left: auto;` or `margin: 0 0 0 auto;`

3. When the `margin` shorthand property has four values, what side of the target element does each value apply margin to, in order?

A. Top, right, bottom, left.

4. What are the three keyword values of the `border-width` property?

A. `thin`, `medium`, and `thick`

5. If the `border-color` shorthand property has three values, what side of the target element does each value apply to, in order?

A. Top, right and left, bottom.

6. Name the shorthand properties that encompass the `border-width`, `border-style`, and `border-color` properties.

A. `border-top`, `border-right`, `border-bottom`, `border-left`, and `border`.

7. If you target IE 6 in quirks mode and earlier versions of IE, which property would you use to align a box?

A. `text-align`

8. If the `padding` shorthand property only has two values, what side of the target element does each value apply to, in order?

A. Top and bottom, right and left.

9. Describe briefly the two situations in which `margin` collapsing occurs?

A. Between adjacent sibling elements where the bottom margin of the top element comes into contact with the top margin of the bottom element, or between nested elements where the top margin of any nested element comes into contact with the top margin of its container element, and likewise when the bottom margin of a nested element comes into contact with the bottom margin of its container element.

10. In the following document, which element's `width` is the `<p>` element's `width` based on if it were to be given a percentage `width` value?

```
<!DOCTYPE html PUBLIC "-//W3C//DTD XHTML 1.0 Strict//EN"
                "http://www.w3.org/TR/xhtml1/DTD/xhtml1-strict.dtd">
<html xmlns='http://www.w3.org/1999/xhtml' xml:lang='en'>
    <head>
```

```
            <title></title>
        </head>
        <body>
            <p>
                Peter Piper picked a peck of pickled peppers.
                Did Peter Piper pick a peck of pickled peppers?
                If Peter Piper picked a peck of pickled peppers,
                where's the peck of pickled peppers Peter Piper picked?
            </p>
        </body>
    </html>
```

A. The `<body>` element.

11. How do you resize an image while maintaining the aspect ratio?

A. Set either the `width` or `height` to `auto` and explicitly set the opposite dimension with a fixed length. If `width` is `auto`, `height` has an explicit length, or if `height` is `auto`, `width` has an explicit length.

12. In IE 6 quirks mode and previous versions of IE, what properties of the box model are included in the measurement specified by the `width` property?

A. `border` and `padding`.

13. What is one method of emulating the `min-width` property in IE 6?

A. Use something like the following declaration in a conditional comment style sheet that only IE 6 can see.

```
width: expression(
    documentElement.clientWidth <= 500? 500 : 'auto'
);
```

14. How is the `min-height` property emulated in IE 6?

A. Set the `height` property in a conditional comment style sheet that only IE can see.

15. What browsers do conditional comments apply to?

A. Internet Explorer, and all browsers that embed IE.

16. If you wanted both `min-width` and `max-width`, what declaration would you use to bring IE 6 on board?

A. Something like the following:

```
width: expression(
    documentElement.clientWidth >= 800?
        800
    :
        (documentElement.clientWidth <= 500? 500 : 'auto')
);
```

17. If you wanted to increase the amount of spacing between lines of text, which property would you use?

A. `line-height`.

18. What are the four keywords of the `overflow` property?

A. `visible`, `auto`, `scroll`, and `hidden`.

Chapter 8

1. When an element is floated, what rule governs its dimensions?

A. The shrink-to-fit rules; the element only expands enough to accommodate the content inside.

2. What happens when an inline element, such as a `<span>` element, is floated?

A. It becomes a block element with shrink-to-fit sizing.

3. What are the three keywords of the `float` property?

A. `left`, `right`, and `none`

4. If an element is floated to the right, and you don't want the following element to wrap around it, what declaration would you apply to that element?

A. `clear: right;` or `clear: both;`

5. What declarations would you use to create subscript and superscript text?

A. `vertical-align: sub;` and `vertical-align: super;`

6. When vertically aligning an inline element to the `middle`, how is the element positioned on the line?

A. It is centered at the center point of the lowercase letter x.

7. What is the difference between the `text-top` and `top` keywords of the `vertical-align` property?

A. In some browsers, nothing. The `text-top` keyword aligns to the top of the tallest lowercase letter, and the `top` keyword aligns to the top of the line box.

8. If you are aligning table cells to the baseline, what determines the baseline?

A. The tallest content in the first row of the table.

Chapter 9

1. Name which keywords of the `list-style-type` property are not supported by IE 6?

A. `decimal-leading-zero`, `lower-greek`, `lower-latin`, `upper-latin`, `armenian`, and `georgian`.

2. What `list-style-type` keywords are supported by IE 7?

A. `disc`, `circle`, `square`, `decimal`, `lower-roman`, `upper-roman`, and `none`.

3. What properties does the `list-style` property render utterly and completely useless?

A. `list-style-type`, `list-style-image`, `list-style-position`.

4. Can size and position be controlled with the `list-style-image` property? If so, how?

A. No.

Chapter 10

1. What are two properties that you can use to specify a background color in a web page?

A. The `background-color` and `background` properties.

2. What are different color values that you can use for a background color?

A. RGB, RGB percentage, hexadecimal, short hexadecimal, color keywords, and the `transparent` keyword.

3. What declaration causes a background image to be tiled only along the x-axis?

A. `background-repeat: repeat-x;`.

4. What keyword value can you use to turn off tiling of a background image?

A. `no-repeat`.

5. What are the three methods of positioning a background image?

A. Length, percentage, and keyword.

6. If you wanted to offset an image ten pixels from the left and ten pixels from the top, what declaration would you use?

A. `background-position: 10px 10px;`

7. Can the different methods of positioning a background image be mixed with one another?

A. Yes.

8. If you wanted a background image to scroll with the document, what declaration would you use?

A. `background-attachment: scroll;`

9. When a background image is said to be "fixed," what (X)HTML element does the background image position relative to?

A. `<body>`.

10. What is the only element that IE 6 supports "fixed" backgrounds on?

A. `<body>`.

11. Write a declaration that contains all five background properties in one.

A. `background: white url('image.png') repeat scroll center center;`

Chapter 11

1. What is the default value of the `top`, `right`, `bottom`, and `left` properties?

A. The `auto` keyword.

2. What are offset properties used for?

A. To control the position of elements with a position value of absolute, relative, or fixed.

3. If the `<body>` element has a sole child that is positioned absolutely, what point of reference is used for its positioning?

A. The browser's viewport.

4. If the `<body>` element has a sole child that is positioned relatively, with an id name of *relative-element*, and that relatively positioned element has a child that is absolutely positioned, what point of reference is used for the absolutely positioned element?

A. The element with id name relative-element.

5. If the element from Exercise 4, *relative-element*, has a fixed position child, what point of reference is used for its positioning?

A. The browser's viewport.

6. Write a rule that you would use to make an element with the following standard CSS work in IE 6 in standards rendering mode.

```
div#element {
    position: fixed;
    top: 0;
    left: 0;
}
```

A. Use the following:

```
div#element {
    position: absolute;
    top: expression(eval(documentElement.scrollTop));
}
```

7. To make fixed position elements compatible with IE 6, what element must you always place fixed position elements inside of

A. The `<body>` element.

8. Write a rule that you would use to make an element with the following standard CSS work in IE 6 and IE 7 in quirks rendering mode.

```
div#element {
    position: fixed;
    bottom: 0;
    left: 0;
}
```

A. Use the following:

```
div#element {
    position: absolute;
    top: expression((document.body.scrollTop +
                     document.body.clientHeight - this.clientHeight) - 2);
}
```

9. The following rule refers to an element that you want to take up all of the space available to it vertically, and positioned to the left. Fill in the blanks.

```
div#column {
    position: absolute;
    _____: 0;
    _____: 0;
    _____: 0;
    padding: 10px;
     border: 1px solid black;
}
```

A. Fill in the blanks as follows:

```
div#column {
    position: absolute;
    top: 0;
    left: 0;
    bottom: 0;
    padding: 10px;
     border: 1px solid black;
}
```

10. You have five elements that are all absolutely positioned siblings, but no z-index is specified for any of them. Name the stacking order that the browser will use for those elements' z-index property. Provide the z-index declaration for each element, in order.

A. z-index: 1;, z-index: 2;, z-index: 3;, z-index: 4;, z-index: 5;.

11. How do you fix the z-index bug in IE 6 and IE 7?

A. You have to specify a descending z-index manually on all of the relatively positioned elements.

Chapter 12

1. Which of the properties discussed in this chapter do not work in IE 6 and IE 7?

A. The caption-side and border-spacing properties do not work in IE 6 or IE 7.

2. Describe what the table-layout: fixed; declaration does.

A. It forces an (X)HTML table to honor explicitly defined widths, instead of auto sizing to accommodate content.

3. When sizing using the table-layout: fixed; declaration, how does the browser determine the width of table columns?

A. First the browser takes into account the width property as applied to the <table> element, then the browser takes into account the width property as applied to <col /> elements. If none is found, it goes to the width property as applied to the <td> elements that appear in the first row of the table. If no width is defined, each column is given equal width.

4. What purpose does the optional <thead> element serve?

A. It contains table headers, when you print a table that spans multiple pages. Its contents are repeated at the top of each printed page.

5. What element would you use if you wanted table column headers that are styled bold and centered?

A. The `<th>` element.

6. In what containing element does the main table data appear?

A. The `<tbody>` element.

7. What browser does not support applying width to table columns? (At the time of this writing, of course.)

A. Safari.

Chapter 13

1. Which media values apply to PC and Mac browsers?

A. Screen, print, and all.

2. Write the opening tag for the `<style>` element, targeting the styles to print.

A. `<style type='text/css' media='print'>`

3. What does the `page-break-before` property do?

A. It forces a page break to happen before the beginning of an element.

4. Write a sample style sheet that includes three rules; the first rule applies to all media types, the second rule applies to onscreen layout, and the third applies to print.

A. Your style sheet may differ, but it should look something like the following.

```
@media all {
    p {
        /* Your declarations appear here */
    }
}
@media screen {
    p {
        /* Your declarations appear here */
    }
}
@media print {
    p {
        /* Your declarations appear here */
    }
}
```

The following is also a valid answer:

```
p {
    /* Your declarations appear here */
}
@media screen {
    p {
        /* Your declarations appear here */
```

```
        }
    }
    @media print {
        p {
            /* Your declarations appear here */
        }
    }
```

Chapter 14

1. What happens when you load an XML document into a browser that doesn't strictly conform to XML structural requirements?

A. The browser will not display the XML document, and instead shows an error message.

2. What are the three pseudo-attributes used in the XML declaration? (Hint: The declaration is the `<?xml version="1.0"?>` bit.)

A. `version`, `encoding`, and `standalone`

3. What is the syntax that you would use to include CSS in an XML document?

A. `<?xml-stylesheet type="text/css" href="stylesheet.css"?>`

4. Name the keywords of the `display` property that have the best browser support.

A. `none`, `block`, `inline`, and `list-item`

5. Name all of the keywords of the `display` property used to emulate (X)HTML table elements (including all optional elements) and their (X)HTML element equivalent. (Hint: `display: table;` = `<table>`)

A.

```
display: table;             = <table>
display: table-row-group;   = <tbody>
display: table-header-group; = <thead>
display: table-footer-group; = <tfoot>
display: table-row;         = <tr>
display: table-column-group; = <colgroup>
display: table-column;      = <col/>
display: table-cell;        = <td>, <th>
display: table-caption;     = <caption>
```

6. Can the `display` property be used on (X)HTML elements?

A. Yes!

7. Which browsers do not support the table keyword values of the `display` property?

A. IE 6 and IE 7.

8. Which browser displays zeros instead of numbers when making a numbered list in XML?

A. Firefox.

Chapter 15

1. What cursor keywords are supported by Mac Opera?

A. `default`, `crosshair`, `pointer`, `move`, `text`, `wait`, and `hand`

2. Write the syntax for including a custom cursor in Firefox.

A. `cursor: url('custom_cursor.png'), default;`

The key is you must specify a fallback keyword after the URL.

3. Write the syntax for including a custom cursor in IE.

A. `cursor: url('custom_cursor.cur'), default;`

or

`cursor: url('custom_cursor.ani'), default;`

The key is you must use either a Windows-proprietary `.cur` or `.ani` file in IE.

4. What browser(s) supports all cursor keywords?

A. IE 6 and IE 7.

5. What browser(s) supports all but one of the cursor keywords?

A. Firefox for Windows and Firefox for the Mac.

CSS Reference

Reference Conventions

The following conventions are used to outline browser compatibility for each CSS feature:

- ❏ **Y = Yes.** The feature is implemented completely per the W3C specification of what that feature is.

- ❏ **N = No.** The feature is not implemented.

- ❏ **B = Buggy.** The feature is implemented but has unexpected side effects.

- ❏ **P = Partial.** The feature is partially implemented.

- ❏ **A = Alternative.** The feature is not implemented but an alternative proprietary feature is available that provides the same functionality.

- ❏ **I = Incorrect.** The feature is implemented but does not conform to the W3C definition of what that feature provides.

The CSS level that reference material refers to is provided in the CSS column. At the time of this writing, there are four CSS specifications:

- ❏ **CSS Level 1:** The reference material provided is outlined in the CSS Level 1 Recommendation made 17 December 1996.

- ❏ **CSS Level 2:** The reference material provided is outlined in the W3C CSS Level 2 Recommendation made 12 May 1998.

- ❏ **CSS Level 2.1:** The reference material provided is outlined in the W3C CSS Level 2.1 Working Draft made 11 April 2006.

- ❏ **CSS Level 3:** The reference material provided refers to a W3C CSS Level 3 Candidate Recommendation (at the time of this writing portions of CSS 3 are still in development; references refer to those parts of CSS 3 in Candidate Recommendation status).

Selectors

Selector	CSS	IE 6.0	IE 7.0	FF 2.0	O 9.0	S 2.0
Universal `* {color: blue;}`	3	Y	Y	Y	Y	Y
Type `div {color: blue;}`	3	Y	Y	Y	Y	Y
Descendant `div p {color: blue;}`	3	Y	Y	Y	Y	Y
Direct Child `div > p {color: blue;}`	3	N	Y	Y	Y	Y
Direct Adjacent Sibling `p + p {color: blue}`	3	N	Y	Y	Y	Y
Indirect Adjacent Sibling `p ~ p {color: blue;}`	3	N	Y	Y	Y	Y
Attribute Existence `input[type] {color: blue;}`	3	N	Y	Y	Y	Y
Attribute's value matches value exactly `input[type=text] {color: blue;}`	3	N	Y	Y	Y	Y

Attribute's value is a space-separated list of words, e.g.
`rel="copyright copyleft copyeditor"`
`a[rel~="copyright"] {`
`  color: blue;`
`}`
	3	N	Y	Y	Y	Y

Attribute's value begins with a value or is the value exactly; value provided may be a hyphen-separated list of words, e.g.
`hreflang="en-us"`
`link[hreflang|="en"] {`
`  color: blue;`
`}`
	3	N	Y	Y	Y	Y

Attribute's value begins with...
`a[href^=http://www.somesite.com] {`
`  color: blue;`
`}`
	3	N	Y	Y	N	Y

Attribute's value contains...
`a[href*=somesite] {`
`  color: blue;`
`}`
	3	N	Y	Y	N	Y

Selector	CSS	IE 6.0	IE 7.0	FF 2.0	O 9.0	S 2.0

Attribute's value ends with...
`a[href$=html] {`
` color: blue;`
`}`
	3	N	Y	Y	N	Y

Class `div.class {color: blue;}`	3	Y	Y	Y	Y	Y

Multiple Classes, e.g.
`class="class1 class2"`
`div.class1.class2 {color: blue;}`
	3	B	Y	Y	Y	Y

IE 6 supports multiple class syntax on the element, but not chaining class selectors in the style sheet.						
ID `div#id {color: blue;}`	3	Y	Y	Y	Y	Y

Pseudo-Classes

Pseudo-Class	CSS	IE 6.0	IE 7.0	FF 2.0	O 9.0	S 2.0
`:link`	3	Y	Y	Y	Y	Y
`:visited`	3	Y	Y	Y	Y	Y
`:hover`	3	P	Y	Y	Y	Y
`:active`	3	P	P	Y	Y	Y
`:focus`	3	N	N	Y	Y	Y
`:target`	3	N	N	Y	N	Y
`:lang`	3	N	N	Y	N	N
`:root`	3	N	N	Y	N	Y
`:first-child`	3	N	Y	Y	Y	Y
`:last-child`	3	N	N	Y	N	Y
`:empty`	3	N	N	I	N	Y
Mozilla incorrectly applies `:empty` to elements that contain white space characters.						
`:not`	3	N	N	Y	N	Y

Pseudo-Elements

Pseudo-Element	CSS	IE 6.0	IE 7.0	FF 2.0	O 9.0	S 2.0
CSS 3 :: (double-colon) syntax.	3	Y	N	Y	Y	Y
::first-line	3	Y	Y	Y	Y	Y
::first-letter	3	Y	Y	Y	Y	Y
::before	3	N	N	Y	Y	Y
::after	3	N	N	Y	Y	Y
::selection	3	N	N	A	N	Y

Mozilla provides a proprietary ::-moz-selection pseudo-element.

Color Properties

Property	CSS	IE 6.0	IE 7.0	FF 2.0	O 9.0	S 2.0
color	2.1	Y	Y	Y	Y	Y
Value:	<color>					
Initial value:	Depends on browser					
Applies to:	All elements					
Inherited:	Yes					
<color> refers to one of the following.						
A color keyword:	body {color: black;}					
A hexadecimal value:	body {color: #000000;}					
Short hexadecimal value:	body {color: #000;}					
RGB value:	body {color: rgb(0, 0, 0);}					
RGB percentage:	body {color: rgb(0% ,0%, 0%);}					
opacity	3	A	A	I	N	Y
Value:	<alphavalue>					
Initial value:	1					

Property	CSS	IE 6.0	IE 7.0	FF 2.0	O 9.0	S 2.0
Applies to:	All elements					
Inherited:	No					

Introduced in CSS 3, the `opacity` property accepts a floating integer between 0.0 (fully transparent) and 1.0 (fully opaque)

Firefox 2.0 incorrectly allows this property to inherit to children elements.

IE 6 and IE 7 provide an alternative, proprietary `filter` property to achieve a similar effect (see entry for the Microsoft `filter` property). Mozilla prior to 1.7 provides an alternative proprietary `-moz-opacity` property (see entry for Mozilla `-moz-opacity` property).

Font Properties

Property	CSS	IE 6.0	IE 7.0	FF 2.0	O 9.0	S 2.0
font-family	2.1	Y	Y	Y	Y	Y
Value:	[[<family-name> | <generic-family>] [, <family-name> | <generic-family>]*]					
Initial value:	Varies from browser to browser					
Applies to:	All elements					
Inherited:	Yes					

`<family-name>` Refers to the name of a font installed on the user's operating system and supported by the browser, for instance: Arial and Times New Roman. A comma-separated list of fonts may be provided, font names containing spaces must be enclosed with quotations.

`<generic-family>` Refers to fonts not native to a particular operating system and provided by the browser. The following are all of the generic font families:

- ❏ serif (Times New Roman, or Times)
- ❏ sans-serif (Arial or Helvetica)
- ❏ cursive (Zapf-Chancery)
- ❏ fantasy (Western)
- ❏ monospace (Courier)

font-style	2.1	Y	Y	Y	Y	Y
Value:	normal | italic | oblique					
Initial value:	normal					

Table continued on following page

Property	CSS	IE 6.0	IE 7.0	FF 2.0	O 9.0	S 2.0
Applies to:	All elements					
Inherited:	Yes					
font-variant	2.1	Y	Y	Y	Y	P
Value:	normal | small-caps					
Initial value:	normal					
Applies to:	All elements					
Inherited:	Yes					
Safari 1.2 does not support the small-caps keyword.						
font-weight	2.1	Y	Y	Y	Y	Y
Value:	normal | bold | bolder | lighter | 100 | 200 | 300 | 400 | 500 | 600 | 700 | 800 | 900					
Initial value:	normal					
Applies to:	All elements					
Inherited:	Yes					
font-size	2.1	Y	Y	Y	Y	Y
Value:	<absolute-size> | <relative-size> | <length> | <percentage>					
Initial value:	medium					
Applies to:	All elements					
Inherited:	Yes					
Percentage value:	Refers to parent element's font size					
<absolute-size> refers to one of the keywords:						
	xx-small | x-small | small | medium | large | xx-large					
<relative-size> refers to one of the keywords:						
	larger | smaller					
font	2.1	Y	Y	Y	Y	Y
Value:	[[<font-style> || <font-variant> || <font-weight>]? <font-size> [/ <line-height>]? <font-family>] | caption | icon | menu | message-box | small-caption | status-bar					
Initial value:	Not defined for shorthand properties					
Applies to:	All elements					
Inherited:	Yes					

Background Properties

Property	CSS	IE 6.0	IE 7.0	FF 2.0	O 9.0	S 2.0
background-color	2.1	Y	Y	Y	Y	Y
Value:	<color> | transparent					
Initial value:	transparent					
Applies to:	All elements					
Inherited:	No					
background-image	2.1	Y	Y	Y	Y	Y
Value:	<uri> | none					
Initial value:	none					
Applies to:	All elements					
Inherited:	No					
background-repeat	2.1	Y	Y	Y	Y	Y
Value:	repeat | repeat-x | repeat-y | no-repeat					
Initial value:	repeat					
Applies to:	All elements					
Inherited:	No					
background-attachment	2.1	P	Y	Y	Y	Y
Value:	scroll | fixed					
Initial value:	repeat					
Applies to:	All elements					
Inherited:	No					
IE 6 only supports the `fixed` keyword when applied to the `<body>` element. The `fixed` keyword may be applied to any element in IE 7.						
background-position	3	Y	Y	Y	Y	Y
Value:	[<percentage> | <length>]{1,2} | [[top | center | bottom] | | [left | center | right]]					
Initial value:	0% 0%					
Applies to:	All elements					
Inherited:	No					
Percentage values:	Are determined based on the size of the element itself					

Table continued on following page

Property	CSS	IE 6.0	IE 7.0	FF 2.0	O 9.0	S 2.0
background	2.1	Y	Y	Y	Y	Y
Value:	<background-color> || <background-image> || <background-repeat> || <background-attachment> || <background-position>					
Initial value:	Not defined for shorthand properties					
Applies to:	All elements					
Inherited:	No					
Percentage values:	Are determined based on the size of the element itself					

Text Properties

Property	CSS	IE 6.0	IE 7.0	FF 2.0	O 9.0	S 2.0
word-spacing	2.1	Y	Y	Y	Y	Y
Value:	normal | <length>					
Initial value:	normal					
Applies to:	All elements					
Inherited:	Yes					
letter-spacing	2.1	Y	Y	Y	Y	Y
Value:	normal | <length>					
Initial value:	normal					
Applies to:	All elements					
Inherited:	Yes					
text-decoration	2.1	Y	Y	Y	Y	Y
Value:	none | [underline || overline || line-through || blink]					
Initial value:	none					
Applies to:	All elements					
Inherited:	No					
text-transform	2.1	Y	Y	Y	Y	Y
Value:	capitalize | uppercase | lowercase | none					
Initial value:	none					
Applies to:	All elements					
Inherited:	Yes					

Property	CSS	IE 6.0	IE 7.0	FF 2.0	O 9.0	S 2.0
text-align	2.1	Y	Y	Y	Y	Y
Value:	left | right | center | justify					
Initial value:	left					
Applies to:	Block-level elements, table cells and inline blocks					
Inherited:	Yes					
text-indent	2.1	Y	Y	Y	Y	Y
Value:	<length> | <percentage>					
Initial value:	0					
Applies to:	Block-level elements, table cells and inline blocks					
Inherited:	Yes					
Percentage value:	Refers to the width of the containing block					
line-height	2.1	Y	Y	Y	Y	Y
Value:	normal | <number> | <length> | <percentage>					
Initial value:	normal					
Applies to:	All elements					
Inherited:	Yes					
Percentage value:	Refers to the font size of the element the line-height is applied to					
vertical-align	2.1	Y	Y	Y	Y	Y
Value:	baseline | sub | super | top | text-top | middle | bottom | text-bottom | <percentage> | <length>					
Initial value:	baseline					
Applies to:	Inline-level and 'table-cell' elements					
Inherited:	No					
Percentage value:	Is determined by the line-height of the element					
white-space	2	Y	Y	Y	Y	Y
Value:	normal | pre | nowrap					
Initial value:	normal					
Applies to:	All elements					
Inherited:	Yes.					

Internet Explorer 5.5 does not support the pre keyword. IE 6 and IE 7 must be in standards rendering mode for the pre keyword to work.

Box Model Properties

Property	CSS	IE 6.0	IE 7.0	FF 2.0	O 9.0	S 2.0
margin-top margin-right margin-bottom margin-left	2.1	Y	Y	Y	Y	Y
Value:	<length> | <percentage> | auto					
Initial value:	0					
Applies to:	All elements					
Inherited:	No					
Percentage value:	Refers to the width of the containing block					
margin	2.1	Y	Y	Y	Y	Y
Value:	[<length> | <percentage> | auto] {1, 4}					
Initial value:	Not defined for shorthand properties					
Applies to:	All elements					
Inherited:	No					
Percentage value:	Refers to the width of the containing block					
padding-top padding-right padding-bottom padding-left	2.1	Y	Y	Y	Y	Y
Value:	<length> | <percentage>					
Initial value:	0					
Applies to:	All elements					
Inherited:	No					
Percentage value:	Refers to the width of the containing block					
padding	2.1	Y	Y	Y	Y	Y
Value:	[<length> | <percentage>] {1,4}					
Initial value:	Not defined for shorthand properties					
Applies to:	All elements					
Inherited:	No					
Percentage value:	Refers to the width of the containing block					

Property	CSS	IE 6.0	IE 7.0	FF 2.0	O 9.0	S 2.0
border-top-width border-right-width border-bottom-width border-left-width	2.1	Y	Y	Y	Y	Y
Value:	thin | medium | thick | <length>					
Initial value:	medium					
Applies to:	All elements					
Inherited:	No					
border-width	2.1	Y	Y	Y	Y	Y
Value:	[thin | medium | thick | <length>] {1,4}					
Initial value:	Not defined for shorthand properties					
Applies to:	All elements					
Inherited:	No					
border-top-color border-right-color border-bottom-color border-left-color	2.1	P	Y	Y	Y	Y
Value:	<color> | transparent					
Initial value:	The value of the `color` property					
Applies to:	All elements					
Inherited:	No					
IE 6 does not support the `transparent` keyword.						
border-color	2.1	P	Y	Y	Y	Y
Value:	[<color> | transparent] {1,4}					
Initial value:	See individual properties					
Applies to:	All elements					
Inherited:	No					
IE 6 does not support the `transparent` keyword.						
border-top-style border-right-style border-bottom-style border-left-style	2.1	P	P	Y	Y	Y
Value:	none | dotted | dashed | solid | double | groove | ridge | inset | outset					

Table continued on following page

573

Property	CSS	IE 6.0	IE 7.0	FF 2.0	O 9.0	S 2.0
Initial value:	none					
Applies to:	All elements					
Inherited:	No					
IE 5.5 and IE 6 render the dotted keyword as dashed.						
border-style	2.1	P	P	Y	Y	Y
Value:	[none | dotted | dashed | solid | double | groove | ridge | inset | outset] {1,4}					
Initial value:	Not defined for shorthand properties					
Applies to:	All elements					
Inherited:	No					
IE 5.5 and 6 render the dotted keyword as dashed.						
border-top border-right border-bottom border-left	2.1	Y	Y	Y	Y	Y
Value:	<border-width> || <border-style> || <border-color>					
Initial value:	Not defined for shorthand properties					
Applies to:	All elements					
Inherited:	No					
border	2.1	Y	Y	Y	Y	Y
Value:	<border-width> || <border-style> || <border-color>					
Initial value:	Not defined for shorthand properties					
Applies to:	All elements					
Inherited:	No					
width	2.1	I	Y	Y	Y	Y
Value:	<length> | <percentage> | auto					
Initial value:	auto					
Applies to:	All elements, but non-replaced inline elements, table rows, and row groups					
Inherited:	No					
IE 6 incorrectly resizes elements if the content inside of the element is larger than its width; this is fixed in IE 7.						

Property	CSS	IE 6.0	IE 7.0	FF 2.0	O 9.0	S 2.0
min-width	2.1	N	Y	Y	Y	Y
Value:	<length> | <percentage>					
Initial value:	0					
Applies to:	All elements, but non-replaced inline elements and table elements					
Inherited:	No					

Versions of Safari previous to 2.0 do not support min-width when applied to positioned elements.

Property	CSS	IE 6.0	IE 7.0	FF 2.0	O 9.0	S 2.0
max-width	2.1	N	Y	Y	Y	Y
Value:	<length> | <percentage> | none					
Initial value:	none					
Applies to:	All elements, but non-replaced inline elements and table elements					
Inherited:	No					

Versions of Safari previous to 2.0 do not support max-width when applied to positioned elements.

Property	CSS	IE 6.0	IE 7.0	FF 2.0	O 9.0	S 2.0
height	2.1	I	Y	Y	Y	Y
Value:	<length> | <percentage> | auto					
Initial value:	auto					
Applies to:	All elements, but non-replaced inline elements, table rows, and row groups					
Inherited:	No					

IE 6 incorrectly resizes elements if the content inside of the element is larger than its height.

Property	CSS	IE 6.0	IE 7.0	FF 2.0	O 9.0	S 2.0
min-height	2.1	P	Y	Y	Y	Y
Value:	<length> | <percentage>					
Initial value:	0					
Applies to:	All elements, but non-replaced inline elements, table rows, and row groups					
Inherited:	No					

IE 6 only supports the min-height property when applied to <td>, <th>, or <tr> elements.

Property	CSS	IE 6.0	IE 7.0	FF 2.0	O 9.0	S 2.0
max-height	2.1	N	Y	Y	Y	Y
Value:	<length> | <percentage> | none					
Initial value:	none					
Applies to:	All elements, but non-replaced inline elements, table rows, and row groups					
Inherited:	No					

Visual Effects

CSS Property	CSS	IE 6.0	IE 7.0	FF 2.0	O 9.0	S 2.0
overflow	2.1	I	Y	Y	Y	Y
Value:	visible | hidden | scroll | auto					
Initial value:	visible					
Applies to:	Block-level and replaced elements					
Inherited:	No					

IE 6 incorrectly resizes element width / height when overflow: visible; is applied in addition to explicit width or height, and the contents overflow. This is fixed in IE 7.

CSS Property	CSS	IE 6.0	IE 7.0	FF 2.0	O 9.0	S 2.0
overflow-x	3	Y	Y	Y	N	N
Value:	visible | hidden | scroll | auto					
Initial Value:	visible					
Applies to:	Block-level and replaced elements					
Inherited:	No					
overflow-y	3	Y	Y	Y	N	N
Value:	visible | hidden | scroll | auto					
Initial Value:	visible					
Applies to:	Block-level and replaced elements					
Inherited:	No					
clip	2.1	Y	Y	Y	Y	Y
Value:	<shape> | auto					
Initial value:	auto					
Applies to:	Absolutely positioned elements					
Inherited:	No					

Under CSS 2 the only valid <shape> value is rect(<top>, <right>, <bottom>, <left>), where rect() provides the dimensions of a rectangle and <top>, <right>, <bottom>, <left> are <length> values.

CSS Property	CSS	IE 6.0	IE 7.0	FF 2.0	O 9.0	S 2.0
visibility	2.1	P	P	P	P	P
Value:	visible | hidden | collapse					
Initial value:	visible					
Applies to:	All elements					
Inherited:	Yes					

No browser supports the collapse keyword, presumably because it essentially provides the same effect as display: none;

Positioning

Property	CSS	IE 6.0	IE 7.0	FF 2.0	O 9.0	S 2.0
display	2.1	P	P	P	Y	Y
Values:	inline | block | list-item | run-in | inline-block | table | inline-table | table-row-group | table-header-group | table-footer-group | table-row | table-column-group | table-column | table-cell | table-caption | none					
Initial value:	inline					
Applies to:	All elements					
Inherited:	No					
IE 5.5 and 6 only support the keywords `block`, `none`, `inline`, `inline-block`, `table-header-group` and `table-footer-group`. IE 6 additionally supports the `list-item` keyword. Firefox does not support the keywords `inline-block`, `run-in`, or `compact`.						
position	2.1	P	Y	Y	Y	Y
Value:	static | relative | absolute | fixed					
Initial value:	static					
Applies to:	All elements					
Inherited:	No					
IE 6 does not support the `fixed` keyword.						
top	2.1	Y	Y	Y	Y	Y
Value:	<length> | <percentage> | auto					
Initial value:	auto					
Applies to:	Positioned elements					
Inherited:	No					
Percentage value:	Refers to height of containing block					
right	2.1	Y	Y	Y	Y	Y
Value:	<length> | <percentage> | auto					
Initial value:	auto					
Applies to:	Positioned elements					
Inherited:	No					
Percentage value:	Refers to width of containing block					
bottom	2.1	Y	Y	Y	Y	Y
Value:	<length> | <percentage> | auto					

Table continued on following page

Property	CSS	IE 6.0	IE 7.0	FF 2.0	O 9.0	S 2.0
Initial value:	auto					
Applies to:	Positioned elements					
Inherited:	No					
Percentage value:	Refers to height of containing block					
left	2.1	Y	Y	Y	Y	Y
Value:	<length> | <percentage> | auto					
Initial value:	auto					
Applies to:	Positioned elements					
Inherited:	No					
Percentage value:	Refers to width of containing block					
top + bottom = height	2.1	N	Y	Y	Y	Y

When both the `top` and `bottom` offset properties are applied to an element positioned absolutely or fixed, height is implied.

	CSS	IE 6.0	IE 7.0	FF 2.0	O 9.0	S 2.0
left + right = width	2.1	N	Y	Y	Y	Y

When both the `left` and `right` offset properties are applied to an element positioned absolutely or fixed, width is implied.

	CSS	IE 6.0	IE 7.0	FF 2.0	O 9.0	S 2.0
float	2.1	Y	Y	Y	Y	Y
Value:	left | right | none					
Initial value:	none					
Applies to:	All elements					
Inherited:	No					
clear	2.1	Y	Y	Y	Y	Y
Value:	none | left | right | both					
Initial value:	none					
Applies to:	Block-level elements					
Inherited:	No					
z-index	2.1	Y	Y	Y	Y	Y
Value:	auto | <integer>					
Initial value:	auto					
Applies to:	Positioned elements					
Inherited:	No					

Table Properties

Property	CSS	IE 6.0	IE 7.0	FF 2.0	O 9.0	S 2.0
caption-side	2.1	N	N	Y	N	Y
Value:	top | bottom					
Initial value:	top					
Applies to:	'table-caption' elements					
Inherited:	Yes					
table-layout	2.1	Y	Y	Y	Y	Y
Value:	auto | fixed					
Initial value:	auto					
Applies to:	'table' and 'inline-table' elements					
Inherited:	No					
border-collapse	2.1	Y	Y	Y	Y	Y
Value:	collapse | separate					
Initial value:	separate					
Applies to:	'table' and 'inline-table' elements					
Inherited:	Yes					
border-spacing	2.1	N	N	Y	Y	Y
Value:	<length> <length> ?					
Initial value:	0					
Applies to:	'table' and 'inline-table' elements					
Inherited:	Yes					
empty-cells	2.1	N	N	Y	Y	Y
Value:	show | hide					
Initial value:	show					
Applies to:	'table-cell' elements					
Inherited:	Yes					

User Interface

Property	CSS	IE 6.0	IE 7.0	FF 2.0	O 9.0	S 2.0
cursor	2.1	Y	Y	Y	Y	P
Value:	[<uri> ,]* [auto | crosshair | default | pointer | move | e-resize | ne-resize | nw-resize | n-resize | se-resize | sw-resize | s-resize | w-resize | text | wait | help | progress]					
Initial value:	auto					
Applies to:	All elements					
Inherited:	Yes					
Safari does not support custom cursors supplied via a <uri>.						
outline-width	2.1	N	N	Y	Y	Y
Value:	<border-width>					
Initial value:	Medium					
Applies to:	All elements					
Inherited:	No					
outline-style	2.1	N	N	Y	Y	Y
Value:	<border-style>					
Initial value:	none					
Applies to:	All elements					
Inherited:	No					
outline-color	2.1	N	N	Y	Y	Y
Value:	<color> | invert					
Initial value:	invert					
Applies to:	All elements					
Inherited:	No					
outline	2.1	N	N	Y	Y	Y
Value:	<'outline-color'> | | <'outline-style'> | | <'outline-width'>					
Initial value:	Not defined for shorthand properties					
Applies to:	All elements					
Inherited:	No					

Generated Content, Automatic Numbering, and Lists

Property	CSS	IE 6.0	IE 7.0	FF 2.0	O 9.0	S 2.0
content	2.1	N	N	Y	Y	Y
Value:	normal | none | [<string> | <uri> | <counter> | attr(<identifier>) | open-quote | close-quote | no-open-quote | no-close-quote]+					
Initial value:	normal					
Applies to:	::before and ::after pseudo-elements					
Inherited:	No					
quotes	2.1	N	N	Y	Y	N
Value:	[<string> <string>]+ | none					
Initial value:	Varies from browser to browser					
Applies to:	All elements					
Inherited:	Yes					
counter-reset	2.1	N	N	N	Y	N
Value:	[<identifier> <integer>?]+ | none					
Initial value:	none					
Applies to:	All elements					
Inherited:	No					
counter-increment	2.1	N	N	N	Y	N
Value:	[<identifier> <integer>?]+ | none					
Initial value:	none					
Applies to:	All elements					
Inherited:	No					
list-style-type	2.1	P	P	P	P	Y
Value:	disc | circle | square | decimal | decimal-leading-zero | lower-roman | upper-roman | lower-greek | lower-latin | upper-latin | armenian | georgian | none					
Initial value:	disc					
Applies to:	Elements with 'display: list-item'					
Inherited:	Yes					

Table continued on following page

Property	CSS	IE 6.0	IE 7.0	FF 2.0	O 9.0	S 2.0
Firefox does not support the georgian keyword. IE 5.5 and IE 6 only support CSS 1 keyword values: disc | circle | square | decimal | lower-roman | upper-roman | lower-alpha | upper-alpha | none						
list-style-image	2.1	Y	Y	Y	Y	Y
Value:	<uri> | none					
Initial value:	none					
Applies to:	Elements with 'display: list-item'					
Inherited:	Yes					
list-style-position	2.1	Y	Y	Y	Y	Y
Value:	inside | outside					
Initial value:	outside					
Applies to:	Elements with 'display: list-item'					
Inherited:	Yes					
list-style	2.1	P	P	P	P	Y
Value:	<'list-style-type'> | | <'list-style-position'> | | <'list-style-image'>					
Initial value:	Not defined for shorthand properties.					
Applies to:	Elements with 'display: list-item'					
Inherited:	Yes					

Paged Media

Property	CSS	IE 6.0	IE 7.0	FF 2.0	O 9.0	S 2.0
size	2.1	N	N	N	Y	N
Value:	<length>{1,2} | auto | portrait | landscape					
Initial value:	auto					
Applies to:	Page (via @page rule)					
marks	2.1	N	N	N	N	N
Value:	[crop | | cross] | none					
Initial value:	none					
Applies to:	Page (via @page rule)					

Property	CSS	IE 6.0	IE 7.0	FF 2.0	O 9.0	S 2.0
page-break-before	2.1	P	P	P	Y	P
Value:	auto | always | avoid | left | right					
Initial value:	auto					
Applies to:	Block-level elements					
IE, Mozilla, and Safari only support the `auto` and `always` keywords.						
page-break-after	2.1	P	P	P	Y	P
Value:	auto | always | avoid | left | right					
Initial value:	auto					
Applies to:	Block-level elements					
IE, Mozilla, and Safari only support the `auto` and `always` keywords.						
page-break-inside	2.1	N	N	N	Y	N
Value:	avoid | auto					
Initial value:	auto					
Applies to:	Block-level elements					
page	2.1	N	N	N	N	N
Value:	<identifier> | auto					
Initial value:	auto					
Applies to:	Block-level elements.					
orphans	2.1	N	N	N	Y	N
Value:	<integer>					
Initial value:	2					
Applies to:	Block-level elements					
widows	2.1	N	N	N	Y	N
Value:	<integer>					
Initial value:	2					
Applies to:	Block-level elements					

Microsoft Proprietary Extensions

The following selections of properties are Microsoft proprietary extensions to CSS and are not part of any W3C standard.

Visual Effects

Property	Supported Since
Filter	IE 5.5
Value:	See below
Applies to:	All elements
Inherited:	No

The filter property is a complicated property that provides effects like transparency, gradients, or an array of other effects that are only available for Windows versions of Internet Explorer. For a complete reference, visit the following URLs.

Introduction to filters:
http://msdn.microsoft.com/workshop/author/filter/filters.asp

Filter reference:
http://msdn.microsoft.com/workshop/author/filter/reference/reference.asp

User-Interface

Property	Supported Since
scrollbar-3dlight-color scrollbar-arrow-color scrollbar-base-color scrollbar-darkshadow-color scrollbar-face-color scrollbar-highlight-color scrollbar-shadow-color	IE 5.5, Opera 7
Value:	<color>
Applies to:	Any object where a scroll bar is applied
Inherited:	Yes

In Opera, custom scroll bar colors are turned off by default. Custom scroll bar colors are only applied if the user has them turned on in the Opera preferences panel.

zoom	IE 5.5
Value:	normal | <number> | <percentage>
Applies to:	Any object where a scroll bar is applied
Inherited:	Yes

Backgrounds

Property	Supported Since
background-position-x	IE 4
Value:	\<length\> | \<percentage\> | left | center | right
Applies to:	All elements
Inherited:	Yes
background-position-y	IE 4
Value:	\<length\> | \<percentage\> | top | center | bottom
Applies to:	All elements
Inherited:	Yes

Gecko Proprietary Extensions

The following selections of CSS features are Gecko proprietary extensions to CSS, which apply to the Mozilla, Netscape, and Firefox family of browsers and are not part of any W3C standard.

When new CSS features are added in Gecko, they usually undergo a testing period where they are prefixed with the Mozilla vendor specific prefix "-moz-", which is the W3C recommended method of deploying proprietary extensions to CSS, or CSS features not yet finalized in an official W3C CSS recommendation. This prefix remains in place until the functionality is finalized in a W3C CSS recommendation, or until bugs can be worked out with the implementation in such a way that Gecko's (or any other browser's) implementation can be expected to follow the W3C definition of what that feature provides.

Features such as these should be used with the understanding that they can be completely changed or removed without notice in future Gecko releases.

The following tables show the version of Gecko in which a particular feature was added. If previous to Mozilla 1.0, Netscape 6 is provided as the version; if the feature was added in Mozilla 1.0 or later (before the arrival of Firefox 1.0), the version of Mozilla is indicated. Be sure to keep in mind the relationships between the Netscape, Mozilla, and Firefox browsers as shown in the tables in Chapter 1.

Pseudo-Elements

Pseudo-Element	Supported Since
::-moz-selection	Mozilla 1.5
Identical to the CSS 3 ::selection pseudo-element.	

Visual Effects

Property	Supported Since
-moz-opacity	NS 6
Value	<alphavalue> | <percentage>\
Initial value:	Visible
Applies to:	Block-level and replaced elements
Inherited:	Yes

Similar to the CSS 3 opacity property, except the CSS 3 opacity property is not inherited. <alphavalue> refers to a floating integer between 0.0 (fully transparent) and 1.0 (fully opaque).

```
table {opacity: 0.9;}
```

Box Model

Property	Supported Since
-moz-border-radius-topleft -moz-border-radius-topright -moz-border-radius-bottom-left -moz-border-radius-bottom-right	NS 6
Value	<length> | <percentage>
Initial value:	0
Applies to:	All elements
Inherited:	No

Applies rounded corners to box borders. Similar to the `border-top-left-radius`, `border-top-right-radius`, `border-bottom-left-radius`, and `border-bottom-right-radius` properties proposed for inclusion in CSS 3.

Property	Supported Since
-moz-border-radius	NS6
Value	[<length> | <percentage>] {1,4}
Initial value:	0
Applies to:	All elements
Inherited:	No

Applies rounded corners to box borders. A similar `border-radius` property is proposed for inclusion in CSS 3.

Property	Supported Since
-moz-border-top-colors -moz-border-right-colors -moz-border-bottom-colors -moz-border-left-colors	NS6
Value	<color>+ | none
Initial value:	None
Applies to:	All elements
Inherited:	No

Provides a color striping effect for borders, where one or more <color> values are provided. Each color is applied in 1 pixel-width increments from the outside border to the inside border. If there are not enough colors specified for each pixel width, the value of the border-color property colors the remaining border.

User-Interface

Firefox version 1.5 and later support the CSS 2 `outline` property, and it's derivatives. Use the following proprietary syntax for versions of Firefox previous to 1.5. There is a slight difference between `-moz-outline` and `outline`, in that the former paints the outline on the inside of the element's border, whereas the latter paints the outline on the outside of the element's border (per the CSS 2 specification).

Property	Supported Since
-moz-outline-color	NS 6
Value:	<color> | invert
Applies to:	All elements
Inherited:	No
-moz-outline-style	NS 6
Value:	<border-style>
Applies to:	All elements
Inherited:	No
-moz-outline-width	NS 6
Value:	<border-width>
Applies to:	All elements
Inherited:	No

Table continued on following page

Property	Supported Since
-moz-outline	NS 6
Value:	<-moz-outline-color> || <-moz-outline-style> || <-moz-outline-width>
Applies to:	All elements
Inherited:	No
-moz-user-select	NS 6
Value:	none | text | element | elements | all | toggle | tri-state | -moz-all
Initial value:	all
Applies to:	All elements
Inherited:	Yes

This property is used in Gecko browsers to control whether a user can select text or elements on the page by holding down the mouse button and dragging the cursor.

CSS 3 Multicolumn Layout

As of Firefox 1.5, the Gecko engine includes experimental support for CSS 3 multicolumn properties.

Property	Supported Since
-moz-column-width	FF 1.5
Value:	<length> | auto
Initial value:	auto
Applies to:	Block-level elements
Inherited:	No
-moz-column-count	FF 1.5
Value:	<integer> | auto
Initial value:	auto
Applies to:	Block-level elements
Inherited:	No
-moz-columns	FF 1.5
Value:	[[<integer> | auto] || [<length> | auto]]
Initial value:	See -moz-column-width and -moz-column-count properties.

Property	Supported Since
Applies to:	Block-level elements
Inherited:	No
-moz-column-gap	FF 1.5
Value:	<length> | normal
Initial value:	normal
Applies to:	Block-level elements
Inherited:	No

Webkit (Safari) Proprietary Extensions

Some of the following Apple Webkit (Safari) extensions have not landed in an official release of Safari, at the time of this writing. Currently, the released version of Safari is 2.0.4. Some of the following features are expected to be released with the next version of Safari, which will be included in Mac OS X Leopard, and will most likely be Safari 3.0.

If you would like to try the following Safari extensions not yet in an official, stable version of Safari, you can do so by downloading a nightly build of Safari from http://www.webkit.org.

All of the following properties appear in the CSS 3 standard currently under development by the W3C.

Property	Supported Since
-khtml-border-radius	?
Value:	<length> <length>?
Initial value:	0
Applies to:	All elements except table elements when border-collapse property is set to collapse
Inherited:	No
-khtml-background-origin	?
Value:	[border | padding | content] [, [border | padding | content]]*
Initial value:	border
Applies to:	All elements
Inherited:	No

Table continued on following page

589

Property	Supported Since
-khtml-background-clip	?
Value:	[border | padding] [, [border | padding]]*
Initial value:	border
Applies to:	All elements
Inherited:	No
-khtml-border-image	?
Value:	none | <uri> [<number> | <percentage>]{4} [/ <border-width>{1,4}]? [stretch | repeat | round] {0,2}
Initial value:	none
Applies to:	All elements
Inherited:	No

CSS 3 Multiple Background Syntax	
Webkit supports the ability to apply multiple background images to a single element, as per the CSS 3 Backgrounds and Borders Module Working Draft.	
background-image	Safari 2.0
Value:	<uri> [, <uri>]* | none
Initial value:	none
Applies to:	All elements
Inherited:	No
background-repeat	Safari 2.0
Value:	<repeat> [, <repeat>]*
Initial value:	repeat
Applies to:	All elements
Inherited:	No
The value <repeat> stands for: repeat-x | repeat-y | [repeat | space | no-repeat]{1,2}.	
background-attachment	Safari 2.0
Value:	scroll | fixed | local [, scroll | fixed | local]*
Initial value:	scroll
Applies to:	All elements
Inherited:	No

CSS 3 Multiple Background Syntax	
background-position	Safari 2.0
Value:	<bg-position> [, <bg-position>]*
Initial value:	0% 0%
Applies to:	All elements
Inherited:	No

<bg-position> stands for: [[<percentage> | <length> | left | center | right] [<percentage> | <length> | top | center | bottom]?] | [[left | center | right] || [top | center | bottom]]

background	Safari 2.0
Value:	[<bg-layer> ,]* <final-bg-layer>
Initial value:	See individual properties
Applies to:	All elements
Inherited:	No

<bg-layer> stands for: <'background-image'> && [(<'background-size'>)]? && <'background-repeat'>? && <'background-position'>? && <'background-attachment'>? && [<'background-clip'> <'background-origin'>?]?

<final-bg-layer> stands for: <'background-image'> || (<'background-size'>) || <'background-repeat'> || <'background-position'> || <'background-attachment'> || [<'background-clip'> <'background-origin'>?] || <'background-color'>

CSS Colors

This appendix references the available CSS color keywords as documented in the W3C CSS 3 candidate recommendation. With the exception of IE 6 not supporting spelling of *lightgray* with an *a*, as in its American spelling, and IE 6 not supporting other gray color keywords spelled with an "e", as in the British spelling, all the following keywords are supported by IE 6, IE 7, Firefox 2, Opera 9, and Safari 2.

Colors Sorted Alphabetically

Color Keyword	Hexadecimal Value	RGB
aliceblue	#F0F8FF	240, 248, 255
antiquewhite	#FAEBD7	250, 235, 215
aqua	#00FFFF	0, 255, 255
aquamarine	#7FFFD4	127, 255, 212
azure	#F0FFFF	240, 255, 255
beige	#F5F5DC	245, 245, 220
bisque	#FFE4C4	255, 228, 196
black	#000000	0, 0, 0
blanchedalmond	#FFEBCD	255, 235, 205
blue	#0000FF	0, 0, 255
blueviolet	#8A2BE2	138, 43, 226
brown	#A52A2A	165, 42, 42
burlywood	#DEB887	222, 184, 135

Table continued on following page

Color Keyword	Hexadecimal Value	RGB
cadetblue	#5F9EA0	95, 158, 160
chartreuse	#7FFF00	127, 255, 0
chocolate	#D2691E	210, 105, 30
coral	#FF7F50	255, 127, 80
cornflowerblue	#6495ED	100, 149, 237
cornsilk	#FFF8DC	255, 248, 220
crimson	#DC143C	220, 20, 60
cyan	#00FFFF	0, 255, 255
darkblue	#00008B	0, 0, 139
darkcyan	#008B8B	0, 139, 139
darkgoldenrod	#B8860B	184, 134, 11
darkgray	#A9A9A9	169, 169, 169
darkgreen	#006400	0, 100, 0
darkgrey	#A9A9A9	169, 169, 169
darkkhaki	#BDB76B	189, 183, 107
darkmagenta	#8B008B	139, 0, 139
darkolivegreen	#556B2F	85, 107, 47
darkorange	#FF8C00	255, 140, 0
darkorchid	#9932CC	153, 50, 204
darkred	#8B0000	139, 0, 0
darksalmon	#E9967A	233, 150, 122
darkseagreen	#8FBC8F	143, 188, 143
darkslateblue	#483D8B	72, 61, 139
darkslategray	#2F4F4F	47, 79, 79
darkslategrey	#2F4F4F	47, 79, 79
darkturquoise	#00CED1	0, 206, 209
darkviolet	#9400D3	148, 0, 211
deeppink	#FF1493	255, 20, 147
deepskyblue	#00BFFF	0, 191, 255
dimgray	#696969	105, 105, 105
dimgrey	#696969	105, 105, 105

Color Keyword	Hexadecimal Value	RGB
dodgerblue	#1E90FF	30, 144, 255
firebrick	#B22222	178, 34, 34
floralwhite	#FFFAF0	255, 250, 240
forestgreen	#228B22	34, 139, 34
fuchsia	#FF00FF	255, 0, 255
gainsboro	#DCDCDC	220, 220, 220
ghostwhite	#F8F8FF	248, 248, 255
gold	#FFD700	255, 215, 0
goldenrod	#DAA520	218, 165, 32
gray	#808080	128, 128, 128
green	#008000	0, 128, 0
greenyellow	#ADFF2F	173, 255, 47
grey	#808080	128, 128, 128
honeydew	#F0FFF0	240, 255, 240
hotpink	#FF69B4	255, 105, 180
indianred	#CD5C5C	205, 92, 92
indigo	#4B0082	75, 0, 130
ivory	#FFFFF0	255, 255, 240
khaki	#F0E68C	240, 230, 140
lavender	#E6E6FA	230, 230, 250
lavenderblush	#FFF0F5	255, 240, 245
lawngreen	#7CFC00	124, 252, 0
lemonchiffon	#FFFACD	255, 250, 205
lightblue	#ADD8E6	173, 216, 230
lightcoral	#F08080	240, 128, 128
lightcyan	#E0FFFF	224, 255, 255
lightgoldenrodyellow	#FAFAD2	250, 250, 210
lightgray	#D3D3D3	211, 211, 211
lightgreen	#90EE90	144, 238, 144
lightgrey	#D3D3D3	211, 211, 211

Table continued on following page

Color Keyword	Hexadecimal Value	RGB
lightpink	#FFB6C1	255, 182, 193
lightsalmon	#FFA07A	255, 160, 122
lightseagreen	#20B2AA	32, 178, 170
lightskyblue	#87CEFA	135, 206, 250
lightslategray	#778899	119, 136, 153
lightslategrey	#778899	119, 136, 153
lightsteelblue	#B0C4DE	176, 196, 222
lightyellow	#FFFFE0	255, 255, 224
lime	#00FF00	0, 255, 0
limegreen	#32CD32	50, 205, 50
linen	#FAF0E6	250, 240, 230
magenta	#FF00FF	255, 0, 255
maroon	#800000	128, 0, 0
mediumaquamarine	#66CDAA	102, 205, 170
mediumblue	#0000CD	0, 0, 205
mediumorchid	#BA55D3	186, 85, 211
mediumpurple	#9370DB	147, 112, 219
mediumseagreen	#3CB371	60, 179, 113
mediumslateblue	#7B68EE	123, 104, 238
mediumspringgreen	#00FA9A	0, 250, 154
mediumturquoise	#48D1CC	72, 209, 204
mediumvioletred	#C71585	199, 21, 133
midnightblue	#191970	25, 25, 112
mintcream	#F5FFFA	245, 255, 250
mistyrose	#FFE4E1	255, 228, 225
moccasin	#FFE4B5	255, 228, 181
navajowhite	#FFDEAD	255, 222, 173
navy	#000080	0, 0, 128
oldlace	#FDF5E6	253, 245, 230
olive	#808000	128, 128, 0
olivedrab	#6B8E23	107, 142, 35

Color Keyword	Hexadecimal Value	RGB
orange	#FFA500	255, 165, 0
orangered	#FF4500	255, 69, 0
orchid	#DA70D6	218, 112, 214
palegoldenrod	#EEE8AA	238, 232, 170
palegreen	#98FB98	152, 251, 152
paleturquoise	#AFEEEE	175, 238, 238
palevioletred	#DB7093	219, 112, 147
papayawhip	#FFEFD5	255, 239, 213
peachpuff	#FFDAB9	255, 218, 185
peru	#CD853F	205, 133, 63
pink	#FFC0CB	255, 192, 203
plum	#DDA0DD	221, 160, 221
powderblue	#B0E0E6	176, 224, 230
purple	#800080	128, 0, 128
red	#FF0000	255, 0, 0
rosybrown	#BC8F8F	188, 143, 143
royalblue	#4169E1	65, 105, 225
saddlebrown	#8B4513	139, 69, 19
salmon	#FA8072	250, 128, 114
sandybrown	#F4A460	244, 164, 96
seagreen	#2E8B57	46, 139, 87
seashell	#FFF5EE	255, 245, 238
sienna	#A0522D	160, 82, 45
silver	#C0C0C0	192, 192, 192
skyblue	#87CEEB	135, 206, 235
slateblue	#6A5ACD	106, 90, 205
slategray	#708090	112, 128, 144
slategrey	#708090	112, 128, 144
snow	#FFFAFA	255, 250, 250
springgreen	#00FF7F	0, 255, 127

Table continued on following page

Color Keyword	Hexadecimal Value	RGB
steelblue	#4682B4	70, 130, 180
tan	#D2B48C	210, 180, 140
teal	#008080	0, 128, 128
thistle	#D8BFD8	216, 191, 216
tomato	#FF6347	255, 99, 71
turquoise	#40E0D0	64, 224, 208
violet	#EE82EE	238, 130, 238
wheat	#F5DEB3	245, 222, 179
white	#FFFFFF	255, 255, 255
whitesmoke	#F5F5F5	245, 245, 245
yellow	#FFFF00	255, 255, 0
yellowgreen	#9ACD32	154, 205, 50

Colors Sorted by Color

The following sections show colors as sorted from light hue to dark hue.

Reds

Color Keyword	Hexadecimal	RGB
lavenderblush	#FFF0F5	255, 240, 245
mistyrose	#FFE4E1	255, 228, 225
pink	#FFC0CB	255, 192, 203
lightpink	#FFB6C1	255, 182, 193
orange	#FFA500	255, 165, 0
lightsalmon	#FFA07A	255, 160, 122
darkorange	#FF8C00	255, 140, 0
coral	#FF7F50	255, 127, 80
hotpink	#FF69B4	255, 105, 180
tomato	#FF6347	255, 99, 71
orangered	#FF4500	255, 69, 0

Color Keyword	Hexadecimal	RGB
deeppink	#FF1493	255, 20, 147
fuchsia	#FF00FF	255, 0, 255
magenta	#FF00FF	255, 0, 255
red	#FF0000	255, 0, 0
salmon	#FA8072	250, 128, 114
lightcoral	#F08080	240, 128, 128
violet	#EE82EE	238, 130, 238
darksalmon	#E9967A	233, 150, 122
plum	#DDA0DD	221, 160, 221
crimson	#DC143C	220, 20, 60
palevioletred	#DB7093	219, 112, 147
orchid	#DA70D6	218, 112, 214
thistle	#D8BFD8	216, 191, 216
indianred	#CD5C5C	205, 92, 92
mediumvioletred	#C71585	199, 21, 133
mediumorchid	#BA55D3	186, 85, 211
firebrick	#B22222	178, 34, 34
darkorchid	#9932CC	153, 50, 204
darkviolet	#9400D3	148, 0, 211
mediumpurple	#9370DB	147, 112, 219
darkmagenta	#8B008B	139, 0, 139
darkred	#8B0000	139, 0, 0
purple	#800080	128, 0, 128
maroon	#800000	128, 0, 0

Blues

Color Keyword	Hexadecimal	RGB
azure	#F0FFFF	240, 255, 255
aliceblue	#F0F8FF	240, 248, 255
lavender	#E6E6FA	230, 230, 250

Table continued on following page

Color Keyword	Hexadecimal	RGB
lightcyan	#E0FFFF	224, 255, 255
powderblue	#B0E0E6	176, 224, 230
lightsteelblue	#B0C4DE	176, 196, 222
paleturquoise	#AFEEEE	175, 238, 238
lightblue	#ADD8E6	173, 216, 230
blueviolet	#8A2BE2	138, 43, 226
lightskyblue	#87CEFA	135, 206, 250
skyblue	#87CEEB	135, 206, 235
mediumslateblue	#7B68EE	123, 104, 238
slateblue	#6A5ACD	106, 90, 205
cornflowerblue	#6495ED	100, 149, 237
cadetblue	#5F9EA0	95, 158, 160
indigo	#4B0082	75, 0, 130
mediumturquoise	#48D1CC	72, 209, 204
darkslateblue	#483D8B	72, 61, 139
steelblue	#4682B4	70, 130, 180
royalblue	#4169E1	65, 105, 225
turquoise	#40E0D0	64, 224, 208
dodgerblue	#1E90FF	30, 144, 255
midnightblue	#191970	25, 25, 112
aqua	#00FFFF	0, 255, 255
cyan	#00FFFF	0, 255, 255
darkturquoise	#00CED1	0, 206, 209
deepskyblue	#00BFFF	0, 191, 255
darkcyan	#008B8B	0, 139, 139
blue	#0000FF	0, 0, 255
mediumblue	#0000CD	0, 0, 205
darkblue	#00008B	0, 0, 139
navy	#000080	0, 0, 128

Greens

Color Keyword	Hexadecimal	RGB
mintcream	#F5FFFA	245, 255, 250
honeydew	#F0FFF0	240, 255, 240
greenyellow	#ADFF2F	173, 255, 47
yellowgreen	#9ACD32	154, 205, 50
palegreen	#98FB98	152, 251, 152
lightgreen	#90EE90	144, 238, 144
darkseagreen	#8FBC8F	143, 188, 143
olive	#808000	128, 128, 0
aquamarine	#7FFFD4	127, 255, 212
chartreuse	#7FFF00	127, 255, 0
lawngreen	#7CFC00	124, 252, 0
olivedrab	#6B8E23	107, 142, 35
mediumaquamarine	#66CDAA	102, 205, 170
darkolivegreen	#556B2F	85, 107, 47
mediumseagreen	#3CB371	60, 179, 113
limegreen	#32CD32	50, 205, 50
seagreen	#2E8B57	46, 139, 87
forestgreen	#228B22	34, 139, 34
lightseagreen	#20B2AA	32, 178, 170
springgreen	#00FF7F	0, 255, 127
lime	#00FF00	0, 255, 0
mediumspringgreen	#00FA9A	0, 250, 154
teal	#008080	0, 128, 128
green	#008000	0, 128, 0
darkgreen	#006400	0, 100, 0

Yellows

Color Keyword	Hexadecimal	RGB
lightgoldenrodyellow	#FAFAD2	250, 250, 210
ivory	#FFFFF0	255, 255, 240
lightyellow	#FFFFE0	255, 255, 224
floralwhite	#FFFAF0	255, 250, 240
lemonchiffon	#FFFACD	255, 250, 205
cornsilk	#FFF8DC	255, 248, 220
khaki	#F0E68C	240, 230, 140
yellow	#FFFF00	255, 255, 0
gold	#FFD700	255, 215, 0
darkkhaki	#BDB76B	189, 183, 107

Browns

Color Keyword	Hexadecimal	RGB
snow	#FFFAFA	255, 250, 250
seashell	#FFF5EE	255, 245, 238
oldlace	#FDF5E6	253, 245, 230
linen	#FAF0E6	250, 240, 230
antiquewhite	#FAEBD7	250, 235, 215
beige	#F5F5DC	245, 245, 220
papayawhip	#FFEFD5	255, 239, 213
blanchedalmond	#FFEBCD	255, 235, 205
bisque	#FFE4C4	255, 228, 196
moccasin	#FFE4B5	255, 228, 181
navajowhite	#FFDEAD	255, 222, 173
peachpuff	#FFDAB9	255, 218, 185
wheat	#F5DEB3	245, 222, 179
sandybrown	#F4A460	244, 164, 96
palegoldenrod	#EEE8AA	238, 232, 170
burlywood	#DEB887	222, 184, 135

Color Keyword	Hexadecimal	RGB
goldenrod	#DAA520	218, 165, 32
tan	#D2B48C	210, 180, 140
chocolate	#D2691E	210, 105, 30
peru	#CD853F	205, 133, 63
rosybrown	#BC8F8F	188, 143, 143
darkgoldenrod	#B8860B	184, 134, 11
brown	#A52A2A	165, 42, 42
sienna	#A0522D	160, 82, 45
saddlebrown	#8B4513	139, 69, 19

Grays

Color Keyword	Hexadecimal	RGB
white	#FFFFFF	255, 255, 255
ghostwhite	#F8F8FF	248, 248, 255
whitesmoke	#F5F5F5	245, 245, 245
gainsboro	#DCDCDC	220, 220, 220
lightgray	#D3D3D3	211, 211, 211
lightgrey	#D3D3D3	211, 211, 211
silver	#C0C0C0	192, 192, 192
darkgray	#A9A9A9	169, 169, 169
darkgrey	#A9A9A9	169, 169, 169
gray	#808080	128, 128, 128
grey	#808080	128, 128, 128
lightslategray	#778899	119, 136, 153
lightslategrey	#778899	119, 136, 153
slategray	#708090	112, 128, 144
slategrey	#708090	112, 128, 144
dimgray	#696969	105, 105, 105
dimgrey	#696969	105, 105, 105

Table continued on following page

Color Keyword	Hexadecimal	RGB
darkslategray	#2F4F4F	47, 79, 79
darkslategrey	#2F4F4F	47, 79, 79
black	#000000	0, 0, 0

User-Interface Color Keywords

User-interface color keywords (CSS 2) enable an author to reference colors present in the user-interface. They are referenced like any other color keyword. These color keywords allow an author to design a website with the same look and feel as the operating system.

Color Keyword	Description
ActiveBorder	Border of the active window.
ActiveCaption	Caption of the active window.
AppWorkspace	Background color of multiple document interface.
Background	Desktop background.
ButtonFace	Face color of three-dimensional display elements.
ButtonHighlight	Dark shadow for three-dimensional display elements (for edges facing away from the light source).
ButtonShadow	Shadow color for three-dimensional display elements.
ButtonText	Text on push buttons.
CaptionText	Text in caption, size box, and scroll bar arrow box.
GrayText	Grayed (disabled) text. This color is set to #000 if the current display driver does not support a solid gray color.
Highlight	Item(s) selected in a control.
HighlightText	Text of item(s) selected in a control.
InactiveBorder	Inactive window border.
InactiveCaption	Inactive window caption.
InactiveCaptionText	Color of text in an inactive caption.
InfoBackground	Background color for tooltip controls.
InfoText	Text color for tooltip controls.
Menu	Menu background.
MenuText	Text in menus.

Color Keyword	Description
Scrollbar	Scroll bar gray area.
ThreeDDarkShadow	Dark shadow for three-dimensional display elements.
ThreeDFace	Face color for three-dimensional display elements.
ThreeDHighlight	Highlight color for three-dimensional display elements.
ThreeDLightShadow	Light color for three-dimensional display elements (for edges facing the light source).
ThreeDShadow	Dark shadow for three-dimensional display elements.
Window	Window background.
WindowFrame	Window frame.
WindowText	Text in windows.

Browser Rendering Modes

As you saw in Chapter 7, the Document Type Declaration of the HTML or XHTML document can be used to trigger different rendering modes in the browser, which in turn affect the CSS features available to you to use in browsers like IE 6 and IE 7. The following table outlines the different document type declarations, and the rendering mode they invoke in the various browsers.

- ❏ S = Standards mode
- ❏ A = Almost standards mode
- ❏ Q = Quirks mode

Doctype / Document	IE6	IE7	FF	O	S
Pre HTML 4.0 DTD	Q	Q	Q	Q	Q
`<!DOCTYPE HTML PUBLIC "-//W3C//DTD HTML 3.2 Final//EN">`					
HTML 4.0					
HTML 4.0 Transitional DTD without DTD URL	Q	Q	Q	Q	Q
`<!DOCTYPE HTML PUBLIC "-//W3C//DTD HTML 4.0 Transitional//EN">`					
HTML 4.0 Transitional DTD with DTD URL	S	S	Q	S	S
`<!DOCTYPE HTML PUBLIC "-//W3C//DTD HTML 4.0 Transitional//EN" "http://www.w3.org/TR/html4/loose.dtd">`					
HTML 4.0 Frameset DTD without DTD URL	Q	Q	Q	Q	Q
`<!DOCTYPE HTML PUBLIC "-//W3C//DTD HTML 4.0 Frameset//EN">`					
HTML 4.0 Frameset DTD with DTD URL	S	S	Q	S	Q
`<!DOCTYPE HTML PUBLIC "-//W3C//DTD HTML 4.0 Frameset//EN" "http://www.w3.org/TR/REC-html40/frameset.dtd">`					

Table continued on following page

Doctype / Document	IE6	IE7	FF	O	S
HTML 4.0 Strict DTD without DTD URL	S	S	S	S	S
`<!DOCTYPE HTML PUBLIC "-//W3C//DTD HTML 4.0//EN">`					
HTML 4.0 Strict DTD with DTD URL	S	S	S	S	S
`<!DOCTYPE HTML PUBLIC "-//W3C//DTD HTML 4.0//EN"` `"http://www.w3.org/TR/html4/strict.dtd">`					
HTML 4.01					
HTML 4.01 Transitional DTD without DTD URL	Q	Q	Q	Q	Q
`<!DOCTYPE HTML PUBLIC "-//W3C//DTD HTML 4.01 Transitional//EN">`					
HTML 4.01 Transitional DTD with DTD URL	S	S	A	S	S
`<!DOCTYPE HTML PUBLIC "-//W3C//DTD HTML 4.01 Transitional//EN"` `"http://www.w3.org/TR/html4/loose.dtd">`					
HTML 4.01 Frameset DTD without DTD URL	Q	Q	Q	Q	Q
`<!DOCTYPE HTML PUBLIC "-//W3C//DTD HTML 4.01 Frameset//EN">`					
HTML 4.01 Frameset DTD with DTD URL	S	S	A	S	A
`<!DOCTYPE HTML PUBLIC "-//W3C//DTD HTML 4.01 Frameset//EN"` `"http://www.w3.org/TR/html4/frameset.dtd">`					
HTML 4.01 Strict DTD without DTD URL	S	S	S	S	S
`<!DOCTYPE HTML PUBLIC "-//W3C//DTD HTML 4.01//EN">`					
HTML 4.01 Strict DTD with DTD URL	S	S	S	S	S
`<!DOCTYPE HTML PUBLIC "-//W3C//DTD HTML 4.01//EN"` `"http://www.w3.org/TR/html4/strict.dtd">`					
XHTML 1.0					
XHTML 1.0 Transitional DTD without an XML Prolog	S	S	A	S	S
`<!DOCTYPE html PUBLIC "-//W3C//DTD XHTML 1.0 Transitional//EN"` `"http://www.w3.org/TR/xhtml1/DTD/xhtml1-transitional.dtd">`					
XHTML 1.0 Transitional DTD with an XML Prolog	Q	S	A	S	S
`<?xml version="1.0" encoding="UTF-8"?>` `<!DOCTYPE html PUBLIC "-//W3C//DTD XHTML 1.0 Transitional//EN"` `"http://www.w3.org/TR/xhtml1/DTD/xhtml1-transitional.dtd">`					
XHTML 1.0 Frameset DTD with a DTD URL	S	S	A	S	A
`<!DOCTYPE html PUBLIC "-//W3C//DTD XHTML 1.0 Frameset//EN"` `"http://www.w3.org/TR/xhtml1/DTD/xhtml1-frameset.dtd">`					

Doctype / Document	IE6	IE7	FF	O	S
XHTML 1.0 Strict DTD without an XML Prolog	S	S	S	S	S
`<!DOCTYPE html PUBLIC "-//W3C//DTD XHTML 1.0 Strict//EN"` `"http://www.w3.org/TR/xhtml1/DTD/xhtml1-strict.dtd">`					
XHTML 1.0 Strict DTD with an XML Prolog	Q	S	S	S	S
`<?xml version="1.0" encoding="UTF-8"?>` `<!DOCTYPE html PUBLIC "-//W3C//DTD XHTML 1.0 Strict//EN"` `"http://www.w3.org/TR/xhtml1/DTD/xhtml1-strict.dtd">`					
Other					
XML Documents	S	S	S	S	S
No DOCTYPE	Q	Q	Q	Q	Q
Unrecognized DOCTYPE	S	S	S	S	S

Index